DATE DUE

'81

PROPERTIUS: "LOVE" AND "WAR"

PROPERTIUS:
"LOVE" AND "WAR"

INDIVIDUAL AND STATE
UNDER AUGUSTUS

HANS-PETER STAHL

UNIVERSITY OF CALIFORNIA PRESS
BERKELEY   LOS ANGELES   LONDON

University of California Press
Berkeley and Los Angeles, California
University of California Press, Ltd.
London, England
© 1985 by
The Regents of the University of California
Printed in the United States of America

1   2   3   4   5   6   7   8   9

Library of Congress Cataloging in Publication Data

Stahl, Hans-Peter.
  Propertius: love and war.

  Bibliography: p.
  Includes index.
  1. Propertius, Sextus—Criticism and interpretation.
2. Love in literature.   3. War in literature.   4. Rome—
History—Augustus, 30 B.C.–14 A.D.   I. Title.
PA6646.S7   1985   874'.01   84-16324
ISBN 0-520-05166-1

To Gisela

CONTENTS

PREFACE

Opposing positions held by the same author are sometimes explained in terms of a development. In the case of Propertius it has been said that the youthful ardor of his love elegies gradually gave way to the mature poetry of the responsible citizen. But what are we to make of recurrent contemporaneous discrepancies? May they not signal lasting conflicts? Perhaps the poet even indicates that his contribution to literature excludes a straightforward view of the human condition. This may be a hypothesis well worth pursuing.

Even more than other classical authors, Propertius has been the property of specialists—for many decades and often to the exclusion of any overall interpretations of his poetry. The reasons for this situation are only too understandable and, therefore, not easily swept aside: Propertius is considered one of the most difficult authors who wrote in Latin, and the manuscript tradition, which has carried his elegies through the centuries down to our times, offers a text which is often doubtful and mutilated beyond repair. Some readers may indeed agree that—as one editor put it—there are as many Propertiuses as there have been editors of his text.

Unreliable text and difficult language: this combination can have the improbable effect of two dynamos inducing each other. One need only think of the two branches of scholarship that are primarily invited to deal with this type of situation. The former is generally called textual criticism, while the latter is probably best characterized by the name of a lexicographical institution: *Thesaurus Linguae Latinae*. Both disciplines, by the nature of their methods and the way they define their objects, display a tendency to concentrate on certain aspects of scholarly and poetical crafts-

ix

manship. Their attitudes are on occasion conducive in themselves to constituting a field of research which appears self-supporting and self-sufficient to those who plough it. (A few critics in this area of linguistic and textual difficulties have been known to develop such self-confident skill that they ventured to fill supposed gaps in the transmitted poems by interpolated verses of their own.)

Such an enclosure is never easily opened from the outside. In the special case of Propertian studies, scholarship itself for a long time blocked an important road to broader understanding by trying to apply historical categories to an important literary phenomenon. Since not a few of Propertius' central poems take an autobiographical form, they were occasionally exploited by adepts of this approach as a sort of quarry from which one might take solid cornerstones for constructing an objective calendar biography of the author's life and love (hi)story. Where the "solution" of such (and similar) problems promises the prizes of scholarship, a poet's entire work may be limited to a kind of closed-circuit reception.

Although some classicists began many years ago to distrust the utterly historical (historistic) orientation of our discipline, we cannot even today claim to be thoroughly aware of the degree to which it permeates our work (a glance at the latest commentaries on Greek and Roman authors proves very revealing). But we should also be aware that we can hardly do any reliable work in our field without making use (however careful) of the tools historistic research has supplied. (We may even one day welcome our traditions as a dike against the tidal waves of fashion in literary criticism.) Craftsmanship is an aspect of literature which was less problematical to ancient authors and was more of a natural prerequisite for writing in their eyes than it is to our time with its annual consumers' book fairs. Publishing less than a hundred elegies (and nothing else) in more than twelve years (as Propertius did) might seem as preposterous by our contemporary standards as spending nearly thirty years of research and writing on a war of about as many years, and nevertheless leaving behind (as Thucydides did) an unfinished work of two rather slim volumes. To assume from these circumstances, however, that either Propertius or Thucydides would have been content to be judged solely or primarily according to standards of literary or scholarly craftsmanship, would be a judgment that reveals less about the author than about the interpreter.

The present book will not be prefaced by yet another hermeneutical theory. It is devoted to one author and wishes to serve him, i.e., the understanding of his poetry, in the times in which today's readers live and this interpreter works, and in which Propertian scholarship is parallel, in some respects, with research done on other authors but displays many features peculiar to itself. A general theory could easily miss the individual author. In fact, it seems that generalization and systematization constitute merits as well as dangers which are characteristic of Propertian studies and their tradition, part of which I outlined above. We possess a considerable number of works with titles such as "Propertius and X," where X means a certain generic entity, e.g., *Properz und das Griechische Epigramm*. We are thus more or less well informed about the poet's use of or relation to, say, meter, epithets, forms of addressing an elegy's recipient, *recusatio* poetry, the gnomic character of the last distich in his elegy, the possessive pronoun, the tradition of Latin poetic language, etc. It could easily be shown how this type of research endangers the individual poetical pronouncement by subsuming it under (and explaining it from) what is supposed to be the poet's general procedure with regard to a certain phenomenon of language. This type of research even can occasionally endanger the poet's whole individuality by measuring his genius in reference to his contribution to (or even participation in) the development and growth of "Latin poetical language". All lexicographical and semantical research into a poet's language is meritorious, but, by its cross-referencing and its search for parallels, it constantly runs the risk of leveling the individual passage with the bulldozer of *index verborum* or concordance. Advanced experts in stylistic research do admit that the speech level (e.g., elevated or low) of a word should be determined by context, and a corresponding statement can be made about research on imagery and semantics. The natural consequence (although I myself do not approach the problems of overall interpretation from this angle) would be the demand that the scholar's uppermost standard be—wherever possible—the complete context of the particular entity or poetical unit which his poet has chosen himself, i.e., in Propertius' case, the single elegy.

But though one can easily find a title such as *Motivkatalog der römischen Elegie*, one cannot find a book on the context and organization of Propertian elegies that would sufficiently and satisfactorily respect the individual elegy. This situation seemed to be one good reason for writing the present book. But the main reason was my repeated experience in reading Propertius of the emphasis placed on an elegy's logical (or even illogical) organization and the clear determination of its parts by the intelligible structure of the whole elegy.

It is my conviction that, by referring my interpretations to the yardstick of an elegy's whole movement of thought, I am able to open (and sometimes reopen) a road of access for my reader which will lead him to central aspects of Propertius' poetry. But apart from performing this service, I hope also to establish a methodological basis for a critical dialogue with my readers: by providing an outline of the disposition of each elegy I interpret in detail, I wish to give those who agree with me a clear summary of my results, and those who disagree the opportunity of defining easily and precisely the point of departure from which a discussion of our disagreement should begin.

Although, for the sake of methodological clarity, I lay emphasis on the train of thought in Propertius' elegies, I do not myself try to introduce a dogma about prevailing structural patterns: this would run the same risk of sacrificing the individual to the general that I pointed out before in speaking of another area of research. In fact, Propertius shows himself to be aware of the problem of patterns as well as of the poetical possibilities they offer. Sometimes he takes pains to build up a long, balanced, even structure—only to break the symmetry by inserting one "odd" distich towards the end. It can be shown that by this procedure he is able to incorporate and describe in his poetry even such things as escape the grasp of a classifying and ordering scheme. Thus the violation of a form which he has built up himself may free him from static description and allow him to make life itself—e.g., the unbalanced thoughts of a worried human mind—a subject for his poetry. A given structure is no end in itself to Propertius but is subordinated to the movement of thought and, as a flexible tool, serves to express meaning. It is, accordingly, in many instances wrong for textual criticism to remove "odd" distichs from their position in the transmitted text and try to insert them elsewhere. A prerequisite for determining the function of any "irregular" distich or group of distichs is a firm grasp of an elegy's whole train of thought. In seeking to attain this, I hope to show that logical connection is much more cogent and plays a more important role in Propertius than is usually assumed.

As my reader will have gathered so far, by referring to an elegy's overall structure as my main tool of orientation I do not wish to exclude, or even unduly limit, any of the traditional tools we possess to approach a text. On the contrary, I would like to dissolve barren rigidities of method and reintegrate them into the task of interpretation. In order to keep this book within readable size, however, I cannot avoid abbreviation and selection. Both contribute to the cause of clear presentation.

Abbreviation has been achieved by compressing the results of textual criticism, linguistic investigation, and traditional commentary into the translations I give of most poems interpreted in detail. The translations are not open-ended but definite and interpretative; they stay as close to the Latin text as it is possible to do without making them unintelligible to the English-speaking reader. This closeness serves two purposes: (a) it is designed to help nonspecialists and students find access to the precise but difficult Latin wording; for their convenience, I have often expanded Propertian brevity by inserting helpful additions in pointed brackets; (b) it is meant to tell the scholar and specialist from the beginning which competing explanation of a given passage I accept. The edition used is Barber's Oxford Classical Text (1960[2]), and readings different from his are listed at the end of each translation. Material contained in the standard commentaries and handbooks of Propertian scholarship is presupposed and is explicitly referred to only when this proves helpful to my own argumentation.

Citation in such instances is mostly by the author's last name only (Shackleton Bailey = SB, Butler and Barber = BB, Camps, Enk, Postgate, Rothstein, Schmeisser, Tränkle).

The number of elegies selected for detailed interpretation has been kept small in order to allow a thorough treatment of the single elegy. The principle of selection has been the interpreter's view both of what is central in Propertius' poetry and of what most urgently needs interpretation for the contemporary reader (whether or not he is a specialist). Both views are open to debate, of course, and it is left to the reader to pass judgment as the book proceeds on the reasons I offer for my selections.

In conclusion I should like to state two points: first, I do not wish to pose as my reader's legal guardian and to exercise judgment for him. All I try to do is to open a way of approach to Propertius' poems and to supply the means for understanding the poet's concerns. In practice this means that I dedicate a large part of my studies to Propertius' first book, the *Monobiblos*, because I have convinced myself that in this book the poet has already envisaged with brilliance and extraordinary intelligence the possibilities as well as the limitations of his life's career—as a poet and as a human being; his early clear-sightedness is what gives the tragic tinge to his later attempts at escape. Having understood his beginnings, we are able to follow him all the way.

Secondly: I felt that it is not desirable to trace once more, as has been done often enough, the slowly declining curve of a once high-flown love all through to its desperate end and—perhaps—even rebirth (moving as this may be); nor did it seem enlightening to depict again the aesthetic development the poet underwent from implicitly Alexandrian beginnings to the open claim to be a Roman Callimachus, and to insist on a political conversion that allegedly went with this development. I have rather, in the second part of my book, preferred to point to the continuity of a tragic constellation (with its "stars" Cynthia and Octavian) which affects even the few periods of happiness the poet professes to have seen in his life. He attests and points to this from the first to the fourth book of his elegies, although with growing caution—and possibly with growing humiliation over the compromises he was making. But the dilemma's continuation may have been as well a criterion for himself that the same suffering being he had always been was still there and alive, and that he had preserved his identity.

The horns of the dilemma have already been well defined by the setting he gives the elegies of the *Monobiblos*. The opening poem and the epilogue, each written in the form of an autobiographical account, cover each a decisive experience of his young life: his torturing love for Cynthia and the massacre of Perusia. To recognize the meaning of these events, we have to allow that they did play a meaningful part in his life, and must believe that, as the reality of the Perusine War is attested by historians, so Cynthia is not so much of a fiction that all the poems which mention her are about the love poetry of a certain Gallus rather than about a personal concern of Propertius.

A few words about the notes are in order. Since my intention in writing the book has been to make access to Propertius easier, the text is designed to be intelligible in itself, and discussion of scholarly opinions has been excluded from the argument as far as this is possible. The book may be read without the notes.

But the more my own methodological position emerges from chapter to chapter, I increasingly add brief accounts of interpretations differing from my own. In this way, I am often able to point out at an earlier stage what consequences will later result (and the reasons why they will result) from a given approach for an overall picture of Propertius' poetry. At the same time, by discussing early a road that may later turn out to be a cul-de-sac, I can both throw my own method into relief and serve my reader's interest in Propertian criticism. For this procedure allows him to have alternative interpretations in mind all the way along with my own argument given in the text. The body of notes in itself forms a companion piece to the book, critically reviewing influential positions held in Propertian scholarship during the last eighty-five or so years. (If a reader judges that one or another work of the most recent years is not sufficiently accounted for, I ask his indulgence for my having found it difficult to keep up with today's rate of publications on Propertius. I am afraid that keeping the discussion in every chapter completely up-to-date would have meant either neglecting the day-to-day duties of our profession or never publishing this monograph at all.)

It remains to express my gratitude for advice received. Professor A. Thomas Cole patiently guided and corrected my early attempts at writing a book in his native language. Miss M. Hubbard, unfailing in her readiness to discuss problems, and Professor M. C. J. Putnam willingly took it upon themselves to help with the final version. In between, other colleagues and friends showed a kind interest. Thus I am further grateful to Professors C. O. Brink, E. Burck, H. Cherniss, J. F. Gilliam, C. J. Herington, W. Ludwig, and to Dr. F. H. Mutschler. I must admit that I have not always followed the good advice I received. The more grateful I am for the indulgence shown to my obstinacy. The mistakes and errors the reader may find in this book are truly mine. Sincere thanks go to Mr. Charles Boggess for his indefatigable patience in checking out references and weeding out errors in quoting, as well as to Mr. Wesley Scott for his help in preparing the typescript, especially the bibliography, for print.

The work could not have been completed without the support it has received from several institutions. Unforgotten is the hospitality of the American Academy in Rome (opening a research leave from Yale University). Two years of membership at the Institute for Advanced Study in Princeton (1974–75 and 1980–81), supported by Fellowships of the John Simon Guggenheim Memorial Foundation and the National Endowment for the Humanities, provided the crucial opportunity for undisturbed scholarly *otium*. In recent years, my work has received generous support from the University of Pittsburgh. Here a special acknowledgment is due to the never failing resourcefulness of Dean J. Rosenberg. To the University of California Press I am obliged for undertaking to publish a large volume in times that do not favor the Classics.

Fox Chapel, Pennsylvania, August 1983   H.P.S.

For advice and help during production of the book I am sincerely indebted to the Editorial Director and members of the Press: William J. McClung, Phyllis Killen, Mary Lamprech, Marilyn Schwartz. Special thanks go to my sponsoring editor, Doris Kretschmer, for patiently guiding the book (and its author) through the complexities of the publication process.

ABBREVIATIONS

Important works cited by special abbreviations:

LEADING EDITIONS

Barber = Barber, E. A. *Sexti Properti carmina*. Scriptorum classicorum bibliotheca Oxoniensis. 2d ed. Oxford, 1960. (All quotations are from this edition except where indicated otherwise. This text is customarily also referred to as OCT.)

Hanslik = Hanslik, R. *Sex. Propertii elegiarum libri IV*. Bibliotheca scriptorum Graecorum et Romanorum Teubneriana. Leipzig, 1979.

OCT   See Barber.

Schuster = Schuster, M. *Sex. Propertii elegiarum libri IV*. Bibliotheca scriptorum Graecorum et Romanorum Teubneriana. Leipzig, 1954. (This edition was taken care of—*postuma cura fungens*, p. XIX—by F. Dornseiff.)

Schu.-Do. = Schuster, M. *Sex. Propertii elegiarum libri IV*. Bibliotheca scriptorum Graecorum et Romanorum Teubneriana. 2d ed. edited by F. Dornseiff. Leipzig, 1958.

EDITIONS AND COMMENTARIES

BB = Butler, H. E., and E. A. Barber. *The Elegies of Propertius*. Reprint. Hildesheim, 1969.

Camps = Camps, W. A. *Propertius. Elegies. Book I*, Cambridge, 1961. 2d ed. 1966. *Book II*, Cambridge, 1967. *Book III*, Cambridge, 1966. *Book IV*, Cambridge, 1965.

Enk = Enk, P. J. *Sex. Propertii elegiarum liber I (Monobiblos)*. 2 vols. Leiden, 1946.

Enk = Enk, P. J. *Sex. Propertii elegiarum liber secundus*. 2 vols. Leiden, 1962.

Fedeli = Fedeli, P. *Properzio. Elegie. Libro IV.* Bari, 1965.

Hertzberg = Hertzberg, G. A. B. *Sex. Aurelii Propertii elegiarum libri quattuor.* 3 vols. Halle, 1843–45.

Lachmann = Lachmann, C. *Sex. Aurelii Properti carmina.* Leipzig, 1816.

Paley = Paley, F. A. *Sex. Aurelii Propertii carmina. The Elegies of Propertius.* London, 1872.

Postgate = Postgate, J. P. *Select Elegies of Propertius.* 2d ed. 1884. Reprint. London, 1968.

Richardson = Richardson, L., Jr. *Propertius. Elegies I–IV.* The American Philological Association Series of Classical Texts. Norman, Okla., 1976.

Rothstein = Rothstein, M. *Die Elegien des Sextus Propertius.* 3d ed. 2 vols. Dublin, 1966.

HANDBOOKS AND BIBLIOGRAPHIES

SB = Bailey, D. R. S. *Propertiana.* 2d ed. Amsterdam, 1967.

Harrauer = Harrauer, H. *A Bibliography to Propertius.* Bibliography to the Augustan Poetry, vol. 2. Hildesheim, 1973.

Phillimore = Phillimore, J. S. *Index verborum Propertianus.* 2d ed. Darmstadt, 1961.

Schmeisser = Schmeisser, B. *A Concordance to the Elegies of Propertius.* Hildesheim, 1970.

Smyth = Smyth, G. R. *Thesaurus Criticus ad Sexti Propertii Textum.* Leiden, 1970.

Tränkle = Tränkle, H. *Die Sprachkunst des Properz und die Tradition der lateinischen Dichtersprache.* Hermes Einzelschriften, 15. Wiesbaden, 1960.

PART

— I —

SETTING THE SCENE

I

BETRAYED LOVE: CHANGE OF IDENTITY

Eventually, this book will address a problem of timeless quality. Specifically, it will deal with a poet's difficulty in raising his unique personal voice in a publicly uniform and therefore homogenizing environment. Historically speaking, the problem touches upon the situation of a nonconformist under the rule of Emperor Augustus, telling of the individual's attempts to preserve his identity by carefully voicing his even most intimate personal concerns. In this respect, the following investigation addresses itself to readers who like to inquire into the recurrent modes of expression in which the *condition humaine* manifests itself over the centuries.

But it will be a long road before the lasting aspects of Propertius' poetry can thus be laid open before the reader's eyes. Questions about his work's literary organization, about the poet's own concerns below the surface of traditional forms, about his personal background and political attitude will have to be answered first as the investigation gradually, chapter by chapter, approaches his central dilemma.

In addition, there are problems resulting from the history of Propertian scholarship itself, which influence and determine the interpreter's presentation. Since our author is best known as the poet of his unhappy love, it would seem only natural to commence where he commences. For in the first line of the first poem of his work (1.1.1), Propertius introduces himself as unhappy in consequence of his love (*miserum me*) and goes on to explain his condition. This elegy, however, although it is placed at the beginning of the book and speaks of the poet's first year of unrequited love for Cynthia, is generally understood to be not an early work but a programmatical prospectus of the *Monobiblos* as a whole, composed for this opening place at a time when publication of the book was in sight. As such, the poem has appeared to many interpreters to be more general in its diagnosis and therefore more difficult than many other elegies, which claim to depict single events in Propertius' love for Cynthia. Its understanding is so obstructed by several unsolved problems of interpretation that it seems to have lost for some contemporary scholars its function of introducing Propertius to his reader.[1]

Accordingly, I shall turn to poems 11 and 12 of Book 1 for an initial elucidation of the unhappiness which the poet conceives of as an indelible characteristic of himself. Here we find a special instance of his unhappiness: Propertius is concerned about the possibility of unfaithfulness on Cynthia's part. And this concern will lead us right into the center of his very existence.

Although nobody would now attempt to arrange Propertius' poems so as to form a chronological record of an autobiographical love story (or history), which he once was supposed to tell about himself and Cynthia, there is no doubt that the poet sometimes does refer to a sequence in time, to one situation which takes place earlier (or later) than another situation, and that he presents such a sequence by a pairing of separate poems, which the reader is asked to see in relation to each other. It would be odd to deny such a technique to Propertius for the only reason that concern with chronological sequence has led to pseudohistorical attempts to gain historical data from poetical situations. If the poet chooses, for example, to present the full impact of the change from (earlier) love to (later) betrayal as it occurs for the first time, the sequence of situations is of the highest poetical importance—no matter when and how it happened historically, and no matter how scholars may have tried to exploit it for biographical data.

1.11

While you, Cynthia, are lingering on in the midst of Baiae,
    where the causeway built by Heracles stretches along the shore,
and while, at another time,[2] you are wondering at the waters
    bordering on noble Miseni[3] that are subjected to Thesprotus'
                           realm,
does concern come over you, ah! to spend nights mindful of me?
    Is there room left for me in a remote corner of your heart?

Or has some unknown enemy, by simulated ardor,
    carried you away, Cynthia, from ⟨your place in⟩ my poems?   (1–8)

Would that a small boat, trusting to its tiny oars,
    were detaining you on the Lucrine lake,
or that the water were holding you enclosed in Teuthras' thin wave,
    —the water, willing to give way to your alternating arms,

—this rather than that there were an ample opportunity for you to
        listen to the flattering whispers of another man,
    softly stretched on the silent beach,
—as is the rule: once the guardian is removed, the girl lapses,
    and, faithlessly, no longer keeps in mind the gods by whom
                        both have sworn.   (9–16)

⟨I say all this⟩ not because I have not recognized you as a girl of proven
                                reputation,
    but because, in this field, I fear any amorous attention paid to you.
Thus you will forgive me if my letters will have
    brought you something sad: that will be the fault of my fear.
Ah, not more anxious is the protection I give my dear mother!
    Or would I, without you, have any concern for my own life?
You and only you, Cynthia, are my home, you and only you my
                                parents,
    you are every moment of my joy!   (17–24)

Whether I appear sad to my friends, or, on the contrary, joyful
    —whatever I shall be, I shall say: "Cynthia has been the cause."(25–26)

You only leave corrupted Baiae as soon as possible:
    to many lovers these shores meant separation
—shores that had been hostile to chaste girls:
    Oh, may the waters of Baiae perish, the stains on Love!   (27–30)

Readings different from OCT: 21: *ah mihi non*; exclamation mark following *matris*. 28: *dabant*.

As the grouping of lines in my translation indicates, I have concluded that the poem's structural unit is the eight-line or four-distich (4D) section, of which we find three instances: lines 1–8, 9–16, 17–24. If we consider this larger unit (4D) to consist of two halves comprising four lines or two distichs (2D) each, we may include lines 27–30 (=2D) as another example of the smaller unit; but then our interpretation will have to account for the exceptional two lines = one distich (1D) at 25/26 and the apparently irregular subdivision of lines 1–8 into 1–6 (3D) and 7/8 (1D). The reader may, with some justification, object that these difficulties are weighty enough to ruin the proposed structure of the poem. And he may well add that there are only too many Propertian poems which do not show a balanced number of distichs, and that attempts to schematize his poems (and books) have seldom shown acceptable results.

    Difficulties of another kind arise when we consult commentaries on the first six lines of the poem, especially 3 and 4. The "realm of Thesprotus" (a mythical king of Epirus in Greece, in whose country an entrance to the underworld was located) presumably refers here to the region where tradition located the Italian entrance to the underworld—in itself an easy transposition of myths from Greece to Italy. But commentators are vexed by a geographical problem: the Italian "realm of Thesprotus" would be the volcanic *campi Phlegraei* (with Lake Avernus) north of Baiae and even north of the Bay of Puteoli. But how, commentators ask, can Propertius say that these *campi* dominate the waters "next to *Miseni*" if Misenum, city as well as promontory, lies *south* of Baiae? Fantastic attempts have been made to remove the contradiction. All (except, I think, Rothstein, who probably did not make himself clear enough) missed the simple solution because they failed to subordinate their search for factual and textual evidence to the expressed thought of the poem and its logical development.

As far as contents are concerned, the first four distichs ask alternative questions: "Are you, while staying at Baiae, still thinking of me or are you not?" The second alternative (7/8) is posed in terms much easier to understand, although it too moves on two different levels with a poetical economy and brevity which is typical of Propertius' linguistic achievements: love and poetry are inseparably connected in Propertius' world, so that he can mention only one of the two and yet mean both of them. By choosing the second here (Cynthia is, possibly, no longer the object of his poetry) he avoids the bluntness of saying that Cynthia (excusingly envisaged not to be the active part, anyway, in this case) may have proved unworthy of his love. Moreover, the choice of poetry could serve, if not as a threat (as in 2.5.3–8), at least as a reminder that her fame depends on the poet's willingness or ability to immortalize her, as in the old argument from epic (implied in 3.1.21–34) that without a Homer the Trojan War and its heroes would long have been forgotten. A third dimension, beyond those of love and poetry, is introduced by *hostis*: only an enemy, unknown to Propertius, might approach Cynthia, and his feelings cannot be honest ones— *simulatis ignibus* (7). True love for Cynthia, claims Propertius, can be felt by himself only; all other men are a priori to be suspected, even discredited. Thus he implicitly warns Cynthia that she can only lose, not gain, from turning to another man. The implied clear-cut distribution of good and evil motives between Propertius, on the one hand, and all other men, on the other, will scarcely convince the impartial reader, and it is not supposed to: the outlook of this poem is distorted by the lover's fear of losing his beloved. Naturally, he now favors (and wishes her to share) a view which would make him the only reliable (and therefore indispensable) factor in a world which is otherwise deceitful to her. The viewpoint of this poem is not objective; its mood is biased; the author's imagination is tinged by fear: so much can be said already without distorting the intention of the couplet 7/8.

In lines 1–6 we expect to find the other alternative in the double question (*Ecquid—an?*), the one more favorable to Propertius: Cynthia may, while absent, still be faithful to him. Instead, we get a grammatically complicated and stylistically elevated description of her stay "in the midst of" (and around) Baiae, that fashionable, sinful, ill-reputed resort. We feel his fear: does she behave as "one" does at Baiae? With his inner eye, he imagines things she is doing, reasons why she hesitates (*cessantem*) to come back to Rome: there, right on the sea, and battered by sounding waves (cf. 3.18.4), is the famous causeway (on which she may be walking or driving—in whose chariot?); or, farther away from Baiae, she may go sight-seeing (in whose company?) and admire the vistas (*mirantem*). Again, to Propertius' sorrow, her mind is fully occupied by what she sees. Clearly, the poet here thinks of some special, absorbing, magnificent view, one which might make her forget that he is waiting in Rome. Therefore, I think that he describes the view one has when standing on the top of, or when climbing only some way up to, the mountain of Cape Misenum, south of Baiae, looking north towards Baiae and Puteoli; the "sea (*aequora*) next to *Miseni*" is "subjected to" (cf. Tib. 4.1.67) the realm of Thesprotus, or appears to "lie at the foot of" the volcanic landscape behind and above it. There is no geographical difficulty in the text[4] if we understand its intention. When the lover tries to ask himself whether Cynthia still thinks of him while at Baiae, his imagination is carried away by the many distractions which Baiae itself and its surroundings offer—and by the unacknowledged, unadmitted fear that not these distractions but another man is the reason why she does not come back: geography disguises emotion. Thus, when he finally sets out to reformulate his question (*ecquid* 1 ~ *ecquis* 6), he asks no longer for her love, but only for a "remainder" (*restat*) of it in a "corner of her heart" (*in extremo . . . amore*, 6).[5] Logically speaking, Propertius has managed to ask an alternative "either-or" question (*ecquid—an*) with both parts of the alternative on the same negative side. Emotionally speaking, that means he cannot convince himself that, in the midst of so many distractions, her heart belongs to him. Poetically, it means that he cannot bring himself to write down the positive side of the alternative; it turns out negatively, once he tries to imagine the circumstances at Baiae. The impression evoked by lines 7/8, that fear rules the writer's views, is confirmed by our analysis of lines 1–6.

Propertius utilizes even the number of distichs employed to paint his picture of the lover in fear of being deserted. While the other two 4D units (9–16; 17–24) are, as will be shown, subdivided in the middle (2D/2D), the first 4D unit (1–8), which could so easily have been divided into two equal halves ("either-or"), is divided in the ratio 3D/1D. The unit is apparently out of balance—as are its contents: the lover can easily believe in and formulate his unhappiness (7/8), but he finds it difficult and has to try twice to write down that Cynthia still cares for him (1–6). For him, the question seems answered in the negative before he has really asked it. The unbalanced ratio of distichs helps to elucidate the lover's unbalanced state of mind and thought and confirms the general applicability in this poem of the 2D/2D rule.

One of the results of our interpretation so far is that Propertius wishes to give us, not a static description, but a means of participating in the worried lover's actual process of thinking or imagining as, step by step, one association follows another and makes him feel more and more certain about his growing, unconfirmed suspicions. The next 4D unit (9–16) shows the same development. It, too, is structured in two different parts, though of equal length. The first half (9–12) contains a wish (Cynthia rowing and swimming) which the faraway lover would like to see fulfilled. The second half (Cynthia on the beach, listening to the seducer, with no one else present, etc., 13–16) describes something which the lover wishes not to happen. So far, the division into a positive and a negative wish seems clear. But we have to understand how, by the way he formulates them, Propertius again makes the negative alternative the more certain one, and the positive a sort of *adynaton*. He himself is not present at Baiae, but Cynthia certainly needs a custodian; so he envisages lifeless objects to take over this function. A rowing boat is asked to "detain" (*moretur*) her on the Lucrine lake, and the water in which she swims should "hold her enclosed in waves" (*teneat clausam . . . in unda*); no doubt, the intention both times is to prevent her by such occupations from making other men's acquaintance, but in both cases Propertius suggests the substitute custodian's lack of power to control Cynthia's will. The "small" rowing boat which is said to "trust" its "tiny" ladies' oars would be subject to Cynthia's will rather than vice versa; and the small waves (*tenui* = "thin" or "liquid") that are supposed to "enclose" (*clausam*) her will hardly hinder her either (the alliteration *teneat—tenui* points to the paradox). They themselves are a product of Cynthia's movements: circles of waves surrounding her. Nor will the water[6] have a tight grip on her (*teneat*), for it is willing to give way to her alternating hand (*alternae facilis cedere lympha manu*), i.e., it allows her to go in whichever direction she is willing to go. Propertius' representatives at Baiae seem to be much weaker than any imaginable rival. Again, his case is lost even before he describes the negative side.

And the negative alternative (13–16) has strong arguments speaking for it: not only would there be present opportunity (*vacet*) opposed to the earlier, futile wish for restraint (*moretur, teneat*); not only do flattery (*blandos*) and relaxation (*molliter . . . compositam*) play their part; not only is the beach imagined as being silent (*tacito*: nobody is around), and the seducer, nevertheless, as whispering (*susurros*: he must be close to her, his mouth next to her ear!)—but, above all: as experience tells, this is a general rule (*solet*): girls do forget their lover when he is absent. With this last distich, lines 15/16 (which Housman should never have tried to push out of its place), the lover reaches the climax of his lonely worries: the general rule, under which he subsumes Cynthia, gives him that degree of sad certainty which he feared from the outset but could not reach without outside

8

confirmation from Baiae; now, reflection on the nature of woman has helped him to a conclusion.

The result seems absurd, and one which only a person deeply in love and deeply apprehensive is able to arrive at (Propertius appears only too well acquainted with this state of mind). The gap between uncontrolled imagination and confirmed reality is wide open, because even a general law of probability (*solet*) cannot grant the same certainty as does eyewitness evidence. Propertius' suspicion, with imagined details (mouth close to ear) and the implied judgment (*perfida*), is close to an unjustified a priori condemnation of Cynthia, and, as such, puts a heavy guilt on his shoulders. This is the turning point of the poem. After his uncontrolled imagination has led him as far away from Cynthia as possible, he now realizes the irresponsibility of his suspicions and sets out to move in the opposite direction, back to and closer to Cynthia. The suspicion, however, can never be fully eradicated, and will finally disrupt the balance of the poem again.

The new movement is again presented in a 4D unit (17–24), subdivided into equal halves. In the first half, the lover rules out the possibility that any of his suspicions are founded in reality (her reputation is firmly established), thus taking back the condemnation of Cynthia which the logic of the foregoing unit had implied. He now acknowledges the difference between imagining and reality, and puts the blame on his imaginative fear (*timetur*, 18, and *timoris*, 20, bind the first two distichs together),[7] so that the *culpa* is solely his. As, however, his fear is nothing but an expression and by-product of his love, he feels entitled to ask her pardon: *ignosces igitur*, we read here for the first time (19), in a wording that reminds us of Catullus (68.31), and of which we will be reminded again, when Propertius will cancel even worse rumors about Cynthia—*omnia me laedent: timidus sum (ignosce timori)*, 2.6.13. If, therefore, his letters to Baiae show something of his depression (*quid . . . triste*, 19),[8] this is a token of his intense love, and may even be welcomed by her (for no reality corresponds to his fears).

Now, however, a new fear overcomes him: once expressed, his suspicions may have given Cynthia the impression that his love has cooled off to some degree. To counter such an untrue impression—or just to expose the roots of his fear—he now feels urged to reassure her of the high rank she possesses in his feelings, and so bursts out into a beautiful, unrestrained confession of his love. Not only does he care for her more than for his dear mother and his own life, but she is all tender human relationships together, every occasion of happiness for him; she is for him, the dependent and fearful lover, what strong Hector is for the otherwise unprotected Andromache (Homer, *Il.* 6.429; cf. Cat. 72.3f). His vulnerability lies open before our eyes, stressed by the reversal of the traditional roles of male and female lover. But what still rings in our ears is, of course, the last line of 21–24, with its stress on gladness: *omnia tu nostrae tempora laetitiae!* (24)— thus compensating any negative impression evoked by 9–16 and the *triste* produced by his fears.

The poem could easily end now with the last 2D unit (27–30). Cynthia is implored on her part to dissociate herself from Baiae, the place which is so hostile to true love. The renewed expression of Baiae's dangers (*discidium, castis inimica puellis, crimen amoris*) could then be ascribed to a fear that is again rising but need no longer be due to suspicion or implicit condemnation; the fear would be, as stated in 17–20, an expression of his love: "purified" fear, so to speak. But it would be even easier, taking notice of the stress on *tu* in *tu modo quam primum corruptas desere Baias,* to interpret as follows: But you, a girl of established reputation and the object of my love, leave a place which is so alien to your character, i.e., bring your outward life into harmony with your inner self by returning to Rome and to me. This would seem a natural consequence of the development which the lover's thoughts have undergone. And it would be, on the whole, a balanced structure if three 4D units, built on the idea of two halves of 2D each, were concluded by the smaller 2D unit. However, this pattern is disturbed by the insertion of one distich (25/26) which gives the whole poem a new twist.

What strikes us first in this distich is the appearance of other people. Hitherto, the poem as a whole has been a personal address to Cynthia; now Propertius suddenly introduces the impressions which third persons may have of him. In this context *amici*, friends, is a rather indefinite group. It may comprise persons addressed in other poems of the first book, such as Tullus, the career politician, Gallus, the deceptive lover, Ponticus, the epic poet. It may even include those who are kind enough to take an interest in Propertius' ever-changing situation, i.e., his readers. Thus this distich is the point of departure from which the private address of the lover to his beloved becomes the public presentation of Propertius, poet of his love. This can, with a high degree of certainty, be inferred from the second half of the pentameter. *Cynthia causa fuit* is the first of a series of sententious coinings, through which the poet tries to pinpoint the core of his love in ever more precise, ever more refined, ever more chiseled formulations. (One of them will be encountered in the following elegy, addressed to an anonymous critic.)

In this distich, Propertius' appearance outside the context of his relationship with Cynthia is certainly startling, but so is the fact that it is not only the loudly ringing word *laetitiae* of the foregoing line which is echoed here (by *laetus*, 25). His depressions (*triste*, 19), which we were led to think of as overcome—overcome because they were unfounded in reality—are considered again as a true possibility:

> seu tristis veniam seu contra laetus amicis,
>   quicquid ero, dicam: Cynthia causa fuit.

Clearly, it is not ruled out here that Cynthia may at some future time be the cause of his depression. Realization of this could lead the reader to a gloomier evaluation of the poem's ending as well as of the eight lines (17–24) that moved from a refutation of suspicion and even *tristitia* to a proclamation of Cynthia's omnipotent meaning in Propertius' life and so to *laetitia*. I would like to see the distich 25/26 as a sort of epilogue to the 4D unit 17–24. The movement of thought from *tristitia* to *laetitia* has led the lover to realize his total dependence upon another human being's behavior. What if that person loses interest in him? It is a possibility, no more; but it has been envisaged. The "odd" distich in the poem's structure contains the key to those aspects that point beyond the situation depicted and fixed in the poem.

Without any attempt to generalize, I would claim that it is impossible to evaluate the movement of thought in this poem without defining the groups of distichs that contain the steps by which the poet's mind proceeds. I would like to emphasize two things: (1) There is a basic structural "unit" or "measure" in this poem, which can be identified several times. We may doubt whether we should define it as the larger 4D unit or as the 2D unit, the subdivision of the former. The latter is used more often by Propertius, and appears in his most elaborate later poems, such as the "elegy" on the death of Cornelia, 4.11. (2) Although the number of distichs which form a group or a subgroup tends to be the same and to occur repeatedly, there is no tyranny of scheme here, and, accordingly, there is no room for any game of numbers on the interpreter's part. Number is not independent, or even autonomous, or the author's goal, but is subordinated to the movement of thought and contributes to a clear presentation of the latter. Thus, when the lover's mind deviates from a clear-cut account of his situation to the unplanned elaboration of one of two alternatives, the deviation can be reflected in the number and order of distichs (the 3:1 ratio of lines 1–8). In the same way, when a certain train of thought leads to the realization of unexpected but vital and far-reaching consequences, this can be underlined by the addition of an "odd" distich [10] (lines 25/26). The poetical gain from such a procedure in the case of our elegy is obvious. The poet can do more than present well-formulated results; he can let us participate in the development of his thoughts, as they are influenced by love and fear, or whatever. His poem depicts this worried development, i.e., it reflects life. With the above in mind, one may

find it helpful to have the bare skeleton of the poem's structure before
one's eyes:

A   1–8: Worried double question addressed to Cynthia.

       a)   1–6: favorable alternative: do you still care
               for me?   3D ⎫

       b)   7–8: negative alternative (of higher proba-   ⎬ 4D
               bility): have you forgotten me?   1D ⎭

B   9–16: Double wish.

       a)   9–12: positive: would that Cynthia would di-
            vert herself by rowing and swimming!   2D ⎫

       b) 13–16: negative (of higher probability): would   ⎬ 4D
            that Cynthia would not be with other
            men!   2D ⎭

C 17–24: Address of recantation.

       a) 17–20: please, pardon my love for being fear-
            ful and therefore suspicious!   2D ⎫

       b) 21–24: let me assure you: you are all I have!   2D ⎭ 4D

D 25–26: Statement of dependence: third persons will be
       asked to ascribe my moods to your conduct. | 1D   1D |

E 27–30: Urgent request: separate yourself from Baiae.   2D   2D

1.12

Why don't you stop raising the unjustified reproach of inactivity
                                     against me,
    because (you say) Rome, witness ⟨of my situation⟩, causes
                         me to procrastinate?   (1–2)

By as many miles is that woman separated from my bed
    as is the river Hypanis from the Venetian Eridanus;
and she neither fosters with her embrace my familiar feelings of love,
    nor does the name "Cynthia" sound sweet in my ear.   (3–6)

Once I was welcome: at that time it was not granted to anyone
    to be able to love with similar devotion (or: trust).
I was the object of envy: has not a god overwhelmed me? or does some
    herb gathered on Promethean mountain-ridges keep us apart?   (7–10)

I am not the one I had been ⟨before her love ceased⟩: a long
                      trip changes a woman's heart.
    How great a love has fled in a brief time!
Now that I am alone for the first time I have to learn how long the
                         nights are,
    and to be myself a nuisance to my own ears.   (11–14)

Happy he, who could weep in his girl's presence:
  Amor very much enjoys being sprinkled with tears;
or (happy) he who could, after being spurned, relocate his ardor:
  there are joys, too, when his servitude has been
                transferred ⟨to another woman⟩.   (15–18)

For me it is not right either to love another or to desist from this one:
  Cynthia was the first, Cynthia will be the end!   (19–20)

Readings different from OCT: 2: *faciat*; no comma (,) before and after *conscia Roma*; 6: no comma (,) after *Cynthia* (but after *amores*, 5); exclamation mark (!) at end of line 20.

The meaning of the first distich is much disputed, but its grammar and logic do yield a satisfactory sense. First, grammar: *faciat* in line 2 is subjunctive of indirect discourse and as such makes it clear that the whole *quod*-clause is part of the faultfinder's reasoning, not Propertius'. [11] This, in turn, makes it improbable that *conscia Roma* should be understood outside the clause's context as a vocative (e.g., Rome being invoked as Propertius' "confidante"); rather, *conscia*, too, is part of the reproach: Rome is a "witness" (or "aware") of Propertius' despicable affairs, i.e., there is open talk about him in the city!

Next, logic: *quod* gives the pentameter, which it introduces, a causal meaning, thus making its contents logically prior to the blame expressed in the hexameter; *because* Propertius hesitates to leave Rome where everyone talks about him, the faultfinder raises the charge of idling. We shall see that, with his usual precision, the poet will explicitly answer both the charge (5f.) and its premise (3f.).

Desidiae has been understood in different ways. Richardson believes that Propertius is being blamed for "'doing nothing', rather than pursuing Cynthia and trying to win her back," i.e., that he is being encouraged to be more active *as a lover*. [12] But this does not do justice to the usual component of social blemish in *desidia* (nor does it square with the context of lines 3ff.). *Desidia*, that alluring (but shameless) "Siren", must be avoided, says the Stoic zealot in Horace (*vitanda est improba Siren / Desidia*, *sat.* 2.3.14f.). Rather, *desidiae* may be taken here not only in general as unmanly, irresponsible inactivity, which contemporary Roman society will not tolerate in a male citizen, but also (with SB) [13] in the special meaning of dedicating oneself to a woman, i.e., being in love and nothing else. For a man of responsibility and dignity is not supposed to give a large portion of his life to playfulness and lighthearted amusements such as love.

Although both the general and the specific tendency of the word thus seem to be clear, some further remarks are in order. For the question arises whether Propertius, when being confronted with the charge, is on his part willing to share the faultfinder's common notion of *desidia* as a (sweet) temptation to be avoided. After all, he does not simply relate in detail the censurer's blame; he rejects it at the same time as unjustified and false (the

13

usual meaning implied in *fingere*). Since he is hardly denying what everybody in Rome knows, viz., that he is in love, he must mean something else. The alternative is that he denies the validity of the faultfinder's conclusion: "From the observation that I do not leave Rome, you must not infer that I am guilty of *desidia*—at least not of *desidia* as *you* understand the word." To him, love may be everything else but *dolce far niente* (see alone his negation of *dulcis* in line 6). This much we can say already without, at this point, going further into the logic of the passage.

The "parallels" adduced by commentators bring out the censurer's view. For an air of social irresponsibility and moral flaw surrounds the word: *desidia* is usually associated with *feriae, otium, languor, amor, inertia*, etc. Even an occasional surface exception to the contrary is fit to confirm this rule. Ovid, after giving a long list of "proofs" that a lover's life and toils are no less hard than a soldier's, resumes:

> Consequently, let whoever called love idleness, stop
> saying so!

> Ergo desidiam quicumque vocabat amorem,
> desinat!   (*Am.* 1.9.31f.)

Ovid's "proof" is sheer fun, of course, sneering at the established position of the soldier as well as mocking that strange creature called a lover. His poem is in fact lighthearted and does not really think of love as a potentially deadly experience. Rather, it confirms the conventional view of love as something not too serious.

This helps us to understand Propertius. He, too, sometimes compares his relation to Cynthia to military service (e.g., 1.6.30; 4.1.135–138), but he is more serious about this, in two ways: love does imply the possibility of suffering and even of death, and, therefore, is to him at least as serious and grave an experience as any of those which a socially established position and recognized career may demand from a man. As far as language is concerned, we may almost speak of a generation gap between Propertius and his somewhat younger friend Ovid. It was a difficult achievement for the older poet to find an adequate description of himself and his position with regard to a society that was newly reconsolidated and to its rigorous code of behavior, whereas the younger can take the inherited vocabulary for granted and use it according to his own talent for artistic virtuosity and playful irony. As far as attitude is concerned, we may also speak of a generation gap, keeping in mind that Propertius himself indicates reservation when he encounters a lighthearted and irresponsible approach towards love among his friends (cf. 1.13, an elegy admonishing Gallus). What the comparison with Ovid establishes is a surprising contrast: Ovid, the poet of erotic elegy, goes together with Propertius' censurer insofar as both show a light and playful attitude towards love. And this is what Propertius implicitly objects to when he refuses to be classified as an example of *desidia* in its usual meaning: his lack of activity is not *dolce far niente* (as his censurer may think), but rather suffering, a permanent paralysis (as he presents it in 1.1 and 1.6, for which see Chapters II and IV). Thus any patronizing advice of the traditional kind, such as "go to see other places so that you will forget your love and become an active member of society" (cf. 3.21.9f.), must hurt him deeply by its lack of understanding—as the rest of the distich (to which we now turn) bears out.

Such repeated (*non cessas*) tactlessness on the part of his self-appointed adviser explains the otherwise unaccountable tone of impatience and even irritation which characterizes the opening line and creates the impression that our poem is an angry retort provoked by a not very congenial friend: "Why don't you give up raising the unjustified charge of *dolce far niente* against me?" A "why don't you stop" question certainly shows no willingness to comply, and the poet's feeling of being annoyed cannot escape our ear. (If line 2 is supposed to echo the faultfinder's wording, Propertius may feel an additional taunt in the paronomastic sequence *ROMA—MORAM*.) We can thus appreciate his discretion in leaving his supposed censurer anonymous instead of calling him "Pontice" (as some conjecture-happy commentators, not recognizing what Ponticus stands for in Propertius' book—see our Chapter III—wish to write for *conscia*) or some other name. After all, an adviser who is being rebuffed while advocating society's claims is (both here and in 3.11; see Chapter X below) likely to feel more seriously about the poet's reaction than, say, friends "Bassus" (in 1.4) and "Gallus" (in 1.5) when being asked not to mingle in Propertius' love relationship. Several scholars, however, have felt that Propertius should be more consistent and *always* address the recipients of his poems *by name*. To ascertain such an unexceptional practice on the poet's part, some try to construe *Roma* (2) as a vocative. The result being linguistically not too attractive, SB (as well as Barber) has no scruples changing the transmitted text (from *faciat* to *facias*).

But it is questionable if this kind of mailman mentality ("no address without the addressee's name!") is rightly imputed to an author who (as we shall see) takes greater liberties elsewhere, as for instance in putting the traditional *sphragis* poem to new and highly personal use (1.22, Chapter V below); subordinating traditional literary elements to a new and individual purpose (1.18, Chapter IV); transforming a Greek epigram and integrating it into a new context not implied in its original design (1.1, Chapter II); etc. Philological desire for strict rules sometimes tends to smooth over ancient texts at the cost of their individuality.

Be that as it may, the identity of an obtrusive adviser is not what matters for the purpose of this poem. The point is rather that the lover's condition appears so manifestly shocking to a patronizing outsider that he can feel invited to interfere, pointing out to the advisee his situation as one of public embarrassment (*conscia Roma*). That gives a forceful background to the personal character of the poem. But the persons whose identities do matter in 1.12 are, as in 1.11, "Propertius" and "Cynthia." As it is generally recognized that our elegy is a supplement to the preceding one, it seems easiest (if an attempt at identification is desired at all) to take the addressee of 1.12 as one of the friends mentioned in 1.11.25. One might also think of the fatherly advisers mentioned in 1.1.25 and 3.24.9—unless the reader decides to hear the voice of an uncongenial general public here.

The most conspicuous change from poem 11 to poem 12 is indeed one which involves the addressee: in 11, third persons, like the friends of line 25, appeared as outsiders from the point of view of Propertius and Cynthia. Now, Propertius faces the outside world and its ways of judging: will it understand him? To judge from his irritation, the prospects are gloomy.

The irritation is not confined to the first line. (I wish to stress its continuance, as interpreters have expressed desire for more coherence between 1/2 and 3ff.) With poignant irony, Propertius reassures his adviser by imitating his conventional way of thinking:

(a) Do not worry! Although both Cynthia and I are in Rome, we are, geographically speaking, as many miles apart as you could ever wish me to travel; let us say, as far away as a river in the faraway East is away from our Po at home. This should satisfy your worries concerning my not leaving Rome: my presence here does not mean what you think it means (3/4).

(b) As to your (mistaken) conclusion about my alleged *dolce far niente*, again you may be reassured. Neither do I enjoy Cynthia's love any more (mine is not a *desidia* enjoying *consuetos . . . amores*), nor does her name sound sweetly (*dulcis*) in my ear [14] (in fact, it makes a bitter sound, causing *tristitia*, not *laetitia*, 5/6; cf. 1.11.25). Again you stand corrected.

Seen as an answer to the censurer's line of argument, lines 3–6 are a perfect match for lines 1/2. We are now in a position to show that the poet explicitly answers both the charge and the premise on which it is based. The chiasmus presenting reproach and retort helps to bring out the inherent logic: the geographical *quod*-clause (2), being logically prior, is answered first, by the mock-geographical argument (3/4). The false (*fingere*) reproach of *desidia* (1), logically a consequent, is dealt with later (5/6) when the censurer is informed that the love affair is over and, specifically, when the poet denies that any "sweetness" is left of it (*nec . . . dulcis* negates any pleasant ingredient the censurer might associate with his charge of *desidia*).

A provoked outburst can often bring more of the truth out into the open than a volunteered statement. We should feel the same about Propertius' retort: in relentless clarity, the two distichs (3–6) spell out his real situation. They can thus serve as a basis for self-communion.

The notion of "not any more" (*nec . . . consuetos nutrit . . . amores . . . nec . . . dulcis . . . sonat*) quite naturally leads to recollection of that past which no longer exists (7–10). It seems long ago (*olim*) now and like an especially gracious and favorable gift. Even the ability to love with utmost devotion was not something within reach of Propertius' conscious will-power. On the contrary, to nobody else "was there granted (*contigit*) the ability (*ut posset*) to love with similar devotion." Considering the fact that poem 1.12 speaks from the viewpoint of later experience and disappointment, we are probably entitled to understand *fides* even in its meaning of "trust in someone's integrity": [15] "Once I was welcome: at that time, none had the gift of being able to love with similar trust (and openness)". This interpretation makes a perfect match: her gracious attitude towards him, as expressed in *gratus*, opened the heart of the young man, who had not loved before, and won his *trust*—trust is outside any arbitrary reach of his, but is a condition that enables him to love with all his heart. Thus the paradoxical expression *contigit ut posset* draws attention to a very tender aspect of his love.

In retrospect, this period of his life does not lose the character of perfectness, of unsurpassable fulfillment that exceeds human boundaries. This is what he alludes to by concluding that it must have been a god's envy that overwhelmed him: traditionally, gods would show signs of envy only when a mortal rose to a superhuman level of achievement or happiness.

The other possible interference considered here (lines 9f.) is likewise from some more than human power (though based on human envy): sorcery which binds men's will beyond rational control. Both causes, sorcery and divine envy, do more than testify to the former greatness and intensity of Cynthia's and Propertius' love: they remove any possibility of attaching blame to human fallibility; there is no room for accusation or even condemnation.

Propertius' present unhappiness, it turns out, is rooted in an excessive, almost divine past happiness (7–10). Being now separated from Cynthia does not, however, mean a simple return to the condition he was in before he met her; it is a threatening experience which again transforms his whole personality. The first attempt at defining the new state of affairs (to be followed by many more in months and years to come) follows the retrospect immediately (11–14), and in the beginning it can only be formulated in the negative: "I am not the one I had been: a long trip changes a woman's heart". The general "rule" which, in the foregoing poem, seemed to confirm his suspicions (*ut solet amoto labi custode puella / perfida*, 11.15f.), but was then dismissed as implying an unfounded condemnation of Cynthia, has by now proved to be correct (*mutat via longa puellas*, 12.11) and applicable to Cynthia (there should be no doubt that *via longa* in 12.11

alludes to her trip to Baiae, where she stayed longer than Propertius wished her to). Also proved correct is what Propertius had said about his own total dependence on Cynthia, about the way, in his life, she had replaced all the other ties and relationships that normally surround a human being (11.21–24). What then sounded like a prophecy beyond the scope of the poem—that Propertius' joyful or depressed appearance before his friends would have its cause in Cynthia's behavior (1.11.25–26)—is now fulfilled: he can speak about himself (the stress is on *ego*) in terms of Cynthia's conduct: *non sum ego qui fueram: mutat via longa puellas*. Poetical achievement (shortest possible formula, precisely defining language, metrical balance of the penthemimeres) and self-knowledge (autobiographical statement) match each other. Her attitude has changed; ergo, I myself lost my identity.

That the change is still hard to believe and difficult to imagine is the message of the next line (12.12). Scholars should not take offense at the imprecise statements of time here, but should try to appreciate time's subjective character in a subjective statement; *olim* in line 7 has already shown that, for Propertius, the period of happy love seems long ago (cf. *illo tempore*). In the same way, Cynthia's "long" trip (*via longa*, 11), was "long" largely because, for the lover, it meant waiting (as described in poem 11), and a wait always appears longer to human beings than the time actually passed and measured on the clock. The same period of time appears "tiny" or exiguous (*exiguo tempore*, 12.12) once again by comparison with the eternal love (*quantus amor*, l.c.) Propertius had hoped for and believed in. Every single word denoting time here is used purposefully, but not, as one commentator would have it, loosely (*"longa* has no emphasis on it, for cf. *exiguo tempore* in the next line"). Actually, a new sense of time seems characteristic of Propertius' changed identity and, therefore, may help him to explain and define his new self: "Now for the first time I am, in my loneliness, forced to recognize the nights as long . . ." (12.13). What better indicator can he give us of his changed self, if at different times and under different circumstances (*solus* or *cum Cynthia*) he measures the same thing differently? An old poetical (and philosophical) phenomenon with a long tradition has once more helped a man to know himself. Another indication of the change lies in the fact that his poetry, which formerly sounded sweet in Cynthia's (and his own) ears, now is a nuisance even to himself (line 14).

Naturally, one may look for remedies (15–18): happy is he who can move his girl by his tears. Often, tears and even quarreling prepare the ground for reconciliation and more intensive love thereafter! But when a woman like Cynthia has turned away from her lover, there is no way to influence her by tears.

Blessed, too, is he who is able to love another girl instead! In many cases, when men call others happy whose fortune they do not share, there is a secret note of refusal implied in the exclamation "happy is he, who . . . !", denoting the happy as simpletons. The same is true with Propertius: not only would he not be able to bring himself to love another girl and forget Cynthia, but he would not even wish to be able to; this for instance is a strong reservation he feels towards his friend Gallus, a renowned girl-chaser (. . . *tibi deceptis augetur fama puellis*, 1.13.5), for whom he outlines the ideal fulfillment of love by the words "to be able to stay happily for good with only one girl" (*poterit felix una remanere puella*, 1.10.29). As it is commonly recognized that poems 1.10 and 1.13 belong together and enclose 1.12 and 1.11 like a shell, we are entitled to draw inferences concerning Propertius from the sort of counter-Propertius whom he depicts in Gallus and tries to convert.[16] Therefore, we must be careful to see the joys (*gaudia*) which men can experience in "transferred servitude" (*translato . . . servitio*, 12.18),[17] not as a happiness which, in Propertius' eyes, would appear desirable.

This becomes even clearer from the poem's last distich (19/20), which unequivocally states the terms that apply to Propertius himself and which distinguish and separate him from other, more "happy" lovers, to whom easier solutions and consolations are open. A sharp *mi*, the first word in the line (19), singles him out from the happy many and finds its emphatic correspondent in *fas est* at the end of the line: his personal fate is neither to love another woman nor to desist from Cynthia, no matter how she may treat him. In thus stating his fate, Propertius achieves an ultimate self-definition and also, after a long explanation, a clear-cut answer to the addressee and his view of a man ("leave Rome, otherwise you are guilty of *desidia*!"). He makes his claims known, claims upon a fate of his own and a life-style that does not bow to the easygoing clichés of "responsibility towards society" which allow for shorter periods of "pleasure" after longer periods of "duty." His position is awkward because it may deprive him of friends and the little human support which is left, support which he needs so much after the human relationship on which he had set all his hopes has failed. Perhaps this fact, that he has not one but two open flanks, explains some of the irritation our poem displays. It also helps explain the impression of exclusiveness and unwillingness to yield which his position creates. In the foregoing elegy he had declared that the way he appeared to third persons would depend on Cynthia: *Cynthia causa fuit*. He now takes up that poetic coinage and recasts it into an even more exclusive and rigid formula: *Cynthia prima fuit, Cynthia finis erit!* What surprises us most, perhaps, is that he already knows himself and his fate so well. In the last poem we have from his hand (4.1), written many years later and after some powerful attempts to change his fate and gain his freedom, he will still reconfirm his position of 1.12, not without the wise self-irony of the experienced. "For, whatever victories you have won by your toils, one single girl, playing her game, mocks them":

> nam tibi victrices quascumque labore parasti,
>   eludit palmas una puella tuas.   (4.1.139/140)

It remains to say a few words about the structure of 1.12. The "ruling unit" is, I hope to have shown, the 2D unit. I would analyze the poem as follows:

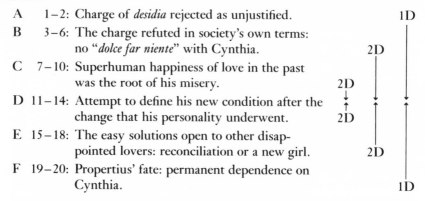

A   1–2: Charge of *desidia* rejected as unjustified.   1D

B   3–6: The charge refuted in society's own terms: no "*dolce far niente*" with Cynthia.   2D

C 7–10: Superhuman happiness of love in the past was the root of his misery.   2D

D 11–14: Attempt to define his new condition after the change that his personality underwent.   2D

E 15–18: The easy solutions open to other disappointed lovers: reconciliation or a new girl.   2D

F 19–20: Propertius' fate: permanent dependence on Cynthia.   1D

The clarity of thought[18] is reflected in the admirable symmetry of structure: no more unbalanced outbursts of fear as in 1.11, but a calm meditation upon the new self, following a provoked retort in the beginning. What we can see only now, at the end of our interpretation, is the movement of thought, which, step by step, approaches this inner self. A contains the reproach from the outside world; B, an answer in the terms of that world; C, a reflection on his happy past; D, on his new self; E, the resulting consciousness of easy solutions open to all others; F, the definition of his unique fate in his own terms and, thus, the final answer to his censurer, which proves that B was only a preliminary answer.

C and D belong together as the poem's core, concerning Propertius himself—a 4D unit, if one so wishes, consisting of two halves of 2D each. This center is surrounded by B and E, again two units of 2D each, concerned with the conventional world and its terms and ways of love. A and F together would form a 2D unit, related to each other as question (charge) and final answer. In this form, they would make a very pointed epigram; but they are split up so that B through E can be sandwiched in as a long explanation. The final answer in F thereby becomes understandable for an outside world that thinks and lives in ways and terms different from those of the poet.

If we view elegies 1.11 and 1.12 together, as the poet would wish us to do, we can now confirm our interpretation of the former. Elegy 11 tries to ban the fear of a future event, but is not wholly successful. The possibility that Cynthia may one day mean not only gladness, but sadness as well, cannot be silenced and is expressed in that prophetic couplet (11.25/26) which exceeds the poem's scope—not only in form (it is first in a series of related short statements about Cynthia) but also in position (as an "odd" distich in the elegy's structure) and content (third persons are introduced into the address to the beloved woman). Elegy 12 speaks of the time after the event has happened; the fear is over, and an attempt is made at a new orientation. Propertius gains insight into the fact that his dependence on Cynthia is permanent (and later years prove this insight to be correct). In trying to explain this fact, he realizes that his values may clash with the norms of society, and that it may be difficult to make himself understood, even among friends. This disagreement with the world and its conventional attitude towards love is a heavy burden, for he may find himself living in complete isolation. But he has no other choice, of that he is convinced.

But disagreement with the surrounding world is consequence, not cause. And the cause, which lies in himself, is more important: the two poems describe a sequence of time, two states in Propertius' life that follow each other. The first is transient, the second permanent (although it does not exclude future periods of comparative happiness, the original trust of his love is gone forever). We may confidently say that the change from the first of the two stages to the second is of highest autobiographical importance to Propertius, as a person and as a poet. By poetically presenting this change, he makes us and himself aware that he now has become the person whom we shall know as Propertius: the poet of disappointed love.[19] For his dependence on Cynthia and his love for her will last (*Cynthia finis erit*), whatever others may think of him, and whatever she may do to him. She may even make him give up what he has felt to be his identity (*non sum ego qui fueram: mutat via longa puellas*). How can he be forced to do this? Because to him love is total, is life itself, at its most intense: were he to succeed in freeing himself, in keeping his identity, he would not be alive so intensely—and his poetry would cover areas which he considers less central to human existence.

— II —

LOVE'S TORTURE: PROPHETIC
LONELINESS

━━━━━━

We have first considered elegies 11 and 12 for two reasons. First, they constitute the turning point of Book 1, and, by their poetic concentration on a single event in the author's experience of love, allow comparatively easy access to the core of his poetry. But the full meaning of this event and the fateful turn it gave to the direction of his life can only be seen (we are asked to understand) if we view his disappointment and hurt feelings against the emotional background which he himself furnishes for the readers of his book in its introductory elegy. There, too, he makes use of the poetical advantages that an autobiographical viewpoint offers.

The other reason for dealing with the introductory elegy not in the opening chapter of this book, is, as I said earlier, found in the current situation of scholarship. Learned opinions on this poem have grown so much in number and have reached such a degree of diversification that it is hard to deal with them and not to lose sight of the poem's purpose in the wider context of Propertius' poetry. But, since this situation points to some real and unsolved problems, the details deserve the attention also of those whose interest lies in the wider framework. Thus readers who find it hard to be confronted with a strictly philological discussion may nevertheless appreciate that in this and in two other chapters of Part One they are being offered a detailed account of the foundation which gives rise to the comprehensive interpretation presented in Part Two.

First, I give my translation of the opening elegy:

1.1

First Cynthia made me, to my unhappiness, her prisoner with her
                    lovely eyes,
    me, who had been touched[1] by no desires before.
Then Amor forced down my eyes, that had shown a firm pride,
    and pressed[2] my head beneath his feet,
until he taught me to hate chaste women,
    that shameless one, and to live without a guiding principle.
And my frenzy already has lasted incessantly for a whole year,
    but nevertheless I must have the gods against me.   (1–8)

Milanion—I am addressing myself to you, Tullus—by shunning no
                    toils whatsoever,
    crumbled the savage resistance of Iasus' haughty daughter
                    ⟨Atalante⟩.
For at times he used to roam about the Parthenian glens in a state of
                    frenzy,
    at times he[3] also[4] went repeatedly to face shaggy beasts.
That hero was even hurt by a blow from Hylaeus' club
    and, wounded, broke into moaning on Arcadian rocks.
Thus he was able to tame and win the swift-footed girl;
    such is the power of prayers and good actions in love.   (9–16)

In my case, however, Amor is tardy and does not devise any crafts ⟨that
                    would help me⟩,
    and he no longer remembers to travel well-known roads, as before.
                    (17–18)

But you, who scheme to pull down the moon
    and labor to perform appeasing sacrifices on magic hearths,
look! go ahead! convert the mind of our mistress
    and make her face paler than mine!
Then I would be ready to believe you that you are able to pull
    the stars and streams by the magic chants of ⟨Medea,⟩ the sorceress
                    from Cytaea.

Or you, my friends, who call me back too late, after I have fallen,
    look for remedies for a heart that is not sound!
Bravely we will endure the knife and the savage fire
    if only freedom be granted to say what my anger wishes to say!
Carry me across the nations at the end of the world and carry me across
                    the sea,
    where no woman can know my way!   (19–30)

You stay behind, to whom the deity has ⟨listened⟩ with gracious ear
                    ⟨and⟩ nodded ⟨approval⟩,
    and—this is my wish—may you always be equal partners in a love
                    that is secure!
In my case our Venus vexes the nights and makes them bitter,
    and at no time my single[5] love ceases.   (31–34)

Avoid this evil, I warn you. May everyone be detained by his own
    dear worry, and may he not stray from his familiar love!
Accordingly, if someone turns slow ears to my warnings,
    alas! with what great pain will he recall my words!   (35–38)

Readings different from OCT: 25: *aut* instead of *et*; 30: exclamation mark after
iter; 32: exclamation mark after *pares*; 34: *amor* instead of *Amor*.

The elegy, serving as a programmatic introduction to the whole book,
has always attracted scholars.[6] But a scholarly approach in dealing with
our poem has not meant guaranteed access to its meaning. Sometimes it
has meant just the contrary: the obstruction of an otherwise open view by
the prejudice that can result from learnedness.[7] Two special dangers have
played their part:

First, the fact that the first two couplets of our poem are, on the
surface, a more or less close translation or imitation of a Greek epigram
(*A.P.* 12.101) composed by Meleager of Gadara, a few decades before
Propertius started writing, has led some scholars into measuring Propertius against his Greek "original" rather than into interpreting the lines in
their Latin context.

Secondly, there exists a long scholarly tradition, with Lachmann as an
outstanding early representative, which has tried to "reconcile" contradicting pieces of information which the poet allegedly furnishes on presumed facts of his life and love. It was mostly scholarly desire for more
solidly biographical information which raised such casual poetical utterances out of their context to the rank of historical data, and it is difficult, I
believe, for a reader burdened with this type of knowledge to take our
poem for what it is meant to be: an opening poem which does not presuppose anything that may be communicated to the reader in other elegies
(even though it may have actually been written later than most or all the
poems contained in Book 1).

An awareness of the methodological problems involved here may save
us from misunderstanding. To give an undisputable example of the second
type of danger: years later the poet says goodbye to his love and love-
poetry (3.24) and declares that Cynthia never was as beautiful as his early
poems depicted her; he claims that that beauty was nothing more than a
product of his loving illusion (*ut, quod non esses, esse putaret amor*, 3.24.6),
and he goes on to allude to the former madness of his love by referring to
(among others) elegy 1.1. Nobody, I assume, would in this case argue that
we would be methodologically entitled to interpret the opening elegy by
retrojecting later disillusionment into an earlier illusion. Even the term "illusion" is not adequate to describe 1.1, because one may speak of "illusion" only from the standpoint of disillusion—which lies outside the categories of the opening poem (in fact, the speaker of 1.1 would certainly call
his present view realistic and that of 3.24 illusionary). This amounts to

another methodological warning: recurrence, even of key notions, would not automatically permit us to equate their meaning in two passages without first checking the context in which they appear.

Considerations similar to ours, but based on a critique specifically of biographical interpretation, led A. W. Allen some thirty-five years ago to evaluate the poem in contemporary terms, i.e., as it would have appealed to the reading public of Propertius' time, which knew as little about the new poet as we know, but which had certain ideas about love and poetry which, according to Allen, Propertius could count on to make himself understood.[8] This meant a new and fruitful approach. On the one hand, it freed the literary critic from the dubious task of being at heart also a biographer of the poet (or a historian of poetry). BB, for instance, being interested, beyond the "precise significance" of the poem, in "the circumstances of its composition", subjected the poet-lover of 1.1 to a situation and a timetable which is unverifiable from—in fact, unknown to—the text of the elegy ("Propertius has enjoyed Cynthia's favour, but his happiness has not lasted long"). Through Allen's critique, the interpreter is cut off effectively from the prejudice of being influenced by any data of subsequent elegies. On the other hand, by locating the elegist's notion of love in one part of a well-known contemporary contrast, viz., that of a self-destructive passion (versus a controlled and philosophically acceptable erotic behavior), Allen was able to prepare the ground for appreciating Propertius' personal isolation. But by emphasizing that the elegy's "personal quality" lies "in the adaptation, through the style, of the traditional conception of love and the conventional motives of love poetry to the analysis of a particular situation" (277), he seems in danger of losing touch again with the unique and individual character he himself makes his reader acknowledge in the poet's experience. In another article (1962), fighting the idea of poetical "sincerity" (the poet as the recorder of his personal history), Allen goes so far as to find Propertius' "excellence" in "his lively personal realization of convention" (146). Here the border line may be blurred between the individual's self-expression (Allen denies that ancient poetic "sincerity" has anything to do with "our interest in individual psychology", 110) and literary convention ("the conventional element in his work is disguised by the personal form", 129). If, as I would tend to see it, the poet senses a communication gap between himself and his audience, this circumstance would be difficult to perceive in Allen's terms, and his results would have a higher significance for understanding the poet's personal message than Allen himself would grant them. Accordingly, the present investigation, though agreeing more often with Allen than with recent interpreters of 1.1, will leave the door open to a more individual interpretation, even if disproval of the generalizing tendency will perhaps result only from the recurrent observation of the individual features which the *Monobiblos* as a whole offers (see especially chapters IV and V).

With the preceding considerations in mind, let us approach the poem itself. The first line tells us how the poet, to his unhappiness, was taken prisoner by Cynthia's eyes. Although Enk grants that the diminutive form *ocellis* (which, in its wider sense, can even denote the poet's own eyes: 1.10.7) is here used meaningfully (her "charming" or "lovely" eyes), *communis opinio* does not grant the same to the words *suis* and *prima*, and in so doing implicitly convicts Propertius of using unnecessary words to stop the holes in the first line of his work.

The case of *suis* is perhaps easier to agree upon. Its positive and emphatic use lies in the pointed opposition between line 1 and line 3: *suis . . . ocellis* and *mihi . . . lumina* form an important contrast, which is underlined by the syntactical variation. More on this below.

This contrast has not been realized because of the generally accepted interpretation of *prima* in line 1—an unconvincing interpretation in which the authority of scholarly tradition overrides the basic Latin. *Prima* is supposed to mean that she was the first woman Propertius ever loved, and *prima* is said to be explained once more by line 2: he had not felt desires before. No justification is given for the apparent redundancy.[9] But a shadow is cast upon Propertius' integrity: he could be suppressing evidence! "*Prima*: This ignores Lycinna" (BB). The words of a more recent commentator (Camps; see also Fedeli) sound like an apology: "At 3.15.1ff. Propertius says that his first experience of love was with a certain Lycinna. But it was not what he now understands by love." Enk in his commentary concurs in allowing the poet the excuse of forgetfulness (originated by K. P. Schulze, but already expressed by Propertius himself at 3.15.9: *cuncta tuus sepelivit amor*). But Enk's annotation to *prima* sounds even stricter: "*non cogitat poeta de Lycinna quam ante Cynthiam amavit* (3.15.5.6.)." Here we hear the heirs of Lachmann, who collected a timetable of the poet's biography and bade scholars as well as Propertius himself adhere to it. Along the same lines one could easily argue that *ocellis* in line 1 is another slight untruthfulness on Propertius' part because he later casually mentions not her eyes but her dress as the quality that first attracted him: *. . . qua primum oculos cepisti veste Properti / indue . . .* (3.10.15f.)! But above all, he does not even say in 3.15 that he loved Lycinna (Enk's *amavit*), but that she introduced him to *amoris iter* (line 4), which means something else.

Prima, however, does not necessarily mean that Cynthia was Propertius' first love in the sense that there was no woman before her in his life. *Primus*, the superlative to *prior*, which means "earlier in line or in time", is a priori looking in the direction of its own opposite *postremus*, and *postremus*, being the superlative to *posterior*, means "last" or "latest", looking backward in the direction of *primus* (*alia prima ponet, alia postrema,* Cic. *Or.* 15.50). Association of *primus* with the preceding state "zero", which modern training in arithmetic makes us think of as the natural antecedent to state "one", would not immediately occur to a Roman mind.[10] Normal use of *primus* is well exemplified by Propertius' own statement at 1.12.20: *Cynthia prima fuit, Cynthia finis erit*. This line is meant to exclude any possibility of another woman's playing a role in Propertius' life (cf. 1.12.19: he cannot desist from Cynthia): *prima* looks from the beginning to all that follows, and *finis* looks back from the end to all that lay before.[11] If we replace the common but inapposite interpretation of *prima* in 1.1.1 with its customary meaning, the result is potentially devastating for a book which, according to the Latin practice of using the first words as titles, is called "Cynthia": "Cynthia was the first ('number one') to catch me . . . with (possibly) more women to follow"! Would the poet allow such a prospect to stay open here?

It is thus proper that *prima* of line 1 should have another point of reference. This is offered in *tum* (line 3) which, meaning "thereafter", usually follows a *primum*, meaning "first". And the adverb *primum* is often enough replaced by a *primus* or *prima* used attributively.[12] In this way, *prima* makes excellent sense and ceases to be a mere doublet of what is said in line 2. And *ante* (2) can take on its proper meaning, denoting a state "zero" which lies before the state characterized by *prima* (1). In other words, the structuring principle of the opening lines is chronological[13] and as strict as we would expect from our reading of poems 11 and 12. Even the subdivisions, expressed by *et*, are carefully marked, as an outline of the structure shows:

stage	key-words	line
0	*ante*	2
I	Cynthia *prima* cepit	1
II	*tum* Amor (a) deiecit	3
	et (b) pressit	4
III	*donec* docuit (a) odisse	5
	et (b) vivere	6
IV	et *iam* toto anno	
	(a) non deficit	7
	(b) cum tamen cogor	8

As can be seen, stages 0 and IV do not, strictly speaking, participate in the chronological development: stage 0 is a neutral period of rest before events occur and bring about change. (That is why it is described in the distich's less important part, the pentameter, while the more emphatic hexameter is reserved for the beginning of action.) Stage IV is a retrospective and summarizing evaluation (present tense in lines 7/8) of the reversal which recent events (past tense in lines 1–6) have brought about in the poet's life. I would like again to lay stress on the precise logical structure, which proceeds step by step, because one can thereby prove Propertius' independence from his Meleagrean "model": from the very beginning (*prima*) he pursues his own train of thought, into which he incorporates only such wording from the Greek epigram as suits his purpose. Any attempt (e.g., Rothstein's) to measure Propertius' alleged shortcomings by the perfection of his Greek "original" betrays poor logic on the interpreter's part and can even lead to gross mistakes (see later on line 4).[14]

A few added remarks on distich structure may be helpful to later interpretation. The first couplet observes, as we saw, the building code of the distich very well. (Action is viewed against the foil of quiet.) The same is true of the fourth couplet: line 7 summarizes the new situation, line 8 seasons the evaluation with a spicy and surprising (*cum tamen*) point. The sentences in lines 3 to 6, to be separated by mere commas, contain the narration proper that follows the law of time: in a narrative connected by *et* (4; 6), there is no point in setting hexameter and pentameter against one another (for *donec*, 5, see later). Viewed structurally, distichs I and IV seem to go together, as do II and III.

After remarks on structure, let us turn to contents. Easiest to understand is probably line 2: the young man had not been in love before, so that when his eyes met Cynthia's, he felt overwhelmed by an experience which he could not relate to anything he had known as yet. Line 2 shows his latent vulnerability as well as his inexperience.

Dispute continues about the meaning of line 1. Steidle, convinced like many others in the Lachmann tradition that in the opening poem Cynthia is already described as the courtesan she later appears to be, sees his thesis partially proved by *cepit ocellis*: the metaphor, if it is to make sense, "setzt es ein aktives Verhalten Cynthias voraus".[15] I doubt the validity of this inference; if active behavior of a courtesan were to be suggested, the present phrase would hardly be adequate.[16] It would be equally convincing (and even more convincing in the light of the following lines) to say that a casual and uninterested glance on her part became to Propertius something which he could never forget. Does not the poem express despair over the lamentable fact that she hardly ever granted him more than a look? The alleged "active" ingredient in the term *capere* quite naturally refers to the loss of activity and freedom which the captive lover feels and which he ascribes—as is still done in modern languages—to a dominating and active element outside himself but inside the object of his love.[17] Line 1 is about *Propertius'* first sensation of love (with more sensations and stages to follow, as our interpretation of *prima* proves), but not about any provocative activities on the part of Cynthia the assumed harlot. In fact, nothing except scholarly tradition necessitates this assumption; and the name *Cynthia*, if any contemporary reader cared to think about it, might just as well indicate a pseudonym such as Catullus' Lesbia,[18] and the latter was known to stand for a member of a high-ranking family.

Interpretation of line 3 is still burdened with the misunderstood *prima* of line 1; Allen, Ahl, and others saw a deliberate ambiguity, produced by the postponement of the sentence's grammatical subject (*Amor*) to the end of line 4: thus, they reasoned, the reader would at first assume *Cynthia* still to be the subject to *deiecit*. This alleged ambiguity is removed by the correct understanding "First Cynthia—thereafter . . . Amor", which leaves no room for *Cynthia* to be understood after *tum*, so that we have to find another reason for the apparent postponement of *Amor*.

The subject is withheld to leave space open for the meaningful contrast of *suis . . . ocellis* (1) and *mihi . . . lumina* (3): while Cynthia's [19] eyes make Propertius a prisoner, his own eyes are forced down (!)—instead of having a similar effect on her. The encounter of their looks has led to completely different consequences. For Propertius it does not simply mean that, being captive, he is no longer his own master; he is humiliated as well (shame is not what makes him cast down his eyes). His eyes had been "of unchanging loftiness", a phrase which indicates the greatness of the change; *fastus* usually means the air of indifference which the uninterested girl displays towards a (or even: any) man wooing her. If Propertius has up to now felt such an attitude to be a firm characteristic of his own behavior, we must apparently picture him along the lines suggested by what is said in line 2, as an almost Hippolytus-like young man who felt molested rather than happy when being addressed or looked at by members of the other sex, and who reacted to erotic overtures by women with a firm resistance. Necessarily he feels humiliated when he sees his beloved pride melting away like snow in the sun, and when, like a slave, he is no longer able to lift his eyes—a permanent inability, according to his later formulation: (*Amor*) . . . *tollere numquam / te patietur humo lumina capta semel* (2.30.9f.). It is the story of Love's merry-go-round: [20] now it is his turn to experience what he unknowingly did to others when his eyes met their eyes and he felt nothing except a desire to show his own repugnance (*fastus*) toward their obtrusiveness. We cannot exclude the possibility that part of the humiliation was experienced when he brought himself to approach Cynthia (the *preces* of the Milanion example in line 16 are perhaps a covert admittance of this)—only to face *her fastus*, as the poem shows.

But it is not only loss of pride (3) which Love causes: that is one side of the coin. The other side (*et*, 4) amounts to downright torture, which Amor applies to replace the former values by his own standards. Here we encounter the third of those instances I mentioned earlier, where we have to correct—or at least to modify—the traditional understanding. It is assumed that line 4 depicts Amor's triumphant gesture of victory: his foot on his victim's neck ("Nacken": "Amor der Sieger", showing his "Triumph" —Rothstein). No offence is taken at the logical contradiction implied in a proposition such as: "Amor triumphed over me *until* I learned the lesson he wished to teach me." The victim's acceptance of the lesson ought to bring about and complete Amor's triumph, not end it.

Thus the question must be raised whether *impositis pressit . . . pedibus* does not signify something more severe (i.e., an *action* rather) than the mere *gesture* of victory, or "Siegergeste".[21] A recent interpretation (assuming the victor to be a gladiator, while others have thought of a warrior) runs like this: "Aufs Haupt des Unterlegenen aber setzte der siegreiche Gladiator den Fuss. Das bedeutet also, dass Properz der Liebe zu Cynthia *nun völlig erlegen* ist."[22] This statement by Hanslik leaves the logical problem raised by *donec* as urgent as ever. For how can Propertius claim to be "now completely defeated" by Amor "*until* he taught me to hate chaste girls"?

Hanslik himself sees a possible difficulty for his interpretation posed by the unexpected plural *pedibus* "an Stelle des Singulars *pede imposito*".[23] He tries to remove the problem by declaring that the plural not only is "Dichtersprache", but is also influenced by the plural ποσσί in the Meleagrian model passage. The latter is perhaps not too convincing since, as Schulz-Vanheyden has observed, "ποσσὶ πατεῖν kann in der griechischen Sprache nicht die Geste des Fussaufsetzens bezeichnen".[24] If there is any influence from the Greek model's phrase ("trample with one's feet"), one would rather assume (as OLD s.v. *premo*, #15, actually does) a harsher meaning of *pedibus premere*, i.e., a nuance which points to an action rather than to a gesture.

As far as "Dichtersprache" is concerned, it is of course true that in poetry we frequently read plural for singular, especially with regard to body parts (though *pedes* is not listed among the many examples given by Kühner-Stegmann).[25] We should, however, take into account that, since it is natural for feet to come two at a time anyway, the plural *pedes* will hardly appear to the reader as "poetic" as, for instance, the more elevated plural forms *terga* or *colla* when used with regard to one person. In fact, a poetic singular for plural, it seems, is what we find more often in *Dichtersprache* (e.g., *Io vaga . . . / fert . . . refertque pedem*, Val.Fl. 7.111f.).

As far as the routine of victory (which includes setting one's foot on the defeated before despoiling him)[26] is concerned, we may cite Vergil, *Aen.* 10.490ff., where Turnus, having killed Pallas, places himself over his victim (*super adsistens*) and gives a haughty speech (491ff.) containing a message to his victim's father. Then, pressing his left foot against the corpse (*laevo pressit pede . . . exanimem*, 495f.), he strips off the spoils. We may also compare Homer, *Il.* 5.620 (pulling out the spear; cf. 16.863). At *Il.* 13.618ff. the order is (1) stepping on the chest of the defeated, (2) stripping off the spoils, (3) giving the self-glorifying speech. In none of these passages does the victor confine himself to a gesture of setting his foot on the defeated.

From the fact that Turnus employs one (his left) foot only, the reader may already anticipate what a survey shows concerning the phrase *pedem imponere* (indicating the routine of victory): the singular number represents the linguistic rule, while the plural form (as used in Prop. 1.1.4) appears to be exceptional. In some cases the singular number may be explained by the "poetic" use. (This can only be decided by interpreting each passage within its overall context—as can the question whether merely a gesture of victory or an action—as part of a sequence of actions—is implied.)[27] The more reason there is to wonder why Propertius' line is, among those cited, the only one to offer the plural. *Thes. ling. Lat.* lists *pede imposito* (Ov. *Met.* 8.425), *urbs . . . victorem terris impositura pedem* (Ov. *Fast.* 4.857f.), *imposito . . . sub pede* (Ov. *Pont.* 4.7.48), *imposito . . . pede* (Ov. *Trist.* 5.8.10), *pedem super cervicem iacenti(s) imposuit* (intending to strike the fatal blow at the defeated, *victum*, Curt. 9.7.22).[28]

Of these passages, one is remarkably close to our passage in question:

> et caput impositis pressit Amor pedibus, (Prop. 1.1.4)
>
> Ipse pede imposito caput exitiabile pressit. (Ov. *Met.* 8.425)

To some readers the similarity (*caput*, *pressit*) may appear so overwhelming that they feel *pede* and *pedibus* are used interchangeably. But the puzzling fact remains that Ovid, when he wished to speak of *one* foot, avoided the kind of "poetic plural" which Hanslik claims for our passage and changed (if he did imitate Propertius here) *pedibus* to the singular—thus leaving Prop. 1.1.4 the only plural form among our passages.

In trying to account for the plural (and foregoing the excuse that Ovid used the singular *metri causa* to fit in the word *exitiabile*), one has, above all, to take into account the difference of situation. In the Ovidian passage, a hunter sets his foot on the *dead* prey's head. (He then proceeds to mention his—and a fellow hunter's—*gloria*, and to strip off the beast's hide and to cut off its head with the tusks, representing the *spolium*, 426, or *exuvias*, 428.) The Propertian line is different (a) from this passage, insofar as the victim—the poet—is *alive*, and (b) from all the passages we cited, insofar as it describes the process from the viewpoint of the *victim* (who is usually not granted a voice): the *caput* is *caput meum* (as *Thes. ling. Lat.* puts it).

It is an extraordinary case that the victim should survive to become the recorder of the event. This feature alone must prevent us from grouping our passage along with the others. Struck by the unusual aspect offered by the poet, the reader is supposed to ask "What does it feel like having one's head under the foot (or feet) of one's conqueror?" The answer must, of course, be "Painful"—especially so if the victor extends the process (*donec*) in order to teach (*docuit*) his victim (*me*) a lesson (*castas odisse puellas*). What on the surface looked like just another case of a victorious warrior's triumph over the defeated enemy has turned out to be a case of torture for the purpose of "brainwashing". In addition to the loss of pride (*fastus*, 3), then, the application of torture (4) has resulted in the loss of principles (5).

Our observations so far warrant a word of comment with regard to interpreting Propertius' poetry. Already on the occasion of lines 1/2 we found the traditional understanding mistaken insofar as it assumes that line 2 merely repeats the content of line 1 in different words (1: Cynthia the "first" woman in the poet's life; 2: no desires before). A similar confusion lies in Rothstein's comment, according to which the poet's habit of crowding vivid similes into a narrow space has led him in lines 4 and 3 "neben dieses Bild noch ein anderes zu stellen". As readers, we must not fall for the easygoing hypothesis that the author may be wasting words (here: by mentioning both the victor's triumph and the victim's loss of pride). The blame that is thus cast on his poetry should rightly come to rest at the critic's door. For his is the linguistic and logical imprecision.

Turning back to the words *pedibus . . . pressit* with an eye on what we have learned about line 4, we wonder whether the rare plural is not used purposefully (i.e., Amor has stepped with *both* his feet on his victim) and why *premere* should not be given a strong nuance like either "press down by one's weight"[29] or "trample"[30] (the latter ascribed to it here by *OLD*). These nuances are well within the range of the verb. It can mean "crush to death" by weight—as does an elephant kneeling on a man (*. . . eumque sub pede subditum dein genu innixus pondere suo . . . premeret atque enecaret*, B. Afr. 84.1);[31] a calf stepping on and squashing young frogs (*pullis vituli pede pressis*, Hor. S. 2.3.314) falls under its range as well as a man "stumping" along the beach (*verso . . . pede pressit harenam*, Ov. Met. 8.869)—the latter then thinned out to a mere "living on" ("lived in Egypt": *Inachias . . . diti pede premit harena[s*, CE 271.11), etc.

Now on the surface the severe nuances "trample" or "crush" correspond of course to the harsh character of Meleager's phrase ποσσὶ πατεῖν. But we must not overlook that Meleager has given the phrase a mitigating twist away from its concrete meaning by making the victim's pride (φρύαγμα) the object of trampling. (Precisely speaking, Meleager's lines 3 and 4, dealing with the philosopher's fallen pride, correspond to Propertius' line 3, which describes the loss of steady *fastus*.) Propertius, on the other hand, has reconcretized the phrase (and thus made it sound harsher again) by making the head itself, *caput*, the object of the feet's action.[32] It is (in combination with the unclarified assumption about a gesture of victory here) possibly the Greek model's metaphor of "haughtiness trampled upon" which made commentators from Rothstein to Hanslik decide that the Roman "copy" must speak of triumph (through humiliation) in line 4: prejudice through knowledge of sources. But once we allow the *victim's* perspective to be in the foreground, the general meaning can no longer be in doubt (though to some it may appear difficult to choose between the two nuances of "trample" and "press"). For it is by inflicting pain or torture that Amor forces his victim to relearn: "He tortured me, *until* I learned his lesson" makes perfect logic.

Communis opinio, which has not recognized Propertius' own strict, time-oriented (and introspective) structure (which starts with the word *prima* in line 1), has also not allowed him a major deviation from his Greek "model" before line 5 [33]—except, of course, where the difference is manifest: in the Greek epigram the captor is not a woman like Cynthia, but a boy called Myiskos; and the captive victim is not a young man like Propertius, but a mature man, even a man of letters or philosophy. The boy's triumph is to see the wise man's pride fall. But the philosopher (Meleager lines 5/6) parries the boy's blow by informing him that there is nothing special about his victory: even Zeus came down from Olympus because of Eros! The point lies in the generalization of an individual experience—and here Propertius (line 5/6) does not follow his "model", for he remains on the individual's level: [34] *donec me docuit*.

As far as I know, the question has never been asked whether Propertius does not make a point of his own—a sort of epigram of his own, so to speak. I believe that he does, and that by phrasing line 4 in a different way from Meleager he prepares the ground. An acoustical device which helps him to drive his message home by heightening his reader's attention is the p-alliteration in line 4: *caput impositis pressit Amor pedibus*, which doubles the number of p-sounds displayed in Meleager's line 4 (ποσσὶ πατῶ). The point itself then is stressed by a sound-pattern of its own: *donec me docuit* (5). Analysis of form thus suggests that the distich 5/6 describes a turn or surprise of epigrammatical character. The word *donec* suggests that the point is contained in an opposition between an earlier state and a later one. The meaning of *docuit* suggests that the point has something to do with the fact that the victim finally relearns by accepting his torturer's creed.

And indeed, the contrast could hardly be greater: Propertius' outlook has made a turn of 180 degrees, so to speak, from one absolute attitude to its opposite. The exclusiveness of his former position was stressed by the apodictic negative and the plural (*contactum nullis ante cupidinibus*, 2) and by the firmness of his refusal (*constantis lumina fastus*, 3): sexuality did not (yet) exist for him. [35] The new position, as formulated here, again appears to be exclusive: hate (the strongest aversion possible) [36] on principle, expressed as if against a whole group—chaste women. Thus Paley and SB, in speaking of the generic plural *castas puellas*, use an abstract: Propertius is now opposed to "chastity in women".

Such wholesale pronouncement, however, should not lead the interpreter to believe that our speaker here has lost sight of the individual in question (". . . his words, though in form a personal narrative, really relate to general experience", SB). In Latin, the generalizing plural may contain a point, especially one of emphasis. Sometimes the speaker, pleading in a state of indignant affect, employs the plural to bring out the greatness of the injustice he feels an individual case does him (or of the obstacle it represents to him)—as when a mother complains that her daughter is given into marriage "to exiled Teucrians" (one man being in question, Verg. *Aen.* 7.359), or when the supreme god finds it unbecoming that "the defeated" should regain strength (*victis*, plural, Verg. *Aen.* 12.799, said with regard to Turnus alone).[37] The consequence of such a mode of speaking is that the individual case in question can be viewed more in focus or in proportion. In keeping with contemporary use of language, we probably should say that the lesson Propertius was forced to learn was "to hate a girl who is chaste". For it is in this form that we pointedly use a general phrase while having in mind an individual. Thus the oracular words *externos . . . duces* signify "a leader who comes from abroad", *externi . . . generi* "a son-in-law who comes from abroad" (*Aen.* 8.503 and 7.98).[38]

Corresponding to the new aversion against a woman who is chaste, the violent teacher, who forced the young adolescent to change his values and convictions, is characterized as *improbus*, "shameless" (the translation coming closest to the point here)—a word whose opposite, "virtuous", goes together with chastity. In 2.19, Propertius resents Cynthia's departure from Rome, but he is glad that she will visit the remote countryside (*devia rura*, 2), because no corrupting young man will "keep you from being virtuous" (*non sinat esse probam*, 4) "in the chaste fields" (*castis . . . in agris*, 3). In 4.4, the Vestal virgin who, by falling in love, has disqualified herself for the service that requires virginity, fittingly calls herself *improba* —the opposite of a *virgo*:

> improba virgineo lecta ministra foco.   (4.4.44)

The emphatic juxtaposition of *improba* and *virgineo* can help us to understand why in Prop. 1.1 Amor's predicate *improbus* is delayed to an emphasized position (first word in the pentameter) which *immediately follows* the words *castas odisse puellas*: the reader is supposed to realize that Propertius' new teacher here receives an epithet that is apposite to his teachings.

In a coordination comparable to Prop. 1.1, Ovid contrasts *casta* and *improba* to show what Agamemnon's immodest sexual behavior has done to his wife's (formerly blameless) morals:

> As long as Agamemnon was content with one woman, she too
>   was chaste: it was by her husband's vice that she became
>   immodest.

> Dum fuit Atrides una contentus, et illa
>   *casta* fuit: vitio est *improba* facta viri.   (*Ars am.* 2.399f.)

As in the passages quoted *castis* and *probam* belong on the same side of the contrast, but *casta* and *improba* represent the mutually exclusive poles of a personal development, so in Prop. 1.1 *castas odisse* and *improbus* go together in signifying the opposite of the speaker's original position. Propertius has changed from one side to the other. At the moment when he saw Cynthia's eyes, a painful development was triggered, that from boyhood to manhood.[39] Both states and their sets of convictions are mutually exclusive. The boy hated sexuality as something strange, and by his nature appreciated chastity. The young man, finding mankind divided into two sexes and himself definitely a member of one sex, is bewildered by his sexuality and comes to hate as unfitting in the opposite sex what he had appreciated before in himself and others as a firm pride and chastity. And although he knows what to decline, he does not know by what principle to guide his life. He must *nullo vivere consilio* (6), because Love has taken away the rules he adhered to, without replacing them by others. What would seem to be able to end his plight lies beyond his reach: it lies in Cynthia's will, of which he is not master (but slave).

Let us recapitulate: It was with her eyes (*ocellis* in line 1 is instrumental ablative) that, to his unhappiness (*miserum* is proleptic or resultative), she (the way he feels it) took his freedom (*cepit*), thus setting in motion a painful development in him (*tum . . . Amor*, 3ff.), which not only made him, the so-far uninterested boy (2), aware of the power of love by humiliating his former pride (3) and even forcing him by torture (4) to hate what he would have appreciated before (5), but has also left him deprived of rational orientation and guidance to master the new circumstances into which he has been plunged (6). Indeed, the development has been so unexpected that the only adequate response for him is to cast the autobiographical statement in an epigrammatical mould.

In a certain way (and here he may hate even the beloved because he loves her), Cynthia has proved deficient. Having (as he would interpret the situation) communicated through her eyes (the organ of recognition par excellence!) an impulse to awareness and painful learning, she later does not respond to the results of this process, but leaves him without the fulfillment which his new state has taught him to consider the natural complement to his own deficiency. While boyhood meant self-sufficiency and autonomy, manhood paradoxically can mean heteronomy and the insufficiency of being a lonely half.

After the account of painful past experience (1–6), there follows a retrospective evaluation of the present situation (7/8), which, by a sudden awareness of the time elapsed ("and *already* for a whole year"), creates a new note: that of despair. This is strengthened by *tamen*, which is usually overlooked by interpreters: "So long already—and *nevertheless* I am forced to have the gods against me." The underlying thought is that suffering is usually limited in time and is soon changed to a more agreeable condition by the divine powers that control man's life (on this principle, a long time of suffering even entitles a man to count on a change for the better soon).[40] The speaker's case, however, seems to defy the consoling rule: so long already—and, nevertheless, no change! And thus fear arises that this madness (*furor*, 7, comprises both sides of stage III: shameless love as well as absence of rational control) may turn out to be a permanent condition. It is not Amor alone, or Cynthia alone, whose adversity (stressed by the double expression: *cogor, adversos*, 8) he has to face—no, it is "the gods", *deos* (8), who are against him, singling him out for a special, non-ordinary fate, as he must see it. Loneliness is the result, in more than one respect.

The reason why I have exposed my reader to so detailed a study of lines 1–8 was to show that the section is logically sound and intelligible on its own merits to anyone who (a) reads it as an introduction by which an otherwise unknown poet introduces himself and his book to the general public, and who (b) thereby tries to avoid mistakes caused by the unguarded introduction of foreign information, even from the poet's own subsequent elegies, into our passage. Such information (not only about the situation, but in some cases about the use of language also) can be called foreign, because the poet chooses to present as his prooemium a very special situation, which predates all situations concerning Cynthia depicted in his book: it is the first year of his unrequited love for Cynthia, the sequel to the fateful moment when the boy Propertius looked into the eyes of Cynthia.

Keeping in mind the results obtained so far, we may now be prepared to deal with the most vexed problem which the first lines have had to offer to many generations of scholars: What is Cynthia's relation to the condition indicated by *castas puellas* in line 5? Although I myself would hesitate to see here a problem of a higher order, I agree that my own interpretation should be subjected to the traditional test of credibility—the more so because I am aware of the consequences some interpreters draw from the interpretation of the word *castas*. I confine myself to a brief survey of opinions, including some names and objections, but excluding more remote interpretations, e.g. that of Vulpius, Bonazzi, and L. Hermann, who believe that *castae puellae* are the Muses:

I *Cynthia casta*
  (1) Cynthia is *casta* because she rejects Propertius.[41]
     Consequences: (a) The state of unhappiness and distractedness Propertius describes; or (b) Propertius hates chaste girls like Cynthia and seeks consolation with prostitutes (still the prevailing interpretation).[42]

Objection to (b): Above all, line 8 and the "helpless passion" displayed throughout the poem exclude this interpretation.[43]

Specifically, prostitutes are considered a remedy of love in antiquity, and thus would not testify to Propertius' suffering.[44] View (b) is in the Lachmann tradition, based on false use of elegies 2.23 and 24 as "evidence" (whereas the poet's words *me quaerere viles*, 2.24.9, actually may be no more than an indirect and sarcastic comment on Cynthia's behavior: "If I have to corrupt my reputation, I can do so at a cheaper price—or rather: with less damage to it—by seeing prostitutes than by seeing Cynthia", 2.24.9/10).[45] Poem 24A says nothing about Propertius' actually seeing prostitutes.[46]

Objections to (1): The meaning of *casta* is being strained, because Cynthia is, as many of Propertius' poems show, not a chaste woman in the strict sense of the word.[47]

But taking *casta* as merely "incompliant" is likewise equivalent to straining the word's meaning.[48]

(2) Cynthia is *casta* in the sense (also found in Propertius) of "loyal to husband or lover."[49]

Objection to (2): This view appears impossible, as there is no trace of a lover in the rest of the poem.[50]

II *Cynthia incesta*

(1) (His love for) Cynthia, the courtesan, has led him to dislike women of his own class.[51]

Alleged support: A scribbler who wrote on a wall in Pompeii: *Candida me docuit nigras odisse puellas.*[52] This, however, is no proof, because the opposition *candida / nigras* may just as well be a one-sided, even purposeful and witty, misinterpretation of Propertius' words, bringing out an ambiguity which the reader normally does not even suspect.

General Objections to (1): The poem does not indicate anything about Cynthia's being a courtesan. Besides, his failure in wooing Cynthia (lines 8 and 17f.) has so far kept the speaker from being in a position to compare the two groups he is said to weigh against each other here.

Specific Objection to (1): It seems unkind and an improbable insult to characterize Cynthia as a harlot in the opening poem of a book that has her name as its title.[53]

Counterobjection: Being a professional courtesan, even if not of the lowest rank, Cynthia did not mind being called what she was.[54]

Counter-counterobjection: The counterobjection amounts to a *petitio principii*.

Consequences of (1): (a) in line 5, "he rejects the approved Roman woman"; (b) line 6 rejects "the approved career for a young Roman man".[55]

Objection: These consequences shift the focus of the given context from the young lover to a young rebel against society.

(2) Propertius' psychological disposition as shown in his poems forbids him to fall in love with chaste girls, attaches him to an *incesta*, bids him injure a third party, etc. (Freud's *Dirnenliebe*). *Odisse castas puellas*, according to this view, is part of a clear-eyed self-analysis.[56]

Objection: The development from boyhood to manhood in 1.1.1–8, including a whole year of unsuccessful wooing, seems still normal enough not to corroborate a psychopathic interpretation of line 5.[57]

So far the predominant interpretations of line 5. Those who declare Cynthia an *incesta* (= II) do so on "evidence" that has been gathered from subsequent elegies (some of them in books that were published years later), but that does not appear in elegy 1.1 itself. The second version of the *Cynthia casta* interpretation (I-2: Cynthia refuses Propertius because she is loyal to another man) is not corroborated by the rest of our elegy; version I-1 (Cynthia haughtily rejects Propertius), however, is consistent with the whole poem's situation (as long as one does not draw the Lachmann-type consequences listed under (b)).

I-1 together with its consequence (a) seems, therefore, to deserve closer consideration. Its alleged flaw is that it strains the strict meaning of *casta*, because Cynthia is said to be far from deserving of the title "chaste". Again we have to object here that such knowledge about Cynthia's alleged status and morals is drawn from subsequent elegies which depict stages of Propertius' and Cynthia's relationship which are unknown and foreign to the situation of elegy 1.1. Our interpretation of poems 1.11 and 12 strongly suggests that considerations based upon the supposed fickleness of Cynthia's love do not enter the poems until some time after the love affair has been established and has lasted for a certain period. Above all, the fact that many years later elegy 1.1 receives a disillusioned counterpiece (3.24), which claims to see through the illusions of 1.1, shows and even proves that the process of painful experience, which starts with the boy's awakening to manhood in 1.1, is not completed so soon but unfolds during the years to come; and a large part of this experience results from Propertius' ever growing insight into the unending possibilities of disappointment in a close human relationship (one instance being the first experience of perfidy expressed in 1.12).[58] If we retroject his later insights into his earlier poems, we are in danger of missing the core of this very human poetry, although we may gain some (questionable) philological equations.

To decide the issue, it seems methodologically correct to ask how Cynthia is depicted in other passages of poem 1.1 itself. Lines 1–8 in general (line 5 excluded) suggest that for a whole year she has not given Propertius the slightest reason for any hope. She is his *domina* (21), he her slave, who has lost the free man's highest quality, free speech (*libertas . . . loqui*, 28). Nothing can change her mind, not even traditional sorcery (*dominae mentem convertite nostrae*, 21); she shows no sign of emotion for him—something he would wish for very much (. . . *illa meo palleat ore magis!* 22). Even if this does not make her strictly *casta*, it puts her closer to the *castae puellae* than to the *incestae* in the eyes of her young admirer (would the idea of a *domina incesta* even occur to him?).

More can be said about the picture the lover fosters of his beloved if we turn to the mythical example of Milanion and Atalante (9–16). This reflects the poet's own situation—but comes to the happy ending which Propertius is denied. Atalante, like Cynthia, is inexorable (*dura*, 10) and shows savage resistance (*saevitia*, 10). The myth, which Propertius does not recount in detail, knows her as a chaste huntress dedicated to Artemis. (To avoid marriage, she even outraces and kills her prospective suitors, and Aphrodite herself has to invent a trick to capture her—a feature which Propertius does not mention, but perhaps alludes to by the word *velox*, 15.) If—and there is no doubt about this—Atalante, symbol of chastity, is to represent Cynthia (with the only difference that Atalante finally gives in while Cynthia does not!), I see no way of withholding here from Cynthia the attribute she is generally denied.[59]

The myth of Atalante indicates two things about our problem: first, that Cynthia cannot be excluded from the *castae puellae* of line 5, and that, if she *has* to be classified (something that Propertius does not directly do in his account of how Love changed him and his life), she will be counted in their number; and second, that *castas* in line 5 may even be taken in its strict meaning and need not be strained (a fault one has found, as we saw, with interpretation I-1 of the word), even if it is to comprise Cynthia also.[60]

The latter result goes together with our interpretation of lines 1–6 as a sort of Propertian epigram, the point of which lies in its third distich and is to be found in Propertius' new condition, which is sharply opposed to his former. This result, too, allowed us to give *castas odisse puellas* its full impact and did not require us to water the phrase down, as some have done, to something like "dislike resistant girls".

The first consequence of our decision in favor of interpretation I is that we are freed from one inherent inconsistency, from which the interpretations of group II suffer. For it seems that this understanding, while trying[61] to acknowledge Cynthia's rejection of the young suitor, must allow chastity to come in again through the back door by according the presumed light-o'-love Cynthia a sort of semivirtuous status like *amica*, "the most respectable sort of courtesan".[62] So is the unprepared reader of the opening elegy to understand that Cynthia is a harlot—but one of highest haughtiness? Once more our earlier objection applies: if Amor is supposed to have taught the young man to appreciate Cynthia's being *incesta*, how could even a god do so with Cynthia's withholding (lines 8 and 17) her favors from the neophyte?

The second and positive consequence is drawn by evaluating what Propertius poetically intends by introducing Cynthia as a girl of inexorable chastity. Here we have to realize first that this presentation is valid on the level and within the context of the opening lines: if the young lover has only recently ceased to be the erotically indifferent Hippolytus-like boy depicted in the first 3 lines, he quite naturally understands his beloved girl's indifference towards him against the background of his own limited horizon, and thus interprets her haughtiness as an Atalante-like chastity and as that aversion to love which he himself until recently felt towards the other sex. He has awakened to a state of conscious, shameless love that bids him woo his mistress as Milanion does. But she, in his eyes, is an Atalante, and has not been subjected to the painful process which he has had to face some time ago.

Of course, this tells us nothing about the historical Cynthia (the alleged Hostia), and it is not supposed to; but it is meant to tell us much about young Propertius' feelings for Cynthia as his beloved—all the more because he will later say that this period of his life was, at least partially, an illusion. When he introduces himself to the reader in the way he does in the opening lines, as nearly a boy himself still, who has fallen in love with a *casta domina*, he means to say that he set out to love her with the highest expectation: he communicates to us the innocence of his love in a way comparable to Catullus' simile of the flower relentlessly cut down by the passing plow (Cat. 11.21–24). From an ideal concept, any path that leads away can lead only downward. For Propertius, love begins by humiliating his innocent pride, and it will go on broadening his view, enlarging his human experience by humiliating and disappointing him ever more— with few periods of happiness in between. He will be ready to settle for less and less, compromising himself more and more, but he will not give up his love for the woman who does all this to him.

For her, too, elegy 1.1 outlines an ideal: it shows what Cynthia could have been, if she had responded to Propertius in the way he intensely wished; she could have become his Atalante. But she was not to; on the contrary, she later became his teacher in the field of human failure, sharpening his sense of affliction by every new move she made. It is worthwhile to quote the words he utters on one such occasion. He is very ill, but she keeps him waiting, taking her time to dress up as if preparing herself to see another man (1.15.1/2):

> Saepe ego multa tuae levitatis dura timebam
> hac tamen excepta, Cynthia, perfidia.

> Often I feared the many hard blows resulting from your
> irresponsibility,
> except however this perfidy, O Cynthia.

Life—and Cynthia *is* life for Propertius—is full of surprises, and not too often good ones. In this sense of growing insight into the ways of human existence, we are entitled to speak of an autobiographical tendency in Propertius' poetry—but it is not stated in calendar terms. Once we have seen that many of his elegies define steps or stages of a process of "education", of growing experience and growing awareness, we can avoid mistakes resulting from too simple a use of cross-references, and we can also read many a poem of his more adequately, because we will respect its special situation. Thus, the long, obstructed way we had to go for understanding eight lines (and for removing misunderstandings about these eight lines), has opened up access to some principal features of Propertius' poetry. As to elegy 1.1, we may sum up by stating that the choice of innocence, youthful inexperience, unworldly trust, in short: vulnerability for the introductory situation of his book infinitely deepens the reader's understanding of the poet's present (and future) sorrowful experiences (and of his happier ones as well). For it shows the unbridgeable distance between hope or ideal and reality.

We now proceed to consider the rest of the elegy, which does not present so many difficulties to a general understanding as it at one time did. The introductory passage 1–8 displays, as we indicated earlier, a transparent structure which agrees well with its contents: the first distich relates the impulse which ends a period of rest; the second and third tell of the ensuing development; and the fourth presents an evaluation of the new situation. A similar, perhaps even clearer organization will be found in the next section (9–16), which again consists of four distichs and thus matches the first. Its structural principle, however, is not progress in time as in 1–8, but logical argumentation: a thesis (9/10) is proved (*nam*, 11) by a climactic narration (11–14), from whose ending the correctness of the initial assertion is then inferred (*ergo*, 15) and confirmed (15/16): a kind of a/b/b/a structure.[63] The presence of so logical a train of thought in our elegy is indicative of Propertius' wish to present a clear-cut, unequivocal case, intelligible to every reader and especially so to his friend Tullus, whom he addresses in line 9 (and to whom he thus, following a Roman tradition, dedicates his Cynthia-book).

Now it is generally agreed that the myth here offers an *exemplum e contrario*[64] to Propertius' own situation: Milanion finally does win Atalante, having gone through hardships and even wounds (although he may beg his beloved like Milanion, a self-sacrifice is probably denied to Propertius). But the myth offers more than that. Atalante is by no means a normal case, but in herself something on the order of an Amazon; still, her example shows that even the most chaste of girls can give in to love—except Cynthia. Here we can grasp one function of the myth which is usually overlooked. It mediates between Propertius' own suffering, which lies beyond imagination, and normal experience, by furnishing an example which stretches the usual concept of a girl's haughtiness towards a suitor without surpassing the limits of common understanding.

In spite of its mediating function, however, the mythical example does not lie in the middle between Propertius and other young men, but, by its happy ending, belongs to the world in which, he feels, he does not participate. This is stressed by the hard opposition between lines 8 and 9 (asyndeton: Milanion, the active, heroic counter-Propertius, is introduced into the poet's self-contemplation without any connective explanation). It is even stressed by the dedication to Tullus, the postponement of which to line 9 should never have been found surprising: Tullus, too, although a friend, belongs to those who need an example which is comprehensible to their limited understanding, who can sympathize with Propertius' despairing love only when and insofar as it is presented to them in the distorting mirror which shows a successful Milanion. Thus the dedication is both an act of gratitude and devotion and, by its context, a mark of distance and a statement of separation.[65] The addressee no less than the myth turns out to be an ingredient in the picture which Propertius draws of his loneliness. The difficulty of communication we found in 1.12 is already expressed in the introductory poem and is linked, here as elsewhere, to his consciousness of having a special fate.

The myth itself is readily understandable; so I pass over here a detailed application of its contents to Propertius' situation (*amens*, 11, corresponds to Propertius' *furor*, 7, cf. 8). On the whole, Milanion's active manliness[66] is stressed (cf. especially *potuit domuisse*, 15) as opposed to Propertius' passive exposure to torture, which leads only to hate, but not to activity. In this respect the emphatic summary in line 16 is interesting because it spells out again the power usually ascribed to *preces* and *bene facta*[67] in love, from which Milanion's victory was naturally derived.

Nothing has changed for Propertius when, with lines 17/18, he switches back to his own person in the same abrupt way (asyndeton) in which he had broken away from himself to Milanion. But the outline of his situation has become much sharper now. He stresses this result not only (17) by again referring to his long, helpless wait (*tardus Amor*, 17, takes up *toto anno*, 7), but also (18) by including a comparison between his present hopelessness and Amor's general helpfulness in a mythical past.[68] If line 17 picks up the thread again from lines 1–8, and line 18 spells out what results from lines 9–16 for Propertius' own situation, the elegy so far has completed one single, coherent circle of description: Propertius–Milanion–Propertius. Again one may marvel at the apparent high degree of logic employed in a presentation of an emotional situation: the whole train of thought so far can be understood as an attempt at self-definition, with the myth serving as a substitute and negative foil for what cannot be expressed clearly in the positive—*definitio sui per negationem*.

The emotional result of the circular movement of thought is that the lover's despair appears even more justified than before. Thus it is with strict consequence of motivation that he now demonstrates the vainness of crying out for help from others (19ff.), addressing two groups: (a) sorceresses (19–24) and (b) friends (25–30), the first with regard to winning over Cynthia, the second with regard to freeing him from the disease of love by employing the harshest measures: surgery and cauterization (27–28), i.e., (I suggest), geographical separation from Cynthia and all women who could remind him of her (29–30).

As the two means of help contradict each other, editors generally replace the connecting *et* of our manuscript tradition in line 25 by *aut* (a minimal "change" considering medieval abbreviations), thus marking (a) and (b) sharply by a near-repetition of sound: *at vos* (19) . . . *aut vos* (25). The *aut* is further supported by the allusion to our passage in 3.24.9f.: *patrii . . . amici . . . aut . . . Thessala saga.* Even if (a) and (b) together will turn out to be a mere accumulation of useless means which would justify the reading *et*, the actual invocation of first one group and then the other (their distinctive functions being observed) by the same speaker demands that we read *aut*—unless we are ready to deny the poet here the logic his poetry usually displays. The fact that the deeper meaning of (a) as well as of (b) amounts to stating an adynaton does not allow us to break the coherence of the poetic language and of the surface conceit. After all, the two groups addressed are assigned different tasks: (a) is to change Cynthia's heart, (b) is to change the poet's mind.[69]

The technique is similar to that which we found in 1.11.1–8 and 9–16, where the poet twice managed to formulate an alternative both parts of which appeared to be negative and pessimistic. In 19–24 (a) the speaker declares his readiness to believe in famous examples of witches' power on the condition that the witches *first* prove their might by converting Cynthia's haughtiness—which is a new way of stating the hopelessness of his love. Reduced to a simple proposition, these three distichs mean: "It is easier to pull the moon down from the sky than to change Cynthia's indifference towards me."[70] Much has been written about Propertius' attitude to witchcraft, whereas the plain truth is that his argument presupposes as a fact that the moon can *not* be pulled down!

In 25–30 (b) the same logic applies to his appeal to friends: of course he assumes that his love cannot be removed from his heart by the kind of "surgery" that his friends would have in mind (we recall 1.12). To call for transportation to a womanless place beyond the limits of mankind is as utopian as calling for the help of sorcery.[71] So what this appeal amounts to is the statement "And you, too, my dear friends with your patronizing but late advice along the traditional lines, are of *no* help to me!" A slight note of refusal, even a shade of blame (*qui sero lapsum revocatis*) may be heard here, very similar to the irony with which we saw him treat his fatherly adviser in 1.12.1/2 (which, of course, does not exclude from *sero* a tinge of tragic hopelessness).

The poetical surprise of lines 18–30 lies in the fact that Propertius has found a still wider range for the expression of his personal isolation: after Cynthia, Amor, the gods, Milanion, Tullus, now even witches (a traditional help in an irrational situation) and volunteering friends are introduced and prove to be of no avail; while the group of "the others" receives accretion, the outline of his loneliness becomes still sharper: *definitio e contrario*.

Recognition of the way the two groups (a) and (b) function in the lover's self-analysis can help us to determine the position of the distich 31/32 in the argument. Editors often continue the train of thought by printing a colon (:) at the end of line 30. And the vocative *vos* (31) as well as the simile contained in *remanete* (31) does indeed seem to tie this distich to the foregoing, which speaks of Propertius' geographical removal from Rome. But this line of interpretation is not satisfactory:

First, the parallel *At vos . . . aut vos* beginnings of (a) and (b) seem to correspond naturally to the equal number of distichs (three each: 19–24; 25–30) employed to address both groups. Moreover, with line 30 the vain appeal for help, addressed to the admonishing friends, has come to its logical end, whether it is taken on the surface level of calling for help or on the deeper level that states the impossibility of help.

Secondly, *vos*, 31, more closely determined by the relative clause *quibus facili deus annuit aure*, denotes a group of happy lovers which is not identical with *vos*, 25, the group of admonishing friends (although, of course, some of the "fatherly friends",[72] as they are called in the allusion at 3.24.9, may be happy lovers . . .).

On the other hand, the distich 31/32 is seen to have a useful function when taken together with what follows rather than with what precedes. Line 33 recalls[73] the beginning *in me tardus Amor* of line 17 by metrical pattern (4 words of equal prosody), by sound pattern (*in me*, 17 ~ *in me*, 33), and even by its contents (Amor, 17 ~ Venus, 33). Thus distich 33/34 completes the second circle of self-definition (19–34), which, like the first (1–18), separates Propertius from other, happier lovers. Lines 31/32 now spell out this separation in most forceful language by taking up the idea of Propertius' removal from Rome (29/30) and working it into a metaphor. "You happy lovers, stay behind!", understood in the way I propose, is a last goodbye to all others, spoken already from the other shore, so to speak (cf. *ferte per undas*), and thus serving as an excellent introduction to the second and final statement of his now utter separation (*remanete*) and isolation. The latter is communicated to us by a description of the despair that fills his lonely nights (33/34). Propertius leaves the country of "safe love" (cf. *in tuto . . . amore*, 32) where couples can be united "always" (*semper*,

32), bound for a different destination which is solitude: "You want to re-move me from Rome? Remove me beyond the known world: that is my place anyway. And goodbye to you, world of happy lovers."

Thus *vos* in line 31 is not said in continuation of *at vos . . . aut vos*, but in contrast[74] to and as the negative foil for the following *in me nostra Venus*. Understanding the couplet 31/32 in this way, one is also able to give a sat-isfactory explanation of the much disputed word *nostra*, 33. As, in the parallel line 17, *Amor* is concerned only with Propertius' situation and not with anybody else, and just as in line 31 *deus* applies only to the other lovers (excepting Propertius), in the same way *nostra*, being *pluralis maiestatis* (or, rather, *modestiae*), refers to Propertius only and means "my"[75] Venus, singling out the poet's singular fate,[76] but hardly means "the Venus we lovers worship",[77] etc.: this elegy lives from the pendular movement of thought which swings to and fro between Propertius and all other lovers.[78]

Once the opposition of distichs 31/32 and 33/34 is recognized, some other problems find their solution also: Propertius' Venus, who does not fulfill his prayers, but renders his nights bitter (*amaras*, 33), is just the op-posite of the deity (*deus*) who has "⟨listened⟩ with merciful ear ⟨and⟩[79] nodded fulfillment" to happy worshippers (31). Thus we get a mean-ingful, intended relationship between the two hexameters 31 and 33.

The same, I think, is true of the pentameters 32 and 34: *semper* in 32 corresponds to *nullo . . . tempore* in 34; the well-meaning wish *sitis . . . pares* corresponds to the despairing "never . . . ceases" (*defit*; there is also some contrasting with *vacuus*); and, last but not least, *in tuto . . . amore* corresponds to *vacuus . . . amor*. The last-mentioned phrase, like the dis-puted *nostra Venus* in 33, represents another old *crux* in Propertian schol-arship. Current rendering ("Cupid is never idle, never absent", Housman, Enk) contains an unsatisfactory duplicate (literally: "ceases unoccupied"). But as an intentional counter-piece to the "safe" love of others ("safe" be-cause protected by a gracious deity), Propertius' own "single love" is a paradoxical expression which excellently describes his paradoxical situa-tion: love—but without a partner! The term *vacuus*, usually employed for *women* without a lover, fits Propertius the better because of his inactive condition: closer to a woman than to a Milanion.[80]

The correspondence with *amore* (32) is against spelling the word with a capital A in 34, as is usually done by editors: Propertius' feelings of lonely love are what is needed in this passage, not the god Amor. The question whether we should understand *deus* in 31 to refer to Venus (in correspondence with *Venus*, 33) rather than Amor hardly arises because their functions are not distinguished here.

To sum up: lines 31/34 are to be taken together; the former distich wishes good-bye to all happy lovers, and thus summarizes the world from which the poet is excluded. This summary serves as a foil to the poet's own sad and paradoxical situation, to which the latter distich returns. There is no *crux*, and no conjecture is necessary.

With line 34, the double movement (1–18; 19–34), by which Propertius has defined his own situation, has come to rest. The assertion about the unhappiness (*me miserum*, 1) which love means to him has been fully elucidated; were the poem about his unhappiness only, we would not desire anything more after line 34. There is, however, something in the nature of a consequence, and it comes in naturally at first, almost casually: the circumstance that his attempt at self-definition has led him to think of himself as separated from other, happier lovers by an ocean (29/30), or of himself and others as located on opposite shores (poetically the two positions were formulated in two different but related distichs: 31/32 and 33/34), of his situation and condition as different from that of others—this circumstance means, as soon as it is realized intellectually, a higher degree of knowledge or consciousness on Propertius' part: he knows of their state and their love; they, however, not only do not understand him but are even unable to appreciate or recognize their own situation in its full meaning.

This difference in the degree of consciousness is present, more latently than openly, in the contrast of distichs 31/32 and 33/34. In the next two distichs, 35–38, it is out in the open, realized and verified by the unhappy Propertius, who bursts out into the *warning* (*moneo*, 35; *monitis*, 37) that none of the others should follow him into solitude because of the pain they might experience. "This evil, I warn you, avoid!" (35). Scholars have wondered what evil, *malum*, he may precisely hint at. I have no doubt that he thinks of the *amor vacuus* (34), which, applied to other, happier lovers, means willfully deserting their beloved one, as contrasted with his own involuntary loneliness: they must be warned by him because they themselves *do not know* the risk they incur.

I hesitate to call Propertius' position here, as some[81] have done, that of the *erotodidascalus*. Although that may be implied (and would be adequate to call Ovid), it is not the important aspect. I do not hesitate to call his position, as he understands it, tragic; it is another instance of the old Aeschylean πάθει μάθος—learning through suffering (*Ag.* 177). Propertius is not so much *magister* but warner, even prophet: the last words *(heu referet quanto verba dolore mea!)* are indisputably prophetic language. *They* are to ring still in the ear of the reader who has finished reading the poem.

Thus, the final four lines give the whole poem a new twist and make all the foregoing (1–34) appear precursory. What seemed to be result (31–34) now turns out to have been, although unexpectedly, the premise to a higher insight, to an inference:[82] his suffering, Propertius realizes, has made him wiser than others. And he not only realizes this within himself, but announces it openly in form of a claim: his singular fate is the title to a tragic gift of prophecy. The poet, of whose love others will read for their own guidance, is born.

We may now proceed to sum up our observations by outlining the elegy's movement of thought: [83]

I   1–18: First circle of self-definition.
   (1) 1–8:   autobiographical statement: helpless love (abbc).   4D
   (2) 9–16: *exemplum e contrario*: Milanion, finally successful
                 (abba).   4D
   (3) 17–18: hope- and helplessness confirmed   ⌐ 1D
II 19–34: Second movement of self-definition.
   (1) 19–24: no help from sorcery (no influence on Cynthia).   │ 3D
   (2) 25–30: no help from friends (his love inextinguishable). │ 3D
   (3) 31–34: hope- and helplessness confirmed: ⌐ 2D (A)
                 (a) 31/32 separation from happy lovers;   │
                 (b) 33/34 his permanent loneliness formulated.   ↓
III 35–38: Consequences of the result as formulated in 31–34:   2D (B)
                 Propertius' higher consciousness is prophetical
                 wisdom. The poet as a warner.

In the poem's context, lines 31–34 (2D where, as the parallel 17/18 suggests, one would expect 1D) serve a double function: (a) they pronounce the *result* of the foregoing double movement of definition; (b) they form the *premise* (A) to a third definition (B), which presents the poet's function as that of a warner.

Again, as in elegy 1.11, the poem's structure turns out to be not rigidly schematic but flexible enough to mirror a live movement of thought, to include even "unplanned" inferences. If a group of distichs appears irregular to us (like the "inflated" 2D group 31–34), we are able to account for such irregularity by reason of contents—as we can in the case of groups of equal length. Propertius' own story of lacking success and that of successful counter-Propertius Milanion are told in 4D each; the failing help from sorcery or from friends is presented in a group of 3D each time.

Forming a group of distichs that belong together and making this group parallel or contrasting with another is an important means for Propertius to present his thoughts clearly. Trying to explicate this inherent structure must be the foremost task of the interpreter. In fulfilling it, he has to proceed as long as possible on the hypothesis that the textual tradition is sound and that this author is able to express himself logically and economically. Such a hypothesis prevents him from rash conjectures and from pushing around distichs, and even from looking for lost distichs, which perhaps never existed (Housman desired very much an addition between lines 11 and 12 of elegy 1.1, and tentatively filled the alleged gap by two lines of his own—therein still finding the consent of Enk).[84]

—III—

LOVE ELEGY AND "HIGHER" POETRY

Of the love elegies contained in the *Monobiblos* (as Propertius' first book is usually called), I have selected for detailed consideration the three which seem to be closest to the poet's own heart. One may question whether this selection is justified, but there is a strong point in its favor: in 1.1 as well as in the pair 1.11 and 12 Propertius chooses the form of auto-biographical statement, and in both cases he not only tells of an event (fall-ing in love in 1.1; experiencing estrangement in 1.12), but also gives a pre-cise account of how the event has influenced his own personality (loss of pride and principles, the prospect of future solitude in 1.1; loss of his iden-tity and consciousness of permanent dependence in 1.12). We hardly ever get closer to what a person considers to be his own center. If, as in our case, the person speaking is a poet, we should be grateful to be granted access, but should not play psychiatrist and try to learn more about him than he consciously and willingly gives us in the medium of his poems. After all, we, not being biographical detectives, wish first and foremost to achieve a better understanding of his writings rather than of his "affair." Certainly, Propertius' love poetry has many more aspects, which may often include a higher degree of sophistication and often present happier subject matter than there is contained in 1.1, 11, and 12. I shall briefly touch on these aspects in the next chapter, for what is involved in nearly every instance belongs to a more marginal sphere of life and poetry (even a love poet may not always be serious or gloomy). There are, however, some decisions and statements in fields other than love which are closer to what appears in the autobiographical elegies, in that they are presented as direct consequences of the poet's awareness of his fate—the necessity that love be the center of his life. (About one possible exception or addition, also an autobiographical issue, I shall speak in the next chapter.)

One of these consequences appears in Propertius' attitude to poetry, others' as well as his own. Having considered his self-definition as a lonely warner in matters of love (1.1), we can say a priori what his judgment on other poets and their poetry will be like, in the first place: it will be just like his judgment on anybody else. Having taught us to judge him by the intensity of his love, and his poetry by the degree to which it reflects this condition, he measures others by the same standard, inquiring how far they possess the human quality of being able to be affected by love. He even goes so far as to do this in the same biographical fashion in which he assessed his own fate: to what extent does love change one's life? This is the way he presents to us his friend Gallus the girl-chaser (see also 1.5): in a sequence, Gallus is first shown (1.10) when he meets a girl who may bind him permanently; then (1.13), after Gallus has fallen in love and is a captive, Propertius predicts Gallus' fate (9ff.) and expresses the hope that from now on Gallus may love only one woman (36)—as Propertius himself does! Friend Tullus, the career politician, is seen as being still young and as having "never" fallen in love (1.6.21), so that he remains a question mark in Book 1 (see the following chapter). His state may be compared to that of Propertius before he saw Cynthia. Ponticus, epic poet, is in the same state when we first meet him (1.7). Propertius predicts what will happen as soon as Amor's arrow has wounded him (15f.). Then (1.9), we see the oracle fulfilled (1ff.), and Propertius can go on to inform Ponticus what he may expect from now on (17ff.).

What these parallels teach us is that Propertius does not show himself interested in Ponticus primarily as an epic poet, but in so far as he is a potential (and, later, actual) lover: the question of this human quality ranks highest, as it does in Propertius himself, in Gallus, in Tullus. Of course, a fellow poet has much more in common with him than, say, a soldier or a politician. But this does not, to Propertius' mind, matter when he decides whether somebody is close to him or just one of "the others", members of that conventional, easygoing, happy world from which he himself is dissociated most of the time. In order to be acknowledged by Propertius, one needs more than poetical skill.

Propertius' outspoken decision in favor of this human quality is of highest importance if we assess his attitude to the tradition of Roman and earlier Alexandrian poetry. It is not his scrupulous dedication to the Callimachean ideal of the small but finely chiseled poem that makes him a poet (it makes him a *poeta doctus*, and even as such he most wishes to be appreciated, not by other learned poets, but by his *puella docta*: 1.7.11). No, what makes him essentially a poet is, as he presents his case, above all his unconditional commitment to Cynthia. Poetry implies personal involvement.[1]

Some of his readers may not see (or may even doubt) that he presents his case "sincerely". Although I see their reasons, I am not persuaded to move my interpretations away from his own words. A good criterion of the picture he intends to give (if there really should be need of one) is that he applies the same standard to Ponticus which he applies to other friends and to himself. Thus, if we find statements about poets and poetry in elegies 1.7 and 9, we may see them also in the larger context of Book 1, which defines Propertius' place in the surrounding world, and we may judge them to be derived from a realm of existence which is closer to or identical with the core of Propertius' poetry and professedly his own self.

1.7

While you, Ponticus, are singing of Cadmean Thebes,
    and of sad arms used in fraternal warfare,
and—as I wish to be happy!—are contending with Homer the master
    (would only, this my wish, fate be merciful to *your* songs!),

We are, as we are accustomed, doing our love poems,
    and looking for something effective to soften our harsh mistress;
and I am forced to serve not so much my talent as my pain
    and to grieve over the harsh times of my youth.   (1–8)

In this manner *my* life's span is worn away, this is *my* fame,
    from here I desire *my* song's glory to spread:
may I be praised as the only one to have won the learned girl's
                                approbation,
    Ponticus, and as having often endured her unjust threats!
May I hereafter be read constantly by the despised lover,
    and may our sorrows, when known, be of help to him!   (9–14)

If you, too, will have been shaken by this boy with his unfailing arrow
    (I would not wish our gods to have decreed this for you),
then, unhappy man, you will realize amid tears that for you the camp is
                           far away, the seven armies far away,
    lying in silence, buried in the eternal rust of oblivion.
And in vain you will long to write a delicate line ⟨of love poetry⟩,
    nor will Amor, at so late a date, come to prompt you any songs. (15–20)

Then you will often admire *me* as no lowly poet,
    then *I* shall head the procession of the Roman literary talents.
And the young men will not be able to keep from saying at our grave:
    "Great poet of our ardor, you lie dead!"   (21–24)

You be careful, and do not despise our songs with your haughtiness:
    often Amor, when coming late, charges high interest!   (25–26)

Readings different from OCT: 10: colon at the end. 16: (*quod nolim nostros evoluisse deos!*). 12, 14, 24, 26: exclamation mark (!) at the end.

The elegy begins by opposing the present concerns of Ponticus (1–4) and Propertius (5–8): while Ponticus is "composing" a *Thebais*, i.e., an epic, Propertius is "busy" with his lowly love verses. As far as contents are concerned, the contrast is clearly one of love, *amores* (5, or of hope for love, 6), and the war, *arma* (2), of fraternal dissent. The way in which the introductory lines of both sections (1/2 correspond to 5/6) characterize the activities of the two poets already indicates that they are working on different levels. This is borne out if we compare the second distichs in the two sections (lines 3/4 correspond with 7/8: the whole group 1–8 is marked by an a/b/a/b structure): Ponticus is contending with the arch-poet Homer; Propertius is concerned not so much with genius (as Ponticus supposedly is) but with his sorrow concerning a difficult woman. What a difference! The incommensurable goals of their ambition (Homer, a woman) make this clear even more than did the foregoing comparison of their activities.

Distinction by language reinforces that by logic: while Propertius continues to describe his own labor in low-key terms ("harsh mistress— harsh life"),[2] he gives his friend the epic poet all the grandeur he can ask for. In fact, Propertius himself rises to the lofty heights of epic style in describing the friend's work (1/2), and he is so successful in imitating[3] the enigmatic way of highbrow epic that we, like his contemporary readers, feel grateful for our education in the classics, because otherwise we would hardly guess that Propertius is speaking of Oedipus' sons Eteocles and Polyneices and their fight for the possession of their paternal (or maternal) city of Thebes.

Thus, what lines 1–8 seem to amount to (and what they have been taken for) is a perfect compliment to the epic poet, paid by his humble colleague, writer of love elegies. This, needless to say, is in complete harmony with the standing clichés about literary genera current in Propertius' own time, clichés which are not only literary but also social ones. Since the day of Hellenism dawned, epic poetry has been considered the adequate way to express the greatness of a powerful man, be he king, consul, or conquerer; and just about the time that Propertius sets out to write his elegies, another epic poet sets out to combine once again the literary and the social prestige of epic poetry to praise another emperor as history's fulfillment (and in so doing, he will be able to have recourse to a few passages in the Homeric *Iliad* that were interpolated at an earlier date to please a local dynasty). Although Propertius will have occasion later to deal with that poet and his court-oriented literary career (2.34, see our Chapter VII), we need not associate Ponticus' epic in 1.7 with any person on the contemporary political stage. For his subject matter, a *Thebais*, seems remote enough from historical times (it may allude to the recent civil war, but of this there can hardly be any proof). We should probably see no more in the compliment than a reflection of the general contemporary esteem for epic.

This in itself, however, may be sufficient to startle us. "Propertius sharing a conventional evaluation?" is a justified question, when we recall his unconditional, even harsh reaction to common clichés elsewhere. Rather, we expect him to take up someone else's language (as we observed him doing in answering the faultfinder's charge in 1.12.3–6) in order to create some common background, before which he can then explain his dissent. That is exactly the case here: the modesty he displays in describing his own poetry is hardly compatible with the relevance he claims it has to his own life (or with the rest of the poem). And comparing his friend to Homer seems more than slightly excessive, the more so as Propertius is prepared to vouch for this statement by risking his own happiness (3; but does he possess any happiness? Line 7 seems to testify to the contrary!). Above all, there is his wish that "only" fate may be lenient to the new Homer's work (no contest here!)—more lenient than it has shown itself to the original one's (of the whole epic cycle, that once circulated under Homer's name, only *Iliad* and *Odyssey* were still much read in Propertius' time—the *Thebais* was among the less well known[4]); which means, in plain English: "Let us hope that your creation will not also be widely forgotten, as is the fate of even the first-rate epic poetry you emulate." Or, in short: "May your work be an exception to the rule!"[5]

Viewed in this way, Propertius' praise of his friend's skills becomes rather ambiguous, while the probable fate of his friend's poetry suddenly appears much clearer. And the first distich's esoteric elaboration—being, on this interpretation, not only an imitation but a persiflage of epic poetry—can perhaps be taken as an explanation of why, in the elegist's eyes, that sort of poetry does not find readers to prevent it from sinking into oblivion.

The above proposed interpretation puts lines 1–8 in harmony with the rest of the elegy, as we shall see immediately. It also makes Propertius' alleged worry, that he is in the service of *dolor*[6] rather than of *ingenium* (7), pretty superfluous: Ponticus should be the one who worries about *ingenium*.

Propertius' own evaluation of his poetry is revealed in the lines immediately following (9–14), where he stops viewing himself through the glasses of a lofty epic poet. Now he claims for himself (10) the term *carmen*, which he had previously reserved for his friend (4), then grading his own products as *amores* (5).

We are supposed to sense his self-confidence, which makes him erect a monument to love elegy right beside that to epic, without regard for convention: fame and glory (*fama*, *nomen*) are connected with his lowly topics, too. And, contrary to Ponticus' scale of values, Propertius even desires (*cupio*, 10) himself to be measured as a poet by his achievements in love poetry. This is the message he hammers (*hic* . . . *haec* . . . *hinc*) into our ears, stressing the point that he—what else could we expect from him? —has a personal set of values, independent from conventional literary clichés: the emphatic series *mihi . . . mea . . . mei* (9/10) initiates the proud statements concerning his own goals, and it is continued by the triumphant and exclamatory parallel beginnings *me . . . me* (11 and 13), which set the tone for the following two distichs.

The whole group 9–14 points to the future, because Propertius here defines the ends he desires to achieve by his beginning poetry—both during his lifetime (11/12) and in times to come (13/14, cf. *post haec*).

Perhaps the possibility cannot be excluded that he ironically over-emphasizes the trifling character (in the epicist's estimation) of his achievement. The praise (*laudent*) which is to result in his lifetime shall be: he alone won his learned girl's approval and showed himself a servant devoted beyond the measure of justice. While the second claim is already known to us from other poems, the first leads, as I indicated at the beginning of this chapter, to another blow aimed at the conventional estimation of literature: it is not only that his fame as a poet will be built on its own subject matter (9–10, picking up 5–8, cf. *hinc*); the critic, too, from whose hands he hopes to receive the first and only prize (*solum*, 11)[7] is not any fellow poet like Ponticus or the elegiac poet whom Horace imagines with horror competing in the Palatine Library (*Epist.* 2.2.91ff.) or an educated general public. No, Propertius' critic, besides possessing the usual qualities of the profession (*docta*), has to be involved personally with his poems: *puella* denotes the object of his poetry not only in the sense that she is depicted in them (like a painter's model), but also in the sense that she is to be moved by them. She represents the "audience" the artist truly cares to satisfy. Again it turns out that Propertius' conception of a poet is not limited to aesthetics.

It is, however, not limited to life either, or even, within the sphere of life, to merely "winning the girl" in the sense of Tibullus' lines *ite procul, Musae, si non prodestis amanti* (2.4.15) and *ad dominam faciles aditus per carmina quaero* (2.5.19). The emphasis of Prop. 1.7.11 does not lie so much—as Stroh (1971, 13) thinks—on his success as a lover (". . . wird Properz durch sein dichterisches Vermögen in seinen praktischen Interessen gefördert"). Both *doctae* and *solum* raise the concern of elegy beyond mere erotic success, the former by addressing the level of literary criticism, the latter by voicing Propertius' personal mark of never-ceasing anxiety (the words *neglectus amator* and *nostra mala* in the following distich are very revealing) and futile wish *placeam tibi, Cynthia, solus.*[8] As far as literary criticism is concerned, the interpreter is, in addition to observing the epithet *doctae*, asked not to neglect the context built up in lines 1–8 where the background was given from which the emphasized *me* in 11 stands out. Because of the implied contrast to his friend the epicist, the words suggest the readers may use the exclusive approbation Propertius (hopes to have) won from this unusual but competent judge as a criterion of his high qualifications as a poet in his own right. In meting out praise to Propertius, his readers are expected to join the poet and make the learned girl's standards their own. This audience is very differently conditioned from the one Ponticus would desire for his epic, both in scope and in standards. Such "literary" goals will be as shocking and paradoxical to the epic poet (who is, we observe, not without a purpose addressed once again here by name) as the idea, expressed in the following line (12), of a glory (*laudent*, 11) based on *endurance* (*tulisse*) of *injustice* (*iniustas* gives *minas* a special flavor). There again life (especially in its painful, less optimistic aspects) does play its part in the appreciation of this poetry and forcefully forbids Ponticus (and the reader), if he wants to be congenial to Propertius, to limit his understanding to the sphere of aesthetics.

The absence of this limitation is stressed even more in the subsequent picture of the general reader whom Propertius desires, beyond his personal and autobiographical situation (*me legat . . . post haec*, 13). The reader is supposed to have been wounded in the same way as Propertius has been (*neglectus amator*), and, recognizing his own sorrow in the mirror of Propertius' elegies, he is supposed to consider this recognition a help (*prosint*)—presumably because it enables him to find an orientation about himself and his incomprehensible plight in addition to bringing consolation which results from being told that one is not alone in one's suffering. F. Solmsen, who has given ample consideration to this notion, finds it unique in antiquity.[9] It certainly is in line with Propertius' position in 1.1, where he wishes to spare others the loneliness to which he himself is exposed. It is also an application to others of the difficult process of reorientation he himself had to go through (1.1) alone. Finally, it is a consequence of his contention that his kind of poetry is meaningful to human beings and not a thing of indifference. If others do find themselves in his elegies, it is the highest confirmation he can desire, source of his pride and his glory (cf. line 24): it proves to him that he can move human beings where they are human.

No wonder that he will stress this poetic goal again at other times, the more so (we may anticipate here his future course as a poet) the harder he feels pressure from others to leave the sphere which he believes to be central. So when Maecenas urges him to write an epic, he writes defensively:

> May these writings of mine burn boys, may they burn girls,
> And may they (the boys and girls) loudly call *me* a god and
>   sacrifice to *me*!

> Haec urant pueros, haec urant scripta puellas,
>   meque deum clament et mihi sacra ferant!   (3.9.45–47)

The passage stylistically recalls the emphasis of 1.7.9ff. (the hammering *haec . . . haec*, the parallel *urant . . . urant*, the stress on Propertius himself: *me . . . mihi*), but owing to the pressure from outside, it appears excessive in the wish to receive godlike honors. Even this feature, however, becomes understandable if we attend to the fact that, if Propertius gave in and wrote an epic, its god would be Augustus, not Propertius: could he make readers "burn" for Octavian? Other reasons apart, he would have to give up his independent judgment.

That he is independent of established standards of judgment is a fact which Maecenas has to face as well as Ponticus. This is the reason, we indicated, why Ponticus is called and addressed by name for a second time in the same poem (line 12, after line 1): "*my* glory be that Cynthia appreciates my poetry. Please, *try to understand*, Ponticus!" But in spite of this injunction, Ponticus is not likely to understand. Will a broader public?

As this second address in line 12 indicates, the emphatic stress on Propertius' own position in lines 9–14 is there to point to a basic difference between Ponticus and himself, which may be as difficult for Ponticus to understand as his friend's goals may appear overstated, even trivial, to him. This difference will have almost certain consequences in the future, so that Propertius' future fame with unhappy lovers (9–14) can be effectively contrasted with Ponticus' future plight in the field of love (15–20; note the beginning *te* in line 15, contrasting with *me* of 11 and 13): if Ponticus, some day late in his life (*serus*, 20), should fall in love (15/16), he will come to realize that his *Thebais*, his life's work, is nothing to him (17/18); it will be lying far, far (*longe . . . longe*, 17) away, in the rust of oblivion (18). Ponticus will himself play that fate to his songs, which Propertius had wished (4) they might be spared!

Even more (19/20): Ponticus will then feel the desire to write the kind of poetry which Propertius writes now (because he will either wish to win his girl's approval or, if rejected, to console himself). However, late Amor will not inspire him with *carmina* (20—the term Ponticus himself will then be ready to apply to *amores*).

If we look over the poem's route so far, we see a double reversal[10] (in chiastic form) between the present and the future: Propertius, now the lower-ranking poet (5–8), desires to upgrade his field as that of true poetry (9–14). Ponticus, now the higher-ranking poet (1–4), will abandon his field as meaningless and turn to Propertius' domain (15–20). In the terms of the opening lines, poetry on love (*amores*, 5) will prove superior to the epic glory of war (*arma*, 2)—even in Ponticus' eyes.

It seems we are now ready for a summation. This is given, as can logically be expected from the foregoing, in two phases:

(a) a final forecast of Propertius' future high ranking in Ponticus' eyes (21/22);

(b) an admonition to Ponticus (based on an even stronger warning) to correct his present attitude towards Propertius' poetry (25/26).

The above summation does not account for the difficult couplet 23/24, which disturbs the well-balanced structure (and which Housman and others wished to move from the place to which our manuscript tradition assigns it). Before approaching the difficulty, I consider the result our elegy produces for the relationship of the two friends.

Easiest to understand is (b): rather wittily, Propertius uses the threat of possible future damage (now raised to extraordinary dimensions— *magno faenore*, 26) to scare his friend out of his haughtiness (25). The word *tuo* is to be taken in its precise meaning: "The haughtiness which is peculiar to you", or "your usual haughtiness". Taken together with the strong expression *contemnas*, it lets us understand Propertius' motive for having himself mocked his friend's poetry in the introductory lines 1–8.

(a) concerns Propertius himself (*tum me*, 21; *tunc ego*, 22) and is a consequence of his prophecy (15–20) that Ponticus will change sides; it contains his triumphant assertion that Ponticus will then look up to Propertius (*mirabere*; *non humilem . . . poetam*, 21) instead of down on him as he does now. The *tum—tunc* emphasis, combined with the stress on *me—ego*, is very similar to that of lines 9–10; but, what was a wish and a goal there (*cupio*, etc.), is now imagined as a fact (future indicative): Ponticus will be included among Propertius' admirers, and, even more, Propertius will be preferred by him (*a te* we have to supply from the closer context with *praeferar*, 22) to "the Roman talents"—a striking expression, the meaning of which, when explicated, is even more striking. The term can only mean that, in favor of Propertius (not, indeed, a "Roman luminary"!), he will abandon his former epic models. Now let us recall from line 3 that Homer is not simply his model but also his rival—in the same way as Vergil will proclaim himself the "New Homer" by the first seven lines of the *Aeneid*. Homer, however, was not a Roman. Therefore, the "Roman talents"—if we then are to speak out the unspeakable—must be called Naevius and Ennius (Vergil cannot yet be among them, since he has just been setting out on his task), the singers of Roman history: Roman luminaries indeed!

If we press the passage hard in order to decide whether Propertius counts himself among the *ingenia* or not, I would, unlike Solmsen,[11] assume that he does: Ponticus is expected to *prefer* him to the *Roman ingenia*, not to *ingenia*. The act of preference itself as well as the proud *ego* point to the same conclusion as the ironic opposition of *ingenio* and *dolori* in line 7. Again, as it turns out, Propertius feels free to think outside established lines. A special point, of course, is that proud Propertius will have incorporated the formerly proud epic poet in the group of his humble admirers. No one can overlook the phase of literary history alluded to here: we face the Alexandrian antagonism of epic and small poem, which biographical tradition (rightly or wrongly) reflected in the memorable story of the friendship between teacher Callimachus and student Apollonius Rhodius. This broke up when the student undertook to write his epic Ἀργοναυτικά. It is worth recalling this to see how different Propertius' position is: we do not hear any aesthetic verdict like "μέγα βιβλίον—μέγα κακόν" from Propertius' mouth, although, needless to repeat, he himself scrupulously adheres to the Callimachean ideals of polished small poetry on the lines of his neoteric forerunners.[12] Rather, Propertius succeeds in giving a new reason of his own for the traditional rejection of epic poetry, thus subordinating the literary tradition (in which he would otherwise appear only as the latest link) to the substance of his own contribution to poetry: Ponticus will have to give up epic, or poetry of war (arma, 2, as opposed to love poetry, amores, 5), because it turns out to be irrelevant when his personal existence is at stake. In other words, it is by its human value, in times of need, that elegy proves its superiority to epic, and not so much by the aesthetic tradition which it derives from Alexandrianism. This is an original and creative achievement, which makes Propertius a poet in his own right—and (within the scope of the Monobiblos) Ponticus another Tullus or Gallus or even Propertius, who will be put to his very life's test—epic or not.

The interpretation proposed is, as I pointed out earlier, in harmony with the set of values Propertius develops in his most personal poems. It will be confirmed, when we view 1.9, which shows the prophecy given to Ponticus in 1.7 fulfilled. What this interpretation can also show is how easily Propertius is misunderstood when he is interpreted exclusively along lines suggested by the examination of the history of Roman literature, the development of Roman poetical language and meter, or the aesthetic ideals of Alexandrianism. It is true that—as for instance W. Wimmel has set out to prove[13]—he can use the Alexandrian creed as an excuse or a pretense to push aside unwelcome demands for an epic praising Augustus' deeds. We must not forget, however, that he claims he is at the same time defending a creed of his own (or, later, perhaps a plight of his own), which ranks first in his thinking and should rank first in his interpreter's.

So far, the surface plot of elegy 1.7 can be wholly understood as an attempt to clarify the relationship of Propertius the elegiac, and Ponticus the epic, poet, proceeding along the line of an argument that moves to and fro between the one and the other. (In a similar way, 1.1 defines Propertius' position by a detailed comparison with other, happier lovers.) The result is that Propertius has no reason to fear Ponticus' haughtiness. (In the end, he can even wittily raise his earlier predictions of a coming storm to that of a possible hurricane, magno faenore.)

But there is one aspect of the poem which, if pursued to its logical conclusion, leads one beyond the surface meaning. This conclusion is formulated in that one distich (23/24) which destroys the poem's parallel structure. We find here the same technique which Propertius uses in 1.11. There, too, one "odd" distich carries the message that exceeds the poem's apparent scope.[14]

The distich 21/22 has brought us the conversion of the epic poet, his incorporation into the number of Propertius' admirers. This adds considerable momentum[15] to the claims of Propertius and his youthful (*iuvenes*) readers as a group: if even a representative of established Roman poetry, in his more mature years (*serus Amor*, 20), abandons his creed and joins them, then they must be right! Ponticus' fate will serve to prove that Propertius is more than a low-level poet of limited range. We now see why the words *a te*, to be supplied with *praeferar* (22), are left out; this opens the road to a more general appreciation of Propertius' poetry, because acknowledgement of his superiority to *Romana ingenia* will not be limited to Ponticus' preference: Ponticus' fall only seals a more general reevaluation.

If, after Propertius' death, the youths will call him *magne poeta* (24), they will be justified in doing so—even by "epic standards". In the end, it turns out, it is not Ponticus who is the rival to *primo Homero*, but Propertius. For while Homer's works after his death (4), and Ponticus' works during his own lifetime (18), may sink into oblivion, the name of Propertius cannot pass into silence (*nec poterunt . . . reticere*, 23). If Ponticus displays haughtiness (*fastu*, 25), Propertius is able to do so too. And the Alexandrian quarrel between the grand and the small form is decided once more in favor of the small form: this time by the involved readers' vote, so to speak, not by the cool connoisseur alone.[16]

Propertius will be close to his readers' hearts because he speaks out and explains to them what they only feel but cannot interpret in words (this is why they call him "great poet of *our* ardor", 24), because he helps them (cf. *prosint*, 14) to understand themselves. This is a very special author-reader relationship: it is vital to the readers. And therefore they lament his death, exclaiming in grief: "You, great poet of our ardor, lie dead!" What lines 23/24 formulate is Propertius' own claim to the poet's immortality.[17]

In the end this poem, too, is an attempt to define his own place in the world by setting it against another, well established one. The full picture becomes more and more visible, each time the artist adds to it another color from his palette. This much we know already: love elegy must claim to be much more than the unobliging, off-duty, limited, irrelevant poetry which convention tends to make it. Its judgments affect the standards of other fields, too.

Before outlining the logical structure of elegy 1.7, I would like to emphasize that there is no reason to suspect, as Housman and others have done, the present position of the distich 23/24 in the poem.[18] It contains a loosely added ("and not") but far-reaching consequence of Propertius' position—a consequence which has just been confirmed by Ponticus' conversion. As in 1.1, what exceeds the poem's narrower context also exceeds its otherwise parallel structure.

I	1–8:	Present contrast (in Ponticus' terms)	
	(1) 1–4:	Ponticus' occupation (a) and high rank as a poet (b)	a } 2D b } 4D
	(2) 5–8:	Propertius' occupation (a) and low rank as a poet (b)	a } 2D b
II	9–20:	Future contrast (in Propertius' terms)	
	(1) 9–14:	Propertius' fame and destination as a poet	3D } 6D
	(2) 15–20:	Ponticus' failure as a poet and his conversion	3D
III	21–26:	Consequences for both of them	
	(1) 21/22:	Propertius honored by Ponticus in the future	1D
	(1a) 23/24:	Propertius' general future: a great poet, unforgotten and even mourned for	1D } 2D + 1D
	(2) 25/26:	Ponticus' present haughtiness is especially dangerous and needs correction	1D

The "odd" distich appears neither as a foreign body nor as unconnected; as it grows naturally out of lines 21/22, explicating a wider horizon, so it adds to the point of 25/26: *tu* and *tuo* (25) in themselves already form a natural contrast to *me* (21) and *ego* (22). But the contrast is enhanced by the interposition of lines 23/24 insofar as through them Propertius' case receives accretion. The *iuvenes* (23), who adore Propertius, help to push the *tu* of line 25, i.e., Ponticus, into a minority position.[19] Imbalance in the number of lines reflects the desired imbalance in the number of admirers that follow epic and elegiac poet.

1.9

I told you, scoffer, that the ardor of love would come to you
    and that not for ever would your words be free.
Lo! you are prostrate and come crawling on your knees to a girl's
                                 jurisdiction,
    and now the first to come, bought only recently, rules over you!

Even the Chaonian doves would not surpass me, in matters of love,
    in telling which boys each girl tames.
Me have pain and tears made an expert, no wonder:
    Oh, would that I might lay my love aside and be called
                  unexperienced!   (1–8)

What does it avail you now in your misery to compose a majestic song
    or to bewail the walls raised by Amphion's lyre?
In matters of love, a line by Mimnermus has more power than Homer:
    civilized Amor looks for gentle songs.

Please, come on and compose "those depressing little books",[20]
    and sing, what any girl wishes to know!
What, if you had *not* easy abundance? Now you,
    in your state of frenzy, are looking for water in the middle of
                  the river.   (9–16)

So far, you are not even pale nor are you touched by the real fire:
    this is only the first spark of the harm that will come.

Then you will prefer to approach Armenian tigers,
    and prefer to know the fetters of the infernal wheel,
than feel the boy's dart so often in your marrow,
    and be unable to refuse your enraged girl anything.

To no one has Amor offered his wings easy to seize,
    without pressing ⟨him⟩ with alternating hands.   (17–24)

And don't let yourself be deceived because that girl is willing enough:
    with more ardor, my Ponticus, that boy steals upon you, if a girl
                  is yours;
certainly so when you may not turn your eyes away at leisure
    and Amor does not allow you to stay awake for any other reason.

He is not detected, until his hand has touched your bones:
    whoever you are, alas! avoid incessant enticements!
Even stones and oak trees might be able to yield to those,
    still less could you resist, light spirit that you are.   (25–32)

Therefore, if you feel shame, confess your errors as soon as possible:
    to say what destroys you, in matters of love often brings
                  alleviation.   (33–34)

Readings different from OCT: 4: *quaevis*; exclamation mark (!) at the end of line
4; 26: *ille*.

As the reader knows, my interpretations rest heavily on the assumption
that Propertius gives his elegies a clear disposition, which renders the
movement of thought logically intelligible—but without slavish formal
dogmatism. Accordingly, as we said earlier, Propertius is able to depict
even the unbalanced course which human emotion likes to take, can successfully communicate to us what resists description because it lacks
intelligibility.

Many of my readers may take the hypothesis outlined above for granted. I would welcome them and be grateful to them. In general, however, it cannot be taken for granted that literary critics check their author for what he seeks to communicate by logical means before they interpret him—even though their own credibility largely rests on the assumption that intelligible communication is possible; and this holds true in Propertian studies. We should not forget that it was once thought that, since each distich is an autonomous poetical unit in itself, the sequence of such units in a single elegy is not a matter of prime importance. One may also recall that the admittedly bad condition of the textual tradition heightened the temptation for interpreters to form better and more plausible elegies by rashly breaking up and rearranging the order of distichs offered by our manuscripts. If I on principle insist on the intelligibility of distich order in Propertius' elegies, I have, of course, to prove my case wherever possible, i.e., in every poem I interpret. This is especially necessary since I cannot discuss all of his poems, but only a small number of them. The results obtained so far might suggest that evenness and a well-balanced, almost parallel structure go with the exposition of circumstances that are comparatively clear and simple. Such are the contents of the elegy we are going to consider now (1.9); they only demonstrate the correctness, in Ponticus' case, of predictions made earlier and of insights which Propertius himself has acquired some time ago, and then under great pains (1.1).

Our elegy even displays a certain amount of serenity, as Propertius, half laughing, sees his haughty friend walk into the trap as predicted. There is always a certain relaxation of tension when we see others go through a difficult but non-fatal experience which we have already been through but which they did not expect to face themselves. This double focus on his own past and the other's present is easily overlooked.

A further question to be posed is whether our insistence on arranging distichs logically in groups can help decide problems which Propertian scholarship has so far tried to solve by using other means independently (semantics, metrical analysis, methods of literary criticism, etc.). Again, this elegy will offer a test case or two.

The understanding of elegy 1.9 depends very much on a correct interpretation of elegy 1.7. Already the opening passage (9.1–8) imitates and thus recalls the structure of the opening lines of 1.7:[21] both times a contrast is shown between Ponticus (first mentioned, lines 1–4) and Propertius (lines 5–8 in both poems). This time, however, the true valuation of the two poets—disguised in the former poem by a pseudocompliment to Ponticus and ironic self-effacement on Propertius' part—is out in the open from the beginning, because the time has now come for what was still future in 1.7 to be revealed and for Propertius' oracle to be fulfilled. Therefore, there is no longer any need to address Ponticus in his own conventional language; he can be talked to in the straight terms that are adequate for fallen pride. The form of lines 1–8 has remained the same (2D/2D); the tone has changed completely.

Propertius starts with a tone of triumph in his voice: "I told you, scoffer . . .". Ponticus is not addressed by name until line 26, but is introduced as the deriding person of the former elegy (cf. *tuo . . . fastu*, 7.25).²² In his new state of humiliation the address *irrisor* is, of course, utterly sarcastic, for now it is Propertius' turn to laugh and play the *irrisor*. And he does play this role with the deep satisfaction of the seer whose oracle has turned out to be correct; he will check off each single point of his prophecy with greatest pleasure, pointing to its fulfillment: "*now* I turn out to be right" (cf. the word *nunc* in lines 4, 9 and 15), even adding a triumphant "lo!" (*ecce*, 3).

His first word (*dicebam*, 1) already²³ refers back to the prophetic section of the former elegy (1.7.15–20, which is section II-2 in our analysis of that poem's structure), or, more precisely, to the first distich (7.15/16) of that prophecy, in which he envisaged his friend shaken by Amor's arrow (although, like a Cassandra, he wished it would not happen). That has become true now; the ardor of love has come to Ponticus, and Propertius has the pleasure of bringing home to Ponticus his new condition in detail, as the repetition of *tibi* in lines 1, 2, 4, together with *ecce* in 3, sufficiently shows.

We may be surprised that he now claims to have predicted something which he actually did not: whereas line 1 is a clear reference to 7.15, line 2 (loss of free speech) has no counterpart in elegy 7. If he nevertheless now makes it part of his earlier prediction (the infinitive *fore*, 2, syntactically depends on *dicebam*, 1), he must mean that it was implied in what he said about the effect of Amor's arrow (7.15). The difficulty is resolved easily by the observation made at the beginning of this chapter: like Gallus in 1.10 and 13, so Ponticus, too, is seen by the standard of Propertius' own experience. And that experience, as described in elegy 1.1 (line 28), does indeed involve the lover's loss of freedom of speech (cf. also his warnings to Gallus: 1.5.14; 17).²⁴ The resulting paradox is that Propertius now watches his own sufferings in another person—not with pain for himself anymore, but with a feeling of satisfaction! This contributes to the atmosphere of serenity I mentioned above.

And his satisfaction could not be greater, because Ponticus' fall from pride to humility could not be deeper; he lost his freedom, not to a lady of distinction (as would befit his distinctive taste in poetry), but, apparently, to a woman he bought recently, i.e., to his own property, so to speak, or to a mere "anybody", as he would have said before he was caught and as Propertius feels free to say now (*quaevis*,²⁵ 4): a true bachelor's fate (cp. *perpetuo*, 2; *serus Amor* 1.7.20); in spite (or because) of all his learnedness (cf. 1.7.1–4) Ponticus finally ends up having an "affair" with his own cook or cleaning-lady! Propertius adds even more spice to the situation by introducing legal terminology: if Ponticus signals his unconditional surrender (*supplex*) and accepts his slave's jurisdiction (*ad iura*, 3)—like a slave himself or as a nation conquered by Rome subjects itself to Rome's rule (cp. *imperat*, 4)—then Ponticus, previously the slave girl's owner and legal master, has moved himself down two steps, from *dominus* to a slave's slave, i.e., a *vicarius*, as a slave's substitute is called. Socially, he is worse off than Propertius, who sees himself as *servus* of a *domina*.

Ponticus' fall is Propertius' rise: as a prophet in matters of love, he now boasts that he is more reliable than Jove's famous oracle at Dodona in Epirus (5).[26] *Non me* (5) and *Me* (7), the opening words of the next two distichs (5–8), show who is in the foreground now. In spite of his triumphal success, however, which just now granted him complete satisfaction against a haughty scoffer, he cannot forget the price he, like many a prophet in Greek and Roman tradition, had to pay and is still paying for this title in the currency of *dolor* and *lacrimae* (7), the companions of his lonely nights. Although he may look on his friend's sudden, strange love with a laughing and knowing eye, deep within himself he must wish (*utinam*, 8) that he had never acquired his wisdom (*peritum*, 7) but had stayed the haughty boy untouched by love (*rudis*, 8) that he once was (cp. our interpretation of 1.1.2–3). The tragic aspect of his love, so prominent in his gift of prophecy (as the retrospection in elegy 1.1 shows), is never absent, and he reminds friend as well as reader of this.

Lines 1–8 are concerned with *love*: love has finally come to Ponticus (*amores*, 1), Propertius has proved a prophet in matters of love (*in amore*, 5). In the following section (9–16), emphasis moves from love to its influence on *poetry*, although the viewpoint of love (*in amore*, 11) is, of course, retained.

The shift of emphasis is rooted in the prophetic section of elegy 1.7 (= II-2 in our outline), where Ponticus' predicted falling in love (15/16) is seen to entail ("if-then") consequences for his poetry (17–20). In 1.9, the first and second distich (lines 1–4) have already elaborated Ponticus' love and thus correspond to 1.7.15–16.

The following distich in 1.7 (lines 17/18) predicted that Ponticus, once in love, would find his *Thebais* irrelevant even to himself in his unhappiness (*miser*). Fulfillment of this oracle is elaborated in 1.9.9–12, where *misero* in line 9 picks up *miser* of 7.17, and line 10 refers to the *Thebais* by mentioning Amphion and his lyre—the latter possibly a subtle reminder to the friend. Ponticus has sung both of the Seven Armies' war against Thebes (1.7.1–2) and the fall of Thebes' walls (*moenia flere*, 1.9.10), which, according to Greek mythology (Homer, *Iliad* 4.404–410), took place in a second war, one generation later. But did he give due consideration to Amphion, who, by playing the lyre Apollo had given to him, made the stones move all by themselves so as to form themselves into walls? (After all, Ponticus may himself soon wish to be able to move a *domina* as unfeeling as rock!) In one of his unrivaled brachylogies, *Amphioniae moenia flere lyrae*, Propertius has condensed and revealed the inner contradiction of Thebes' mythical history: founded by Muses' power, destroyed by military power. There can be no doubt which kind Propertius favors, as the opposition of *arma*, 7.2, and *amores*, 7.5, has taught us. At present, we should only recall that, since the day of Euripides' *Antiope*, Antiope's sons Amphion and Zethos have been the ancients' symbols of *vita contemplativa* and *vita activa* (Euripides' play was so powerful that even Plato drew upon it when, in his *Gorgias*, he opposed philosopher and politician in the persons of Socrates and Kallikles). Ponticus so far has dedicated himself to the side represented by *durus Zethus*. Has he at all thought of paying due tribute to *Amphion mollis* (as Propertius calls him at 3.15.29)? "What does it help you now to bewail the fall of Thebes' walls— walls that had been raised by the *lyre of Amphion?*"

Having clarified the implications of line 10, we may now explain the *grave . . . carmen* of line 9. It cannot, as is assumed, be identical with Ponticus' *Thebais*. Apart from our hypothesis that Propertius hardly ever says things twice without a cogent necessity, the *aut* at the beginning of line 10 prevents us from the identification because *aut* usually demands an alternative. The alternative to line 10 (his *Thebais* is of no avail to him now) is that he vainly tries to apply his epic skills to his present situation (*nunc*), i.e., to write a "love epic"! "What does it now help you in your misery to sing a majestic song?" is a perfect mockery—perhaps even imagining Ponticus trying to impress his slave girl by a boring and pompous epic? What a lover, whose girl may fall asleep long before he has ended his overture! Whichever the details may be, the elegist's prediction has become true: epic poetry or the fall of Thebes can no longer be Ponticus' central concern.

Propertius emphasizes in the next distich (at line 11, which corresponds to 9, while 12 will take up 10) that, in the field of love, a single verse of Mimnermus (supposedly the Greek founder of love elegy) has more power than all of Homer's works (this is the meaning of *Homero*): bulk and gravity do not count in love—nor does war, the subject matter of epic (12; cf. *flere*, 10). Here for the first time we should indicate that there is a deeper root of Propertius' antipathy to epic. In elegy 1.7 he implied that his personal experience allows him to give a new meaning to the Hellenistic contrast of small poem and epic—by expressing his love in the elegiac form for involved readers, i.e., by ranking *amores* (5) over *arma* (2). From this point of view, epic appeared as a form which is irrelevant to man's serious emotion. The new point of view which we may add to expand on 9.10 and 12 is that epic serves the arch foe of mankind: it is glorification of war (*"bella canere"*, as he will call it positively in 2.10.8). Again, a personal experience is involved here (as our next chapters will show), one which will lead him even more in the direction of love poetry and dissociate him even more from the kind of values honored by his contemporaries. Amor stands for civilization (*mansuetus*, 12) and looks for gentle and peaceful (*lenia*[27], 12), not warlike songs: *Pacis Amor deus est, pacem veneramur amantes* (3.5.1, see our Chapter VIII). We get barely a glimpse at this aspect of love poetry in 1.9, but we should know about it in time in order to understand Elegy's claim on civilization and humanity. To Propertius, elegy is always more than "mere" love poetry.

The three prophetic distichs in 1.7 (lines 15–20) envisage three aspects of Ponticus' future fate:

(1) he might fall in love (7.15/16); this part of the oracle is now fulfilled (9.1–8; cf. *nunc*, 9.4)
(2) his epic would then mean nothing to him (7.17/18); this, too, is fulfilled now (9.9–12; cf. *nunc* 9.9)
(3) his attempt to turn to love poetry would then be futile (7.19/20); this aspect of the prophecy, too, is to be considered fulfilled now, and must be treated in 9, lines 13–16 (cf. *nunc*, 9.15), if logical arrangement of thought has any meaning at all in Propertius' poetry.[28]

The first distich of subsection 9.13–16 bids Ponticus (9.13/14 ~ 7.19; *compone* 9.13 ~ *componere* 7.19) attempt to write love poetry, i.e., the critical moment in his poetical career has come as predicted—though, it must be said, a "desire" (*cupies*, 7.19) is apparently not yet manifest, and is, so far, replaced by Propertius' imperative *compone!*, 9.13. What has also been predicted, but fulfillment of which has so far not been stated either, is the circumstance that Ponticus' attempt at love elegy will be *in vain* (*nec . . . subiciet*, 7.20; cf. *frustra*, 7.19). This, then, is what we must expect to be the contents of 9.15/16, corresponding to 7.20. The problem of this distich is that it first offers a *si*-clause, which can only be defined as "contrary to fact" (*esset*), preceded by an abbreviated main clause (*quid*; = "what, if?"). Then follows (*nunc*, marked by bucolic diaeresis) a main clause in the indicative (*quaeris*). This is a rare juxtaposition, which must not be passed unaccounted for. Now, if we, following the lead given to us in 1.7.20, take the terminology here to be that of literary criticism (and not of sexuality), we find the key terms of the Alexandrian quarrel between epic and small form, Apollonius Rhodius and Callimachus—as I briefly outlined the quarrel above in connection with elegy 1.7; the pompous and rich vocabulary of large epic is usually compared to a (polluted) big river (cf. *flumine*, 16), while the small form demands the (potable) water (cf. *aquam*, 16), presumably of a crystal-clear small well. Only a few years before Propertius started writing, this terminology had been restated by Horace, among others, when he proudly compared his New Satire with the bulk of Lucilius' production (Hor. *Sat.* 1.4.11; cf. 1.10.50: *cum flueret lutulentus*, sc., *Lucilius*).

Therefore, what Propertius says in line 15 seems to be this: what would you do, if it turned out that you do not possess the exuberance of language (*copia*, sc., *verborum*[29]), which you, as an epic poet, believe yourself to have? This is spoken in the person of Ponticus who does not yet realize that his epic skills are actually worthless (the same way as he has not yet felt the desire to write love elegies): therefore, it is expressed in a contrary-to-fact statement.

The following sentence gives Propertius' view (analysis) of the case and states the actual helplessness Ponticus is about to become aware of himself (therefore stated in the indicative): now (*nunc* for the third time points to the fulfillment of Propertius' oracle) you actually are in the position of one who is floating amidst his stream of epic vocabulary and is looking (*quaeris*) for the clear well of love poetry—and ⟨is about to experience that he⟩ does not find it: a "tantalizing" situation, which corresponds to the prediction of 1.7.19/20.

There is no difficulty in our text if the larger context of the two elegies is kept in mind. The chronology is such that Propertius again is ahead of his friend's self-perception, claiming to know more about his condition than Ponticus himself is aware of. This, by the way, is in harmony with the higher state of awareness we saw the poet claim in 1.1.35ff. (cf. 31ff.).

With line 16 we have reached the end of a major section. Propertius' prophecy of 1.7.15–20 has found an application in each of its three points. "But what about the climactic warning at the end", we may ask, "the possible hurricane (*magno faenore*, 7.26) that allegedly exceeds the dimensions of an ordinary rainstorm?" The following section, again comprising 16 lines (17–32),[30] brings an answer (of sorts), insofar as it contains a new prophecy, so to speak. For it tells Ponticus what to expect next (17–24 = 4D), and tries to keep him from seeing his situation too optimistically (25–32 = 4D). Clearly, Propertius himself has an ax to grind here. For it was, after all, he himself who outlined (7.26) to Ponticus that love, when coming late in life, often charges excessive interest. If the dire warning is not convincing to the—so far, not unhappy—victim, the prophet sees his own reputation at stake and must reinforce the warning by predicting further details.[31] What moves still more into the foreground now for readers acquainted with elegy 1.1, is the impression that we see Propertius' own fate reflected in a case that is described in the second person singular, a case which, as already Rothstein has felt, is not quite as hopeless as Propertius' own.

At least the victim seems to see it that way, for Propertius' advice appears more offered than asked for. (We may recall that in the foregoing section, too, Propertius appeared slightly ahead of Ponticus, telling him what to do now and what he was about to realize.) Therefore, the next lines take on the shape of a demonstration, with the prophecy proper (19–22) framed by a foregoing diagnosis (17/18) and a following statement of the general "law of love" (23–24). This is the same a/b/b/a structure Propertius uses when he tries to open up Tullus' understanding of the extremes of love (1.1.9–16).

The first thing Ponticus is told is that he is mistaken if he believes that it is love that he now feels: no, he shows some early symptoms, a "spark"[32] compared with the disastrous fire to come. He is not yet even pale (we recall Propertius' futile wish that Cynthia turn more pale than he himself, 1.1.22). With "then" (*tum*, 19) the prophet turns to the future and gives a detailed account of the deep-seated pains of love (21) and the lover's loss of freedom (22, cf. 1.1.28) as well as of his futile wishes to escape to less terrible dangers: wild beasts (19; we recall Milanion's willing bravery 1.1.11ff.) and infernal torture (20; we recall Propertius' own willingness to undergo painful surgery, 1.1.27f.). Strictly speaking, 21 corresponds to 19, and 22 to 20.

In his present state, Ponticus may doubt that what so far has been a not unpleasant type of slavery on his part will really become a torture when time moves on. Propertius must therefore bring home to him the inescapability of his situation by invoking the general law of love which does not admit of any exception. This aim is achieved by the expression *nullus* Amor (23), which amounts to the meaning "Amor *never*." The cogency of the ensuing development is further stressed by the consecutive force of *nullus . . . ita, ut non*, which results in the connection: "never state I . . . without state II". Insight into the distich's logical function may ease the difficulty of its interpretation: an easy introductory phase (indicated by *facilis* and the hexameter as a whole) is followed by a tortured one (*presserit* and the pentameter as a whole. *Presserit* perhaps makes us recall the second, torturing stage of Propertius' own love, after he had been caught by Cynthia's eyes: *Tum . . . caput impositis pressit Amor pedibus*, 1.1.3/4.).

In describing what Amor and what the lover do to each other, Propertius apparently has in mind a precise picture of their actions, but none of the interpretations so far proposed is satisfactory.[33] Logic of the situation demands that lover and Amor *face* each other and that the lover hold Amor by his wings (hoping to hold him in his power and to keep him at a distance at the same time, i.e., have his cake and eat it too), while Amor has allowed (*praebuit*) such easy capture (*facilis . . . alas*) so that he can get close to and torture his victim—but *alterna manu*, i.e., not close enough to use both hands at the same time: he must stretch out one arm to reach the lover (while the other arm and shoulder move backward). This seems plausible because the lover's arms are longer than those of Amor who is a boy.

A situation satisfying these conditions is given if we imagine Amor caught by his wingtips, but fluttering over the lover's head, pressing the lover's throat which is exposed because the lover bends his head backwards to look up. The play and counterplay of powers can be seen 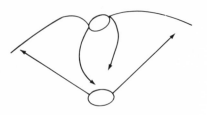 from the sketch. As the lover will move his left shoulder backward and try to avoid being choked, Amor will react by using his other (= left) hand. We can now see that *ille* (24) is not just another case of postclassic use of the word in the unemphatic sense of "he"; *ille* is emphatic as it should be, stressing the paradox: *that* one, who allowed himself to be seized, is the one who really applies pressure—bringing out the ambiguity in Ponticus' situation, which Propertius wishes him to recognize: he believes himself to be in control, but is being controlled. I cannot find anything wrong with our distich's text. One can only admire Propertius' precision in distributing the tensions or powers involved on hexameter and pentameter. Although I do not know of any example, I can imagine that he was inspired by a work of sculpture (or even by two scenes from real life: a human holding a bird, a human holding up a child).

The following subsection (25–32) tries to prevent Ponticus from cherishing another illusion (*nec te decipiat*, 25) and thus, by an evident parallelism (*nec*, 17, corresponds to *nec*, 25), confirms our view of the function of the preceding subsection (17–24). The two differ in that the first warns the lover not to take the early symptoms for the sickness itself that will befall him, while the second warns him not to take the woman's present willingness or her willing presence for any easy cure of his passion.[34] On the contrary, whenever *she* is there, *he* sneaks in (note the pointed use of the repetition *illa . . . ille* referring to the girl and Amor, and marking the sequence "stage I–stage II", cp. 1.1.1–4 again), and, as she is *always* there, Ponticus (note the address, 26) is in a special danger: he cannot open his eyes without seeing her—and he sees nothing but her. The freedom of choice (*vacuos seducere ocellos*) he still believes himself to possess no longer exists (25–28).

Again, however, Ponticus himself may not see the seriousness of his situation, so that Propertius has once more to take recourse to pointing out the general character of Ponticus' sickness: it is not revealed before it has reached the bones and before it is too late for a cure. Therefore everybody (*quisquis*, 30) has to avoid infection, which comes through constant enticement. Even the hardest and most dead products of nature (hardest stone and hardest wood) cannot resist constant enticement. How could Ponticus? (29–32).

We cannot know for sure whether the elaborate eloquence of a Propertius was able to convince Ponticus of the serious consequences his present situation was to entail, or whether Ponticus persisted in the erroneous belief that his present and not uncomfortable situation could be extended into a lasting and not uncomfortable arrangement. But we can see the beautiful clarity and skill of Propertius' argumentation: having proved his credibility by the threefold fulfillment of his oracle, and having simultaneously warned his friend again that love elegy requires more than part-time work of a moonlighting, off-duty epic poet (1–16), he goes on to prove to him in two separate, but parallel, movements of thought that, from his present condition, it is not possible to step back any more, and that future disaster is imminent and inescapable (17–32).

"But is this a nice thing to do?" we ask ourselves. "Why give a friend who cannot avoid going out the depressing forecast that it will inevitably rain cats and dogs?" The answer of any practical Englishman would doubtless be: "To make him take an umbrella along".

Thus, what the structure of elegy 1.9 makes us look for in the remaining distich (33/34) is a piece of friendly advice, following the prediction of a rainstorm of love: "*Therefore*, hurry to get an umbrella lest you be absolutely unprotected!" Upon checking, we find that our expectation gives us a perfect explanation not only for the very first word: "Therefore" (*quare*),[35] and the last, "alleviation" (*levat*), for the urging "as soon as possible" (*quam primum*) and "in the rain" (*in amore*)—not only for these, I say, but also for the rest of this well-known philological riddle. The sentence "Confess your errors as soon as possible: in the field of love, to say what makes you perish often brings alleviation" means again nothing else than what the first half of the poem had amounted to already: hurry to acquire the umbrella of love elegy—you have no more time to lose. "Confess" (*fatere*, 33) is used in the same way as in 2.34.89 (*confessa*), where it is said of Calvus' page that it "confessed" when he sang of his love, and *dicere* means "to write poetry" as it does in line 9 of our poem or in 7.1. Apparently, the notion that writing down one's worries (or reading of similar ones in others, cf. 1.7.13f.) helps to master them is not so recent an invention of mankind (cf. Theocritus 11.1ff., 80f., e.g.) as it is sometimes thought to be.

So far, our overall view dispenses us from all interpretations along the lines "confess your sins to me, for goodness' sake: it helps to unbosom yourself to me and to confide"—as if Propertius were eager to get a name and erotic details.[36] However, there still remains the question whether the words *si pudor est* can be accounted for by our interpretation. They are today usually explained as a mere formula, like "for goodness' sake"[37], with "parallels" from other poems and even authors. But I think they serve a definite purpose. There is a subtle but important difference between the two halves of the poem; the first (1–16) shows the epic poet unable to win a girl (*et cane quod quaevis nosse puella velit*, 14, cf. 11); the second shows Ponticus unable to help himself against his growing passion (17–32). Therefore Propertius bids him write love elegies as soon as possible "in case you feel shame". Is it not a logical and quite natural assumption on Propertius' part that Ponticus should feel shame about a development that takes away his former pride (cf. 9.3), his self-mastery (cf. 9.4), and defeats his resistance (*nedum tu possis*, scil. *resistere*), as if he were nothing (*spiritus iste levis*, 32)? We need only recall what Propertius says about his own humiliation in the introductory poem (1.1.3ff.) and elsewhere, to understand what he alludes to here. This is the second aspect of love poetry: one concerns the beloved, the other yourself. The latter helps you to go through those inescapable situations, actions (or reactions), and types of behavior you are ashamed of (with *pudor*, we therefore have to understand *erratorum* or *erravisse*, as the prosaic word order would be: *quare quam primum fatere errata, si pudor est*, scil. *eorum s. erravisse*). This interpretation also solves the last difficulty of our distich: *quo pereas* is *not* a masculine form of feminine meaning "by which girl (her name, please!) you perish", but is neuter and refers to his love[38] which causes Ponticus' shame. My explicit translation would run: "Therefore (i.e., because you are too weak to resist your growing passion) hurry to confess in elegiac writing your errors if you feel shame about them. For (causative asyndeton) in matters of love, if often brings alleviation to express in poetic form what makes you perish". Again, regard for the larger context of an elegy's disposition has permitted us to approach a much-vexed passage from a more adequate point of view. The main gain is our insight into the logical structure of Propertian elegy and the artistic movement of its thought.

The elegant and serene eloquence which Propertius employs to convince an infidel and erring friend of the serious danger he is in could easily raise the question whether a responsible umbrella specialist would go so far as to make the weather outlook even gloomier than it is—just to induce a friend to acquire an umbrella? Our answer will depend on the degree of sophistication we concede Propertius when he is dealing with erotic subjects outside the vital (and possibly fatal) sphere in which they involve himself. One certain example of his playful ambiguity will be mentioned in the following chapter (1.18).

The structure of elegy 1.9 is as balanced and crystal clear as any we have evaluated so far, comparable in its relation to the more complicated 1.7 as is 1.12 to 1.11. In 1.7, Propertius still fought to establish his own immortality as a poet against established but lifeless epic. At the time of

1.9, life has supposedly spoken, and Propertius' first line already begins with a serene "I told you so", communicated from superior to inferior. The air of established superiority is kept up through all of the poem and crowned by the final "therefore hurry to follow me: in my domain lies the possibility of help". A brief outline of the elegy's structure may indicate the direction of its argument more clearly.

I 1–16:   Earlier Oracle fulfilled: Triumph
   A   1–8: Love
                (a)   1–4: Ponticus' fate fulfilled as pre-   2D ⎫
                             dicted (= 1.7.15/16)   ⎬ 4D
                (b)   5–8: Propertius confirmed as a   2D ⎭
                             prophet of love
   B   9–16: Poetry
                (a)   9–12: epic is of no avail to Ponticus   2D ⎫
                             (= 1.7.17/18)   ⎬ 4D
                (b)   13–16: elegy is not easily within his   2D ⎭
                             reach (= 1.7.19/20)

II 17–32:   New Oracle issued: Warning (~ 1.7.26)
   A 17–24: Torture by Amor unavoidable (early
            symptoms entail later stages of disease)
                (a) 17–18: light early symptoms   a   1D ⎫
                (b) 19–22: future pains   bb   2D ⎬ 4D
                (c) 23/24: Law of Inescapability   a   1D ⎭
   B 25–32: Ponticus' false illusions revealed (no cure
            available)
                (a) 25–28: Ponticus in special danger   2D ⎫
                (b) 29–32: escape no longer possible   2D ⎬ 4D

III   33–34: Friendly Advice: Alleviation through
               Love Elegy   1D

It is an attractive thought that an ironical meaning is hidden under the smooth surface. Elegy 1.9 clearly and distinctly demonstrates what *ought* to be Ponticus' experience provided his heart could be as deeply affected by love as Propertius' own. In case the epic poet should turn out not to measure up to the human standards of his friend the elegist, this circumstance would hardly appear as a blemish on Propertius' second prophecy because it only confirms his basic judgment, viz., that to write epic poetry is not an occupation relevant to man as a human being. But it would also confirm a message which the other poems my reader has so far been acquainted with appeared to convey: in the way he himself experiences love, Propertius feels alone and isolated from other lovers.

CHAPTER

——IV——

LOVE AND FRIENDSHIP:
POET AND POLITICS

▬▬▬▬▬▬

The poetic form of Propertius' *Monobiblos*, as it is gradually revealed to the reader, is: setting the scene of the poet's life. In his first book, he presents himself primarily as the unhappy lover finding a voice for his suffering (our Chapters I and II above) or, beyond the central sphere, as the elegiac poet asserting a superiority over his friend the epicist to whom tradition would assign the higher rank of the two (our Chapter III). Looking around farther, we find that he portrays himself in other roles too. He is the poet of Alexandrian narrative, the critical observer of others as well as of himself, the loyal friend and adviser, the long-mourning member of a family involved and hurt in the civil war, even the (albeit inactive and withdrawn) citizen—in short, the human being Propertius who is exposed to multifarious kinds of influence exercised by his contemporary environment.

Though every word of his we read is fiction, there may be different degrees of closeness to or distance from the realm of historical facts. When varying a traditional motif of love poetry, his work may appear to us (though we can never be sure[1]) less likely to reflect features of his real life and actual circumstances than when, say, his elegies approach the nonfictional sphere of contemporary politics.

In addressing friends who are presented as pursuing different walks of life, he explores different sections of his intellectual and historical environment, and then goes on to stake out his own claim, leaving the frontier open to some of his neighbors, closing it to others, himself paying visits outside and fending off intruders from his own territory. As his own domain is, in a way, terra incognita to the new settler himself, he finds border disputes (as for instance with Ponticus) helpful in exploring his own property. Each time he is able to draw the line between another outsider and himself, he becomes more sure of the extension, shape, and topography: of the map, in short, of his own territory.

An interpreter is obliged to start out by allowing his author the broadest scope possible. To see in Propertius a poet with a central interest (as unfolded in elegies 1.1 or 11/12) is only one side of the coin. The other is that, as he shows a critical perception of himself and his own growing experience, so he reveals an open eye for the world around himself. To look on him only as the representative of a genre ("love elegy") may be as limiting as the extreme that would define him as a sort of antiestablishment rebel. On each single occasion, we should leave it to him to tell us of his decision what and who—besides his love—may be called dear and relevant to him, and what and who may not be included in his work. Only by granting him this independence in choosing his own company can we fruitfully explore the world of his poems—as an interpreters' truism says.

Border clashes can be implacable and incessant; some inroads may even turn out to be wounds that stay open permanently and form a permanent threat to the heartland. Propertius experiences such a threat to the core of his poetry from the beginning to the end of his career (it will represent a major subject this book will have to deal with). He has the courage to face and answer the challenge already in his *Monobiblos* (1.22; cf. 21; our Chapter V below), signaling its priority by granting it an autobiographical expression corresponding to the one he gave to his hopeless and disappointed love. The danger originates from that same outside world of success and action to which he demonstrates his "unsuccessful" love in the introductory poem. To understand the way he feels, let us first see what he says when he views and measures this other world by his personal standards (1.6). But, still before that, we should look at some of the other, especially the lighter, aspects of his book in order both to get some methodological leads for our interpretations and to give our picture a balanced background—provided there is a balance of darkness and light in his *Monobiblos*.

The encounter with Ponticus was a borderline clash, but proved to be a lighter one in the end than in the beginning. In 1.7 Propertius took pains to assert his own, if only future, fame against the epic poet. In 1.9 Ponticus has stumbled, but turns out to be of a lower rank in the field of love than might be expected from his poetry, settling down to a "relationship" with the first (*quaevis*, 9.4) servant to come into his household. Naturally, Ponticus' disappointing development perfectly matches Propertius' expressed opinion of epic and an epic poet, but, also, makes it easier to keep up his poetical claims in a more friendly and less polemical manner: perhaps, we said, he even bids Ponticus come under the wings of superior love elegy in spite of a suspicion that his friend will never be able to fall in love so deeply as to need this protection. Thus the second prophecy (9.17–32), by its possibly overstated warnings, would turn into an indication of Ponticus' human shortcomings. I leave it to my reader how far he would follow me on this road of playful, perhaps even ironical, ambiguity, but ask him to observe with me our poet's sharp eye for human weakness as well as for poetical pomp.

There are poems, it is true, that seem to speak on a less sophisticated, even simple level. When, for example, Propertius reminds his girl not to overdress (1.2), we can hardly avoid the impression that a standard topic of erotic poetry is being treated. Some poems serve complementary but transparent functions, such as 1.4, where friend Bassus is asked to stop praising other girls to Propertius if he wishes to avoid Cynthia's wrath, and 1.5, where Gallus is warned not to woo Cynthia because, if successful, he would suffer the same fate as Propertius. As in 1.9, a certain cheerfulness appears in 1.5 as Propertius pictures the friend suffering Propertius' own sorrows: self-irony is not alien to our poet. But a shadow of sorrow lies over the playfulness of 1.4 when in the end the poet prays (*adoro*, 27): would that Cynthia would always remain as jealous! The same may be said of 1.2: for whom does she overdress? The cloud of fear is sometimes not even visible, but barely suggested, as in 1.8b. There, after Cynthia gives up her plan to go to Illyria with another man, Propertius exults joyfully: neither gold, nor jewels, but the homage of his song alone was powerful enough to make her stay with him.

> Hanc ego non auro, non Indis flectere conchis,
> Sed potui blandi carminis obsequio.   (8.39–40)

In spite of the emphatic *ego* and *potui*, the reader is not sure that love of the poet was her only motive to stay in Rome (and that Propertius feels this, but does not openly admit it to himself—as in the beginning of 1.11). Having once become sensitive to the vibrations of uneasiness in the elegies, the reader rarely enjoys an undivided cheerfulness. Rather, he believes that he has a direct hold on the poet's intentions whenever he encounters an openly pessimistic view, as in elegy 1.19. There Propertius expresses fear greater than that of death: that Cynthia would, even at his grave, surrender her love to his successor. In the same way, elegy 1.15 is convincing prima facie by its revelation of Cynthia's *perfidia* (line 2): Propertius' serious illness notwithstanding, she keeps him waiting while she dresses up as if for another man, making him recall numerous similar occasions.

For the less gloomy and more cheerful aspects of love, there is not

much room in his book's experience. This does not exclude a subtle sense
of humor,[2] which again reveals the keen observer of his own and other
people's peculiarities, the one we found him when painting his iridescent
portrait of Ponticus. Humor, according to Propertius' painful experience,
is only too often connected with ambiguous situations and different levels
of understanding (as in true comedy). One of his most brilliant pieces in
this genre is 1.3, an elegy of strict and austere architecture[3] which uses
parallelism to bring out how a misunderstanding may arise from bad
timing of otherwise converging intentions. The scene opens with a picture
of Cynthia lying asleep, seen through the eyes of her just arriving and
slightly inebriated lover, to whom she seems (*visa*, 7) in sweet, quiet sleep
(*mollem spirare quietem*, 7). Neither reader nor lover learns before the end
that Cynthia had been waiting for Propertius all evening, finally falling
asleep among lonely tears; i.e., had the lover only come earlier, it would
have been a very happy evening. Now, however, there is the difference of
time: the lover, not knowing of the girl's earlier yearning for him, desires
to approach her but, in spite of his alcoholic condition, resists, being
afraid to wake her for fear of her well-known wrath. Thus, he unexpectedly finds himself in a contemplative and unerotic attitude towards her,
protecting her peaceful sleep—and misinterpreting her longing sighs as
her dreaming fear of an importunate stranger. She, however, when awakened hours later by the slow-moving moon shining on her face, suspects
him of having just come in after staying out all night, and lets him experience the full power of her wrath for having neglected her for so long, possibly even in favor of another woman (as she rashly concludes from the
fact that it is shortly before morning, 37f.)—in short: a vivid counter-piece
of the peacefully sleeping girl she was before, and exactly the fury he
wished to avoid by not waking her from her "sweet" sleep. The peaceful,
"unknown" (cf. *ignotis cornibus*, 20) Cynthia he stared at for hours with the
hundred eyes of an Argus (20) was an illusion which has yielded again to
the real-life, abusive woman, the one who will stay in his memory forever—as her visit in a dream from beyond the grave will show (4.7), still
years from now. The second half of her speech is more calm, recalling the
hours of futile waiting for Propertius—hours which correspond to those
which he spent waiting for her to wake up by herself. Bad timing produces unexpected results, and, beyond simple misunderstanding and a
"lost" evening, even misapprehension of characters (a peaceful Cynthia,
an unfaithful Propertius)—and all, of course, at the cost of unlucky
Propertius, who willingly pays the bill for our smile. The richness of this
elegy in poetical color and human insight is not easily exhausted (and can
be brought into the open only if the poem is read aloud). The only way to
structure the elegy lies, to my mind, in setting off the four "scenes" against
each other:

I 1–10: The inebriated poet's straying vision, due to his corrupted (cf. 11) senses, of Cynthia as a softly sleeping Ariadne, Andromeda, and, finally, a bacchant.

II 11–20: The initial courage of his drunkenness, urging him to approach Cynthia, is defeated by his rising fear of her well-known wrath.

III 21–33: In a meditative (and probably sobering) phase lasting a longer period of time, he tries to become acquainted with the "unknown" Cynthia. The scene ends with Cynthia opening her eyes (. . . *patefecit ocellos*, 33).

IV 34–46: This scene opens with "The following words she spoke . . ." (*Sic ait* . . . , 34) and contains the outburst of the misinterpreted woman's wrath.

The structure (5D / 5D; 6½D / 6½D) is remarkable because of the strong *caesura* between sleeping Cynthia and Cynthia awake (thus harshly emphasizing the difference between illusion and reality): an asyndeton tears hexameter (33) and pentameter (34) apart, a device rarely used by Propertius.[4]

I would like to illustrate the playful opposition of illusion and reality from one more elegy, which, unlike the Ponticus elegies and the Cynthia poem 1.3, extends the deception to include the reader, giving him no key to the true situation until shortly before the elegy ends. The elegy I have in mind is 1.18,[5] last in a group of three that discuss aspects of the same experience: the lover despised by his mistress. In 17 Propertius, shipwrecked while on his way to Greece and facing a lonely death, bitterly repents having left Rome and having fled from his mistress's humors, because dying at home would at least have meant that Cynthia would have mourned at his funeral. In 16, we hear the front door of a formerly well-reputed house complain about the present lady's morals, especially about the night-long songs (i.e., *paraclausithyra*) of the *exclusus amator*, who directs his outbursts of wrath against the poor door, hoping however that his voice may travel beyond the door and reach the ears of his mistress (27/28), whom he believes to be in the arms of another man inside.

Elegy 1.18 introduces Propertius bewailing his hard fate as a despised lover.

He has withdrawn into a silent and deserted place, where nobody, except loyal rocks and gentle winds, can hear him, in order to pour forth his sorrows "unpunished" (1–4=2D).

Then he announces, in a sort of *prooemium*, his plan to lament over Cynthia's haughtiness (*fastus*) and reflect on what possibly caused the sudden change of his lover's luck (5–8=2D).

The following middle part of the poem (9–26=9D) contains his futile search for causes:

(1) His search for possible errors on his part (9; I read *crimina* instead of Barber's *carmina*) is first specified by the question (10): have I been unfaithful? The answer comes in the negative, in three distichs fervently acquitting him of such a crime (11–16=3D).

(2) The second possibility (again the question is formulated in one single distich, 17/18) is: has he ever given any signs that his love has cooled off? The answer, coming in two distichs (the foregoing answer needed three distichs), is in the negative again: the trees shall be witnesses for his unceasing love; in their bark, he writes the name Cynthia! etc. (19–22=2D).

(3) The third offense he could think of (again formulated in one distich: 23–24):

Or ⟨are you cross with me⟩ because your injustice caused me worries
   —something, which is known only to your silent door?

An tua quod peperit nobis iniuria curas,
   —quae solum tacitis cognita sunt foribus?
Different from OCT: punctuation.

The question seems to carry the answer in itself, and so is answered by one distich only ("I have endured all orders the haughty mistress gave me without complaining", etc., 25/26), instead of two distichs for the foregoing question, or three distichs for the first. Clearly, we have an *anti-climax* before us: three questions, all formulated in one distich each and introduced in every instance by *an*—but the answers becoming shorter every time, according to the weight of the crimes (the first, possible unfaithfulness, weighed heaviest) (25–26=1D).

Thus the search for a reason for his sudden change of luck has proved unsuccessful—he appears innocent (9–26).

If he now once more describes his unfriendly and inhospitable surroundings out here in wild nature and in a deserted place (27–30=2D), it sounds much more pessimistic and undeserved than in the two introductory distichs of the elegy.

But, nevertheless, whatever her behavior, Propertius will praise her name, and even trees and deserted rocks out here shall resound with her name! This is what one last and desperate distich tells us (31–32=1D).

The overall impression we receive from reading this elegy is that Propertius has given a magnificent and beautiful new version of a well-known traditional topic: the despised lover's lament in the loneliness of deserted nature. Upon second thought, however, we ask ourselves if he really is as innocent as he claims. Does not the third question (23/24) admit that he *has* voiced his complaints, viz., before her "silent" door? What, if the door was *not* silent (let us recall that in 1.16 the lover expressly wishes that his voice travel beyond the door and reach the ears of his mistress inside!), but passed the outbursts of his anger on to the lady inside? In that case, there would be a perfectly understandable reason why Cynthia so suddenly (*modo*, 7) withdrew her favor from him! Reread along these lines, the whole elegy changes its meaning: the lover's misgivings about the loyalty (*fidem*, 4) of inanimate rocks (4) originate from bad experience with an inanimate door. His desire to lament "unpunished" (3) out here is understandable after he received his punishment elsewhere. The anticlimax of a lover's possible crimes means: "Look, what I *could* have done! Why punish me for so light a fault? Moreover, it was meant for your door 'only' (*solum*, 24), not for your ears. And besides: was I not always obedient and willing without complaining? (25/26)". The law court vocabulary (trees as witnesses for Propertius, etc.) suddenly makes sense if the poem's real purpose is a defense and a plea for mercy. Apparently, Propertius has used traditional elements for a new purpose; this is not a lament poured forth in deserted nature, but a love letter, admittedly written at home at his desk, and asking pardon for last night's behavior, as well as for a next rendezvous. To state it in modern terms: using romantic scenery, Propertius plays a rococo game.

In elegy 1.18, the ambiguity is intended from the beginning (whether or not the elegy was really once sent to "Cynthia" as a love letter after "Propertius" really spent a noisy night in front of her house). Its revelation is purposefully postponed because not before line 24 do the two words *solum* and *tacitis* give us the key to the opening scene and its enigmatic words (*certe* 1 = "finally", *taciturna* 1, *vacuum* 2, *licet* 3, *impune* 3, *fidem* 4), as well as to the anticlimax of 9–26 and its legal vocabulary. The demonstrable ambiguity of 1.18, based on a logical structure and on giving a new sense to traditional literary elements, may, because of its comparatively narrow range, be more easily discernable to our eye, than is, say, the pseudorespectful attitude towards epic in elegy 1.7 (and 9), where, too, we saw Propertius fill traditional literary elements and theories with a new meaning. If we include in our present consideration the tragicomic elegy 1.3 with its skillful handling of the time element to produce two levels of understanding, one illusionary and one realistic, side by side and in two persons, we may round off our picture of Propertius' sophisticated and ambiguous humor and realize to what degree his interpreter must be aware of possible irony (or self-irony) and intellectual playfulness. Of course, such masterful handling of given materials for original purposes goes beautifully together with, and may well have grown from, what the *Monobiblos* claims to be his original painful experience, viz., that in his own life things do not seem to fit together as smoothly and orderly as they do for most people (1.1).

78

Having gained a general impression of the *Monobiblos*, its lighter and more refined aspects as well as its gloomier and more direct ones, we may take up a distinction introduced in the foregoing chapter: that between more central and more marginal poems, considered in relation to Propertius' primary decisions. It is now, I think, easier to see that some elegies, such as the humorous one about the lovers' misunderstanding (3) or the lament allegedly sung in a desolate environment (18), though artfully contrived and participating in the tradition of erotic poetry, may be less close to his work's central concerns than, say, the assertion of his values and poetic goals against Ponticus in 1.7—although, strictly speaking, 1.7 is not a "love elegy" in the precise sense of the term. The reason for this situation is, to say it once more, that love and its central expression in elegy would, according to Propertius' concept in the *Monobiblos*, leave no part of a man's condition untouched (provided he does not suffer from a crippled or undeveloped personality as does friend Ponticus without knowing it). Now his poetry also explicates the consequences which love entails for various areas of the individual's life. So elegy occasionally has to stake out a wider claim than some neighbors would like to grant it in order to be able to communicate its widely involving message. Viewed from Propertius' standpoint, it would therefore be more adequate to say that others try to claim his territory than vice versa. Once we are willing to grant his viewpoint, we will no longer be surprised about his independence of judgment, his many poetological elegies, his competition with Roman "luminaries", his seemingly disrespectful attitude towards society's conventions, etc. We will realize the self-protective character of such utterances: as he feels it, he is defending his poetry's human core and consequences against incursions by interfering, less essential forces. How he came to think so is a question well worth asking. An initial and guiding answer can, as I said earlier in this chapter, be found in elegy 6, where he deals with a special and lasting challenge to his position and its implications. Our methodological findings about different spheres of illusion and reality in some of his poems may be helpful here in distinguishing the surface occasion from the successively revealed deeper message. The poem concerns and clarifies Propertius' relationship to his friend and (probably) early patron, Tullus.

We have seen Propertius' peculiar way of defining his own position by trying to realize what he has in common with others and—more often as it turns out—what separates him from them. The others include happy lovers, bachelor Ponticus, easygoing Gallus, fatherly and Philistine (and nonunderstanding) advisers, and even Tullus his probable patron: the way he is addressed in 1.1.9 showed us that he, too, belongs to those who can hardly understand Propertius' desperate situation. They follow him only insofar as his plight is presented to them in the form of a story that tells of a difficult, but in the end yielding, girl and an enduring, but finally successful, lover. This seems a good starting point from which to view Tullus' role in Propertius' poetry. Historically, Tullus can be seen to stand close to the rule of the new Emperor. His uncle was a consul in 33 B.C.—the other consul then was Octavian, the later Augustus, himself. Accordingly, Tullus is active in the politics of the new regime—and his family have kept their riches, whereas Propertius has suffered heavy loss at the hands of the victorious side and now possibly depends on the support of people like Tullus. In a frank poem (1.14) Propertius defines his financially poor but emotionally rich situation by comparing it to Tullus' wealthy, but loveless life. The contrast is unproblematical because there is no doubt about the distribution of nuances in this clear-cut, black-and-white picture. The architecture offers three stanzas of 4D, each one being subdivided between the third and fourth distich. The poem amounts to the thesis that, with Venus on his side, Propertius feels able to despise realms and riches (23/24), while Tullus must hear that Venus wins even hard heroes from within and cannot be frightened away by wealth (17–22). There is no indication that Tullus is suffering from love now, but lines 17ff. might be interpreted as a warning to Tullus of this as a future possibility,[6] and that the introductory picture of Tullus calmly viewing the world from his estate may prove to be an illusion. However, this standard of measurement does not apply to the Tullus of Book 1, as we shall see; here he will turn out to be the active man who cannot easily be influenced by or succumb to love, the man with whom duty and country rank first. Thus he may once more serve as a contrast to Propertius (1.6): Zethus against Amphion, so to speak.

I first give the poem in translation:

> It is not so that *I* am afraid now to experience the Adriatic sea together
> > with you,
> > Tullus, or to set our sails in the Aegean:
> with you I could bring myself to climb the Rhipaean Mountains (in the
> > icy North)
> > and go beyond Memnon's palace (in the ardent South).
> But I am held back by the words of my girl when she embraces me
> > and by her frequent weighty entreaties, her changing color.   (1–6)

> *She* talks to me for whole nights of her love's ardor
> > and, in her abandonment, laments that no gods exist.
> *She* already denies that she is mine any longer, *she* utters the threats
> > which, when in a state of gloom, a girlfriend usually utters
> > > towards an ungrateful man.
> I am not the person to be able to last one single hour under these
> > > laments.
> > Ah, may the lover perish who can be indifferent to his girl!   (7–12)

Or would it be worth so much to me to see learned Athens
    and to look at Asia's ancient riches,
that, when the boat has been launched, Cynthia should give me
    a rating and mark her face with insane hands,
and assert that she owes kisses (not to me but) to the adverse wind[7]
    and that there is nothing more cruel than an unfaithful man?   (13–18)

You set out to march in front of your uncle's well-earned fasces
    and restore the old jurisdiction to forgetful allies!
For in all your life you have never taken time off for love,
    but your concern has always been the fatherland in arms;
and to you may that boy never bring our labors
    and all the torments known to my tears!   (19–24)

Let me, whom fortune wished to lie forever name- and fameless,
    surrender this life to worthlessness right through to my end!
Many have perished gladly in a long-lasting love:
    as one of them may I, too, be covered by the soil!
I am not the person who is born for fame, nor apt for arms:
    this is the sort of military service fate wants me to undertake.   (25–30)

But you, whether where effeminate Ionia extends herself, or where
    Pactolus' water tinges Lydian fields;
whether across the lands on foot or the sea with oars
    you will travel and be part of the governmental power conferred
                                            (upon your uncle):
if there comes to you then an hour when you remember me,
    you will be sure that I live under a harsh star.   (31–36)

Readings different from OCT: exclamation marks at the ends of lines 20; 26; 28.

Although, when the elegy opens, the speaker's decision has been reached already, preceding considerations are still reflected, even rectified in the present attempt to explain a compelling situation to a friend. Apparently, Propertius' final refusal to join Tullus and his uncle's suite has elicited the friend's mocking comment: "Now[8] it is fear of the sea that keeps you from coming with me". The poet's answer (1) reads like this: "I am not now afraid of the sea—for together with *you* I would gladly endure even worse hardships (3/4), but my mistress's entreaties detain me here." So far, a misunderstanding has been corrected: not sudden fear of the stormy seas, as you seem to (or: may) think, but my mistress's words prevent me from going with you (1–6).

But the simple correction "not A but B" will not do, Propertius feels. What needs further explanation for skeptical Tullus is the power of the woman's words: *illa . . . illa* is the emphatic introduction to the two distichs (a third *illa* in line 9) which describe her irresistible argumentation (7–10). Although the poet describes in broad and moving terms the despair and feeling of loneliness which Tullus' invitation has already caused his beloved girl, we cannot be sure that Tullus is as impressed as Propertius. The effect of her words on Propertius (*his* is emphatic again: "under this kind of lament" we might insufficiently say in English) is stated in line 11; a condemnation of indifferent lovers raises Propertius' attitude to the level of a general maxim (12). What he has achieved towards Tullus by this stanza (7–12) is a sort of moral (*nullos esse . . . deos*, 8; *ingrato . . . viro*, 10) and human (*non horam possum durare*, 11) *justification* of his decision, that allows him to set values of his own (12) against claims of friendship Tullus might assert. We can now see the reason why line 11 begins (*his ego non*) by echoing the elegy's opening words (*non ego nunc*). Distich 11f. summarizes his true reasons for not joining Tullus, and thus definitively corrects Tullus' mistaken guess rejected in lines 1ff.: it is not the savage sea that Propertius cannot bear, it is his girl's lament. The verb *durare*, "bear", fitting the situation in line 11, simultaneously points back to the alleged fear mentioned in line 1. Consequently, Tullus faces a serious, and apparently unexpected, situation: his friend Propertius is shying away, not from dangers he may encounter at Tullus' side while traveling, but from hurting a human being other than Tullus! The striking repetition of *illa* (7; 9a; 9b)—the pronoun usually points to a person not participating in the communion of "I" and "you"—then serves to drive home a striking fact: our relationship, my dear Tullus, is impinged on and superseded by a person whom you would (and I, insofar as I am your friend, perhaps should) call an outsider, *illa*. I am hers, not yours.

In summarizing what the reader, along with Tullus, learns from lines 1–12, let us state that the decision made by the poet recently was not the choice discussed in lines 1ff., of safety at home over the dangers of a voyage across two seas to Greece and Asia Minor, but of another person—a woman—over Tullus. And Propertius wants his friend not to be mistaken about the true reason. Why be so direct?[9] Why avoid hurting the beloved at the cost of possibly hurting the friend? Would mal de mer, as suggested by Tullus, not constitute a more polite *propemptikon*? The elegy postpones an answer to the reader who may ask these questions.

On the scales of the newly defined moral position (12) Propertius may even, tentatively, weigh the advantages of his participation (13/14; they are, admittedly, great: an educational visit to the spiritual and cultural "museums" of his time) against Cynthia's—strongly expressed—disappointment at the time of departure and her—then justified—reproach of his infidelity (15–18). The result is already indicated by the way in which he presents his consideration: as a question introduced by *an* (13). He thus lets his friend know immediately that he is no longer willing to grant this voyage more reality than is involved in giving thought to it. The price (*tanti*, 13, is *genetivus pretii*, picked up and explained by the *ut*-clause, 15ff.) he would make Cynthia pay in pains would be too high. And that simultaneously means that the price he would have to pay himself (*mihi*, 13) would be too high. For he would cause the deplorable scene and would carry the picture (15–18) of distressed Cynthia, being left behind on the shore, in his mind all the way to "learned Athens" and to Asia Minor, remorsefully and guiltily recalling the expression of her despair: *nihil infido durius esse viro*. Thus, merely exploring (13–18) the alternative to his recent decision makes him feel confirmed in the position expounded in the preceding stanza (7–12).

In summarizing our elegy's first movement (1–18), we may say that it, in its three steps, reflects and clarifies arguments, considerations, and circumstances that have contributed to Propertius' decision (as well as perhaps delayed its birth) even though the decision itself has been made before the first line is uttered. From now on, the near future of the two friends is discernibly determined, so that the poem's second half (19–36) can spell out the separation of Tullus and Propertius. As it turns out, the separation involves still another question deeper than whether to go on a trip together or not.

The first two subsections (19–24; 25–30) in the second half are as bluntly introduced (asyndeton) and opposed to each other as possible: the division "*tu* . . . (19)—*me* . . . (25)" truly draws the line. In going or not going, it will turn out, a decision of principle is involved. In the future, the two friends will be following different vocations. Recognition of the new level reached in lines 19ff.—from now on, the accent lies on difference in basic attitudes—may help us to see a few difficult passages in perspective.

The section concerning Tullus is opened by a distich that sends him out to participate in his uncle's political mission. In the hexameter (19), every word except for the first has been disputed with regard to its precise meaning. The pentameter (20), more general, gives us background information about the task in which friend Tullus will participate. Here, too, interpretation runs into problems, but they allow easier access.

General agreement seems to have been reached about the uncle's (*patrui*, 19) identity. In all probability, he is L. Volcacius Tullus, who (as we said earlier) had been consul together with Octavian (the later Augustus) in 33 B.C. and who, in 30/29 or 29/28,[10] went to Asia Minor as a proconsul. If one considers any political aspects to the elder Tullus' assignment, then two things are a priori certain: after Octavian's naval victory at Actium (September 2, 31 B.C.) and the capture of Alexandria (August 3, 30 B.C.), (1) no proconsul would go to Asia without Octavian's consent or even his orders (Octavian himself is in Asia Minor in the winter of 30/29, entering his fifth consulate on January 1, 29, in Samos); (2) the proconsul's primary goal, at present, would be to help to ensure again Asia's dependence on Rome as the head of the Empire, and to eliminate any remains of Antony's rule.

The second aspect I see reflected in the injunction of line 20: "Restore the old jurisdiction to forgetful allies!", where I take "forgetful" (*oblitis*) to point, as it often does, to an act of—if not deliberate, so at least—morally reprehensible forgetfulness (cf. *oblitos famae melioris amantis*, Verg. *Aen.* 4.221). After all, the "allies" had, albeit involuntarily, cooperated with Antony. I can offer no direct parallel for the phrase *vetera iura referre sociis*, but the situation itself addressed by Propertius is unique and therefore not easily paralleled. (We may understand *iura*—"a symbol of sovereignty", *OLD* s.v.—as in *triumphatisque possit / Roma ferox dare iura Medis*, Hor. *C.* 3.3.43f.; *iura dabat legesque viris*, Verg. *Aen.* 1.507; *Roma an Carthago iura gentibus daret*, Liv. 30.32.2; and (*vetera iura*) *referre* as in *antiquum . . . rettulit morem*, Suet. *Caes.* 20.1; *relatis quibusdam ex magno intervallo caerimoniis*, Liv. III 55.6; *institutum referri ac renovari moleste ferunt*, Cic. *Div. in Caec.* 21.68).

Commentators are usually inclined to see *iura* here, not as Rome's jurisdiction reimposed on "forgetful allies" after their cooperation with Antony has been ended (viewpoint: from ordering Rome), but as the privilege and benefit of Roman order (as once instituted by Pompey) restored to them (viewpoint: from happy recipient). Historically, this appears not completely convincing. After all, Roman administration had meant decades of payments exacted successively for Pompey, Caesar, Trebonius, Dolabella, taxes ten years in advance for Brutus and Cassius (the same for Antony), etc.[11] Shall we assume the poet to say that the allies have "forgotten" about their beneficial "ancient rights"? Within the elegy's context, it would seem to me that active restoration of Rome's leading position after years of disorder and disputed loyalty is much more likely to be Propertius' focus when he envisages Tullus' participation in his uncle's political task than dwelling on a prospective favorable reception to be given friend Tullus by the ruled Asians as the bringer of Rome's jurisdiction. The fact that Tullus' participation is derived (*nam*, 21) from his continuous concern for his country *in arms* (22) likewise points rather to active, even military restoration (we cannot bring in at this point the luxuries of life in Asia the poet will mention in lines 31ff. when giving his train of thought a surprise turn).

Specifically, my interpretation can stand without forcing the meaning of *oblitis* in 20—a difficulty the alternative interpretation runs into. Enk seems to understand that Tullus will restore to the allies what they have missed and desired for such a long time that they have "*nearly* forgotten" about it: *socii iura sibi adempta paene obliti sunt* (Enk *ad loc.*). There can be no doubt that this interpretation does force the text by stretching the meaning of *oblitis* (neither is Enk's "*paene*" in Propertius' text nor are the words *sibi adempta* to be supplied by necessity). Now one may of course maintain that Roman rule, when viewed after Actium and especially from official Rome, includes a beneficial effect for the ruled (and Octavian, in the situation of 29 B.C., actually showed prudent self-restraint in granting tax relief and avoiding both Caesar's and Antony's religious claims[12]). But still the question remains whether this view can be extracted from *oblitis* as being that of Propertius. Would not *oblitis* naturally point out that an urgent reminder and even strong action is required of Rome's new master and his helpers in the East? Do we, in the elegy about Propertius' choice of a woman over Tullus, expect or even understand any hint at all concerning the mood of the natives in the Eastern provinces?

Several commentators (among them SB, BB, Camps, Enk, Richardson) find a positive attitude of the Asian provincials towards Octavian's rule, and Tullus the elder's (or even the nephew's) mission anticipated in Propertius' words in line 34. When he tells friend Tullus that, wherever he will be traveling at ease in Asia Minor, he will be *accepti pars . . . imperii* (34), this means, we are for instance informed, that he will be "a welcome part of a welcome administration" (Richardson *ad loc.*; echoed by Petersmann 1980, 60: "ein willkommenes Mitglied einer willkommenen Administration")—similar to the way in which there is nothing more "welcome" in Propertius' own life than his beloved mistress (*te nihil in vita nobis acceptius umquam*, 2.9.43, compared by Richardson, BB, and SB).

The underlying thought is again that, after Antony's heavy rule, the provincials welcomed Octavian's regime. This is of course compatible with historical facts, especially when viewed from Octavian's angle (cf., e.g., *Res Gestae* 24). The provincials on their part were eager to demonstrate loyalty to Octavian the victor because they had only recently fought for Antony his now defeated opponent and, in the present situation, wished to place themselves under his protection. The prospect of lasting peace, i.e., of an end to war and war contributions, was reason enough to show gratitude to the victor whatever his name.[13] An indicator of their mood in 30/29 is the request (granted and modified by Octavian) of the councils of the Greek cities in Asia and Bithynia (cf. Dio Cass. 51.20.6ff.) that they might establish cult and temple for the victor (as they had done for his forerunners; Octavian's moderating contribution apparently was to include *Roma* in the cult).

It can neither be confirmed nor excluded that the "allies" were on occasion given a helping hand in finding ways of welcoming the new regime. In the case of Tullus the elder, we only know it was under his proconsulship[14] (i.e., either simultaneous with Octavian's own restorative activities in the East in 30/29 or in the following year 29/28) that the council of the Greek cities of Asia at Smyrna offered a prize (a wreath) for the best suggestion to honor Octavian "the god" (τῷ μεγίστας γ᾽ εἰς τὸν θεὸν καθεὑρόντι τειμὰς εἶναι στέφανον, line 43). Nothing is mentioned about Tullus influencing this decision. But it sets one thinking to learn that the prize lay unclaimed for about twenty years until a late successor to Tullus, the Roman proconsul Paullus Fabius Maximus himself, hit upon the glorious idea of naming the year's first month after Octavian (by then Emperor Augustus) and by letting the new year begin on the Emperor's birthday. In acknowledgment of his inventive suggestion (formulated in a proconsular letter which he ordered to be published in Augustus' temple together with the council's anticipated positive response to it, both inscribed on the same pillar), Paullus Fabius Maximus was awarded the wreath by the council—for having "found in honor of Augustus even what the Greeks have not known up to now" (καὶ τὸ μέχρι νῦν ἀγνοηθὲν ὑπὸ τῶν Ἑλλήνων εἰς τὴν τοῦ Σεβαστοῦ τιμὴν εὕρετο, lines 47ff.). The superb disclaimer of Greek inventiveness in favor of the Roman proconsul's intellectual achievement, together with the fact that, for two decades, Greek minds had failed to produce a solution worthy of the prize, might lead us to believe that in 30/29 (or 29/28), too, the initiative for offering the prize originated in the mind of the Roman proconsul (Tullus) rather than spontaneously in the Greek council (after all, the Greek cities already had offered divinity and cult to the victor).

These considerations can tell us little about Tullus the elder, less about his nephew's expectations when planning to join his uncle's suite, and nothing at all about Propertius' thoughts and intentions in expressing his anticipation that friend Tullus will be *accepti pars . . . imperii*. For, as in the case of line 20, so in that of line 34, we again have to ask the question: is the single word *accepti* sufficient to document an intention on Propertius' part of introducing into his elegy the view that Octavian's (or his proconsul's) rule will be welcomed in the Eastern provinces? In giving a positive answer to this question, are we not, perhaps without noticing it, carrying unverified political preconceptions into his poetry?

There is another explanation, given by Rothstein—supported in recent years by Atkinson (1958) and Cairns (1974)—which takes *imperium acceptum* as the governmental power "granted" to (or "assumed" by) the holder of an office (cf. the technical term *provinciam accipere* or the Vergilian parallel *consulis imperium . . . accipiet*, Aen. 6.819f.).[15] Does it fit the context better? Yes, according to our interpretation which found the elegy's second half offering a new characteristic of the two friends' relation, rooted in their different vocations. Let us assume that Tullus is here said to be "part of the *imperium* granted" to his uncle—and granted, no doubt, by the final authority of Octavian the victor himself: in this case he is even more socially elevated because integrated into the political framework of the leading figures of the day (no matter whether young Tullus himself will exercise an official function of his own or not). The nephew is here defined by and seen in the light of the high position held by his uncle. This fits—notwithstanding the ironical touch of the last six lines we shall describe later—very well into the thematic contrast of passive, lowly, hopeless Propertius (25ff.) and active, elevated, hopeful Tullus (19ff.) that characterizes the elegy's second half. In case the poet had really gone out of his way in this elegy to slip in the compliment that Octavian's administration (as exercised through his proconsul) will be welcome in the eyes of the ruled Asians, it would be highly important for his interpreter to take such a bow to the new regime into his account. But if the word *accepti* finds its functional explanation within the elegy's thematic set of characters and circumstances, it is equally important for us not to call in standards of appreciation which later times almost automatically associate with the "Augustan Age". As things stand, line 34 neither "makes excellent sense if *accepti* be understood as *grati*" (SB *ad loc.*)—this would divert the focus from the younger Tullus' participation in his uncle's political glory—nor can the line supply undoubted support for securing for *oblitis* in 20 the meaning *paene oblitis* assumed by Enk.

Thus, in returning to distich 19/20, we will be even more cautious about verifying an alleged political consent which so far we have seen Propertius not explicitly confess to. If Vergil (*G.* 4.560ff.), at about the same time of Tullus the elder's proconsulship, refers to Octavian's repossession of the East for Rome by saying

> Caesar dum magnus ad altum
> fulminat Euphraten bello victorque volentes
> per populos dat iura viamque adfectat Olympo,

then it is not only the addition of *volentes* to *populos* that distinguishes him from Propertius, but in the first place the fact that Vergil introduces praise of Octavian into his context at all, and secondly that he pays tribute to him comprehensively through the words *magnus, fulminat, volentes, victor,* and *viam adfectat Olympo.*[16] In Propertius 1.6, neither *oblitis* nor *accepti* are found in a context that would a priori support a pro-Octavian interpretation. Propertius' language merely suggests that he refers to the official goal of the mission ("restore Rome's sovereignty!") without further comment (except for telling his friend "you will be part of this governmental power assigned to your uncle"). If he then bids Tullus go without him, this appears to be another instance of that independence of stance and of judgment which we found to be so characteristic of Propertius in other areas too.

In proceeding to discuss the hexameter line (19)

> Tu patrui meritas conare anteire securis,

we note that a first-sight understanding sees the poet encourage his friend to go about to precede his uncle's lictors. For the *secures,* being part of the *fasces*, are carried by the *lictores*, who precede the proconsul in single file when he appears in public. The axes are the visible sign and grim expression of the uncle's powerful authority—well described in their context by Nisbet and Hubbard (*ad* Hor. *C.* 1.35.17): "*anteit* suggests a grim squad of Roman lictors, carrying the fearsome symbols of *imperium*, subservient to their arrogant master and implacable to everyone else." In our case then, young Tullus would precede the lictors who precede his uncle. Such a concrete surface understanding, however, has for various reasons appeared faulty to a number of scholars, and so the line has been interpreted more or less as an encouragement to young Tullus, asking him to outdo his uncle's achievements as a proconsul.

To my mind, this understanding of *anteire securis* is not without difficulties either. Although *secures* (referring to the *fasces*) may express Roman supremacy or dominion (e.g., *Galliam, quae . . . securibus subiecta perpetua premitur servitute*, Caes. *B.G.* 7.77.16), even point to the authority and power of the consular office (*consulis imperium hic primus saevasque securis / accipiet*, Verg. *Aen.* 6.819; cf. Prop. 3.9.23), I do not find a parallel passage that would describe the *secures*, while standing for and symbolizing a magisterial *office*, as belonging to an individual ("your uncle's proconsulship") —not to mention the special meaning implied here by commentators: "the uncle's axes" = his "*achievements* in office". Even if we follow K. P. Schulze —see Enk, SB *ad loc.*—in taking *meritas* to mean *bene meritas de re publica*, the problem would not be removed.[17] And besides, the uncle's "achievements" would be given a rather dire connotation by *secures* (= "axes that served the country well"). Signifying the executioner's tool, the word regularly suggests killing: *saevumque securi / aspice Torquatum*, Verg. *Aen.* 6.824f. (Torquatus put his own son to death). When used metaphorically, it approximates our "death-blow" (*quam enim illi iudices . . . graviorem potuerunt rei publicae infligere securim . . . ?* Cic. *Planc.* 29.70; *quam te securim putas iniecisse petitioni tuae . . . ?* Cic. *Mur.* 24.48). Ovid combines the concrete executioner's axe and the nuance of Roman dominion when he imagines a triumphal procession in which personified Germania, her hands tied and her hair disheveled, is being displayed on a chariot, sitting at the victor's feet: *collaque Romanae praebens animosa securi* (*Trist.* 4.2.45; the Roman reader of course expects her to be put to death in the *Mamertinum* as soon as the procession reaches the *clivus Capitolinus*). Cp. also the association of fear in Hor. *CS* 53f.: *manus potentis / Medus Albanasque timet securis.*

To sum up: both the unparalleled individual genitive (*patrui*) and the forced meaning ("achievements") commentators assume here for *secures* speak against the abstract understanding. It further seems—considering the word's underlying and always present associations—improbable that Propertius would, while simultaneously urging friend Tullus to "outdo" his uncle, choose the bloody "axes" to characterize the elder Tullus' prospective (or even past)[18] administrative activities.

Thus nothing should keep us from trying to understand *secures* here as we would naturally do anyway—as long as the difficulties raised by this understanding are not too great to be overcome. In its concrete meaning, we said, the word stands (*pars pro toto*) for the *fasces* that are carried by the *lictores* in single file in front of the proconsul. The axes (=lictors) in our context then are the visible sign of the uncle's governmental authority (*imperium*), illustrative of his magisterial rank rather than of his achievements made while holding this (or, as some would have it, an earlier) office.

A similar statement can be made about *anteire*. Among the examples given in *Thes. ling. Lat.* for the metaphorical meaning "*antecellere*", "*superare*", our passage appears—*pace* Petersmann 1980, 59, n. 9—out of place. For, as a rule, Latin authors indicate the metaphorical meaning by unmistakably establishing a context of competition, either by indicating the area (mostly ablative) in which superiority is sought or achieved (e.g., *qui*—sc. *equi*—*candore* nives anteirent, *cursibus* auras, Verg. Aen. 12.84; si quis vult *fama* tabulas anteire vetustas, Propertius himself 2.3.41), or simply by relying on the apparent nature, drive, or relationship of participants in the competitive situation: *virtus . . . anteire priores cupit*, Sen. Benef. 3.36.1; *dum aequales, dein superiores, postremo suasmet ipse spes antire parat*, Tac. Ann. 3.66.4; *qui te . . . longe . . . antisse patris mei amicitias ferunt*, Tac. Ann. 4.40.5; *nec cursus anteeat illa tuos*, Ov. Ars Am. 2.726). I do not find an example of *anteire* = "outdo", "surpass", in a context ambiguous enough simultaneously to allow the concrete understanding ("go in front of"). Therefore the juxtaposition *anteire securis* in Propertius 1.6.19, as understood by most commentators, would be an unusual phenomenon: (a) no area of competition indicated (usually ablative; sometimes, in unmistakable situations of competition, etc., accusative of direct object)—unless we are willing to admit as object an accusative of unparalleled abstract meaning: *securis* = "achievements in office"; (b) a concrete understanding ("precede the lictors") not precluded by the immediate context.

These features in themselves suggest reconsidering the passage. What makes for instance SB (*ad loc.*; the same objection is also voiced by Paley *ad loc.*), decide in favor of metaphorical *anteire* = "*superare*", "outdo", is a negative argument, viz., that concrete *anteire* (as Hertzberg took it) would "stultify" *conare* (line 19). Shackleton Bailey himself seems not too confident about his decision, since he is simultaneously warning us—in the case of the aide-de-camp being asked to outdo his chief—not to take his solution too seriously (in SB's words: not to take *anteire securis* "more solemnly than Propertius probably intended").

But (as Camps has indicated *ad loc.*) *conari* is not limited to meaning "attempt". It may approximate our "dare" or "undertake" ("You undertake = prepare to take up a marching position in front of your uncle's lictors"), in which case it would contrast Tullus' active, politically oriented spirit with Propertius' fated inactivity (*Tu . . . conare*, 19—*Me sine, quem . . .*

iacere, 25). *Conari* may even (as is accepted in my translation of the poem) point to the stage when one has made a decision and "sets about" carrying it out. *Helvetii id quod constituerant facere conantur*, . . . (Caes. *B.G.* 1.5.1, cf. 3.1; different from later passages like 1.8.2;3;4, where their *attempts* are futile because Caesar will check them). Lewis and Short offer Nep. *Dat.* 7.1: *qui . . . prius cogitare quam conari consuesset*, and translate "before he *proceeded* to the undertaking" (italics mine). (*Thes. ling. Lat.* is not explicit, but apparently subsumes this nuance under "*incipere*"; Georges does specify "*zur Unternehmung schreiten*"; the *Oxford Latin Dictionary* is silent).

In Propertius himself we read *conari* (with infinitive) meaning "to set out to do, set about doing" in 1.3.12: *hanc ego . . . conor adire*, followed by: *non tamen ausus eram dominae turbare quietem* (line 17). Here the poet does not "try" to approach his mistress, but "sets out" to, then breaks off his undertaking immediately upon beginning. And in 2.26.19 Propertius was not "already attempting" to throw himself from the cliff, but was "already preparing" to jump ("on the point of", Camps)—when his dream suddenly vanished.

This nuance, needless to say, is well compatible with the concrete understanding (which I favor) of the difficult phrase *anteire securis*. The combination *anteire securis* is so close to similar expressions of concrete local meaning like *anteire agmen* (Tac. *Hist.* 2.5.1), *hi currum regis anteibant* (Curt. 3.3, 15), *cum iam tua vexilla, tuas aquilas magno gradu anteires* (Plin. *Paneg.* 10.3), that I am hesitant about attempts (Rothstein, BB, Enk, Richardson, Cairns 1974; see also Petersmann 1980, 59, n. 9) to see here a one-time juxtaposition of two individual, abstract metaphors (allegedly conveying, as we saw above, something like "outdo the proconsul's achievements") with no connection between their original, concrete meanings. Rather, we should first take the two words together as one concrete phrase ("precede the lictors"), the meaning of which is understood by Camps (*ad loc.*) literally as either marching ahead of the proconsul as part of a military escort or as walking ahead of him as a member of his suite. The *metaphorical* meaning of the *combined* phrase, then, I take it, presumes for Tullus a visible position and/or distinguished function within his uncle's political task of helping to restore Rome's sovereignty in the East—the pentameter (20), as we said, giving as a background the general meaning of the uncle's proconsular mission. If we picture Tullus preceding his uncle's lictors when the elder Tullus appears in public for official business, we may understand that Propertius envisions his friend, too, imbued with and participating in that awe-inspiring atmosphere of Roman government symbolized by the *secures* (see also what we said above on *accepti pars eris imperii*, line 34). There seems nothing "bizarre" (Richardson *ad loc.*) in this picture, even if an exact parallel for the situation cannot be offered (Camps *ad loc.* compares Ovid, *Pont.* 4.9.18).[19] Even if certainty cannot be reached concerning the phrase *anteire securis*, its concrete understanding supported above by us both relieves us from interpretations such as "outdo your uncle" or "go to Asia some time ahead of your uncle", and also allows us to leave *conare* the full power of the nuance explicated above: "You prepare to take a marked position on your uncle's staff!" makes good sense in itself—and it can be seen to fit perfectly in its context as we analyzed it because "you" (*tu*, 19) from now on at the same time means: "not I". The poetic purpose of assigning friend Tullus a conspicuous position among his high-ranking uncle's retinue is clear. The poet begins to unfold the contrast between elevated friend Tullus and lowly Propertius. As I said before, Tullus' participation in active political life is to find its incompatible counterpart in a Propertius whom fate has condemned to permanent, helpless inactivity.

The word left to explain in line 19 is *meritas*, which, when taken to mean "deserved" (or "well-earned", Camps)—rather than in the dire (and impossible) connotation of *de patria bene meritas* mentioned above—points to the continuity of the uncle's political career. The word would refer to Tullus the elder's consulate (33 B.C.) in which he, we presume, cooperated so smoothly with his colleague in office Octavian that his present proconsular governmental authority of Asia (of which the "axes", i.e., lictors, are the visible expression) seems "deserved". This understanding makes the whole distich 19/20 a consistent concession to Tullus, spoken in Tullus' language, to participate and distinguish himself in his uncle's pro-Octavian mission.

But the distich can hardly be claimed as an expression of approval of Tullus' plans. We may even watch a tendency to the contrary gradually reveal itself; as in modern languages, so in Latin a phrase like "you go and . . . !" can, if a community of only two persons is in question, be a statement of separation and difference, meaning: "your road is not my road". That we have to understand lines 19/20 in this way is brought out by *nam* (21), which logically derives and explains Tullus' decision to go (the aspect has shifted since lines 1–18: it is no longer Propertius' behavior but that of Tullus which receives an explanation now!) as a result of his continuous disinterest in love and from his longtime involvement with politics. The emphasis lies on continuity of attitude (*non . . . umquam . . . , semper at*, in this a parallel to *semper*, 25, *longinquo*, 27, etc.). This is important for us to observe, because here Tullus' present project is derived from permanent features in his life. In other words, his participation in restoring provincial administration and Rome's sovereignty, in securing the transition from Antony to Octavian, is not accidental in the poet's eyes but reveals an underlying pattern.[20] Propertius' language becomes pointed here. In defining Tullus' so far exclusive dedication to his country in arms, he plays out here for the first time the paronomasia *armatae* (22)—*amori*

(21), as we shall see him do again in later years. The opposition of arms and love is not new to my reader: we met it in a similar form in 1.9: as there Propertius' *amores* (5) are contrasted with the *arma* (2) of fraternal dissent, so "civilized" Amor does not like warlike epic but gentle songs (12). Then I pointed out that this opposition is essential to Propertius (cf. 3.5.1, our Chapter VIII). Elegy 1.6 is more specific, insofar as not only arms in epic but concern for the country herself, *armatae cura . . . patriae*, is considered an occupation of a man who has not (yet) met with an essential personal involvement. It is clear that Tullus is measured by the same standard as is Ponticus (1.7.15ff.) or Propertius himself who describes his own early period as untouched by love (1.1.2). In 1.6 the implied judgment on and attitude toward national politics seems indifferent, even unfriendly at a time when the new master of Rome wishes his past and present actions to be esteemed as the salvation of Rome. The reserve of elegy 1.6 must not however be taken to be a political attack; it is rather an evaluation of human qualities, leaving a back door open to the friend, or, better, asking him not to be too certain about his future:[21] the contrast *non . . . umquam* (21)—*semper at* (22) is wishfully extended into the future (23f.): "May your *non umquam* (23, picking up *non . . . umquam* of 21) persist for ever!" (Otherwise, the reader of 1.7 may supply, your uncle's mission or the country in arms might become to you what a *Thebais* can become to an epic poet!). This again is important: by specifically adding the wish (23/24) that his friend's attitude may continue without interference from "this boy" Amor, i.e., by trying to stave off a possibility unwelcome to Tullus' present plans, Propertius (the "wiser" of the two) implies that the possibility of change does exist as a potential threat to Tullus' principles. The poet will not allow a similar possibility of change when discussing his own permanent attitude (25ff.).

In subsection 19–24, Tullus is subjected to Propertius' yardstick (*nam tua non aetas umquam cessavit amori*, 21). In the following subsection (25–30), Propertius sets out by presenting his own way of life in the words a Roman career politician would use to describe it: let me hand over my life to "life-long" (I follow Rothstein's understanding) worthlessness (as you, Tullus, and people of your class would call it). To lie forever fameless and nameless is my fate—exactly the opposite of an ambitious young Roman's like you. Looking ahead from his present position, we already see how Propertius may tentatively favor Antony over Octavian (2.15; our Chapter IX), the "worthless" over the "savior",—or, to express the contrast in Vergilian terms (*Aeneid* IV), would favor Aeneas staying with Dido over Aeneas leaving Dido (see our Chapter VI on 2.7).

We have seen other cases where Propertius uses an opponent's terminology in order to make his own dissent understood to the other person: in 1.12.3–6 he picks up his faultfinder's language in order to tell the critic in his own words that his assumptions about Propertius are wrong. In

1.7.1–8 he employs, with a strong touch of irony, Ponticus' epic language (1–4) and uses his friend's low opinion of elegy to depict himself (5–8), but immediately changes his tone to say to Ponticus: what you despise, I desire to be the source of my fame (7.9–10). The same procedure is followed in 1.6. After asking Tullus not to interfere but to leave him to his *extrema . . . nequitia* (25/26), he turns around and proceeds to tell him that many have *gladly* perished in this way, and that he, Propertius, too, even *wishes* to be *buried* under this title (27/28). In this distich, we face another reevaluation of standing values: despicable unmanliness becomes a desirable, openly declared human condition, well worth dying for.

This makes the spiritual separation complete, and Propertius' final refusal of Tullus' world comes forth with great pungency: for arms and (civic[22]) glory he is not born (29; "born": a biological, unchangeable destiny, an *entelecheia* philosophically speaking. Cp. 3.9.19f. and Chapter VIII below). Line 29 (*non ego sum*) again, as did line 11 before (*his ego non*), echoes line 1 (*non ego nunc*). The reason for the echo is the same both times. As 11 corrected Tullus' mistaken guess (denied in line 1) concerning Propertius' alleged fear of the sea by, in summing up, emphasizing the true reason (Cynthia) for his refusal, so 29 bases the correction on a deeper understanding of Propertius' own innermost nature which can have no part in Tullus' world of *laus* and *arma*. And while Tullus' future was left open (23f.), that of Propertius (28; cf. 25f.) appears closed to any change. His decision in favor of Cynthia and against participating with friend Tullus in a proconsular mission of state is rooted in his personal constitution and is therefore final. Perishing gladly *in amore* (27) entails ineptitude for *armis* (29). Love excludes war, as (1.9.2 and 5) love poetry excludes war poetry. We have moved from the shell to the serious core of the elegy. A difference in outlook has come to light that was not visible to (though triggered by) Tullus when inviting Propertius to come along.[23]

At this point, the poet goes still one step (a decisive step) further: he even wrests one of Tullus' characteristic values away from his friend and paradoxically claims it for himself and his "worthless" way of life (and death): "This is the *military service* (*militia*) fate has in store for me" (30). Here a reversal clearly takes place and a reevaluation of one of society's points of honor, a reevaluation which must shock the normal Roman mind. For, by assigning the term of honor to his own miserable condition, Propertius gives the impression of upgrading it to the level of (or valuing it as high as) the official career,[24] declaring the lover's wounds to be, in his eyes, as honorable as the soldier's. He seems to imply that he wants his choice (or should we say: "necessity"—cf. *fata*, 30—?) of a way of life respected. In his eyes, his own commitment is as unconditional and as adequate for a man as a human being as is Tullus' so-called *cursus honorum* in the eyes of contemporary society.

Again, in spite of its bluntness, Propertius' outspokenness should be seen not so much as an attack upon Roman social values but as a protective reaction to secure his individual freedom of choice and human responsibility (as exemplified in the reasons for his decision not to desert Cynthia—a behavior which among Tullus and his peers would hardly be worth thinking twice about). As we said at the beginning of the preceding chapter, his poetry claims to present a central experience, which entails a few direct cogent consequences; whoever denies their validity denies the importance of the central experience itself. We must not forget that our poem starts out as a defense against Tullus' reproach ("you are afraid of the sea") and that the subsection we just considered starts by asking Tullus not to interfere: "let me . . ." (*me sine* . . . , 25).

The positions are now clear. *At tu*, line 31, is spoken against the foil of *non ego*, 29, and *hanc me*, 30 (*at tu* does not refer to Tullus in 6.2, as Petersmann 1980, 59, n. 10, citing Abel, thinks). But stating the contrast between the two friends does not mean breaking up their friendship; it means a new relationship or, at least, a new nuance to it, which Propertius, returning to a lighter tone and to the subject of traveling, can now accentuate (31–36). Tullus is here pictured in Asia Minor, and this painting offers surprising aspects because the transference of concepts does work not only one-way, from civic to erotic, but also vice versa, from erotic to civic.

The notoriously effeminate life-style (*mollis . . . Ionia*, 31, contrasting with the harsh *militia* of line 30) and the suggestion of rich, cultivated farmland, watered by the famous river which once carried gold (we think of King Croesus; although, in Propertius' time, it only makes the fields green—or gold?—with its waters), arouse certain associations of luxury that we have so far not connected with Tullus' patriotic traveling plans in this poem. Rothstein thinks Lydia and Ionia are mentioned because their wealth and luxury are able to catch a traveler's interest and make him forget his friends back at home. This comes close insofar as the trip as a whole is pictured to be absorbing for Tullus. But there may be an application *ad hominem* here. The poet's own viewpoint at line 14 was quite different, aiming at the *ancient* riches of Asia Minor, while contemporary abundance and riches are contained also in the picture which Propertius draws of Tullus' luxurious life in Rome (1.14). This helps to understand the ironical implication: your way of life need not change over there (6.31/32).

The implication is perhaps also borne out by a closer look at line 33. Naturally, the poet's Roman contemporaries tend to find the true hardships with Tullus' exhausting expedition rather than with Propertius' unmanly love life. But, as his use of the word *mollis* (31; to be countered, as we shall see, by *duro*, 36) has already suggested, the elegist may again prove capable of reversing the established standards.

At first glance, the line (unlike the two preceding it) is all toils and hardship:

whether you will be going to push your way on foot across the lands or
by oars across the sea. . . .

Naturally, the reader tends to understand *pedibus* of poor Tullus' own feet
that have to do the walking—as one may in Plautus (*St.* 292) sympathize
with Pinacium, who, crying for a vehicle, complains *nam pedibus ire non
queo*. But what are we to think of *remis*? Certainly Tullus is not going to
handle the oars himself when crossing the sea (*pontum*), is he? No, he will
be rowed by slaves. Ergo, the relieved reader concludes upon second
thought, Tullus is certainly not going to use his own feet walking the lands
either (especially since in so doing he will be "part of the governmental
authority bestowed" on the uncle, 34; authority rarely travels on its own
feet), but *pedibus* must point to a mode of land travel as *remis* points to propulsion by oars. Actually, these modes (the general inconveniences of traveling for once set aside) might be not too uncomfortable, as even the inferior alternatives permitted in Claudius' edict (Suet. *Cl.* 25.2) illustrate:
ne per Italiae oppida nisi aut pedibus aut sella aut lectica transirent (here, of
course, *pedibus* is used in the sense which we first assumed but then had
to exclude from line 33). Though one may in the first place think of
Tullus' horse, one should not believe that a sedan chair is less common in
times when it is less often mentioned in our scanty sources (cf. Lamer
in Pauly-Wissowa s.v. *lectica*)—not to mention the possibility of four
wheels. A member of the Roman authority may very well travel in style.

Pedibus, then, if taken in its narrow sense, is misleading (it may cover
the common soldiers, but hardly Tullus and his uncle). The point is that the
word may be purposefully misleading here, giving the line just that small
amount of gravity and ambiguity which is sufficient to make the trip
sound impressively toilsome while really it is not quite so. For *pedibus* also
means "by land", its opposite being "by sea", as in 2.27.5 where it is answered by *classe* (almost as "army" is answered by "navy"), and both
words are complemented in a chiasmus by *et maris et terrae* (27.6):

> seu pedibus Parthos sequimur seu classe Britannos,
> et maris et terrae caeca pericla viae.

A similar chiasmus is presented in 1.6.33: *pedibus—terras—pontum—remis*.
But in 2.27 the earlier part of the chiasmus (line 5: *sc. sequimur*) and the
later part (line 6: *sc. pericla viae*) serve each its own distinctive semantic
function. In elegy 1.6 this can be said only of the second half, which distinguishes the traveling medium (*pontum*) from the mode of propulsion
(*remis*). In the first half the distinction is minimal, if at all existent (*pedibus
terras* = to cross "the lands on land"). If we do not believe that Propertius
merely filled in an empty slot in his otherwise completed line with a tautology (a hazardous assumption to make for the experienced reader of his

elegies), we must assume that he used *pedibus* to enhance the (pseudo-) heroic picture of his friend's toils in service abroad. The solemn balance[25] of the line

$$\overline{\text{seu pedibus te}\underbrace{\text{rras se}}\text{u po}\underbrace{\text{ntum}}\text{ carpere remis}}$$

turns out to carry a playful piece of irony under its extraordinarily smooth surface. I do not think that one need understand *carpere* ("to push one's way or press along", *OLD s.v.*, no. 8) in a special sense (*carpere* "covers a wide range of actions pursued with enjoyment", Richardson *ad loc.*) to bring out the friendly irony in the picture of patriotic Tullus not overexerting himself but observing the requirements of convenience by leisurely traveling on land (on horseback? in a sedan chair? in a chariot?) or by sea (in a smooth-riding boat, 33/34).[26]

The ambiguous tone in line 33 is suggested by *pedibus* as well as by the context of the two preceding lines. Does it continue? The answer is yes, I believe. Under such prospects, Propertius ends his argumentation wittily, his friend—in case Tullus should at some time think of him being in Rome—should know: Propertius is not the one who is better off, for Propertius lives under a *harsh* fate (35/36; harsh, *duro*, being the epitheton usually applied to warlike deeds of epic character, while effeminate, *mollis* —in line 31 used to characterize Tullus' target area—usually is the epitheton of soft love elegy, cf. 1.7).[27] The contrast of "you" (*tibi*, 35) and "I" (*mei*, 35; *me*, 36) has found its final pointed expression based on a reversed application of value terms.

The turn our elegy has taken is certainly surprising. And had I not introduced elegy 1.7 before, with its swift change from elegiac humility and respect towards epic to disrespect towards epic and self-praise of the elegist, my reader would perhaps follow a scholar who finds the picture of the patron and friend in Asia, surrounded by luxury and traveling at ease, so "highly unflattering to Tullus" that he concludes: "Such an interpretation must . . . be wrong".[28] Therefore, he devises a way to understand lines 31–34 against their literal wording and out of context: they, he informs us, represent a topos of *propemptikon* poetry, introduced here as "a form of laudatory congratulation of Tullus". In other words, Propertius is said to mechanically mix here genre elements which are usually found grouped together, and he is assumed to do so at the cost of destroying the train of thought of his own text ("Since the topos so occurs the author is excused from producing explicit links with its context . . .").

My experience with the poet's insistence on logical presentation makes it hard for me to accept Cairns' theory. Therefore I return briefly to my initial question (asked at the occasion of lines 1–12) why, in a farewell poem to a friend, one should be so direct? The obvious answer I am now in a position to give is: what we have in 1.6 is more than the usual send-off poem. If one posits that 1.6 is a *propemptikon* and nothing more, one deprives oneself of getting to know Propertius' deepest concerns in this elegy, viz., to define his own exposed but unnegotiable position in the light of an unfavorable contemporary environment. The artefact's essential message is found in its individualizing—and perhaps even offensive—features, but not by way of reduction to genre elements. By no means must we make 1.6 into a "*propemptikon*", explaining allegedly unintegrated parts from our knowledge of the genre or even making passages whose wordings resist our understanding comply by reinterpreting them as unintegrated inserts of generic topoi. The interpreter's freedom is much more limited to the text than Cairns' hypothesis allows. To see in the poem excusatory tendencies on Propertius' part and an encomium for Tullus, as Cairns does, takes away from the creation its creator's specific ingredients, and that is its raison d'être.

Thus, in coming to the end of our interpretation, we should say that the situations of the two friends turn out to be the opposite of what Tullus had originally (1) surmised: by not going, Propertius does *not* anxiously avoid hardships. And by going, Tullus does *not* necessarily undergo hardships. So much for the common trip to Asia Minor and the hardships of traveling.

More important, of course, is the message below the surface, the definition of the different spiritual roads the two friends are traveling. As the smooth architecture (6 stanzas of 6 distichs each [29]) might suggest, the difference is not hard to outline. The elegy comprises two movements of three stanzas (a b c ; a b c). The first movement, ending a past period of irresolution, runs as follows:

I (a) 1–6: Tullus' false surmise about Propertius' motive is corrected and Cynthia's influence on the poet mentioned.
  (b) 7–12: Cynthia's desperate argumentation is presented and shown to be binding on Propertius.
  (c) 13–18: A hypothetical comparison between the advantages the trip would offer Propertius and the heartbreak it would cause Cynthia confirms his decision as right.

The second movement reveals a difference of standards underlying this decision:

II (a) 19–24: Patriotic Tullus, (so far) not overcome by love, is seen in the shining light of his high-ranking uncle's political mission.
  (b) 25–30: Propertius, inactive and permanently determined by his love, demands noninterference and reveals his own standards to be competitive with those of society.

(c) 31–36: Tullus, while being in luxurious Asia, is asked to think of Propertius' fate as harsh.

The surprise our elegy offers its reader lies not so much in the light way (from the addressee's point of view), in which Propertius dismisses a great trip offered at a low price (in fact, those invited by the proconsul usually hoped to do better than break even[30]), but also in the independence the poet shows in setting the limits within which friend (and patron?) may communicate with him. For in the end it is not Propertius any more who is being judged for his alleged fear of the sea and blamed for letting his friend go away alone; in the last instance it is Tullus who is being shown understanding for pursuing goals that befit an immature young man: the judge finds himself being judged (a similar aspect is offered in 1.14, where the pauper poet holds the key to a door which might prove locked in case rich Tullus should try to open it).

For Propertius, of course, Tullus is, as a participant in his uncle's mission, the greatest challenge we have seen so far: greater than Ponticus the epic poet, Gallus the unstable lover, the faultfinding Philistine, even Tullus himself the rich man (1.14). For in his present function, Tullus represents something which has conventionally been thought in Rome to be a man's highest possible pride and self-fulfillment and the lack of which has always been thought to prove a man's unworthiness (cf. *nequitiae*, 26). Propertius now openly claims this lack as a desirable destiny (*libenter*, 27; cf. 28). Although for methodological reasons I would not here feel free to call in an association with Antony (Richardson, *ad loc.*, feels "the context reminds us of Antony and Cleopatra"), the question certainly arises: why does he carry his point to such extremes? Was it really necessary to draw the line so clearly as in the contrast of lines 19–30? It must have been, and he must have felt a severe threat to his position. In Tullus' invitation, two things came together: one is, of course, the suggestion that the poet would be willing to desert Cynthia, from whose side this trip would have pulled him.[31] The other is that joining Tullus meant more than seeing beautiful "museums": it meant paying tribute to the life of patriotic political and military action; and yes, in the last instance—not mentioned in 1.6 itself—it meant joining a cause whose victims were likely to be closer to his heart than the victors. To see this point, we have to turn to the last poem of his *Monobiblos*.

EARLY MEMORIES:
CIVIL WAR

1.22:

What kind of a man I am as far as family is concerned, where my
    family comes from, what the gods of my house are,
you keep asking me all the time, my Tullus, in virtue of our
        friendship.

If the country's graves at Perusia are known to you,
    Italy's funerals in harsh times,
when Rome's discord drove her own citizens   5

    (thus you, dust of Etruria, are a cause of pain to me especially:
you have let my relative's limbs be cast away,
    you cover the poor man's bones with no dole of soil):
The land that borders ⟨on Perusia⟩ with its underlying plain, Umbria
        in closest neighborhood,
    rich in fertile fields, has brought forth me.   10

The elegy has been tantalizing to many a reader because it does not
deliver what it seems to promise, viz., precise answers to Tullus' three
questions. Some scholars have explained the "vagueness" (BB) by assuming
that the text we read is not the original one. Housman's remedy [1] was to
add to the poem some lines which he removed from the second (30.21–22)
and fourth (1.65–66) books. Leo, likewise unpersuaded that the final
poem (after initially announcing what his learnedness felt to be the typical
βίος καὶ γένος which Alexandrian scholars used to add to their annotated
editions of classical authors) should "send the readers home" [2] with such

scanty information, believed 1.22 as we have it to be a fragment of which the important part is missing. The assumed gap even led this critic to write "Textgeschichte"[3], positing a mutilated text of the *Monobiblos* even before books 1 to 4 were published together. Enk, on the other hand, unimpressed by the poem's seeming incongruity, introduces it: "Hac elegia . . . Propertius ubi natus sit exponit. Eodem modo Vergilius quartum librum Georgicon claudit" (!), and goes on to list Greek and Latin examples of the traditional σφραγίς—by which ancient authors used to seal their works, secure the authorship against theft, and give some details of the author's life. It seems to me that one should not pass over in silence the problem that stirred Housman, Leo, and others. But before imposing generic demands which the poem possibly cannot fulfill, we might first wish to ask whether the incongruity was perhaps intended by the author, and further, whether the elegy contains features that tie it to the book to which it forms the epilogue. In pursuing this line, it is worth recalling Rothstein's introductory remark that the poet, even when following the custom of including some biographical data in the sealing poem of one's work, was completely free to select whichever data he wished to see published about himself.

Let us begin by stating that in the questions which Tullus is portrayed as asking here a certain insistence seems to manifest itself. "What kind of a man are you with regard to family background? Where do you come from as far as your family is concerned? What *Penates* do you have?" One is tempted to sense a degree of obtrusiveness[4] from the fact that he asks three questions, not one. We further observe that these do not represent the kind of questions that together would lead to fuller biographical information—questions we might easily make up from our knowledge of sealing poems composed by other authors, e.g.: "When born?" ("Under the Consuls X and Y"). "Where?" ("Sulmo"). "Which people?" ("Paelignians"). "Place of residence while writing?" ("Naples"). "Family?" ("Father a freedman"). Among such and similar bits of information, which are easily obtained from well-known examples, Tullus' interest appears to be rather single-minded in its concentration on the last-mentioned type. For all three of his inquiries involve Propertius' family background, i.e., his social origins. However, when seen against the background of the *Monobiblos*, Tullus' questions appear very much in character. As readers, we understand immediately why a friend's family and social rank should be of interest to him: being of great wealth (14) and highest political connections (6), he himself has so far dedicated his life exclusively to armed service under Octavian, the future Augustus, and presently seems destined for a postwar career under the auspices of the victorious régime. Naturally, social background must mean a lot in his eyes. Coming from Tullus' lips, the questions provide the reader with a different setting than if they were asked by Ponticus.

Propertius himself, on the other hand, has already told his friend (1.6) that he would "gladly" end his life in the passive and socially despicable role of the "unworthy" lover, and that the *cursus honorum* fails to appeal to him. Why then, if he does not care for his own social standing, does the poet compose an elegy the opening lines of which make his reader's expectations vainly converge on this feature? To make us think that he would have to be ashamed of the answer in case Tullus (and we with him) heard it (so he would be less self-confident than Horace in *Ep.* 1.20)? This consideration may safely be excluded since, when çoming back to the subject years later, he is able to describe himself as the descendant of a well-known family (*notis . . . Penatibus*, 4.1.121; so in 1.22 he chooses to be less self-assertive than Ovid in *Amores* 3.15). We also may exclude that in 1.22 he wants to indicate once more that the love poet is not interested in the social hierarchy. For, besides having already said so to Tullus in 1.6 (and what purpose would be achieved in the epilogue by a mere repetition?), he does give an answer to Tullus' urging questions, viz., in lines 3–10. If the answer does not fit the—after all, fictitious—questions, we can only assume (provided the poem has not been mutilated in the long manuscript tradition) that he wants us to be aware of the discrepancy.

In other words, in first composing a threefold precise request for information and then dodging it, although he has no reason to be ashamed of his origins, the poet may indicate that he does not see fit to answer questions of this kind. This explanation gives us an advantage over interpretations advanced by others: if the poem is designed to demonstrate that Tullus insists but Propertius hesitates to answer, then its structure *must* result precisely in the kind of incongruous, evasive response which some interpreters found offensive to the degree of declaring the elegy mutilated.

Our explanation may even allow us to take sides in an old controversy: does *semper* (line 2) go—in the manner of the Greek language (example: ὁ ἀεὶ χρόνος)—with *nostra . . . amicitia* (Rothstein) or with *quaeris* (BB)? *Communis opinio* today recommends the former, because "Tullus would not have needed to ask the question continually" (SB, following Enk) or, in Camps' words, because "the thought of constant repetition of this simple question is ludicrous." What if this is not a "simple question" for our poet to answer? Camps himself, on the other hand, when investigating Tullus' three questions (and Propertius' single answer), concludes: ". . . so there cannot be much difference in meaning between them." Why then does Tullus ask the same simple question three times? In suggesting for our elegy a dramatic situation that consists of a pressing and urging Tullus and a reluctant Propertius we are able to offer a sufficient explanation. "You keep asking me all the time by virtue of our friendship" is a legitimate translation of line 2, and it is much more in agreement with Tullus' three (!) almost identical (!) questions in line 1 and with the ensuing "somewhat vague" (BB) answer in lines 3–10 than it would be with a set of biographical data as offered by traditional *sphragis* poems. Besides, the grouping of related words in the pentameter 22.2 (it is almost the same as, e.g., in 21.2) is much more up to Propertius' artistic standards if the two word groups are formed by nos. 1, 4 and 2, 3, 5, respectively, than by nos. 1 and 2, 3, 4, 5.[5]

The problem raised by my explanation is of course: *why* would Propertius not see fit to answer? Because the answer, if given, might bring up facts unwelcome to Tullus (or to an influential part of the general audience thinking like Tullus)? Or because the customary answer would appear trifling and irrelevant in the face of the superseding substitute answer actually given in lines 3 to 10? Or perhaps both? The circumstance that Tullus can invoke the solemn right of friendship (2) makes Propertius' evasive reaction almost appear impolite, if not rude. Or does it not? Is perhaps the opposite possible, viz., that Tullus, with his continuous insistence, is the one who has gone too far, beyond the border line of tactfulness? We recall that once before (1.6; Chapter IV above) a seemingly innocent advance made by Tullus led Propertius to examining and redefining their relationship, and to uncovering a difference in basic attitudes. We possess enough historical and biographical information to state a priori at least one reason why an inquiry by Tullus concerning Propertius' family background should touch a sensitive area and reveal another contrast between the two friends: while Tullus' family, having actively favored Octavian's now victorius party during the recent civil war, have kept their wealth and are presently in good political standing, Propertius experienced the loss of his family's fortunes and suffered a deprived childhood (4.1.121ff.) when the same Octavian in 41/40 executed the triumviral land expropriation program in favor of the veteran soldiers. (And, let us add, neither has the Propertius of 29 B.C.—as is assumed to be the case with Vergil—been swiftly reinstated into his property by Octavian, nor do we know of any material compensation or support he may have received as Horace meanwhile has from Octavian's friend Maecenas.) The fact that Propertius' answer to Tullus' alleged questions mentions Perusia—the city in which Antony's brother Lucius Antonius, leader of the revolt against Octavian and against the expropriations—had been besieged by Octavian in 41/40 and finally forced to surrender, seems to confirm that, this time, the contrast between the two friends is rooted in the fact that their families espoused opposing political causes in the civil war. Thus the historical background—only too painfully present to the reader of the year 29 B.C. —can help us too to see even better why Tullus is chosen to be the mouthpiece for fictitious questions Propertius does not wish to answer frankly, but apparently does not wish to leave unasked (and unanswered) either. Tullus, the counter-Propertius already in 1.1, 1.6, and 1.14, once more helps to further the difficult process of *definitio sui per negationem*. The poem's procedure, appropriate in the face of possible delicate political implications, is no longer open as in 1.6, but comparable to that of 1.18 discussed in our previous chapter, where the servant-lover, being in no position of directly blaming the ways of his overbearing *domina*, likewise expresses himself in a circuitous manner.

If my assumption is right, viz., that the poem's notorious incongruity is due to an underlying but veiled political contrast, then we would have another case in which Propertius puts a traditional form (that of a *sphragis* poem) to a new, personal use by avoiding to give the stock information his reader expects from the genre. In similar fashion, we said at the occasion of 1.18, he may use traditional scenery to play his own rococo-like game; or, in the case of 1.1, he may use a Greek epigram, when dealing with his own inner development, to introduce an autobiographical statement. The problem arising for my hypothesis is, of course, how to verify it. Would the poet, in the difficult situation after Actium, dare to give his reader a glimpse of his true attitude if he does not agree with the new régime? Among scholars, this question is hotly contested, and thus cannot be answered categorically. Much depends on the interpreter's evaluation of the climate at Rome after the civil war has been decided: could a dissenter feel free to speak openly or not? Unanimity on this point seems out of reach. If "yes", then Propertius' epilogue hardly contains any opposition, for, as we shall show, he does not voice any (i.e., not openly). If "no", do his words express the cautious reserve of the politically disagreeing writer? Historians tend to answer the question differently from literary critics; the latter often see Propertius in the light of Horace and Vergil, who found their way early to feeling reconciled to Octavian's cause. But it may be methodologically doubtful if we define an individual's political convictions by subsuming him under the Zeitgeist represented by the contemporary members of his guild. The question of political attitude has to be decided anew in each single case.

In the preceding chapter (when comparing 1.6.20 to Georgics 4. 559ff.) we already saw how far removed Propertius' position is from Vergil's admiration for *Caesar . . . magnus*, who "is on his way to Olympus." A position like the one taken in Vergil's first Eclogue, which alludes to Octavian as to a *deus* (6; qualified in 7; cf. 18; 41) seems inconceivable in the terms of the *Monobiblos*. Agreeing with a cautious critic,[6] we may also point to the difference between Propertius and Horace. The *Monobiblos* has no word of praise for Rome's new master. Horace, on the other hand, widely acknowledges Octavian's value for Rome. In *C.* 1.2 (composed probably at the end of 28 B.C.[7]) the lyric poet, convinced that mortal prayers no longer reach the ears of the nation's gods, calls for an immortal to achieve expiation of Rome's civil war crimes. The divine mediator is found in Mercury-

Octavian, who is implored not to return to heaven too soon in wrath about "our crimes" (*nostris vitiis*, 47; "our" hardly refers to Horace's former individual opposition against Octavian, but, according to the poem's scope, covers all who have raised their arms against C. Julius Caesar and the cause of his adopted son, Caesar Octavian). Rather, Horace prays, may the mediator stay on among the Roman people and be pleased to be called Father (sc., of the Country) and *Princeps*. In his human manifestation, we hear, Mercury-Octavian permits himself to be called *Caesaris ultor* (44), the avenger of his adoptive father's death (the last of C. J. Caesar's killers were executed after Octavian's victory at Actium in 31 B.C., more than thirteen years after the deed). In the *Monobiblos*, Caesar the adoptive son is far from being appreciated as *Caesaris ultor*. The only reference is to his hostile swords, *Caesaris ensis* (1.21.7), from which a relative of Propertius barely escaped while fighting *against* Octavian in the Perusine War of 41/40 B.C. Each of the two authors records the view which one of the two opposed civil war parties held of Octavian: C. J. Caesar's pious avenger and now Rome's divine savior beyond mortal hope to one, he manifests a fatal threat to a family member in the eyes of the other. Side by side with Horace's praise should of course be listed Vergil's slightly earlier promise to carry the fame of Octavian's name into the far distant future by singing his victories (*G.* 3.47f.).

A similar, perhaps even more striking difference can be seen if we make a comparison concerning time, taking another look at the first Eclogue, traditionally believed to be written in 40 B.C. (but even the date of 35 B.C., suggested by Clausen 1972, will do for our purpose). Vergil here sees fit to visualize the victor of Perusia, who expropriated Italians from their land, in terms of a merciful *deus*. Propertius, in a work published *twelve years after* those same events, still recalls Octavian as the threat which his swords once posed to his family. If any guidelines can be gained from our comparison of disparate passages, then in two points: first, the *Monobiblos* should not be measured by the standards of the "early Augustans" Horace and Vergil, but deserves individual consideration; secondly, Propertius presents himself as a person of a long memory.[8] The offensive "vagueness" of his answer to Tullus' questions—Tullus, we keep in mind, is espousing the same cause as are Horace and Vergil—may consequently result from an unwillingness or even inability to forget. In that case, the question of open speech may not be dismissed easily.

Let us then see whether elegy 1.22 bears out any of the implications which might be suggested by the *Monobiblos*' silence about the glorified events and the celebrated victor of the day. Two problems arise: first, since Propertius manifestly avoids a direct answer to the questions he puts into Tullus' mouth, what kind of positive clues would he incorporate for his contemporary reader to understand the central concern of his epilogue? Secondly: are we, two millennia later, in a position to verify such hints? Necessarily, the interpreter walks on a thin line here. And, whenever introducing the poet's contemporary scenery, he should try to make sure that any event he adduces is seen from Propertius' viewpoint, not from a (post-) Augustan angle. (Many a historian has failed to grasp Thucydides' central concerns because he would impose modern imperial attitudes on his ancient "predecessor's" analysis of Athens' imperial age).

The poet's singular way of recording in 29 (or 28) B.C. Octavian's swords of 41/40 B.C. may give us a lead in another case. Why does he dwell on the feature that his homeland Umbria was *"rich* in *fertile* fields", using the (perhaps untranslatable) abundant collocation *fertilis uberibus* (10)? What is his personal view in this? According to 4.1.127ff., Propertius lost his wealthy possessions in Umbria (*tua . . . rura, multi . . . iuvenci, excultas . . . opes*) to the confiscations of 41/40 (in the context of the Perusine War), and so was forced into narrow circumstances (*in tenues cogeris . . . lares*). Is it too farfetched to say that, in mentioning to Tullus the wealth of his[9] home district, Propertius cannot but also recall the fact that his own wealth there was taken from him by the party which wealthy Tullus is serving today? This would add a new emotional feature to the contrast of propertied Tullus and lover Propertius who is not so well off (1.14). The stylistic abundance *fertilis uberibus* finds a sufficient explanation if it is used for the purpose of nostalgically emphasizing a personal loss—a loss understandable to the informed contemporary.[10]

The category "personal loss" can be confirmed as an appropriate viewpoint because it will make another appearance in the epilogue's artful composition (6–8). But before coming to it, the poet outlines a more general condition (*si . . .* , 3–5) which Tullus must be aware of (*tibi . . . nota*) if he is to understand his friend's final answer given in 9/10. This condition can hardly be taken merely (or at least predominantly) as a geographical guide to describe the location of the poet's little-known hometown, like "fifteen miles to the east of better known Perusia" ("Allgemein bekannt dagegen durch die traurigen Ereignisse. . . war die Bergstadt Perusia. . . . So konnte Properz die Schilderung seiner Heimat an Perusia und den perusinischen Krieg anknüpfen."—Rothstein. "Propertius brings it"— sc., Perusia—"into the present poem simply because it was a famous place, as Assisium at that time was not, and so a reference to it would afford a generally intelligible way of indicating the area in which he was born."— Camps). For the reference is not so much to Perusia's location on the map (or Assisi's location in relation to Perusia) but to fatal events that happened there (*Perusina . . . sepulchra*); also, not to the year of the poet's birth (as in a *sphragis* poem) but to a later time (*temporibus, cum*) of civic sorrow; not even to the sad events of Perusia alone, but to them as a symbolic nucleus of far broader destruction: *Perusina . . . patriae . . . sepulcra*, a phrase in itself leaving the local level, is quickly widened geographically into *Italiae . . . funera* (4), which itself again involves the whole political range of Rome's self-destructive civil war (*Romana . . . discordia, suos . . . cives*, 5). So what Propertius wants to say by this answer is apparently: "If you know the deaths of Perusia, the symbol of our recent civil war—close-by I was born," i.e., "I am a child of the civil war. Amidst its sorrows I grew up." The sinister contents of the long *si*-clause modify the meaning of the emphasized first word (*proxima*, 9) in the dependent main clause. Along with geographical proximity to a neighboring town, the reader cannot but understand: closest physical and emotional vicinity to the theater of war.

It seems strange that interpreters should have found the poem's message "vague" (BB), especially if one includes the personal part (6–8). "It" (sc., the poem) "contains an account, not very precise, of the poet's birthplace, with a parenthesis lamenting the melancholy fate of his relation" (Postgate). The form of a broad parenthesis (6–8), however, as Rothstein has seen, "ist für das Verweilen bei einer schmerzlichen Erinnerung, die alle anderen Gedanken zurückdrängt, . . . geeignet." Recalling our observations in the preceding chapter on 1.3.33/34, we may add that 1.22.5/6 provides us with another one of the few Propertian examples where the pentameter opens a new movement of thought within a poem. The artistic purpose is transparent beyond doubt: the emotion of personal loss and sorrow is so overwhelming that its expression is presented as disrupting the balanced flow of regular syntax and meter (but not of poem structure, as our outline will show; we will be able to offer a similar case when dealing with 2.15.1ff. in Chapter IX below). By its disruptive force, the lament forms the epilogue's emotional climax (following it, the original grammatical construction is picked up again and continued). This finding should make a strong case for our thesis that Propertius in 1.22 is not so much out to fulfill a traditional custom (information on birthplace, family rank, father's name, year of birth, ancestral honors, etc.), but rather utilizes it for concerns of his own. If here—as in 1.21—he centers his compassion on a loved one who died years ago in the Perusine War, the critic has no right to find—as some readers have done—such long-lasting grief strange or even alien to human nature. To decide whether or not a loss experienced during the formative years of childhood is in later years felt to have grown into a permanent wound, lies, in this case, not within the interpreter's range of arbitrament.

What it meant to ancient feeling if a close relative lay unburied (Propertius' words reach the level of accusation against the unfeeling Etruscan soil when describing in detail his poor relative's deplorable fate), may to moderns probably best be communicated in the lively words of drama. Antigone expresses this feeling—not so much when she discursively reacts to Creon's newly given laws (νόμοι) by herself referring to the gods' always valid unwritten laws (ἄγραπτα . . . νόμιμα) (Soph., *Ant.* 450ff.), but when she expresses her unbridled and original desire to give protection in afterlife to him who shared with her the protection of the same habitat (her mother's womb) before this life:

> ". . . Thus it is no pain at all for me to meet this fate
>   (of being executed) myself.
> But, if I endured that the son born from my own
>   mother, upon dying, would be a corpse
> unburied—about that I would indeed feel pain . . ."
>
> (Soph., *Ant.* 465ff.)

Feelings of utter anguish, not dissimilar to Antigone's, are what Propertius wishes to convey to his reader when addressing the soil of Etruria that has allowed his poor relative's limbs to be dispersed and lie unburied.

It seems to me that one can hardly find fault with a composition that purposefully avoids answering questions concerning the social background of the poet's family by substituting a lament on his childhood experience of civil war and death within his family. Only one must grant the poet the liberty to modify existing generic forms in order to put them to an individual use so as to achieve his own purposes. As classicists we are perhaps too easily inclined to allow rules of genre to override individual creativity even in cases where non–fulfillment of genre expectations can be as poetically important as staying within the "rules". That personal grief can outweigh biographical data, and that painful memories can prevent a person from precisely answering questions asked of him, is humanly so convincing that dramatic presentation of these reactions in a *sphragis* poem should not need an excuse—especially so if (a) the uncustomary contents result in a logically consistent presentation ("For you, as my friend, it is more important to know that my childhood was exposed to the Perusine War than to be informed about my family background"), and (b) the poem's form as read today can be proved to be intentionally designed and final. In favor of (b) we may cite not only the broken distich and the interrupted syntax but also the fact that this disruption itself is well integrated into the overall structure and thus visibly made a part of the whole (a similar observation was made in Chapter I above when we analyzed the overflowing emotion in the opening six lines of 1.11 within a general framework of subunits comprising four lines each). To show my point, I outline the epilogue's clear-cut disposition:

I 1–2: Tullus' detailed request (threefold) to hear about   1D
Propertius' family background

II 3–8: Provisions (*si*) under which an answer can be
given:

(a) 3–5: knowledge (*nota*, 3) of the Perusine deaths as a national disaster — 1½D

(b) 6–8: the poet's personal sorrow in connection with this war — 1½D

} 3D

III 9–10: Answer: Propertius was born in the neighborhood closest to Perusia, viz., in fertile Umbria. — 1D

A structure the verifiable elements of which are presented in logical sections counting 2 : 3 : 3 : 2 lines deserves to be intensively investigated before being discarded as mechanically mutilated by an unmerciful tradition of its manuscripts.

So far, we have laid bare the human core of this difficult poem, but we still have not encountered the proof we were looking for of an implied political attitude or even bias. Thus the question to be taken up again is whether, in addition, the concluding poem of the book necessarily contains a political statement. Although some interpreters have felt it does,[11] I think such a case is hard to prove on the basis of 1.22 alone. For a sceptic might argue that Propertius almost completely avoids any expression that could be taken as tendentious. In fact, the sceptic might feel tempted to argue to the contrary, i.e., that the poet is neutral with regard to the warring parties. We do not learn on which of the two sides his deceased relative fought, that of Octavian or that of Lucius Antonius. "Rome's discord", driving her citizens, and "Italy's funerals in harsh times" are phrases that in themselves do not seem to favor one side over the other.[12] Even the reference to the fighting over a single city can perhaps be said to be couched in a more general context by the addition of *patriae* to *Perusina . . . sepulcra.*[13]

Shall we then accept the conclusion that the poem does not bear out any of the potential political implications we mentioned earlier? Yes and no. "No" insofar as all the material I introduced to point out the undeniable contrast between Tullus' attachment to the new régime and Propertius was not taken from 1.22 itself (but from 1.6, 1.14, 1.21, 4.1, even Horace, Vergil). And the poem's core can easily be outlined in nonpolitical terms as a long-felt sorrow about personal loss in war. But "yes" insofar as the doubtless existing contrast between the friends Propertius and Tullus, easily defined by their families' opposing party affiliations, cannot simply be forgotten. I suggest that to those contemporaries who read the whole book carefully (the more so if they even knew about the poet's circumstances from knowing him personally) the epilogue could seem to say more than it did in the eyes of those who read it as a single, unconnected poem. My readers, for instance, already introduced to the contemporary and personal background early on in this and the preceding chapter, are in a position to see that, beyond our interpretation given on the foregoing pages, elegy 1.22 may easily contain the message: "Tullus, my friend, do not press me to reveal my family background to you. ⟨In case you force me to answer, I would have to speak out that your and my families have fought on opposing sides and that still today I cannot forget the harm done to us by your party. Be it enough that I give you a circumlocutory answer:⟩ I am a child of the country's Perusine War and am still suffering from personal loss." This wider interpretation, unnecessary to say, would also explain the lack of any praise for Caesar Octavian we observed when comparing Propertius with Horace and Vergil.

In terms of methodology, I still owe my reader proof that the author wished such political overtones, in addition to the private core, to be understood by his reader. The first issue I shall discuss is a word contained in 1.22 itself, which I have so far left aside: Perusina (3).

Earlier, I had said only that, in Perusia, the opponents of the veterans' settlements and the expropriation program were besieged by Octavian and finally forced to surrender. The term *sepulcra* thus might at first sight be taken to point to the losses suffered by both sides or especially to the deaths from starvation among the besieged (Appian, *BC* 5.5.38; 39; *et passim*; Dio Cass. 48.14.3). But Perusia was remembered later for other deaths as well, which occurred *after* the city had been surrendered. Whereas Appian (5.5.48f., drawing on Octavian's—the later Augustus'—own Memoirs?) reports "only" the Perusine town council (τῆς βουλῆς μόνης) not pardoned but killed by Octavian (and his chief personal enemies by his soldiers), Dio (l.c.) has it that "some" were pardoned, "but the majority of the senators and knights were put to death", as were "the majority of the Perusines and the other captives" (14.5; cf. Suet. *Aug.* 15). He adds the "story" (λόγος; some details are mentioned by Sueton, l.c.) that the Roman senators and knights, a multitude of 300, were sacrificed on the Ides of March (i.e., about two weeks after the surrender), at the altar of C. J. Caesar (a way for "Caesar's avenger" to remember the day of his adoptive father's assassination?). Even Velleius (usually pro-Augustan) admits savage treatment of the Perusines (although more by the soldiers than by Octavian's will, 2.74.4). Whatever the truth value [14] of the "story", Seneca already can presuppose it as well known when mentioning merely *Perusinas aras et proscriptiones* (*De Clem.* 1.11.1) while exemplifying Augustus' early cruelty (*ego vero clementiam non voco lassam crudelitatem*). Definitely, Perusia was remembered as a high point in the activities of *Caesaris ultor*. Even if we, being sceptical, discount the sacrifice, those reports nevertheless leave us wondering if *Perusina . . . sepulcra*, for the contemporary reader, would arouse associations of neutrality only and not of partiality. The fine point of course is that Propertius does not make any allusion to the name of the man who, assuming the authority of judge (App. 5.48), ordered the killings, but points only to the graves of the victims. Whoever would wish to denounce the poet would himself have to name the name first. But who would like to name the name in 29 B.C.?

The phrase *Perusina . . . patriae . . . sepulcra* may perhaps reveal even more than is suggested by the concrete understanding "the graves of our (or even: my) countrymen who died at Perusia". If in Lucretius (5.259) Earth can be *rerum commune sepulcrum* (because she who brings forth also buries all things); or if for Catullus (68.89, opening of a passage which Kroll *ad. loc.* defines as a model for Prop. 1.22.6ff.) Troy can be *commune sepulcrum Europae Asiaeque* (certainly not only because men of both continents died there fighting, but because their youth, rank and number—*Ad quam tum properans . . . undique pubes Graeca*, 101f.—were the essence or life-blood of the two continents themselves); if Scylla, betraying father and country, can be *patris miseri patriaeque inventa sepulcrum* (*Ciris* 131)—could not then *Perusina . . . patriae . . . sepulcra* be the graves in which, so to speak, the fatherland itself was buried,[15] or rather the graves that meant the end of the fatherland (because, in our poet's eyes, those defeated and killed by Octavian, and their cause, represented the true—Republican— country)? (And would the killer of Perusia not be the country's grave- digger rather than its saviour?)

And, in similar fashion: if a leading man's political destruction can be said *funus esse rei publicae* (Cic., *Prov. Cons.* 19.45); if a person could be said to prepare *funus . . . imperio* (Hor., *C.* 1.37.8); or if Horace (C. 1.8.14f.) could speak of the *lacrimosa Troiae funera*, cannot then *Italiae . . . funera* mean the end of Italy? "Denied justice and liberty, Italy rose against Rome for the last time", R. Syme (1974, 208) rightly characterizes the opposition against Octavian and his veterans' settlements, implying a wider historical background. A "war . . . most harsh and long-lasting for Italy", Appian (*BC* 5.5.49) summarizes the—meanwhile justified—prewar expectations when finishing his report on Perusia.

It seems to me that, once Propertius' contemporary reader visualized the political and historical facts about Perusia and Italy (after all, eighteen cities were scheduled to cede lands to the triumvirs' soldiers, and many others joined their resistance)[16], it was hard for him to exclude a political dimension from his understanding of elegy 1.22, and to read the epilogue merely as the nonpartisan expression of private grief which our earlier in- terpretation of its restrained surface brought out.

"The country's graves at Perusia" (or especially when understood to mean "*my* country's graves at Perusia"; after all, the poet is supposed to answer about his own family's home district), being a childhood mem- ory, do have the potential of pointing to more than the pitiful victims of the famine and of the carnage that was the result of Lucius' attempts to break the siege: locally (and, beyond that, also for a wider area), they do mean the end of "the fatherland" (the republic) as well as of "Italy". If you know the graves of Perusia, you know all that is important to know about my origins. This is a strong statement considering the fact that it was made in the years that follow Octavian's victory at Actium, and it cannot but color the reader's view of the author's political attitude.

Let us review also lines 5ff. within this time frame (after 31 B.C.). We are dealing with the aftermath of a period which Rome's new master will proclaim to have been one of national unity, when allegedly *all of Italy* had *voluntarily* sworn allegiance to him (cf. *R.G.* 25.2f.: *iuravit in mea verba tota Italia sponte sua*, etc.; Augustan Vergil loyally voices the same sentiment at *Aen.* 8.678ff.). Propertius, however, speaking a year or more after Actium, publicly recalls memories of civil discord, *Romana . . . discordia* (5), and explicates their lasting meaning for his own life (*mihi praecipue*, 6)—up to this very day (even if written earlier, the reader cannot but understand the concluding poem to state the author's feelings as of the time of publication): *tu nullo miseri contegis ossa solo* (8) is *present* tense, as must be the auxiliary verb—*es*—to be supplied with *dolor* (6). For the poet's heart, the dire events of the civil war and of Perusia especially are by no means already a matter of the past.

Sceptics (and their number is not small) may still object that Propertius in 1.22 does not *himself* point out any of the associations or connections I have made. To them I would respond, beyond invoking the word *Perusina* (and the name *Italiae*) in 1.22, by introducing another issue: the fact that Propertius did include poem 1.21 with his collection. For (as we indicated earlier) there he resigns the neutrality observed in the final poem and does identify the party his deceased relative (*mei . . . propinqui*, 22.7) had fought against: Octavian, i.e., the victor over Perusia then, and the master of Rome and Italy now, at the time when the poem is being published as part of the *Monobiblos* in 29/28 B.C.

In comparison with the "epilogue" 1.22, poem 1.21 is sometimes called an "epitaph" because it claims to record the last message of a dying man to his beloved, in a fashion similar to sepulchral epigrams (especially such written as if for cenotaphs, empty tombs erected for deceased persons whose bodies were never found) as we find them in the *Anthologia Palatina*. I shall deal with its generic aspects later, for now only asking my reader to recall our finding that in 1.22 it was not the generic aspect which turned out to be the essential one, but its individualizing modification.

A question to be considered beforehand is whether dying Gallus (by this name he identifies himself in line 7) is identical with Propertius' unburied relative of the epilogue. In general, scholars have, though with different degrees of conviction, presumed that this is the case (cf. Postgate, Rothstein, BB, Enk, Camps, Hubbard 1975, 40, Hodge and Buttimore

1977, 213). Today, as far as I can see, apart from Bodoh (1972, 241) only Richardson in his commentary assumes (without stating his reasons) this identity to be "unlikely". In both poems the deceased is assumed to have died in connection with the Perusine War; in both poems also the problem of later burying the remains is touched upon (*dispersa . . . ossa*, 21.9; *proiecta . . . membra*, 22.7, etc.).[17] Since, as we have seen, the dedicatees in the *Monobiblos* fulfill the function of helping the poet define—though more often by contrast than by agreement—a sector of his own life or self, it seems a good procedure to ask what features the words of dying Gallus add to the picture Propertius gives us of himself (or, for the reader who would wish me to be more precise, of the speaker of the book's poems). By subject matter, time reference (41/40 B.C.), size (the exceptional brevity of precisely ten lines—in 1.22 part of the overall design, as we saw) and position, the "epigram" coordinates itself to only one other poem in the book: the immediately following "epilogue" 1.22. The methodological question to ask, then, is: what does the reader learn in 1.21 that gives him a better preparation for understanding the poet's grievous memories voiced in the ensuing poem? Already, we can give a preliminary and guiding answer: 1.21 not only provides us with the name and political affiliation of the poet's deceased relative mentioned in the epilogue, but also deals with the tragic details of his death and the effect of the sad event on his beloved—details directly conducive to understanding the outcry of grief that forms the emotional climax of 1.22.

Unfortunately, the poem's text—and, depending on the text, its interpretation—has been subject to such hot debates that unanimity about its meaning will hardly ever be reached. Only recently Richardson has presented another new edition which almost certainly will trigger a wave of criticism. Luckily for our purpose, however, Gallus' central message (lines 7/8) can be phrased clearly without any change in the transmitted text. In the rest of the poem, I differ from Barber's OCT edition in two places for reasons of syntax and logic. In both instances the difference is minor in view of the manuscript tradition.

Because of the difficulties, I precede my translation with an outline of my understanding of the speaker's situation: Gallus, one of the defenders of Perusia under Consul Lucius Antonius, has escaped from the immediate danger of being killed by Octavian's soldiers (whether during one of the sorties described in Appian[18], or from the executions after the surrender, or even from the sacrifice at C. J. Caesar's altar[19]—we cannot know). On his way home to Assisi, he has been attacked and fatally wounded by unknown assassins. Awaiting his death, he beholds another soldier—his bride's or wife's brother—making his way home from Perusia[20], likewise wounded. Gallus addresses the frightened man, reassuring him by identifying himself as the member he is of the same side and even family. He wishes his kinsman luck in reaching home and staying alive (so his parents may rejoice) and asks him to let his[21] sister know about her fiancé's (or husband's) death without telling her the whole, sad truth.

> You, who hurry to escape the common destruction,
>> soldier, coming wounded from the Etruscan mounds,
> why, at our moans, do you roll your eyes so they protrude?
>> I am part of your campaign—the part most closely related
>>> ⟨to you⟩!
> Thus save yourself that your parents can be joyful,   5
>> and that your sister does not, from your weeping, become aware
>>> of what happened ⟨viz.⟩:
> that Gallus, although snatched to safety from amidst Caesar's swords,
>> has not been able to escape unknown hands;
> but may she know that, whatever bones she will find scattered about
>> on the Etruscan mountains, these are mine.   10

Readings different from OCT: *nec*, 6; *at*, 9 (cf. Schuster-Dornseiff *in app. crit.*).

The first thing to register is, of course, that here, differently from the epilogue poem, Caesar Octavian is mentioned by name: the campaign in which Propertius' relative Gallus participated was directed against Octavian. Thus the reader of 1.21 gains more information for understanding 1.22 than he who reads the epilogue for itself as merely representing the traditional *sphragis*. To realize the connection between the two poems is however left to the reader's acuity. Again, the poet can hardly be denounced for something he does not say openly. Now I have already indicated that the information which 1.21 supplies for understanding 1.22 is not only factual but, above all, emotional—in this corresponding to the emotional climax of 1.22 (lines 6 to 8). Scholarship has not been very kindly disposed toward this aspect of 1.21. BB, convinced that a last request in an ancient sepulchral poem can only concern burial of the remains and nothing else, take offense at the double aspect of Gallus' entreaty; that the nature of his death should be concealed, but the location of his bones (as BB understand lines 9f.) be revealed, is unacceptable to them: "This partial revelation is incredibly feeble, and may be rejected out of hand." "BB's comments hold good", SB holds, while (rightly) rejecting E. Reitzenstein's (1936, 7) and Enk's notion that what the sister should be prevented from knowing is "the disgrace of flight".

But Reitzenstein and Enk have at least acknowledged that the negative part (lines 7/8, introduced by line 6) of Gallus' entreaty to his kinsman is distinctly twofold, according to the poem's transmitted text: (a) *ereptum* . . . (b) *effugere . . . non potuisse*. It was, however, unfortunate that Reitzenstein (occasioned, as one may easily suppose, by his contemporary sociopolitical environment[22]) introduced the notion of "*auf dem Felde der Ehre gefallen*" (o.c. p. 7), assuming that it would have been "bei allem Herzeleid ein Trost" for the woman to know that Gallus died fighting in battle and not, as is the truth (allegedly to be concealed from her), after leaving the battle-field (cf. Enk: *Gallum non cecidisse in acie, sed a latronibus occisum esse*). By introducing the patriotic motif (the woman's concern for her man's honor) into Gallus' last message, Reitzenstein falsified his own correct find-ing, viz.: "Was soll die *soror* denn nicht erfahren? Nun, dass er eigentlich gerettet war, dass er aus der Schlacht entronnen war und erst nachträglich den *ignotae manus*, der dunklen Mörderhand, doch noch zum Opfer gefallen ist" (l.c.). This simple contrast of "escaped (survived)—and yet killed" un-folds a human tragedy [23] which can only be obfuscated by the introduction of additional explanations. For the sorrow must be immeasurably harsher for anyone who loved the deceased, in case it became known to him or her that Gallus was safe already after escaping almost certain death (*per medios . . . ensis*, 7)—only to face death again, this time without escaping. Is it not to the eye of a close one as if Gallus had to encounter (suffer) death twice? And does it not, on his part, reveal a degree of love rarely ex-pressed, if he, himself at the point of dying, asks that his beloved bride be *not* informed about the tragic circumstances [24] because he wishes to spare her the increase in pain and despair which awareness (*sentiat*, 6) of the facts [25] (*acta*, 6; detailed in 7/8) would add to her mourning? (A similar tact-fulness and regard for others lies in his wish that his kinsman's parents may be granted the joy of seeing their wounded son live). [26]

It would seem unfortunate if the humane voice of ancient poetry should not be heard today because the terms of our scholarship limit its sepulchral or related poems to a certain set of subjects. Camps, going far-ther than BB and SB, even finds it "hard to conceive such a request being imagined by Propertius and made the subject of a poem, and impossible to reconcile such a request with the concluding request in line 10". Conse-quently, Camps changes the manuscript text to make it agree with "an-cient sentiment". But once we take the alternative route of interpretation and do permit the ancient poet to express feelings like those uttered by dying Gallus in lines 7/8, we are almost able to deduce logically what the second part (lines 9/10) of his entreaty will contain. If Gallus desires to spare his bride (or wife) any awareness of his vain escape from and final encounter with death, he will also wish to put her mind at rest (at least as far as is possible in a case where she cannot have the sad confirmation that lies in burying his remains), i.e., leave her in no doubt about the fact that she can no longer hope to see him alive. This is the function of lines 9/10 within the message entrusted to his kinsman, as we shall see. I do not however wish to give the impression of deducing my interpretation of the poem's ending beforehand. Rather, I wish to open a road to understanding the final distich. Commentators so far have set the tracks of their inter-pretations in such a way that they no longer review the textual evidence for alternative interpretations when they arrive at explaining the last two lines. The double aspect of

> (a) death in spite of escape (7/8)

and (b) death (corpse) without[27] burial (9/10)

is clearly expressed in the text, and two different verbs are used by Gallus in conveying his twofold request. He separates

> (a) what the bereaved woman should *not* (*ne* codd., OCT; *nec* ς, Postgate, Rothstein *et al.*) *become aware of* (*sentiat*, 6), viz., the tragic circumstances preceding his death,

from (b) what she is to *know* (*sciat*, 10), viz., the fact itself of his death at a location unknown to her.

Although Quintilian (10.1.13) says that the two verbs (and some others) "often" mean "the same", we must by no means fail to weigh the individual case and to distinguish here between *sentire* (become aware of, feel the negative impact of the *acta*) and *scire* (know). The distinction is neglected still in one of the more recent treatments of 1.21 done by Tränkle who paraphrases both verbs by the identical word "erfahren" (= learn).[28] It is observed by Kunihara (1974).

The possible difference in *intellectual* nuances may be verified from sentences like . . . *hoc etiam sunt timendi magis quod quid cogitent me scire sentiunt neque tamen permoventur*. . . . *Omnia superioris noctis consilia ad me perlata esse sentiunt* (Cic. *Cat.* 2.3.5f.), or *scio ego* (I know) *et sentio ipse* ("realize" myself, i.e., need not be made aware of by you), *quid agam* (Plaut. *Trin.* 639). Cf. *nescis heu, perdita, necdum / Laomedonteae sentis periuria gentis?* (Verg. *Aen.* 4.541f.).

The particular *emotional* nuance carried by *sentiat* in Prop. 1.21 is not slight, considering Gallus' desire to spare the woman's "feelings" (as we say): the negated verb (*sentire*) that originates in the realm of sensual perception is much more appropriate to express Gallus' purpose of preventing her from having an additional painful experience than would be *scire* or any "synonym" of it. In the same way, *scire* is appropriate where only the full intellectual grasp of the fact (of Gallus' death) can prevent her mind from indulging in self-tormenting, eventually vain hopes that she might see Gallus again alive. We shall comment below on the sorrowful paradox which mixes certain knowledge (of the loved one's death) with lasting ignorance (concerning the identity of his remains).

If the difference between the two finite verbs in lines 6 and 10 is observed (and the negative opening of line 6 maintained against editors' attempts to replace the manuscript tradition by a positive conjunction[29]), a contrast results between lines 7/8 and 9/10. Enk (who, though aiming at a different interpretation, likewise sees the contrast here, paraphrasing it:

"*ne . . . sentiat . . . sed sciat . . .*") writes *et* in his commentary *ad* lines
9/10, but prints *sed* in his edition of the text as the first word of line 9. It
seems easier (as far as manuscripts go, the difference belongs to the minor
ones; cf. 1.6.22) not to introduce *sed* but to read *at*—which Schuster-
Dornseiff (cf. *app. crit.*) even consider as possibly the true manuscript
reading.

The final distich offers a special question, which has been answered
differently by interpreters. Does *haec* (10) refer (a) to *quaecumque*, making
both pronouns point to identical contents? Or does *haec* mean (b) the
speaker's remains as distinguished from all others the *soror* may come
across, i.e., does Gallus in these words—in agreement with the tradition
of certain sepulchral poems—ask the passerby that he reveal the location
of his bones to the *soror* (so she may find and bury them later)? The latter
(b) is accepted by Housman (1893, 184), BB, Enk, Damsté (1924, 5ff.),
Helm, Camps, Tränkle (1968, 565f.), Bodoh (1972, 239f.), Hodge and
Buttimore (1977, 213). My own observations have (as my translation
shows) led me to decide in favor of Rothstein's answer (a) (shared by Paley;
Hommel 1926; E. Reitzenstein 1936, 9; Quinn 1969, 22; Postgate, sharing
(a) but finding it inappropriate, changes the manuscript text). We have
seen that both in 1.22 and in 1.21 (as elsewhere) Propertius feels free to
vary and modify traditional forms for his own poetical purposes. The
train of thought in 1.21 does not lead straight up to the standard request of
sepulchral epigrams for the ritual burial, but is in the first place directed at
alleviating the fate of the bereaved woman (lines 6 to 8)[30]. The interpretation "These bones—the ones here in this place—are mine", although perhaps not wholly impossible (if one reads "*et*" at the beginning of line 9)
within the framework of our findings, would certainly risk giving away the
fact the speaker wishes to see concealed, viz., that Gallus died upon escaping from the circumvallation of Perusia, i.e., while already on his way
home. Thus (b) must rank second to (a), i.e., the understanding prevails
which accepts the (as even Housman seems to imply) not unnatural grammatical connection and sees *quaecumque* (9) picked up by *haec* (10).

In this way, the poem's last two lines ("But may she know that mine
are whichever bones she will come across scattered about on the Etruscan
mountains!") convey the fact not only of Gallus' death (*ossa*) but also of his
remains being lost to her. We may paraphrase: "My bones and their location will be unidentifiable (and therefore the consolation of giving *me* burial will be withheld from her). May she know that my remains may be any
bones she finds."[31]

There is a sad oxymoron (reflecting the paradoxical situation) implied
in Gallus' last words: although they contain the certain information that he
is lying dead (= "bones", *ossa*) on the Etruscan mountains, they cannot
remove the uncertainty (*quaecumque*) that she will never be able to identify

his remains. This is in agreement with Gallus' purpose to spare her feelings as much as possible: she must be told ("*know*") that he is no longer among the living, and she has to *know* also that she cannot expect to receive the customary confirmation of his death, viz., an identified corpse that can be buried. But she is not to know how, and that includes (according to line 7; cf. 2) where, he died—except for the vague description "on the Etruscan mountains". This vague indication may even be taken to include the devastated mountain city of Perusia itself, so no suspicion is aroused in her that might lead to "becoming aware" (*nec . . . sentiat*, 6) of the truth (*acta*, 6).

As a confirmation and postscript let us remark that the interpretation given above of Gallus' words is in complete agreement with the lament voiced in Propertius' own *persona* in 1.22, viz., that his relative's limbs were cast away and are not covered with any dust by the Etruscan soil (lines 6 to 8), i.e., a burial has *not* taken place later (*dispersa* 21.9 ~ *proiecta* 22.7).

What does the "epitaph"—doubtless a worthy specimen of its author's refined art and humanity—tell us about Propertius, speaker of the *Monobiblos?*

First, we have learnt about the family's party affiliation: anti-Octavian, pro-Republican. This will keep us from reading both 1.21 as a politically neutral, general civil war memorial (cf. Richardson) and 1.22 as the politically "objective" poem which its restrained surface suggested at first glance. It seems impossible that the Propertius whose family we are acquainted with in the epitaph poem should be impartial in the epilogue poem when recalling the Perusine War and his personal loss.

Although we do not have the vivid memories which his contemporaries had, it is perhaps possible to get still closer than we have so far come to the intellectual environment which the boy Propertius was exposed to at the time of the Perusine War and which he has in mind when recalling his childhood experience. Appian, toward the end of his report on the siege of Perusia in 41/40 B.C., gives us three speeches: two, similar in their arguments, by Consul Lucius Antonius when contemplating surrender (one to his soldiers, another one addressing his conqueror Octavian), one by Octavian (answering Lucius). Since Appian claims (*BC* 5.5.45) to have translated the latter two from "the Memoirs"—of Augustus himself, as is usually understood—, there may well be some, albeit filtered, historicity to the arguments put into Lucius' mouth, especially so since Octavian, in answering them, seeks to weaken them by accusing Lucius of artful slander against himself (ὅσα σὺν τέχνῃ μου κατεψεύσω, l.c.). I shall give my quotations from the consul's first speech (*BC* 5.5.39). In Appian's account, Lucius Antonius, in resisting Octavian, considered himself fighting not for the threatened landowners (ἐλέῳ τῶν γεωργῶν) but "for the country" (ὑπὲρ τῆς πατρίδος), trying to restore "the republic" (τὴν πάτριον

. . . πολιτείαν), against "the tyrannical government of the triumvirs" (τυραννίδα τὴν τῶν τριῶν ἀνδρῶν ἀρχήν). Worst of the triumvirs he considers to be (with the two colleagues Lepidus and Antony out of the way) Octavian, to whom "the ancient Roman government was nothing but a pretext and a laughing-stock" (τὰ δὲ πάτρια ῾Ρωμαίοις πρόσχημα μόνον ἦν καὶ γέλως). Thus Lucius maintains he tried to turn things back "to the inherited freedom and democracy" (ἐς τὴν ἄνωθεν ἐλευθερίαν τε καὶ δημοκρατίαν), attempting to end Octavian's "monarchy" (μοναρχίαν), even by force, "in virtue of my office" (ἐπὶ τῆς ἐμῆς ἀρχῆς) as a consul.

Would not the patriotic harangues ascribed to Lucius here naturally express the kind of ideas which young Propertius heard in his family (perhaps together with other, more local ones), viz.: fighting under the rightful consul (Lucius) for freedom and the republic, against tyranny and (Octavian's) monarchy? The same *Caesaris ultor* whom Horace praises in the above-mentioned poem (*C.* 1.2) as the god-sent (god-on-earth) Father of the Country was by them experienced as a harsh enemy. For the only exception "Caesar's avenger" was willing to make from the executions after the fall of Perusia was in favor of a certain Lucius Aemilius—who had, while serving on a jury at Rome, openly voted to condemn Caesar's assassins to death (τὴν καταδικάζουσαν ἤνεγκε φανερῶς) and bidden his fellow-jurors to do likewise (App. *BC* 5.5.48). The other defenders of Perusia, who had fought for (as young Propertius would hear the case) freedom all along, did not meet a judge so merciful.

Can there be any doubt on whose side young Propertius did feel at the peak of the civil war? We can hardly escape the conclusion that the boy's sympathies were with the ideas and the party his lamented relative had fought for and with the neighboring town and its sufferings. Looking across the valleys from his hometown, Assisi, perhaps even while waiting for his relative to come home, he probably could see [32] the smoke rising over burning Perusia. (Although we may have no archaeological evidence of Perusia burning down, both Dio—ἡ πόλις αὐτή, πλὴν τοῦ ῾Ηφαιστείου τοῦ τε τῆς ῞Ηρας ἕδους, πᾶσα κατεκαύθη, 48.14.5—and Appian—καὶ ἐνεπρήσθη χωρὶς τοῦ ῾Ηφαιστείου μόνου, 5.5.49—report the fire, and I find it hard to take in any other way Propertius' own description at 2.1.29: *eversosque focos antiquae gentis Etruscae*). Are the alternative positions at all conceivable, viz., either that he admired the author of the executions, or that the last two poems of the *Monobiblos* mean that the boy was a neutral observer of the Perusine War?

Secondly, what—beside the family's party affiliation and the implications for young Propertius' political attitude—do the loving thoughts of dying relative Gallus in 1.21 tell us that would facilitate our understanding of the ensuing epilogue poem?

Definitely the reader's mind is prepared to participate in the outburst of grief in 1.22.6–8. For, when turning to 1.22, the reader has impressed in his mind both the sad result (21, lines 9/10) and the tragic circumstances (21, lines 6–8, i.e., the emotional climax) of Gallus' death.

An attractive hypothesis (Kunihara 1974), explaining equally well the poet's lasting pain of more than ten years and the political reserve expressed in 1.22, would be to assume that dying "Gallus" (a surname used in several families, among them the *Cornelii* and the *Sulpicii*) was Propertius' own father (whom he lost early, before putting on the *toga virilis*, and who is the only man of the elder generation he mentions with sadness elsewhere, 4.1.127f.). The *soror*, in that case, would be the poet's mother. But such a hypothesis can lay no claim to verifiable reality. For in 4.1 the poet also tells us that he did bury his father. It may, however, bring us nearer to answering the question what Propertius wishes his reader to understand to have been his part in the events described. Is then perhaps Rothstein's consideration, that the kinsman addressed by dying Gallus was Propertius' father, worth repeating? In a way, yes. For it allows us to stay within the boy's immediate family when visualizing his early experience of loss. Should one perhaps even surmise that his father's early death (4.1.127f.) was caused by the wound which dying Gallus is referring to (*saucius*, 21.2)? We have to discount this as pure speculation (although some readers might think it would heighten the poetic density of the sorrow expressed).

Whatever the historical facts, the reader is asked to share and feel the poet's own (*mei*, 22.7) commiseration (*miseri*, etc., l.c.) with the deceased —a commiseration which is unceasing (*contegis*, present tense, 22.8, cf. *dolor*, sc., *es*, 22.6). Rothstein's hypothesis may help considerably in fulfilling this purpose of the poem. For, if the anonymous kinsman who brought home the news of Gallus' death was the poet's father, then the bereaved woman was Propertius' aunt (his father's sister).[33] This means that the boy Propertius not only lost an uncle (or an uncle-to-be, if Gallus was not yet married to his aunt, but betrothed) whom he loved and to whom he felt especially close. Above all, it means that the boy witnessed the bereaved woman's grief, her desperate questions about the manner of Gallus' death, about the location of his remains, his father's reluctant answers—everything within the closest family circle, and at a time when the threat of expropriation by Octavian's soldiers, of being driven from their estate and their home, was about to be carried out (or even had become true already) for all of them.

We may go even one step further. Why should the poet present Gallus as concealing the circumstances of his death (21, lines 7/8) but conveying the fact of his death at an unknown location (lines 9/10), if not to make the reader, too, feel and realize the impact of this split communication on the family's situation? What if the poet's "father" (to continue Rothstein's identification hypothetically) did fulfill Gallus' request? What if young

Propertius did get to know that part of Gallus' last words which was with-held from his "aunt", i.e., the *soror*? We have every reason to interpret the poem consistently. Enk's paraphrase (*"Deinde petit ab eo, ne soror eius praemature suam miserandam mortem comperiat, sed ut postea demum eam edoceat, ubi ossa sua iaceant"*) evades answering this question, by arbitrarily insert-ing the words *praemature* and *postea demum*, which cannot be accounted for in the poem's transmitted text. It is hardly a compliment paid to the author by the commentator if the latter feels he has to clarify a poem's text by himself providing the crucial time plan that would make its parts logically compatible with each other. Why not rather understand and accept that the boy Propertius did learn about the truth (the *acta* of 21.6), perhaps from his "father", while the same truth was, according to Gallus' wish, withheld from the "aunt"?[34] This means that, in addition to seeing the woman's sorrow, the boy himself was exposed to the full measure of grief inherent in Gallus' fate—that full measure which is expressed in the epitaph poem written (and published) years later by the grown-up man. I would not wish to be misunderstood as claiming that there is any histor-ical truth to the family relations I have, following Rothstein's suggestion, tentatively assumed above. What I wanted to do was to fill the framework of the two final poems with that degree of reality which the speaker of the last one claims to have been affected by in the formative years of his child-hood (and ever since).

Thus 1.21 puts the politically informed contemporary reader in a bet-ter position to understand Propertius' intense lament in 1.22. It even helps to set up a sort of calendar of the personal impressions which stand behind the mention of the Perusine graves and his relative's death in 1.22: the boy watched the Perusine War with the anxiety which is created by the partici-pation of a family member (or members) in the losing but (as the family felt) "just" cause. He would hear about the famine, the fall of the city, the massacre. He saw the impact and himself felt the pain over the death of a relative who had fought against Octavian. He experienced loss of the fam-ily home and estate (*fertilis uberibus*, 22.10[35]; cf. 4.1 where we read that he thereafter grew up in narrow circumstances and also was relatively young when his father died). All this Tullus (and the contemporary reader) un-derstood when asked to understand the long condition ("If you know the graves . . .") formulated in 1.22.3–8 and the answer given to Tullus' ques-tions in lines 9/10. It may (perhaps) be an objective statement, but cer-tainly not the impression the poet, by including 1.21 with his collection, wishes to give of his early situation when Richardson writes (*ad* 1.22.7): "all things considered, P. and his family would seem to have got through what must have been terrible times for that part of the country with rela-tively light losses."[36] This would wrongly allow us to move Propertius more easily into the vicinity of Horace and Vergil, but would block the way to understanding the lasting attitude of mourning and reserve expressed in 1.22 and detailed in 1.21.

In all, by preceding the epilogue poem with the epitaph, the poet has gained a manifest advantage for the latter poem. His reader may, thus well-prepared, be much more certain about the character of the closing poem. Not only is the climax of personal sorrow in 1.22 easier to understand, but also the political overtones we thought we heard in 1.22 earlier but could not prove immanently are definitely there and can no longer be ruled out. This however does not mean that the first interpretation of 1.22 we arrived at (above p. 107f.), before introducing the political implications, was wrong. For there can be no question that the epilogue in the first place is a personal not a political poem.[37] But, since the political forces of the time have left their inextinguishable mark in the author's life, any statement in autobiographical form that would not include his civil war experience (if only in the veiled form the present political situation allows) would be lacking in an essential area of his personality and development. The negative balance we registered when comparing Vergil's and Horace's praise for Octavian with Propertius' silence does turn out to be significant. By once more choosing, from all the characters addressed in the *Monobiblos*, Tullus to ask the question concerning the poet's background, and by then avoiding a straight answer, the seemingly hesitant poet has become surprisingly outspoken, at least to a reflective reader who has lived through the end of the forties and the thirties B.C. Tullus is the one friend who most definitely marches in a political direction which is opposed to that of the poet, whose eyes are looking "backward", not in a direction which Tullus and his political friends would call "forward". Beyond the message of 1.6 (our Chapter IV above), Tullus (and the reading public) may understand that it is not only Cynthia who keeps Propertius from the Active Life, but also his own early political experience. The opposition of lover and politician in 1.6 is given a very specific background in 1.22. Let us realize that at the time Propertius is writing his epilogue (29/28 B.C., roughly), Octavian has won his complete victory over Antony and all other opponents inside and outside Italy, and is indisputably the most powerful man on the contemporary political stage. It could be unwise at this time to allude openly to what many considered the crowning cruelty of his bloody career. Here a separate and preceding poem can certainly provide helpful though indirect clues.[38] If free speech was not contained in the restoration program now beginning, it was already ambiguous and an indication of courage to introduce oneself publicly as a child of the Perusine War. The least Propertius' *sphragis* itself indicated about its creator's political attitude (to those who had an ear for political overtones—and who had not at that time?) was that the doors of a human heart could not be opened to the new peace program as easily as the gates of Janus' temple were closed. The latter took place in January of 29, after the end of the civil war. In August of the same year, Octavian the future Augustus celebrated his threefold public triumph.

Before ourselves investigating the contribution the two last poems make to the overall impression of the *Monobiblos*, we should reflect on the function some interpreters have assigned them (or denied them) within the setting of the book. In general, scholarship after the time of Housman and Leo has not seen fit either to give the epilogue (and the poem preceding it) better marks, even when refraining from declaring it a fragment, as those two scholars did. E. Reitzenstein, trying a new way, saw in the poem's core (22.3–8) "die in einem einzigen Crescendo gegebene Darstellung seines Seelenschmerzes beim Gedanken an die Heimat, also ein Gefühl, eine Empfindung in einer inneren Spannung und Bewegung, wie ich das als Aufgabe der Elegie für Properz aufstellte" (1936, 15). But this influential work has no word for Propertius' painstaking efforts to communicate his *Schmerz* in an intelligible and logically stringent, even concrete (*Perusina . . . sepulcra, proiecta . . . membra, nullo . . . solo*) way. Reitzenstein, in spite of his discovery of *Gefühl*, can make no better use of 1.21 and 22 than to see them as "*künstlerische Versuche*" (!), "*wegen ihres hohen poetischen Wertes*" deserving a place in the *Monobiblos*, "*auch wenn sie äusserlich gesehen nicht ganz in das Buch passten*" (o.c.p. 16; italics mine).

Here, of course, we may raise the question whether the interpreter's idea of a book does match the author's idea of his *Monobiblos*. This is true also about several later attempts to determine the internal order of Propertius' first publication, especially about those who see him pursue patterns of numerical proportions. Camps' plan of the *Monobiblos* (1961, 10) stops before reaching our two poems, at 1.19, the "natural counterpart" of 1.1. Skutsch (continuing from where Leo's disciple Ites had left off in 1908), though allowing 21/22 (along with 20) to be "part of the *Monobiblos*", nevertheless states: "The coda or superstructure of three poems, 20 to 22, stands entirely apart" (1963, 239). Courtney, following Skutsch, declares 20 to 22 "early poems, which Propertius did not wish to discard" (1968, 254). Otis, calling 1 to 19 "the *Monobiblos* in the strict sense" (1965, 7), does not even deal with the two final poems. Hubbard, though not trying to establish any numerical schema, likewise excludes 1.21/22 from the book's main body: 1.20 "is indeed in a sense the last poem of the book" (1975, 40). Barsby (1974, 134: "an autobiographical tailpiece") and Hodge and Buttimore (10: 21/22 among the "early poems", cf. 215[39]) follow along, as does Petersmann (1980, 220f.: no thematic connection).

Among the aforementioned, Otis goes farthest in drawing method-ological consequences from Skutsch's numerical findings which may be characterized briefly as follows: poems 1 to 19 = 89 + 71 + 70 + 88 distichs; if one adds poems 20 to 22 (= 36 distichs) to the inner numbers, the sum (= 177 distichs) equals the sum of the outer numbers—provided one distich is missing from poem 1.1 (Skutsch o.c.p. 238). Otis draws the consequence that "any attempt to consider single poems in isolation from the *ensemble* can quite well lead to serious errors of interpretation" (o.c.p. 2). Although his warning does not apply to 1.21 and 22 (since Otis does not include the two concluding poems with what he calls the "quite intri-cate unity" of poems 1 to 19), we should at least point out the danger that lies in predetermining the meaning of single elegies from their position in a presumed numerical *"ensemble"*. In hardly any elegy we have interpreted in the preceding chapters except for the most obvious ones, the structures of which were generally acknowledged anyway, as in 1.6, could Otis' nu-merical analyses of single elegies, as reported in his tables 3 and 4, be confirmed.

Opposition against the numerical schemata has been voiced by Hering, who reunites the last three elegies with the book: "Die Hauptbedenken müssen sich gegen die Absonderung der drei letzten Gedichte als eine Art Coda richten" (1973, 70). In rebutting Skutsch, he reinstates the weight of a poem's contents into its right within the balance of interpretation, and thus is much freer to acknowledge on principle the Catullan richness of Propertius' poetry, which is not limited to his love but deals also with his life, poetry, friends, family; even historical and social aspects are not ex-cluded: "vielmehr scheint seine Dichtung aus dem persönlichen Erlebnis der Bürgerkriege sehr bewusst als eine Chance zum Leben zu erwachsen" (Hering 1973, 72). This approach allows the two last poems to have a legit-imate place in the book. Our own account has likewise shown that form serves to express thought in Propertius, not vice versa. Thus some gener-ally recognized groups (among them 1.7 and 9, see Chapter III above; 1.11 and 12, see Chapter I above; and, surrounding the latter and in contrast with them, 1.10 and 13) helped us to interpret the elegies' meaning. But the order of poems in the book can hardly have been formed merely or even predominantly to please any scheme of symmetry or numbers' game[40].

In the same way, I would like to recall here, the friends addressed in the single elegies (like Tullus, Ponticus, Gallus) are chosen not at random (and not merely, as Otis, o.c.p. 25, unnecessarily limits his findings con-cerning 6 to 14, because the poet is "defending his ideal of love . . . against the criticism of the three friends"), but because—and I include Bassus here, too—, apart from their possible concept of love, their life-style, po-etic goals, personal attitude, political conviction, etc., could or do overlap or even interfere with Propertius' own domain and convictions and therefore demand a clarification from his own lips so his own position may be defined more precisely. Once this purpose is recognized, we may stop looking for external motivations for our poet's selection of addressees. That Bassus in 1.4 is the iambic poet known under this name is hardly a matter of relevance, for Propertius does not make a point to address friends of his "literary circle"[41]: the poem claims that Bassus is addressed because he wants to estrange Propertius from Cynthia—as in the next elegy (1.5) Gallus is claimed to be addressed because he wants to estrange Cynthia from Propertius. Here is a clear relation, defined by complementary functions, and fully understandable from the given context. The only justification, to my mind, for introducing into the interpretation the circumstance that the Bassus of 1.4 is identical with Bassus the iambic poet would be a desire to prove that Bassus wants to convert Propertius from elegiac to iambic verse writing (something I do not intend to hypothesize). The case of Tullus in 1.22 was different because the material we adduced from other sources had a direct bearing on clarifying his function within the epilogue poem itself for the modern reader.

A related consideration may be included here. Much has been written about a possible antagonism of Propertius and Tibullus. One argument (*ex silentio*) is that Propertius does not mention Tibullus among his "literary friends"[42]. Our observations cause us to ask why he would wish to address someone who does not contest his claims if his principle is to illuminate his own sphere himself and show their proper place to those who tend to cripple elegy's range as he defines it? Along the same lines we may, looking a few years further ahead, understand both that Vergil will be among the addressees and why Vergil the author of bucolic eclogues will be much closer to meeting Propertius' approval than the writer of the *Georgics*—not to mention the problem posed by the later Vergil who turned epic poet—a new Ponticus—(2.34, our Chapter VII below).

The idea of defining his own position in a multifarious environment is essential to the young poet, and, without showing ourselves receptive to the manifoldness of subjects actually presented in the *Monobiblos*, we cannot verify his intentions in designing the book.

With the requirement formulated above in mind, I finally turn to the question what, according to our interpretation, the last two poems add to the reading experience of the *Monobiblos* as a whole. Under the aspect of form, three preparatory observations can be made:[43]

(1) The dedication of 1.22 to Tullus, referring back to the opening dedication of 1.1.9 (and the intervening addresses in 6 and 14) certainly helps to create a unifying frame for all the poems contained within the setting. (Besides, Tullus is, as we said before, here—more so than in 1, because here the poet goes back in time beyond his love to his early

roots—cautiously being acquainted more closely with the other side of his friend, the one that does not appear, e.g., in his love poems. There is a polar relationship for Tullus between 1.1 and 1.22.)

(2) The fact that the sorrowful climax of 1.22.6–8 receives detailed treatment in a special poem (1.21) which is incorporated in and therefore part of the *Monobiblos*, makes it impossible for the reader to consider the allusion to the killing in 22.6–8 as an isolated and therefore incidental piece of biographical information. We face a section of Propertius' life considered essential by the author himself.

(3) 1.22 is similar to 1.1 in pointing to an event which, at the time of writing, lies back in time (roughly, twelve years preceding), but apparently must be considered to have been of high formative power in the author's life, up to the day of writing (and of publication). In a similar way (as the comparable positions of 1.1 and 1.22 at the beginning and end of the book suggest), the fact that he met Cynthia has had a lasting and immeasurable influence on Propertius' life. The avoidance of any name (author, family, birthplace) in the *sphragis* and the emphasis on personal experience move 1.22 close to the account of his inner development given in 1.1. In fact, in both poems the author has chosen the form of an autobiographical retrospect which explains his present condition. Prologue and epilogue complete each other, giving a firm setting to the contents in between.

These formal considerations suggest that the importance of the final poem (and the one preceding it) has generally been underestimated. Propertius shows that, in spite of the deep-searching introduction he gave his book (1.1), the self-portrait the reader could and should gain so far from the *Monobiblos* would be incomplete without the last two poems. This does not mean that they are alien additions to an otherwise homogeneous setting, with no connection to the book's contents. They are in line with other self-definitions addressed to friends, related in spirit especially to 1.6 and its good-bye to political activism, but go deeper, to the childhood roots of that attitude. They may be important even for the author's views displayed in the love poems which cover a later stage in his development. Let us then see if, in combining the basic aspects the poet gives his reader of himself, a direction can be discerned into which the literary self-analysis is pointing.

Before meeting Cynthia, the boy's mind was imbued with the experience of war and the sorrow about a near relative's lonely death. If these are the prominent and determining events of his youth as he sees it still in 29 or 28 B.C., he makes his reader understand much better the absorbing love and unconditional attitude towards Cynthia which his poems pronounce. The fear of losing her would naturally be much more intense after the lover had experienced the loss of a loved one [44] already. We are now put in a position to see how his early impressions (not to mention what he later, in

4.1, tells us about his early years) could drive the young man in the same direction as his love and intensify the dependence on Cynthia (and on "Cynthia poetry" as a central form of self-expression). We are probably entitled to see here the "real life" root of his literary statement that Cynthia, besides being his love, is also his home and his parents to him (1.11.23ff.; cf. Homer, *Iliad* 6.429; Cat. 72.3f.; see our Chapter I). What he also makes his reader see better by disclosing his childhood impressions, is how her fickleness would drive him into despair, even at the price of losing his own self-esteem. Another result—or a by-product—of our present considera-tion is a further insight into how irrelevant, even abhorrent the writing of warlike epic poetry (including an epic on the fall of Thebes) may have been to him. "Propertius' distaste for war was well-founded"[45]. And this, fi-nally, opens our eyes in time to his belief (stated later; see our Chapter VIII) that love goes together with peace (*pacem veneramur amantes*, 3.5.1.), and that Amor, representing civilization, desires gentle songs and rejects war poetry (1.9.12): *amores* (7.5) rank higher than *arma* (7.2; cf. our Chap-ter III above).

So far as the grown-up man, i.e., the poet, is concerned, the "self-portrait" of the *Monobiblos* is set before the background supplied by Rome's political and intellectual scenery of the year 29/28 B.C. By addressing him-self in 1.22 to Tullus again, who is an active participant in the new régime, Propertius once more defines himself and claims his ground against pos-sible or actual interference. As in elegy 1.6, discussed in the foregoing chapter (cf. *me sine*, 6.25), the poet in 1.22 does not launch a political at-tack, but utters another request to be left alone. This time, the intruding force seen behind Tullus is manifestly the victorious military and political power of the day, being the precise continuation of that danger which sad-dened and threatened his early years. Far from being a mere foil for remi-niscing childhood sorrows, the same political realities add a whole dimen-sion to his present situation as a poet. In all probability, a defeat of the individual is predictable, should the individual insist on keeping the vic-torious force off his ground.

Coping with this force thus is a matter of survival, now, after Actium, even more than ever, intellectually perhaps even more than physically. For its representation is overwhelming. Vergil, having (like Horace) espoused the Julian cause for many yeai s already, is prepared once more to assign to Venus' offspring Octavian a place among the immortals, this time through the mouth of Rome's highest god, Jove (*Aen.* 1.289f.;[46] cf. *G.* 4.560ff., Chapter IV above; *G.* 3.16). The recent end of the civil war between Octa-vian and Antony was officially the end of Rome's war against Egypt's Cleopatra. On Octavian's interpretation it was a case of "peace achieved by victories" (*parta victoriis pax*, *R.G.* 13) all over the empire (*per totum impe-*

rium populi Romani, l.c.), which he proudly sees symbolized in the closing of Janus' Temple (through senate action). It also was about to be celebrated accordingly in the *Aeneid* (1.292ff.; this is from Jove's prophecy to Venus):

> Aged Fides and Vesta, Romulus reconciled to his brother Remus
> will give laws; the dreadful Gates of War will be closed
> by iron and tight joints; impious Rage, sitting inside
> over savage arms, his hands tied behind his back
> with a hundred brazen knots, will bellow horribly with bloody mouth.

To Vergil the Julian, the process of national reconciliation of Romans with Romans has begun with the closing of Janus' gates in early 29 B.C., half a year after Antony's suicide in Alexandria. The *Monobiblos'* closing elegies tell us how Propertius, coming, if not from a pro-Antonian, at least a Republican family, was neither able to forget so quickly nor to join readily in the spirit of forgiveness and fraternization. Will he be able to share the *Aeneid's* view, which will see Octavian's rule as impartial, objective, and god-sent, or will he rather feel like being one of the defeated and conquered victims in the "peace achieved by victories"? (Our ensuing chapter will, among signs of political consent, uncover some evidence in favor of the latter alternative.) Would he be able to understand that *impius Furor* comprises both warring parties, or would he suspect—since piety has been claimed all along by *Caesaris ultor* for what the victor would term defending "the republic" and its "liberty" against alleged oppression by a "faction" (cf., e.g., *R.G.* 1)—that the "impious rage" of civil war is meant to point alone to the side of Mark Antony, and Lucius Antonius, and the dead relative Gallus of his own family who had fought against Octavian for home, liberty, and republic? Which terms will still be left for him as a poet to express in them his deeply rooted abhorrence of war and love of peace if the new master, by closing the Gates of War, does annex the title of peacemaker—twelve years after Perusia?

Here we realize that for Propertius the step to joining the régime will, since it takes place later, be larger and more problematical than for others; but above all and for the present, we see the problem unfolding of surviving intellectually in the face of an all-pervasive political rule the exclusive claims of which are pronounced by the ablest contemporary writers. How will a dissident individual avoid feeling the charge of being petty and querulous at a time of national renaissance?

Besides, the victorious master of Rome has the power to decree a final *damnatio memoriae*, i.e., kill a poet as a poet outright (as happened recently to Cassius Parmensis[47] or will happen soon to Propertius' "forerunner" Gallus, of whose work only by a chance finding[48] more than a single line has come down to us); he also, by controlling public communications, can kill a poet partly, by stating conditions for allowing or not allowing him publicity, i.e., an audience (the story about Vergil having to delete from his *Georgics* the praise of Gallus would have to be listed here). Pressure, as readers of Propertius' later books may observe, will become stronger in years to come, even after (or, perhaps, because?) he has started paying tribute to the new régime, driving him deeper into disguises and deeper into compromises, further and further away from that already evasive, but still dignified and proud attitude in which he addresses his new patron, Maecenas, at the beginning of Book 2. If I were a great enough poet to write epic, he says,

> I would tell of wars and deeds of *your* Caesar, and you
> would be my second concern, just below great Caesar.

> bellaque resque *tui* memorarem Caesaris, et tu
> Caesare sub magno cura secunda fores. (2.1.25/26)

Already the necessity of using cautious language and displaying willingness to adapt oneself can clearly be felt. But the poet's distance from his hypothetical subject matter can still be shown (as our next chapter will do) even to one who looks at the poem from the outside: *your* Caesar—not mine; for *your* sake—not his. It was, at one point, already "*my* leader" (*mei* . . . *ducis*, 2.10.4)—in a poem which "postponed" (of all genres) an epic on his supposed leader. But in the introductory elegy to the book, which was (as our next chapter will show) written later, it is "your", no longer "mine". More and more often from now on, Propertius will require that his reader understand him from indirect hints, without being led by the clear-cut oppositions and open contrasts which mark most poems of the *Monobiblos*. The reader who wishes to go on hearing his poet's innermost voice will often have to go back to and draw on the standards and values expounded in Book 1; he also will have to recall both the mastery of handling ambiguity and the technique of speaking simultaneously on more than one level— two features that were developed in the more complex and sophisticated elegies of the earlier work. Our following chapters will be dedicated to the new situation.

It is evident that unfavorable political circumstances must drive Propertius (as one should not hesitate to call the speaker of the *Monobiblos*[49]) even more into the isolation which he has already felt as resulting from his unhappy love, for his love, following the early experience of war, has cut him off even more from the world of success and achievement in which his happier friends and counterparts move so easily. Naturally, the political situation will make him cling to Cynthia even more intensely (see our interpretation of elegy 2.7 in the following chapter), as she is pictured as the only hold he can grasp at. And vice versa: the more unreliable this hold proves (possibly draining his productivity at the same time), and the more he is humiliated by her (and compromises himself), the more he might try, from sheer desire to survive, to find a modus vivendi with the régime and the sort of prizes it awards—possibly at the cost of new compromises, and possibly only to discover that, after all, he is not able to shift the center of his poetry or to change the core of his human values. Should he be able to lift even this new and ambiguous experience into the intelligible sphere of words, it would certainly confirm and even heighten his rank as a poet.

Considerations such as these, though based on indications the early poems give of the direction his work is going to take, transcend the constellation actually expressed in the *Monobiblos*. But if they are (as the following chapters hope to show) a correct account of his later development, they can help us to appreciate once more the intellectual precision of the early self-analysis, which depicts his love and his poetry as centered on Cynthia (in herself, an unstable center), and as threatened from the outside by the forces which he associates with the name Perusia. Indeed, it seems that in his first work already he has been successful in setting the complete scenery of his life's play.

PART

—— II ——

THE PLOT UNFOLDING

PREFATORY NOTE

Interpreters who wished to deal with the total of Propertius' work have often felt that they faced a discontinuity when penetrating to the core of his poetry: how can the two sides, presented in the extremes of Book 1 and Book 4, be "reconciled"? To formulate the problem more pointedly: what has the unhappy lover and victim of Octavian's Perusine War (1.1 and 1.22) in common with the poet laureate of 4.11, who writes a moving elegy (some call it *regina elegiarum*) on the death of a Roman mother and member of the royal family, and who finds in her person an opportunity to call the cruel victor of Perusia a "god" (*deo*, 11.60)? It appears impossible indeed to reconcile such (and similar) contradictions in an author's work.

But do we necessarily have to speak of discontinuity? Perhaps the question is how to explain rather than how to reconcile, and how in doing so to take advantage of the poet's own indications that his thoughts can travel on different roads and levels. A poem such as 4.1, introduction to and program piece for the last book, in my eyes openly calls for such a procedure. The method would allow us to stay close to the poet even when he feels his situation to be ambiguous and not easily described. It would allow us to see continuity even below the changing surface (provided, of course, that he wishes his reader to perceive continuity behind changing appearance).

In this way, we would not have to resort to the hypothesis of development, a hypothesis which, in the case of Propertius, can take two complementing and therefore very persuasive forms:

(1) From a poet of passionate love (Book 1), Propertius develops, when his love has slowly ceased (by the end of Book 3), into the poet of Roman national themes (Book 4). This development may be evaluated in two different ways: (a) From the unsurpassed height of its love-inspired beginnings, his poetry sinks to bloodless versification of Roman myth and history, the latter being a surrogate after he ran out of his original subject

133

matter. A poem such as the powerful visualization of Cynthia's spirit (4.7) would accordingly have to be classified as a sort of leftover from an earlier period. (b) A positive evaluation would argue that the poet, from youthful ardor and impetuosity, has found his way ultimately to a mature responsibility which allows him to participate in his country's spiritual renewal under Augustus. Again, a poem such as 4.7 or 4.1 could not really be integrated into the scheme.

(2) The second form of development posited is stylistic. This may be, specifically, a growing interest in the Callimachean ideal (a creed which we were able, however, to confirm for his earlier period already: 1.9.15/16). The result is the "Roman Callimachus" (4.1.64), poet of Roman aetiological myths (who seems to blend perfectly with the mature citizen of (1)(b) above—but perhaps not quite with the Callimachus invoked in 2.1 and elsewhere to attest to the love poet's inability to write an epic on national themes). Seen more generally, the development may involve a growing mastery of language, i.e., of artful expression of his heart's concerns as well as of topics that imply a wider range. Their contents and meaning, however, can hardly be determined by a reader's stylistic perception alone.

By hypotheses of "development" interpreters try to give an account of what seems, to their understanding, to be shifting emphasis or incompatibility between parts in an author's work. This is a justified and natural procedure, because every man appears, in the course of his life, to undergo certain changes of interest or even of creed. Experience tells us, for example, that unconditional love, in most people's lives, dominates for a comparatively short period, and also that love poetry, practiced exclusively, may quickly run out of themes. Similarly, we may, after a period of *Sturm und Drang* in a person's life, count on greater compliance with society's demands; and, in a poet, on a higher effort at stylistic perfection as well.

It is only right, then, to assume that Propertius, too, is subject to natural human changes, so long as we grant him the freedom of living an individual life within these general limits: he himself tells us often enough about the painful changes he had to undergo. Therefore a biographical account of his poetry, symbolized by two complementary, crossing curves, may well convince us: one curve, signifying his love, would steadily fall, while the other, signifying the national Callimachus, would steadily rise all along the axis that represents his development from Book 1 to Book 4.

But it may be wrong and a false simplification to assume "development" whenever (and because) we do not see emphasized in his later poetry a specific feature that appeared prominent in his earlier work, or when we find a later statement that seems to exclude a position formerly held. Alongside inner change and development, we must always be aware of the possibility of outward change while personal attitude remains the same—especially so if, as our interpretation of Book 1 has shown, Propertius' inner life is exposed to two forces that move independently from any control of his. In other words: a hypothesis of development, being in itself one-dimensional and a one-way street, may well lead the interpreter into a cul-de-sac, from which the poet was able to steer away and free himself again as soon as he discovered its dead-end nature. If his poetry (and his life) at its liveliest was a tension or even a zigzag movement between poles (and not a movement from one pole to another), the interpreter must try to cling to the movement itself more than to the poles, lest he lose contact with his poet's real concerns. We ourselves have tried to keep various channels open by pointing to the fact that, from the beginning, elegy cannot, in Propertius' eyes, be confined to themes of love alone, but is a vehicle for all aspects of a loving individual's outlook and thought and self-expression. It is with this expectation of diversity again, that we approach the second book and its sequels.

Let us remark in advance that a slight change in the mode of presentation appears appropriate for Part Two. The opening chapters, which introduced the reader to our methodology, offered complete translations of the central elegies, and many a detailed discussion was included of traditional ways in which Propertius' work has been approached, especially on the level of verbal annotation and textual criticism. This was necessary in order to establish the thesis that an elegy's logical organization and total argument are of primary importance whenever an interpreter desires to determine the intrinsic intentions of this admittedly difficult poet. No case was made, let us recall, in favor of discarding any of the traditional tools of our discipline.

Part Two will, wherever possible, restrict discussion of philological problems (the word "philological" here taken in its narrower sense) in favor of emphasizing the literary aspects that help to formulate a plausible hypothesis concerning the poet's long-range outlook. Such reviewing on a larger scale and surveying is necessitated by the goal (as stated above) of reaching an overall understanding of Propertius' poetry, which also includes the troublesome and well-known contradictions contained in and displayed by Book 4. All along, however, the reader is asked to understand that the change is one of presentation rather than of methods.

DEALING WITH THE ZEITGEIST: REFUSAL AND DISGUISE

─── VI ───

NO EPIC FOR THE MASTER OF ROME

Book 2 certainly is different from the *Monobiblos* in more than one respect. Propertius himself is aware of this, and gives his new collection of elegies an introduction (2.1) that emphasizes the continuity of his goals under changing conditions of life and love. A major problem for him from now on is to define his crucial position under the new political realities of Augustus' rule. This raises another difficulty for his interpreter, that of distinguishing lip service from true attitude. The following pages will approach this new aspect of Propertius' poetry, which reaches beyond the limits of Book 2, through the terms of elegies 2.7 and 10. But before going into the details of his relation to the Zeitgeist, we should view it alongside some other symptoms of the change that occurred between completion of Books 1 and 2—symptoms which can be more easily stated:

(1) The most striking feature which Propertius' poetry now displays (this is true also for Books 3 and 4), is the size of certain elegies: e.g., no. 1, comprises 78 lines (while even the "epyllion" on the death of Hylas, 1.20, had no more than 52 lines!); the last elegy in Book 2 (34) has 94. Again we may observe, as we did earlier, that Propertius does not schematize. Short elegies (the shortest is 2.11 with six lines) are found along with the new type, and the large elegy itself does not display a uniform structure; some show the highest possible balance (e.g., 2.25 is arranged: 5D; 5D; 4D; 5D; 5D), others show balance in their corresponding subgroups only. Although general interest in poetic structure has grown during the last decades, and has led to increased investigation of thought structure in the larger elegies, we must still confess to much uncertainty in this area.

(2) The second symptom, which goes together with the first and often accounts for it, is the increasingly theoretical character of the contents. The movement of thought is often that of discursive argumentation, discussing the various ramifications of the pro's and con's, alternatives, and consequences of a given subject. Again, this may lead either to a structurally uneven statement of unchangeable difficulties or contradiction (such as 2.1), or to a clear formulation of a theoretical assumption and its application to an individual problem (e.g., 2.12, the two halves of which are of equal length (6D), and subdivided into three equal thirds (2D) each). Again we may say that this feature is characteristic also of later books—or at least of Book 3.

(3) If we move closer to the contents of Book 2, we realize an increasing consciousness of death: death is present as the natural terminal stage and consequence of Propertius' own way of living (cf. 2.1; 8; 9; 13; 15; 24; 27; cf. 1.19). This motif cannot be confined to serving a tactical function against outward pressure ("life is too short to write an epic"), but rather appears as a philosophical awareness (close to the Epicurean attitude) that death's continuous presence intensifies life. If we once more apply our distinction of central and marginal (derivative) themes, we classify the stylistic defense ("a Callimachean does not live to write epic") as marginal, and death's meaning for lovers as substantial.

(4) The Zeitgeist and its managers unmistakably make themselves heard in the new book, almost against the poet's will. Prooemium and epilogue, two of the book's latest elegies, both refer to Vergil's growing *Aeneid* and the favor its subject already enjoys in the highest circles. I cannot follow any interpretation that sees the existence of Vergil's epic as a source of relief for Propertius (because he may feel free from having to write an epic himself now that someone else does it).[1] On the contrary, official acknowledgement of Vergil's undertaking only further belittles Propertius' claim to offer his own true and meaningful interpretation of man's life. And the circumstance that an enterprise such as Vergil's ("to found Caesar's glory on his Trojan forefathers", *Caesaris in Phrygios condere nomen avos*, 2.1.42) may a priori count on the régime's support and a wide publicity is, in my eyes, largely responsible for the defiant tone one hears in some poems of the second book.

A prime example of the poet's refusal to yield (and, at the same time, of his undisguised true attitude) is elegy 2.7, which may serve to introduce my reader to the new book. I first give my translation:

2.7

Certainly you were happy, my Cynthia, that the law was withdrawn
    about which, when it was issued, we both once wept for a long
                                                                time,

fearing that it might separate us; though not even Jupiter himself is able
    to make two lovers part against their will.   (1–4)

"But Caesar is great". Certainly, Caesar is great—in *war* (arms):
    defeated nations count nothing in *love*.
For sooner I would suffer my head to be severed from my neck
    than be able to waste my passion ⟨for you⟩ in love for a wife,
or—*I* a husband!—pass by *your* door (then closed),
    looking back with moist eyes to the threshold I betrayed.
Ah, what kind of lullabies would then my flute sing for you,
    my flute, then sadder than the trumpet at the funeral!   (5–12)

Why should I ⟨marry and⟩ offer sons for the country's triumphs?
    There will be no soldier from our blood.
But if my girl had a real camp and I followed her camp,
    Castor's charger would not be great enough for me.
For this is the source from which *my* glory has earned so great a name
    —my glory that has been carried to the people on wintery
                                  Dnieper.
You alone please me: may I alone please you, my Cynthia:
    this love will be worth even more than the blood of my family.   (13–20)

Readings different from OCT: 1: *es* instead of *est*;˥comma (,) before and following
Cynthia; 3: semicolon (;) following *divideret*; 8: *amore* instead of *more*; 13: the
manuscript reading *patriis* is kept against Ruhnken's conjecture *Parthis* printed in
OCT; 20: the manuscript reading *sanguine* is kept against Postgate's conjecture
nomine accepted in OCT.

In a recent interpretation, F. Cairns has maintained that the poem's anti-Augustan surface is refuted by its deeper message: in attacking the Emperor's marriage legislation, Propertius is assumed to justify it and prove its moral desirability; by presenting himself, "the degenerate lover-poet", as "a morally tainted individual", he is said to undercut his own arguments against the law in question; etc.[2] If Cairns were right, then Propertius must have changed his values radically from the time of elegy 1.6 when he counted himself among the number of those who "gladly died in a long-lasting love" and asked Tullus to leave him alone to follow his—thereafter positively evaluated—*nequitia* right through to the end of his life (see Chapter IV). Also, the contemporary Augustan literature as represented through Horace and Vergil makes it highly improbable, as we shall see, that 2.7 should be understood in the renunciatory way in which Cairns wishes us to see it. It seems we have reached another crucial point where the interpretation of a single elegy may set the track for achieving or missing a correct overall understanding.

    Let us be aware that, before Cairns, the poem has been a difficult obstacle to Augustan Interpretation, and we shall have to ask whether its core does not represent a refusal on principle and of wider meaning rather than the partial and isolated piece of opposition to which Boucher (quoted by Cairns) appears to reduce it when saying: "Mais *il reste un point* où Pro-

perce s'est opposé au prince de façon visible et indiscutable: celui de la ré-
forme des moeurs. Pour rester l'amant de Cynthie il refuse le mariage et la
paternité", etc.[3] Boucher, though a just critic of Paratore's over-politicizing
"hypothèse d'un Properce anti-augustéen", perhaps underestimates Propertius' central concerns when he refers to "passages patriotiques où le
poète chante la gloire de l'empire", etc. It is precisely in the area of political praise that the interpreter cannot a priori exclude that sophisticated
ambiguity which we encountered when analyzing Book 1. Can we assume
that the message of 2.7 is wiped off the board by the poet's pro-Augustan
utterances in other poems, or do the contradictions imply an essential opposition and thus call for a more subtle evaluation?

As far as the piece of legislation opposed in 2.7 is concerned, we cannot be sure of its contents. Livy (*Praef.* 9: *nec vitia nostra nec remedia pati
possumus*) perhaps provides testimony that, because of protests, Octavian
had to withdraw an early form of his marriage legislation.[4] Since our poem
itself belongs to the scanty source material we have about the ruler's supposed legislative endeavors of 28 B.C., its understanding is not facilitated
by its legal background. As far as the *lex edicta* and *sublata* of lines 1 and 2
is concerned, Mommsen's sceptical suggestion of 1899, that the poet is
speaking not even of a repealed law but only of a withdrawn proposal
("nicht . . . ein erlassenes und wieder aufgehobenes Gesetz . . . , sondern
ein zurückgezogener Gesetzesvorsschlag"), has found its followers up to
this day.[5] Cairns, extrapolating from the later laws (of 18 B.C. and A.D. 9),
goes so far as to assume that "Propertius is simply exaggerating"[6] (sc., the
effects that threatened to result from the measures of 28 B.C.). His ra-
tionale is that, the more powerful the Emperor became in the course of his
career, the harsher were the laws which he was able to impose. This is not
necessarily so, since "There can be no doubt that the *lex Papia Poppaea* [sc.,
of A.D. 9] was milder than the *lex Iulia*"[7] (sc., *de maritandis ordinibus*, including the legislation *de adulteriis coercendis*, of 18 B.C.), and the later law nevertheless caused an unprecedented protest demonstration from the *equites* (if
it did not itself represent a concession to protests that resulted from intervening legislation[8]). Thus one may credibly argue against Cairns that the
second legislation (of 18 B.C.) was probably more moderate than the aborted
first attempt of about 28 B.C. Be this as it may, the truth is that we do not
know enough of the legislative background to evaluate the Propertian position independently and on a firm basis.

Thus we have to understand the situation from the poem itself. Cairns
suggested that Propertius here follows a *progymnasma*, i.e., a rhetorical exercise of attacking a proposed law. The fact that in our case the law had
been withdrawn does not appear as an obstacle to him: "Augustus' withdrawal of the law was tactical only . . . : he returned to his plans for marriage legislation as soon as he could."[9] Here precisely is the point where

Cairns' "generic" approach can be shown to go wrong from the beginning. For within the poem itself and on the level of poetical reality presented in it neither the speaker nor his beloved girl show any knowledge of the withdrawal's temporary or "tactical" character or of Octavian's long-range legislative plans. In fact, when Cairns introduces such depressing foreknowledge, he is in danger of falsifying the poetical situation of joyful relief depicted in the opening (*gavisa*, 1) in the same way as the introduction of a technical *progymnasma* changes the elegiac situation from one of love threatened by political interference to a juristic discussion of (imminent or even recent) legislation.

But the gravest misconception resulting from Cairns' sentence as quoted above concerns the character and quality of the poet's defiance. For, far from opposing a more or less continuing process of legislation, Propertius makes it quite clear that he is raising his voice *after* the measure has been withdrawn, i.e., technically speaking, he is reviving a dead issue in the present, more hopeful situation, and he tells us so. Here his reader is supposed to ask: "Why bother about something which has turned into a matter of the past without factual consequence?" The answer suggested by the poem's tone is: because, to the speaker of this elegy, the factual success or failure of Octavian's attempt is, though important, not everything. The threat to the individual contained in such legislation is so basic that, as a response, a statement of principle is required, independently of the law's enactment or realization. This poem may reach the level of a personal manifesto. (Of course, it is also easier to protest in a climate of liberal thaw than at the time of the law's issuance.)

A related issue of much speculation is highlighted by the question why the law (if it was a *law*) would have separated Propertius from Cynthia. It is often held that the poet could not marry his *puella* because she was a *meretrix* or "courtesan",[10] though perhaps of highest standing ("*amica*").[11] But not long ago G. Williams[12] has persuasively shown that one may with equal justice build a case in favor of Cynthia (her real name, of course, being Hostia) the married woman, with whom to have an affair made Propertius guilty of adultery (at least under the terms of the *lex Iulia de adulteriis* of 18 B.C.). I think it must be conceded to Williams that the poetic situation in many an elegy is not inconsistent with Cynthia's being a married woman. This is especially true if on the other hand one considers that some of the poet's strongest incriminations against her (Cynthia in 2.6 compared to the famous courtesans Thais, Lais, and Phryne) are admittedly feeding less on facts than on his own unbridled jealous imagination which (he says) does not stop at a girlfriend who stays overnight with Cynthia (Propertius suspects a man in disguise) or at a little boy in the cradles (2.6.10 and 14). As we saw it happen before in 1.11.18ff., his jealous fear again goes so far that he feels he has to apologize: *timidus sum* (ig-

nosce timori), 2.6.13. Cairns, it is true, has meanwhile objected against Williams' seeing Cynthia in a position comparable to that of Catullus' Lesbia (the historic Clodia who was married to Q. Metellus Celer): "Catullus' Lesbia is irrelevant to elegy since the conventions of Roman lyric were different from those of elegy."[13] But Cairns' generic approach apparently overlooks the fact that Propertius not only lists Catullus' Lesbia among his poetic models (2.34.87f.), but even asks for impunity for his immoral Cynthia on the grounds that, being the successor, she is less guilty than her forerunner Lesbia (2.32.45f.; see our Chapter VII)! Why bother at all about excusing Cynthia's scandalous behavior if she were always depicted as a professional light-o'-love?[14] (I wish to emphasize that I do not claim that Cynthia is always represented as a married woman; the poetic reality changes, and so does the degree to which the poet allows historical reality to be reflected).

Thus the possibility cannot be excluded that the law might have separated the two lovers for the reason alone that Cynthia was married and both feared the punishment of adultery (which possibly would—if it was like the law of 18 B.C.—have left them on different islands for the rest of their lives). But the specific situation of elegy 2.7 demands that Propertius himself is forced to become the husband (*maritus*, 9) of a woman (other than Cynthia). We cannot know what the material disadvantages of disobedience would have been. But we can hardly (with Cairns) assume, contrary to line 3, that there would not have been any grave sanctions and that Propertius is just "exaggerating". Beyond this, it is the most unfortunate misunderstanding to maintain that the poet "would not have been forced to *abandon* Cynthia" (italics mine) for the reason that "a married man could have as many affairs as he liked", etc., and to derive from this inappropriate statement the equally misguided consequence that "Propertius' reaction to the law therefore destroys his credibility as a critic of it", etc.[15] If the modern interpreter believes that the Propertius of 2.7 would ever have allowed his beloved Cynthia to have to put up with the part of an extramarital concubine (i.e., to be the mistress in today's terms), then his concept of elegiac love—both individual and generic—can hardly be more wrong. Suffice it here to recall the ending of the preceding elegy (2.6)[16] to remind ourselves of the genuinely Propertian idea of his relationship with Cynthia:

> Never will a wife, never a mistress seduce me:
> you will always be my mistress, always also my wife.

> nos uxor numquam, numquam seducet amica:
> semper amica mihi, semper et uxor eris.

It must be considered a fundamental quality in Propertius' concept that his love does not admit of the traditional split between love and marriage.

Any reference to the many "affairs" allowed to the "married man" in Rome undermines the human seriousness of the stand he wishes to propound in elegy 2.7 (as well as in others). Thus our methodological critique of Cairns' generic approach has helped us to bring out the premises on which an understanding of this difficult elegy has to be built.

The consequences of underestimating the lover's commitment to the beloved woman in 2.7 reach as far down as to the level of textual criticism, as an example may show. The precise meaning of line 8 is far from secured. It must cover the case that Propertius would marry a woman other than Cynthia. But the nuance given to this circumstance? The translation "waste marriage-torches" (or similar ones) for *perdere . . . faces* has generally been given up today (though perhaps not quite impossible) in favor of "lose my passion". Three readings are found in current editions: *more* Barber (⟨*e*⟩ *more* G. Williams 1958, 28); *in ore* Hanslik (so also SB); *amore* Schu.-Do. Each of the three has something going for itself, but each is also under some aspect or other unsatisfactory. If *more* comes out the winner, we should perhaps translate "at the bidding of a wife" (cf. Scheidweiler 1960, 77: "nach dem Willen einer Gattin") rather than "at the whim of a bride" (which Scheidweiler believes to translate by his phrasing).

What is of methodological interest here is the reason why *amore* (*D*, *V₁*, *Vo*, etc.) has fallen out of favor in recent years. Let us hear SB: ". . . *amore*, once the vulgate, is clearly no more than a misguided conjecture. Propertius might say 'Caesar will never make me love a wife'; he cannot be supposed to say 'Caesar will never make me marry for love'." That the situation is not quite as clear-cut and uncomplicated as to be circumscribed by "marry for love", SB might have learned by raising his eyes to the last distich of the preceding elegy where, as my reader has seen, the poet for his part refuses to accept the traditional[17] division of *uxor* and *amica*: marriage itself to another woman would be an intolerable offense to Propertius' concept of his love. But also a glance at the line which immediately follows (2.7.10) might have convinced SB that the reading *amore* deserves closer consideration: if Propertius feels that a "betrayal" (cf. *prodita*) of Cynthia is involved in obeying the ruler's measures, then *amor*— once reserved for Cynthia—is just the right term to denote the new relationship with a legal wife. After all (one may add), such a marriage, since entered into for the purpose of procreation (line 13),[18] can hardly go without a certain violation of his exclusive dedication to Cynthia as he has repeatedly defined it. For these reasons I found it difficult not to base my own translation on the reading *amore* in line 8: ". . . than to waste (ruin?) my passion ⟨for you⟩ in love of a wife". In fact, in order to bring out what such a marriage would mean to him emotionally, the poet might find the word *amor* just strong enough to convey his feelings of concern, but not so strong as to outshine the term *faces* that covers his passion for Cynthia.

After dealing with the poem's uncertain legal background and its emotional premises, we may review the structure of its thought sequence. It opens with a double view of the past. Each of the two lovers (*uterque*) is said to have once been filled with fear of separation, but today their reactions are different. Cynthia is assumed to feel joyful relief at the removal of the threat, while Propertius has apparently changed his mind and now denies the possibility of political interference against the will of the two lovers. Thus lines 1–4 not only inform the reader of the former plight and its recent elimination, they also outline a difference of opinion in judging a matter formerly agreed upon. The poet wants to give us his "second thoughts". What are they? Does he now deny Augustus the power he and Cynthia were formerly so afraid of that they wept "for a long time"?

That can hardly be the case since Octavian is, if anything, politically as strong as ever. And thus the new section (5–10) will point to a change in attitude rather on the part of the *lover*. Propertius throws his new position into profile by introducing a brief dialogue in which Cynthia retains the fearful attitude experienced by both of them before (A: "*At magnus Caesar*") while he himself, in contradicting her (B: *sed magnus Caesar in armis*), limits and corrects their former timidity by merely adding two words to her objection: *in armis* (5). The result is not only a claim to freedom for the loving individual, but a challenge to the ruler who has infringed on the citizens' rights, acting as if he were mightier than almighty Jove (the comparison is hardly a flattery as Hertzberg and Paley think).

By being referred and confined to the area of *arma* (5), Caesar has been pushed out of the overall position of power granted him in Cynthia's statement A. The ground Caesar has lost is not void, but is held by *amor* (6). The antithesis of *Love and War*, *amor* and *arma*, known to my readers from chapters III (1.7) and IV (1.6), apparently is again a valid means for the poet to define his own position—this time in confrontation with the most powerful man of his time. The strong, even contemptuous "nothing" (*nil*, 6) should prevent us from seeing the words *devictae gentes* merely as a loose circumscription for "military victories". No: the passive phrasing of the sentence "Nations *defeated to the end* count *nothing* (mean no power whatsoever) in love" views the *victims* of Augustus' military victories in line with the victims of his legislative endeavors.

This is defiant language, and it is not enough to point to Propertius' unforgetting sadness in poems 1.21 and 1.22 (Chapter V above) to account for his comparing his own situation to that of the country's foreign enemy (the difference being that nations, upon defeat, will ask for peace and, in order to survive, will accept Caesar's "mercy", while the poet, being the more inexorable enemy, is willing to die rather than to comply). While we may state continuity (as in Book 1, so Propertius here too finds himself and his life located between the two poles Cynthia on the one hand and the victor of Perusia on the other), we must understand that, after the civil war, the victor's additional measures on the home front, though repealed, have incited the poet to announce his alienation and resistance. Apparently Propertius realized that the intrusion of politics into the domain of love had in new ways threatened the individual's freedom—or what was left of it after long before already e.g. the oath of allegiance sworn to Octavian's person had made everybody—at least morally, if not physically— liable with his own family.[19] We can judge only by the effects of the later laws of 18 B.C. to which degree spying and prying could invade the citizen's privacy—even on the part of his own servants who (this is one of the laws' specialties) might be used to testify against him. "Thus a reign of terror was established in the realm of Aphrodite."[20]

Perhaps our time is more inclined than other periods to let the threatened individual have our ear—even if the whole Zeitgeist stands against him. Cairns' thesis that, under the guise of the degenerate poet-lover, Propertius intends to justify Augustus' legislation, still goes together with those schools of interpreters who (perhaps conditioned by the pyramidal structure of the societies they themselves lived in) found morality and justice on the side of the all-powerful victor of the civil war and his new design, and felt they could bestow on Propertius the praise of greatness as a poet only where he finally seemed to join the political course of Horace and Vergil, i.e., in Book 4. In this context it is worth contemplating the reasons why, in the 1930s, elegy 2.7 and its refusal "to breed soldiers" plays no role in the discussion of Augustus' laws on marriage and adultery: "In the background always are Fascist and National Socialist attitudes towards race, the family, procreation," etc.[21] Scholarship at times has rated the rank of poetry by the degree of support it gave to the Emperor. For Propertius, love·always means more than vacationing from society's obligations. It can on occasion, as we shall see, mean to him the last, though weak, bastion of the individual for defending himself against the homogenizing forces of an authoritarian rule. Whenever an interpreter a priori restricts the message of an elegy, his preoccupation can cause him to let an ancient voice of humanity go unheard.

These considerations may prepare us for the unyielding course (B) Propertius is ready to follow in lines 5ff. Of course his change of mind (which has led him to deny the Emperor the power to interfere with his love affair) has not brought about any change in the realm of facts or physical necessity. And so the sad truth about the lover's alleged invincibility is that he, unlike subdued nations, can continue his resistance right to the end of his very existence. His freedom turns out to be the freedom to choose death over forced marriage (7). This hardly means that Propertius felt that the Emperor might apply the death penalty to him by having his head cut off (line 7: the type of execution used on free men in contrast to slaves). In the law *de adulteriis* of 18 B.C. killing as a penalty was apparently limited. It could be used only against an adulterer who was caught with a married woman by her husband or her father (the latter, if he killed, had to kill both lovers), and the husband was allowed to kill the criminal only if the adulterer was an actor, freedman of the family, etc. (A free man could be detained by the husband for a certain time to ascertain proof of the crime.) Otherwise, husband or father were expected to prosecute, and a public trial would lead to loss of (half of) the criminal's property (dowry) and exile, etc. Equal penalties applied to *stuprum* between consenting free individuals. (All this makes G. Williams' thesis [22] convincing that, if the historical Cynthia was not a courtesan but a married woman, Propertius would be eager to give the impression that there was no husband involved.) It is not before the third century A.D. that adultery is subject to capital punishment. [23]

Thus the statement of line 7, anyway made after the removal of the threat, is, like the contrary-to-fact subjunctive it is expressed in, of a non-factual nature: the case of capital punishment is a hypothetical assumption. But this does not lessen the seriousness of the message. Augustus may even go so far as to kill the individual, but he cannot force him to stop loving in the way he can defeat the resistance of nations. One can see how much weight Propertius attached to his statement by reviewing (as we did earlier) the literary technique by which he has introduced it. After referring to the two lovers' common former fear and his own new spirit of defiance (1–4), he makes Cynthia repeat their earlier position (5a) as an objection (A) to his new stand (B). This arrangement affords him the opportunity, by on his part contradicting her objection (A), to defend and explicate his new position (B) in fuller detail (5b to, at least, 12). Analysis of form clearly reveals a desire for being explicit. The logical connection (*nam*, 7) bases the Emperor's failure to conquer and subdue on the lover's readiness to face death rather than to betray (cf. *prodita*, 10) his love. In an unexpected and bitter way, Propertius' newly solidified determination has made him a soldier in the service of love (cf. 1.6.30).

The poet's decision in favor of death may irk Cynthia (and the reader). And so he gives room (8–12) to explaining that the alternative which consists in compliance (and acknowledgement of statement A) is unacceptable. The rejected alternative is in itself twofold: it would, on the one hand (8), mean that Propertius waste himself (or his real self) by wasting his passion in a forced marriage. He might as well be dead. On the other hand, [24] he would suffer the pain of separation while living in physical vicinity to Cynthia: "*I* (a husband!) would pass by *your* door, then closed to me" (the opposition of *ego* and *tua* helps to bring out the incredible implication, as that of *mea* and *tibi* does in line 11): he would have to look back (*respiciens*), to weep (*udis . . . luminibus*), to live with the awareness of having betrayed her (*prodita*. This word is placed near *respiciens* to indicate his later remorse. Rothstein). Again, under this aspect, too, circumstances turn out to be so unbearable that death must appear preferable to him. We do not know why her door would be closed to him—probably because she would feel betrayed. But it is also possible that, if she is to be considered a married woman, the dangers resulting from the fateful law or edict would have forced her to give up Propertius—as it would have compelled him to betray her by marrying another woman.

The thought of their both being alive but separated (9f.) is clearly even more formidable to the poet than the prospect of having to marry a woman other than Cynthia (8). This is why it is mentioned in the second, more climactic, place, spun out broader—two lines (9/10) versus one (8)—, and emphasized by an attached special climax (11f.) of rare onomatopoietic structure, where the threefold *tib-* of the flute is ominously reinterpreted by the gloomy sound *tub-* contained in *tuba* (with the dark *u* introduced by the very word *funesta*, as the t's and i's of *tibia* are echoed in *tristior*):

> a mea tum qualis caneret tibi tibia somnos,
> tibia, funesta tristior illa tuba!

Clearly, the final extension of position A in the distich 11f., underlined as it is by a disconcerting sound pattern, is designed to leave the reader, who so far has been led on by the steps of a logical argument, in a state of emotional affectedness that allows him to feel himself the pain (and nothing but the pain) connected with this dreadful prospect. Thus the section 5–10 ends (as will section 13–18) in a climactic distich, the emotional intensity of which outshines all that preceded. It is above all important to see that in these lines Propertius envisages himself communicating with Cynthia spiritually through his elegies (*mea . . . tibi tibia*) even *after* their relationship has been cut off. If by *tibia* he points to his poetry,[25] then there are two possible interpretations: (a) that the poems he once wrote for her will, though read by her before going to sleep still after their separation, bring her nothing but sadness; or (b) one may understand that he would continue to write new poems for her which would reach her hands and so let her know that he still thinks of her and bring her sleeplessness rather than sleep (*qualis . . . somnos*). Interpretation (a) is probably more in keeping with the hypothetical situation. Besides, this interpretation would add to the pain of separation Propertius feels his awareness of the pain she must feel when reminded of him by his poems—he himself must then be to her as good as dead, though still being alive.

Some readers may feel that the poet's imagination is carrying him too far away from reality—but, then, what other appeal can the powerless individual invoke against overwhelming power ("*At magnus Caesar*") than the pain inflicted upon human beings? Jupiter himself would not be able to separate the two lovers against their will—and he would probably not even wish to. Though many a reader has not seen fit to grant Propertius' position serious consideration, it may nevertheless be possible to acknowledge his human stand in the face of authoritarian rule.

With lines 11/12 the train of thought which has shown that compliant survival would be more painful than defiant death has come to an end. The following lines (13ff.) switch from the dire consequences which Caesar's edict had in store for the lover to the principle that underlies Propertius' resistance: the pro-Augustan alternative (A) is now challenged by an unsubdued spirit with regard to its justification. It turns out that, to the independently thinking individual, there appears to be no reason "why" he "should offer sons for the country's triumphs" (13). Understood in this context, lines 13ff. go well together with the preceding distichs (the defiant attitude of lines 5ff. continues) and justify modern editors who join together what the manuscript tradition offers in two pieces.

The lines fit less well if *unde* (13) is rendered by "how," as SB, pointing to a number of passages, wants to translate. For this would lead to a sort of *recusatio* (or *excusatio*), in which the poet, willing to comply, first wonders *how* he might provide future soldiers (13), and then regrettingly resigns by pointing to the lack of military qualification in his biological potential (14). Such a fainthearted though obliging despondency is out of character in this elegy, both with regard to the earlier defiance and, as we shall see, with regard to the self-assertion that follows. It is much better to leave *unde* its natural meaning (*qua ex causa? cur? quare?* Forcellini *s.v.* II.1.b.δ) and have the defiant question ("why should I . . . ?" 13) followed by the categoric statement: "There will be no soldier from my blood!"—the reason for the denial, of course, being that Propertius refuses to oblige by marrying and begetting children (14).

Understood in this way, the refusal to breed soldiers is in harmony with the following outline of conditions under which Propertius would be willing to play an active military rôle: if—of all possible commanders in chief!—Cynthia had a real[26] camp (like Caesar, we may supply), then Propertius' will to go to war would be so great that only a charger trained by a more-than-mortal horseman could give him satisfactory service. This is both a superb spoof of the Emperor's ambition for military grandeur (a—his—girl in Augustus' place,—and Propertius would be ready to go!) and, below the jocular surface, a pronouncement of loyalty: not Augustus, but Cynthia has Propertius' allegiance.

Again, as on the occasion of 2.7.7, it must be pointed out that lines 15/16 do not offer a statement without a context, but the logically coherent justification for it is supplied in the following distich (*etenim*, 17). For Cynthia Propertius would go to war *because* (*etenim*) it is from the service performed for her (*hinc*) that his fame ("so great a name!") has resulted. The poet appears very egoistic: service for great Caesar would result in glory for great Caesar—but he thinks of his *own* (*mea*, 17, is emphasizing) glory, and of glory alone, as the cunning series *gloria nomen, / gloria* suggests. It would be a misunderstanding par excellence if, guided by the jocular surface (a woman's military camp seems to be a less than serious *contradictio in adiecto*) which is designed to take the potential political sting out of the poem, we would underrate the hot desire for autonomy that erupts here. (Realizing the poet's desire to protect his own fame, one may even wonder whether the transmitted form *comitarent*—sc., *me*—should really be changed to *comitarem*, because the poet might wish himself to be viewed in the rôle of Queen Cynthia's military leader and warlord on horseback, who is accompanied by her troops and baggage.[27])

Along the same lines one may have to take the mention of the faraway, hardly known *wintery Borysthenides*. Neither does Propertius wish "to send his glory *somewhere*, to give it 'a local habitation and a name'" (Postgate, still followed by Enk), nor—and here I agree with Postgate—does he mean "that the legionaries take his poems with them on their expeditions". If the latter were the case, Propertius' poetry would be nothing but a modest companion to the Emperor's military campaigns (a self-effacement not favored in this elegy). But this does not mean that the exotic name (and country) is chosen arbitrarily. To see the poet's geographical terminology in historical proportion to the contemporary climate, one should compare the imperial and expansionistic language of Augustus' *Res Gestae* (26–33), especially his recurrent pride in having gained influence in areas reached by *no Roman before* him (26; 30; 31; 32). It turns out that the poet does not mind rivaling the Emperor and stating his own claim to fame in those terms of geographical extension in which mighty Caesar himself would define his realm (and his ambitions).[28] Only after giving this "imperial" definition of his poetry, does the poet turn to an evaluation in his own terms (19/20)—which now clearly defines the different relevance of the two spheres.

The procedure is not unsimilar to the way which we found him using when he addressed Tullus (1.6) and Ponticus (1.7) and the faultfinder of 1.12 first in their own jargon before stating his claims in his personal language. Thus the final distich in the section (13–20 = 3D plus 1D) is again accorded the personal climax.

> tu mihi sola places: placeam tibi, Cynthia, solus:
> hic erit et patrio sanguine pluris amor.

Rightly Rothstein remarks that through *sola*, 19, Cynthia is opposed not only to other women but also to the military glory suggested by the preceding lines. Besides, the distich picks up his love experience in the form it has taken since the turning point of Book 1 (elegy 12, our Chapter I): there is no doubt about his own faithfulness, but much doubt about Cynthia's. The threat of political interference in his life is again complemented by the instability of affection he experiences on the human level. Thus Book 2 suggests a precarious continuity in the poet's condition.

Propertian scholarship has experienced great difficulties in interpreting the elegy's last line, and there has hardly been an editor in recent years who was willing to print (as I have done above) the text as transmitted in the manuscripts without alteration. But the main objections can be met by our interpretation, I believe. It is said that the manuscript reading demands an unacceptable change of meaning in the adjective *patrius, -a, -um* within close neighborhood: in line 13, the word is adjective to *patria*; in line 20, to *pater*. But the same difference of meaning at even closer distance is found (and generally accepted) in Vergil's *Aeneid* (4.598 and 602). Against *sanguine*, "corrected" to *nomine* already by Postgate, Jachmann (1951, 180) held that *sanguis* here can only mean *gens*—which did not make sense to him. But *gens* was rightly accepted by Camps: "i.e. 'line' or 'stock'; Propertius is willing even that his line should end with him." Perhaps one may phrase: Propertius is not willing to continue his family line in order to breed soldiers for the Emperor's armies—"There will be no soldier from my blood" (14). Seen under this aspect, the poem's last line ranks Propertius' and Cynthia's love higher than society's claims (i.e., than the task of procreation, which is the traditional function of marriage, about to be reemphasized by Augustus: *liberorum procreandorum causa*). In so doing, the conclusion once more confirms the categorical refusal of lines 13/14, now under the viewpoint which is the only one essential to the poet: "This love will be worth even more than (preserving) the blood of my family". A bold idea is born: the individual ranks higher than the race. In the name of true love, Propertius feels entitled to cut the production line on which mighty Caesar and his power, in the long run, depend.

It is easy to see how ill elegy 2.7 fits into the picture of the opening Augustan Age. One need only cite Horace's desire, expressed again and again over the years (and more and more officially inspired), for a leader who restores moral and religious traditions and especially the purity of childbearing marriage. Before Actium already Horace had excluded Medea, the *impudica Colchis* (*Epod.* 16.58), who had left her father's house for her lover, from his Island of the Blessed and Pious. In *C.* 3.24 (generally considered an early ode, written soon after or even before Actium), the prospective Father of Cities (*Pater urbium*) is advised first of all to curb unchecked license, *indomitam . . . refrenare licentiam* (28f.). And, in later years, Horace is eager to confirm the positive effects of Augustus' marriage legislation (as well as before he was willing to pray for its success, *C.S.* 17ff.):

> No unchastity pollutes the virtuous house,
>> custom and law have completely conquered sin.

> nullis polluitur casta domus stupris,
>> mos et lex maculosum edomuit nefas.   (*C.* 4.5.21f.)[29]

So Horace may well serve as a foil which offers a sharper picture of Propertius' un-Augustan position in elegy 2.7.

But what cannot be demonstrated from Horace is the seriousness implied in Propertius' challenge of Augustus' ideas. For to Horace, love never meant a force that might change the course of his life (at least not for long) or sweep away his loyalty to the state of mighty Caesar. For Propertius, love leads the individual to being aware of his own worth and to replacing the heteronomy exercised by the autocratic state with the autonomy of the free man. The degree to which elegy 2.7 denies what was to become the official concept can only be demonstrated by comparing Vergil.[30] Such a comparison is not out of place since in the opening and in the epilogue of Book 2 Propertius (as we shall see) clearly (though cautiously) deals with the growing *Aeneid*, the spirit of which he contradicts in advance.

When in *Aeneid* 4 Aeneas, reminded of his political task by Mercury, has decided to leave Carthage and Queen Dido (his hostess and mistress), he answers her fervent pleas with arguments that to modern readers have seemed worthy of a divorce lawyer. But one must not forget that, as far as Roman morality is concerned (reflected also in an "official" poem of Propertius, 4.11.35f.), the widowed queen has violated the ideal of the *univira*, of the woman loyal to the one man who is her husband. Dido is repeatedly shown to be aware of her moral flaw, and her lacking morals are exposed by her creator:

> She calls it marriage, with this name she embroiders her guilt.

> *coniugium* vocat, hoc praetexit nomine culpam.   (4.172)

Accordingly, when confronted with Aeneas' intention of leaving, she complains that she can now call him only "my guest" but no longer "my lawful husband" (323f.). Dido shows an attitude similar to that of Propertius in elegy 2.7 by expecting of an "extramarital affair" the human weight and obliging consequence of a lawful marriage. Augustan Aeneas, on the other hand, like Vergil himself, has never intended his relationship with the Phoenician Queen to be more than temporary:

> Let me say a few words for my case. Neither have I for my part
> (don't make this up!) hoped to conceal my departure like flight in
> secret, nor have I *ever* held before me the wedding torches of the
> rightful husband or have entered this kind of binding alliance.

> pro re pauca loquar. neque ego hanc abscondere furto
> speravi (ne finge) fugam, nec *coniugis umquam*
> praetendi taedas aut haec in foedera veni.   (428–430)

From Aeneas' point of view, the matter is quite clear: *he* never claimed the position of the rightful *coniunx*, *she* was wrong in calling their relationship *coniugium*. No marriage treaty—no damage claim. The fault, if there is one, is hers if she (like Propertius in 2.6.41f.) fails to distinguish *uxor* from *amica*.

The disappointment this unyielding position means to Dido is even enhanced by the following lines (340–344) in which Aeneas informs his mistress that, if he could act according to his own will and liking, he would now be busy tending a rebuilt Troy. This shocking (shocking for Dido, that is) revelation of Aeneas' priorities (cf. *primum*, 342) is not mitigated by his later assurance (i.e., when he sees Dido again in the underworld) that he left her shores against his will (6.460; cf. 4.361). For the pronouncement of his priorities makes clear to her (and to the reader) that his desire aims at more than merely the survival and physical well-being of his people (after all, the Queen of Carthage had offered the shipwrecked Trojans lasting hospitality and even an equal share in her young city, 1.572–574). What he in the long run aspires to (Dido must learn) is the restoration of a national identity, either (a hope unfulfilled) in Troy or (as fate allows) in Italy. Unlike Propertius in 2.7, Aeneas ranks the national restoration under his family's leadership higher than the individual human relationship or even the happiness of his people (the latter rôle is left in the *Aeneid* to Antenor and his city, Padua, 1.242–53, to mention one example).

Aeneas goes on (345ff.) to point out that it is divine guidance (Apollo of Gryneum, the Oracle of Patara) which orders him to leave and to go to Italy, following up his explanation with the most extraordinary piece of personal compliance: "This is my love, for this is my country" *hic amor, haec patria est* (347). For Aeneas (truly the opposite of Propertius), love is clearly subordinated to the political mission, is a servant to the task of founding the new country. Even if one understood *amor* at 4.347 to refer to the royal consort, *regia coniunx* (i.e., Lavinia), as announced by Creusa's ghost in 2.783, love would still be subsumed under the political task. But *amor* (not even mentioned in the prophecy of 2.783) might as well or better refer to the sort of *amor patriae* (6.823) displayed by Consul Brutus which overrides all personal ties. Aeneas is comparable to Tullus in 1.6 (Chapter IV), whose "life has so far never yielded to love" (*amori*), but whose "emotional concern has always been for the country in arms" (*armatae . . . patriae*; see also 2.7.5 and 6). Only Aeneas is more of an Augustan hero because he does experience the temptation of love and then conquers it— unlike Tullus, whose patriotism will fizzle away (3.22, Chapter VIII below).

Before concluding his speech by pointing to Jove's orders which Mercury transmitted to him (356ff.), Aeneas mentions a two-sided argument favoring his departure: on the one hand, his *father* Anchises appears to him in his dreams, admonishes (*admonet*) and even frightens (*terret*) him; on the other hand, he is afraid of the injustice that he, by staying on in Carthage, may do to his *son* Ascanius, whom "I defraud of his kingdom and the soil of Italy". Nothing can make clearer the contrast of Vergil and Propertius. Aeneas views himself as a link in the chain of his family, between his father and his son Ascanius-Iulus (a chain which will one day extend as far as Iulius Augustus), destined to pass on the entrusted penates of imperial Troy to the next generation. Propertius, while denying his country any sons for its triumphs, disrupts the chain and ranks the individual higher than the race: "This love will be worth even more than the blood (line) of my family". Defined in terms of Vergil's Augustan epic, the speaker of elegy 2.7 must be called an Anti-Aeneas.

It is evident that the full impact of elegy 2.7 (though in itself a poem of surprisingly and extraordinarily strong language—the fruit of recent relief from political pressure) can be fathomed by modern readers only against the background of its contemporary environment. The unforgetting young poet from Perusia (1.21 and 22) has matured into the unyielding defender of personal freedom against authoritarian interference. Unwilling to allow his personal life to be used for imperial purposes, he reassures the beloved woman by explaining to her that the freedom of choosing one's own death renders the single human being (unlike nations) politically invincible. Will he be able to proclaim this defiant message for long? Clearly not (unless he chooses to speak in disguise), since the relief of line 1 will turn out to be brief and the demand for compliance will increase for those who wish to speak. How is literary criticism to deal with an independent poet like Propertius? To do him justice, we evidently must not measure his achievement in the terms of Horace and Vergil. In that case he would be in danger of coming out the minor poet, since being the lesser Augustan. About Aeneas' uncompromising farewell speech to Dido, which we discussed above, one commentator remarks: "His speech, though we may not like it, was the Roman answer to the conflict between two compelling forms of love".[31] One wonders where this leaves Propertius. Would in these terms his choice, which sets love of the individual over love of the Emperor's country, not necessarily have to be called "the *un-Roman* answer to the conflict between two compelling forms of love"? Suffice it here to have asked the question. It seems certain that a fair appreciation of Propertius' poetry may have some difficult problems in store for the tradition of our discipline.

In itself, elegy 2.7 gives a clear enough account of Propertius' attitude, which appears consistent with what we read in Book 1. Difficulties may arise when we compare 2.7 with the new tone of solemn praise for Augustus, which is found here and there from Book 2 on. As an example, I introduce here elegy 2.10. The interpretation of this elegy is burdened with a discussion of style and genre because its last lines (25/26) allude to Vergil's sixth Eclogue (64–73) and possibly to Gallus. But this fact, important as it is for considerations about aesthetic tradition, should not serve as an escape route that leads away from the solid problems which a surface reading of its contents seems to indicate: the first major break in the poet's so far homogeneous attitude.

2.10

But it is time to move around Helicon with different dances
    and it is time already to give the field to the Haemonian horse.
Already it pleases both to tell of squadrons bravely moving into battles
    and to sing of *my* leader's Roman camp.
But if my powers should fail, my boldness certainly
    will earn praise: in great things it is sufficient even to have wished. (1–6)

Let youth sing of love, old age of fighting:
    I shall sing of wars when (since) writing abut my girl is done.
Now it is my wish to move ahead more gravely with my brows raised,
    now my Muse teaches me (to use) another cithara.
Rise already, my soul, from lowly song! Assume powers,
    Muses: now there will be need of a powerful voice. (7–12)

Already the Euphrates refuses to protect the Parthians' horseman
    in the rear and regrets having contained the Crassi.
Even India, Augustus, is offering its neck to your triumph,
    and the house (land) of undefeated Arabia is trembling in fear of
                      you;
and if some country keeps aloof on faraway shores,
    may it, captured, feel your hands hereafter! (13–18)

This is the camp that *I* am going to follow; by singing of *your* camp
    I shall be a great priest-poet. May the fates keep this day in store
            for me! (19–20)

As with large statues (where one cannot touch the head)
    the wreath is placed down here before the feet,
thus we now, unable to climb up to the peak of praise,
    are offering cheap frankincense in a poor shrine.
So far my songs have not even known the springs of Ascra,
    but Amor has just recently bathed me in River Permessus. (21–26)

Readings different from OCT: line 6: *veneres*; lines 11f.: *surge, anime, ex humili iam carmine! sumite vires, / Pierides: magni nunc erit oris opus*; line 14: period (.) at end of line; line 20: period (.) after *ero*; line 21: *ut*; line 22: *hic* (no satisfactory conjecture has so far been presented); comma (,) at end of line; line 23: *culmen*.

The poem displays all the marks of high and elevated style, and these—like the contents—seem to indicate a complete turn in the direction of

Propertius' poetry: youth shall sing of love, but age of fighting (7): of wars I will sing, since writing about my mistress is done (*bella canam, quando scripta puella mea est*, 8). Although for a moment we may hesitate to believe that Propertius' *aetas prima* is already over and his *aetas extrema* has arrived, our doubts are silenced by the direct address to Augustus (15) and the expressed desire to sing of "my" leader's military campaigns for Rome (*libet . . . Romana mei dicere castra ducis*, 3f.), as well as by the delusive scheme of time indications which all seem to point to one fact only: the hour of change and conversion has come for our poet. The series runs: *tempus . . . iam . . . tempus . . . iam . . . nunc . . . nunc . . . iam . . . nunc . . . iam . . . postmodo*, the last two words pointing to the political present and immediate future. Thereupon follows the full-fledged new credo:

> Haec ego castra sequar; vates tua castro canendo
> magnus ero: servent hunc mihi fata diem! (19–20)

Where, the surprised reader may ask, is the idea of Cynthia's camp now—expressed in the *vera meae . . . castra puellae* of 2.7.15? Deserted and forgotten? Is this a palinode? *Ad* line 19 Postgate annotated: "*haec castra*, i.e., not those of Venus". As it seems impossible to reconcile the two passages directly, shall we then, by stating that elegy 7 belongs to an earlier stratum of Book 2, and elegy 10 to a later one, allow for a biographical development from love to patriotism—in agreement with the linguistic development from alienated (*castra puellae*) to correct metaphor (*castra Augusti*)? But how—to mention only one inherent difficulty—are we to account for the considerably cooler "*tui Caesaris*" of 2.1.25, which is almost certainly later [32] than 2.10?

Perhaps we should remember the technique of elegy 1.18 (Chapter IV) and feel invited to take a second look at 2.10, especially lines 19–20: [33] nothing is said there, if we look closely, about Propertius actually following Augustus' camp at the present time—everything is left to the *future*! Strictly speaking, it is left in the hands of fate whether Propertius will see the day of Augustus' worldwide victory, which presumably would be the last day to be incorporated in his new poetry. Propertius hangs his writing of epic on the peg of Augustus' still incomplete victories. [34] Nothing is certain so far, and for the present the poem concludes with a "not yet" (*nondum*, 25), resulting in nothing more than a promise or a sign of goodwill; as line 6 indicated it: *in magnis et voluisse sat est*. Applying the strict logic of the biographical timetable which Propertius sets up in line 7, we have to say: it is still the time of the *aetas prima* (line 7) whose task is to *canere veneres* (and of the attitude expressed in 2.7). The period of epic poetry (*aetas extrema*) is so far away that the poet may not live long enough to see it (*servent . . . fata diem!*). The actual present (not the fictitious impression of the first 18 lines) is marked by *nunc* (23) . . . *nondum etiam* (25) . . . *sed modo . . . Amor* (26).

What, therefore, remains in our hands, is a deceptive indication of immediateness (*tempus . . . iam . . . tempus . . . iam*, etc., 1ff.), an expression of goodwill (*voluisse*, 6; cf. *volo*, 9) and inability (*deficiant vires*, 5; cf. 21–26), and an enthusiastic and stylish confession of loyalty (19f.). But the last carries with it no immediate consequences—or, let us say: carries consequences that are as immediate as is Augustus' domination of the whole world (18). The irony contained in this "immediateness" comes out more fully if we consider that Augustus had just recently given up his plan of subduing Britannia—an "*extrema tellus*" (cf. 17) indeed!

By strict logic, we might even infer that what are by the standard of 2.7 compromising words (line 4: <u>mei ducis</u>) can only be seen in the context of the planned future epic (*dicere castra*, 4) on Augustus' future exploits (cf. *vates tua castra canendo / magnus ero*, 19f.) and do not apply to Propertius' attitude at the time of writing elegy 2.10. I suppose that this is really what he wishes his observant reader to understand—but what a price he has already paid by giving that first impression of enthusiastic praise, which hardly any simpleminded reader (to say nothing of Lachmann and his followers) can avoid having! What pains it must have cost him to write down that he will be *vates . . . magnus* by praising (*canendo*)—of all men—great Augustus, who, as we were told before (2.7.5ff.), though *magnus in armis* and threatening enough to bring the thought of execution to the poet, cannot extinguish his love. Can we really believe that Propertius ever wholeheartedly or voluntarily intended to switch from love poetry to war poetry for Octavian? We cannot, because the opposition of love and war, Cynthia and Augustus, remains valid in his subsequent poetry, and there is no uncertainty as to on which of the two sides we find Propertius (see our next chapter). We are therefore prevented from offering the explanation that he gave to Augustus what was Augustus', and otherwise kept to his own quarters.[35]

Where we can neither harmonize opposites nor convincingly hypothesize development, we can only try to explain. I suggest that what appears as the first major breakthrough of loyalty towards Augustus really is a first breakdown of the individual's power of resistance—at least of open and public resistance. The motive is easy to find. Homage paid to the ruler buys breathing space for the subject, which means for the poet: opportunity to go on announcing his own message—if necessary, in disguise. One may well imagine that 2.10, which contains a direct address (*Auguste*, 15), was sent to the Emperor, while 2.7, which addresses itself to Cynthia (line 1),[36] was not. And unmasking the disguise is less easy if one reads 2.10 by itself—though it is possible. One may point, for example, to the elusive and ambiguous impression the poem gives. While the extraordinary series of time particles (*tempus . . . iam*, etc., 1f.) seems to indicate imminent or even present happenings, the grammatical structure unobtrusively points to the future: the first three subsections, of 3D each, all move from these indications of present tense to grammatical forms with future meaning (*erit*, 6; *erit*, 12, preceded immediately by an ambiguous *nunc*; *sentiat . . . postmodo*, 18),[37] a meaning which then dominates the peak of distich 19/20. This distich (another "odd" distich), acts like a sponge in absorbing all foregoing indications of the future, and makes the true *future* character of Propertius' alleged intentions explicit, thus fully revealing and simultaneously ending the ambiguity. A surprise door can now be opened (21–26 = 3D) in the paneled wall to let in the actual and true present and its "cheap frankincense" (24). The technique, of which there are more examples, is to offer with one hand and to take away (or fail to support) with the other.[38] Whether this is enough to keep the poet from compromising himself is for his reader to decide—who may well think that the limits of sincerity have already been violated in this elusive elegy. But if he is willing to go along, he may sense two consequences which remain unspoken. First, the painful process of humiliation and subjugation which characterizes Propertius' relationship to Cynthia is being extended to the other force that has power over his life. And second, although tone and style of almost every line in elegy 10 (except lines 21–26) indicate the qualifications of an epic poet (in a similar way as did the address to Ponticus 1.7.1f.), Propertius is going to deny this potential—true to his destiny, as even his *obtrectatores* will concede. By "postponing" for himself the development of Gallus as visualized in Vergil's sixth Eclogue (or even the development of Vergil himself), the elegist nothing but cautiously emphasizes his decision.

The final distich has given interpreters much trouble and should provide a touchstone also for our own understanding. For this purpose, I give an outline of the poem's structure as suggested by the foregoing observations.

A. A call for change. Lines 1–6 pretend that the subject of contemporary events (the *magna* of line 6) calls upon Propertius to write an epic (surface reading), but imply the poet's insufficiency (= deeper meaning).[39]

B. The poet's timetable. Lines 7–12 appear to announce Propertius' subjective readiness, even enthusiasm, to comply with the "objective" contemporary situation (surface reading), but contain an unfulfilled "maturity" clausula (*aetas . . . extrema tumultus*, 7 = true meaning).

C. The state of the Empire. Lines 13–18, returning to and now naming the *magna* (surface), find them still too incomplete for epic praise (= deeper meaning: *dolet* 14; *intactae . . . tremit* 16; *se subtrahit* 17; *postmodo* 18).

D. Decision concerning the future. Lines 19/20 offer a solemn (or pompous) promise which is as empty as the Emperor's future conquests are incomplete.

E. Consequence for the present. Lines 21–26 depict reality: the poet may, after offering cheap frankincense to Augustus' colossal toes, happily stay in the "lowly" region which he, after all, has never left.

From the train of thought, it seems likely that the last distich is designed to underline the author's *recusatio*. I believe that this expectation is indeed fulfilled if one follows up the literary allusions.

The reference is, of course, to Vergil's sixth Eclogue, not to the actual geography of Greece (as introduced by some interpreters). There Vergil (the follower of Callimachus) himself declines to write an epic on Varus' deeds, since Apollo does not allow the bucolic poet (*pastorem*, 4) to "sing of kings and battles" (*cum canerem reges et proelia*, 3). Further, Vergil there has Silenus sing of elegiac poet Gallus who, when wandering by the river Permessus (64), is led up into the Boeotian mountains by a Muse and presented (by Linus)[40] with the reed-pipe of Hesiod, "the old man from Ascra" (*Ascraeo . . . seni*, 70). With this pipe the ancient poet (Hesiod) used to lead trees down from the mountains (*quibus ille solebat / cantando rigidas deducere montibus ornos*, 70f.). Gallus in turn is asked to use the pipe to sing of the origin of (Apollo's) Grynean grove (*Grynei . . . nemoris origo*, 72)— certainly not an epic this either.

What Propertius, then, wishes to indicate by keeping Vergil's locations (Ascra, Permessus; while changing Vergil's similes: pipe → spring; wandering → bathing) is how far he really is away from writing an epic on Augustus' feats: he has so far not even (*nondum etiam*, 2.10.25) reached the stage of the Ascraean well from which presumably the old man from Ascra drew when writing his *Works and Days*, but is still at the stage of Gallus when Gallus was wandering along Permessus, before being presented with Hesiod's pipe (a gift which the historical Gallus perhaps made use of to write "*epyllia*", but hardly to write an epic: will Propertius ever get that far?). Or, in terms of Vergil's development: Propertius has not even reached the second level of Vergil, i.e., that of the *Georgics* (which correspond to Hesiod's *Works and Days*). How could he seriously think of now attaining Vergil's third level, that of an epic on Augustus? (We may add that he characterizes the *Aeneid* as "to found Augustus' fame on his Trojan forefathers," 2.1.42).

Thus a well-read contemporary may have concluded that the literary allusions to Gallus and Vergil in the final distich amount to the same statement that is embedded in the elegy's twisted train of thought: Propertius has no intention whatsoever of writing the kind of court poetry which he on the surface pretends to be so eager to produce. In fact, the encoded message of lines 25/26 informs the reader, he is not one but two stages away from writing an epic on Augustus—even more: he has only "just recently" (10.26) entered that first stage which would be equivalent to the *Eclogues* in Vergil's development (or to the love poetry of Gallus). That is, he is not going to make use "now" (or any time soon) of the epic talents displayed in 2.10.

Why then does he take upon himself the toils entailed in producing a deceptive form of surface promise and subsurface denial? My answer is that he was exposed to considerable pressure—more pressure than some critics today are inclined to ascribe to Maecenas or Augustus in their dealings with contemporary writers.

Looking back on the interpretations given of this elegy, we must state especially that Lachmann and his followers[41] have not shown a lucky hand in deciding that 2.10 must be the opening poem of a new book of *Augustan* poetry. The one tell-tale word "enough" ("in great things, it is *enough* to have wished", 6) should have been sufficient to make them suspicious regarding the author's true intentions. For the perceptive reader who analyzes the poem's line of thought and literary allusions will not expect any change in Propertius' poetry within the foreseeable future.

Thus it may well be that the poetic excuses of lacking talent and incomplete victories conceal a personal reason: his unwillingness to give up the independence which he so fiercely defended in 2.7. The adjectives "forced" and "insincere" used by Richardson to characterize Propertius' alleged readiness in 2.10 to write an epic on Augustus may, after all, be well chosen. (Rothstein already found it necessary to emphasize that the poet did not intend "den Leser im allgemeinen oder seine vornehmen Gönner im besondern über seine wahre Absicht zu täuschen"). Then Enk's trusting attitude towards the poet's fearful modesty ("In hoc carmine audacia quaedam vel superbia cum *pavore quodam minimaque sui fiducia* mixta est"; italics mine) may not reach deep enough below the Augustan surface so as to touch the personal core.

In the final distich (10.25f.) the poet's feelings become quite clear (the distich has a causal function in the context, the causal asyndeton having the same meaning as an introduction by *enim*): his concern with love poetry, his recent (cf. *modo*, 26) vocation, is far from being over. This attitude, no need to say, has no difficulty going together with the creed of undefeated freedom expressed in 2.7. There may be a tragic note involved—a note struck in the final distich of elegy 2.7—viz. that the love for the free expression of which he is fighting may be hollowed from within, by Cynthia's less than responsive attitude (Book 2 offers enough examples to confirm this concern). This, however, though making his situation similar to that of a soldier fighting for a lost cause, does not (yet) change Propertius' stand (as expressed in 2.7) against authoritarian interference with his personal and poetic sphere to a pro-Augustan position. Moreover, the introductory poem to the whole book will, as we shall see shortly, set the poet's priorities straight in a way that leaves no room for a mistake on the part of the reader (and of recipient Maecenas). On occasion (for instance when sending a poem to court) he may seem to bend over very far and to leave the interpretation of his true intention on knife's edge. But he must trust his reader to distinguish the historically necessary from the individually possible.

Both elegies, 2.7 and 2.10, may give us an introductory picture of the degree to which the Zeitgeist threatened Propertius and forced the direction of his poetry, emotionally as well as intellectually, and of the degree to which we should expect a covered and guarded way of expression before coming upon the bare core of his intentions.[42] We shall meet poems (especially one in our last chapter) the core of which seems to be nearly unapproachable, like a nut in an unbreakable shell. As building a protective shell is a skill difficult to acquire, we should certainly not carelessly break but rather appreciate these new and artful devices, for they form an increasingly larger part of Propertius' poetry. We must, however, not mistake the shells for the hard core just because he made them hard, too.

If we now turn to the introductory elegy, 2.1, we may draw on the difference of tone we found between 2.7 and 10. But we cannot expect the same clear and balanced structure which makes even the insertion of a single "odd" distich meaningful so that the interpreter can account for its existence. There have, it is true, been attempts to find an even balance in 2.1, but so far they have hardly been convincing. Camps in his commentary suggests the following pattern: if one views lines 1–16 as only loosely prefixed, and adds an allegedly lost distich after line 38, one ends up with a remainder of 24 + 8 + 24 + 8 lines. There is a punctuation after the first 10 lines in each larger section, and the middle of the whole sequence falls between lines 46 and 47. Attractive as this pattern may appear, I do not think that it (and others) is corroborated by the elegy's logical structure, which demands continuity at 46/47.[43] Working from the structure of the contents only, I propose the following overall sections:

I   1–16: On the source of Propertius' elegies and the reasons of their success.

II 17–38: A false destination for Propertius (mode of speaking: "contrary to fact"): to be an epic poet.

III 39–56: Propertius' true destiny: a lifelong poet of his love.

IV 57–70: Incurability of his love.

V   71–78: Consequences for Maecenas to draw.

The survey already indicates the theoretical and argumentative note, characteristic of the new long elegy. It also shows that, for the expression of his love proper, there is comparatively little room (section III). Besides, even those sections, which do not address Maecenas by name as do II (line 17) and V (line 73) and do not directly fend off his request that the poet write an epic on Octavian's civil war deeds, can easily be seen to serve the same defensive purpose. There is no doubt: by having won Maecenas' attention and favor, the poet's life as a poet's has not necessarily become easier. But his problems are too solid, I am afraid, to be explained predominantly in terms of *Stoffkritik* and *Callimachus-Nachfolge*.[44] These categories may even obstruct access to the elegy rather than open it, in the same way as knowledge of Meleager's epigram has done to Book 1's introductory elegy. I believe that a more adequate basis for viewing 2.1 is provided by the poet's own attitude as expressed in all of Book 1. After all, he himself refers us to the *Monobiblos* (2.1.1f.). I proceed to give a short paraphrase and comment upon passages important to our subject, according to the divisions of the outline above.

I.   1–16: Propertius protests (1–4), in frank directness, that the source (*unde . . . scribantur amores*, 1) and success (*unde meus veniat mollis in ora liber*, 2) of *his* love poetry lie not in a superhuman mythical power to which earlier (or "higher") poets referred their *ingenium*, but in the beloved human being herself. The examples he gives to confirm this thesis (5–16) leave nothing to be desired in silliness and lack of dignity. A see-through gown, curls on her forehead, her fingers moving over the lyre, etc.: innumerable (*mille*) themes, right up to his and her naked wrestling-matches, his description of which he dares to compare to the endless scenes of fighting heroes in old Homer's venerable *Iliad* (14)! "Épatez le bourgeois!" But who is the bourgeois here? That epic poet and wretched lover of 1.7 and 9 again? No, that guess was (half) wrong. The next distich (15f.) is more outspoken. His girl's doings and chatterings (what can be more silly and indignant to a serious, male Roman mind?), he makes it all from the nonsense it is into something even more dignified than epic (because epic, after all, is only fiction): into something comparable to real deeds and real speeches of responsible, masculine men of the type we will soon read about in Livy's new and growing work and we Romans think of in our hearts when we are proud of our country's recent (civil war) history and when we feel grateful to divine Caesar's already semidivine son Augustus. What is this last, highest, unsurpassable form of human memorial, no: of divine glory? We call it by a Greek name, history: *maxima de nihilo nascitur historia* (16).

Already in Book 1 Propertius had claimed that, through him, Cynthia can become *nobilis historia* (15.24); but the ludicrous discrepancy between allegedly trifling contents (*nihilo*) and claim to the utmost (*maxima*) in serious glorification of human achievement (*historia*) is not stressed before 2.1, and therefore it probably helps to underline the poem's special purpose. Now, the epic which Maecenas hopes for from Propertius is not a mythical *Iliad* but a historical epic on Augustus' deeds of arms, as our elegy's next section (17ff.) bears out. The disrespectful persiflage of epic and history in 1–16, then, as well as their incorporation into Propertius' own "silly" claims to fame (we know this type of reasoning from 2.7.15ff. and elsewhere), secures Propertius' independence in advance from the posters of national values that are just being set up in these years by the Augustan Zeitgeist that is largely connected with Maecenas' name. Both Vergil and Livy (and, to a degree, Horace) have already set out on their tasks, and Propertius is now expected to join them. Implicit ridicule (even self-ridicule) is often the only weapon of the weak. But even this weapon cannot be used too openly against an established emperor's desire for glorification. It may be wiser to allow for the impression of jokingly upgrading one's own "clownish business" to the level of serious poetry. Serious readers will like that and not take offense.

II.   17–38: Contrary to its outspoken assumption (and its "contrary to fact" mode of speech), this section bears highly convincing testimony to Propertius' faculties as an epic poet. It is grand style all over, and, as such, forms the sharpest contrast to its ludicrous antecedent. Its train of thought runs like this: Maecenas, if fate had granted me epic talent, I would sing neither of the traditional themes of myth nor of past Greek or Roman history, but would select as my topic *your* (*tui*) Caesar's wars and achievements, *and you* (*et tu*) would always be my next thought after mighty Caesar; for (*nam*), whenever I sang of Mutina, Philippi, etc., right through to his crowning triumphs (in 29 B.C.), "my Muse would always interweave *you* (*te*) with those arms", etc. Over the impressive ornamental characterizations of civil war places and victims, that stand for mighty Caesar's victories, one easily loses sight of the grammatical construction which allows mighty Caesar (together with his victories) to come into the picture only as a friend of Maecenas' (a similar ambiguity between stylistic emphasis and strict logic we found in 2.10).

Of course, the whole passage can literally be taken to be a grand compliment paid to Octavian's power (the force of which Propertius would be the last to deny anyway!) by one who is sorry that he cannot pay a greater one. But the foregoing persiflage of epic and history, together with the reserved "*tui*" *Caesaris* (25) and "*illis*" *armis* (35), as well as the passage's grand style itself, make us ask whether really fate's alleged stinginess in granting him talent (17) is the reason for Propertius' *recusatio*, rather than his love and something his readers remember from his *Monobiblos'* last two poems, but which to say openly would be even less advisable today, at least three years later, and with the régime determining what should be grand poetry. The key-word in 1.22 was *Perusia*. It does not appear here openly, but the event is duly characterized.[45] Propertius would have to sing of "the overthrown hearths of the ancient Etruscan nation",

eversosque focos antiquae gentis Etruscae   (29)

Is this a victory for Augustus to be proud of, one that resulted in a razed city? (Fireplaces used to be sacrosanct, and Augustus himself will later rebuild the town under the name of *Perusia Augusta!*) Does the expression "the ancient nation" really help to heighten Octavian's glory?[46] Or is it possibly a barbarism to be involved in the destruction of something ancient that had a long tradition? Which is the effect of the word *Etruscae* upon the addressee, a well-known descendant of a well-known Etruscan family (*Maecenas, eques Etrusco de sanguine regum*, Propertius addresses him in 3.9.1)? Could it mean: in this case at least you ought to be on my, i.e., the other side? Is it really desirable for Maecenas to be *always* (*semper*, 35) connected with "those" arms (*te mea*, 35, go together against *illis . . . armis*, with which Maecenas would be "interwoven" if the epic were to be written)? Nothing is said openly, of course, and all the victories Octavian would like to hear about are mentioned. But a sharp eye finds nothing that would point to a revision of Propertius' attitude of 1.22, and some indications that it may still be the same.

To secure a correct understanding of section II, a word must be said about the last two lines and their relation to the train of thought. The truth about this splendidly diplomatic couplet, unrecognized by deferential Augustan scholars, is: the lines end the passage on the imaginary epic (25–38)[47] by citing two famous examples which once more and in a way easily understood explain the procedure and sum up the effect of the hypothetical epic. Thus, in a ring composition, lines 37/38 confirm the opening statement of lines 25/26, viz. that Propertius would praise Caesar in order to commemorate Maecenas. In the same way, Pirithous and Patroclus (background figures, like publicity-shunning—cf. 3.9.21–30—Maecenas himself) need their better-known partners Theseus and Achilles to bear witness of them and to keep their names from falling into oblivion. If Propertius wrote an epic, he would do so to eternalize Maecenas' name. But to achieve that purpose, he would have to put Caesar into the foreground. He would be a Homer writing an *Achilleis* for Patroclus' sake, so to speak: *Maecenas* (17)—*tui* (25)—*et tu* (25)—*te . . . semper* (35).

If lines 37/38 pick up and restate in general terms (i.e., through mythical examples) the important (and delicate) point of 25/26, they give a clear setting and direction to the intervening lines (27–36, introduced by *nam*) and their selection of topics for an Augustan epic. The train of thought being complete, no lacuna should be assumed after 38 (as is still done in Barber's text). The *sed* (39) is needed to indicate Propertius' breaking away from his contrary-to-fact hypothesis and returning to reality.

The special meaning of *testari* (37) accepted here ("to bear witness of something and to keep its memory alive") was recognized by Housman,[48] but not utilized correctly by him. For Housman, in his line-to-line procedure, looked back only one distich (35/36), then diagnosed that the couplet 37/38 "has no relation to the sentences around it". Thus he tore a distich (3.9.33f.) out of the third book and transplanted it into elegy 2.1, hoping thus to supply the missing filling for a lacuna that others had stated already before him. But along the way he changed the meaning intended by the poet. For 3.9.33f., though (as Rothstein saw) similar, is not equivalent to 2.1.25f. To the reader who recalls the final note to Chapter II above, Housman's mistake(s) may appear not atypical of his method. First, he compares the problematic distich 37/38 to the immediately preceding distich only, not checking out the logical context, which could have shown him that 35/36 are the main clause of a long sentence introduced by *nam*. Since *nam* gives logical support to what precedes it, Housman might have easily found what he was looking for in the distich preceding the *nam*, i.e., in lines 25/26. Secondly, Housman himself found some fault with the distich he introduced from the third book: his missing-and-found distich should have contained expressly a "*tu*". Instead of looking back a little further, viz. to lines 25/26 of elegy 2.1 where he would have found the "*tu*" (plus a "*tui*") and might have realized the futility of inserting a "missing" distich taken from another book, he embarked on gathering examples (not all convincing to this writer) to prove that poetry may drop the personal pronoun where prose would require it.

Our analysis of Housman's procedure is of methodological importance, not only for understanding the distich in question (2.1.37/38), but for Propertian criticism in general. Housman has had an occasionally baneful influence on his imitators. His own example shows that even the best linguistic training in Latin is at times not sufficient to deal with a logically demanding text. If, with some of his followers, the scholar's unwarranted self-confinement to textual criticism and word investigation—in itself a perspective directed to the line rather than to the paragraph or to the whole poem—is combined with a hypothesis ascribing a lack of logical coherence to the ancient author and his design, then the door is opened to a development in which early on already the attitude of the interpreter is no longer that of a servant to the piece of poetry but that of a master and a judge.

In the understanding outlined on the foregoing pages, lines 37/38 implicitly underline once more the poet's cool reservation toward the Emperor and his supposed achievements. Maecenas, by being the person loyal to Augustus he is (*fidele caput*, 35), becomes the intermediary who makes Propertius think about the possibilities of an epic on his patron's friend for his patron's sake. In similar fashion, the phrasing *tui . . . Caesaris* (25) indicates a much less immediate approach than (and none of the alleged enthusiasm of) the wording *mei . . . ducis* in 2.10.4. The new book, it turns out, is dedicated to Maecenas personally and exclusively to a degree the recipient had apparently not asked for.

III.   39–56: This section returns from "contrary to fact" to the reality of Propertius' love poetry as it had been characterized in section I (1–16). With a poignant "but" (*sed*, 39) he ends his unfulfillable speculations about an epic on Augustus: "but" neither does Callimachus in his "narrow chest" sing loudly of the giants' mythical fights, nor does it fit Propertius' mind "to found Caesar's fame on Trojan forefathers" (as it now fits Vergil's mind!). The allusion is on the one hand to the growing *Aeneid*, on the other to the prologue of Callimachus' Αἴτια,[49] where Callimachus likewise refuses to sing a long epic on kings[50] or mythical heroes[51]—against the demand of the grumbling Telchines, who "in their ignorance" (νήιδες) are "no friends of the Muse". The ideal of the "narrow" chest may, if one wishes to pin it down also, refer to Callimachus' wish to sing among those who like the soft sound of the cicadas, but not the noise of the donkeys,[52] and *intonet* almost certainly refers to Callimachus' βρονταν οὐκ ἐμόν, ἀλλὰ Διός (line 20).

Thus the references to Callimachus, when verified, turn into a manifest reproach of epic poetry (including, by the frank reference of line 42, Vergil's *Aeneid*), and Maecenas himself, by desiring an epic, comes dangerously close to being a grumbling Telchis—a disrespect which deferential interpreters have not ventured to credit Propertius with,[53] although it fits in perfectly with the hoax which section I makes of epic and history— and with the kind of mockery we could see Propertius use against his epic friend Ponticus in 1.7 and 9.

In the two elegies of the *Monobiblos*, however, the opposed aesthetic categories of Alexandria (Callimachus' pure water against Apollonius' muddy stream, 1.9.16: *insanus medio flumine quaeris aquam*) were filled, we said in Chapter III, with a new meaning, insofar as the large form seemed indifferent and useless to a poet's own life and experience, whereas the small form proved helpful in reflecting his own worries and concerns as a human being. The same is (though perhaps less prominent and visible in a more complex poem) still true in 2.1; after what looks like a *stoffkritisches* rejection of epic poetry on Callimachean grounds (39–42, 2D), Propertius ties the themes one sings of to the sort of life one has made one's occupation (or to the essentials one's survival depends upon): the sailor talks of winds, the soldier of wounds, etc., Propertius of the (two) people fighting their battles in a "narrow" bed (*angusto lecto*, 45, a new twist to *angusto pectore* of line 40!). Everyone should spend his life in the profession in which he can: Propertius' battlefield is not Philippi or Actium as is Octavian's, it is his bed (the word *proelia* keeps the contrast with Augustan epic before our inner eye, but also points back to lines 13f.). Tying his poetry in with his life is the main function of lines 43–46 (= 2D).

One thing however has not yet been said about his poetry: that confinement to small forms and a lover's life is *not* meant to be confinement to a lower life and a lesser kind of glory. So far, Propertius has spoken of elegy's aesthetic superiority (39–42); its close relation to true life (43–46). Now (47–50 = 2D), he speaks of the fame of his life and poetry: we are reaching the core of our elegy. The initial exclamation "a glory to die in love!" (47) still looks back to the *proelia* fought in bed (45) and sets their glory side by side with the honor of death on the battlefield (this connection, similar to the description of the love poet's literary fame in the terms of the Emperor's military fame in 2.7.17f., would be lost if we separated 47ff. from the foregoing). This is again the poet's way of claiming established honors of society for his own sphere, after first seeming to adapt himself to society's standards (very similar, as my reader knows, are his own unexpected claim for glory against Ponticus' epic 1.7.9ff. and his claim to use the term *militia* for his own *nequitia* against Tullus 1.6.25–30, where he also states that "many gladly perished in a long love").[54] It is thus quite clear that "narrow" chest (40) and "narrow" bed (45) do not entail "narrow" fame.

The second exclamation, as in 2.7.19, is already far away from a glory that could be expressed by military metaphors: "another glory, if one is granted to be able to enjoy *one* love (only)!"

Then follows the final climax: "Oh, would I *alone* enjoy my love!"

> Laus in amore mori; laus altera, si datur uno
> posse frui: fruar o solus amore meo!   (47/48)
>
> Reading different from OCT: ; 47.

This is another one of the single distichs or lines in which Propertius tries to compress an essential and overall understanding of his love. The first we encountered was 1.12.19/20 (itself pointing back to 11.26), ending in *Cynthia prima fuit, Cynthia finis erit*. What a further condensation now! His claim to fame added as a prelude, the position of 1.12.20 (Cynthia the only woman he ever loves) restated, and now his greatest sorrow (Cynthia's lack of faithfulness) included as a necessary ingredient of his experience. Here, too, we can see that continuity which was the subject of the introduction to this chapter. The desire to be her only lover is the exact expression of the situation that was developed in elegies 11 and 12 of Book 1 (which we termed the turning point of the *Monobiblos*) and which by now has proved to be permanent. The brachylogy and intensity of expression seem unsurpassable. But what a long time it has taken our elegy to reach this point! Although the attitude and the priorities of feeling and thought are still the same, the poet has to spend even more time and lines in bridging the gulf between his heart and his contemporary audience than in the introduction he gave to the *Monobiblos*. The change of addressees, from Tullus to Maecenas—the one close to the future Augustus' colleague in office of the year 33 B.C., the other close to the established Emperor Augustus himself—tells better than anything else in which direction the reading public has been pushed in the last few years: there are more Τελχῖνες around. Necessarily, this is reflected in the writings of an author who, after all, wishes to be read (and who knows the conditions of the market: "It is by singing of your camp that I shall be a great seer-poet!" 2.10.19f.).

The following distich (49/50) is ambiguous. First, it seems to be concerned with Cynthia's faithfulness alone and to indicate that his wish to be the only one to enjoy her love may be fulfilled. She does not like girls of light morals and rejects the whole *Iliad* because of Helen's sinful behavior (here, however, he is not quite sure about his inference: *si memini* admits that doubt which the reader of the *Monobiblos*, too, feels about Cynthia's faithfulness[55]). Secondly, he states flatly, using intentionally one of those "silly" arguments which made lines 5–16 so provocative, that Cynthia—for a poetically inadequate reason—does not appreciate the "whole" *Iliad*. And that, we are to understand along the way, is reason enough for Propertius himself not to be interested in Homer (or epic), because *illa*, not the connoisseurs, is the judge he acknowledges. He resumes in other words what he had stated in 1.7.11: *me laudent doctae solum placuisse puellae—she* is his "learned" critic—as *she* is responsible for his *ingenium* (2.1.4). If she dislikes epic, he will not write epic. This certainly is a drastic way of refusing Maecenas, but it also is softened by its humor; and we should be aware that elsewhere, in a less "official" context, Propertius chooses to be even more drastic when he distinguishes his poetry's goal of moving Cynthia from the more traditional poetic ideal associated with the names of Orpheus and Linus, pointing to the pure ears (*puris . . . auribus*) of his *doctae puellae*: her approval (*probasse*) makes him say good-bye to the babble of the crowd (*populi confusa valeto / fabula*), "for with my mistress as judge I shall be safe" (*nam domina iudice tutus ero*, 2.13.11–14).

What results[56] from his position as stated in 49f. is that nothing but death will separate him from his love (51–56). Whether one uses poison or sorcery (both open to interpretation) to try to turn him away from Cynthia,[57] his funeral procession will start from Cynthia's house! This is one of the dominant issues of Book 2 mentioned earlier: even his death is predetermined as a consequence of his lover's destiny. I do not know why the simple message behind these words has not been understood (perhaps because people have not seen that lines 39–56 speak coherently of his love

and his kind of poetry). His commitment to Cynthia and to elegy is necessarily lifelong. There will be nothing, not even an epic on Augustus, between his love's end and his life's end (we may compare 1.6.26 again): *laus
in amore mori* (47; cf. 46).

IV.   57–70: The new section is introduced by what I would like to
term a thesis.[58] Its message, given in one distich and then elucidated by the
six that follow, is that there is a remedy for all human pains (57; explained
in 59–64), but not for love (58; explained in 65–70). The reason for this
situation is stated in the pentameter, but is, as far as I can see, constantly
overlooked: love itself does not *want* the doctor, i.e., the patient wants to
keep the disease. The doctor would have to attack the patient's will before
attacking the sickness. Without understanding this, we cannot understand
the following examples: four mythical cases of miraculous cures (Philoc-
tetes, Phoenix, Androgeon, Telephus, 59–64 = 3D) are contrasted with
Propertius' incurable disease (*vitium*), which is compared to (a) Tantalus'
apples, (b) the Danaids' leaky water-pots, (c) Prometheus' bird-eaten but
regrowing liver (65–70 = 3D)—three perfect parallels to the never satisfied because ever regrowing appetite of love. The passage says the same as
do the vain cries for the help of sorceresses and friends in 1.1 (19–30),
thereby pointing out another continuity between Books 1 and 2. And the
miracles (59–64) serve the same purpose as does the Milanion story in
1.1.9–16; by way of the extraordinary they prepare the addressee (Tullus
there, Maecenas here) for hearing of Propertius' own situation, which
seems downright inconceivable to the "normal" mind. In both passages,
myth mediates between Propertius' singular fate and his addressee's normal common sense. The solemn, highly stylized, and mythological character of the passage helps underline Propertius' serious determination: his
love is *incurable* because he *himself* does not want to change from love to
war, from elegy to epic: *solus amor morbi non amat artificem.* Understood in
this way, the passage makes perfect sense in the overall context of refusal
(with Maecenas appearing as the potential uninvited *artifex* who would try
to cure Propertius of his love), even without the following *igitur* (71), which
invites Maecenas to draw certain consequences from the whole elegy.

V.   71–78: What Propertius has made clear so far is that love and elegy will be his only occupation, through to his death. Of course, he does
not say directly, "Never in all my life am I going to write you an epic on
your Augustus". He says it in a more polite (and cautious) way, inviting
(*igitur*) Maecenas himself over to understand his, Propertius', side. When
you one day pass my tomb, cry over my ashes: "This unhappy man's fate
was a hard mistress. *Huic misero fatum dura puella fuit.*" The allusions in
this last line (78) are numerous: *misero* recalls *Cynthia prima suis miserum me*

cepit ocellis of 1.1.1 and stresses the continuous presence of the most prominent characteristic of his love. His fate at the hands of an "inexorable woman" recalls another appeal to another member of the régime, Tullus: *vivere me duro sidere certus eris* (1.6.36). The determination implied in *fatum* recalls line 17: his *fata* have not allowed him to become an epic poet. And *dura puella* finally (along with *in exiguo marmore*) reminds Maecenas that not only the heroes of epic but also the author of a *mollis liber* (2.1.2) lives a hard life, perhaps by contrast with Maecenas' own life of luxury, indicated by the reference to his rich *esseda* (76; cf. the similar ending of 1.6, Chapter IV above). Above all, it is his determined resolution not to leave love and elegy which is brought out by the epilogue. The idea of death helps to formulate this firm consistency. Therefore we should not be surprised that Propertius mentions his own *iuventa*, *vita*, and *mors* within two lines (73/74) and a few lines earlier, in 71, the time when *vitam mea fata reposcent*: a man's *fate* cannot be influenced, even if he is still a very young man, and even if the name of the *Telchis* who tries to influence him is Maecenas.

My understanding of this introductory elegy allows for unbroken continuity in the poet's priorities. What changes is the way of presentation; it is less direct, more careful, covered, disguised. This is largely owing to mounting political pressure from the outside. But the changing (or hardening) political situation has not been able to bribe him into changing his métier (although he doubtless would be able enough, in spite of his denial). All his adaptations serve the purpose of allowing him to go on announcing the same message as before. But, doubtless, he does allow adaptation and does not avoid the superficial impression of paying homage to the Emperor.

If, in the end, we outline the elegy's train of thought once more, we do come up, I think, with a coherent argument. The source of Propertius' *Monobiblos* and the reason for its success are Cynthia; her person and his love for her are subjects which he raises to the importance of epic and history (I). Had fate given him the ability to write epic, he would, for Maecenas' sake, sing of the deeds done by Maecenas' friend Caesar (II). But, like Callimachus, he rejects the large epic. Instead, he speaks of his own experience, which, after all, is not without glory; its glory, however, may be impaired by Cynthia's inconstancy (although she seems to reject the *Iliad* for moral reasons). Propertius' own commitment to his love, anyway, is lifelong (III). Attempts to influence him in another direction are useless. His love is incurable, and, unlike other sick people, he does not want to be healed (IV). Therefore, his life's course is unalterable and predictable to the end, and Maecenas is asked not to refuse to understand Propertius' harsh fate, in case he one day, surrounded by the luxuries of his life-style, happens to pass by the poet's small tomb (V).

—VII—

WEIGHING THE NEW HOMER

All in all, the introductory poem of Book 2 presents itself as a cautious but firm and even witty refusal to cooperate with the Emperor's wish, communicated through Maecenas, to be glorified in a historical epic. The artistic argument openly given for the refusal (lack of skill) is not too convincing in the face of the grand style employed in section II (17ff.), and there is room for seeing the old resentments of the poet's early youth still alive just as they were at the end of Book 1. This ambiguity between pretended and true reason goes well with the double aspect of his Callimachean creed. Of course Callimachus demands from his followers that they adhere to the small form (and avoid epic), and no serious interpreter will ever doubt Propertius' toils and achievements in this field. But it would be wrong to conclude that Callimachus made him hit upon Cynthia as adequate subject matter. The truth is the opposite: the Callimachean Pure Water (1.9.16) is first introduced as an adequate artistic expression for (Ponticus' already existing) love (we should not, before Ovid, automatically argue in terms of "poetical conventions"). For Propertius himself, too, the priority goes to his love—to such a degree that Cynthia is able to create his *ingenium* (2.1.4), as well as to function as his sole literary critic (*domina iudice tutus ero*).[1] The crowd's babble is of no interest to him, as he also says in 2.13 (lines 13f.: *populi confusa valeto / fabula*), venturing a more explicit judgment in the field of elegy than he does when dealing with the delicate question of a contemporary epic. Below the surface arguments of "lacking epic skill" and "Callimachean Principle of Small Form", there lie solid motivations associated with the names Octavian Augustus and Cynthia.

"What then was Propertius' attitude towards the poet who did fulfill the Emperor's desire?" is a question we may like to ask because the knowledge of Books 1 and 2 we gained so far from our interpretations indicates the possibility of a conflict. The issue is indeed so important to Propertius that he dedicates the larger part of the Second Book's epilogue to explaining his relationship to Vergil: a natural counter-piece to his own introductory refusal to write an epic on Augustus' deeds, and another vivid testimony to the increasing difficulty Propertius encountered when trying to make his own message publicly known against the Zeitgeist. In his lifetime, already, he stood in the shadow (as of the new régime so) of Vergil, and later generations, from antiquity to modern times, have confirmed this. I do not here intend to reassess the two men as to respective poetical rank, but I wish to point out a tragic overtone: Propertius has been termed an "Augustan" poet so definitively that even where he cautiously opposed Vergil he has been understood to admire him. At least, his true voice has a right to be heard.

Two reasons are mainly responsible for the inadequate appreciation of elegy 2.34: first, the general prejudice of 'Augustan Interpretation' which did not expect to find in a contemporary of Vergil's anything other than its own admiration for the *Aeneid*; secondly, a methodological approach which ranks style and genre higher than content and arrangement of thought. In this area, the categories that proved fruitful in our detailed interpretations of the elegies in the *Monobiblos* should provide a firm foundation on which to build an understanding of elegy 2.34.

The poem begins with generalizing reflections on an embarrassing incident. Amor severs the closest ties between men; for friend Lynceus (a fictitious name?), apparently a guest of Propertius, has, like another Paris or Jason, approached the mistress of the house, and is now exposed to the poet's accusations (1–12 = 6D; the reproachful questions: 9ff., producing a subdivision of 4D + 2D). A series of strict admonitions to stay away from the jealous poet's love (13–20 = 4D), leads to an act of forgiveness, accompanied, however, by cautious distrust (21–24 = 2D).[2]

Separated from the smoothly balanced introduction by an asyndeton (which does *not* indicate a new elegy, as is still assumed in Barber's OCT), lines 25ff. evaluate the same incident from a new point of view, which transfers its meaning from the sphere of the regrettable to that of joy, even triumph:[3]

> Even my Lynceus is mad with late love:
>   I am glad that you of all[4] approach our gods!
>
> Lynceus ipse meus seros insanit amores:
>   solum te nostros laetor adire deos.
>
> (25/26)

The tone of these and the following lines is well known to my reader: "late" love (cf. *serus Amor*, 1.7.20) of a longtime bachelor was a strong point in the *Monobiblos* to prove elegy's vital superiority to epic (1.7 and 9; see Chapter III). If Propertius now chooses to state the case once more (both times, a mature person's serious convictions and values are overthrown by his experience of love), on an even broader scale, he apparently feels the continuing presence or intensification of the situation he faced when defining the contrast between his own love and poetry and that of Ponticus. The situation of Lynceus in love in 2.34 corresponds to Ponticus' situation in 1.9, after the fulfillment of Propertius' prophecy (cf. 1.7; no prophecy has preceded Lynceus' fate). The dramatic situation has been intensified insofar as not a slave girl (as with Ponticus) but Cynthia herself (as with Propertius, cf. 1.1) has triggered the inebriated bachelor's overture, and so initiated the turn in the tide of his life. The context is further broadened by the fact that Lynceus is not only, like Ponticus, the author of a *Thebaid*, but also an adept of philosophy. This circumstance reintroduces a feature of the Meleager epigram (*A.P.* 12.101.3f.) which Propertius had also utilized in the account of his own love in 1.1.1–8: the wise man's fall from his lofty pride (which causes the boy in Meleager's poem to triumph), τὸ δ'ἐπ' ὀφρύσι κεῖνο φρύαγμα / σκηπτροφόρου σοφίας ἠνίδε ποσσὶ πατῶ. This time, it is Propertius who has reason to exult—even more than when Ponticus fell in love.

It may be useful to point out beforehand a few more parallels between Ponticus and Lynceus, beyond the fact that their loves come "late" in their lives (2.34.25 ~ 1.7.20; 26). Both have thus far shown disrespect for Propertius' poetry (2.34.58 ~ 1.7.25), but now (*nunc* 2.34.27 points to the new situation as in 1.9.4, 9, and 15) both receive no "help" (*prodesse* is the verb in 2.34.28, 29, and 39 as well as in 1.9.9) from their *Thebaid*, nor Lynceus from his books on ethics and physics (2.34.27/28. The name in line 29 of the author supposedly read by Lynceus cannot be safely restored in our manuscripts). Like Ponticus 1.9.13ff., Lynceus is asked to abandon his present pompous style (the words *Aeschyleo . . . coturno*, 41, need not point to the writing of tragedy, but may well be an exaggerated characterization of epic by the scoffing elegiac poet Propertius) and turn to "soft" love elegy (2.34.41ff., cf. 1.7.19 *mollem versum*; respect for the girl's taste is recommended in 2.34.46 as it is in 1.9.14). Wild (*trux*) Lynceus will have to be "tamed" or "civilized" (*domandus*, 50) by Propertius (*a nobis*, l.c.), as Ponticus had to recognize Propertius' authority (1.7.21f.) and to learn that "tamed" or "civilized" (*mansuetus*, 1.9.12) Amor prefers "gentle" (*lenia*, l.c.) poems. Lynceus must cease to be a "*poeta durus*" (2.34.44) and become a poet of his own love (*tuos ignis* 2.34.44), as Ponticus was admonished to desert his *copia* (sc. *verborum*, 1.9.15) and to prepare himself for the "true fire" (*vero . . . igni*, 1.9.17) to come by "confessing" his love in writing (1.9.33f.). Even where the words are not exactly the same, the similarity of Ponticus' and Lynceus' situations is so evident that we may safely draw on our knowledge of Ponticus for help in interpreting Lynceus and the higher dramatic intensity of his case—another welcome instance of continuity between Book 1 and Book 2.

Again we hear Propertius' claim of 1.7 and 9 that elegy, unlike epic, serves a vital need of its author (as it does of its reader). To achieve that purpose, he must undergo a hard poetical and stylistic training. This once more establishes the priority of love over style, of life over learning—a point I would like to stress because as philologists—understandably perhaps, given the nature of our tools—we tend to overstate the contribution of style and learning to the totality of a poem.[5] For similar reasons, I do hesitate to see in our poem a catalogue of the writings of L. Varius Rufus—a catalogue which can supposedly tell us more about his works than we know from other sources.[6] In my eyes, Lynceus' occupations, as far as they are mentioned in 2.34, fulfill so evident a function in the elegy's argument that they can no more be claimed as literary historical signposts than (as we said) Bassus' works can contribute to an understanding of Propertius' intentions in Book 1 (elegy 4).

These preconceptions together with the mutilated manuscript tradition have made it difficult to understand the structure and the purpose of the section that deals with Lynceus' conversion. It helps a great deal if we see that, after the initial distich stating Propertius' joy over his friend's conversion (25/26), the section proceeds in units of 2D (with the exception of lines 31–38, where we find its larger relative, the 4D-unit) through to line 58—a structure which is quite comparable to the 2D and 4D units of lines 1–24. For our present purpose, it seems sufficient if I paraphrase my understanding of the section, indicating the logical connections between subunits wherever possible.

The first subsection (27–30) is dominated by Propertius' feeling of triumph over his wise and serious friend's unexpected helplessness (*quid . . . tibi nunc . . . proderit? . . . quid . . . tibi prosunt . . . ?*): philosophy, moral as well as natural, is no reliable bulwark against love. Nor does it help *in magno amore* to read an old Athenian's (?) songs.

31–38: The only way for Lynceus to deal with the unavoidable is to prepare himself for it: not philosophy, but rather (*satius*, 31) imitation of Philetas and "not puffy" Callimachus' Αἴτια, i.e., elegy in its Hellenistic form. For (*nam*) small subjects only are "allowed"[7] to the adept of love: Achelous' punished passion for Heracles' love Deianeira (a horn broken off)[8]; River Meander's self-deceiving, "meandering" pattern (almost a theme for embroidery); and of the *Thebaid*-story, only the delicate and marginal theme of a speaking racehorse's victory and mourning at an infant's funeral games;

39–42: but (asyndeton) do *not* expect help from the *Thebaid*'s grander themes:[9] Amphiaraus and his whole *quadriga* swallowed by the earth (it was opened by Jove's lightning), or, equally "puffy", Jove smashing the aggressor Capaneus with his lightning. βροντᾶν οὐ σόν, ὦ Λυγκεῦ, ἀλλὰ Διός! You *must* abandon (*desine . . . desine*) writing with Aeschylean pomp,[10] and turn to "softer" dancing!

43–46: On the positive side, you must now (*iam*: this apparently is going to be stage II after the Hellenistic elegy that formed stage I in Lynceus' new education) work on verses inserted in the narrow (*angusto*, cf. 2.1.40 and 45) lathe, and come to write of your *own* passion (*inque tuos ignis . . . veni*). For (asyndeton) you will fall for a girl ⟨—see only your recent error!—⟩ as did Antimachos, author of a *Thebaid*, for Lyde, or as did Homer himself for Penelope (according to Hermesianax' account): a beautiful girl disrespects even (*et*) the great deities of epic poetry (not to mention you)!

47–50: But (*sed*) you cannot start right away: like a savage bull before pulling the plough, so your wildness will first have to be tamed and domesticated by me because you cannot, through your own resources and by yourself, endure so hard, i.e., so inexorable, love(s).

It can be said at once that two of the main functions assigned to elegy in Book 1 (see Chapter III) remain intact: elegy (a) tries to move and win the girl (2.34.46; cf. 1.7.11 and 9.14); and (b) helps the author to endure the sorrows and sufferings of love (2.34.49; cf. 1.9.34).

Otherwise the section is difficult. First, we must realize that Propertius again has wrested away from his friend, the *durus* (i.e., epic) *poeta* (line 44), one of his principal claims: hardships, as he told Maecenas in 2.1 (*dura puella*, 78) or Tullus in 1.6 (*vivere me duro sidere certus eris*, 1.6.36), are experienced by lovers at least as much as they are by men of action or epic heroes. In the lover's life, they originate with the inexorable women who are the incarnations of what love can do to men. It is in this sense that we have to understand *duros . . . amores* (49): the plural refers not only, as in line 25, to the insane condition of a lover, but at the same time to the inexorable person[11] (or persons) who drives the lover mad, i.e., causes his (or her) insane condition; cf. *meos . . . amores* 4.4.37, said of Tarpeia's "love" Tatius (as being carried on his horse's back!). In Lynceus' case we have to understand a plurality of persons because Propertius is certainly going to prepare him, not for winning Cynthia, but rather—now that love has been able to get hold of him briefly—for another woman (or women) he may soon fall in love with.[12]

51–54: (Your own resources are weak.) For (asyndeton) no woman is interested in the nature of the universe, the possibility of an afterlife, or arbitrary exceptions to causality.

The outline of Lynceus' new curriculum is thus concluded with a statement of the inadequacy of his education through philosophy, one which recalls the earlier (27–30) exposé of the helplessness of theoretical learning in the face of real life. The same triumph which we were supposed to sense there as an undertone comes fully into the open now as Propertius, in sharp contrast (asyndeton) to Lynceus' helplessness, sets himself up as an example of resourcefulness worthy of imitation by the friend.

55–58: Look at me (*aspice me . . .*)! With only a small fortune left and no *triumphator* in the family (two important presuppositions for social success in Rome) I am king (*regnem*: another social term with haughty overtones) among the girls at the party: by means of my *ingenium*, which you now (still) despise!

We should not be too surprised to find Propertius, lover of Cynthia and Cynthia only, here as a ladies' king:[13] the picture is drawn to impress Lynceus, whose future love-life can well be guessed from the swift way in which he tried to conquer Cynthia, and who has so far not recognized Propertius' *ingenium*. Like Ponticus, he is not the type for whom love will be a possibly fatal experience. This may give us an important hint on how to judge Vergil through Propertius' eyes in the next section of our elegy.

It is not easy to define where the new section begins and even more difficult to see how it is related to the curriculum recommended to Lynceus. (Damon and Helmbold went so far as to regard line 59 as the beginning of a new elegy.[14]) To elucidate the connection, I paraphrase the argument of the poem thus far:

Lynceus has shown himself a disloyal friend by making an inebriated overture to Propertius' mistress (1–24). The other side of the coin is that, by doing so, he has justified Propertius' way of life and discredited his own; studying philosophy and writing epic are illusory goods that do not pass the test of real life, once a man's vital interests are involved. Even more: if he wishes to survive, he must give up his literary genre as well as his philosophical principles (or "wisdom") and turn, via Hellenistic poetry, to Propertian elegy—as well as surrender to love's rule.

Roughly, Lynceus is, as we said before, another Ponticus, but more fully realized dramatically. Why the doubling? Is it only to prove continuity, that Propertius' standards (poetry's rank is defined primarily by its significance for human needs) have not changed since the last time he published a book? This may well be the reason, because the general public's conditions have changed a lot since then! Or is there in addition a new need for stating his claim once more? The answer is obvious once we include the rest of the elegy in our considerations: a mature epic poet who turns to love and elegy, thus recognizing Propertius' superiority, is, it turns out, the ideal foil for dealing with Vergil, who started from Hellenistic bucolic poetry, but is now going to end up with the sort of historically (and politically) oriented epic which Propertius, in the prologue of Book 2, refuses to write.[15] Even if a new elegy began at line 59, the mere juxtaposition of Lynceus' and Vergil's antipodic careers would lead me to see the later poem in the light of its antecedent. In a similar way 1.21 certifies the meaning of 1.22, and for similar reasons. Propertius may feel that one cannot too openly oppose someone who is prepared to declare that the bloody victor of Perusia is history's own golden fulfillment and will be invoked in prayers as a bringer of peace (cf. *Aen.* 1.286–296; 6.791ff.). The apparently fictitious name Lynceus may suitably point to a merely fictitious existence of this *Ponticus redivivus* and, thus, to his function as a foil in the elegy's train of thought—rather than to the pseudonym (why?) of a contemporary writer who, besides being a historical person, would *also* happen to be the negative from which to print the positive called Vergil.

These considerations allow us to see lines 59ff. as part III of the same poem of which we have so far viewed sections I (1–24) and II (25–58). We only have to grant distich 59/60 its character as a transition. Lynceus and Vergil are opposed to each other because of their contrary developments: away from epic the one, towards epic the other. But as epic poets, both are in opposition to Propertius the love poet so that in one and the same distich he can contrast his own person both with what went before (Lynceus) and with what follows (Vergil). Formally, lines 59/60 correspond to the introductory distich (25/26) of section II (in between, we found mostly 2D subsections) and give the *summa* of Propertius' life (at which the last subsection, 55–58, had just arrived). But in the same way (linked by virtue of being part of the same grammatical construction), distich 59/60 forms a contrast to distich 61/62 which formulates the Vergilian ambitions (*posse*) that are so utterly opposed to Propertius' own. Such a doubly functioning unit within a progressive train of thought is not unfamiliar to my reader: in 1.1, lines 31 to 34 absorb the sum of what has been said before; at the same time, they form the basis for the final realization of Propertius' claim to speak for others (see Chapter II). In a similar way, lines 59/60 in the epilogue of Book 2 can be a summary and at the same time an adequate basis for the syncrisis of Propertius and Vergil.[16] Knowledge of this thought structure should be a great help in determining the meaning of lines 59ff., of which I first give a translation:

> May it be my pleasure to lie relaxed among yesterday's garlands
> —I was hit by a shot from the unerring god right through to my
> bones;
> May it be Vergil's ⟨pleasure⟩ to be able to sing of the shores at Actium
> that Phoebus guards,
> and of Caesar's brave ships,

(Vergil's) who now rouses ⟨from sleeping memory⟩ Trojan Aeneas' arms
    and the walls founded on Lavinian shores.
Yield, writers of Rome, yield, writers of Greece:
    something (I don't know how to say it) greater than the *Iliad* is
                       being born! (59–66)

You sing under the pine trees of the shady Galaesus
    of Thyrsis and Daphnis with the well-worn pipe,
and how ten apples are able to seduce girls,
    and a young goat, sent right from its mother's teats.
Happy you, who buy love cheap for apples!
    To such a girl, although she may be ungrateful, even Tityrus may
                       sing!
Happy Corydon, who tries to steal inaccessible Alexis,
    the delight of his farmer master!
Although he is (now) tired and rests from his pipe,
    he is (still) praised among our indulgent native nymphs.   (67–76)

You sing the precepts of the ancient poet of Ascra (= Hesiod):
    on which field the seed grows, on which hillside the grape.
Such a song you produce on the learned lyre, as
    Cynthius (= Apollo) plays when his fingers touch the strings. (77–80)

Nevertheless these ⟨poems of mine⟩ will not come unwelcome to any
                       reader,
    whether he be uninitiated in love or experienced.
Nor am I, because of these, inferior in spirits or inferior in voice—
                     certainly [17] not:
    in the field of the gander's learned song, the tuneful swan has
                     yielded.   (81–84)

Such playful poems were also composed by Varro—after he had
                    finished his epic on Jason,
    by Varro, intense fire of his Leucadia.
Such poetry was sung also in the writings of wanton Catullus,
    through which Lesbia is even more widely known than Helen.
Such was also what learned Calvus' page confessed,
    when he sang of unhappy Quintilia's death.
And recently, how many wounds from beautiful Lycoris
    did the dead Gallus bathe in the water of the underworld!
Cynthia, too, ⟨will be⟩ praised by Propertius' verse,
    if Fame will be ready to place me among these men. (85–94)

Readings different from OCT: 65: colon at the end of the line; 66: exclamation
mark at the end; 83/84: no conjectures, different sentence structure (see below);
93: comma (instead of dash) at the end.

The first part of the passage translated (lines 59–80, they form section
III in the elegy) is usually taken to be a tribute paid to Vergil, in a spirit of
due deference. I hope that I have already prevented my reader from shar-

ing this prejudice. Rather, I should like him to expect another of those self-definitions *e contrario* which Propertius gave in the first book when he felt challenged to stand and defend his ground. For there should be no doubt about the provocative contrast between what is Propertius' desired pleasure (*iuvet*, 59) and what is Vergil's "pleasure", who has not been touched *ad ossa* (cf. 60) by Amor (rightly, Propertius does not repeat *iuvet* in line 61, but leaves it to his reader to supply the word from line 59); Vergil's "ability" (*posse*, 62) (which Propertius in 2.1 says he himself lacks) to glorify Octavian's victory at Actium can hardly be seen as something desirable if we try to define it in terms of Propertius' own "ambitions". If both halves of our elegy are kept together (especially sections II and III), it is hard to make the mistake of taking the following lines (65–66) at their face value. Rather, they take on an added spice—similar to that we extract from the mere juxtaposition of Propertius' relaxed morning after (59) and Vergil's drum-beating eagerness to praise Octavian's "brave ships" (62).[18]

There is no doubt that Propertius refers to the *Aeneid*, though less to the "Roman *Odyssey*" (*Aen.* 1–6) than to the "Roman *Iliad*" (*Aen.* 7–12): he must have known at least a rough outline of what Vergil intended.[19] The phrasing *Aeneae Troiani . . . arma* (63) and *Lavinis litoribus* (64) even suggests the *Aeneid*'s proem (*Arma virumque cano, Troiae qui,* etc., and *Lavin(i)a . . . litora*), as perhaps does the comparison (66) with Homer's *Iliad*. In the first seven lines of the *Aeneid*, Vergil imitates by several devices the first seven lines of the *Iliad*, and so reveals—as he does elsewhere—his claim to be the New Homer—at least to the connoisseur. What Propertius' exclamation about something greater than the *Iliad* being born reflects is, therefore, Vergil's self-assessment.[20] No commitment on Propertius' part is involved—except for that unexpected and ambiguous "I don't know what" (*nescio quid maius*, 66), which the Latin language uses to denote the extraordinary, in the positive as well as in the negative sense. Nothing keeps us from understanding *nescio quid* in the positive sense here, though with an ironical tinge. For what has Homer with his alleged greatness been to Propertius, so far? A poet whose works are partly forgotten (1.7.3/4), who talks of uncivilized war and is of no use in love (1.9.11), who finally falls for a girl called Penelope (2.34.45), as his followers fall for a slave girl (Ponticus, 1.9.1ff.) or for Cynthia (Lynceus, 2.34.1ff.), etc. We should also not forget that *arma* (2.34.63) has an ominous meaning in Propertius' own mouth.[21] But above all, we must not forget that the *Monobiblos'* emphasis on the artistic and human inadequacy of epic has just been restated in part II of our elegy and reconfirmed on a larger scale in the fictitious figure of Lynceus. What reason does the elegist have to consider Vergil's growing epic an exception to the rule? None whatsoever. It does not cost him anything to hand out (or grant Vergil's claim to) the first prize (66) in a genre in which he himself has publicly refused to contend (2.1), and the pretenders to which (Ponticus, Lynceus) he has declared potential proselytes to his own domain, to be eclipsed by his own future fame (1.7.21f.). Coming from Propertius' lips, the exuberant tribute to a New Homer and an epic even greater than the *Iliad* is a very dubious, because ambiguous, compliment. (The opening of Book 3—see Chapter VIII—will once more confirm this.)

This is borne out by the way in which Vergil's poetical career is reviewed in the following lines.[22] For the simpleminded among his contemporaries, however, Propertius has satisfied the requirements of Augustan poetry and society by paying lip service to Vergil's epic and its contents. He fulfilled the task so well that his distich (65/66) could be quoted as an early testimony to the greatness of the *Aeneid*: *Aeneidos vixdum coeptae tanta extitit fama, ut Sextus Propertius non dubitaverit sic praedicare: "Cedite Romani scriptores,"*[23] etc. What strikes me most in Donatus', or rather Suetonius', account, is the wording that Propertius "did *not hesitate* to praise" the unborn *Aeneid*: it suggests that the praise has excessive form and that hesitancy was what could be expected from Propertius in this affair. It thus confirms that here truth and misunderstanding lie within a hair's breadth. It highlights Propertius' situation that one can misquote him by reciting one of his own distichs—in isolation, of course.[24]

For, in spite of the irony, the context is—for those who care for context more than for slogans—clear and unmistakable. After pointing out the contrast between himself and Vergil in his present determination to rival Homer, Propertius reviews Vergil's past works. Naturally, the *Eclogues*, and the bucolic love, strike a friendly note with the elegiac poet: the genre is similar to that which he had, earlier in our poem, recommended to Lynceus as a preparation for love elegy. However, we should not overlook implied criticism. While alluding to scenes in the *Eclogues*, Propertius takes the liberty to mock Vergil's bucolic idea of love: ten quinces are able (*possint*) to win a girl (in Vergil, we actually read of a boy), or a young goat will do the same—unbelievable to someone who has to cope with a *dura domina*! Knowing the despair of Propertius, we sense the irony when we hear him recall once more (69 ~ 71): "Happy you who buy love cheap— for apples!" As already in 1.12.15, so again here the exclamation *felix* (71; 73), superficially a praise of someone's happiness, carries the undertone of "how naïve (simple) you are!"[25] and is far from stating true happiness; and as in 1.12.15, where a lover is called happy if he can transfer his love to another woman, so here *felix* Corydon (73) cannot really be taken seriously by Propertius—no matter how unhappy (the opposite of *felix*!) he appears in the second eclogue. For Corydon, when his attempt (cf. *temptat*, 73) to win Alexis proves unsuccessful, will not suffer for too long: *invenies alium, si te hic fastidit, Alexin* (Verg. *Ecl.* 2.73—a line which, like its context, only gains if taken as the comment of the author himself and not of the shepherd). Propertius' position is, as my reader knows, exactly the contrary: *mi neque amare aliam neque ab hac desistere fas est* (1.12.19). Propertius' attitude resembles that of Gallus as he is presented in Vergil's tenth eclogue. He realizes that Corydon's relative love for Alexis (*Ecl.* 10.38/39 recall *Ecl.* 2.14–18) is irreconcilable with and therefore inapplicable to his own absolute love for Lycoris, and that, accordingly, bucolic poetry cannot grant him a poetic homestead, not even if he drove his sheep to the farthest north and the farthest south (10.64–69), i.e., made the fullest use of the genre's possibilities. (But Gallus' love will have a place in Propertius' own pedigree, 91f.).

The criticism that Vergil's idea of love is too superficial (not *ad ossa*) also shines through the last distich (75/76) that deals with the *Eclogues*. There it is said that the *compliant* (*facilis*) Italian nymphs miss Corydon's songs; for the *durae puellae* of real life, and elegy, something stronger than apples is required. But the criticism is minor, of course, in the face of the fact that Vergil should once practice a small art form dealing with love at all. The greater criticism is that Vergil turned away from it: Corydon (= Vergil), although now silent, is still being praised among the light Hamadryads (*inter Hamadryadas*, 76)—as Propertius, by his *ingenium*, is similarly a "king" among the girls (*inter . . . puellas*, 57). And they, we recall, are to be considered the judges of poetry. Will the same lasting praise be granted to the *Aeneid*? Or will it suffer the fate of Ponticus' or Lynceus' or Homer's *Thebaid*? Contemporary Propertius, we must not forget, did not have the benefit of historical hindsight which we enjoy.

A third subsection (77–80), introduced by another direct address (*tu canis*, 67 ~ *tu canis*, 77), deals with the third aspect of Vergil's poetry: his sequel to Hesiod's Ἔργα καὶ Ἡμέραι is still allowed the predicate "learned" (*docta testudine*, 79) because the elegiac poet can recognize in it his own ideal of learned poetry. The *Georgics*, however, are inspired by Cynthi*us* (80)—not by Cynth*ia* (as we easily supply from the introductory elegy's distinction between *Apollo* and *ipsa puella*, 2.1.3f.)!

This ends what is section III (59–80) in our analysis of the epilogue's structure. For in the rest of the elegy (81–94, section IV) Propertius erects a monument to his own poetry and gives it a pedigree of its own.

We may sum up what Propertius has to say about Vergil as follows: Propertius' criticism of the *Aeneid* is not open (and we easily understand why: Vergil's patron is too powerful), but must be inferred partly from the foregoing judgment on "Lynceus", which reconfirms Propertius' low opinion of epic and shows his appreciation of a personal development which runs counter to Vergil's. In his review of Vergil's career as a poet, Propertius does not avoid the surface impression of praise for the *Aeneid* (65/66), although he sets out by picturing provocatively the contrast between himself and Vergil (59ff.). His true attitude is revealed by the fact that the only aspect of Vergil's poetry with which he can personally become involved seems to be the bucolic, and even there Vergil appears slightly naïve and superficial, not to say remote from life. Nevertheless, Propertius can dedicate five distichs to the *Eclogues*—as many as he is willing to grant the *Aeneid* and the *Georgics* together.[26]

As the reader of the foregoing chapters knows, Propertius hardly ever undergoes the toils of describing another person's position if it does not serve him as a foil to clarify his own claims. He does the same in the epilogue of Book 2. Having pointed to the fork where Vergil left the path of the true poet (as Propertius defines it), Propertius can now show how he himself stepped in and exceeded Vergil in the deserted field of learned Small Poetry. This is the simple meaning of a famous *locus valde vexatus*, lines 83/84.

First, let us see the context. We saw already that "Cynthius-inspired" (80) poetry is not the highest form of praise, measured by the Propertian standard (which is inspiration through Cynthia). Propertius, however, keeps his pseudodeferential disguise, saying that "nevertheless" (*non tamen*, 81), i.e., in spite of the Apollonic quality of Vergil's poetry (on farming), "*haec*", i.e., Propertius' lowly elegies of Book 2,[27] will meet a favorable and grateful audience everywhere—whether the readers are uninitiated (like "Lynceus" and Vergil the new epic poet) or experienced (like the *iuvenes* of 1.7.23f.) in love:[28] the special relationship of the elegiac poet and his reader, his open access to his reader's heart, is here hinted at again (cf. 1.7, Chapter III).

The point of the following distich (lines 83/84) is that Propertius defines his own success in Vergilian terms. In his bucolic period, Vergil had once likened himself to a gander, whom he distinguished from the lofty epic "swans" Varius and Cinna (*Ecl.* 9.35; cf. 29). At that time, Vergil was in a position similar to the one Propertius is in now: Vergil declined to write an epic on his patron Alfenus Varus and justified his refusal by saying that he was "so far" (*adhuc*) only a gander among swans (his refusal is far less rigid and less exclusive than Propertius' towards Maecenas in 2.1). Now, if Propertius takes up the metaphor to describe his own present situation in relation to Vergil, I see no other way to understand it except by taking today's swan to be Vergil (who left his Small Poetry for the *Aeneid*, i.e., joined the "swans" Cinna and Varius) and today's gander to be Propertius, who practices the Small Form (and that in a more meaningful way than Vergil did when in his *Eclogues* he sang of that strange phenomenon, bucolic love).[29] My interpretation allows me to leave the transmitted text unchanged:[30]

> Nec minor his animis aut sim minor ore: canorus
> anseris in docto carmine cessit olor.   (83/84)

> Nor am I, because of these songs, inferior in spirits or in voice—
> certainly not:
> in the field of the gander's learned song, the tuneful swan has
> yielded.

In other words, in what was once his own field, Vergil has given way to Propertius (*cessit* is used as *cedite . . . cedite* in 65 tells Greeks and Romans alike to "give way" to Vergil's supposedly all-surpassing epic; similarly, *docto*, 84, takes up *docta testudine*, 79, granted as a compliment to Vergil's *Georgics*). And as this is the only field in which Propertius really cares for a contest (cf. *me iuvet*, 59), we understand the emphasis he gives to his "superiority": he does not simply now abandon the Callimachean's alleged modesty and "narrow chest" and claim enthusiasm and a resounding voice (we note in 83 the subjective certainty which a potential subjunctive [*sim*] often expresses[31]). He goes right on to prove it onomatopoietically by letting the strong-voiced *or*-sound appear five times in this one distich! As in many other passages which we have seen so far, and especially in 2.1, so here in 2.34 the pseudodeferential attitude, which first uses the partner's or opponent's vocabulary for stating the case, is unexpectedly dropped, and the other's set of values is triumphantly claimed for describing Propertius' own glory (cf. 2.1.47: *laus in amore mori!* etc.). The epithet *canorus*, "tuneful", which Vergil may find fit for an epic poet, is downright ironical if applied to an epic poet by an elegiac one. Only *Telchines* will sense a compliment here. Irony also looms in the fact that learnedness (*docto*, 84) goes with the gander, not with the "tuneful" swan—as Vergil would call himself now.

An apparent bow to ruling convention is rarely unequivocal in Propertius, and may prove before long to have been ironical: a concession to the régime's tastes, which is corrected and replaced by a true evaluation before the elegy ends. The situation is most delicate, of course, if the epic poet's customer and most distinguished listener is the Emperor himself. In this case, it may be wiser, before making claim to one's own fame, to play the stereotyped rôle of a gander who looks up to and admires the tuneful swan, and to express one's criticisms either indirectly by appreciating Vergil's earlier career or by welcoming the conversion to love elegy of another epic poet, who bears the fictitious name "Lynceus".[32]

That Lynceus is not "forgotten" in the later part of the elegy, as Roth-stein and others assumed, is clear from the way the last section of our elegy proceeds: having established himself as no small poet, even in the face of Vergil's achievements (81–84), Propertius now goes on to give his elegies an ancestry to be proud of. If we do not understand that this pedigree is drawn up with an eye on the *Aeneid*'s royally sanctioned publicity, we miss its essential function: to help Propertius build up a degree of recognition for himself which is independent from the ruling forces of the Zeitgeist.[33]

The first name he mentions already serves as a link to the Lynceus-complex of section III: Propertius' "unserious" type of poetry was prac-ticed also by the epic poet Varro Atacinus, *after* he had *finished* his epic *Argonautica*: *perfecto . . . Iasone* (85). Why emphasize the biographical se-quence if not to point to our elegy's main thesis, viz., that true fulfillment of a poet's career is found not in an epic but in love poetry? There should be no doubt that Propertius takes Vergil on as he took on Ponticus in the *Monobiblos*. Having come so far in our understanding of Propertius, we may confidently say that, at the time of Book 2, he would not seriously have considered the project to *Caesaris in Phrygios condere nomen avos*, and that the autobiographical sequence outlined in 2.10.8 (*bella canam, quando scripta puella mea est*) was indeed no more than a hypothetical concession, made to preserve his personal freedom at that time. It goes without saying that his objection was directed not only against epic poetry as such, but especially against the *bella* (and the *bellator*) of his time.[34]

The second in the line of ancestors is Catullus (87f.), whose writings have made Lesbia, we hear, even more widely known than famous Helen herself (*ipsa*), the *cause scandaleuse* of the Trojan War that constitutes Ho-mer's epic.[35] Clearly, this proves the love poet (read: Propertius) to be more widely read than his epic colleague (read: Vergil).

But there is more to the name Lesbia, especially in connection with Catullus' epithet *lascivus* (87), than an allusion to Vergil the epic poet. The prudish and moralizing attitude of the Augustan restoration (well repre-sented in *pius Aeneas* and the later laws on adultery) is a threat to Proper-tius. For his idea of love, although far from being irresponsible, is not se-cured by any institutional safeguards. He is thus virtually defenseless when he is called upon to defend his liaison before the tribunal of the Zeitgeist (2.32 et passim). His tragic situation, as I said in Chapter IV, is that he has two open flanks, not one: pressed from outside by the régime, he finds no support from the human being whom he has allowed to be the center of his life. In this situation, he refers to Lesbia as a precedent for judging a poet's love outside conventional moral lines (2.32). His original pride (*fastus*, 1.1.3) has by now been humiliated so often that he pretends not to mind any longer when Cynthia now and then spends a night with another man (*non me crimina parva movent*, 2.32.30). But on the other hand he defends her ways (and his love for her) in the sharpest conceivable tone against moralizing attacks, mounted by Rome's "Nouvelle Morale":

> Oh Rome, exceedingly happy in our time,
> > if only one single girl acts against what is considered decent!
> Lesbia, too, has already done these same things unpunished before
> > > > > > > > > > Cynthia:
> > she who follows is certainly less shocking.

> O nimium nostro felicem tempore Romam,
> > si contra mores una puella facit!
> haec eadem ante illam iam impune et Lesbia fecit:
> > quae sequitur, certe est invidiosa minus.   (2. 32.43–46)

Propertius then, as he does elsewhere, goes on to mock Augustus' romantic ideas about the moral purity of early Rome (the "custom" of sinning already existed among the girls of King Saturnus' times! 52). Similarly, he mocks at anyone who looks for "Tatios veteres durosque Sabinos" in contemporary Rome; he must be new in town, Propertius infers with his peculiar sense of realism (47/48).[36]

Taking elegy 2.32 into account, we observe that the reference to *lascivus Catullus* and the comparison of Lesbia and Helen allude not only to Vergil but beyond him to the reforms of Augustus himself, which threaten to curb a lover's and writer's freedom: *semper vive meo libera iudicio!* (2.32.62). The request for impunity (*impune*, 2.32.45) is in spirit not unsimilar to the call for independence and freedom in 2.7.

Next in line is a poet who represents, besides the claim of the chiseled Small Form (*docti*, 89) against the large epic, the personal dimension of elegiac poetry. Calvus' page "confessed" (*confessa*, 89, revelation in words of the most intimate feelings, cf. 1.9.34) his mourning sorrow (something which a man of self-discipline should be able to overcome in silence, according to society's inhuman rules) at his Quintilia's death: elegy as a place where a man is allowed to be a human being.

The fourth (91/92) author of elegy whom Propertius claims as his direct ancestor here, died only recently—a suicide following the fall from royal grace: C. Cornelius Gallus. Propertius does not mention the true cause of his death (he makes it look almost as if Lycoris were the reason, but only almost), but he shows courage in honoring him, even in mentioning his name at all. Vergil, obeying royal orders, is said to have canceled the *laudes Galli* from the fourth book of his *Georgics*. Here would be another important issue, where we can see the different reactions of Vergil and Propertius to the Emperor's preferences. Apart from this, we may acknowledge what is, to Propertius' eye, most worth observing in Gallus: the wounds Lycoris caused him, are washed (i.e., assuaged) only by death.

Once again, Vergil's tenth eclogue is relevant here. We have seen earlier that Gallus' despairing love for Lycoris could not find a bucolic setting among shepherds such as Corydon (who, after wooing without success, will turn his affection to someone else: *invenies alium*, 2.73). In eclogue 10, Gallus is introduced as trying in vain to think like Corydon (10.37–41 correspond to 2.14–18), whose love is neither exclusive nor unconditional. For Gallus, Corydon's easy consolations are no solution—nor are they for Propertius, as our interpretation of *felix . . . Corydon* (Prop. 2.34.73) tried to show. Therefore, Propertius can now claim (in 2.34.91) to be the true heir to Gallus' love poetry: the wounds caused by Cynthia, like those by Lycoris, do not heal in this life (cf. 2.1. 57–70; *Ecl.* 10.60f.).

Last but not least, Cynthia appears as the woman glorified by Propertius. The name Propertius, not mentioned in the *Monobiblos*, finally appears in a conspicuous place, marked by a clear-cut pledge of allegiance. If *Fama* is requested to place him among *these* names (*hos inter* is the emphatic beginning of line 94), we should bear in mind that "these" men, in the context of our elegy, were defined as the alternative to contemporary epic. Although on the whole more concealed than in the epilogue of the *Monobiblos*, the consciousness of the fact that his own position and poetry are evaluated and defined independently from the tide of the Zeitgeist betrays more self-certainty and pride than his misery would lead us to expect. This is well worth emphasizing because a superficial reading may see only the breakdown and near-surrender, which are signaled by his increasing compromises with Cynthia's ways, on the one hand, and, on the other, his public bows to Augustus' grandeur. Part IV of the epilogue is a firm indication that the individual is still struggling to preserve his independence from the victor of Perusia who has by now become almighty, and to concentrate on·features essential to the life of human beings: *perfecto . . . Iasone; maxima flamma; lascivi, Lesbia . . . notior . . . Helena; docti confessa est pagina, cum caneret miserae funera . . . ; multa . . . mortuus inferna vulnera lavit aqua: hos inter si me ponere Fama volet.*

To sum up briefly: I see no difficulty in understanding the epilogue of Book 2 as one coherent, logically consistent elegy, if allowance is made for the necessity of disguise created by the oppressive, conformist, anti-individualistic climate of the time. The elegy's casual appearance[37] thus rests on an uncompromising structure:

I   1–24: A certain "Lynceus", so far a mature man of strict morals, violated the tie of friendship by approaching Propertius' mistress.

II 25–58: Lynceus' error means that his philosophical *sapientia* and epic writing have proved worthless for real life and true existence;

he must, therefore, via Hellenistic poetry, turn to love elegy, the province of despised Propertius, king of the girls at the party.

III 59–80: Propertius, wounded by Love, likes to lie relaxed among yesterday's garlands—but Vergil, to sing of Actium and write an epic greater than the *Iliad*. He, too, once wrote of love, however naïvely, and his *Eclogues* are still being read. Beside that, he wrote a learned imitation of Hesiod, worthy of Apollo himself.

IV 81–94: Nevertheless, Propertius is welcomed by his readers, and does not have to yield in voice or spirits. In fact, the tuneful epic swan (= Vergil) had to give way to the learned gander (= Propertius) in the realm of the small poetic form; Propertius claims to be the true heir to Varro Atacinus, Catullus, Calvus, and even Gallus, whose love was lifelong.

—VIII—

A FAREWELL TO PROMETHEAN MAN

I am aware of the possibility that, to some of my readers, Propertius' opposition to contemporary epic and his rejection of Augustan Zeitgeist is not as fundamental as I have outlined. They may claim that the outward submissiveness Propertius occasionally displays towards Vergil and Augustus is more sincere than I assume, and that, consequently, the signals of inner withdrawal and independence do not reflect anything vital, but stem from a rather marginal desire not to be bothered. In short, my reader may question whether the flame kindled by Octavian's Perusine massacre in general (1.22) and by the early loss of a close relative specifically (1.21) is still alive in our poet's breast and, rekindled by threatening new interference with his personal life (2.7) and poetry (2.1; 10), has led to a firm and permanent position. The answer to this question demands nothing less than an evaluation of Propertius' attitude towards Augustus' imperial ideology—an attitude which, if it amounts to a rejection (as I think it does), can hardly be expected to be open and comprehensive, but rather offered symbolically and in disguise. But an answer can be given. For this purpose I turn to some passages in Propertius' third book of elegies.

In parenthesis, it may be said that Books 2 and 3 are the two most closely related and most homogeneous, so that there is no difficulty in extending discussion of a topic from Book 2 into Book 3—provided, of course, that the context of the individual elegies discussed corroborates such continuity. The characterization I gave of Book 2 (as compared with the *Monobiblos*) in the beginning of chapter VI is valid for Book 3 also: prominence of the long elegy; a theoretical and argumentative character;

preoccupation with the Zeitgeist in order to set off an individual poetical message against it; increasing surrender to the political facts through lip service to the régime; loud self-advertisement of the elegist's greatness. Of new or newly prominent features, I mention the beginnings of objective elegy [1] and the growing emptiness of the personal love-theme, which finally leads to an outspoken farewell to Cynthia (the slow death of his love is, as I said in the Preface, an aspect of Propertius' poetry which this book will not treat in detail). Although a shift of emphasis doubtless takes place—a movement to and fro of certain themes between foreground and background—I do not see a change of basic attitudes, but rather a desire to express personal continuity in a changing environment.

To emphasize the continuity and, at the same time, to confirm my interpretation of Propertius' attitude towards Vergil (which, after all, is part of his attitude towards Augustus) I would like to draw my reader's attention to the proem of Book 3. It is certain that elegies 2.1 and 2.34 were purposefully conceived as a setting and guideline for the contents of that book, and we may accordingly be sure that elegy 3.1, as an introduction to Book 3, picks the reader up from the spot where elegy 2.34 left him.

In the opening lines (3.1.1–6),[2] Propertius, using almost religious language, introduces himself as the first poet to dress his Italian content in the forms employed by Callimachus and Philitas—the two Hellenistic writers of learned Small Poetry whom he had recommended to "Lynceus" in the epilogue of Book 2 (line 31f.) as a pre-stage that would prepare him for the writing of personal love elegies (43ff.) in the Propertian manner (55ff.).

More interesting for us than the literary link Propertius sees between himself and Alexandrian Form are the manifest implications and guidelines (hardly a matter of style alone) he finds for his own poetry in this pedigree:

> Ah, away with him, whoever wastes Apollo's time in arms!
>
> A valeat, Phoebum quicumque moratur in armis!   (3.1.7)

The observant reader, I am afraid, cannot but individualize the innocent, general word "whoever" (*quicumque*) when he recalls the "pleasure" Vergil was alleged to find (2.34.61ff.) in being able to sing of Apollo's participation in the battle of Actium—Vergil

> who now rouses Trojan Aeneas' *arms*
>
> qui nunc Aeneae Troiani suscitat *arma*.   (63)

If we still had some doubt about how to take the "compliment" paid to the new Homer (*nescio quid maius nascitur Iliade*, 2.34.66), we may now claim that degree of certainty which irony allows without losing its fun.

Not very humbly, Propertius goes on to depict his own Fame as the master of the chiseled Small Form, even the triumph[3] of the poetry which he himself (!) has created (*a me / nata . . . Musa*, 9f.), followed by the "crowd of the authors"—his rank-and-file army, we assume![4] There will be "many" (*multi*, 15), to add Rome's new glories to history's annals (as once written by Ennius?), by singing of Bactra's incorporation into the *Imperium Romanum*, i.e., of the fulfillment of the old expansionists' dream that Parthia be added to the Roman domain—a dream just now revived under the slogan "vengeance for the two Crassi". But Propertius sets a new goal for Rome (it is Rome as a whole that he feels entitled to address!): peace poetry.

> But offering a work *which you* (sc., Rome) *may read in peace*, our page
> brought this
> down from the Muses' mountain by an untrodden path.

> sed, quod pace legas, opus hoc de monte Sororum
> detulit intacta pagina nostra via.   (17/18)

The contrast between arms (7; cf. *laudes*, 15) and peace (17), *arma* and *pax*, comes into the open sharper than ever because it is now coupled with the contrast (*sed*, 17) of the "many" (among whom we must count Vergil, too) who sing of Rome's military glory, and the one Propertius, who tries to introduce something which he feels is completely new (*intacta . . . via*, 18, as opposed to the *lata via* of 14) to the Roman scene: love elegy as the poetry of peace—not so much peace which has been won through arms (peace as a postwar period, so to speak), but peace as the expression of a basic human attitude—love—which is conceived without the idea of war as its complement (cf. *pacis Amor deus est*, 3.5.1).[5] This of course does not mean that Propertius' idea of peace cannot be enhanced or even given a sharper profile against the background of the threat of war—one need only think of its biographical origin as described in Chapter V above. It was, as we pointed out earlier, an unlucky circumstance for Propertius that the term *pax* had already been claimed by the victor of Perusia and Actium. This made it extremely difficult (and delicate) to outline a *Pax Propertiana* in the face of the *Pax Augusta*. Who would listen to a poet who could neither swim with the stream of his contemporaries nor spell out his message too openly? The sense of isolation that results from these conditions is voiced once again in 3.1: to ask for *mollia serta*, the garlands of the love elegist (19), because the *dura corona*, the wreath of the epic poet, does not fit one's head (20), is no way to earn acknowledgment from the "many", who approach the Muses on the "broad road" (cf. *lata via*, 14) and who allegedly try in vain to compete with Propertius (*quid frustra . . . certatis . . . ?* 13). On the contrary, Propertius' exclusive poetry (honored by the Muses: _vestro_ . . . _poetae_, 19), like Callimachus', even arouses envy among the "crowd"—in this way he, showing no lack of self-confidence,[6] understands and interprets contemporary reaction to his work:

> But what the envious crowd has detracted from me during my lifetime,
>   the deity of Honor[7] will return to me with double interest after my
>   death.

> At mihi quod vivo detraxerit invida turba,
>   post obitum duplici faenore reddet Honos.   (21f.)

There is no shyness when he speaks about his own future fame. He even ventures to liken his situation to that of Homer (!), whose poetry grew more famous after its author's death (33f.), and then proceeds:

> I, too, shall receive Rome's praise among later generations:
>   I myself prophecy that day after my death.

> Meque inter seros laudabit Roma nepotes:
>   illum post cineres auguror ipse diem.   (35f.)

The situation is clear: Propertius has something to say to Rome, but Rome is not yet mature enough to listen. The _Pax Augusta_ still prefers the glorious annals of war to the unglorious poetry of the _Pax Propertiana_. It is the daring generalization of his love's claim which lifts him above the heads of the forerunners mentioned in 2.34.85–92. They would never have dreamt of seriously recommending to Rome the lover's life as a human ideal which is difficult to attain. But of course they did not yet face a uniformed Rome, ruled by one strong hand. Now, the poet's lot truly is to be _unzeitgemäss_.

Propertius' refusal to join the _multi_ (3.1.15) who will glorify Rome's victory over the Parthians leaves nothing to be desired in clarity. If further explanation is needed, Propertius gives it once more in 3.3, where Apollo himself is introduced, telling our poet in no uncertain terms (cf. _demens_, 3.15) not to think of writing a historic epic and becoming a successor to Ennius (cf. 6ff.), but directing him on a peculiar "new path" (_nova_ . . . _semita_, 26), which reminds us of the _intacta_ . . . _via_ of 3.1.18. That the new poetry envisaged by Propertius means Alexandrian Form, but personal (and appealing) contents, is the message we have understood continuously from elegy 1.7 through to 3.1 where we finally see the distinctive program of peace poetry announced (1.17; see also _cara legenti_, 3.2.15).

We are therefore surprised to find, in 3.4, our poet functioning as a priest and seer who prays in public for a successful outcome of Augustus' expedition against the Parthians. We are, however, in for a second surprise: the next elegy (3.5), taken by some as the last in a series of five coherent introductory poems,[8] denounces, if we can read on as well as between the lines, the spirit that leads to the Parthian expedition, in a voice shriller than ever—thus rendering the gap between the poet's public concessions to the régime and his personal standpoint wider than ever before. In the case of elegies 4 and 5, the contradiction between the views presented is so obvious that one may presuppose its existence without having to prove it,[9] and may proceed immediately to a detailed evaluation of its meaning in the context of Propertius' poetry. Both elegies can be read in themselves, especially 3.4. This poem is similar to 2.10 in starting on a high level—the speaker is a future epic poet there, a religious prophet here—and ending in an anticlimax: the end (or the other hand, as we said then) does not back up the beginning (the offer presented with one hand). The presence of two levels of meaning, the one promising, the other retracting, has been found in so many poems by now that we may rightly call it a Propertian technique. This time we shall find it enriched by a new twist: the retraction contained in the poem itself is outdone by an outright about-face in the following poem.

Elegy 3.4 displays a structure that can be easily described.[10]

A   1/2:   Augustus' plan for an expedition to the east   } 1D

B   3–10:   Propertius predicts great rewards to the soldiers and victory to Augustus: the ends of the world will yield triumphs, Parthia become a Roman province.
Poet and seer Propertius sends out the soldiers, sings of favorable omens: "wash out the shame of the two Crassi's death (in 53 B.C.) and serve Roman history well!"   4D

C   11–18:   Prayer (*precor*) to Mars and Vesta that Propertius may live to see the day of Augustus' return and triumphal procession, of which (and of himself, reclining against his girl's bosom and watching) he gives a vivid picture in advance.   4D

D   19–20:   Special prayer to Venus, to grant eternal life to Augustus, her latest descendant in the line originating from Aeneas.   1D

E   21–22:   The poet leaves the expedition's booty to the warriors: for him it will be enough to be able to applaud the triumphal procession on the Sacra Via.   1D

It can be shown that elegy 3.4, like 2.10, implicitly contains the refusal of an epic praising the Emperor's deeds. The elegist will be present at the triumph, and he will applaud—but no more. The last section (E), like an epilogue, draws the line. This refusal, however, is in no way aggressive: it points to modesty and lack of ability (*posse*, 22), but not to lack of will. Even the disrespect we sense in the picture of Propertius watching the Emperor's triumph from the viewpoint which his girl's bosom allows him (*inque sinu carae nixus spectare puellae*, 15) is, in my eyes, not necessarily an insult if read by the Emperor, especially not in the face of the flattering prophecy preceding it: it may be taken to be the cheeky expression of devotion of a court clown who knows that a continuous panegyric tone is not expected from his lips. Once before already (2.1.1–16) we saw Propertius clownishly ridicule himself in the eyes of Maecenas and Augustus, without revealing his real attitude.

His lip service to the Emperor, on the other hand—most visible in unbalanced ("odd") section D which eternalizes Augustus—has here reached a degree of submissiveness which will be exceeded only by his elegy on the battle of Actium (4.6) where Julius Caesar will find his own deification confirmed by Augustus' victory over Cleopatra. In 3.4 Augustus himself is called *deus*—a fact that cannot be got around even by the most cunning interpretation, so striking is its singularity (even Horace and Vergil rarely went that far) and its insincerity (3.5 leaves no doubt that Propertius' *deus* is *not* the Emperor). The breakdown of the public resistance, or at least of open reserve, which made itself felt already in the change of tone from 1.22 to 2.10, is complete long before the unsuccessful poet of national themes announces himself in 4.1.

For elegy 3.4 certainly contains more than mere acknowledgment of the Emperor's power to use force (as did the unintimidated poem 2.7); even more than 2.10, it contains consent (*plaudere posse*, 22) and, beyond consent, active participation by the "seer-poet" who encourages the Emperor's troops to go to war (*magna, viri, merces . . . ite agite . . . date lintea . . . ducite . . . omina fausta cano . . . piate . . . ite . . . consulite!* 3–10). This incitement to war is as flagrant an offense to the program of peace poetry (3.1.17f.) as is the poem's first word, *arma*, which, occupying the most emphatic position of all, makes the reader rightly expect something related in subject matter to the opening line of Vergil's *Aeneid* (alluded to but rejected as non-Propertian in spirit in 2.34.63, cf. 3.1.7). In the same way, the subject of punishment of the Parthians for killing father and son Crassus (3.4.9) in itself suggests a deviation from the range of subject matter set up in 3.1.15ff. (*multi . . . , qui finem imperii Bactra futura canent*). So does Propertius' interest in the promotion of *Romanae . . . historiae* (4.10), for which Camps rightly compares the spirit of Livy's *praefatio*.[11] Precisely this spirit had been superbly mocked in the opening poem of Book 2 (*maxima de nihilo nascitur historia*, 1.16, Chapter VI). And—to mention one more matter—the prayer to Venus (3.4.19f.) displays, beside a surprising interest in Octavian's longevity (or even eternal existence), an unexpected endorsement of his official pedigree, the epic realization of which Propertius had termed *Caesaris in Phrygios condere nomen avos* a few years ago, 2.1.42.

There is no denying that elegy 3.4, if viewed against the general background of Propertius' poetry and independently from its pendant 3.5, is at odds with what we have learned to take as Propertius' personal attitude and outlook. In its approval of the Emperor's person and politics, it far exceeds even the sort of lip service an unsuspicious contemporary Augustan might have appreciated in poems like 2.10, 2.1, or 2.34; and its reserve, where pronounced, is soft, and does not appear to be a matter of principle. The principles are banished to and discussed in a separate elegy (this is the new[12] twist I mentioned above; the true rejection is uttered separately and fended off by some soft mock opposition). For my own interpretation, I must emphasize the increasing abyss between what has by now become public adulation and, on the other hand, the proud, but disguised denial of any common ground with the adulated. If we refuse to acknowledge the abyss (or ridicule it by calling it schizophrenia), and if we fail to see the pain and self-torture entailed by appearing in one's own book of peace-poetry as a priest blessing the arms of Octavian, we are bound to miss the vital interest which poems dealing with the Zeitgeist possessed for their author. It is hardly sufficient to ascribe the large part of his work that is concerned with its own function merely or even predominantly to his poetological interests. He must (to formulate a working hypothesis) have been under severe pressure to write something like 3.4 and to include it in the collection.

If one turns to the next elegy, one is surprised how soft the reserve voiced at the end of 4 seems in comparison with the new criticism contained in 5. For, once the character of 3.5 as a disguised recantation of 3.4 is recognized,[13] the meaning of 3.4 is reversed into the opposite of what it originally seemed, from blessing and praise to curse and condemnation.

I begin my interpretation by decoding the message of the first line, which, read for itself, appears rather harmless:

> Of peace, Amor is the god, peace is what we lovers worship.
>
> Pacis Amor deus est, pacem veneramur amantes.   (3.5.1)

That love and peace go together is suggested also in the introductory poem of Book 3. Spice is added when we take into account the official imperial program of "peace", which means, rather, pacification. About ten years from now (13 B.C.), a symbol of this official "peace", the *Ara Pacis Augustae*, will be built when the Emperor will have returned from "pacifying" Spain and Gallia—a situation well comparable to the present one in which the Parthian expedition of 3.4 (and 5) is expected to bring Parthia under Augustus' "jurisdiction" (cf. *sub tua iura*, 3.4.4) and make it a *provincia* (4.5) of "peacetime" Rome. The Zeitgeist, background for Propertius' formulation, once more finds its adequate expression, as in Augustus' *Res Gestae* (26ff.), so in the *Aeneid*, where *Augustus Caesar, divi genus, aurea condet / saecula, qui . . . super et Garamantas et Indos proferet imperium; iacet extra sidera tellus*, etc. (6.792ff.), his worldwide (cf. *nec . . . tantum telluris*, 801) exterminator's activity being compared, among other things, to Heracles' "pacifying" (*pacarit*, 803) act of killing the Erymanthian boar. By restoring the Golden

Age (792f.) in this and similar ways, Augustus fulfills the Roman's mission in this world. It consists not so much in promoting the arts and sciences (847–850) as in "ruling nations" and "*imposing* (the) order on (of) peace" (852). As we have seen Propertius to be conscious of the growing *Aeneid*'s spirit (2.1; 2.34; 3.1), it may be worthwhile to imagine in what way the famous lines about Rome's destiny must have impressed him:

> tu regere imperio populos, Romane, memento
> (hae tibi erunt artes), paci(s)que imponere morem,
> parcere subiectis et debellare superbos. (*Aen.* 6.851–853)

As we said earlier, Augustan peace may be defined (especially by those affected) as a postwar period in which the defeat (*debellare*) of independence (*superbos*) is followed by a grant of humiliating survival (*parcere subiectis*)—almost precisely what young Propertius and his family had experienced from Octavian the victor over Perusia (1.21; 22)—except for the fact that *parcere subiectis* had not at that time been an obligatory part of the peace program. Later, in 2.7, we heard Propertius assert that even powerful Caesar is unable to handle the loving individual the way he treats nations (*devictae gentes*), for (*nam*) the lover is willing to face execution rather than give in (2.7.5–7). This passage can help us understand why there is no difference in principle—but only in degree—between a pacified nation and Propertius himself in his precarious situation, and why the Parthian expedition—in my view, almost a matter of foreign policy—and the public enthusiasm surrounding it (which, moreover, Propertius himself felt obliged to join) are able to trigger a personal confession which may become dangerous once it is decoded and deprived of the disguise of popular philosophy.

The wording "Of Peace, Amor is the god" (3.5.1) sounds as incomplete in Latin as it does in English, because, by its emphatic early position in the line, the notion "of Peace" seems to point to an unmentioned but implied contrast, e.g., "of War" or "of Arms". That war is in the air is proved by line 2, where we have to supply this meaning: hard enough, for my person, are the battles I fight with my lady (sc., in bed). *Sat* [14] *mihi cum domina proelia dura mea.* The contrasting form has actually been supplied already and is still in the ear of the reader who recalls the foregoing poem's first line "Arms God Caesar" (. . . intends to raise against the East . . .). The mutual logical complementation of the two head-lines (Arms—Love), in itself a reminder of a Propertian *leitmotiv* ever since elegy 1.6, is underlined by an artful employment of positioning, sound, and word play:

Arma *deus Caesar* (3.4.1)

Pacis *Amor deus* (3.5.1)

While "God Caesar" is tied up with arms, "God Amor" is connected with the peace that Augustus would like to make his trademark. Something of Propertius' peculiar way of thinking, observed by us again and again, shines through here also: his inclination to state his own case in the terms in which his opponent is accustomed to think, even to wrest key terms away from the opponent in order to show that they belong to the elegist as well if he is to fulfill his task of interpreting essential aspects of man's destiny. In the present case, Propertius claims the term *pax* for his world of Love, while leaving to Augustus the sphere of War.

In a similar way—a parenthesis may strengthen my point—he can even wrest deification from "God Caesar" and claim it for himself. When in 3.9 he refuses Maecenas an epic on Augustus, on the cheeky grounds of having chosen as his young life's model Maecenas himself (who always prefers to remain in the background: *in tenuis humilem te colligis umbras*, 29), he also adds, in his "innocent" modesty, that the kind of appreciation that Callimachus and Philitas receive will be enough (*sat erit placuisse*, 43f.) for himself, and then proceeds to add that "tiny" further touch of personal achievement which he has always claimed for his poetry: [15]

> Let these writings (of mine) kindle passion in boys, kindle passion in
> girls,
> And *me* let them call a god, and to *me* offer sacrifices!

> Haec urant pueros, haec urant scripta puellas,
> *me*que deum clament et *mihi* sacra ferant!   (3.9.45f.)

In the context of epic themes (35–42 and 47–56), which lead up to Augustus' success over the Parthians (54) and his defeated opponent Antonius' suicide (56), Propertius himself would hardly appear as a god, but would have to leave this honor to Augustus. He rather prefers, however, to receive it himself. The words *meque deum clament* can be appreciated fully only if seen before the background of Augustus' heroic deification in the epic which is requested by Maecenas but refused by Propertius.[16] And it is only logical in a poem such as 3.9 that we find repeated (cf. 1.6.29f., Chapter IV above) that other claim of our poet, viz., that peace is his, and war does not go with his "nature":

> "This one is born for *peace*, that one is useful for the *arms* of the camp:
> everyone follows the seeds of his nature."

> Hic satus ad *pacem*, hic castrensibus utilis *armis*:
> naturae sequitur semina quisque suae.   (3.9.19/20)

By introducing the philosophical notion of *entelecheia*, he expresses here in one line what took him twenty-two in his other poem dedicated to

Maecenas (2.1.57–78): every attempt to divert him from his destiny, which is the peace of love, is doomed to failure.[17]

I return to elegy 3.5. The categories of 3.9 provide a parallel example which helps explicate the overlapping notions of the beginning lines of elegies 3.4 and 5: *deus* Caesar faces competition from *deus* Amor; *pax* is the preserve of Amor and not so much of Augustus, who is characterized through *arma*. In fact, it looks as if Augustus gets his spelling wrong when claiming to be the lord of peace: for that purpose, one should spell *AMOR* (5.1), not *ARMA* (4.1). It is along these lines that we should look for the meaning implied in the paronomasia.

Once we realize that the opening of 3.5 wishes to refer the reader back to that of elegy 3.4, we cannot help keeping our eyes open for further allusions hidden behind the façade of moral philosophy displayed in 3.5.[18]

That Propertius claims the term *proelia* (2) for his loving embraces, and that he terms these battles hard, *dura* (2), like real battles, fits into the pattern of, e.g., 1.6 (36) and 2.1 (13f; 45.). But what is new is that, in the present poem, he goes on to denounce the attitude that leads to *proelia* in their original meaning (i.e., he castigates what he himself, in the rôle of an Augustan *vates*, has encouraged in the preceding poem!). For his own "battles" are, in spite of the military metaphor, "nevertheless" (*tamen*, 3) removed from the world of materialistic greed (3), senseless luxury (4), large estates (5), and, above all, profitable gains from other people's miseries (6). The series of four *necs* successfully drives one point home: the peace of love and lovers (1) is, in spite of its "battles", free from the guilt and crime of war—unlike all other *proelia* and the motives leading to war. Philosophically speaking, the τέλος, i.e., the wise man, of whom the *sapientes* of various popular schools try to talk more or less convincingly, is— the lover! He is the true opposite of the *miser* (6) castigated by every street preacher! Moral philosophy is another realm whose terms Propertius may claim for his own "philosophy" of love, especially when he wishes to define what separates him from men of *arma*. The *pax Propertiana* turns out to be a philosophical position and a basic human condition rather than a political situation (1–6).

And that is exactly what he needs, because a definition of his position in philosophical terms grants him that degree of general and theoretical certainty (a *punctum Archimedis*, so to speak) which permits him to criticize man's given nature (7–12): in creating man, Prometheus showed neither a lucky hand nor the sense of foresight which his name implies (7/8). It seems to me that Propertius here purposely discredits Pro-metheus (cf. *parum caute*, the better MSS' reading in 8), who is seen elsewhere, in a hardly more optimistic interpretation of man's condition,[19] as the helper who finds amendments for the mistakes his brother Epi-metheus committed. Propertius is like those pessimistic moral philosophers who see that man has made evil use of the tools of survival which Prometheus gave him: Prometheus cared for the body's "straight way" (9/10), not for the mind's. The one example (*nunc*, 11) Propertius introduces of Promethean man's perverseness is that we go far over the sea,

> . . . and search after an enemy,
> and tie new wars (arms) to wars (arms).
> > et hostem
> quaerimus, atque armis nectimus arma nova. (11f.)

I have no doubt at all that the poet here (as in lines 47f.) gives his condemnation of Augustus' plan for a Parthian expedition. The expedition is the natural point of reference, once we allow that 3.5 comments on 3.4. Augustus has literally to go overseas in search of an enemy (. . . *meditatur . . . freta gemmiferi findere classe maris*, 4.1f.), since at home everything is quiet; but prestige demands another victory, and so one has to dig up the defeat of the Crassi (by now, after all, thirty years ago) in order to find a cause for raising war, for "tying new wars to wars". If the poet cannot openly criticize the royal enterprise (which he even blessed in 3.4), the mask of philosophical preacher is probably the one most unlikely to be offensive (or even to be decoded) (7–12). He can be more open when he confines himself to his "unserious" love subject matter—as in 3.12, where he blames Postumus, who left his wife Galla to follow Augustus (*Augusti fortia signa sequi*, 2) against the Parthians:

> If it is right to say, may all you greedy ones perish together
> > and anyone (else), who ranked arms higher than a faithful wife!
>
> Si fas est, omnes pariter pereatis avari,
> > et quisquis fido praetulit arma toro! (3.12.5/6)

Application to the concrete political situation is also in order for the following section—again three distichs (13–18)—in which, like a philosophical *diatribe*, the sermon finds its climax by addressing an imaginary listener: *stulte* (14). Concrete interpretation is supported by the fact that the addressee will subsequently have as his concrete counterpart the poet himself (*me*, 19 . . . *me*, 21). Logically speaking, the new section (13–18) states the *reasons why* human behavior (as described in 7–12) must be considered wrong.

The first distich points to the fact that none of the riches acquired by Promethean man will accompany him to the underworld (13/14). This need not in itself be a reference to the Emperor's expedition, because the feature would apply just as well to, say, the nonpolitical businessman, who likewise, to Propertius' eyes, betrays man's true destiny. In a poem of similar fundamental importance (3.7), the money-chasing, worried life (*sol-*

licitae . . . vitae, 7.1) of his friend Paetus is contrasted with his own condition of being *iners* (72), and Paetus' death at sea is to the poet a death caused by human guilt:

> Go, build curved boats and thus create causes of destruction:
> this death is caused by human hands.

> Ite, rates curvas et leti texite causas:
> ista per humanas mors venit acta manus. (29f.)

But in spite of his obsession with money (1ff.), and in spite of having neglected Propertius' advice (43–46), Paetus does not lose the poet's warm compassion, because the crime he committed against himself is, after all, not of the kind considered in 3.5. The *stulitia* of the merchant is exceeded by that of the warlord.[20] It is therefore not before the second distich of our section (5.15f.), that the full impact of Propertius' judgment is expressed:

> The victor's shade will be thrown together with the shades of the
> defeated:
> you, captive Iugurtha, sit together with consul Marius.

> Victor cum victis pariter miscebitur umbris:
> consule cum Mario, capte Iugurtha, sedes. (3.5.15/16)

Who, exemplified by Consul Marius, can be the *future* (*miscebitur*) victor to share Iugurtha's fate as a shade? If we refrain from any speculative drawing of parallels and confine ourselves strictly to the situations outlined in elegies 3.4 and 5, we cannot but compare the shade of Marius—who led defeated Iugurtha in his triumph and had him killed in the Tullianum at the end of the Sacra Via—to Augustus, whose triumph poem 4 predicts by vividly painting the procession on the Sacra Via, including the captive Parthian chieftains (*captos . . . duces*, 18) who, like Iugurtha, will be killed in the Tullianum, as soon as Augustus' triumphal procession has left the Sacra Via and the Forum Romanum, and before the Emperor climbs up the Capitoline Hill. Augustus is nothing but a shadow, like Marius, pursuing an empty and unworthy goal—this has been the poet's thought behind the splendid scene of 3.4![21] In retrospect, the vision of Augustus' triumph as seen in 3.4 now turns into a painting of his *stultitia*; for in the same way as the consoling address to defeated Iugurtha (5.16) points to Augustus' Parthian victims (and, finally, perhaps—we recall 2.7 and 3.5.6—to Propertius himself), the address to the *stultus* (14), who pursues the riches of this world, comes to include the conquering Emperor,[22] once it is viewed in the whole context of lines 13–18. The poet's refusal of any part of the booty (3.4.21), then, did have a deeper reason.

It is a daring deed to mention Marius (whose victory over Iugurtha was supposed to have wiped out a national disgrace and whose victories in general could be, for "official" use [2.1.24], summed up as *benefacta*) as a shade among shades in a poem that refers (47/48) negatively to Augustus' Parthian expedition (which likewise was supposed to wipe out a national disgrace). The historical example is probably as close to Augustus as Propertius could ever dare come when disclosing his true feelings. Thus we should not be surprised that the following distich (17/18), like the one preceding the crucial lines, is remote from Roman history: it denies that a difference exists between the fate of the rich king Croesus (almost a mythical figure) and that of the Homeric beggar Irus. Philosophically, of course, the distich makes the same point as its two predecessors, and it concludes by praising "a natural death as opposed to drowning or death in battle".[23]

So far, elegy 3.5 has proceeded on a well-balanced course: lines 1–6 declare the peace of love as free from all greedy motivations that are the causes of war; 7–12 blame Prometheus' creation for its emphasis on physical welfare instead of soundness of mind; 13–18 explain the *stultitia* involved in the pursuit of riches and military victory (and secretly condemn Augustus by way of correcting the false impression created by the foregoing elegy).

As often, the well-balanced structure of the beginning (3D; 3D; 3D) is purposefully interrupted by apparent disorder, stemming this time from the poet's introduction of his own person into the context. To express the contrast, he chooses the same formula he used to distinguish his own position from that of "Lynceus" and Vergil (2.34.59; similar is 2.13.11): *me iuvat* (19) . . . *me iuvat*[24] (21). It is *his* joy to have spent his early youth with poetry as it is *his* joy to have his head always (*semper*) crowned with the convivial wreath of roses (cf. 2.34, 59), and to "*chain* my mind with lots of *loosening* wine", *multo mentem vincire Lyaeo* (21). The apparent paradox, that the wine-god, Dionysos "Lyaeus", who is usually believed to bring relaxation from worries, is said to "chain" the poet's mind, must be taken together with Propertius' criticism of Pro-metheus' creation and interpreted along the same lines. It is not the happy relief from worries or any exuberant excesses of alcohol that Propertius appreciates in wine; rather, the paralyzing effect of wine is seen as a means of restraining the human mind from committing the outrages that are part of man's Promethean constitution.[25] The phrase *mentem vincire Lyaeo* (21) refers back to the defect of the mind (*mentem*) described earlier in lines 9/10, and shares the same basic pessimism about human nature. The emphatic *me . . . me* shows that 3.5.1–18 is not an irrelevant catalogue of opinions held by popular philosophy, but that, so far, notions of popular philosophy have helped to express the poet's own position and led up to the personal statement of lines 19–22. That enervation or diversion by alcohol means prevention of crime, and thus, under the circumstances of man's condition, comes close to being a moral achievement, is, as we shall see (2.15, see our

Chapter IX), a serious thought of the poet's which is most easily understood if we recall the political conditions that formed and threatened him in his younger years—years which he consciously dedicated to the Muses (*me iuvat in prima coluisse Helicona iuventa* etc., 19f.). What we read in 3.5 is, taking into account the conditions of "free" speech at Rome in the late twenties B.C., still the same rejection of the Active Life that forbade him to join his friend Tullus on his official mission to purge Asia Minor of any remnants of Antonian rule (1.6), and made the poet defend his own *militia*, which denounced *arma* and *laus* in favor of *extrema nequitia* (1.6.25–30, see above Chapter IV).

But such open and unrestrained claims would, when Book 3 was being written (ca. 24–21 B.C.), sound almost revolutionary. They cannot be maintained, therefore, except in the disguised and indirectly alluding form of 3.5, which mentions Marius and means Augustus. We may even, as in the case of 2.7 and 2.10, conjecture that 3.4 was destined for the Emperor and the court to read, whereas 3.5 was not. The lengths to which Propertius could go in complying with official wishes and in disowning his true position will be seen from elegy 3.22, an invitation to his friend Tullus to come home from the East. A short description of this poem at the end of this chapter will help us to appreciate the relative openness of 3.5.

After three sections of 3D each, the reader may well expect that the fourth section, which deals with the poet's own views and attitude, may also be limited to 3D. We are surprised, however, that the third distich (23/24) introduces a lengthy description (11D) of the philosophical subjects which the poet may choose to concern himself with at a later date. After speaking of his youth (19f.), and the unchanging (*semper*) present (21f.), he is going to speak of his future life (23f.), when love will have yielded to grey hair:

Then may it please me to learn thoroughly the ways of nature,

Tum mihi naturae libeat perdiscere mores . . .   (3.5.25)

The list of possible subjects of investigation comprises a surprisingly wide variety of philosophical problems, ranging from natural philosophy to men's fears about an afterlife. The large number of topics presented in these eleven distichs has eluded all attempts to find a convincing pattern of balanced subgroups. This has not prevented inventive philologists from seeing here an announced program (never realized, alas) for future philosophical writings—as if *perdiscere* means "to write". (In a similar way 2.34 has been made into a catalogue of Varius' writings.)

No one, as far as I can see, has taken this pile of philosophical problems for what it is: an unordered mass of difficult questions that present themselves to a thinking mind, engaging it in such a way that a thorough and detailed investigation (*per-discere*) will certainly take up more than one lifetime. What the poet means to say by this impressively long list is this: "For the rest of my life (if I shall live longer than I love), I am already booked up completely for philosophical studies: may no one try to bother me with the occupations of Pro-methean man!" This interpretation (a) allows the list of questions to be long because the poet *wants* it to be long— just as in 2.1 he lengthily demonstrates to Maecenas (lines 57–70) that absolutely nothing can distract him from his love; and (b) preserves a logical connection between the three distichs that precede (19–22) and introduce (23/24) the list and the one distich (the last in the poem, 47f.) following it:[26]

> This is what remains for the rest of my life. But you to whom war
> (arms)
> is more pleasing, bring home Crassus' standards!
>
> Exitus hic vitae superest mihi: vos, quibus arma
> grata magis, Crassi signa referte domum! (3.5.47/48)

If he is ever forced to retire from the innocence of love, it will be in the direction of the pure contemplation of philosophy but there is no room in his life for the crimes of arms. They will not even be his δεύτεραι φροντίδες! He wants to have nothing in common with the man whose drum he felt urged to beat in the foregoing poem (*Arma deus Caesar . . .*), and when he now utters another of those imperatives (cf. *ite . . . ducite . . . piate . . . ite et Romanae consulite historiae!* 4.7–10), the meaning is no longer *omina fausta cano* (4.9), but rather like *omnes pariter pereatis avari* (12.5), i.e., "have done with you" (who leave their love for Augustus' Parthian expedition, 12.1–4). I interpret *Crassi signa referte domum* (5.48) in exactly the same way as I interpreted the imperatives addressed to Tullus in 1.6.19/20 (cf. Chapter IV above).

> tu patrui meritas conare anteire securis
> et vetera oblitis iura refer sociis! (1.6.19/20)

Propertius is sending the other away on a road on which he would never be willing to follow: "You go!" can mean (if two parties only are involved), as we said, "Your way is not my way". And the reason given in 1.6 was already the same—and expressed by the same paronomasia *arma—amor*— as years later in 3.5:

> nam tua non aetas umquam cessavit *amori*,
> semper at *arma*tae cura fuit patriae. (1.6.21/22)

It is this kind of continuity I had in mind when, in the prefatory note to Part Two of this book, I expressed concern about rashly established hypotheses of "development" which are introduced to reconcile surface contradictions in an author's works, but which fail to account for the possibility of personal and inner consistency in the face of a changing environment and mounting outward pressure. We fail to understand a major part (by sheer number of lines, perhaps the major part) of Propertius' poetry if we do not recognize the precautionary facades he erected, which allowed his true attitude to hide behind them and peep out only occasionally. We are now entitled to say that he never intended to write epic court poetry in the event his love poetry gave out (but he did give that false impression in 2.10. Lines 7/8 of 2.10 are refuted by 3.5.23ff.);[27] that he probably never had any detailed plan of studying certain philosophical problems in his later years (although, it must be said, his nature is not unphilosophical); that he never appreciated Augustus' Parthian expedition (though, as seer-poet, he pretended to bless the arms of the departing soldiers in 3.4). We would fail to see one tragic aspect of his life if we took the tribute paid to Caesar Augustus at its face value, and not as mere lip service rendered with greatest reluctance and performed under the severest emotional pain. An interpreter is obliged to observe the small bores of dissent hidden in the facades of praise and submission. We may not like the insincerity involved; but before passing a negative judgment and diagnosing a character flaw, we should recall three points in favor of the defendant: he is a victim of the régime and doubtless feels strong pressure upon himself;[28] there are not many poems of adulation that fail to give the attentive reader a key to the author's true attitude, either by their own structure and content or by some sort of pendant; addresses of submission are not written for their own sake (or to support the official political program), but are used as a protective cover that allows the channels to remain open through which the poet's personal message may reach the public.

I do not deny the possibility that, with his love's hopes slowly dying, he may have been in danger of shifting his position. While the return from insane love to *Mens Bona* (3.24.19) does not necessarily mean more than recovery from sickness to health, the wish to end his torture by leaving Rome and Cynthia for Greece and philosophy (3.21) might in some way be seen to reflect the philistine faultfinder's line of thinking in 1.12 (see Chapter I above); and the acceptance into his own vocabulary of society's judgment on his "dishonorable" or "ignominious" love (*turpi fractus amore*, 3.21.33, see Chapter IX on 2.16.36 and 39) can be seen as a partial surrender—as can his hope that the day of his death will be *honesta* (3.21.34).[29] At least we know that he suffers from the contempt he meets. But we also know from the fourth book (4.1) that even the announced end of his relationship with Cynthia (end of Book 3) could not fundamentally change, at least not for long, the direction of his life and poetry, but could only modify it—although he himself had apparently believed the change might happen. And we shall find his old outlook cautiously restated (4.4, see our Chapter XII). But before that the increasing discrepancy we have observed between public lip service and personal reserve reaches a final peak that, in my eyes, even surpasses the one between elegies 3.4 and 5, because it must sound like a palinode inside his own personal domain of poetry. This is, as I indicated before, his attempt to call friend Tullus home from the East.

Elegy 3.22 is composed in the well-balanced manner that is found already in poems of the first book. Its structure almost surpasses the smoothness of its counterpart 1.6 (above Chapter IV), which dismissed Tullus on his political mission. A short outline of the contents may lead us to the poem's core: [30]

A   1–4: Tullus, you have preferred to stay at cool Cyzicus for many years. }2D

B   5–16: Though you may travel in any part of the world (in the West, East, South, etc.) ⟨let me tell you⟩: }6D

C   17–26: 17/18: Rome's advantages will prove unsurpassed: 1D
              (1) 19–22: its history,   2D }5D
              (2) 23–26: its natural attractions.   2D

D   27–38: Crimes (of Greek myth) that are unknown in Rome.   }6D

E   39–42: Tullus, you should come home where you belong and found a family! }2D

The elegy almost reverses the situation of the two friends at the time of Tullus' departure: Propertius, then dedicated to *extremae . . . nequitiae* (1.6.26), refused to join the friend on his uncle's political, pro-Octavian mission. Since then, several years have passed, and Tullus, whom we knew as the privileged young career man of high family and high prospects, has chosen not to return home (to continue his career) but to stay at pleasantly (*placuit*) cool (*frigida*)[31] Cyzicus on the Propontis. Now Propertius of all persons calls him home, not so much for the sake of their friendship (the personal ties, although enhanced by the address *Tulle*, are mentioned in one line [6] only, and then in the negative: *si . . . nec desiderio, Tulle, movere meo*), but rather by on his part outlining to the friend those patriotic values and motives by which the poet once characterized nephew and uncle in 1.6.

   ˙ I see two possible lines of interpretation:
   (1) Propertius is longing for his friend Tullus and tries to sweeten the idea of homecoming by describing Rome and Italy in the patriotic terms which Tullus himself will appreciate—at least the Tullus whom we know from elegy 1.6.
   Two points make me reject this line of interpretation:

(a) At the time when Propertius asks him to come home, Tullus has been away at least six (at most nine) years, i.e., he overstayed the return of his uncle's *cohors* for so many years that no real interest in a further political career on Tullus' part can any longer be assumed; on the contrary, an appeal to patriotic motives might even contribute to making him stay at Cyzicus.

(b) In the foregoing elegy (3.21), Propertius himself takes leave of Rome for Greece; if he really desires to see Tullus again, it would be better to ask him to expect the poet's arrival in Greece than to come to Rome. This consideration does not hypothesize a greater consistency than there actually is between the situations of poems 3.21 and 22. For 21, besides taking into account other passages of the *Monobiblos*,[32] also contains a revocation of Propertius' refusal in 1.6.13–18 to leave Cynthia for Tullus and Athens; and it also refers literally to the fear of the sea which had been earlier alleged as the reason for Propertius' refusal to accompany Tullus (*Non ego nunc Hadriae vereor mare noscere tecum*, etc., 1.6.1ff.). The echo cannot be missed: "So it is now that I will go by boat as a guest of the rough Adriatic Sea" (*ergo ego nunc rudis Hadriaci vehar aequoris hospes* . . . 3.21.17).

It is thus doubly improbable that Propertius in 3.22 is formulating a serious personal call to a friend he has been missing for a long time.[33] From all we know about Propertius, he must have been delighted rather than disappointed to see his friend give up thinking in patriotic terms of a public career; perhaps (it has been assumed) it is even love which keeps Tullus in the East and has destroyed his taste for politics. After all, he would in this way only fulfill Propertius' earlier diagnosis:

> Nam tua non aetas umquam cessavit amori,
>   semper at armatae cura fuit patriae.   (1.6.21f.)

Surely, love would, in Propertius' eyes, be a valid motive for staying away from Rome—even at a time when the poet himself thinks of freeing himself from his own *turpis amor* (cf. 3.21.33). We are not informed, however, about Tullus' motive for staying, and I therefore exclude this speculation from my train of thought.[34]

(2) The other and more convincing hypothesis is that Tullus' family (we recall from our fourth chapter that his uncle had been a consul together with Octavian, and had, as proconsul of Asia Minor, served Octavian's interests) would like to see the young man back in Rome and active in politics (possibly the Emperor himself has indicated a gracious interest in Tullus?). Why not exercise a soft pressure on Tullus' old friend (and former client?) Propertius to use his poetical talents and personal ties for the good purpose of reminding Tullus of his Roman obligations? My hypothesis would sufficiently explain the strange reversal in Propertius' atti-

tude towards what Tullus is doing: the poetic letter to Cyzicus is in the first place written to accommodate certain circles in Rome—while the addressee may be sure of the correspondent's deep-seated understanding for his extended stay in Cyzicus. Thus viewed, the letter becomes another document of the disguises (or self-denials) Propertius was forced into, in his effort to survive as a poet of personal goals.

The words of elegy 3.22 speak for themselves,[35] as does the structure which I outlined before: in the center (17–26 = 5D) we find the praise of Rome, surrounded by two shells. The outer shell (1–4, 39–42, 2D each) addresses Tullus in his actual and in his proper environment; the inner shell in its earlier half (5–16, 6D) describes the rest of the world as contrasted with Rome, and in its latter half (27–38, 6D) contrasts some horrors of Greek mythology with Rome's more benign character.

The center itself, in an introductory distich (17/18), makes Rome's miracles surpass everything else in the world. Its second main part (23–26) praises Rome for its healthy (and cool) waters (so Rome can rival "cool Cyzicus", 1—an advantage the contemporary reader cannot adequately appreciate). The first of the two main parts (19–22) brings a positive evaluation of Roman history:

> Land more apt for arms than fit for crime:
> *Fama*, oh Rome, is not ashamed of your history!
> For as through our sword, so through our piety powerful
> we stand: our anger restrains its hand in victory.

> Armis apta magis tellus quam commoda noxae:
> famam, Roma, tuae non pudet historiae!
> Nam quantum ferro tantum pietate potentes
> stamus: victrices temperat ira manus.   (3.22.19–22)

Here, finally, we see Propertius publicly signing the *pax Augusta*. He clearly joins the pattern we find in the *Aeneid*, especially the programmatic lines cited earlier in this chapter (6.851–853): reinterpretation of Rome's bloody history in terms of an ultrareligious, all-pervading piety (we may compare *pius Aeneas*), self-moderation after victory as a Roman characteristic, a distinction drawn between arms and crime. This is the language of 3.4 raised to the level of principle, with no pendant like 3.5 to show the reader the reverse side of the coin where we would find Iugurtha instead of Marius, the defeated nations instead of the Roman soldiers, Propertius instead of Augustus.[36] More than anything hitherto (but like some later poems), these lines mean Propertius' political surrender—whatever his feelings may have been. Perhaps he hoped that he himself would experience Augustus' moderation in victory and be allowed to continue in his vocation. But—for other reasons—that was hardly possible, for—if we may draw a conclusion from the position of elegy 3.22 in the neighborhood of poems that say farewell to Cynthia[37]—the time of final surrender to political pressure seems to have coincided with a period when he felt that his love must cease to be his life's center if he was to survive. The crisis sets in on both flanks of his endangered personality at about the same time.

The crisis even invades the poet's own world of similes and imagination. The following section (22.27–38) reminds Tullus that the horrors of Greece, especially of Greek myth, do not exist in Rome. Examples are: a daughter in chains, suffering for the hubris of her mother (for the benefit of a monster); a father being served his two sons for dinner; a mother killing her son by magic; a man chased and torn to pieces by his mother and her associates; a father sacrificing his daughter (to satisfy his political ambition); a goddess changing her human rival into a cow; etc. It was often, and especially in times of heightened national consciousness, fashionable in Rome to characterize the Greeks as inhuman, unreliable, treacherous. And it was part of Augustan ideology that Rome's domination of Greece (accompanied perhaps by feelings of guilt in some educated minds) was justified because it only paid back to contemporary Greeks what their ancestors had done to Rome's—i.e., the Iulians'—alleged Trojan ancestors by capturing Troy (the *Aeneid* relies heavily on this scheme).[38] How crudely this line of thinking could be pursued at times, we may see from the table of horrors that Propertius feels free to offer his Augustan readers. But the question which the more educated among his readers must raise is this: "How could he thus betray the world in which not only his much-praised forerunners Philitas and Callimachus but also his own mind and thoughts were so much at home that he seriously considered the study of Greek art (together with Greek philosophy and literature, 3.21.25–30) as an alternative to his life of a love-poet now ending?" Had he not from the very beginning—we need only recall Milanion and Atalante as symbols for Propertius and Cynthia in 1.1—used Greek myth to help him express what he wished his readers to understand? The alternative interpretation—Propertius was suddenly and truly converted to seeing Greek myth as a collection of nightmarish excesses—will not hold, especially in the face of the foregoing poem 3.21, and must be excluded. Therefore, I can only ascribe this cheap and almost rhetorical declamation to the pressure and taste of the circles who ordered the poem. Perhaps Propertius felt he could count on the addressee and the educated among his contemporary readers to understand his reasons for including yet another patriotic piece in his book.

The pledge of loyalty to Roman values is still incomplete. The peak of self-denial is reserved for the last four lines:

This country has given you birth, Tullus, this is the most beautiful of
                                                countries,
here you must strive for honor and office worthy of your noble
                                                family,
here are the citizens to listen to your oratory, here you have rich hope
for offspring, here you find the proper love of a future wife.

Haec tibi, Tulle, parens, haec est pulcherrima sedes,
   hic tibi pro digna gente petendus honos,
hic tibi ad eloquium cives, hic ampla nepotum
   spes et venturae coniugis aptus amor.   (3.22.39–42)

This passage mentions the family (which, according to my hypothesis, urged the poet to write this elegy) and its ambitious hopes for Tullus' career. Moreover, by speaking of marriage and begetting children, it also lays a bait for Tullus which Propertius himself has, so far, never found alluring; on the contrary: *Unde mihi patriis natos praebere triumphis?* (2.7.13). But the bait is definitely in line with the Emperor's reforms. The discrepancy cannot be denied: there is no bridge leading over the abyss between the poet's true feelings and the public statements he has felt obliged to make. The argument of this chapter—which shall not be repeated here at length— has been that we must acknowledge the discrepancy if we are to understand the poet's personal difficulties and to see the extent to which his creative powers were involved in dealing with the Zeitgeist.[39] That some of this involuntary investment came back, with interest, will be shown in the following chapters. But first, a few remarks on scholarship are in place.

. The failure of Augustan Interpretation to recognize a discrepancy between Augustan surface and personal attitude has resulted in a tragic misunderstanding which takes the façade poems as indicators of a true and smooth development towards Augustanism, "passaggio dalla poesia erotica ad un' altra quasi epica o meglio civile", as Alfonsi's chapter on Book 3 puts it (1945D, 65). Because of the implications for correctly understanding Book 4, I ask my reader to compare my above results with two statements on 3.4 and 22. First, La Penna (1951B, 50) with regard to 3.22: "L'invito all' amico è la cornice, le lodi dell' Italia sono l'essenziale. È evidente che Properzio ha davanti à se e cerca di rifare, variando, Virgilio, Georg. 2, 136sgg." . . . "3,22 è già un avviamento abbastanza netto verso la poesia etiologica nazionale dell' ultimo libro, dove Virgilio è spesso presente."

Next, Haffter (1970, 61f.): "Die Elegie 22, was gibt sie anderes als *laudes Italiae* und zugleich *laudes Romae*? Natürlich ist dieser Lobpreis nicht für sich allein vorgebracht, sondern irgendwie [*sic!*] mit der Nennung einer Person verbunden, mit Tullus, dem das erste Buch gewidmet ist." (Then follow remarks on Propertius' being in agreement with Vergil's *laudes Italiae* in the *Georgics* and with the *Aeneid's parcere subjectis et debellare superbos.*) The poem's final call to Tullus for fulfillment of his civic duties and for marriage at Rome elicits the following comment: "Dieser unmittelbare Gedichtschluss, wie sehr weist er auch für sich allein wieder voraus auf das vierte Buch!" Generally, Haffter says, in Books 2 and 3 "wird das Römische mehr und mehr ausführlich beschrieben und es verliert mehr und mehr seinen negativ-distanzierten Ton. Betrachten wir gleich im dritten Buch die kurze Elegie 4 . . . den Soldaten ruft Properz zu, sie sollten . . . für die römische Geschichte sorgen. Dieser römische Tenor füllt bis auf zwei oder drei Verse das ganze Gedicht", etc. (o.c. p. 60f.).

We see once again that it was not only contemporary opinion which the poet successfully eluded by his game of political hide and seek. Even Paratore (1936, 157ff.; cf. 1942), usually anxious to avoid a patriotic interpretation, goes into the trap. Dismissing any search for a logical argument in 3.22, he explains the poem on the basis of opposition to Vergil's *laudes Italiae* , but finds in the last distich (but only there) "una nota di più umana romanità" (o.c. p. 169). Paratore goes out of his way to prove that Propertius writes *laudes Romae* (or *Latii*), but not, as Vergil does, *Italiae*. The reason for this, he says, is that egoistic Propertius is interested only in the joys of the capital, where his mistress resides ("dove era trascorsa la sua vita di avido gaudente", 1936, 166) . . . I prefer to stay with the poem's argument which implies that it was Tullus' noble family who wanted to see him back in Rome (and not only in Italy). This keeps another road open for interpreting Book 4.

Philologically speaking, the most instructive misunderstanding of 3.22 is again provided by G. Williams (1968, 417ff.; cf. his misreading of 1.21 and 22, analyzed in Chapter V above). Eager to explain the poem in terms of a poor copy depending on a superb model (i.e., Vergil, *Georg.* 2.136–174), he finds it "weak and trivial", its logic "not powerful", etc. Once more he is blind to the fact that the main deficiencies he finds are caused by his own method, which does not verify the alleged copy's immanent and independent train of thought. Let us hear him on 3.22.23–26: ". . . the lakes appear in what is mainly a review of Italian water resources which has little point and no logic" (p. 422). But already by the emphatic first word in the poem's first line (*Frigida*) Propertius voices concern that friend Tullus is not returning to Rome because of Cyzicus' attractively (*placuit*) cool climate[40] which results from its being surrounded by water (cf. *isthmos, aqua, fluit,* line 2)! How can it be a "mistake" if, in inviting Tullus to come home, Propertius undertakes "a review of Italian water resources", to point out that Rome is able to rival Cyzicus' sea climate? ". . . essentially the same mistake as he made when he adopted the theme of Italian lakes from Virgil, but ignored the way in which Virgil had set them" (p. 425). Williams' faultfinding words turn against himself, because not Propertius but he is the one who "ignored the way in which" the elegist "set them". Unable to understand a passage within the logical context designed by its author, the scholar is quick to see in it a mere stylistic reference to a passage in another, earlier author; then proceeds to declare the alleged copy poetically and logically inferior to its alleged source.

The other alleged "mistake" our censorious literary critic finds is that (in 3.22.27ff.) for Vergil's "monsters he substitutes a series of monstrous acts from Greek mythology" (p. 424). Again the critic misses Propertius' point, which is not a mere stylistic substitution but the argument that Tullus should leave the alien Greek world, which is here represented as being dominated by a crime-ridden religion, and return to where he belongs, i.e., to Rome's innocent religiosity (cf. *armis—noxae*, 19; *pietate potentes*, 21—terms unintelligible in their context to our mistaken critic, p. 424). There is no way the poet could possibly have integrated Vergilian monsters into his argument—except to justify Professor Williams' theories. Obsessed with searching for models and copies, Williams blurs the difference between stylistic devices (some of which do indeed, in this official poem, imitate Vergil praising fertile Italy and her presumably greatest fruit: *te, maxime Caesar, Georg.* 2.170), on the one hand, and discursive thinking (which here demonstrates to Tullus the superiority of Roman healthy climate and Roman piety over Greek pleasant climate and Greek crime), on the other.

Once more it turns out that stylistic investigation, when practiced without proper regard for logic, cannot even explain the surface level of the artefact (not to mention its true meaning). If the critic nevertheless feels entitled to develop his mistaken understanding into a theory of "Tradition and Originality", and, by means of his theory, condemns the innocent poem as lacking, one might rightly despair of philological interpretation. This·is especially true because a political, pro-Augustan attitude, an "emotion for patriotism" (o.c. p. 425) on the poet's part, is taken for granted by Williams all along (and not by Williams only). A poet's dissent is a priori limited to matters of style and, if discovered, blamed lavishly: "The result is feeble and silly. The reader who knows the passage of Virgil is astonished at the tasteless ineptitude of style and content in Propertius" (p. 425). It is interesting to see how swiftly the word "content" (i.e., the not understood argument of 3.22) is slipped into the sentence just quoted along with the judgment of style.

From another viewpoint, it may be remarked that the approach which my interpretations try to keep open is one which theoretical literary criticism often considers naïve and uncritical (cf. Allen 1962, passim). The poetical "ego" speaking in the elegies, we are told, must not be confused or identified with the poet's own. This is, as far as our present chapter is concerned, true for instance insofar as Propertius never did as a *vates* bless the arms of Augustus' soldiers. Kraus (1965) has in this manner checked through all the poems in the first book of Tibullus and concluded about its bitter core that it "eben nicht wörtlich als ein einzelnes, individuelles Erlebnis genommen werden soll" (p. 163). This may be true about Tibullus 1, and, to a degree (as we saw), even about Propertius 1. But set absolute, the demand to exclude the poet's ego from his poetry would a priori prevent the interpreter from even considering as real the dilemma of façade and personal poetry to which our present chapter is dedicated—in short: the literary theory would wipe out the essential conflict reflected in the work of art.

Let the preceding pages be enough of a necessary exercise in dealing with existing scholarship. Today's reader of Propertius faces difficulties that arise not only from his author's text (and personal situation) but also from the fixations of scholarship, which can perhaps be roughly outlined in two opposing opinions. On the one hand, "Propertius, the lesser Augustan, comes to imitate his greater contemporaries Horace and Vergil because he has recognized their superiority". On the other hand (a position less widely discussed so far), "Propertius, though somewhat individualistic, has not as obligingly presented the lonely individual as has Vergil in the hero of his *Aeneid*". May the elegist's interpreter be forgiven if, in this situation, he has taken a detailed route to show, in Part Two, Section A of this study, how the old dilemma of "love" versus "war" is alive and continuing. The new forms of public disguise and personal consistency (or opposition), once analyzed, will help us in approaching the poet's later work in Part Two, Section B of this study. Also of help will be the knowledge we acquired of the elegist's growing artistic and personal loneliness. The situation of Book 3 does not even allow for an opening address to a Tullus or a Maecenas any longer.

PART II

SECTION

— B —

LOVE: A PEACE NOT WON THROUGH ARMS

——IX——

DISTRESSFUL HAPPINESS: A COMPLEX VIEW OF LOVE

Having read to the end of the foregoing chapter, my reader may well have decided that he has received all the help I can give him for understanding the central aspects of Propertian elegy, and that anything which follows can only interfere with his own reading. Such a decision would be consistent with my basic intention stated in the Preface, not to develop another lengthy and dogmatic thesis on Propertius, but to give a series of single interpretations which in themselves constitute an argument. The train of thought should at every point allow my reader to state his own reasons for consent or disagreement, and my interpretation should never obstruct a direct approach to the poet's text.

What I naturally wish to draw my reader's attention to next is the repercussion of the Zeitgeist on Propertius' presentation of his love. Having seen how creative the elegist is in exploiting his encounters with the surrounding world for ever-sharper definitions of his own point of view, a reader of the *Monobiblos* may expect that the large and numerous elegies of the following books in which the poet cautiously denies the ruling forces of the day any influence on the goals of his poetry will in some way or other pay back the poetical capital invested in them. In fact, it is only in the interest of clarity that the political aspects in Propertius' first three books have been considered separately from those concerning his love; both sides are almost always present, and it is only the necessity of defending his territory which makes Propertius give temporary prominence to the former. I have accordingly made the results of the investigation in the foregoing section (Chapters VI to VIII) into a heading for the section which follows (Chapters IX to XII): once the notion of love as a peace not won through arms has been conceived, and, with the passage of time, formulated more clearly, it turns out that the contrary, Augustan idea of peace can be used to give Propertius' own concept a broader scope, just as Tullus' patriotism (1.6) once helped to bring out more sharply Propertius' own *nequitia* as a new form of *militia*.

The most poignant rejection of the Zeitgeist found thus far is elegy 3.5, which is obviously in danger of being negative only. It remains to be seen how the political aspect of Propertius' poetry can be part of an integrated whole, in which it plays no more than a merely contributory role, like other characteristic motifs of the second and following books (e.g., the awareness of death) that we have mentioned before. Not all poems are central, of course, and the emptier the love theme becomes during the course of Books 2 and 3, the more frequent are pieces that display a virtuoso mastery of the genre rather than a concern for personal self-expression (in the way the *Monobiblos* had claimed to reflect its author's growing human experience). Two things, however, must be kept in mind: (a) elegy never ceases for long to be the poet's characteristic tool of self-orientation (in fact, this function is intensified towards the end of Book 3), and (b) the (preliminary or final) end of Propertius' love and of his activity as a love poet towards the end of Book 3 is not to be equated with a sudden termination of those basic views on life and human behavior which the poet has expressed more and more distinctly over the years. The reader's task is once again twofold: to distinguish the central from the marginal, and to see the complex character of what is central (i.e., to avoid any one-dimensional treatment). By way of example, I have chosen elegy 2.15 for a detailed interpretation.

2.15

Oh, happy me! Oh night, bright to me! And oh you,
    bed, made happy through my delights!
How many words we exchanged when the lamp was close by,
    and what a great fight it was when the light had been removed!
For now she wrestled with me, with her breasts bare,
    and then, in between, she delayed, covered with her *tunica*.
It was she who opened my eyes, that had closed in sleep,
    with her mouth, and said: "Do you lie thus, lazy one?"
In how manyfold embrace we shifted our arms! How long
    did my kisses tarry on your lips!   (1–10)

It is no joy to mar love in sightless movement:
    in case you do not know: the eyes are the guides in love.
Paris himself is said to have been stricken with love for the naked
                                  Spartan,
    when she rose from Menelaus' bed;
naked also Endymion is said to have impassioned Phoebus' sister,
    and to have slept with the naked goddess.

If therefore, stubborn in your mind, you lie dressed,
　　your dress will be torn and you will experience my hands;
yes, even, if my emotion carries me further,
　　you will show your mother your hurt arms.
So far, no hanging breasts hinder you from playing:
　　let her attend to this, whatever woman feels shame to have borne
　　　　　　　　　　　　　　　　　　　　　　　　　　already.
As long as fate allows us, we will still our eyes' craving with love:
　　a long night is coming to you, and day will not return.　　　(11-24)

Oh, that you felt the wish to bind us, hanging on to each other, with a
　　　　　　　　　　　　　　　　　　　　　　　　　chain
　　in such a way that never a day loosed it!
The pigeons united in love may offer you an example,
　　male and female a complete couple.
He errs, who seeks an end of mad love:
　　true love does not know moderation.
Sooner will the earth deceive the farmers with false fruit,
　　and the sun-god drive black horses,
and rivers start to recall their waters to the source,
　　and the fish be dry in a drained channel,
than I be able to transfer my pains elsewhere:
　　hers I shall be alive, hers I shall be in death!　　　(25-36)

If therefore she on her part is willing to concede me such nights with
　　　　　　　　　　　　　　　　　　　　　　　　herself,
　　even a year of my life will be ⟨a⟩ long ⟨life⟩.
If she grants many, I shall be immortal in¹ them:
　　in one night, anyone is able to be even a god.
If all men desired to pass their life in this way,
　　and to lie, their limbs weighed down with lots of unwatered wine,
there would be no cruel iron nor any warship,
　　nor would the sea near Actium churn over our bones,
nor would Rome, so often assaulted everywhere by victories hurting
　　　　　　　　　　　　　　　　　　　　　　　her own flesh,
　　feel tired of putting down her hair in mourning.
Rightly (there is no doubt!) later generations will be able to praise *this*
　　　　　　　　　　　　　　　　　　　　　　　way of life:
　　no insult has been done to any gods by our goblets.　　　(37-48)

Do you only neglect not the joy of life, as long as it is daylight:
　　if you give all (your) kisses, you will give few!
And, as the petals have left the withering wreaths,
　　—the petals which you see floating here and there in the bowls—
thus for us, who now breathe deeply in love,
　　the morrow will perhaps contain the end of our lives.　　　(49-54)

Readings different from OCT: semicolon at the end of lines 14 and 18; exclamation mark at the end of line 36; colon at the end of line 49; exclamation mark at the end of line 50.

The difficulties which this elegy has seemed to pose stem at least partially from the ways in which it has been approached. Two especially must be mentioned here: (1) As both elegy 2.15 and its antecedent, 2.14, refer to a night of happy love, the night in both cases has been assumed to be the same and the two poems to be concerned with the same subject, as if Propertius had set himself the poetical or rhetorical exercise of writing variations on an identical motif.[2]

The preceding elegy is triumphant and optimistic in tone, even humorous; the poet, barely able to find an adequate comparison for his overwhelming joy, happily announces that he has finally won the unhoped-for victory over his mistress' resistance. His secret recipe: disdain. Exulting over this "victory", he again does not mind borrowing (as elsewhere— e.g., 2.7.15–18) from the stock vocabulary that military Rome uses for occasions like these: he is going to nail the "exuviae" (supposedly torn from his defeated "enemy's" body) to a column in the temple of—Venus! He also goes out of his way to tell us that this "victory" means more to him than: defeat of the Parthians, spoils, captive kings, triumphal chariot:

> Haec mihi devictis potior victoria Parthis,
>   haec spolia, haec reges, haec mihi currus erunt.   (2.14.23f.)

In short, all those grave and patriotic notions that lend dignity to, e.g., the Augustus poems 2.10 and 3.4 are here utilized for a hilarious presentation of *Imperator Propertius*. And were it not for the possible ambiguity and pessimism of the last two distichs (29–32: a final interpretation has not been found),[3] one would feel tempted to view the whole elegy as a surprising hoax.

However one decides to understand the last four lines, one will hardly end up with a poem that ranges through more than three or four basic movements: unexpected joy (1–10), secret recipe (11–20), pseudomilitary victory and triumph (21–28), greater or lesser degree of certainty about his love's future (29–32). Once elegies 2.14 and 15 are assumed to run along the same basic lines, the narrow scope of 2.14 precludes a proper interpretation of 2.15—should it turn out that the viewpoint of the latter is different or its angle of vision wider.[4] Methodologically speaking, an independent investigation of 2.15 is called for.

(2) The other approach concerns elegy 2.15 directly. It has been maintained that the frequent change of grammatical person—the speaker's mistress is sometimes addressed directly as "you", sometimes referred to in the third person, sometimes contained in the plural "we"—indicates different dramatic situations that follow each other in the course of the night: if the poet speaks of "her", this indicates that "she" is asleep while he is monologizing, but the use of "you" points to a conversation between the lovers, etc. Stoessl, the originator of this interpretation,[5] even feels compe-

tent to say what the lovers are doing (and how often) in the course of the night, thus making the supposedly unspoken outspoken. The structure his interpretation extracts from the elegy appears seductive indeed—so far as balance goes (3D; 9D; 3D; 9D; 3D). But it is open to objections: (a) Propertius' use of apostrophe, including swift changes of addressees, increases over the years without contributing to the establishment of more precise poetical situations;[6] in our elegy itself, we find a switch from "she" (15.7) to "your" (15.10) without any change of situation. It is possible, therefore, that confining the shift of grammatical person to use in connection with a change in mimetic situation deprives us of appreciating varying degrees of emotional intensity and poetical vividness in the lover's words. (b) The shifts of grammatical persons do not define (although they twice coincide with) the sections which constitute the elegy's train of thought. Stoessl constantly points to "Lässigkeit" in expression and thought, assuming that the poet describes his own sleepiness in this way. The assumption strikes me as improbable in itself—my experience as a reader would lead me to expect clarity even here—and the passages cited by Stoessl are ones where a logical argumentation can, I believe, be discerned. It is hardly justifiable to print—as Enk does—a mimetic and a logical (or what Enk considers to be a logical) disposition side by side without reconciling them.

In what follows, I shall give priority to argument over mimesis, more because of poem 2.15 itself than any expectations resulting from earlier chapters. The analysis which I wish to present (and which may already be seen from the sections into which my translation was divided), can draw on a kind of evidence not yet introduced: from Book 2 on, and increasingly in the larger elegies of Books 3 and 4, Propertius occasionally uses the device of cyclical composition ("Ringkomposition") to mark off sections or units within the larger context of an elegy. Although the unit thus emphasized is usually the favorite 2D (on the prominence of which throughout all four books I remarked when discussing poems 1.11 and 12 in Chapter I), this structural device is like others used by Propertius in that it is never employed dogmatically or mechanically. In its simpler form, it underlines a section's unity by repeating a key word from the section's first line in the last. In the elegies so far mentioned, there is only one striking example. When speaking of his friend's Paetus' death by drowning, Propertius classifies it, as we saw in the foregoing chapter, as a death caused "by human hands" (3.7.30), because the motive for Paetus' voyage was his craving for money. Propertius even implies that punishment is deserved by those who trespass on the sea because the land is "not enough" for them:

> *Terra parum* fuerat, fatis adiecimus undas:
>   fortunae miseras auximus arte vias.
> ancora te teneat, quem non tenuere penates?
>   quid meritum dicas, cui sua *terra parum* est?   (3.7.31–34)

There can be no doubt that in this extremely artful 2D group (I only point to assonance and alliteration, rhyme and metrical parallelism) the cycle, running from *terra parum* at the beginning of 31 to the same words at the end of 34, serves the purposes of unity as well as emphasis. The emphasis is heightened by the fact that none of the other fifteen 2D units in the elegy displays cyclic word or thought composition. Although we shall see that cyclic construction is far from having consistently the same importance as in the two distichs quoted above—which affirm a basic philosophical position of the poet's—, recognition of the new structural element is certainly another welcome means for basing Propertian interpretation on something sounder than the guesswork of arbitrary associations.

As to the first section of elegy 2.15, I concur with most interpreters by limiting it to lines 1–10. Its argument proper is preceded by a highly unusual distich (1/2): three exclamations pressed into two lines, all three introduced by the same inarticulate "o" with no verb added to complete a proposition, the first even ending in an apparent offense against the rules of meter (*hiatus, brevis in longo*). The form gives us the impression of someone trying to say the unspeakable, stammering because his stupefaction appears beyond intelligible communication, and this impression of form is confirmed by the paradoxical content. To the speaker (he views everything in relation to his own elated condition: *me . . . mihi . . . meis*) everything in the world is out of its usual order. His "sweet little bed", *lectule*, is called happy (because it has been allowed to bear him and his love); to him, the night lost its darkness (its main objective, scientific characteristic); but above all and in the first place: Propertius himself is *happy*—he whose constant epithet from the first line of his first book on has been "unhappy" (*miserum me*, 1.1.1)! A truly extraordinary situation—and one in which even a poet may be pardoned for temporarily losing his mastery of chiseled speech (and for committing a *hiatus . . .*).

The human way of intellectually accounting for an overwhelming emotional experience is to relive, i.e., recount, that experience. This is what the speaker of our poem does or, rather, tries to do. For he fails to come to grips with the abundance of his memories. *Quam multa* (3, emphatic because of its unusual form) and *quanta* (4), both used here to introduce another set of exclamations, certainly do not subsume emotions under ordering categories of the mind; they point rather to lack of words. But order comes with the next distich, which substantiates (*nam*, 5)[7] its antecedent by establishing a sort of pattern, but what a pattern! It states nothing but the alternation (*modo—interdum*) of love's fast pace and periods of hesitation. Only one fact is present—the asyndeton (7) signals a climactic new event—which the lover can single out from his recollection and nail down (7/8): the unbelievable truth that *his* own love was not only requited but even exceeded by *her* desire. We must grant the juxtaposition *illa meos* (7) its full weight (and not see here another case of postclassical *illa* = "she"): "It was *she* who opened *my* eyes (and not me who woke her)!"

Almost necessarily, the thought of her slightly reproachful words (*Sicine, lente, iaces?*) makes him recall the ardor of their mutual (*mutamus*) response, foremost the endless time during which his lips pressed hers—or rather, "yours" (*tuis*, 10) because his recollection has by now reached such a degree of vividness that he imagines the beloved to be present. He can now directly refute the charge of being languid, and counter his memory of *illa meos* (7) with the straight answer *nostra . . . tuis* (10): "It is true, she woke me up. But it was *I* who would not stop kissing *you*!" The increasing vividness of the lover's recollection begins to restore past events as if they were happening now at this very moment. The poetical purpose is not mimetic, it is rather to show how the lover tries in vain to cope with a recent overwhelming experience. Instead of mastering it, he is being mastered by it—again! The attempt at rationalization ends (9/10) where it started (3/4), in the expression of innumerable joys, the sheer multitude of which escapes the grip of an ordering mind. The lover returns to the same dyad of stupefied exclamations with which he started his "account": *quam vario . . .* and *quantum . . .* in line 9 correspond to *quam multa . . .* and *quanta . . .* in lines 3/4. Similarly, the tenses move from immediate visualization (the parallel forms *narramus*, 3, and *mutamus*, 9, both preceding the bucolic diaeresis, should doubtless be taken as "historical presents") to implicit admission that the happy night is now over and only relived (perfect tense in the pentameters 4 and 10: *fuit, sunt . . . morata*).

To sum up our interpretation of lines 1–10 so far: they are to be understood as a futile attempt to express in words the recent experience of overwhelming happiness. A distich of paradoxical and barely articulate exclamations (1/2) is followed by a cyclic movement of thought (3–10), in which imaginative recollection ("you") proves stronger than present reality ("she"). Instead of clarifying his thoughts, the lover sinks back into the transport of love. Once more—as, for example, in 1.11—we accompany the lover through the actual movements of his thoughts and emotions. Poetically, this means that Propertius here immortalizes his love in his own peculiar way: by putting in writing the process through which he tries to approach the events and impressions of this memorable night. If an indication of time is really needed (as many readers have felt), I would say that the dramatic situation presents the lover on the next morning, not too many hours after his night of love. This fits best with Propertius' striving for immediateness. Nothing else has occurred in between, so that the impressions are still fresh and pure—so vivid indeed that they seem incapable of being collected into the narrow confines of language.

The second section, lines 11–24, picks up one aspect of the introduction and elaborates it. We recall that the only "structure" which the
lover's recollection could find in the night that passed was the alternation
(*modo . . . interdum*) of naked love (*nudatis mecum est luctata papillis*, 5) and
of covered delay (*duxit operta moram*, 6). Each of the two phases was also
marked by references to light: periods of delay meant talk under the lamp
(3), periods of naked love meant *rixa* with the light removed or extinguished
(4). Lines 3–6 display a chiastic order (comparable to that in the other subunit 7–10): 3 ~ 6: light and covered delay; 4 ~ 5: darkness and naked love.

The new section (11–24) insists on breaking up this order and on co-
ordinating light and naked love, while the other two ingredients, darkness
and covered delay, disappear from consideration. My reader will, I hope,
forgive this schematic presentation. It helps to reveal the climax at which
the poet is going to aim: a more intensive poetic presentation of his love as
well as a more concentrated approach to love's essence as he sees it. He
further heightens the intensity of this section by keeping the level of imaginative address which he had reached in line 10 (*tuis*), as if the beloved
were present.

The first three distichs (11–16) take the form of an argumentative admonition to his mistress, introduced by a thesis: it is no joy to mar love by
sightless movement (11). The term "blind" (*caeco*) refers not only to the
darkness of night when the lamp is extinguished, but also—as the next
lines, with their stress on *oculi* and nudity, show— to the cover mentioned
in the foregoing section. The beloved girl should know (*si nescis*) that love is
not appreciated fully through movement, i.e., the sense of touch alone; it
must be guided by the sense of sight, which in turn depends on light.
Thus the new section starts with a formula of general scope, which can be
confirmed by the following examples (13–16) and also serves as a basis to
which the cyclic train of thought returns at the end (23/24).

The two mythical examples (13–16) form a climax: the first (13/14)
shows Paris' ardor for *naked* Helen, the second (15/16) shows Selene, female counterpart to the man Paris, delighted at the sight of naked Endymion, *and herself* naked when Endymion lies with her. (If a commentator is
worried because such a nude version of a certain myth is not indicated in
other literary sources, we must console him by saying that our poet believes only the most perfect actions to be appropriate for mythical times,
and that this belief determines his account.)

Having proved the correctness of his thesis by referring to the "ideal"
world of myth, the lover is now in a position to judge and even forcefully
institute what is right. If his beloved should show obstinacy (*pertendens an-
imo*, 17) and, unlike the goddess (*nudae . . . deae*, 16), should lie (*cubaris*,
17, ~ *concubuisse*, 16) dressed (*vestita*, 17) as she did before (*operta*, 6), then

he will be entitled to tear her dress or even bruise her resisting arms (thus revealing an impetuosity that does not deserve the addresss "lente").

Moreover, his mistress' resistance to nudity lacks the only justification one could possibly think of ("moral" reasons, as defined by, e.g., the censurer of 1.12, are clearly out of the question). Her youthful figure has absolutely nothing to be "ashamed of" (i.e., to hide, 21/22).

The poet has established his point, perhaps not without letting us see a twinkle in his eye. But the frivolous air is misleading because the happy and joyful aspect of love which he wants to present at its most intense is always exposed to threats, extending from the first loss of youth's bloom (*si quam iam peperisse pudet*) right through to the inescapable end of life (*nec reditura dies*, 24). Once we recognize the dark background which is first implied, then made explicit, the whole section from 11 to 24 appears in a new light. Not eyesight and nudity alone form the main topic, but love (as expressed through them) in the face of death. The underlying pessimism comes unexpectedly and takes the reader by surprise because no hint has prepared him for the metaphorical association of light and dark with life and death. The only indication foreshadowing the gloomy utterance 23/24 comes late in the passage (21/22): our nature is subject to decay (cf. *nec-dum;*[8] *iam*; and see the logical asyndeton between the two distichs).

First, let us see how the cycle of composition is completed: *in caeco . . . motu* (11), love in the darkness of night, is taken up by *nox* (24); the statement *oculi sunt in amore duces* (12) corresponds, as commentators have seen, to the words *oculos satiemus amore* (23).[9]

Let us, then, view the widening of meaning. The prefixed clause *dum nos fata sinunt* (the thought itself is derived from the idea of vanishing youth implied in the preceding distich) alludes explicitly to death, and so makes the subsequent *oculos satiemus amore* contain above and beyond its erotic meaning an affirmation of life itself: love, as the peak of life, is the true opposite of death. The attribute *longa* (24), added to *nox*, might still point to nothing more than the lover's night, which has thus far prevailed through the poem. But its negative foil, *nec reditura dies*, by saying that daylight will not return, gives *nox . . . longa* the meaning "*eternal* night", i.e., death. Is it too farfetched to surmise, on the new level of understanding, that the paradoxical phrase *nox . . . candida* of line 1 has been chosen not so much because the night is lit by the *lucerna* but because it is to be contrasted with the *nox longa* at the end of the second section (24)? In other words, in the terms reached at line 24, a lover's night, being life's essence, indeed amounts to a bright and shining period of time, however short, in the eternal night of death before and after it.

I sum up my understanding of lines 11–24. They build on the unsuccessful attempt of lines 1–10 to express in words a night of happy love,

insofar as they single out from it the elements of eyesight (3) and naked-
ness (5) and combine them with the direct address and presence ("you")
reached in line 10, to give a more intensive account of love itself.. The
joyful (and even playful) surface, dressed in the form of an "instruction" to
the mistress, is soon shown to conceal a sad fact: love, being life's highest
self-expression, is threatened by the fact of death. When, therefore, the
cyclical train of thought returns to its initial position (11 ~ 24; 12 ~ 23), it
is no longer quite the same, because pessimistic overtones are now included. Even the "bright" night of line 1 must be seen against this background, and the rare instance of happiness (*o me felicem*) is heightened by
the lover's knowledge of the human condition—almost in the Epicurean
sense.[10] But Propertius' *carpe diem* contains more tragic aspects than have
been mentioned so far.

The third section, lines 25 to 36, develops another negative aspect to
the experience of love, and this one will appear more characteristically
Propertian to my reader. Not only is love threatened by death as man's
natural limit; the short period of our lives during which we are permitted
to love can be further shortened and marred by the lovers' own doings and
behavior. And the account of what love's essence is would not be complete—as we have known ever since we read elegy 1.12—if Propertius did
not incorporate the cruel possibility that the lover's desire for love to last
eternally is not shared by the beloved. The different attitude of the two
lovers is indicated by the subdivision of our section. The first three distichs (25–30) speak of his vain wish that Cynthia (as I do not hesitate to
call the beloved woman here, although no name is mentioned) should always stay with him; the other three distichs (31–36) tell of his never-
ceasing love for her. In short, the section is a well-balanced and clear-cut
differentiation of the two lovers and their attitudes towards each other.[11]

Nevertheless, there have been difficulties about how to interpret the
first half, lines 25–30. Commentators have at times overlooked the fact
that *ut* in line 26 introduces, not another independent wish, but a consecutive clause announced by *sic* (25: *sic* goes *not* with *haerentis* but with
vincire). More often, they have failed to see that *utinam vincire velles* is
something very different from *vellem vincires*: the former (which is Propertius' text) expresses the poet's unrealizable wish (imperfect subjunctive)
that Cynthia *on her pàrt* felt desire to chain them both together forever.
The Latin form (equivalent in meaning to "contrary to fact") implies the
sad knowledge that she actually does *not* foster such a wish. There is no
difficulty in our couplet if we understand it according to the precise rules
of Latin grammar.[12]

The following distich (27/28), presenting a realizable wish, or rather
an exhortation (present subjunctive), should not be taken to say the same

as the foregoing with its stress on never-ending love (cf. *ut numquam sol-
veret*, 26). I take it to refer not so much to the lifelong faithfulness of
pigeons as to the other characteristic ascribed to these birds: their erotic
passion, as supposedly expressed through continuous kissing[13] (cf. Propertius' express appreciation of this activity in lines 9/10). *Coniugium*, then,
refers to physical union rather than monogamy.

My interpretation, which distinguishes between vain hope for Cynthia's indissoluble, everlasting love (25/26), on the one hand, and, on the
other, a realizable desire for her passionate love (27/28), is confirmed by
the third distich (29/30), which, on a general level, claims that the one
should not be without the other: the words *vesani . . . amoris* (29) take up
the pigeons' exemplary passion, while the words *errat, qui finem . . . quaerit* refer back to the idea of the eternal chain.

But there is more in our distich than a mere synthesis of the two ideas.
The general phrasing *errat, qui* already points to the fact that the speaker is
in the possession of correct knowledge and is able to judge the errors of
human beings, almost like the philosophical *sapiens*. This feature comes
out more strongly in the pentameter (30), where the *verus amor* is defined.
Our speaker indeed knows the truth of love. It is not, however, the dry
and lifeless truth of moral philosophy. On the contrary: *verus amor* (30)
takes up *vesani . . . amoris* (29, stressed by alliteration). *True* love is *mad*
love,[14] which "does *not* know any measure or moderation"! Propertius'
"philosophy" of love, which is life's essence, dismisses the philosophical
ideal of temperate love because it lacks the "moral" quality of lifelong
faithfulness.

While lines 25–30 amount to a judgment on Cynthia's attitude, lines
31–36 show Propertius himself in agreement with the law of true love. As
in 2.1 (65–70), he again chooses the form of an *adynaton* to point to the
unchangeable loyalty of his own love: the laws of nature would have to be
overthrown before he would be able "to transfer my pains". Pains, *dolores*,
is the essence of his love's experience (in spite of *me felicem*, 15.1) and of his
poetry as he has already told Ponticus (1.7.7). But, as he has already told
his censurer when disappointed for the first time (cf. *mutare calores, translato . . . servitio*, 1.12.17ff.), to find release by turning to another woman is
not a possibility open to him.

The result of his thoughts on the eternal duration of love is once more
pessimistic. When the circle is closed (25/26 ~ 35/36), his futile wish for
her eternal love is answered by a statement of his own eternal faith: *huius
ero vivus, mortuus huius ero*—another of those precise coinings into which
he sometimes presses the essence of his experience. We find him again in
that lonely isolation that has characterized him from the beginning (see
Chapters I and II above). When comparing himself with Cynthia he finds
more that points to separation than to lasting unity. The resulting despair

is indicated by the fact that the elated "you", which originated from the recollection of his tarrying kisses (10), ends with the introduction of wishful thinking about their love's future. From the beloved's imagined presence and from direct address to her, he is thrown back upon himself and monologue (from 31 onward it is "she" again, cf. *huius*, 36). His sense of happiness (*o me felicem*) is heightened not only by the ever-present knowledge of death (11–24), but even more by the awareness of Cynthia's fickleness (25–36).

Taken as a whole, lines 25–36 broaden further the elegy's scope by introducing the future as a touchstone for the two lovers' different attitudes to their love and to each other. Propertius' tragic happiness receives a new dimension.

For a last time the elegy's view is broadened (37–48) as the lover reflects on the true purpose and meaning of life (*vitae*, 38; *qualem . . . vitam*, 41; *haec*, 47; cf. *vitae*, 49), and on what the word "immortality" truly means for human beings: not the allegedly "eternal" glory achieved through the crimes of warfare, but rather the innocent, intense dedication of a lover's life. If all men were motivated like Propertius and desired this kind of life (*qualem si cuncti cuperent decurrere vitam*, 41), one would not now have to face the cruel and murderous results of Rome's bellicose history (43–46). This view, which makes Propertius' life a potential model for all (*cuncti*) to strive after, but makes Roman history a series of pollutions, is so shattering to the Augustan poetic ideal, that Rothstein, sensing some of the implications, apparently felt lost. He saw in this passage homage to Augustus(!), but nevertheless warned against taking the argument seriously. In fact, blindness towards Propertius' position continues to prevent interpreters from seeing the section's unity of thought. I hope in the three preceding chapters to have laid a foundation for understanding the passage in itself and in the context of elegy 2.15. I shall draw on this foundation in the commentary that follows.

Lines 37/38 offer a reevaluation of common notions about time, according to which a long life is a desirable life. Propertius replaces length by meaningfulness, i.e., by the use which is made of time.[15] Measured by this standard, such nights as the one described in our poem (here line 37 picks up line 10) can make a year of his life long, i.e., completely fulfilled. If such a woman (*haec*) grants *many* such nights, Propertius will receive more fulfillment than is usually contained in a human lifetime: through[16] them, he will become *immortalis*. As in 1.12 (lines 11–14), man's relation to time serves as an indicator of his condition. In 2.15, Propertius is even playful and haughty when he compares his own high demands to "anyone's" concept of becoming even a god by only *one* night (*nocte una*)—Propertius himself started with the plural (*talis noctes*). In spite of his peculiar way of measuring time by the intensity of lovers' nights, we should not wrongly assume that his immortality can be founded on a small number of them (39/40)!

Line 41 brings us the generalization from *mihi* (37)—via *quivis*, 40—to *cuncti*, which hypothetically (*si*) sets Propertius' understanding of life (*qualem . . . vitam*) and of human immortality as a model to all mankind. The pentameter (42) merely explicates: *et pressi multo membra iacere mero*. The language (*pressi multo . . . mero*) reappears in a later poem (*multo mentem vincire Lyaeo*, 3.5.21), with the same implications. Strong alcohol, as we found in our analysis of that poem (Chapter VIII) is conceived of as subduing the violent and criminal nature of Promethean man. The phrasing also reminds us of the contrast between the things which delight (*iuvet*, 2.34.59ff., see Chapter VII above) Vergil and Propertius: *hesternis positum languere corollis* (essentially identical with 2.15.42) for the latter, but for the former, "to be able to sing of Caesar's brave ships" and of Actium—an event which in the terms of 2.15 is an instance of the cruelty (*crudele*) and war (*bellica navis*) which receive wholesale condemnation in 2.15.43ff. Propertius' life-style would have prevented the drowning (killing) of Roman men at Actium, *nec nostra Actiacum verteret ossa mare* (2.15.44). If there should still be any doubt that Propertius' opposition to Vergil is primarily directed not against his writing of un-Callimachean epic but against his poem's connection with war, especially with contemporary or recent civil war, this doubt should be dispelled by 2.15: it is not form but content (the historical event Actium) that drives Propertius away.

The close relationship between 2.15, 2.34 and 3.5 (one may also compare 2.1 and others) raises the question whether 2.15, by mentioning Actium and civil war, does not also imply a more definite judgment on Rome's master himself[17]—comparable perhaps to the denunciation of a Parthian expedition found in 3.5. Chapter VIII has argued that Augustus is by no means excepted from the poet's condemnation of Promethean man, so that for us the name Actium does not necessarily, as it did to Rothstein and others, strike a note of homage. It reminds us of Octavian's role as a participant in civil strife, even presents him as warlord and victor, the one who declared the war and had come "across the vast sea in search of his enemy to join arms" (to use Propertius' language of 3.5.11/12) with him or, rather, her.

Perhaps a mere mention of Actium as the last of the regrettable events of civil war is harmless in itself, especially so since royal propaganda officially favored civil peace over war.[18] But for one who lies with his limbs heavy from much wine (42) to call the deaths of Actium regrettable, and even avoidable (*nec . . . verteret*), leaves no room for the official version of Actium as a combined act of national heroism, one which saved Rome by extinguishing the threat from the East posed by an oriental queen and a profligate former triumvir, who, as a favorite slave, was wax in the hands of her political ambitions . . . On the contrary, if Propertius here (as elsewhere) presents himself as sluggish from too much undiluted wine (42), he must, so far as the two opponents at Actium are concerned, be linked to Antony rather than Octavian. He himself once characterizes Antony as "a tongue continuously buried in wine" (*assiduo lingua sepulta mero*, 3.11.56),[19] hinting at the official propaganda,[20] the excesses of which are still echoed by writers as late as Pliny the Elder (*Nat. Hist.* 14.147f.) and Seneca the Younger. The latter writes (*Ep. ad Lucilium* 83.25): *M. Antonium . . . quae alia res perdidit et in externos mores ac vitia non Romana traiecit quam ebrietas nec minor vino Cleopatrae amor?* "What else destroyed M. Antonius and made him accept outlandish customs and un-Roman vices, except his drunkenness and, no less than the wine, his love for Cleopatra?" This un-Roman profligate is similar to Propertius, not only in his surrender to wine (which the poet, however, ranks as a moral achievement: it keeps man from murdering his fellow man), but also in his surrender to the beloved woman (an act which, however un-Roman, is to the poet another instance of peace not won through arms). Is it possible, we must ask now, that Propertius occasionally dresses his rejection of the Zeitgeist in the garb of Antony as he was pictured in official propaganda? If, for a moment, my reader credits my reasons and allows me to answer the question positively,[21] I should like to point out a consequence which can confirm an interpretation offered earlier but which could not be introduced at that time (Chapter VII above). The syncrisis of Propertius and Vergil (2.34.59ff.), a passage whose close relation to 2.15.41ff. has struck us already, would make even more sense if Vergil, happy to sing of Octavian's brave ships and the battle of Actium, i.e., to be the partisan of Octavian, is contrasted with Propertius the follower of Antony, i.e., imitator of Antony's alleged effeminate life-style, lying "relaxed among yesterday's garlands", 2.34.59. (The other characteristic of Propertius, "whom the unfailing god [of love] touched with his shot through to the bones", 34.60, likewise applies to Antony.) Having, as a poet, no official support and no influential public to welcome his untimely message, Propertius will find it enormously helpful if he can capitalize upon the widely publicized contrast of Octavian and Antony, of Roman and un-Roman behavior. This loan works in two ways. First, it makes it easier for him to define his own dissenter's position in the language of his time; he has only to make sure to dissociate himself from the third element (beside wine and love) in the official picture of Antony, the alleged thirst for blood (on which Seneca also dwells in the above-mentioned passage). Here Propertius, as we saw, finds a place for his own thesis that love, as a peace not won through arms, is (like wine) innocent of the crimes of warfare—a thesis which includes a tacit condemnation of the Emperor. Secondly, the chances for being heard at all are better if he expresses himself in categories which have already been widely publicized and are common knowledge. If we see behind the different joys of Propertius and Vergil in 2.34.59ff. the opposing "models" Antony and Octavian, we can better realize how total Propertius' refusal of the Zeitgeist is to be taken as being.[22]

My reader will ask for further evidence, and a passage where Propertius indicates an at least partial identification of himself with Antony. In reply, I would refer him to elegy 2.16.[23] It repeats a situation of the *Monobiblos* (1.8) insofar as the *praetor*, whom Cynthia then almost followed to Illyria (before, as Propertius boasted, being prevented by the poet's songs from leaving Rome), has come back and now ranks first in Cynthia's favor. Propertius deplores Cynthia's corruptness, but also (31ff.) reflects upon his own disgraceful inability to free himself from a humiliating attachment or at least return to his usual daily schedule. He then proceeds to answer a fictitious critic, who is perhaps himself:

> "But you ought to be ashamed!"[24] Certainly, so I ought—except
>   perhaps that, so they say,
>   a disgraceful love usually shows itself to be deaf:
> look (for instance) at the leader who with an empty roar lately filled
>   the sea near Actium with doomed soldiers:
> his infamous love ordered this man to turn his ships and take to flight
>   and to search for an escape at the end of the world.
> This is Caesar's manliness, and Caesar's glory is this:
>   with his victorious hand, he laid war to rest.   (2.16.35–42)

Readings different from OCT: exclamation mark after *at pudeat*, 35; em dash only after *certe, pudeat*; colon at the end of line 36.

There can be no doubt that Propertius' own *turpis amor* (36) for Cynthia is paralleled with Antony's *infamis amor* (39) for Cleopatra. What surprises us is that Antony is *not* chosen *by the critic* as a deterrent example to warn Propertius of his disastrous future. Antony is *Propertius' own* example to show the critic that any attempt to interfere with abject love by appealing to a sense of shame is useless. Antony is the model that explains Propertius' case! Potentially, Propertius, too, after an empty roar (= his poems), may possibly leave his troops (i.e., his honor) at the mercy of his opponent, himself following his abject love whatever humiliation it leads to— just as Antony deserted the battle of Actium to follow Cleopatra in her flight.[25]

Antony's defeat and flight is Caesar's manliness (41)—this is the other side of the coin.[26] But the praise, though in accord with the official evaluation, is dubious. Propertius is no admirer of manliness but rather sympathizes with unmanly surrender to love. Does the mention of Caesar's *clementia* (42) perhaps reveal Propertius' request for tolerance (it is Propertius who has survived to experience *clementia*, not Antony)? Possibly, but my reasons are too weak to allow me to attach yet another unproven interpretation to the much-vexed lines 41/42. I can point, however, to the parallel at 3.22.22, which is likewise far from sincere or deeply felt.[27]

The evidence of 2.16.35ff. appears, to my eye, certain enough to prove that Propertius occasionally[28] does liken himself to Antony. The fact alone is sufficient to give additional support to the interpretation of 2.34.59f., offered in Chapter VI, as well as to allow the name of Actium in 2.15.44 to play a similarly ambiguous role—ambiguous in that official Augustan and Propertius' own evaluation of the motives behind the event do not necessarily go together. The same ambiguous role is played by Augustus' Parthian expedition elsewhere, especially in 3.4 and 5.

I now return to the third section of elegy 2.15. If all men would pursue the Propertian life, Actium could have been avoided (44), and Rome would not have become tired of letting her hair down in mourning for her own triumphs (45f.), i.e., triumphs over herself. (Instead of enemies—or: no people at all—Romans were the victims of Roman attacks.) The language is, though more general (*totiens*), close to 1.22.3ff., which picks out Perusia (*Perusina . . . sepulchra*) as a symbol for the victims of civil war,

> Italiae duris funera temporibus,
> cum Romana suos egit discordia civis . . .

Both passages view the civil war from the viewpoint of the victims and do not allow for a proud victor. Poem 1.22 (6–8) refers to a source of special sorrow for the poet: a close relative of his had been murdered after having fought against Octavian for the cause of L. Antonius at Perusia (see Chapter V). Is it possible that the personal sorrow which moulded the outlook of his youth is at least partially responsible for his later judgment on the opponents at Actium? It is not difficult to see how an early antipathy towards Octavian (and sympathy for Antony?), originating in family sorrow (both political and human), may have led, under the influence of later dedication to Cynthia and his persistent rejection of the Augustan Zeitgeist, to an even closer feeling of identification with Octavian's silenced opponent. Like Propertius, Antony had given away his honor for his love; he had even given up his own life upon receiving the (false) news of Cleopatra's death. Doubtless there was more than one thing about Antony that would strike a chord in Propertius.

On the other hand, although Antony and Octavian have negative qualities in common, especially a reckless drive for power, Octavian's character has little to offer in compensation that would make him appear *humanus*[29] in the eyes of a Propertius. Although in his own time the victor of Actium receives all the glory and all the praise (because right is might, and the might is all his), the attitude of future generations, i.e., history, is less certain. Will they judge him and his career according to his own standards of glory (founded on the defeat of others) and peace (won through arms), or will his drive for power seem to put him into the same class as his opponent—another Marius or Iugurtha (cf. 3.5.16)?

One thing at any rate is certain (*certe*, 47): so far as Propertius' own life and "career" (*haec*) are concerned, later generations (*minores*) will *not* feel like withholding their praise (*poterunt laudare*)—and in doing so, they will judge according to right and merit (*merito*)! "For (*asyndeton*) our goblets (i.e., my life as a lover and banqueter) have not insulted any gods (48)"— as have the victories of Romans over Romans at Actium, Perusia, etc.

I must again ask my reader's pardon for having dwelt so long on so few lines. But this was necessary in order to secure them the meaning intended by their author. *Pocula nostra* should never have been understood as a contrast to Antony's drunkenness, as Augustan Interpretation understands them still today owing to the false belief that mentioning Actium must mean praising Augustus, and that mentioning goblets must hence point to his drunken opponent Antony.[30] If either of the two is able to strike a sympathetic chord in our poet, then rather Antony than Augustus. As scholars, we should free ourselves from the aftermath of Augustan propaganda. The truth is that *pocula nostra*, with *nostra* meaning "my" (or perhaps "Cynthia's and mine"), points by way of summary to the *vita Propertiana* (cf. *qualem . . . vitam*, 41), and this is opposed to both Augustus' and Antony's[31] careers, as it is to those of all who employ *ferrum crudele* and *bellica navis* (43) for achieving their goals. The *vita Propertiana*, applied to *cuncti*, may be an Epicurean *utopia*, considering man's Promethean origin (and Propertius would be the last to deny it), but its author is convinced that, in the judgment of history, he will be found innocent of the crimes of his time. This is a proud conviction, the more so if we compare it to the humiliation in the face of which it was formulated.

Understood correctly, the section's last distich (47/48) maintains the innocence of Propertius' life, and thus, at the end of the circular movement of thought, confirms from another viewpoint the basic correctness of the thesis about true longevity and true immortality developed in the first two distichs (37–40; *pocula nostra* in 48 and *talis noctes* in 37—the latter picked up by *qualem . . . vitam*, 41, and complemented by line 42—correspond to each other, being the two aspects of Propertian life). In between (41–46), Propertius' life as a lover is contrasted with, and even seen as an alternative to, Rome's civil war and its deadly peak at Actium. The section as a whole, then, is about the meaningful life: it distinguishes true human immortality, the measure of which is time dedicated to love, from the false afterlife of military glory as aspired to by the participants in Rome's civil war.[32]

This result is important for my understanding of Propertius in two respects:

(a) It shows that his dissent from the Augustan Zeitgeist (cf. Section

A, chapters VI–VIII above) can be integrated into the picture of his love when he wants to define his love against a broader background and in a more general setting—just as the many encounters with his environment described in the *Monobiblos* all helped him, in one way or another, to see his own situation in focus.

(b) It shows that it was appropriate for me to try in Part One of this book to see Propertius as basically defined by two complexes (presented in proem and epilogue of the *Monobiblos*), Cynthia and Perusia, experience of love and of war. Both complexes undergo surface modifications in later years (Cynthia's inaccessibility moves from haughtiness to fickleness; Perusia is followed by Actium and the developing pax Augusta), but both continue to make up the constellation in relation to which Propertius must be seen if we want to understand him.

Having dealt with the external, non-Propertian world, and having found it lacking and guilty, the poet returns to the inner circle of his own world, into which only one person beside himself is admitted: the beloved "you" (the grammatical person switches again from third to second in the elegy's last three distichs, lines 49–54). Against the background of the wrong life described in the preceding lines, the exhortation not to neglect the fruit of life, *fructum . . . vitae* (49), now carries with it the weight of certified truth, and it receives urgency both from the *tu* and from the *modo* that stresses the imperative's function and, above all, from the time indication "as long as it is daylight" (*dum lucet*), which seems to indicate that night is within sight, i.e., the *nox longa* (24) of death, as the passing day (*lucet*) is the day that will not return, *nec reditura dies* (24).

It is evident that the last section intends to return to the immediate experience of love from which the first section had set out. The long way traveled by the poet's thoughts in this elegy has in the end confirmed the position expressed in the opening distichs, both in its intensity and in its innocence. Thus, the kisses of the initial section (10) find a pendant in the kisses of the last (50)—though with a significant difference: whereas the lover's kisses the night before could tarry (*quantum / oscula sunt . . . morata . . . !*), his present hortation betrays haste. There is the danger that the lovers will be overtaken by death (cf. *dum lucet*) before realizing how tiny even the full share of love allotted to them is: *omnia si dederis oscula, pauca dabis!*

Thus, the last two distichs are solely dedicated to heightening the consciousness of love in the beloved by giving her an awareness of death. The literary topos comparing human life to that of leaves is here given a pointed precision: flowers or branches for wreaths are plucked at the time of their full blossom or freshness to rejoice the human eye. But being plucked is the beginning of their death, and the banqueters can actually see the wreaths wither and the petals fall in the course of the night. Propertius bids Cynthia turn her eyes to this decay (*quae passim calathis strata natare vides*, 52) with the same directness he had used earlier in pointing to the bloom of her own youth (21/22). Death has visibly been present since the beginning of the night, and the lovers themselves, although they are expressing life's highest self-manifestation through their love, may already be bound to meet their fate tomorrow.[33] One may say that the end of our elegy, by the intensity with which it addresses and entreats the beloved, reaches the same degree of vividness and imaginative reality as the opening section.

It remains to point out the scheme of the elegy's structure:

I 1–10:   Stammering, incomplete account of a night of love.   5D
II 11–24: Eyesight and nudity: love in the face of death.   7D
III 25–36: Propertius' unfulfilled desire for an everlasting union.   6D
IV 37–48: The true and the false way of seeking immortality: 6D
           Propertius' peace of love and Rome's civil wars.
V 49–54:   A call for living the right life.   3D

As usually, we find that Propertius does not feel any compulsion towards exact formal balance.[34] Sections III and IV adhere to the prevailing movement in 6D units, and even the epilogue V seems to confirm the existence of such a unit by offering exactly half its size (3D). The first and second sections only approximate the general pattern, by virtue of counting, respectively, one distich too few and one too many.

This skeletal structure can even clarify certain details of our earlier interpretations. Elegy 2.15 is not just a double version of 2.14, but is a complex presentation of Propertius' love, a single survey, including many facets, which thus far have been seen separately: the irrational nature of the passion of his love, which seems to be beyond words; its exposure to Cynthia's fickleness and to the decay of human nature in general; its innocence and its opposition to the murderous forces in contemporary politics; its utter homelessness and awareness of death. These features unfold the tragic background implicit in a rare cry of Propertian happiness.

AGGRESSIVE SELF-PRESERVATION: FROM CYNTHIA TO CLEOPATRA

The interpretation of elegy 2.15 in Chapter IX has, I believe, justified the section subtitle "Love: A Peace Not Won through Arms". This definition comes to the poet whenever he tries to express his love in categories drawn from his contemporary environment. Basically, we face the same process of *definitio e contrario* that we observed in the *Monobiblos* often enough to make it a primary element in our overall interpretation of Propertius (perhaps any human being tends to become known to himself by formulating the repercussions he feels resulting from encounters with the world around him). By the time of Book 2 the environment has, as we said, both changed and remained the same: Cynthia's haughtiness (1.1) has yielded to fickleness—but she remains a characteristically unaccountable factor in Propertius' life. And the cruel victor of Perusia (1.22) has, since Actium, evolved into the self-appointed lord of "peace"—while continuing characteristically to pose a threat to the uncomplying individual's freedom. On the whole, Propertius has achieved great precision in defining his situation: unconditionally dedicated to a hopeless love, he feels further endangered by society's contempt as well as by the régime's demand for political poetry.

As elegy 2.15 shows once more, the nature of the surrounding world and of Promethean man confirms Propertius in his conviction that his way of life is right—so much so that his environment can be worked into the picture of his love and serve as an effective negative background and setting. But, we may ask, can he endure the situation in which he himself is always on the defensive (and his poetry a *turpis . . . liber*, 2.3.4) when, morally, it is the other side which should be in this situation? In Chapters VI to VIII, I described his technique of first pretending to grant the régime the grandeur it demands but then retracting his grant and revealing his own standards. This procedure implies, at least temporarily, a submissiveness towards the powerful which is irreconcilable with moral superiority. But if both his unyielding loyalty to his love and his abstinence from the crimes of his time speak in his favor, why should he not now and then take the offensive and interpret the facts of history and Rome's political scenery so as to support *his* standpoint? He will never be in a position where he can speak completely openly for long and drop all ambiguity. But he can turn the tables on Rome's official standards and virtues so long as he leaves room for a surface understanding that is at least benevolent towards the Emperor.

The most conspicuous such counterattack of his is contained in elegy 3.11. It, too, alludes to the notion suggested in 2.16, but implicit also in 2.34 and elsewhere, that Cynthia is to Propertius what Cleopatra is to Antony. If further instances can be added of men who have been dominated by women, his own case will lose its allegedly abnormal character—the suggestion of un-Roman "unmanliness"—and the contemporary ideal of Roman virtue insensitive to weaknesses like love will implicitly lose its monopoly. Elegy 3.11 displays the usual ambiguity. Both views are offered, but in the fashion for which we have ascertained elegy 2.34 as a methodological precedent (Chapter VII): the beginning—a refutation of yet another censurer—clearly measures by Propertian standards; but the end admonishes an anonymous Roman sailor to show gratitude to Augustus for his victory at Actium. Somewhere in between the surface emphasis changes, from the Propertian to the Augustan point of view. There are two ways to look at things.[1]

> Why are you astonished if a woman governs my life
>   and leads me (a man!) captive to be her bond servant,
> and why do you unfairly raise shameful charges of cowardice against
>   me
>   because (you say) I cannot break the yoke and tear the chains? (3.11.1–4)

The blame is similar to that in 1.12.1ff. (discussed in our first chapter), but the answer is completely different. In 1.12, Propertius denied the "facts" of the charge. In 2.16, we recall, the charge of *turpis amor* was acknowledged, but answered by pointing at Antony's *infamis amor* (2.16.39). But already in 2.30 he has struck back by denying that his being defeated by love is something abnormal (*communis culpae cur reus unus agor?* line 32). This line of defense, or rather: of attack, is also pursued in 3.11. The phrase *quid mirare* clearly indicates that there is nothing astonishing in Propertius' condition, but rather in his faultfinder's way of thinking. This is confirmed by lines 5–8 (= 2D), where Propertius judges his censurer to be inexperienced (as he himself once was) in human affairs: he should *learn* fear from Propertius' example: *tu nunc exemplo disce timere meo!* Propertius himself no longer claims to be master over his condition, to know better than others when and what to fear (*timere*, 8) ⟨and perhaps to avoid⟩ like the experienced (*vulneribus*) soldier (*metum*, 6), and the experienced (*praesagit*) sailor (*mortem*, 5).[2]

There follow examples. Medea put fire-breathing bulls to the yoke, sowed the seed of the dragon teeth, and removed the threat posed by the dragon—all so that Jason could take the golden fleece to Iolcus and regain his father's throne—a woman handling the tasks which properly belonged to her protégé (9–12, 2D).

Penthesilea the Amazon dared (*ausa*) attack the Greek ships; defeated, she won a victory over her conquerer, the hero of heroes, Achilles (*vicit victorem . . . virum*)—through the beauty which she possessed still in death (13–16, 2D).

Queen Omphale of Lydia was so beautiful that the victorious Heracles, who had pacified the *world* and set up his trophies in the far west (Gibraltar; *qui pacato statuisset in orbe columnas*), helped her spin wool— with his warrior's hands (*dura . . . manu*) (17–20, 2D)!

Semiramis built the strong city and citadel of Babylon and bade Bactra bow its head to her power: just as, we recall from line 2, Cynthia has extended her jurisdiction over Propertius (21–26, 3D).

> ⟨I better say no more.⟩ For why shall *I* drag heroes, why *I* drag gods
> into court?
>   (Jove disgraces himself and his house!)
> Why the woman, who lately brought disgrace upon our arms,
>   and—a woman who looked for lovers among her own servants!—
> demanded as the price of her obscene marriage the walls of Rome
>   and the senators, led as bond servants under her power?

> Nam quid ego heroas, quid raptem in crimina divos?
>   (Iuppiter infamat seque suamque domum!)
> Quid, modo quae nostris opprobria vexerit armis
>   et, famulos inter femina trita suos,
> coniugis obsceni pretium Romana poposcit
>   moenia et addictos in sua regna Patres?   (27–32 = 3D)

The examples of Medea, Penthesilea, Omphale, Semiramis have, in varying ways, confirmed Propertius' answer to his censurer: there is no cowardice and nothing astonishing or abnormal in his surrender to Cynthia, because enough instances are known, in which women ruled not only unimportant figures like poets, but held sway over undefeated warriors (Achilles, Heracles), handled a man's affairs (Jason), acted as successful statesmen (Babylon), even bade other countries bow to their own (as Semiramis bade Bactra). Indeed, it is so embarrassing (for the faultfinder, of course, not for Propertius!) to see how many men have succumbed to women, that our defendant prefers not to continue his enumeration (27): why should *he* (*ego* is stressed) lend his hand to exposing (still more) heroes and even gods to such *crimina* (27) as were unjustly raised by his Philistine critic against him (*crimina . . . mihi turpia fingis*, 3)? Not to mention the "worst": Jove himself, god of gods, ruins his family's reputation (*infamat . . . suam . . . domum*, 28)![3] The last instance almost declares male defeat through love and male subjugation to female rule a cosmic law, one whose universal character makes one feel sorry for our faultfinder: what foundation is left for his morality?

So far, we seem to have witnessed a splendid hoax, practiced by a self-confident, superior Propertius upon the hypocritical reproaches of contemporary moralists, similar in mood to the opening of 2.30:

> Ista senes licet accusent convivia duri . . .

The line of the poet's argument has been so clear thus far that we are completely taken by surprise when the third *quid* (29) in a series turns out not to continue its two antecedents (in 27), as our reading eyes naturally expect it to do (and my translation wrongly suggests), but apparently means something like "why mention her, who . . . ?" After a group of able and dominating women (admired rather than blamed by the poet, cf. *honorem*, 17), and after a series of male examples (blamable perhaps to the censurer's eye, not the poet's: *heroas, divos, Iuppiter*), it appears strange that the *woman* shall be considered a possible object of *crimina*; even more strange that the poet allows her man (*coniugis*) to share the blame (*obsceni*, 31)—has Propertius not been on an excusing mission for himself, the man, rather than on an accusing one? We do not see how the way in which he presents this new instance of male subordination under female rule can continue Propertius' defense—especially if we regard the moral accents: *opprobria, trita, obsceni, Romana poposcit moenia* . . . Is Propertius torpedoing his own argument? Has he suddenly changed sides and accepted his censurer's terms? Is it possible that he cannot go on in the way he wished (and his argument demands), because his final example, if pursued along the same lines as its forerunners, would involve unwelcome consequences?

The question to ask, then, is: "What is so special about this example?" And the answer must be: (a) with it, he has moved from myth and ancient oriental history into the field of recent Roman history (*modo*, 29, *Romana*, 31), of which (b) there already exists an official contemporary evaluation, not to say version, which the poet feels called upon not to contradict but rather to support. This is why he refrains from subsuming the couple in question under the powerful law of *nature* (which was first invoked to explain and defend the poet's own situation), but rather changes his viewpoint (*nostris* . . . *armis*, 29) in the middle of an argument[4] and joins the official *moral* condemnation of the two (thus running the risk of allowing his own liaison to be judged in the same way!).

Even without knowing Propertius' affinity to Antony as expressed, e.g., in elegy 2.16, my reader, familiar with the strict logical structure favored by Propertius, will be reluctant to believe that in 3.11 the poet carelessly ran his argument aground; rather, he would assume that an open break in the train of thought serves as a hint that from this point on open thought (and speech) stops and disguise begins. (For we cannot accept the alternative that from now on the poet rejects his own initial standpoint!) We are thus invited to see whether the original argument continues under the new surface of political adulation. Elegy 3.11, then, is similar to elegy 2.10 (as interpreted in Chapter VI above) in that it contains two contradicting viewpoints; but it is much more impertinent than 2.10 insofar as in its first part it takes the time to establish the poet's private position as a natural one, before switching to the viewpoint of public-patriotic "morality". In this latter aspect, it resembles 2.34, which first degrades epic poet Lynceus before "praising" Vergil's epic (see Chapter VII). If in the second half the patriotic and moral viewpoint ("*our* arms", 29) goes unchallenged and is even embellished, this does not of course mean that the poet shares it.[5] His own moral position has always been that responsibility towards the beloved ranks higher than responsibility towards the régime, or, as he once told Tullus when he refused to desert Cynthia and join him on his uncle's pro-Octavian mission: "*You* set out to march in your uncle's entourage; *for you* have never yielded to *amor* but always concerned yourself with *armata patria*" (1.6.21/22). The same contrast of (the censurer's) youthful interest in public standards and (Propertius') mature dedication (submission) to the beloved appears also in 3.11 (*ego praeterita . . . iuventa* 7, and *tu nunc* 8).

The surface meaning of lines 29–32, then, is simple. They take seriously the "infamy" implied in erotic dependence (*Iuppiter infamat se*, 28, was intended by Propertius to be not too serious in tone), and reproduce the standpoint of official propaganda: to win Cleopatra's love, Antony even traded in his fatherland and allowed her to wage war against Rome. To understand the supposed outrage fully, one must consider the male chauvinist ingredient in Roman political thinking. The point in our passage is that a woman who selects her own lovers from the flock of her slaves (30) and even includes a Roman citizen in this group (31) annihilates the traditional position of the Roman *pater familias* by inventing a female counterpart to it. But the worst possible insult is her next step. By fighting against Rome she showed her desire to incorporate the whole sacrosanct set of Roman *Patres* (sc., *conscriptos*) like slaves into that kingdom of hers (*addictos in sua regna Patres*, 32). We see that a supposed military threat can be defined as an attempt to deprive Rome of her (or rather *his*!) virility. Horace (C. 1.37; *Ep.* 9.11f.) and Vergil (*Aen.* 8.688) confirm this kind of sexist language.

It is this official phrasing and thinking on which Propertius plays. For to him, Cleopatra indeed has done to Rome just what Cynthia does to Propertius. The phrase used of Cynthia—*trahit addictum sub sua iura virum* (2)—was clearly chosen with regard to and as a preparation for the characterization of Cleopatra: *poposcit . . . addictos in sua regna Patres.*[6] The noun *femina* (1) instead of the name *Cynthia* also points to male-oriented Roman thinking. Indeed, we may say that Propertius' aggressive self-defense has, at the time of elegy 3.11, expanded its scope *from Cynthia to Cleopatra*—although he may not say so aloud. The conclusion his reader is asked to draw silently is well prepared logically: what has happened to Propertius happened also to Antony and almost happened to Rome as well. It can now be seen that Semiramis, the successful female statesman and conquerer (no dominated lover is mentioned in her case), must have been introduced (21ff.) to broaden the view from private (erotic) to public (political) rule exercised by women over men, thus preparing the way for Cleopatra's political challenge to Rome. For when we compare the scope of 3.11 with that of 2.16, we see that Cleopatra's role has been widened from that of a woman controlling the dependent Antony to that of a woman who dares to face Rome. Propertius, correspondingly, can implicitly compare himself not only to Antony but also to threatened Rome herself (58). If, then, at 29ff. we ignore the break in the surface direction of Propertius' argument and continue the sense of lines 1–28, we find him saying that there is nothing astonishing (cf. *quid mirare*, 1) in subjugation to (or by) a woman, since, apart from the cases already mentioned, this has recently (*modo*, 29) happened to a Roman *triumvir*, and would have happened to Rome itself and its senators if this other woman had only had her own way . . .

The following apostrophe to a guilty Alexandria (33ff.) interrupts the argument ("guilty Cleopatra!" is what we expect, knowing of her men-enslaving role in Roman politics), but it appears in place to guarantee the surface patriotism and anti-Egyptian tone of the continuation of our elegy. From Cleopatra's fight against Rome at Actium in 31 B.C., Propertius now goes back seventeen years to Pompey's assassination on the shores of Egypt in 48 B.C.—another inextinguishable disgrace (*notam*, 36 ~ *opprobria*, 29) for Rome (*tollet nulla dies hanc tibi, Roma, notam*). Indeed, it would have been better for Pompey if he had died on his sickbed near Naples in 50

B.C. (37), or bowed his head to C. J. Caesar, his father-in-law (*si socero colla daturus eras*, 38), instead of having it cut off by king Ptolemaeus' Secretaries (33–38, 3D).

From Pompey, the elegy returns to the impertinence of Cleopatra facing Rome's fleet near Actium—i.e., it again swiftly crosses and supersedes the same period of seventeen years. Why was Pompey mentioned? Is he so important to Propertius' argument? But he is neither pro-Octavian nor a slave to a woman. Did Propertius perhaps just want to utter another accusation against Egypt in order to give geographical background to the evil character of Cleopatra? This may suffice as a surface explanation. But what is the reader to make of *totiens*, 34? To fill the notion of "so often" with meaning, more than two instances (Pompey's assassination, the battle of Actium) are required.

At this point, I believe, Propertius provides the reader who looks deeper than the surface with an argument *ex silentio*, which hardly any contemporary of his could overlook when he considered Rome's dealings with Egypt: had there been no event, that would be worth mentioning in the context of our elegy, between Pompey's assassination in 48 B.C. and the defeat inflicted on Cleopatra (and Antony) by Octavian in 31 B.C.? Of course there had been, and its protagonist is, so to speak, the missing link between Pompey (who was murdered when he fled from him) and Octavian (who officially called himself his son): C. J. Caesar! Caesar has just been mentioned by Propertius (although not by name), at the end of the passage on Egypt's never extinguishable guilt: he is the father-in-law of Pompey mentioned in line 38. And his liaison with Cleopatra was, as every contemporary knew, not too dissimilar to Antony's.[7] Would all the lines on Rome's disgrace (33–38) not be more suitably dedicated to Caesar and Cleopatra than to Pompey and Alexandria? Two further things should be noted: (1) When Caesar, after Pompey's assassination, came to Egypt, he fell so deeply in love with Cleopatra and under her spell that he not only reinstated her as queen into her former rights, but also, when being besieged with her in Alexandria in the winter of 48/47 B.C., was himself on the brink of having to give up Rome, political career, and even his physical existence. (2) From that time on until Caesar's death, Cleopatra had her residence in Rome, in the *horti Caesaris*. Both issues are less important for Propertius' attitude towards C. J. Caesar himself than for the feelings they evoke when viewed from the angle of elegy 3.11, i.e., of Octavian's propaganda against Antony and Cleopatra.

My reader will perhaps object that, although C. J. Caesar is mentioned in our poem, the two aspects of his relationship with Cleopatra stressed above are not. I would have to concede that they are not mentioned openly, but suggest that they are hinted at indirectly, in two passages the logical function of which I would otherwise find hard to explain.

(1) To evaluate the first passage, one should perhaps recognize that the traits of superiority ascribed to women of the past in lines 9–26, do reoccur in one way or another in Cleopatra's political career (29ff). I hesitate to pin them down in detail because there can be no real proof that Propertius had this or that event in mind. But, on the other hand, I cannot believe that the four women of the past, who must openly lend support to the poet's thesis (viz. that a man's subjugation to a woman is nothing extraordinary) do not foreshadow their great Egyptian successor about whom the poet admittedly must follow the official version.

Now Cleopatra can be compared to *Medea* (9–12) insofar as each of them handles her protégé's affairs. Medea uses her power to fight the obstacles that lie between Jason and his father's throne: she helps him to get the golden fleece; Cleopatra fights the obstacles that lie between Antony and his possession of Rome (it is she on whom, as the enemy, Rome officially declares war in 32 B.C., not Antony).

Penthesilea's daring (*ausa*, 13) fight against the camp of Greek ships (*ratis*, 14) finds a parallel in Cleopatra's daring (*ausa*,[8] 41) war against Rome and its Liburnian *rostra* (44; may one also compare the ablatives *sagittis*, 13, and *contis*, 44?). Cleopatra, too, after being defeated, *vicit victorem . . . virum* (16), although, this last time, not through her beauty (as does deceased Penthesilea). She deprived victor Octavian of his final victory, interfering with his plans for a triumph by her suicide (the latter mentioned by Propertius in lines 53f.).[9]

Cleopatra resembles *Semiramis* (21–26), as I have indicated already, in successfully safeguarding her kingdom through many years of Roman attempts to interfere with her country's independence. What Semiramis did to Bactra (*iussit et imperio subdere Bactra caput*, 26) is almost what Cleopatra tried to do to Rome (*Romana poposcit / moenia et addictos in sua regna Patres*, 31f.).

The comparison of Cleopatra's actions and those of Medea, Penthesilea, Semiramis does not result in an equation, but the similarities I mentioned appear striking enough to me to suggest the existence of a purposeful composition. What Propertius was kept from saying openly and directly about Cleopatra may be concluded indirectly from the features emphasized in lines 9–26. In this way, we can understand Cleopatra's dealings with Rome as yet another instance confirming Propertius' original thesis—in spite of the fact that, on the surface, i.e., the literal level, he sticks to the official version.

A problem presented by my interpretation is that, although I find Propertius' accounts of Medea, Penthesilea, Semiramis more or less confirmed and reflected in his narration about Cleopatra (29ff.), I do not find any echo of the Omphale story (17–20)—except as it applies to her affair with C. J. Caesar: as Omphale of Lydia teaches Heracles (who had pacified the world and set up his trophies at the far end of Spain) to spin wool, so Cleopatra teaches the victor of Gaul, Italy, and—just recently—Spain to be a prisoner of love, i.e., a servant to an oriental queen.

Now it is obvious that Propertius could not openly even mention the affair of Caesar and Cleopatra:[10] that would have been nothing short of making Caesar another abject Antony—to be precise: Antony's forerunner (which, after all, he was!). On the other hand, it would be the most beautiful confirmation of Propertius' original thesis that surrender of a man to a woman, even at the price of his career, is nothing extraordinary if the poet could include Caesar (especially in the situation of winter 48/47) among his examples. I herewith propose that he actually has included Caesar: by mentioning him apropos of Pompey's death (this is the deeper reason why Pompey is mentioned) and by the *argumentum ex silentio* which I explained above. For the emphasis he is not allowed to give, we are referred to the story of Omphale and Heracles. It must have been a deep satisfaction to the poet that his talent allowed him to enlist the Emperor's "father" as a witness for the defense against the charges he had to face from circles close to Augustus' moral restoration because of his all-consuming love for Cynthia.

Of the two resemblances mentioned between C. J. Caesar and Antony concerning their affairs with Cleopatra, I have so far dealt with the first: like Antony, Caesar, too, "forgot" and almost lost his political career in Rome during that winter of 48/47 which he spent with her in Alexandria. Propertius seems to refer to this fact through the myth of Omphale and Heracles as well as through the mention of Pompey and his father-in-law. Moreover, the Alexandrian War of 48/47 gives meaning to *totiens* (34) by providing a third instance of Roman blood lost in Egypt (= "Memphis").

(2) The second resemblance I mentioned involves her stay in Rome during the following years (she lived, as I said, in the *horti Caesaris*) and her supposed influence on Caesar and Roman politics. I believe that this, also, is alluded to by Propertius, viz. in that subsequent section in which, after the "digression" on Pompey (33–38), he returns to the subject of Cleopatra threatening Rome in 31 B.C. (39–46 = 4D).

One has remarked that this section basically repeats what was already said about Cleopatra in 29f. On the surface, this is true; but if we include the *argumentum ex silentio* I outlined above (viz. that Caesar's appearance in the antecedent section has set the Roman reader to thinking about his affair with Cleopatra), two allegations gain additional weight: line 39 returns

to Cleopatra by calling her "the meretricious queen of incestuous Canopus" (Canopus being the Egyptian counterpart to Baiae or Acapulco):

> Scilicet incesti meretrix regina Canopi.

The abusive and base nomenclature becomes poignant if it makes us not
only think of Antony (3) and her own slaves (30) as Cleopatra's lovers, but
if, through it, we are also made aware that one lover of this "meretricious"
and promiscuous woman (as Augustan propaganda would see her) has
been mentioned *just in the line before* (38): C. J. Caesar!

Distich 39/40, again characterizing (cf. 30) Cleopatra the whore, forms
the beginning of a long sentence (39–46, 4D). While the two inner distichs
(41/42 and 43/44), plushy with patriotic indignation about her military
threat against Rome in 31 B.C., basically repeat and embellish what lines
29–32 said about her war actions and goals, the last and fourth distich
(45/46) speaks of her desire to put up her mosquito net on the Tarpeian
Rock (monument of punished unchastity!) in Rome and to exercise jurisdiction on the Capitoline Hill (Rome's national shrine!), taking up and
varying the theme of lines 31f. This distich has caused interpreters to
wonder, because it refers to alleged hopes of hers (which never trans-
gressed the stage of imagination) *as if* they had become true. As a solution
to this difficulty, I propose that the fourth distich, like the first, refers under the surface to C. J. Caesar rather than to Antony: while, together with
Antony, she waged war against but never reached Rome; as Caesar's mistress she actually did come to Rome (although she did not put up her
mosquito-net precisely on the Tarpeian Rock but in Caesar's house), and
her presence showed that she actually did exercise influence—if not on the
Capitoline Hill, at least on the dictator's mind.[11] Her renewed plans cannot
but make the Roman reader recall her earlier accomplishments.

Once we understand that section 39–46 superficially refers to the time
of her liaison with Antony, but also means to remind us of Cleopatra the
mistress of Caesar, it fits smoothly into Propertius' original argument by
supplying yet another instance of female influence. And, Cleopatra's alleged desire to exercise jurisdiction (*iura dare*, 46) can without any difficulty be seen to be parallel to Cynthia's jurisdiction over Propertius
(*trahit . . . sub sua iura virum*, 2), which troubles his faultfinder so much.
The poet's answer, then, seems to be: before blaming me, direct your criticism against the influence which Caesar's mistress exercised in Rome!

If distich 45/46 refers to Caesar as well, and Cleopatra's presence in
Rome can be taken in the elegy's context as a historical fact (and not only a
dream of hers), then the subsequent section (47–50 = 2D) gains enormously in sense: "What does it, under these circumstances, help" (*Quid*

nunc . . . iuvat), that tyrant Tarquinius Superbus was driven out of Rome, "if a woman was to be endured" (*si mulier patienda fuit*)? Beside this, with Cleopatra's Roman residence in the back of his reader's mind, Propertius can superbly undercut his "official" argument because Octavian has done nothing else than save Rome from his father's mistress: "Seize, Rome, the triumph, and, saved, pray for a long life for Augustus!"

> cape, Roma, triumphum
> et longum Augusto salva precare diem! (49f.)

Whereas another subsection (51–54, 2D), in direct apostrophe, follows Cleopatra's fate after Octavian's victory to being a Roman prisoner and finally committing suicide, a final 2D group (55–58) first allows her to acknowledge her defeat in her own voice, pay tribute to victor Octavian, and express contempt for Antony:

> "With this great citizen (= Octavian) alive, you had not to fear me, o
> Rome,"
> she said, "and (not) the tongue that was constantly buried by pure
> wine."

> "Non hoc, Roma, fui tanto tibi cive verenda,"
> dixit, "et assiduo lingua sepulta mero."[12]

In the second distich (57/58), the poet himself takes the floor to summarize and put on record what this woman meant to Rome:

> The city, high on seven hills, which rules over the whole world,
> did, frightened by war, fear the threats of a woman!

> Septem urbs alta iugis, toto quae praesidet orbi,
> femineas timuit territa Marte minas. (57/58)

On the surface, these lines, like the foregoing acknowledgment of defeat from Cleopatra's own lips, contribute to the heightening of Augustus' fame: the greater Rome's fear of Cleopatra, the greater the relief he brought about.

But at the same time, of course, the poet's statement is the keystone in the architecture of his own defense, and his censurer should by now be disarmed completely: while the mythical examples proved Propertius' case to be anything but abnormal, the "victims" of Cleopatra have shown that he cannot even be called un-Roman. Proceeding first from Antony to C. J. Caesar, our elegy's range has now widened to include Rome herself: if the world power trembled with fear of a woman's threat (*femineas . . . minas*), how can one be so unjust (*fingis*, 3) as to reproach (*crimina . . . turpia*) a loving poet and call him a coward (*ignavi capitis*, 3) because a woman (*femina*, 1) overturns his life, too (*versat . . . vitam*, 1)? Propertius has used this type of reasoning in other places, too: if greater persons or even institutions cannot overcome wounds inflicted by love, why, then, blame little Propertius? For an illustration, I quote the last distich of elegy 2.8, a poem in which the poet compares his inability to cope with Cynthia's estrangement to Achilles' behavior when Briseis is taken away from him, and concludes:

> Inferior multo cum sim vel matre vel armis,
>   mirum, si de me iure triumphat Amor?   (2.8.39/40)

From the train of thought in 3.11, as initiated in the first half (cf. *quid mirare*, 3.11.1, and *mirum*, 2.8.40), I conclude that he has very much the same thing in mind when he stresses Rome's fear of a woman. When allowed to speak openly, he would always claim that his own behavior is not only normal and natural but also more human and even well within the Roman tradition; and he might as well claim that the isolation and embarrassment which the outsider ("the exception to the rule") feels so heavily ought to be not with him but with the other side. For, after all, as 2.15 informed us, he is the one who enjoys the innocence from the crimes of his time!

I assume that the personal train of thought, containing Propertius' "defense", has come to an end with the statement on the fear of a woman felt by Rome: the broadest scope possible has been achieved. What remains is to bring the elegy to an end on its "Augustan" level (59ff.), which will indignantly correct *timuit* (58, itself picking up *verenda*, 55) by *vix timeat* (66).[13]

The woman's war against Rome almost overturned the proud picture which patriotic Romans have so far fostered about their history: three distichs (59–64, I take them in the transmitted order of our text) indignantly recall famous names of Roman victories and Roman bravery, which were all in danger of being negated and extinguished by Cleopatra. Reassured by the glorious past, three more distichs (65–70) show that Augustus' Actian victory not only saved this glory for the future but even surpassed the grandeur connected with names like Scipio, Camillus, Pompeius. Thus, beginning and "end" (i.e., Augustus' rule) of Roman history correspond:

> Gods (=Romulus) founded these walls, and gods (=Augustus!)[14] do
>   save them:
> With Caesar safe, Rome need hardly fear Jove.

> Haec di condiderant, haec di quoque moenia servant:
>   Vix timeat salvo Caesare Roma Iovem.   (65/66)

Do we or do we not see a twinkle in the poet's eye in this lofty context of adulation? Is Jove, whom Augustus' Romans (formerly terrified by a woman, 58) need not fear, the one threatened by barking Anubis (41) or the one who brings shame on himself and his whole house (28)?

The interpretation presented here of lines 59–70 tries to understand the sequence of distichs as it is offered by our manuscripts. The present interpreter feels that rearrangement of lines (influenced mostly by Housman) has not borne fruit worth harvesting. SB prints 57/58 as a question, followed by 67f. (understood as "an indignant question, reinforcing the note of shame and anger struck by *femineas*"): Rome's fear of a woman's threats has wiped out heroic deeds, such as Scipio's sailing against Carthage, etc. I have doubts that *nunc* here, *after* the poet's tribute to Octavian's victory (49b–56), can be understood in any function other than temporary, referring to the time after the Actian victory. Distich 67f. must not be taken to vary (or repeat) the idea of 47f., where the context leading up to *nunc* (47) is very different.

Once one recognizes that Rome's fear is *not* shameful in Propertius' eyes but a welcome argument to him, it is better to print an exclamation mark after 57/58, indicating the poet's triumphant emphasis. His original train of thought requires that Rome's fears appear justified and are not a sign of cowardice (the blame falsely raised against the elegist himself in line 4). Accordingly, there is no way of belittling Octavian's victory over the (powerful) woman, as SB's transposition of 67f. after 57f. would easily suggest to the reader (considering 49b–56). His triumph does not disgrace (or fail to measure up to) Rome's earlier military fame, but excels it: Octavian is the rare exception, indomitable by the woman as she herself is forced to admit grudgingly: *hoc . . . tanto . . . cive* (55).

The transmitted sequence (as, for instance, retained in Schu.-Do.'s edition) has more recently been defended by Nethercut. He observes[15] that (a) lines 57–65 go upwards in Roman history, while (b) 67–70 move down from past to present. I would confirm the upward movement for my section 59–64 in which the poet, in an indignant "Augustan" exclamation, points to more glorious earlier feats of Rome. (The emphasis is on the feats, not—as SB thinks—on the memorials which help to recall them.) The viewpoint changes in the following section (65–70), which, now drawing fresh confidence from the Roman history just reviewed, judges everything, including past—earlier (67) as well as recent (*modo*, 68), following Nethercut's pattern—and future (*memorabit*, 69) by the standard of the events that (70) have given shape to the *present* time: *servant*, 65; *timeat*, 66; *nunc ubi* ("a commonplace of encomium",[16] 67); even the disputed pluperfect *condiderant* (65) is correct from the viewpoint of the present tense: it points to something that, having happened before the events narrated in lines 63/64, helps to explain their outstanding character.

The elegy ends by addressing itself to a sailor assumed to be crossing the sea between Italy and Greece, admonishing him to be mindful of Augustus:

> At tu, sive petes portus seu, navita, linques,
>> Caesaris in toto sis memor Ionio! (71/72)

According to line 5, the sailor knows the deadly danger better than his passenger (and therefore also knows to appreciate its removal): so he may be grateful to Augustus for having pacified the sea on the shores of which Actium lies! But, also, the sailor's dangerous situation cannot, to the degree that it is manageable, be compared to the uncontrollable danger of love which threatens Propertius (7f.). Along these lines we should probably try to understand the last distich: the Emperor's victory and rule may be appreciated by a Roman sailor and his like, who live in a pragmatic world of order and accountability. To such subordinates the poet addresses the "Augustan" surface of the elegy's second half. But for himself he reserves the freedom to suffer the risks of his own life—and the freedom to challenge current standards by an independent judgment of his own.

The two different addressees of elegy 3.11, then, correspond to the two different levels on which the poet speaks. His censurer addressed in line 1 receives as an answer Propertius' own opinion: a man living in servitude to a woman is nothing monstrous; his case is humanly understandable and can be confirmed by instances from myth and history, even Roman history. The sailor addressed in line 72 receives the official[17] answer: praise of Augustus, who saved Rome from servitude to a woman. The poet has by no means forgotten in the end what he said in the beginning. Rather, the apparent self-contradiction warns his reader not to be satisfied with the surface succession of two different standpoints, the second of which, as in elegy 2.10, rises to the heights of deification, but to look for the poem's turning point and to see whether the original argument continues and is completed under the new rhetorical surface.[18]

247

──XI──

SURRENDER ON TWO FRONTS:
THE ROMAN CALLIMACHUS

―――――――

The four books of Propertian elegies which we read today were published successively by the poet himself in his own lifetime—not by some
arbitrary posthumous editor.¹ The authenticity of the existing arrangement of poems can be of considerable help to the interpreter, the more so
as Propertius progressively clarified and reassessed his views in programmatic elegies. Not only did he, with each new book, redefine his positions
towards his love, the reading public, the changing political environment,
and the rival poets of his time, but he also referred his readers back to his
earlier books and to single elegies in them. Thus he established a continuity of communication with those readers who were patient and willing to
follow him through successive stages of his life and his talent's unfolding.
To a considerable degree, we may conclude, Propertius wishes his poetry
to be appreciated as autobiographical, an accounting for successive steps in
his development.

In this book, I have tried to honor the poet's wish by building my progressive argument exclusively on the basis of Book 1 of the elegies, and by
being especially cautious about introducing passages from later books into
the interpretation of earlier elegies. One welcome result of this method has
been that I have been able to state continuity rather than its opposite, identical core rather than deluding change of surface. A few of our observations may be summarized and repeated now so that I can interpret the
poet's concerns in Book 4 against the background of his earlier indications.

The elegist had opened his career in 29/28 B.C. with a pointedly composed book, the setting of which pictured him between two poles: the announcement (1.1, our Chapter II) showed how his helpless dependence on uncontrollable Cynthia had made him a poet. The epilogue (1.22, Chapter V) commemorated another formative experience, of still earlier years: the murder of a member of his family who had opposed Octavian in arms and the destruction of Perusia, a city of his homeland, at the hands of Octavian, the later Augustus. In the light of the following books it appears like clairvoyance that already then Propertius could diagnose his life as being ruled by two forces: powerful Cynthia, and powerful Octavian.

By the time Book 2 is published (roughly, 25 B.C.), Cynthia has risen to represent the poet's only source of inspiration, and Octavian has consolidated his political victory to the point that his wish has begun to control what the public gets to read. Propertius moves between surface reverence paid to the Emperor ("my leader", 2.10.4) and personal resistance: "I would rather let my head be cut off" (than allow Augustan interference with my love: 2.7.7). But at the time of publication, he settles for cautious independence, programmatically (2.1) refusing Maecenas an epic on "your" Caesar (2.1.25) and claiming lifelong, exclusive obsession with his love (Chapter VI). The epilogue (2.34, Chapter VII), a partly encoded message, establishes a special rank and a worthy pedigree for his own poetry and implicitly rejects Vergil's poetical development towards epic, as well as his drum-beating for Octavian. Propertius' own life is seen in sharp contrast to Vergil's, and, from a more complex point of view (2.15, Chapter IX), turns out to be the tragic life of innocence, which refuses to participate in the crimes of its time (Actium is among them) but is threatened from two sides: political ambitions (e.g., of Octavian, who ranks lower than his opponent Antony, the self-destroying lover of Cleopatra: 2.16) and human failure (Cynthia's unfaithfulness). Life's highest and most intense fulfilment, which love is seen to be, appears to be a utopia.

Book 3, published about the year 21, i.e., a decade after Actium, leads the twofold autobiographical crisis to its climax: opening where Book 2 ended, it overstates Propertius' claim to poetical eternity in a shrill voice (3.1ff.): his poetry of love means peace, not glorification of war, and posterity must grant him the fame which his own time withholds. A semi-adulatory praise of *deus Caesar* and his plans for a Parthian campaign (3.4) is followed by a condemnation of this and similar criminal undertakings of Promethean man (3.5). If there should ever be an alternative to the innocent peace of love, it would be the philosopher's life—not the conqueror's (Chapter VIII). The poet's moral superiority even allows him to criticize contemporary worshippers of the manly hero (3.11): the Propertian self-subordination to a woman's will has always been a natural male attitude, ever from mythical times down through past history to the present, with

Augustus' "father" and Mark Antony as the most recent examples. If openly pursued to the end, the argument would make the *pax Propertiana* the rule, and Augustus the unhuman exception (Chapter X).

With this kind of isolated resistance to the Zeitgeist, the poet is hardly gaining access to the régime-supported publicity of his time (cf. 3.1). At the end of Book 3, we see his resistance break down. Disillusionment about Cynthia's true character leads him to turn against his own earlier love poetry (3.24) and seriously to consider the alternative which Greece (philosophy, literature, arts) offers (3.21); the pressure of isolation makes him surrender and revoke his earlier good-bye (1.6, our Chapter IV) to career politician Tullus, and now employ the régime's official ideology (i.e., poetically speaking: Vergilian language)—which includes a denigration of his earlier beloved Greek mythology in a made-to-order poem (3.22, Chapter VIII). Does the open surrender result in a true conversion? Does the polarity of *amor* and *arma*, love and war, elegy and epic, disappear from the poet's life? Or does the tension survive somewhere, but necessarily dressed in a new form? With the autobiographical dimension in mind, we return to the elegist's last book.

The bold proclamation of the *pax Propertiana* (3.1) with which the elegist published his third book, could hardly outweigh the fact that he had already, although ambiguously, signed the terms of the *pax Augusta* (3.22). This development is continued in Book 4: more adulation with less accompanying ambiguity. The sterility of which the established Augustan Age was capable may well be seen from an elegy (4.6) which "is fundamentally unserious, a professional poet's manipulation of conventional symbols."[2] I introduce the poem not for its dubious aesthetic qualities but because it throws light on Propertius' personal situation, as he has entered the fourth decade of his life, about six years after he published Book 3. Politically, nothing has changed (except that the Emperor has become even more divine than he was five or ten years ago). But precisely this hopeless monotony, inherent in the absence of any change, will have contributed to wearing out what little remained of Propertius' personal resistance. The poet without a public of 3.1, who did not expect to earn fame on the "broad way" (*lata via*) of his time (in fact, he seemed to deny that there *is* a broad way in poetry), is finally seeking contemporary recognition through recognizing Augustus' divine connections.

Much can be deduced from the subject itself: Propertius praises Augustus' victory at Actium, which is the αἴτιον for Apollo's temple on the Emperor's residential hill. Our poem may even have been a contribution to the official anniversary festival. This is the last thing we would expect from a poet who once (2.15.41–48) defined true human immortality and his own guiltless life in opposition to political ambitions which created the bloodshed of Actium. This is not the only surprise the elegy has in stock for readers of Propertius' earlier books, as we shall see.

On the whole, the hymn shies away from the historical Battle of Actium; no account of the fighting (except for a hint at 25f.), no individual name, no eminent deed of heroism is recorded. Even Agrippa's name, still mentioned in the *Aeneid's* account of the battle (8.682), is dropped. Fifteen years after the actual event, the facts have become irrelevant, perhaps even disturbing. The only value which Actium can have today, in the reality of the year 16 B.C. (and especially in the face of two embarrassing recent military defeats), lies in its contribution to the understanding (and reenforcing) of the Emperor's greatness, which is so far beyond the capacity of the normal human mind. The remoteness of Caesar Augustus from common mortality can best be communicated through a religious atmosphere and mythical elevation of the past. "Already then," the Roman audience is supposed to conclude, "his eternal mission was fated." Accordingly, Propertius' account (which roughly equals the official account we read in Vergil's *Aeneid* 8) lays all its stress on Octavian's divine connections after the poet has first stylized himself into an Augustan priest-poet of the purest literary ancestry (6.1–10).

Twelve years earlier, Propertius had found a place for the same temple in his love poetry by fictitiously telling his girl that he was late for a date because "great Caesar" had opened his marvellous Temple of Apollo (2.31). No such erotic context is possible any longer. Now Jove himself is asked to take time off while songs are being spun on Caesar's name:

> Caesaris in nomen ducuntur carmina: Caesar
> dum canitur, quaeso, Iuppiter ipse vaces! (13f.)

An anthology of the numerous gods appearing at mythical Actium reads like a concentrate from fate-loaded passages in the *Aeneid*: from the beginning, the enemy was condemned by deified Romulus of Trojan origin (*sic!*, 21), the Augustan boat had its sails swelled by Jove's omen (*sic!*, 23), Nereus arranged the fighting lines (25). Phoebus, coming in person from Delos, addresses Octavian as "Saviour of the world, Augustus (*sic!*[3]), sprung from Alba Longa, proved greater than your Trojan forefathers of Hector's family" (37f.). Romulus' founding of Rome is seen by seer god Apollo as equivalent to Augustus' victory (43f.). And after Apollo (who, bow in hand, stands next to Caesar, spear in hand, 55f.) has struck ten of Cleopatra's ships with one single arrow (68) and the woman has paid her penalty (*dat femina poenas*, 57); even deified C. J. Caesar, looking down from his star, but apparently not yet at home in his immortality, feels his own divinity confirmed:[4] "*Sum deus; est nostri sanguinis ista fides*" (60). And "Triton and all the marine goddesses" (61) applaud eagerly.

As one can hardly assume that Propertius, by exaggeration, ridiculed the Emperor's desire for deification outright, one must conclude that he felt sure of a welcoming reception for his adulation. The latter alternative is confirmed by the repeated associations of the Julian family with established gods: surely, the Julians have been a divine race for a long time, the public is once more invited to believe.[5] If this is what is expected (and we have convincing parallels) of a prize-winning poet who seeks contemporary recognition because he would otherwise fall into oblivion, then we may assume that humiliated Propertius is paying political lip service, which will allow his nonadulatory poetry to survive as well. What aggravates his situation, on the other hand, is that he has meanwhile lost the source of inspiration for his nonpolitical poetry. So far, however, we can only surmise.

Is the poem purely impersonal, telling nothing of the author's feelings? We mentioned already that the attitude differs from that of 2.31. The official outrage in *dat femina poenas* (57) recalls indignant language in the Augustan facade of 3.11'(*urbs . . . femineas timuit . . . minas*, 57f., etc.), as does the grief over Cleopatra's escape through suicide (3.11.51ff. ~ 4.6.63f.). But this time Propertius goes a step further. The Emperor is being consoled: the gods knew better and therefore permitted Cleopatra to commit suicide. For a triumphal procession with a woman alone as the captive on display would not have been appropriate in the streets "through which a Jugurtha had once been led!" (65f.). Is the reader supposed to think back? In 3.5, we recall from Chapter VIII, Marius' victory over Jugurtha (standing for Augustus' expected victory over the Parthians) had symbolized the vain *stultitia* of Promethean man, whose ambition forgets that in the underworld victor Marius and his prisoner Jugurtha sit at the same table (13ff.). Is 4.6 to be seen as a partial recantation of 3.5? It clearly seeks to gratify the Emperor. Another instance of reconsideration on the poet's part may be found in lines 80ff.: one of the fellow poets at Propertius' table (not Propertius himself) sings of the Parthians' future defeat at the hands of Augustus or—in case he decides in favor of a merciful delay—at the hands of his sons. 3.5 had refused to participate in the spirit of a Parthian campaign: *vos, quibus arma / grata magis, Crassi signa referte domum!* (48; cf. 2.14.23f. before). It looks as if the publication of 3.5 (which itself wiped out the drum-beating call for a Parthian campaign in 3.4) has had some repercussions, which are smoothed away in 4.6.

The new melody, especially its reference to the Emperor's sons (just adopted), is played for the ears of the royal family itself. We can hear it replayed without any noteworthy variations about fifteen years later, when Ovid, seeking the same kind of recognition as Propertius, predicts a Parthian victory for C. Caesar (*Ars Am.* 1.177ff.), who is one of the two *pueri* Propertius has in mind in 4.6.82. Ovid not only mentions Augustus' posthumous divine status, and his blessing *numen*, together with that of Mars (203f.), but raises young C. Caesar to the same divine level:

> You cowards stop counting the birthdays of GODS:
>   to Caesars, manliness comes before the usual day.

> Parcite natales timidi numerare *deorum*:
>   Caesaribus virtus contigit ante diem.   (183f.)

It appears that Propertius is in complete agreement with court customs.[6] There is no built-in counterargument to be found as in the earlier praise of Octavian for saving Rome from domination by a woman (3.11, Chapter X above). And there is also no balancing or corrective pendant for 4.6 that would reveal the poet's true personal attitude as 2.7 did for 2.10, or 3.5 for 3.4 (Chapter VIII above). No wonder then that Propertius in lines 41f. makes even god Apollo allude to[7] and endorse one of the Emperor's favorite ploys: still in his "Achievements", Augustus proudly records that, before the battle of Actium, all the inhabitants of Italy had "demanded" his leadership and "voluntarily" sworn an oath of loyalty to his person, *iuravit in mea verba tota Italia sponte sua et me belli quo vici ad Actium ducem depoposcit*, *R.G.* 25.2. The poet's service in elegy 4.6, it seems, provides the divine sanction for the wishful royal self-portrait.

Conditions in Rome have now reached the stage where the excessive rhetoric of adulation has become unconvincing by its own totality, but has throttled all possibilities of expressing deviation.

A third and more complex example of Propertius' changed manner of speaking may illuminate my point. In the proem of Book 3, he had, as elsewhere, proudly rejected the misuse of his art for military poetry (with an eye on Vergil, as we saw in Chapter VIII):

> a valeat, Phoebum quicumque moratur in armis!   (3.1.7)

Now he *himself* introduces Apollo not (*non*) with his lyre to play a *carmen inerme*, but (*sed*) with the grim face he displayed when killing Agamemnon's Greeks in the plague before Troy or the Python at Delphi (to protect the Muses—another kowtow? 4.6.31–36). This may sound as if Propertius were aware of having alienated his art from its true purpose, but no hint is given about his own feelings. And the high-flying introduction (1–10) certainly does not suggest unwillingness.

Only once is a slightly impatient sigh of relief heard—when praise is over and the αἴτιον has been established:

> Enough have I sung of wars: already victorious Apollo
>   demands the lyre and lays aside his arms for placid dances.

> Bella satis cecini: citharam iam poscit Apollo
>   victor et ad placidos exuit arma choros.   (4.6.69/70)

253

If the elegist had written what would have, in the eyes of his contemporaries (not in our view), amounted to a parody of court poetry—an unlikely assumption considering the parallels from *Res Gestae* and *Ars Am.* mentioned above—, lines 69/70 would be the turning point where we would expect at least a hint of his true feelings. But nothing more comes forth.

This is the closest the reader comes to the Propertius he has known, who now and then gave a surface note of official praise, but returned to the private sphere as soon as possible. Now, however, a new surprise is in store for the reader, even in the poet's personal circle. In the following lines (71ff.), the *placidi chori* announced in 70 are revealed to be not love poetry but a formal dinner party following the ceremony. Participants are formally dressed contemporary poets, who, as soon as the wine shows effect, take turns in singing of the empire's military victories (Rothstein took these lines to be a promise to deliver an epic on Augustus). Propertius no longer stakes out any freedom space for personal poetry. As if this were not enough, he closes with an even more intimate assurance:

> Thus let me spend the night with the *patera*, thus with singing until
> the day throws its rays on my wine cups.

> sic noctem patera, sic ducam carmine, donec
> iniciat radios in mea vina dies!   (4.6.85f.)

The *patera* goes beyond the topics about which Propertius and his colleagues will allegedly sing at the party: it is the vessel from which libations are poured for the gods. In our context, the recipient is god Augustus. For, since his final victory over Cleopatra in 30 B.C., everybody was supposed to pour libations for him even at *private* parties (ἐν τοῖς συσσιτίοις οὐχ ὅτι τοῖς κοινοῖς, ἀλλὰ καὶ τοῖς ἰδίοις, Dio Cass. 51.19). Propertius seems to indicate personal compliance with this requirement by the possessive pronoun *mea*: in mea vina—thus making the last distich balance the spirit of the first (cf. *meos*, 2).

The assurance that even his night life (*noctem*) will be dedicated not only to national poetry but to veneration of Augustus grants the last distich a special effect. The elegy leaves its reader with the impression that the New Propertius knows no loyalty other than to his Emperor and his country. There is no longer any visible split between façade and core, because all his speech is homogeneously patriotic. Once before the innocent life and true immortality for men had been defined through wine, the wine that lovers drink, separated from the crimes of Actium:

> haec certe merito poterunt laudare minores:
> laeserunt nullos pocula nostra deos.   (2.15.47/48)

And the final distich of 4.6 sheds light on still another transformation. In lines 71–74, the party to be given in honor of Augustus is characterized not only by reference to choice wine and precious saffron perfume, but also by the wish "may (wreaths of) sweet roses sink down from my head over my neck". In earlier years, the dissolving wreaths had been a symbol of untimely death threatening the lovers (2.15.51ff., our Chapter IX) as opposed to death suffered at Actium and of opposition against Vergil's praise of Actium (2.34.59, our Chapter VII). They (together with wine) even helped to define Propertius' stand against Promethean man's crimes and the spirit of a Parthian campaign (3.5.21f.):

> me iuvet et multo mentem vincire Lyaeo
> et caput in verna semper habere rosa.

iuvat OCT.

All that appears to be over, perhaps even revoked. If the conversion to the Augustan ideology is true and thorough, we must assume that the Propertius whom his readers have known for a dozen or so years is dead, and we must accept as valid his self-representation in 4.6 (the only place in Book 4—except 4.1—where he speaks about his present state, since the Cynthia poems 4.7 and 8 point to the past). But before writing an epitaph on the love poet who suffered under the limitations placed upon him by the Zeitgeist, we should carefully consider whether the new political enthusiasm may not after all turn out to be something else: another symptom of progressive political pressure; and we should look to see if there still is a live spark under the ashes. For, having watched Propertius through so many years of conflict, we shall not easily be content with a smooth change of labels, like Alfonsi's (and others') "from youthful love, to mature patriotism".[8] So far, we have always discovered life and tension behind the labels. To determine the degree of his new dedication, let us turn to the last poem we have from his hand—his last will and testament, so to speak: the introduction he wrote to his fourth book.

The poem offers two sections: one serious in tone, the other ridiculous. The serious one (A = 1–70) introduces the New Propertius and recommends him with a refined piece of adulation: a review of Rome's history from the viewpoint of the Julian family. The spirit here is in line with the Actium poem 4.6, so our interpretation of 4.6 may help us understand the homogeneous argument critics have sometimes failed to see in this section.

In order to make the Julian achievements in leading Rome to greatness appear as impressive as possible, Propertius combines two devices. First, he confronts a fictitious stranger with the vast, overwhelming sight (*Hoc, quodcumque vides*) of the huge contemporary city (*maxima Roma*) by placing him on the Palatine Hill, i.e., on the site of Augustus' residence—the viewpoint is Augustan[9] in the most literal way—not far from the Temple of the Actian Apollo celebrated in 4.6. Secondly, he heightens the grand impression still further by contrasting the splendid present vista with the desolate conditions (*collis et herba*) which prevailed here when for the first time a member of the Julian family, Aeneas, paid a visit to the area (*ante Phrygem Aenean*, 1.1–4; the reader cannot but recall *Aeneid* 8). And although most of the conditions and institutions mentioned (5–36) are of early Roman, i.e., post-Aenean, origin, the resulting overall picture appears homogeneous: aboriginal as well as early Julian Rome was the poorest place imaginable. The contrast between Rome once and Rome today is worked out climactically in three areas,[10] starting with what is in view: (a) today's "golden" temples and splendid buildings do not have any pendant in early Roman antiquity (5–16). Indications of ancient poverty are these: *fictilibus* (sc., *deis*) (5); *sine arte* (6); *nuda de rupe* (7); *unus . . . focus* (10); *pellitos . . . Patres* (12); *bucina* (13); *centum* (14, "only one hundred"); *in prato* (14). (b) Early local religion is characterized by recurrent features of poverty (17–26): *nulli . . . externos* (17); *faeno* (19); *Vesta . . . pauper* (21); *macrae . . . boves, vilia sacra* (22); *parva . . . compita* (23); *calamos, ovis* (26). (c) The ancient military lacked splendor (*nec . . . radiabat*, 27) as well as technique (*rudis*, 27) and even "big" hostilities and affairs were on a tiny scale if compared with Rome's later dimensions (27–36). King Tatius ruled among his sheep.[11] The only possible exception[12] among the small proportions of older times was offered by "powerful" (*potens*, 35) Alba Longa, i.e., the Julian family's first (after Lavinium) and fateful settlement (*albae suis omine nata*, 35; again the *Aeneid* looms in the background) on Italian soil before they founded Rome through Romulus (cf. 4.6.37). Lines 37/38 sum up the area's pre-Julian and early Roman period:

> No inheritance except a name has the Roman nursling:
> > but it is no shame that a she-wolf is the foster-mother of the race.

> Nil patrium nisi nomen habet Romanus alumnus:
> > sanguinis altricem non pudet esse lupam.　　　　　　(37/38)
> *putet:* OCT

In Propertian breviloquence, the couplet not only, through *lupa*, alludes to Romulus the nursling of a she-wolf. It also views the Roman in general[13] (*Romanus alumnus*) in relation to what his homeland originally offered him: nothing, except the ravenous spirit a beast of prey may communicate through her milk. In other words, the poor country, underdeveloped but prepared for fighting through the spirit symbolized by Mars' wolf, was ready to support the Julians (themselves deprived refugees) on their fateful mission of restoring the splendor of Troy.

It reveals consistency (and is by no means a parenthesis) that, after the summary, Propertius now turns to the Julian newcomers on Italian soil and reviews their prosperous growth:

> It was for a better destiny,[14] Troy, that you sent your refugee gods
> > precisely to this land.

> Huc melius profugos misisti, Troia, Penatis.　　　　　　(39)

To a mortal eye, it may seem a hopeless situation if the refugees from Troy reach the area of refugee Evander (*profugos*, 39, picks up *profugae*, 4). But, as the Roman reader knows, Evander is their relative (*sic genus amborum scindit se sanguine ab uno*, Vergil, *Aen.* 8.142). And, in retrospect, divine guidance is revealed to have been at work from the outset (41ff.). It made the fire spare pious Aeneas (or, with synecdochical precision: his patrophoric shoulders—this time, the ghastly scenery of *Aeneid* 2 is evoked before the reader's inner eye) and led the refugees, unscathed by the invaders, away from Troy. Akin to Aeneas' heroism, the courage of a Decius (self-sacrifice) and Brutus' self-discipline (no pardon for his own flesh) are claimed for the Julians along with Venus' help[15] for her Octavian in the final battle of Actium which completes the rebirth of the Trojan-Julian Empire from the ashes (46f. Line 47 should be ended by a period, not a colon, as in OCT). Thus the Julians have been granted their fated goal on Italian soil:

> A fortunate[16] land has welcomed your gods, Iulus;
>
> Felix terra tuos cepit, Iule, deos; (48)

"if" (or rather "since," as the condition expressed by *si* has meanwhile been fulfilled; *si*, 49, is parallel to *quod*, 41) the Cumaean Sibyl once voiced Fate's demand for Rome's founding, or "since" Cassandra's prophecy to aged Priam has been correct, viz., that the arms of revived Troy would defeat the Greeks (*melius*, 39 ~ *male*, 53).

Some comments are called for here. First, a remark on *arma* (54). The word need not be restricted here to avenging Troy on the Greeks, but it may cover other victories (e.g., Actium) as well. But it is significant of Propertius' Julian attitude in this poem that he picks out and endorses the feature of Augustan ideology according to which the contemporary political servitude of Greece is a deserved punishment for the ancient Greeks' conquest of Troy.[17]

Further, it must be said that the passage under discussion (48–54) has posed problems for interpreters, regarding its structure as well as its function. While it is still useful to read Rothstein's comments, SB's notes suffer both from insufficient regard for the gerundive form *pianda* in line 50 and from his usual concentration on isolated passages, which here causes him to print the lines that announce Cassandra's words (51–52) separately from what editors take to be her prophecy (53–54). Accordingly, he finds a prophecy not only in 53f. proper, but another one ("she foretold Priam's doom") in 52—in spite of *sero rata* (51) which words clearly point to her correct prediction of Troy's revival in imperial Rome (rather than once more to Priam's longevity).

A view less confined than SB's would see that the two subsections 39–47 and 48–54 end on the same note. The victorious arms (we note the emphasis: *arma . . . arma . . . victricia*, 46f.) of Troy reborn (*resurgentis . . .*

Troiae) complete the victories that were once announced in Cassandra's late-fulfilled (*sero rata*, 51) prophecy *huic cineri Iuppiter arma dabit* (54). That is, reflection on the Julians' history, its bravery, and, above all, its richness in miracles (39–46) leads the poet on to see the fortunate development under the aspect of divine announcements preceding it (48–54). From the circle of oracular utterances he selects two which complement each other: Cassandra's less specific announcement to Priam of Troy's revival is narrowed down in the Sibyl's revelation to Aeneas that (and where) Rome shall be founded. By no means should one follow SB who hopes to certify a "theme" for Propertius by imputing to the Sibyl a prophecy "which she may be presumed to have made at the same time", but which is not mentioned by the poet. A commentator's freedom of interpretation is surely limited by the contents of the ancient text he is annotating.

In lines 39 to 54, then, the vatic poet, far from offering a "parenthesis" (Camps), has provided his reader with the key to understanding the unexplained contrast (5–36) of Rome's ancient poverty and contemporary splendor: the driving force behind this progress has been the Julian race who, in pursuing their fated mission, have developed the unimportant rural place into the world's leading power. In other words, Rome has become great because the land has been the vehicle which carried the Julians on their way to restoring Troy. This new aspect of the subject is included when the summary of 37/38 is rephrased in the lines 55/56: the *lupa* (38) is now revealed as the *lupa Martia* (55), and the not embarrassing foster-mother (38) as having proved the "best of foster-mothers" (55) for "our affairs" (*rebus*, 55), which are so different from old Tatius' affairs (*rerum*, 30) among sheep. Even the word "our", formerly applied to primitive "Rome" (8), now expresses the speaker's identification with the Julian concept:

> Best of foster-mothers to our affairs, O Mars' she-wolf,
>> what walls (i.e., what a city) have grown from your milk!
>
> Optima nutricum nostris lupa Martia rebus,
>> qualia creverunt moenia lacte tuo!   (55/56)

Of the two ideas connected in 37/38, only the general one is retained in 55/56: the fighting spirit which Mars injected into the have-not inhabitants of the pauper place has given the walls founded by Romulus their lasting character, i.e., Rome its survival. Perhaps one may go so far as to say that the indigenous population has turned out to be a worthy substratum for the imported Julian leadership.[18] At any rate, the closeness to the *Aeneid* we repeatedly observed in lines 39–54 must be viewed as a consequence of the section's pro-Julian character. It was Vergil who showed Propertius the road of imperial poetry (even if Tib. 2.5 be an intermediary).

The compliment to Augustus, who crowned and finished his family's task of rebuilding Troy (46/47), is almost grand and unobtrusive (because indirect) if compared with the empty pomp of 4.6. And it appears impossible to doubt Propertius' loyalty when he now announces his own "pious"[19] attempt (57) to sing of the city walls which are the essence of New Troy and whose holiness has been established ever since Remus' death. The word "attempt"[20] (*coner*) itself purposely leaves the question open whether the proposed goal will be reached or not. The following "alas!" (*ei*, 58), with which the poet deplores the inadequacy of his poetical skills (his "thin voice"), seems to drag down his professed enthusiasm once more to the well-known level of artful apology and *recusatio*, the deceiving surface of which my reader has first met in elegy 2.10. This time, however, there is no indication of the poet's backing out of his elaborate scheme—as there is none in 4.6. On the contrary:

> But nevertheless, whatever of a brook will flow from my tiny chest,
>> this in its totality will serve my country.

> Sed tamen exiguo quodcumque e pectore rivi
>> fluxerit, hoc patriae serviet omne meae.   (59/60)

Grammatically, the suspicious reader of 2.10 may object, this is again nothing more than a promise concerning the future (which, we must admit, will not be fulfilled). But through the Alexandrian terminology we can see a new attitude not formerly professed in similar contexts. It is true that "my" country may do nothing more than restore the word "my" to the phrase "my leader" of 2.10.4 (which had been neutralized in 2.1.25: "your" Caesar; Chapter VI above). But beyond patriotism goes the assurance that Propertius' inadequate powers will be wholly (*omne*), i.e., exclusively, dedicated to Troy Rebuilt. This again agrees with 4.6 (even his night and his wine-cups will be dedicated to the Emperor), but breaks with his former practice when his "small" skills served as an excuse for not writing an epic on Augustus (2.10) or even for refusing any epic on the principle that epic was incompatible with his Callimachean creed (2.1.39–42):

> Sed neque Phlegraeos Iovis Enceladique tumultus
>> intonet angusto pectore Callimachus,
> nec mea conveniunt duro praecordia versu
>> Caesaris in Phrygios condere nomen avos.

Now, in or about 16 B.C., a *pectus angustum* or *exiguum* is no longer a sufficient excuse: if the elegist does not have the breath to switch to an epic on Augustus, then Augustan Rome will present a subject matter fit for elegy. There is no longer room for privacy and love, even in elegy itself, according to the exclusive concept of 4.1A and 4.6. Once the poet found bold words to assert a freedom space for the individual:

> "At magnus Caesar". sed magnus Caesar in armis:
>> devictae gentes nil in amore valent.   (2.7.5f., Chapter VI above)

Now even this space, vacant since Cynthia and Propertius' love for her have left his poems, has been occupied by mighty Caesar. With Julian Rome now inside elegy, not simply outside as before, all walls of personal self-protection have been demolished. The importance of *tamen*, *quodcumque* (59), and *omne*, together with the emphatic *meae* (60), can hardly be stressed enough. For their combined effect, which confirms our interpretation of 4.6, means that Propertius' own poetic vehicle has finally been invaded and conquered by the Zeitgeist, and that, in case his patriotic conversion should not be genuine or quite spontaneous, he would have no medium left through which he could voice his dissent or even his personal viewpoint. It is clear that his insistence on this new "total" dedication is intended to make amends for all earlier halfhearted or superficial declarations of loyalty (and for the more or less well disguised mocking opposition still present in Book 3). Part A of elegy 4.1 could go right up to the Palatine Hill and be read to the Emperor upon his return—even before volume IV as a whole was finished. The desire to please is expressed in echoes of official concepts (piety, 57, is loyalty towards the Julian mission) and goes along with the more excessive Actium poem 4.6 and the Letter to Cyzicus 3.22, both of which betray the presence of high-ranking interest in Propertius' poetical services.

The much discussed topic of *Callimachus Romanus* (64) should be viewed from more than one angle. First, it classifies Propertius as an Augustan poet, in that he fills a slot, so far open, in contemporary Roman imitation of Greek genres. In similar fashion Vergil claims to be the New Homer and Horace the New Alcaeus or Sappho. This should silence his contemporary critics. Secondly, the patriotic nuance in *Romanus* (64) also points back to the pious poet of 57/58 who wishes nothing else than to serve his country. All of lines 5–56 form an example of "national" Roman poetry. In the third place, the fact that Callimachus (whose adept he had claimed to be before) himself used distichs to write aetiological poetry (the Αἴτια) supplies the most desired self-justification for Propertius against the imminent charge that he is now alienating elegy from the personal sphere which he himself had earlier assigned and almost exclusively reserved for it. It is a difficult position for him to say that his homeland Umbria shall exult, swollen with pride, over him—yes, even become known through him, the Roman Callimachus:

> Whoever sees the citadel (of Assisi) rise from the valleys,
>   let him value the walls by my talent!

> Scandentis quisquis cernit de vallibus arces,
>   ingenio muros aestimet ille meo! (65f.)

For still as late as in 3.1 he had claimed Callimachus (1.1ff.) for love poetry, e.g., *at mecum in curru parvi vectantur Amores* (1.11). Callimachus, Philitas, and love poetry are perhaps even more closely connected in 3.9 (43–46), a *recusatio* to Maecenas. But as the source of his fame, Book 4 announces a subject completely different from Cynthia as he once saw her: *ingenium nobis ipsa puella facit* (2.1.4). Now he will sing of Roman rites, festivals, and old place-names (69), with Rome as his pious audience (*Roma, fave*). It is true that even now he avoids mentioning arms. But his new subject has just as little in common with the peace poetry he asked Rome (*Roma, . . . quod pace legas*) to listen to about six years ago (3.1.15ff.). The peace he serves now is that of the successful *gens Iulia* and its ruling member, Augustus. No word (cf. 3.5) about philosophy succeeding love poetry.

I would be the last to doubt that, as an Alexandrian poet, Propertius felt justifiedly proud of his Roman *Aetia*. They are among the most elaborate and artful products we have from his hand. But I wonder if he himself thought them the rightful capstone of his career. All the personal poetry of his earlier years speaks against it—as far as contents go. Moreover, we know three things: (1) At one time he realized that—in spite of many earlier protestations to the contrary—he could not go on being the poet of his love for Cynthia and nothing else. This left him without his main personal inspiration and subject matter. (2) When publishing Book 3, he considered himself to be a poet without an audience. He must have suffered from the lack of response, for why else should he try to console himself with posthumous glory (3.1)? (3) He was exposed to mounting pressure from very high up in the hierarchy to lend his talents to the régime (Maecenas, Tullus' family; young Marcellus, commemorated in 3.18, was Augustus' son-in-law and designated successor; the epitaph on Cornelia, 4.11, is on the Emperor's stepdaughter and mentions Augustus' own tears).

All three kinds of pressure were removed the moment he gave in to sing the *Aetia* of Troy Rebuilt: (1) a new subject matter was found to replace Cynthia; (2) the Emperor and his circle should feel pleased; (3) an audience and recognition in his own time seemed guaranteed. Why then did he not finish his new program? My answer will be—as my reader is probably aware—that the new program was to its author only a substitute undertaking, a second-best, because it lacked the all-decisive quality his creativity needed: his personal involvement. Never would he be able to say that *Caesar ipse ingenium nobis facit*. I think one may convincingly argue that Propertius did not feel able to continue his rejection of the tenets he had professed earlier. A single instance, in which his earlier position is reconfirmed, will be sufficient to suggest that, in the long run, self-consistency was stronger with him than change for the sake of shining success—even if in the end it meant, once Cynthia was banished from his poetry, falling into silence.

A first glance at the evidence of Book 4 seems to point in both directions, love elegist as well as Roman Callimachus, with perhaps even more consistency among the national poems (if we set 1B aside for a moment).[21] Summarily, we may say that 4.1A, which culminates in praise of the city walls, finds the causes for Rome's greatness in the Julian mission to rebuild Troy; 4.2 presents several explanations of the god Vertumnus' name and in the end tells of the origin of a certain Vertumnus statue; 4 derives the *cognomen* (93) of the Tarpeian Rock from the high treason committed by the Vestal Tarpeia; 6 gives us the αἴτιον of Apollo's Temple on the Palatine Hill (viz., his rôle in the battle of Actium); 9 makes sense out of Heracles' *cognomen* Sancus and tells of the origin of the *Ara Maxima*; 10 reveals the *causa* (45, cf. *causas* 1) of the cult of *Iuppiter Feretrius*; 11, although not easily classifiable as an αἴτιον, certainly shares the national features which the New Callimachus gave to his Roman cycle. It also is related to 1A and 6 by its closeness to the top of the political pyramid (in this respect, it is in line with the Letter to Cyzicus and the Marcellus Eulogy): so intimate is this epitaph on the Emperor's stepdaughter Cornelia that it mentions Augustus' mourning as a point in her honor (58) and even testifies to his tears: "and we saw tears falling from the god's eyes", *et lacrimas vidimus ire deo* (60). On the whole, by warmly painting Cornelia's affection for her family and the purity of her entire life, the poem describes an ideal turned reality. At the same time, it serves the Emperor's purpose: by showing a flesh-and-blood paradigm of the legislated Augustan womanhood, defined by pious loyalty towards ancestors, marital integrity (lines 36 and 68 specifically point to monogamy), dedication to child-rearing. If then, the collection's last poem does not offer another αἴτιον, it at least contains reference to the First Family, thus complementing the Palatine viewpoint of 4.1A in still another dimension. Also, by making it the last poem in his last book, Propertius appears to seal his career with a last-minute conversion from the type of woman Cynthia represented. Some, unoffended by the rhetorical makeup, have called this epilogue the "Queen of Elegies".[22]

The viewpoints of the Roman poems appear so closely similar and their tendency is so homogeneous that one must ask why their author abandoned them before completing the cycle (he could hardly have run out of cults, causes, or *cognomina*), the more so as the other five elegies of Book 4 in no way represent an alternative poetical program. Only two of them are concerned with Cynthia: 4.7 conjures up her memory from the dead—a powerful portrait, but no doubt one that excludes any revival of the earlier Cynthia poetry (although her appearance makes eternal claims on Propertius). The same may be said about 8. Although pretending to describe an event of "last night", it seems years apart from the intense relationship of "I" and "you" we read of in the earlier books. One would rather classify it as another attempt at narrative elegy, objectifying rather than intensifying, in spite of the poet's being himself its main character: a late and more elaborate echo of the misunderstanding depicted in 1.3, so to speak. 5 is the genre portrait of a procuress, comic and self-revealing, an exercise in dramatic elegy (related to the astrologer of 4.1B), with a realistic vulgar note. Still another portrait (but "portrait" is hardly meant to be a valid counter-program to the Roman *Aetia*) is presented in elegy 4.3— perhaps the most informative one because it most clearly shows the transformation of earlier poetry.

During Propertius' earlier phase, other persons would appear in his poetry largely to help him clarify his own position by way of contrast. Experience of true love was limited to himself and his relation to Cynthia, narrated as the poet's own feelings ("I") towards the beloved woman ("you"). If other lovers were introduced at all, they were to be measured against Propertius' own standards. Gallus' happy love (1.10 and 13) serves as an encircling contrast to Propertius' worries (1.11 and 12); Ponticus (1.7 and 9) or Lynceus (2.34) are not to be taken seriously as lovers. Propertius' position is especially exposed because of his total dependence on Cynthia. To describe it, he exceeded even Catullus, who once (72.3f.) had applied Andromache's total dependence on Hector (*Iliad* 6.429) to his own feelings by saying that his love for Lesbia included the protective love of a father, too. Propertius went further by exchanging the rôle of the sexes in this context: he was to be the exposed Andromache, and Cynthia was the protecting Hector:

> Tu mihi sola domus, tu, Cynthia, sola parentes.
>
> (1. 11.23; Chapter I above)

To express his love's suffering, for which there is no room in the conventional Roman picture of a man, Propertius cast himself in the socially abject rôle of a woman, thus opening up new ways of expression for himself.

The first time we find him seriously arguing the case of a loving being other than himself, it is that of a woman, Aelia Galla (3.12), whose husband Postumus (both names may be historical) has gone on a Parthian Campaign for Augustus. The poet voices the deserted woman's complaints and sorrows, her condemnation of those who rank arms higher than love, and he tells Postumus to be as sure of his wife's fidelity as Odysseus could be of Penelope's. Whoever the real Aelia Galla may have been, her situation is so close to Propertius' own loneliness and aversion to arms that we easily understand his identification with her sorrows. Nevertheless, we must state that here for the first time he objectified his own experience by dressing it in another person's, a woman's, thought. Poetically speaking, he is not simply going back to the Catullan stage of Homer's Andromache. For Andromache was Hector's booty, but Aelia Galla is a Roman matron: marriage is another new accent.

Turning to Book 4, we see that the change has become permanent: love is (except in the recollections of his own earlier love, 4.7 and 8) confined to women, meaning once more: married women (4.3; 11). Only once do we read of unhappy, unrequited, deceived love as we used to. But this time it is not Propertius' own but the treacherous and criminal love of an unchaste Vestal priestess for her country's enemy (4.4). In the epitaph on the Emperor's stepdaughter (4.11) love is, as we said already, strictly defined as marital love, being one aspect among many others of a woman characterized mostly by a sense of duty. Love as a human being's central concern is found in 4.3, a fictitious letter from an Arethusa to her husband Lycotas (both possibly pseudonyms of historical persons, like those in 3.12.?) who has been away from home as a Roman soldier or officer for several years. It is not necessary to point to Ovid's *Epistulae Heroidum* to understand this letter. Rather, we sense a welcome opportunity for Propertius to display some of his long-standing views in an unoffensive setting. For who can take it ill if a loving wife is upset by her husband's long absence and thinks she might die from loneliness before he comes back? Nevertheless, it is—to say the least—surprising when a Propertian *puella* argues that marital love is the most intense of all:

> omnis amor magnus, sed aperto in coniuge maior:
> hanc Venus, ut vivat, ventilat ipsa facem.   (49/50)

The only feature that may remind us of the Propertius we have known can be found in Arethusa's wish that a Roman camp should be open to *puellae* like herself so she can be a "faithful baggage pack for your military service":

> Romanis utinam patuissent castra puellis!
> essem militiae sarcina fida tuae,   (45/46)

The pointed coinage reminds us of the technique used in elegy 1.6 when Propertius himself wrested the term *militia* (30) from friend Tullus and claimed it for himself.

But once more we must state that, for Propertius, this letter has not become a poetical alternative, either to the Roman Callimachus or to his earlier love poetry. It is an objectified, weak echo of earlier, more direct sounds, so to speak: Cynthia, finally married to Propertius, faithfully waiting for him to come home from Augustus' military campaigns . . .

CHAPTER

—XII—

ABANDONING A PROGRAM:
RETURN INTO SILENCE

_____

With our survey of Book 4 in mind, we turn now to the "unserious" second half (4.1B)[1] of the introductory elegy. One problem raised by the solemn and homogeneously Augustan character of the first half would be: how can Propertius undercut this position or retreat from it without provoking the ruler whose view of Rome's history he has just now so enthusiastically accepted? Although it is conceivable that 1A alone, together perhaps with some of the Roman elegies, was originally presented to the Palatine Hill to announce a whole cycle, we must deal with the fact that, by the publication of a mixed collection—seven poems related to the cycle (if we include no. 11 here), four unrelated ones plus a retraction (1B) of the first cycle poem—the national program was made to appear not only unfulfilled but expressly terminated by the author's own statement (1B). No interpreter is free to circumvent the elaborate negation of 1A which 1B represents, and so make Propertius end his career as a court poet. Propertius himself abandoned the idea of becoming the Roman Callimachus—in spite of having no other program to offer to himself and the public, aside from a few attempts at narrative or portrait elegy. The lack of a poetical alternative makes his decision to resign seem even more grave because he now faces again the same situation outlined at the end of Book 3 (21): the end of his Cynthia poetry is also the end of Propertius as a poet. The only difference is that, once the new attempt of Book 4 failed, his silence would be final and therefore even more tragic. All the more reason to admire the humorous façade he gave his abdication.

However, before submitting a detailed interpretation to my reader, I

265

find it necessary to set out a systematic and summary account of existing scholarship. A number of interpreters have tried to neutralize the impact of 1B. Though the burden of proof is theirs, not mine, the arguments advanced by them deserve our attention. They are fit to shed light on a problem of literary criticism that has pervaded almost every discussion of interpretative methodology offered in this monograph. With regard to 4.1A the problem may be addressed by asking the question if and (if yes) why Latin scholarship has been insufficiently prepared for dealing with an ambiguous poet of the Augustan Age.

Let the survey be opened by the presentation of a more sophisticated view. Lefèvre (1966), although suspicious about Propertius' new patriotism (p. 442), thinks it would be strange ("merkwürdig", p. 429) if Propertius, perhaps even ironically, wiped out in 1B the impression given in 1A. According to Lefèvre, 1B is a justification of the new aetiological poetry, an *excusatio* instead of the customary *recusatio* (p. 441; for the latter, see Wimmel 1960, 277ff.): Propertius proudly looks back on his mastery of love elegy (= Apollo's past prediction of his poetic destiny, 135–146), but declares himself to have been aware of the dangers inherent in the new genre and of overextending his powers while composing the new work (= Horos' warning, 71–74 and 147–150, p. 440). Some of my objections are that this reduces the contradiction of B and A to a matter of style and genre only, and that the subordination of 1B to 1A takes away the compositional independence of Horos' speech and argument, thus watering down their force. Further, Lefèvre fails to recognize that the logical connection between Apollo's earlier prophecy (which *confines* the poet to love elegy!) and Horos' present warning (cf. *aversus Apollo*, 73, etc.) is causal ("therefore" do not enter the new field, 147–150), not (as he thinks) adversative ("but now when" moving in the new field, beware!). For more details, see my interpretation later on in this chapter.

Lefèvre has presented an advanced interpretation insofar as he realizes the possibly detrimental consequences resulting from Horos' argument for the Roman program. He seeks to neutralize this effect by making Apollo's call for love poetry a matter that concerns merely the past ("unverbindliche Brechung", "nur noch die Funktion einer Erinnerung", o.c. p. 432). In doing so, he takes 1B less seriously than did his predecessor Dieterich (1900) to whom he pays tribute. Dieterich ascribed 1B to a different (later) biographical stage than the core of 1A, after the poet had given up the aetiological elegy and allegedly returned to love poetry (o.c. p. 220f.).

Today, the most widely held view on 4.1 still depends on Dieterich. The view is simple but, to my mind, wrong. It considers 4.1 to be the announcement of two programs side by side (they are supposedly executed in Book 4), 1A of the Roman aetiological poems, 1B of the love poems. See, for instance: Dieterich (1900, 220): "beide fast gleichen Theile des Buches werden durch die beiden fast gleichen Theile des Gedichtes angekündigt"; Hanslik 1963: 4.1 announces "den zweigeteilten Inhalt des Buches" and gives "eine Verteidigung dieses Inhaltes des Buches" (p. 180); Michelfeit 1969: Book 4 "führt beide Themenkreise gleichrangig nebeneinander", p. 359; 4.1 "programmatisch vereinigt" both subjects, p. 358; cf. "betont gleichgewichtig", l.c.; Haffter (1970, 54f.): two "Programme"; Pasoli (1967B, 4f.): A and B, each a *prooemium* to a genre, show the poet's intention "librum mixtum . . . componere"; Becker (1971, 474): 4.1 "führt die beiden Leitthemen vor"; "beide Themenkreise" (479); das "Nebeneinander von Properz- und Horosrede" (460; cf. 1966, 442); Baker (1968B, 349, n. 3): "Propertius' particular achievement in bringing both his themes to their conclusion, in this book of dual character, without detriment to either"; Celentano, although finding the poet's "dualismo" and "incoerenza" not in two different groups of elegies, nevertheless sees in 4.1 "due programmi di poesia", or, rather, "due monologhi" of the poet with "una doppia personalità" (1956, 36; cf. 45); Burck (1966, 411): 1B is to "rechtfertigen" (justify) "die Vereinigung" of Roman and love poetry in the same book; Grimal (1953, 46): "Properce, en son poème liminaire, a pris soin de définir cette dualité essentielle de son livre"; MacLeod (1976, 146) envisages "a compromise" between "the two genres" after the opening introduces "a book which contains both poems about origins (2; 4; 6; 9) and poems about love (3; 5; 7; 8)." Most recently, see J. F. Miller (1982, 382).

Naturally, most of these interpreters consider the whole book to be composed and published by the author himself, and 4.1 is accordingly assumed to be the (almost) latest (even last) elegy Propertius wrote, intending to introduce with it his new collection to the public. To many of them, the dual character of the book and its introductory poem is not incompatible with a preponderance of the national over the erotic theme. So, e.g., Burck (1966, 414): "das 'römische' 4. Buch"; Grimal 1953 (the uniting bond is *Fides*, p. 53): Book 4 amounts to "un véritable Évangile de Rome" (p. 35). But this preponderance can only be established at the cost of 1B. In fact, Horos' objection to the Roman Cycle (*aversus Apollo*, line 73, etc.) has often been discredited because it is not announced by Apollo himself (as for instance in 3.3): "statt Apollos nur der Astrologe" (Becker 1971, 460; this classicist would even enjoin Apollo himself not to retract from nationalized poetry: "Dem Apollo . . . stünde es auch schlecht an, von der Behandlung solcher Themen abzuraten."); Horos' speech "gar nicht ernst gemeint" (Suerbaum 1964, 358), Horos himself "unglaubwürdig *because* he takes Apollo's place (o.c. p. 359); "But it is only Horos, a rather ridiculous figure . . . , not the god himself" (Fontenrose 1949, 386); Burck (1966, 410) does not grant Horos the "Verbindlichkeit der Einwürfe Apolls". Wimmel (1960, 282) is exceptional in seeing the function of the "Warner" as more serious: by not only refusing an epic, but offering not even a full book of aetiological poems ("ein Kompromiss im Kompromiss"), Propertius disappointed the Emperor's expectations and so needed a strong apologetic figure; a voice in favor of Horos is a rare case (cf. Sandbach 1962, 267: "Horos offers first-rate credentials and justifies his claims").

A homogeneous interpretation of Book 4 hardly ever occurs. Fontenrose saw an aetiological element in every elegy of 4, and 1B according to him does not announce a second program; through 1B, Propertius merely "hedged himself against possible failure" (1949, 386). More recently, Pillinger (1969) tried to conceive a homogeneously Hellenistic and Callimachean impression of Book 4, but in doing so was unable to overcome the apparent dualism of content: 1B has the "effect of polarizing the contents of the book into two broad categories—etiological and amatory poetry" (p. 174). The dualistic view of 4.1 must be considered *communis opinio*, held at least theoretically, while common practice favors an overall description of the book based on the national features contained in it.

The readiness with which the thesis (1A) rather than the antithesis (1B) has—contrary to the rules of rhetoric—commonly been given priority in ascertaining the poet's last will is at least partly rooted in the scholarly tradition which we in earlier chapters tentatively characterized as "Augustan Interpretation". Interpreters of the "Augustan Age", we recall, tend to see a Propertian development from erotic passion to spiritual Augustanism. In the words of Hanslik (1972, 102): "L'amore per Cinzia e sostituito dall' amore per Roma". Thus Alfonsi does nothing but draw the consequences of this view when he maintains that in Horos (whose prophetic warnings he summarily dismisses as *post eventum*) the poet ironically ridicules his own earlier love elegies and his past resistance against heroic poetry (1945D, 81). However, he fails to prove that all elegies (he excepts only no. 8) can be subsumed under the program announced in 1A (*sacra diesque* and *hoc patriae serviet omne meae*, 69 and 60). But Alfonsi is not alone in his attempt to find a homogeneously Augustan outlook. Haffter, for instance (1970, 55), expressly warns us not to read Book 4 as if the poet broke away from his Roman program and returned to his earlier love poetry. No, we are assured, love itself is generally different in Book 4 ("eine andere Liebe" than in Books 1–3), Augustan love, so to speak: "eine Liebe, die sich verbinden lässt mit den Werten der römischen Umwelt in Gegenwart und Vergangenheit" (59). In short, Book 4 is a work "welches Rom und die Liebe nebeneinander oder ineinander beisammen hat" (p. 59; my reader, who may wish to point, for instance, to the coarse procuress in 5 or Tarpeia's treacherous love in 4, may stay calm: for these two unworthy ones, we are told (o.c. p. 58), are condemned by their creator himself). Let us compare a voice of moderate dualism (G. Williams 1980, 123): "The poem, taken as a unit, is thus programmatic to Book 4, which combines both the type of poetry that Propertius proposed for himself and also the type that the astrologer enjoined."

Now the truth is—and it is being more and more acknowledged—that the love poems in Book 4 are miles apart from the poet's earlier elegies and their "I-you" relationship. We have pointed to this and other differences in our survey in the preceding chapter. But it should also be acknowledged that Apollo's prediction to young Propertius, as recapitulated in Horos' speech, points to Cynthia poetry ("one single girl will pull you like a fish on the hook wherever she wishes . . ."), not to the love poems of Book 4. Lefèvre, to whose essay I now return, was therefore right in insisting that Horos does not announce the erotic elegies of the last book. The question I wish to ask and answer is whether Lefèvre (and not only he) was therefore also entitled to reduce the meaning of Apollo's old prophecy to an unobliging memory ("nur noch die Funktion einer Erinnerung"; see the beginning of this excursus). Only by granting Horos, at least hypothetically, that his message is potentially serious, can we ascertain whether the mention of Apollo's early prediction is in any logically demonstrable way connected with the present warning (as I think it is) or not, and whether or not 1B can help us to a better understanding of the book's contents.

If I fail, there will still be time to make use of the worst of all interpreter's excuses and to ascribe all remaining inconsistencies and incompatibilities of content to the immortal "posthumous editor". See, e.g., Postgate, p. liv; Damsté 1928, 214; Herrmann 1951, 137ff.; Fedeli 1965, xxii ("la prematura morte di Properzio") and xxx ("Un amico di Properzio, non identificabile, raccolse alla morte del poeta *quanto trovò*," etc.; italics Fedeli's); Becker 1971, 475f. ("unfertige Stellen" left untouched by the *Herausgeber*).

The "editor" plays the same part—with regard to method of interpretation—in large-scale "inconsistencies" (i.e., when whole elegies or parts of books appear incompatible to an interpreter) which is played in the case of the single elegy by Propertius' alleged disregard of "die kalte Logik" in favor of "Einheitlichkeit der dichterischen Inspiration" (Pasoli 1971, 83/84): "Er strebt keine logisch konsequente Entwicklung in der Darstellung an, sondern bietet vielmehr verschiedene Szenen und 'Momente'." Many problems, we are told, cease to exist if we keep "jene Eigentümlichkeit in der Kompositionskunst des Properz" (in plain English, his logical incoherence) in mind (Pasoli, o.c. p. 83). It was left to Celentano (1956, 68) to raise this position to the level of principle by instructing interpreters: "La coerenza di questo poeta è infatti nella sua incoerenza," etc. I refrain from listing more followers of this dogma here and refer my reader to my discussions in earlier chapters. Instead, I suggest that the Propertian consistency found by us in preceding chapters may serve as a guide to approaching the core of 4.1B and its presumed difficulties.

I return to the question of how to retract and counteract the enthusiastically patriotic impetus of 4.1A without incurring royal displeasure (and possibly a *damnatio memoriae*). Propertius solves the problem more or less as he did in the proem of Book 2. There he appeared to ridicule himself in epic terms (and epic poetry in his terms) before declining to write an epic (*maxima de nihilo nascitur historia*, 1.16). Here too he can neither directly ridicule the lofty enterprise which he wishes to abandon nor his own position as patriotic poet (except perhaps for confirming his "short breath" of 1A.58). Thus he must weaken the negative impression which the Roman Callimachus' resignation may leave on court-related circles. He does it by discrediting the seriousness of his messenger. This allows him to communicate the message without appearing responsible for its potentially serious implications. According to my interpretation, Horos' Ianus-like character of evidently speaking the truth but not being a serious prophet is rooted in the ambiguous situation of his inventor. In Horos, silly mediator between poet and public, another mask has been found, behind which the inventive poet may hide (or reveal) his true face.

After distinguishing messenger and message, let us turn first to the messenger. The larger part of Horos' speech is concerned, at least on the surface, with his own credibility: lines 75 to 146 = 36 distichs, i.e., everything except two introductory and two concluding distichs that deal with Propertius' future. The disproportion in the sheer number of lines between prophecy and self-justification is enhanced by the strange contents. Nevertheless—as sometimes seems to happen with extreme specialists— the strange material is well integrated into the logic of an argument. In the first section (75–88) of self-praise Horos (an ambitious name!) tries to remove any doubts about his qualifications:

> I shall report certain data from certain sources—or else I personally
> > as a prophet
> > do not know how to move the signs (of the zodiac)
> > > on the brazen sphere.

> Certa feram certis auctoribus, aut ego vates
> > nescius aerata signa movere pila. (75/76)

Horos, like a cheap seer in the streets of Rome, tends to overstate his case. The repetition *certa . . . certis*, the insistence on his own person (*ego*), on professional pride (*vates*), and on distinguishing his competence from the ignorance which does not know how to handle the basic tools—all this does not sound like a star professor who considers himself and his science generally accepted. His alleged pedigree, going back hundreds of years, includes even Plato's friend Archytas, and he claims not to have dishonored his ancestors. The gods are to be his witnesses,

> that in my books nothing ranks higher than reliability.

> inque meis libris nil prius esse fide. (80)

These are the few concepts around which his thinking is centered, *fides* being his greatest asset. His claims are massive, and his talents—if lines 87/88 are in their right place—cover the same historical range as Propertius' own in the poem's first half: from predicting Troy's fall to predicting its Roman resurrection.

Does Horos the warner want to rival—perhaps even mock—Propertius the Roman Callimachus? Horos knows that claims alone do not make a seer's credibility but that fulfilled prophecies do. His first success story concerns two young men, whose death during a military campaign he had predicted (89–98; we note his pride in the words *dixi ego*, 89, as well as in *nempe meam firmant . . . fidem*, 92).

> Ill-fated boys, two victims of a mother's avarice:
>   confirmed as true—although against my will—
>   was my reliability in this case.

> Fatales pueri, duo funera matris avarae:
>   vera, sed invito, contigit ista fides.   (97/98)

Tactless as the astrologer may appear, his attitude of condemning avarice that seeks to gain profit, especially from war, is genuinely Propertian. Besides 3.12.5 (*omnes pariter pereatis avari*), we may quote the first six lines of 3.5 (both poems turn against the spirit of a Parthian campaign), which culminate in the protestation:

> nec miser aera paro clade, Corinthe, tua.

The surface paradox, that the seer employs a Propertian *Leitmotiv* to bolster his own shaky credibility (*vera . . . fides*,[2] 98, reinforces *fide*, 80), is resolved if we respect the double function which our interpretation assigns to him: to communicate his inventor's ideas without giving them their full weight.

His second successful prediction appears still less convincing (99–102): that in the opposite field, too (not death, this time, but birth[3]), he, the same Horos (*idem ego*, picking up *ego*, 75 and 89), master in two fields, was able to score a success, by helping a woman in childbirth:

> She gives birth, but the prize is given to my books.

> Illa parit: libris est data palma meis!   (102)

As *fides* in 98, so *libris* in 102 refers back to line 80: the thesis set up in 80 is now triumphantly proved.

His success affords the astrologer a condescending look at rival disciplines (103–118): Jove's Oracle at Ammon, *haruspicium*, hydromancy—none of them can compete with the "true path" of astrology (*verusque per astra / trames*, 107f.) and its peculiar reliability (*fides*, 108—once more the key word). What is documented here is the pride of the specialist who has nothing in mind but the success of his own method in his own narrow field. The outcome of Horos' persistence is that the public may take him and his claims even less seriously—even in the event he is right. He ends his criticism of the unsatisfactory competition by picking a *cause célèbre* (109–118). Seer Calchas' advice helped Agamemnon's Greeks set sail for Troy, it is true. Nevertheless, Calchas was shortsighted because he did not see the further implication for the Greek campaign (here in Augustan fashion characterized as impious—cf. *pia saxa*, 110—, set between an innocent girl's killing 111/112 and the rape of a priestess 117/118): the shameful undertaking came to an inglorious end when the Greek fleet, after sacking Troy, was—through a father's revenge of his innocent son's death—wrecked on its way home, and the Greeks were sunk by the weight of their booty. We note that for the second time Horos uses an example from the same sphere which Propertius himself treated in 1A. This time, with his story of death coming to the victorious Greeks at sea, he is close to Cassandra's *dictum* to the Greeks (53 above): *male vincitis!* (cf. also the words *bene haerentes*, 110). Once more we ask: Does Horos (1B) wish to rival his creator (1A)? A certain rivalry between the two is beyond doubt; Horos, being Propertius' alter ego, wishes to divert him from his recently assumed role as poet of patriotic destiny. No wonder that he dwells on the same sort of "evidence".

I am afraid, however, that Horos' claim about Propertius is more serious than appears at first sight from his narrow-minded professionalism. If we assume that he could exercise the same function in Propertius' life as he did in the successful episodes which he brags about, we must surmise that, as a helper in difficult childbirth, he could also help Propertius in creating a new type of poetry (perhaps the portraits of 1B, 3, 4, 5, 7?)—a spiritual childbirth, so to speak. As a warner against avarice (greedy Arria gave her sons their arms *vetante deo*, 90, almost precisely as Apollo is *aversus* from Propertius' Roman cycle, 73), he might mean to restrain Propertius from seeking secular glory. His most serious example is clearly Calchas (*exemplum grave*, 109), whose narrow prophecy favors short-term success at the price of long-range ruin. Does Horos hint that the New Propertius, too, sacrifices a poet's long-term fame (Propertius himself has often claimed eternity as a love poet) to the dubious goal of a short-term success? This or something close to it must be implied in Horos' warning to the Roman Callimachus, if his methodological example of shortsighted Calchas is to make sense. No wonder that Propertius seems to hide more than he reveals. We shall return to Horos' claims later, remarking here only that his seemingly Augustan view of the Greek campaign against Troy does not necessarily result in subsurface pro-Augustan advice to the Roman Callimachus: a new level of poetic ambiguity?

After displaying his professional skills in the field of past events (*hactenus historiae*), Horos now turns to seeking individual recognition from

Propertius himself by divining highlights of Propertius' past biography (119–134 or 146). "Do I lie?" (*mentior*? 122) is his triumphant question when he believes to hit upon a truth.[4] In this way he seeks credibility for his warning, which is first hinted at in rather general terms:

> You, with composure, start to be ready for new tears.
>
> incipe tu lacrimis aequus adesse novis. (120)

For now, it is not clear whether the "new" tears are tears "unheard of" so far and equal to those announced in line 73, or a renewal of the "old" tears shed over Cynthia's behavior. We shall argue in favor of the former.

The biographical facts, of course, though in line with Horos' character and argument, serve at the same time as the poet's self-introduction to his public—a resumption of the first book's epilogue, which makes us think that Propertius at this point was aware that the fourth would also be his last book of poetry ever. It is worth listening to, because once more he draws the picture of a deprived childhood: early loss of his father (occupying the place here which Gallus' death had there), straitened circumstances in his mother's house after his large inheritance had been lost during the confiscations of 41 B.C. Still today, although there is no direct mention of Perusia, the aftermath of the civil war is necessarily on his mind when he remembers. The passage, however, according to Horos' self-assumed "higher" viewpoint, is not without irony. There is the astrologer's reference to Propertius' homeland, where

> the wall of climbing Assisi rises on its hilltop,
>> that wall (which you mentioned before), more known
>>> from your talent.
>
> scandentisque Asisi[5] consurgit vertice murus,
>> murus ab ingenio notior ille tuo. (125/126)
>
> *Asis*: OCT.

As has been seen, Horos alludes to Propertius' wish

> whoever sees the citadel that climbs from the valleys,
>> may he esteem the walls by the measure of my talent!
>
> scandentis quisquis cernit de vallibus arces,
>> ingenio muros aestimet ille meo! (65f.)

"Talent" and "climb" and the twice used "wall" in the later passage are quotations from the earlier, but they receive a potentially devastating meaning through the ambiguous comparative *notior*:

> that wall you mentioned, more notorious from your talent . . .

That could mean: the wall is already known only too well, is known more than it would itself wish to be. Propertius has brought a dubious sort of fame to his hometown. My interpretation goes well together with

273

Horos' critical attitude towards Propertius' new enterprise, and also makes sense of the otherwise puzzling stress in the repetitious quotation *murus / murus . . . ille*, 125f.[6] It means a lack of response similar to the one he complains about in 3.1 if his hometown so far has not indicated much pride in its son the elegiac poet. And it shows superb irony if Propertius makes his critic point to this lack of past recognition at the very moment when he is supposedly embarking upon another poetic venture, one which, he hopes, will make his homeland swell with pride over him (*tumefacta superbiat*, 63) . . .

Having finished his report on the poet's childhood (121–132), Horos in due course (*tum*, 133, *mox*, 131) resumes his irony about the ambiguous "success" of Propertius' poetical career. Apollo turned the young man from a public life to elegiac poetry. Horos recalls Apollo's injunction in a long direct quotation[7] (135–146), thus making it the weightiest part so far of his biographical account. At the same time, the god's earlier order to write elegies, combined with his interdiction (*vetat*, 134) against public speaking, makes a strong case for seeing Propertius' erotic-elegiac vocation as permanent and his new patriotic course as human insubordination (cf. *aversus Apollo*, 73) similar to Arria's ill-fated greediness, which likewise disobeyed the god's order (*vetante deo*, 90).

Before pursuing the overall argument further, I wish to point out that Apollo's alleged address to young Propertius is, of course, a *vaticinium ex eventu*, which refers to characteristic, identifiable pieces of Propertius' earlier poetry. Thus he is even more unequivocally defined as the love poet he has been so far to his readers:

> But you write elegies ⟨instead of pursuing a public career⟩, that deceiving genre ⟨"deceiving" because it will never fulfill its purpose of winning Cynthia for you⟩: this is your camp ⟨you will realize that it is not by praise of Augustus' camp (*haec ego castra sequar, vates tua castra canendo / magnus ero*, 2.10.19f.) but by praise of Cynthia's (*quod si vera meae comitarem castra puellae*, 2.7.15), that you will found your claim to fame (*hinc etenim tantum meruit mea gloria nomen*, o.c. 17)⟩; so let the rest of the crowd write following your example ⟨as you will say in your third book's proem: *scriptorumque meas turba secuta rotas*, 3.1.12⟩.

> At tu finge elegos, fallax opus: haec tua castra!
> scribat ut exemplo cetera turba tuo.   (4.1.135f.)

In typically Propertian brachylogy, the couplet mentions only those alternatives which he has realized in his poetry, but not the contrasting ones which he has rejected. His longtime reader of course understands this selective procedure and easily fills in the gaps (which I have marked by ⟨ ⟩). We see that "Apollo" refers to elegies (2.7 and 10, 3.1) which played a decisive rôle in Propertius' earlier attempts to define his own position (accordingly, we gave full consideration to them in earlier chapters of this book). The same is true about the next distichs:

> YOU will experience your military service under the flattering arms
> of Venus ⟨and not those of Mars or Augustus⟩,
> and to Venus' boys you will be a useful ⟨because easily defeated⟩
> enemy ⟨as in 2.9.37 or 2.29A⟩.
> For whatever prizes of victory you have prepared by your toils,
> one single girl (sc., Cynthia) will mock them.

> Militiam Veneris blandis patiere sub armis
> et Veneris pueris utilis hostis eris.
> Nam tibi victrices quascumque labore parasti,
> eludet palmas una puella tuas.   (137–140)

Line 139 cannot be separated from 138, because it gives the reason (*nam*) why Propertius is a "useful" enemy to the *Erotes*: because he is always defeated (one of Horos' ironical triumphs), never gains the upper hand, is conquered by *una puella*, who—as the following lines explain—holds him, hook in mouth, like a fish on her rod (Horos exults in picturing Apollo's predictions), and is master of his every single moment, day and night, even of his tears. Again, the reader feels reminded. A long time ago, when defining his tragic love for the first time, Propertius had formulated the same plight:

> seu tristis veniam seu contra laetus amicis,
> quicquid ero, dicam "Cynthia causa fuit".   (1.11.25f.)

Continuity, even in his often troubled relations with Cynthia, seems in the end stronger than disruption, even after the "final" break we read of at the end of Book 3. The same is true with his *militia* (137). My reader knows that this term, too, points back to an important self-definition of Book 1: he had used it for the first time when he told friend Tullus, the Octavian career politician (as at that time he still was), that from now on they would travel on different roads:

> non ego sum laudi, non natus idoneus armis:
> hanc me militiam fata subire volunt.   (1.6.29f.)

By recalling that early (and later often confirmed) decision in his last poem of all, and especially by including it in "Apollo's" early prophecy, Horos, i.e., Propertius, makes even clearer the rift which the Roman poems have meant for his elegiac poetry: a deviation from the path of his destiny which had been revealed to him by the voice of poetry. Rothstein (introduction to 4.1) was right in seeing a parallel to 3.3 where Apollo called the poet back to love poetry from the road of Roman epic. Only we must understand the tragic consequence: the reenactment of Apollo's prophecy at this point condemns the poet to silence, since Cynthia is now "dead" (4.7) and since he is not free to court honestly any other Muse. It may well be that it is in this way, too, that we are to understand Cynthia's last words from beyond the grave:

> Now others may possess you: soon I alone shall hold you.
>   You will be with me, and I will rub bones with mingled bones.

> Nunc te possideant aliae: mox sola tenebo:
>   mecum eris, et mixtis ossibus ossa teram.   (4.7.93/94)

Without Cynthia, he cannot survive for long, either as a human being or as a poet. Her death means that his death will come soon (*mox*). But once he has died, he will be exclusively hers forever; eternity will know him as the lover of Cynthia, not as the sometime Roman Callimachus. Or, using the words of 4.1B.139f. to look back on his life: his past attempts and present toils as a patriotic poet (*victrices quascumque labore parasti . . . palmas*) have always been snatched away by a single girl (*eludet . . . una puella*). The books of love, now to be towed by the hoped-for fame of his Roman elegies (*libris*, 4.1A.63, is plural and so includes Books 1 to 3 along with 4), will one day be the source of his everlasting glory.

We should distinguish two things: (1) the fictitious situation of 4.1B is one in which Horos, overriding and cooling Propertius' present enthusiasm for a program of Julian poetry, mockingly reminds the poet of his inescapable destiny. (2) The biographical situation at the time of writing is gloomier. The poet has been aware for some time already that he will never finish his Roman cycle; but he knows also that there is no poetical alternative. So he signals the breakdown of his attempt (cf. *coner*, 57) and indicates the reasons for his abdication. His personal situation and the unsparing account he gives of it lead me to understand that 4.1B was written in full knowledge that he would not publish another book of poetry again. The final raison d'être of the Horos comedy is to communicate the personal tragedy of its author in an acceptable way. If my interpretation is right, then, it was not death, as many have thought, but Propertius' own decision during his lifetime which made him put down his pen.

My interpretation runs counter to many existing ones, but I claim that I can explain the separate sections which scholarship has found in the poem and their relationship to each other in a way which does not hurt but brings out the logic of the argument. Having explained the long and circumstantial way of Horos' reasoning and given reasons why Propertius created this strange character, I turn now to those eight lines—four in the beginning and four at the end of Horos' speech—which, according to *communis opinio* among scholars, contain the warning proper administered to Propertius:

Where are you rushing uncautiously, straying Propertius, to sing of
fateful topics?
Your poetry's threads are not spun from a propitious distaff.[8]
You are calling for tears by your singing, Apollo has turned away
from you:
Against the lyre's will you are demanding words (from it)
which you must regret.

Quo ruis imprudens, vage, dicere fata, Properti?
non sunt a dextro condita fila colo.
Accersis lacrimas cantans, aversus Apollo:
poscis ab invita verba pigenda lyra.   (71–74)

Basically, all four lines tell the same message four (or even more) times:
everything speaks against Propertius' wish that *inceptis dextera cantet avis*
(68)! The words *non . . . a dextro . . . colo* (72) directly reject his wish by
using the same kind of metaphor ("left" and "right"). Propertius' enthusiasm (*ruis*) is inconsiderate (*imprudens*), roaming far from his erotic-elegiac
destiny (*vage*) by concerning itself with Rome's Julian history (*fata*).[9] The
repetitive oracular style well serves the purpose of cutting off any argument Propertius might bring forward in defense of his Roman poetry. The
consequences are made only too clear: tears for himself, the god of poetry
standing against him, the lyre unwilling to cooperate, his own future regret announced. I do not see any way to interpret these lines except as a
condemnation of the Roman Cycle. As the time of writing is close to that
of publication (4.1B justifies the collection's mixed character: Roman plus
post- or non-Roman elegies), we must assume that the fictitiously predicted "regret" (*pigenda*) has already become reality, that dissatisfaction,
which led him to break off the cycle, has long been the poet's companion,
that the predicted tears have been shed by now (and are thus identical with
those mentioned in 120). Horos' warning to Propertius is, as we said before, basically a *vaticinium ex eventu*, which cautiously tells the reader why
the Roman Callimachus did not finish his *Aetia*. Lines 71 to 74 do not say
anything directly about contents, so we might find in them just another
dichtungstheoretische consideration. The *fata*, however, clearly point to the
adulation of the Julian mission and the Palatine viewpoint of 4.1A. More
could hardly be said, except indirectly in the examples which Horos introduces in his self-praising speech.

The last four lines (147–150) appear even more oracular and void of
meaning, so that Housman found many followers when he highlighted his
insights into Propertian thought by declaring that "Propertius had no definite idea what he meant". Should the point of Horos' long and otherwise
conclusive argument really be that there is no point? Or is the point too
sharp to be published without a wrapping? After all, it must contain an
attack on Propertius' latest court-related poetry.

Now either your boat is allowed to struggle in the middle of the sea
 or you, an unarmed enemy, are free to meet armed men,
or the earth, shaking, may open a wide gap—
 be afraid of the eight-footed Cancer's sinister back!

Nunc tua vel mediis puppis luctetur in undis,
 vel licet armatis hostis inermis eas,
vel tremefacta cavom tellus diducat hiatum:
 octipedis Cancri terga sinistra time!   (147–150)

To solve the riddle, we evidently have to turn to the last line. In 71–74, Horos had piled up phrase after phrase to indicate fate's aversion to Propertius' Roman Cycle. In 75–146, he had done everything to prove his own qualification as a prophet, ending with a direct quotation from Apollo's former (tum, 133) prophecy to young Propertius: he was to be a poet of his love for Cynthia—throughout his life. The word "now" (nunc, 147) defines Propertius' present opportunities as a consequence of that old prophecy,[10] so that we understand: Propertius is now free to experience all the dangers which are conventionally considered harmful or even fatal. They will not be dangers to him. But one thing is indeed "sinister". Viewed from Apollo's prophecy, this thing can only be poetry other than Cynthia poetry. In addition to this, it must be said that sinistra, 150, takes up again the metaphors of "left" and "right" employed in 68 and 72,[11] where they concerned the lucky or unlucky outcome of the planned Roman Cycle. This makes it even more unavoidable that the final warning is aimed at the New Poetry or some aspect of it, alluded to by the "eight-footed Cancer".

All attempts, however, to find an astrological solution have been unconvincing, and they are perhaps a priori so; for, although we easily understand that the poet prefers to speak cautiously and enigmatically when he has to make a highly personal decision in matters which are of interest to the Emperor himself, it would hardly serve his purpose if he dressed his message in astrological terms which any court astrologer could easily retranslate into everyday colloquial Latin.[12] No, it would better fit his purpose to veil and present his message in such a way that an attentive and thinking reader could understand it without being able to nail Propertius down and make him responsible for the interpretation. Our train of thought makes us look for the solution in less professional quarters than those claimed by Horos (although Horos himself, joker that he is, might perhaps choose to shift his perspective unexpectedly). As such a less esoteric interpretation of "Cancer", one lying literally before every contemporary's eyes, we may claim that which according to Camps may point to a rich rival of Propertius, but which according to our understanding must point to his Roman Elegies. The gold coins of about 18 B.C., which carry a crab on their reverse side,[13] may very well turn out to be the only real danger for Propertius the elegist, if Horos means to hint that Propertius might—

like others—receive financial remuneration for his services in spreading
the Julian ideology. This is not only a materialistic temptation to impov-
erished Propertius (Horos has just mentioned the loss of his wealth in
41 B.C., lines 129f.). Far worse, it could be seen as a bribe for which the
poet has finally sold his freedom and his long-standing position as an individual withstanding the Zeitgeist. This latter point, however, can hardly be
maintained on the grounds of one ambiguous line in his poetry. Although
possibly implied, it needs further proof. In the poem itself (A.61–70) Propertius speaks of the *Aetia* as the crowning success and fame of his career
as a poet, and it is at that point that Horos, his alter ego, interferes and
tries to dampen his enthusiasm (B.71–74). When exemplifying his own
competence, Horos warns of the unbefitting avarice of a mother who
sends her children to fight for the empire (as Propertius is about to send
his elegies, i.e., his spiritual children), but claims that, as the same Horos,
he can help with "fulfillable" birth labors (Propertius' present "preg-
nancy" would hardly be termed "fulfillable" by Horos). And Horos makes
a lengthy final point about his knowing what is good in the long run by
contrast with seer Calchas' short-term success at the cost of later ruin, i.e.,
drowning caused by the heavy weight of one's booty. Here once more we
see another parallel concerning Propertius: by changing the source of his
fame from Cynthia to Julian Rome, he may in truth have earned short-
term recognition at the cost of his longtime, eternal fame as a love poet.
Seen in this perspective, any payment received in the freshly coined currency of the day (i.e., about 16 B.C.) may obliterate the rewards he may
otherwise expect from generations to come (cp. 3.1) for his true achievements as a love poet.

The nature of Horos' horoscope leaves it uncertain how far we may go
in applying details of his lengthy speech to Propertius' own situation. Additional evidence is especially desired to elaborate on my interpretation
that, in his latest stage, Propertius considered his Roman Cycle a cul-de-
sac from which he had again pulled out. If the poet's Julian period was an
episode rather than a lasting conversion, one feels dissatisfied that he simply resigned by including in his last book a number of heterogeneous
poems together with the incomplete Roman Cycle. Was he really unable to
go beyond Horos' oracular language and indicate, however cautiously and
enigmatically under the given circumstances, that he still sympathized
with his former position towards the Zeitgeist, or at least point more
clearly to the dilemma posed by the claims of subjective love poetry and
presently required national poetry? Now the review of Book 4 we made in
the preceding chapter has shown that all his Roman Elegies are emotionally (i.e., erotically) cool—except one: 4.4, describing the treacherous
love of an unchaste Vestal. Tarpeia's monologue marks the only time that

the burning human voice of unrequited love is heard in a way comparable to Propertius' own, as his readers have come to know it over the years. They should not feel at a loss, because the person speaking is not Propertius himself but a woman of the past. This may well go together with the sad process of objectifying his own experience, to which I have pointed in the foregoing chapter. But what should startle us is the harsh condemnation of her illegitimate love right from the opening line, which associates even her name with shamefulness by the sound pattern *TARP . . . TARP . . . TURP*:

> Of Tarpeia's grove and Tarpeia's shameful end
>   I shall speak . . .
>
> Tarpeium nemus et Tarpeiae turpe sepulcrum
>   fabor . . .   (4.4.1f.)

From the beginning, it appears, Propertius has looked at his subject matter from the perspective of patriotism and honor. This may be confirmed indirectly both by line 89, where even the enemy is shown to condemn the traitor:

> At Tatius (neque enim sceleri dedit hostis honorem) . . .

and by comparing Livy (1.11.7), who likewise conjectures the honor code to be Tatius' possible motive for killing the traitor: *seu prodendi exempli causa ne quid usquam fidum proditori esset.* "Does not Propertius' opening verdict then clearly set the national tone in which the poem as a whole must be understood?" my reader will ask, with some justification. "Has not Propertius himself finally come to condemn love which disregards society's obligations?" A satisfactory answer can, of course, be given only by a detailed interpretation. But a few preliminary remarks may serve as a warning against too clear-cut expectations. Ever since the opening of Book 2, we have encountered the new type of long elegy, which, except for subsections, cannot a priori be expected to build up a precisely symmetric overall structure or at least a numerically traceable balance, as do many of the shorter elegies, in which even an "odd" distich can be accounted for by the interpreter. All the elegies of Book 4 belong to the long type. Besides, Book 4 gives a prominent role to the Alexandrian narrative, which favors detailed, ornamental description over logical argumentation. This is especially true of the Roman Cycle, to which the Tarpeia Elegy belongs. The long poem also allows for a change of viewpoint or even opposing viewpoints within one elegy, as 3.11 or 4.1 have shown us. Personal outlook is represented especially in the new portrayal type, which characterizes a person through his or her own utterances (we have seen star professor Horos and loving wife Arethusa, and we should also think of both the businesslike procuress and the casuistic god Vertumnus). Tarpeia, pleading her case in a long monologue, reveals her whole personality—thus adding a soft individual viewpoint to the rigid social standards of the poem's setting. It may well be that, upon close inspection, this elegy, like others, can be shown to contain a valid counterargument below its Augustan surface. But the core may be hidden deeper than in earlier poems, because, as we learned from 4.1A, the Zeitgeist by now has invaded elegy itself and deprived the poet of the sole ownership of his own medium. This difficulty does indeed account partly for the elegy's complicated introductory structure, which comprises five sections:

(a) The poem opens, as we have seen, with a sounding condemnation of Tarpeia. She is of course known to every contemporary Roman reader as the traitor who opened the Capitoline Hill to Romulus' Sabine enemy under their king Tatius. But it is not only through the patriotic verdict that the first line announces a poem of the Roman Cycle; by mentioning the "Tarpeian Grove" and the "Tarpeian Tomb", Propertius reminds us of his programmatic promise (4.1A) to sing of *cognomina prisca locorum* (69). The identification of the elegy as an aetiological poem is completed beyond doubt in line 2 (*antiqui limina capta Iovis*). For it was Tarpeia's help in capturing the hill and her subsequent death which gave its name to a corner of the hilltop which was otherwise dedicated to *Iuppiter Capitolinus* (lines 1/2).

(b) Having appealed to well-established associations and created firm expectations about the elegy's military contents, Propertius surprises his reader by a change of tone and unrelated scenery (3–6): stylistically, we observe not only the asyndetic opening as if a new story is to be told ("There was a grove"), but also the lyric language which appeals both to our eyes (3) and to our ears (4) in order to help our imagination envisage the hidden, remote *locale* and its *flora*. In lines 5/6 the description reaches its pastoral destination and climax, complete with spring, sheep, and "sweet-sounding" (a positive quality) shepherd's pipe. The main literary function of this whole emotional and lyrical enclave in the elegy's military opening will not be revealed before line 19: it is from this hidden grove that Tarpeia will see Tatius for the first time and fall in love with him. By setting up pastoral scenery, Propertius gives his poem a new identification and an independent tableau of action on which the tender story of Tarpeia's sorrowful affection can be developed.

(c) Another result of the lyrical passage is that the initial report on Tatius' military action does not originate in a void, but breaks into the peaceful landscape in a truly hostile manner:

> It was this spring which Tatius surrounded in front
> with a maple palisade . . .

> Hunc Tatius fontem vallo praecingit acerno . . .[14]　　　　　　(7f.)

(d) After Tatius and his strategical action have been introduced, the reader faces still another asyndetical break, the third break by now, in the elegy's flow. This time Propertius introduces his contemporaries to the conditions of early Rome, by confronting past with present (9–14, cf. the sequence *tum . . . nunc . . . nunc*). This is precisely the method announced and used in 4.1A when Propertius explained to the stranger the vistas of Rome as seen from the Palatine Hill. His geographical viewpoint is not clear in elegy 4, but the national viewpoint is clearly that of 4.1A. The author's patriotic indignation is heard when he reports that "Sabine spears stood on the (later) Forum Romanum, where now jurisdiction takes place over subjected countries":

> atque ubi nunc terris dicuntur iura subactis,
> stabant Romano pila Sabina Foro. (11f.)

The couplet tells something about Roman and Augustan self-righteousness, because the ignorant Sabines' position is judged as an offense against the future world mission of Trojan Rome. The spirit is related to that of the *Aeneid*.

(e) A fifth section finally introduces the person who had been announced in line 1, Tarpeia herself.

Correct analysis of our elegy's five introductory sections and their proper functions helps to avoid some long-standing difficulties about the arrangement of the text. I believe that the manuscripts' sequence of lines 1–14, as printed by Barber and Schu.-Do., does not require any change.[15] Given the background of the foregoing chapter, especially as it pertains to elegies 4.6 and 4.1A, my reader will easily classify four of the five sections: (a) announces an aetiological poem, (c) begins its military narrative (and presents a major character), (e) introduces the story's negative heroine. (d) adds the program's Julian viewpoint of past simplicity and today's splendor, and could be printed as a parenthesis because it contributes information necessary for the reader, but does not lead the ancient story a single step forward.

Only (b) appears as a truly foreign body, because gentle pastoral poetry had not been a part of the program announced in 4.1A (the fact that Tatius did much of his ruler's business among sheep, 4.1A.30, was a sign of ancient poverty but not of pastoral inclinations). And, nevertheless, (b) offers the topographical crystallization point from which both sides of our story originate. Tatius guards glade and spring (or stream) with a palisade, Tarpeia comes to the same glade and spring to draw ritual water for Vesta. The two lover-antagonists are introduced through their respective activities at the spring, and this relationship is emphasized by a degree of linguistic and metrical parallelism:

> hunc Tatius fontem vallo praecingit . . . (7)
> hinc Tarpeia deae fontem libavit. . . . (15)

I suggest that, by inserting a lyrical passage (b) foreign to the Roman Callimachus' national program, Propertius indeed gives an additional dimension to the story and, for his reader, a means of orientation. Both actors, Tatius as well as Tarpeia, can now be measured not only from the patriotic viewpoint of arms and enemy, but also by reference to their attitude towards peaceful pastoral landscape. We have met the contrast of (Julian) arms and pastoral lover once before in Propertius' work (2.34), when he weighed Vergil's *Eclogues* against Vergil's *Aeneid*. At that time he indicated his preference for the Eclogues (Chapter VII above).

After line 16, with both the major characters now known (and Tarpeia's sense of duty perhaps already questionable: "But, the earthen vessel weighed heavy right on her head", 16—or is this the first sign of the author's sympathy?), we expect the story to begin. But another *fermata* brings delay: the patriotic author, presupposing his reader's general acquaintance with the story to follow, premises another condemnation, even more outspoken than the sound-pattern in line 1:

> And could one death be enough for the evil girl,
> who wished to deceive your flames, Vesta?

> et satis una malae potuit mors esse puellae,
> quae voluit flammas fallere, Vesta, tuas?

The phrasing appears somewhat strange because *puella* in Propertius (as can be easily verified from Schmeisser's concordance) is generally a woman capable of sexual love, regardless of her social status. Such a "girl" may be a matron like Arethusa (4.3.45; 54; 72) or even a goddess like Aurora (2.18.17). If we further consider that *fallere* generally does of course not only apply to deceiving gods (as *fallere deos*, Ovid *F.* 2.262), but to deceiving human loved ones as well (*virum . . . fallere*, Ovid, *Ars Am.* 1.310; cf. Prop. 1.13.4; 4.1.146), and that the *mala puella* naturally is the unfaithful one (although the elegiac lover-servant wòuld never call his mistress *mala*), we cannot exclude that Propertius' indignation is voiced here not merely in patriotic or religious but rather in elegiac terms: the *puella* was unfaithful to the goddess who, by demanding virginity, took the place of a lover in Tarpeia's life. If the elegiac interpretation is correct, lines 17f. are not a mere repetition of the condemnation in lines 1f. For the choice of *puella* instead of *virgo* (or any other less technical word) to denote Tarpeia indirectly points to an inherent conflict: being potentially a woman in the full sense of the word, Tarpeia would necessarily become a "bad" woman if she ever actualized and fulfilled her human potential. Faithfulness, in her case, must be nonfulfillment. Already we note a possible similarity between Tarpeia's and young Propertius' own experience of love—once we understand and admit the elegiac viewpoint, which will surface completely in the lines that follow.

Up to line 18 everything has been preparation. Now the scene belongs so exclusively to Tarpeia that Tatius is a silent character, seen only through

Tarpeia's eyes. The poetical subunit which conveys her lonely experience and thoughts is the same group of two distichs (2D) which long ago served to communicate the poet's own feelings and fears of love (1.11 and 12, our Chapter I). By now, the poet has added a couple of touches to mark the units visibly.

The elegy's composition is such that, after condemning the *mala puella*, it slowly shifts and moves to a more understanding position, until it finally approaches her own feelings and lays bare her inner self by granting her the monologue which forms the work's central piece. The reader, being taken along, himself experiences a change of viewpoint.[16]

The initial 2D unit (19–22), itself added asyndetically to the foregoing, at first sight appears asyndetic in itself because there is no connective particle between the two sentences that fill the two distichs. But this structure admirably pictures the abruptness of what happens to Tarpeia: "She saw (sc., Tatius): she was stupefied", *vidit . . . : obstipuit*. Besides, a closer look reveals the link. What she beholds is Tatius practicing (*Tatium proludere*, 19) and brandishing his colorful arms (*picta . . . arma levare*, 20). And what stupefies her are precisely these same two objects of her gaze, viz., Tatius' person and his arms (the repetition is meaningful, but not "suspect", as BB claim):

> obstipuit regis facie et regalibus armis   (21).

Thus it turns out that line 21, by stating the second stage in her enchantment with Tatius, at the same time specifies her impression more clearly: it is a numbing, twofold impression of kingliness that finds its way through her eyes into her heart.

Her physical response is like that of a fainting person. Her hands lose their grip on the jar, so that the jar, drawn by its weight, pursues its own independent movement and falls to the ground (grammatically, the change is indicated by *urna* becoming the subject in line 22). At the same time, the fact that she lets the jar go is symbolic of her changed orientation, from Vesta to Tatius. Propertius indicates the symbolic character by naming her weakened hands "forgetful", *oblitas*.

Finally, we are asked to observe that *urna* in 22 is a repetition from 16, and that *urna manus* in 22 metrically occupy the position held in 16 by *urna caput*. Thus, what happens to the vessel each time is indicative of what happens to Tarpeia, and the double mention of *urna*, like that of *arma*, far from showing bad taste on the poet's part (as Butler and Barber think), is a means of structuring which shows us that 19–22 belong together and form a subunit. In them a new stage of the action is reached, which was not yet actualized in 15–18 when the jar was still on her head and not yet in her hands. The method of picking up a key word immediately and presenting it in another, more precise context is similar to that of dramatic stichomythia.

The following 2D unit, 23–26, is easily identified by the repeated hexameter openings *saepe . . . saepe. . . .* Tarpeia makes it her habit to come to the spring and the hidden glade, finding all sorts of excuses for coming. Although her behavior is in no way excused (on the contrary, the moon is exculpated, *immerita*, because misused by the Vestal),[17] the poet nevertheless grants her conduct sympathetic overtones by adding another lyrical touch to her place of refuge (cf. lines 3–6):

Saepe tulit blandis argentea lilia Nymphis   (25).

To the goddesses of the pastoral world, so remote from the present war of Romans and Sabines, Tarpeia voices her prayer "lest Tatius' body be hurt by Romulus' spear", with *faciem* (26) pointing back to *facie* (21), object then of her love and now of her care, and rounding out the 2D unit. Tarpeia's thoughts are not at home in her country, but in an apolitical, individual, lyrical and pastoral world of her wishes.

But it is not at the spring that we hear her speak her monologue. One evening,[18] when returning to the hilltop from one of her frequent visits to the Nymphs, Tarpeia, her arms scratched by the brambles, bewails her wounds (here again the physical represents the emotional), "wounds intolerable to neighboring Jove". While these latter words show in topographical terms her crime against her community and its religious foundation, at the same time "her" corner of the hill (i.e., the one later to be named after her) is chosen for the monologue because it involves geographical separation from Tatius while it allows her loving eyes (and her longing thoughts) to travel freely over the otherwise unbridgeable abyss to Tatius' camp. This is the reason why she is said to moan "from" the Tarpeian Rock (*Tarpeia . . . ab arce*, 29). Thus her conflict, expressed in local terms, is that, though physically on her state's territory (in the neighborhood of Iuppiter Optimus Maximus), she emotionally longs to be in the enemy's camp. It is worth noting how once more Propertius chooses the scenic as a vehicle for the emotional. (Again I ask my reader to recall 1.11.) For throughout her monologue, she will try to "overlook" the abyss between hope and reality and regard the impossible as possible.

Before interpreting the monologue, it may be worth asking why the poet chose to expound Tarpeia's unhappy love. I cannot satisfy myself with the conventional explanation that, as an elegist, Propertius would not accept the version in which Tarpeia was bribed by the Sabines' gold bracelets, and therefore changed her motive to falling in love with the Sabine king. Considerations of genre alone have too often turned out to be superficial in the case of Propertius. Besides, the current explanation accounts only for the love motive, not for Propertius' insistence on Tarpeia's being a Vestal, nor for his making her sorrows the central part of the poem. The latter two features are more easily explained against the background of his autobiographical poetry. In elegy 2.7, to pick one of many possible examples, Propertius himself, as a loving individual, denied the Emperor's marital legislation any interference with his personal life and love. In 2.15, and even more openly in 3.11, he used the figure of the Emperor's opponent Antony to indicate that, for him, individual love ranked higher than country or society on the scale of human achievement. This position, to give only one more example, found an almost philosophical expression in the polarity of *arma* (3.4) and *amor* (3.5).

Seen against the biographical background as presented in the poet's work, Tarpeia is a poetical invention that leads the old polarity of love and war to an artful extreme. Being a Vestal, she is not only forbidden to love but also obliged to keep the imperial flames of Vesta alive—much more so than the Roman Callimachus himself. By not only falling in love, but by loving the country's enemy, she as an individual violates the life of her political community, again even more than Propertius, whose love only ordered him to withdraw into his private world of love and lyric, but not to betray his country to an enemy. The elements of Propertius' Tarpeia story look like an encoded and polarized revival of his earlier autobiographical lyrics. Then his life appeared to be exposed to two uncontrollable forces: Cynthia and Octavian's rule. The poet and his creation appear even more closely related if we compare Tatius' breach of faith to Cynthia's fickleness. Is it possible that Propertius has depicted part of himself in the loving Vestal Tarpeia?

With this question in mind, at least as a possibility, let us view the monologue. By now the reader is supposed to feel so close to Tarpeia that he can look with her eyes from the Capitoline Hill across the valley to Tatius' camp, where now—as announced by *primo . . . fumo* (27)—the evening fires are clearly visible:

> O fires of the camp, and headquarters of Tatius' troops,
>   and Sabine arms, beautiful to my eyes,
> would that I might sit as a prisoner at your hearth,
>   provided as a prisoner I can see my Tatius' face!

> Ignes castrorum et Tatiae praetoria turmae
>   et formosa oculis arma Sabina meis,
> O utinam ad vestros sedeam captiva Penates,
>   dum captiva mei conspicer ora Tati! (31–34)

Although her affection now seems to widen from Tatius (19; 21) and his arms (*arma*, 20, *armis*, 21) to Tatius' soldiers and their arms (31/32), this plural is rather to be seen psychologically as a multiplication of beloved Tatius himself, so that, with "my" Tatius mentioned once more in the fourth line of the subdivision, we are entitled to say that the 2D unit 31–34 is marked by an enclosing, circular composition.

There is another purposeful repetition in these lines, viz., that of *captiva* (33/34), which may serve us as an indication of the way in which her wishful thinking tries to reconcile the conflict of loyalties in which she is caught and of which she is aware—*pace* Rothstein—right from the beginning. For, if she were a prisoner, she would have come to Tatius' camp by outside force, and her conscience could feel free from any guilt towards Vesta and Rome. The repetition is a fine psychological touch: it emphasizes the only condition (unreal but hoped for) under which Tarpeia could be close to Tatius without causing any damage to her country or to her honor.

> Roman mountains, and Rome built on the mountains,
>> good-bye! and you, Vesta, bound to be an object of shame by my
>>> disgrace, good-bye!
> That horse will carry back my love to the camp, that one over there,
>> whose mane Tatius himself brushes to the right side.

> Romani montes, et montibus addita Roma,
>> et valeat probro Vesta pudenda meo:
> ille equus, ille meos in castra reponet amores,
>> cui Tatius dextras collocat ipse iubas! (35–38)

The asyndeton from 34 to 35 conceals her step from wish to imaginary fulfillment. Although she identifies the horse as the one which she now sees every day from her rock ("that one") and which enjoys the privilege of Tatius' personal care (how much she herself would like to receive his attention!), she actually pictures herself as being (a continuation from her situation in 33/34)[19] in Tatius' camp. Thus, the horse will bring her love (i.e., Tatius) "back", i.e., to the camp—as a victorious warrior, we must assume. And her resounding "good-bye" is likewise spoken as if she is looking back towards Rome from the camp or already from farther away (she can see the Roman mountains and the city on them). One thing, however, betrays her knowledge deep within that wishful thinking alone will not bring her anywhere, and that she will have to commit an act of disloyalty: this is her admission that her departure will be a disgrace and will bring shame upon Vesta (36).

However, awareness of wrongdoing (as defined by the categories of her upbringing) does not keep her from proceeding—on the contrary: she feels strong enough to make a case for herself. The two parallel rhetorical questions *quid mirum* (39) . . . *quid mirum* (41) make it clear enough that she finds nothing "marvelous" or extraordinary with Ariadne betraying (*prodita*: the ominous word is first applied to someone else) her "brother" (the Minotaur) in favor of foreigner Theseus or with Scylla who surrenders her father to his enemy (39–42). Perhaps the "unpleasing repetition" (BB) *saevisse* . . . *saevos* should be interpreted along these lines: there is nothing strange in Scylla's case, neither in that she "acted in fury" against her father, nor in that "her beautiful body was turned into furious dogs". The dogs' rage is to show that even after her punishment and metamorphosis Scylla is dominated by the same original "fury", which by its survival proves inextinguishable; the madness of love is stronger than the identity of the individual possessed by it. Tarpeia feels this as Propertius himself once did (1.12).

With her line of argument, Tarpeia is on good Propertian ground. He has defended himself in similar ways. Because he lost beautiful Briseis (*formosam*), Achilles allowed the Greeks, his allies, to be defeated and his friend Patroclus to be killed:

tantus in erepto saevit amore dolor   (2.8.36).

If even Achilles, hero of heroes, is conquered by love, what is so "marvelous" about Propertius' defeat?

mirum, si de me *iure* triumphat amor?   (40)

We may also compare 2.30.31f.: if nobody can resist Amor, why accuse me alone?

communis culpae cur reus unus agor?

But above all, we should think of 3.11 (Chapter X above):

quid mirare, meam si versat femina vitam . . . ?   (1)

In that poem, we recall, Propertius refuses the shameful charges of cowardly unmanliness (*crimina . . . ignavi capitis . . . turpia*) by turning the tables on his accuser: complete surrender of the lover to the beloved is nothing extraordinary and can be confirmed by examples from mythical times down to contemporary history: Heracles was Omphale's slave, Antony was conquered by Cleopatra—as was even C. J. Caesar (as the poet hints but does not say openly). Shameful as this law of nature may appear (the *crimina . . . turpia* of line 3 correspond to Tarpeia's *turpe sepulcrum*), it is seldom broken (Octavian is the rare exception). Under C. J. Caesar, Cleopatra even dared "to set up her abominable mosquito tent on the Tarpeian Rock" (3.11.45),

foedaque Tarpeio conopia tendere saxo . . .

which means, in the light of 4.4, that Cleopatra's adultery took place in the face of the unworthy Vestal's punishment. There is no stopping a lover through punishment or an appeal to honor.

Form (*quid mirare*, 3.11.1 ~ *quid mirum*, 4.4.39ff.) as well as goal (self-justification in the face of public accusation) of the argument in 3.11 and 4.4 are so much the same that the poet may be said to have granted Tarpeia his own earlier defense for her monologue. The old personal conflict be-

288

tween pressure exercised by society's political masters, on the one hand, and the individual's striving for human self-fulfillment through love, on the other, still attracts his talent. But while 3.11 started in open self-defense but ended in public praise of the Emperor, 4.4 condemns the loving individual from the beginning—but then allows her to make her own voice heard.

Tarpeia, like Propertius in 3.11, does not waver (43–46) or become hesitant when she thinks of the charge (*quantum ego sum . . . crimen factura*, 43) which her own behavior will create. She knows that she is unworthy in the eyes of Rome (*improba virgineo lecta ministra foco*, 44), yet she dares ask for pardon—by referring to her former statement that there is nothing extraordinary about women like Ariadne and Scylla (*si quis mirabitur* in 45 picks up her premise *quid mirum* of 39 and 41):

> If someone will wonder that Pallas' fire is extinguished
> —may he forgive me: the altar is sprinkled with my tears.

> Pallados exstinctos si quis mirabitur ignis,
> ignoscat: lacrimis spargitur ara meis.   (45f.)

Public standards (*crimen, improba*, 43f.) must be suspended for her (*ignoscat*, 45f.), she feels. The alliteration *ignis ignoscat* underlines her striking wish, so frivolous to any patriotic Augustan because Vesta's fire guards the *Palladium* brought by Aeneas from Troy, i.e., the very symbol of the Julian mission to restore and rebuild sunken Troy in imperial Rome (*Vesta, Iliacae felix tutela favillae*, 4.69). Tarpeia's attitude in 43–46 amounts to a denial of the "Palatine viewpoint" presented by Propertius in 4.1A to the *hospes*. Once more we ask: does he emphasize Tarpeia's being a Vestal in order to give her ampler opportunity to sin against her country through love? It is by the tears of her unhappy love that the fire is extinguished, and the *Palladium* which should be guarded by her is, in Cicero's words (*pro Scauro*, 48), *quasi pignus nostrae salutis atque imperi*! Being a Vestal, Tarpeia is definitely aware of her love's implications for the central Roman (Julian!)[20] sanctuary. Nevertheless, she goes right ahead with her plans, as the subsequent 2D unit (47–50) reveals.

The harsh *cras* at the beginning of line 47 indicates a new move, as if from thought to application: a definite time for action is at hand and so her mind centers on concrete advice. Her urge to help Tatius is underlined by a stylistic feature which I find in the fourth book only and which here well serves the injunction she intends to give to Tatius. I mean the doubling of key terms: *terga iugi* (48) both emphasize the ridge of a mountain; *lubrica . . . perfida* (49) both stress the unreliability of his path; *fallaci celat* (50, cf. *tacentis*) both mark the danger as difficult to recognize. In these lines, her imagination again pictures her as being in Tatius' camp. There-fore she can address him directly (*tu*, 48) and explain to him personally the dangers he will encounter on his way to Rome. Again her thoughts (*spinosi*, 48) reflect her environment (*hirsutis, secta*, 28).

Her excitement, owing to her wish to protect the beloved, is in my view the reason also for the first break in the well-balanced 2D structure. For the inserted distich 51/52, with its exclamation, results from her aware-ness of the dangers Tatius faces: as Medea used magic to neutralize the dangers (dragon, fiery oxen, seed of warriors) Jason had to face, so Tarpeia bursts into a sudden wish to help her "fair one" (*formoso*) by means of magic spells. Fear for Tatius' life makes her lose her balance.

Her speech oscillates between facts of the day and hot phantasies be-yond any facts. As the fires of Tatius' camp had induced her to picture herself first as a prisoner in Tatius' camp, and then as Tatius' personal ad-viser, so the thought of "tomorrow", i.e., the day of the fighting, carries her away still further. Her vision: Tatius, king of Rome, and Tarpeia, his beloved queen (interestingly enough, she passes over the Romans' defeat in silence):

> It is you whom the purple robe befits—not him whom, without
> > the honor of a mother,
> the harsh nipple of an inhuman she-wolf has nursed.
> Thus, my host, shall I give birth under your roof as your queen?
> As no humble dowry, betrayed Rome comes to you.

> Te toga picta decet, non quem sine matris honore
> > nutrit inhumanae dura papilla lupae.
> Sic, hospes, pariamne tua[21] regina sub aula?
> > dos tibi non humilis prodita Roma venit. (53–56)

55: hic; patria metuar: OCT

She gives no explicit reason why Tatius is worthier to be king, but from her negative thoughts on Romulus we may infer that her love freely (and mistakenly) attributes to the Sabine what she misses in the Roman leader: gentle humanity in the first place.

Almost more striking than her love for the enemy is her criticism of Rome's founder—at least to the ears of the poet's contemporaries who have been witnessing the restoration of so-called early Roman virtues and hu-manity under Romulus' greater successor, Augustus of Julian race. And as, after 43–46, this is the second time that her monologue reaches a con-frontation, supported by undeniable references, with the Palatine view-point of the program outlined in 4.1A, the question arises: why did Pro-pertius allow her to go so far? Is Horos' oracular opposition to the spirit of Roman Elegies not outspoken enough? Did the poet perhaps wish to voice the feelings of unconditional love once again? Is that voice so dangerous that it can be made heard only in a setting which condemns it? Are the setting and complex introduction perhaps written only to enable the poet to give us Tarpeia's speech? For—to ask the counterquestion—why vainly describe heart and feelings of a traitor for whom "one death" cannot "be enough" (17)?

In 4.1A, we recall, the Roman she-wolf was first declared a foster-mother one need not be ashamed of (38). Then, after a review of Rome's history which led up to Troy's revival (*huic cineri Iuppiter arma dabit*, 54; *arma resurgentis . . . victricia Troiae*, 47), the she-wolf's rôle was evaluated once more, in even higher praise:

> Optima nutricum nostris lupa Martia rebus,
>   qualia creverunt moenia lacte tuo!   (4.1.55f.)

Let us first say a word about *moenia*, because they are the Roman Callimachus' subject matter (*moenia namque pio coner disponere versu*, 1.57). In elegy 4, the situation is such that the walls have not yet been built: *murus erant montes* (4.13). And to these substitute walls Tarpeia bids good-bye: *Romani montes, et montibus addita Roma, / et valeat . . .* (4.35f.). The walls turn out to be another issue on which Tarpeia crosses her creator's, the Roman Callimachus', never-finished poetical program. In the terms of 4.1A, she is truly impious (cf. *pio . . . versu*, 1.57). The question arises again: why depict impiety in detail if the program announces piety? Or could the elegy have been composed at a time when the Roman Callimachus already knew that he was going to abandon his plan? Is it possible that Tarpeia tells us his reasons for not continuing his Roman Cycle? Tarpeia's reference to the *lupa*, so prominent in 4.1A, cannot easily be dismissed, even less if we look at the epithets: *Optima nutricum, lupa Martia*, in the program, but *inhumana lupa*, with *dura papilla*, to Tarpeia. The program enthusiastically endorsed the martial expansion of imperial Rome (the she-wolf is best nurse *nostris . . . rebus*, i.e., for the Julian Empire of Troy rebuilt, 4.1A.55)—as the introduction of 4.4 still does (we pointed to line 12 before). Tarpeia's understanding of Rome's founder, however, stresses the beast in the wolf: *inhumana*, inhuman, almost in the sense of not yet human, sub-human. *Dura* is of course not a physiological predicate, but, in loving Tarpeia's mouth, it is the opposite of *mollis*, the word which has always represented Propertius' poetry of innocent love in opposition to Augustan epic and crimes of war, as my reader knows. Thus, we are not surprised to find Tarpeia almost literally quoting her creator's own opinion, as stated in elegy 2.6.

There Propertius complains about Cynthia's promiscuity (1ff.; at the same time he admits that his own jealousy is excessive: 9ff.), which gives him an ambiguous chance to moralize and join the chorus of Augustan censurers: Rome's present decadence results from neglect of inherited religion (25–36). Tough as his position may appear, it has been undermined beforehand. For the poet had first exemplified seduction of women from Greek myth (15–19; a statement quickly neutralized [23f.] by a reminder about faithful Penelope and faithful Alcestis), but had immediately moved on to a massive case of forceful abduction committed in precisely that early Rome which Augustan official interpretation praises as the source of purity and the paradigm of old-fashioned morality:

> Why shall I look for Greek examples? You are the beginner of the
> crime,
>   you, Romulus, nursed by the hard (!) milk of the she-wolf:
> You have taught ⟨the Romans⟩ to rape the innocent Sabine women
>   without punishment:
>   through you it has come so far that nowadays Amor dares anything
>   in Rome.

> cur exempla petam Graium? tu criminis auctor,
>   nutritus duro, Romule, lacte lupae:
> tu rapere intactas docuisti impune Sabinas:
> per te nunc Romae quidlibet audet Amor.   (19–22)

Apart from the anti-Augustan realism, which cynically denies the ancient Romans a superior morality when compared to their descendants of today, our passage contains a genuinely Propertian concern: identifying himself with the Sabine women in their sad situation, he says that it is the crime (*crimen*) of an unfeeling (*duro . . . lacte*) beast (*lupae*), and one which deserves punishment (*impune*), to interfere with another human being's love by abducting (*rapere*) his or her innocent ("untouched": *intactas*) beloved. Propertius equates inhumane Romulus with Cynthia's promiscuous lovers by making him their teacher (Cynthia, as we remark in parenthesis, at the same time moves closer to the rôle of an innocent victim). To Propertius, as to Tarpeia, the fact that Romulus was nursed by a she-wolf serves to condemn rather than to idealize him.[22]

When Tarpeia develops her second proposal (4.4.57), she will sympathize with the deprivation of the Sabine women in almost the same way as Propertius himself found his own deprivation reflected in their lot (4.4.57 verbally alludes to 2.6.21, inescapably confirming the equation Propertius = Tarpeia). But we have no indication that at the time when she points to Romulus' inhumane upbringing (4.4.54 recalls 2.6.20), Tarpeia already has the Sabine women on her mind. Rather, she is still thinking of her own love, which must remain unfulfilled where Romulus' harshness rules. Therefore, the words *sine matris honore* must not be taken too narrowly as pointing to the disgrace of Rhea Sylvia, Romulus' mother, but rather in the wider sense "without the honor which consists in a mother": if Romulus had had a human mother as his nurse, he would be less savage and more human. As things are, Romulus and humanity are mutually exclusive, and the loving Vestal ominously rejects the contribution which the she-wolf's milk made to Troy's resurrection (*qualia creverunt moenia lacte tuo*, 4.1A.56).

Tarpeia's rejection of the beastly foster-mother and her inhuman foster-son goes well with the following distich (in which I follow codex N, as Schuster and Fedeli do) in which she pictures herself as a mother—a human counterpart to Romulus' inhuman nurse—bearing a child to the man she loves. And besides, she will be a worthy queen to him—with betrayed Rome her dowry (56). Only now and almost casually, as Rothstein saw, the word treason (41; 56) is applied to herself. Treason against Rome is apparently of no concern once her heart has spoken. Rome's value to her lies in giving support to her love. It is not necessary that I take my reader back once more to my former chapters to show how close her ranking love over country is to that offered by Propertius himself in his earlier books. This is no question. The problem is: to what degree does Tarpeia stand for the Propertius of Book 4 *after* he decided to break off his Roman *Aetia*? Perhaps we need to go one step more before answering the question. But we may already state that Tarpeia's thinking, dedicated to love and averse to the harsh inhumanity of war, is in agreement with the pastoral enclave of lines 3–6, which form a foreign and independent body in the elegy's long introduction.

> If you decline my proposal, at least—lest the Romans have raped
> > the Sabine women without punishment—
> ravish me and pay them back in turn, according to the law
> > of reciprocity!
> I personally am able to dissolve the fighting lines:
> > you ⟨Romans and Sabines⟩ make a mediating pact by way of
> > > my marriage!
> Hymenaeus, you add the wedding songs—you, trumpeter hush
> > your inhuman (beastlike) sound:
> believe me ⟨both sides⟩, my bed will mitigate your arms.

> Si minus, at raptae ne sint impune Sabinae,
> > me rape et alterna lege repende vices!
> Commissas acies ego possum solvere: nuptae
> > vos medium palla foedus inite mea.
> Adde Hymenaee modos, tubicen fera murmura conde:
> > credite, vestra meus molliet arma torus.   (57–62)

Si minus, at introduces a less preferable alternative, but "less preferable" to whom? To Tatius? Yes, but on the surface only, we must assume. For the first priority in Tarpeia's monologue goes to the fulfillment of her love, not to Tatius' strategic or political goals. So what is the difference resulting for *her* situation from the two alternatives? In the first, more preferable one, she is treated as an honored guest (cf. *hospes*) at Tatius' court; even more, she faces humane (53) King Tatius on a basis of equal rank, as his *regina* (55), with a splendid *dos* (56) to guarantee her unimpaired dignity (to be a *regina*, Tatius' female counterpart, is a wish that flows naturally from the deep impressions his royal appearance made on her inexperienced young mind; cf. the repetition *regis . . . regalibus*, 21). This, to sum up then, would be the ideal fulfillment of her love: to be Tatius' beloved consort, humane mother of his children,[23] with Rome the queen's dowry. It is incomparably bolder than her initial dream of being the king's *captiva* (33f.). And because her bold vision (as she realizes) may be asking too much of beloved Tatius, she offers him the new, less-demanding alternative (she can easily give up being his queen, but not being his beloved): he may avail himself of her services both to wipe out the disgrace (the rape of the poor Sabine women, with whom lonely Tarpeia can sympathize as Propertius himself once did, 4.4.57 ~ 2.6.21) that led to the present war and—if 59ff. are taken to continue the thought—to end the war by a peaceful settlement. In this way, her love for the enemy as well as her being loved by the enemy would not only atone for Roman force used against Sabine loved ones, but at the same time achieve a political end: to win peace through love and not through war. And in this case she herself, although not having reached her ultimate ideal,[24] would in the end be innocent even in the eyes of her own countrymen (and much more innocent than she would be as Tatius' beloved *captiva*, 33f.), because she would be the honored peacemaker.

What Propertius does here is to make Tarpeia invent a counter-version to the story of the peacemaking Sabine women which everybody could read (and probably had read) in Livy's first decade. Why did he do it? Just to show to his Livy-trained fellow Romans how confused the unpolitical, uncontrolled phantasies of a loving girl can be? Or to show that she really deserved the penalty she received? That alone does not explain the special turn her train of thought takes. Propertius picks up the "historical" situation as everyone knows it, at a point shortly before Tatius' attack against the Capitoline Hill, and from there bends it towards an imaginary ending: it is not the abducted Sabine women who will separate the fighting lines (*dirimere infestas acies*, Livy 1.13.2), but Tarpeia pictures a story of "The Rape of the Roman Woman" as a countermove against the abduction of the Sabine Women (the repetition *raptae . . . rape* emphasizes her point, as does the logically redundant but emotionally intensifying duplication *alterna . . . vices*, 57/58). And as her abduction and/or[25] her marriage (*nuptae*, 59) with beautiful and humane (as her love apparently pictures him) King Tatius is supposed to bring about peace, we must assume that she plans to do what the Sabine Women do in Livy: she will throw herself between the fighting lines and implore both her father not to kill his son-in-law and her husband not to kill his father-in-law, and both of them not to become murderers of their kin—which would be a stain on her children's future (*ne parricidio macularent partus suos*, Livy o.c.). Naturally, she will—taking the place of all the Sabine women in Livy—extend her argument to all Sabine fathers and to all Roman husbands of Sabine women, and so bring about the intended peace treaty—just as if she had read Livy's account before inventing her own. How else can she be so self-confident and convinced that her plan will work out (*commissas acies ego possum solvere*)?

The truth, of course, is that Propertius, in presenting a counter-version to Livy's existing story, cannot quite avoid making Tarpeia's plan appear anachronistic. But his point is not to correct Livy; his point is rather to show that Tarpeia is unrealistic (historic reality took a different turn, as everyone knows, and perhaps Livy's version, too, would appear too beautiful to be true to Propertius). He emphasizes her disregard for the political realities of the day once more by allowing her wishes and planning to overrule even her actual sense-perception:

> adde Hymenaee modos, tubicen fera murmura conde: (61).

In one and the same line, centered around the penthemimeral caesura, her phantasy fills her ears with the sound of the imaginary wedding music and at the same time hushes and silences the "beast-like", inhuman sound of the trumpet which, because it is actually heard now and bursts into the dreamlike world of her wishes, could so well serve as a wakening corrective to her feverish plans! Instead, it reminds her to impose her plan on reality.

Both the *tubicen* (9) and the sound (*lento murmure*, 10) of his instrument have appeared in the description which the parenthesis (d) of the introduction gave in order to help the contemporary Roman reader envisage the factual background of our elegy. By picking up the same words again in 61 and replacing the objective *lento* by the subjective and condemning *fera*, the author indicates to his reader that the heroine abandons the reality of her environment in favor of a personal and wishful interpretation of her situation. The fact that she is carried away once more shows most clearly in her call for action "on with the marriage song" (as Camps rightly translates).

The unreal character of her reasoning as presented in the hexameter also invalidates the consequence which she desires to be drawn from it in the pentameter:

> credite, vestra meus molliet arma torus. (62)

Nobody who knows the true situation will accept her injunction "to believe" (*credite*) her: her intended peace mission is truly out of the world.

But precisely here, where to the reader's eye the ship of her plans is already visibly running aground, Propertius deals with an idea that he himself has often pursued with great zeal: his conviction that *love means a peace not won through arms*. If, therefore, Tarpeia's juxtaposition *arma torus* appears paradoxical, and her claim that arms will surrender to love seems clearly utopian, we must ask what precisely separates her from Propertius' position. First, the similarities. He himself, like her, we recall (see Chapter IX), although feeling ashamed (*pudeat*), would not save his honor by giving up his "shameful love": *turpis amor surdis auribus esse solet*; he even accepted a similarity between himself and Antony's *infamis amor*, that led to cowardly defeat and national shame (2.16.35–40). Antony, like Tarpeia, was willing to make Rome itself the price paid to his beloved Cleopatra: *pretium Romana poposcit / moenia*, 3.11.31f. (Chapter X). Also like Tarpeia, Propertius would claim that love prevents the crimes of war (e.g., of Actium): *qualem si cuncti cuperent decurrere vitam . . . non ferrum crudele neque esset bellica navis* (2.15.41; 43; Chapter IX above). And, the most striking parallel: Propertius would claim Amor as the god of peace, as opposed to Augustus, god of arms, and would call lovers exempted from the crimes of war: *Pacis Amor deus est, pacem veneramur amantes* (3.5.1ff., cf. 4.1, our Chapter VIII). Where then is the difference between the Propertius of Books 1 to 3 and the Tarpeia of Book 4?

It seems to lie in Tarpeia's greater naïveté. It is true that Propertius himself constantly asserted his right to use established terms of the political and military spheres for depicting his own exposed situation as a lover: *militia, amicitia, pax* are among them. But he never demanded, not even of friend Tullus, that love should impose its rules upon and try to influence politics, for, according to his theory, arms (the means of politics) and love are related like crime and innocence, and must not mix; they are incompatible. Tarpeia errs if she naïvely thinks that her love can supersede and restructure political reality (*ego possum solvere*, 59). The opposite of what she expects will happen, because "humane" Tatius will think exactly along the same lines as does the nursling of the she-wolf (89 ff.).

So Tarpeia's reasoning is mistaken, while Propertius himself never extended love's peace into the political field. Is "disclosure of falsehood" sufficient reason in itself for expounding the "traitor's" error in her monologue? Hardly. We have seen earlier how much Propertius intensified her conflict, on the one hand by making her a Vestal who, serving at the national shrine, is forbidden to love at all, and on the other hand by making her fall in love with—of all people—the king of the enemy. This construction necessarily leads Tarpeia into confrontation with political forces, a confrontation which, then, must be intentional. And if Tatius was not willing to let his kingdom go (which history tells he was not) and elope with her to some idyllic refuge, her situation as outlined by Propertius prevents her love and her peace plan from succeeding and can result in nothing but disaster for Tarpeia. Her mistake, therefore, is an essential ingredient of Propertius' version.

From the Palatine viewpoint of the Roman Callimachus, the disaster will be called a just punishment of the traitor. But judging from Propertius' own love poetry in Books 1 to 3, we have already acknowledged the extended polarization of his personal dilemma and must call Tarpeia's suffering tragic. For her illusion, which will end in fatal disappointment, springs partly from lack of acquaintance with worldly ways and therefore contains a degree of innocence which she herself feels and claims when she dares ask Rome to forgive her (45f.). It is an illusion similar to that which Propertius himself, inexperienced and overpowered by love like Tarpeia (1.1), once fostered. For him, disillusionment did not come—as it comes to Tarpeia—in the form of sudden death from the beloved's hand, but it caused what he felt to be a change of his identity (1.12) and triggered a long and painful process of unwelcome awakening to the truth—mirrored in three books of elegies.

In summing up we must say that what Propertius, lover of Cynthia, and Tarpeia, falling in love with Tatius, have in common is more than what separates them. And as long as she is speaking, the elegist lends her every nuance of his mature art to bring out to the full her way of looking at things, no matter how harshly the Augustan setting of the poem condemns her. Therefore, we must not take it lightly if the poet takes pains to show how and where Tarpeia's love transgresses reality and overlooks the political situation, when she naïvely (a brutal word) believes that love can bring to fighting people a peace that is not won through arms. For her error sadly confirms his own earlier finding, as stated for instance in the complex poem 2.15, viz., that the innocence of true love is always threatened, both from within by failure to reciprocate and from the outside by the world's murderous lust for power. Thus it may well be that, by drawing the picture of Tarpeia's extreme dilemma, he wants to state for a last time that there is no room for unconditional love in the world of Promethean man— be he of Roman or Sabine origin: love which leaves the private sphere is bound to be killed.

Of course I am aware that our poem does not acknowledge Tarpeia's peace plan anywhere outside her speech. Therefore I must leave open the question whether in Tarpeia Propertius has reproduced his own views of the past only to show that he now condemns them. A final answer is perhaps not yet possible, but the sum of our findings already points to the opposite suggestion, viz., that through Tarpeia's suffering in a loveless, Promethean environment the poet has revealed the reason why he felt unable to continue playing the prophet of Julian Rome. If the essence of his own life could not be incorporated in his new work except in a disguise of a girl's lonely, unheard monologue, it was perhaps better for him to resign from his task.[26] Thus, the incompatible ingredients—love and war—of this singular Roman elegy may also lead us to understanding why the Roman Callimachus subjected his proud program to the oracular criticism of astrologer Horos.

In lines 61/62 the monologue has reached its final climax. A concluding 2D unit (63–66) momentarily takes Tarpeia back into the real world: the sound of the *bucina* reminds her that dawn is close and she should try to find some sleep—and dreams, in which, she hopes, Tatius will appear to her, "a friendly shadow", *umbra benigna*.

Again, her hope is mistaken (*nescia*, 68), because she is vexed by "new madness" (*furiis . . . novis*),[27] and "Vesta, propitious guardian of Troy's embers, nourishes her (feelings of) guilt". Her experience is almost like that of Venus in the *Aeneid*. In broad daylight Venus readily follows father Jove's plan and herself encourages her son Aeneas to enter Carthage and see Dido. But in the following night she *nova pectore versat / consilia* (1.657f.), because her old worries and her old fear of Juno, friend of Carthage, are aroused to new life.[28] In a similar way Tarpeia, after having reasoned out a clear position of her own towards Vesta in her monologue (45f.), is in her following sleep haunted again by uncontrolled thoughts of Vesta, whose priestess she after all has been. "Vesta" need not be a living deity in our passage, but rather is an externalization of Tarpeia's conflict of loyalties ("the *thought* of Vesta nourishes her feelings of guilt"[29]). Against the pardon (*ignoscat*) for *extinctos . . . ignis* (45f.) stands Vesta as *tutela favillae*. In unguarded moments, her older allegiance will try to overthrow her recent position and bring "new" madness. Out of her senses, Tarpeia gets up and rushes to nowhere—like a Bacchant[30] (67–72).

In the same way in which the elegy slowly approached its center, i.e., Tarpeia's inner world, as expressed in her own words (first person singular), the poem's course now moves slowly away from Tarpeia and back to the impersonal, "objective" viewpoint of the Roman Callimachus, whose guiding principle is the Julian mission. Although lines 67–72 still tell of Tarpeia's emotions, she is already spoken of in the third person, described from outside, as she was before the monologue began (cf. 19ff.). And as before the monologue her behavior, especially towards Vesta, was narrated not without due condemnation (17f.), so after her monologue we again hear relentless judgment, beginning once more with Vesta (69), who intensifies Tarpeia's *culpa* (*plures condit in ossa faces*, 70). And as, before the monologue, the contemporary reader was acquainted with conditions in early Rome (9–14), so now in another parenthesis (73–78) the poet informs him about early Rome's *Parilia* festival, which celebrates the founding of the

city walls. *primus . . . moenibus . . . dies* (74) refers to the Roman Callimachus' program (*moenia*, 4.1A.57, *dies*, 69) in the same fashion as did
lines 9–14 both with *murus erant montes* and the contrast of *tum . . . nunc*
(for which we may compare, e.g., *olim* or *nunc* in 4.1A.9 or 11). The *Parilia* themselves were mentioned 4.1A.19f. The narrative of 4.4 leans as
closely as possible on the program of 4.1A—whereas the centerpiece moves
away from it as far as possible. Our earlier description of a complex type
of Propertian elegy as a personal nucleus surrounded by one or more
almost unbreakable shells that are destined to deal with the Zeitgeist,
may be applied to elegy 4.4. In 4.1 the Julian program (A) is followed
by an enigmatic warning against it (B). In 4.4 the program itself is sym-
metrically wrapped around its very negation. In both elegies, the inherent
self-contradiction is superficially mitigated because the seriousness of the
program's opponents is discredited: Tarpeia may be dismissed as being a
"traitor" (and "only" a girl); Horos is characterized as a narrow-minded
specialist.

Just as "early Rome" (9–14) served as a background for Tarpeia's story,
so the theme's resumption in 73–78 serves as a time indicator for the military action which the reader has been expecting ever since line 2 (*limina
capta Iovis*), but which, playing a subordinate part in Propertius' account,
is confined to a few distichs in the poem's last third: because of the festival,
Romulus has withdrawn the guards from their posts.

> This, Tarpeia thought, was her time and she met the enemy:
> she made a pact, herself meaning to be a companion to the pact.

> Hoc Tarpeia suum tempus rata convenit hostem:
> pacta ligat, pactis ipsa futura comes.   (81f.)

Her being herself a "companion" to the pact of course refers to her planned
marriage with Tatius (*regina*, 55; *nuptae*, 59; cf. *nube*, 90). However, the
narrative does not respect her viewpoint any longer, but represents the
official line of the Roman Callimachus. Tatius is now "the enemy", *hostis*,
and the pact, especially since Tarpeia herself is part of the deal, appears
disgusting and unethical. The same is true of "her" individual time (*suum
tempus*): an abominable deviation from her nation's *communis opinio*.

She leads the enemy up a difficult mountain path—probably the
same that she so ambiguously called *via . . . perfida* in her monologue
(49)—and helps them surprise the unsuspecting Romans. Jove alone—
Rome's supreme god and her outraged neighbor, according to line 30,
whose "threshold" (2) was in the danger of being "seized" (2)—watches
lest she go unpunished (83–86), thus by his "decision" (*decrevit*, 86) pro-
pitiously correcting the harmful outcome of Romulus' "decision" (*decrevit*,
79) to withdraw the guards. The situation, shortly before her death and

punishment (cf. *poenis*, 86), calls for an "objective" evaluation (in keeping with the way Jove would look at her crime):

> She had betrayed the reliability of the gate and her sleeping country,
>   and she tried to name her own marriage day.

> Prodiderat portaeque fidem patriamque iacentem,
>   nubendique petit, quem velit, ipsa diem.   (87f.)

Indignation spills over in the sound similarity of the three words beginning with *p* (87; here we recall the sound pattern of line 1). The patriotic tone by way of contrast reminds us how much less weight the charge of treason carried in Tarpeia's thinking (39; 41; 56), in which love not only had priority over state, but even wished to exercise a peaceful influence on matters of state (59f.). Our present couplet takes just the opposite position. It not only expects loyalty to the community (hexameter), but, in genuine Roman tradition, even demands subordination of the individual's personal life under the established authorities—especially so if the individual happens to be female (pentameter). Propertius himself, as my reader knows, has from his early days rejected the claims which the ruling powers laid on him, and he often has cast his love's feelings in a feminine mold, because this was the only way to express "soft" suffering in a "hard" Roman environment. Above all, he refused the attempt of Rome's head of state to interfere with his love, and our earlier interpretation (Chapter VI) of, for instance, poems 2.10 and 2.7—the latter taking a stand against imperial marriage legislation—has shown the way in which he tried to preserve personal freedom against official pressure. Then it was said that Jove himself is not able to separate lovers against their will (*diducere amantis . . . invitos*, 2.7.3f.), and "*magnus*" *Caesar* was told to confine himself to *armis*, as being powerless in *amore* (5f.). Propertius would rather be decapitated than marry to order (and desert Cynthia, 7f.). The poet of 2.7 would side with Tarpeia's monologue rather than with Jove's judgment as expressed by the Roman Callimachus in the couplet under consideration. Let us not forget that, already at the time of Book 2, the fresh protest of elegy 7 was published only together with the embarrassing adulation of elegy 10. At the time of Book 4, Tarpeia's monologue, in spite of being surrounded by harsh condemnation, must have appeared much bolder. For we have seen the degree of adulation (or should I say: "profession of loyalty"?) that could be expected of a poet by now when we interpreted the Actium elegy 4.6.

Core and shell of elegy 4.4 are truly incompatible, and the irreconcilable difference of viewpoints appears clearer and clearer, the closer the narrative draws towards its factual ending. A surprise is effected when beloved Tatius, too, is granted a few words in direct discourse. In spite of representing the Sabine side (we observe the strong *at*, 89), he may be called the tool of Jove's punishment.

But Tatius (for the enemy did not honor her crime)
    said: "Here, get married, and climb onto the bed of my kingdom!"
Thus he spoke, and had her covered with his companions' arms:
    "This, virgin, was a dowry worthy of your services."

At Tatius (neque enim sceleri dedit hostis honorem)
    "Nube" ait "et regni scande cubile mei!"
Dixit, et ingestis comitum super obruit armis:
    "haec, virgo, officiis dos erat apta tuis."   (89–92)

In his usual drive for poetical economy, Propertius employs as few words as possible, leaving it to the reader to fill in the whole picture. *Nube* (90) probably points to the first and more preferable (55f.) of Tarpeia's two proposals: "marry me" rather than "*si minus . . . me rape*" (57ff.: *nuptae*, 59, then appears subordinated).[31] Marriage was implied both in her suggestion that she might be humane mother to Tatius' children (55) and in her wish to be his *regina* of equal rank (55), to which Tatius now sarcastically refers with the circumscription *regni . . . cubile mei* (90).

What we have to understand then, is that there are three steps: (1) Tarpeia's lonely monologue, in which she develops her plan; (2) her conversation with Tatius, in which she submits her suggestions (81), and, apparently, finds his consent to the more preferable alternative (82); (3) Tatius' poignant sarcasm and new interpretation of his earlier consent at the time when Tarpeia has fulfilled her part of the deal (90). Contrary to the usual interpretation, I would like to suggest that line 92 also is spoken by Tatius, addressed to her dead (*erat*) body, because the words *dos . . . apta* indicate the same type of sarcastic reinterpretation of her original words (*dos . . . non humilis*, 56) from the same original continuous context (55/56).[32] With Tatius as speaker, the address *virgo* (92) also serves the same ironical purpose of degrading Tarpeia's motive: Tatius addresses her by what Rome and Vesta demanded her to be but she, because of Tatius, did not want to remain any longer (*improba <u>virgineo</u> lecta ministra foco*, 44). Finally, *officia*, duties or services rendered, points in the direction of the same ambiguity. Weighing her behavior not in the terms of the service she desired to render to himself (cf. *opem*, 52) and which she actually did render, but rather ironically in terms of the disservice to her country or as the act of neglected duty which it was from Jove's (*sceleri*, 89) and Vesta's (*quantum . . . crimen*, 43) point of view, Tatius the enemy reveals that he shares with his Roman enemy the same honor code (the juxtaposition <u>hostis honorem</u>, 89, is as purposeful as was the other one <u>ignis ignoscat</u>, 45f.). *Tuis* (92), then, continues the "you" contained in *nube* and *scande* (90).

Why, then, the repetition of key words from phase (1) in phase (3)? Only to show (as Livy does) that the enemy thinks along the same lines as his opponent? This, of course, is important for understanding Tarpeia's miscalculation (an ugly, "objective" word, appropriate to strategy rather than love). To her, the real Tatius turns out to be just as hard and inhumane as Romulus, the foster-son of the she-wolf. He has no understanding whatsoever of her motivation. Her self-confident attempt to exercise a mitigating influence on the world of politics (*molliet arma torus*, 62), to set love over war, is shattered because her love is accepted only as long as it is useful for acquiring power. After that, she is simply dropped and excluded from that "honor" (89) which counts in combat and in the struggle for power, but is so different from the kind of "honor" (53) which she associated with love, motherhood, and humanity.

But from Tatius' lips, the twisted repetition of key words from Tarpeia's monologue and from her subsequent offer to him reveals not only the fact that the political enemies have more in common with each other than one of them has with a girl who loves him and risks everything she is for the sake of her love. In Tatius' mouth, these words are deliberate misquotations and brutal distortions of a tender original, to whose echoless meaning the poet has lent his own, almost autobiographical voice. The reader, trained to see the other side and introduced to Tarpeia's thoughts by her monologue, cannot avoid picturing Tarpeia's reaction to Tatius' words, even if the poet lets her die mute. Her eyes must have been opened to the fact that "fair" and "humane" Tatius was nothing but a product of her loving imagination, so that one is tempted to quote Propertius himself: *noster amor talis tribuit tibi, Cynthia, laudes* (3.24.3). To Tarpeia, Tatius is something much worse than a peer of his enemy Romulus. By holding her love in derision (*nube*) and willfully scorning her girlish hopes (*regni scande cubile mei*), he transgresses the political sphere and goes beyond punishing a traitor. His sarcasm enjoys hurting the individual, the human being in Tarpeia. When he insults her corpse and mocks her readiness to give up her ritual virginity for him (the ironical "virgo" practically declares Tarpeia a whore), he characterizes himself as incapable of receiving love, i.e., of being humanized.

Tatius' scornful behavior occupies the final two distichs of the narrative; after them, only one more distich, different in its orientation, follows. That is to say, from the viewpoint of composition, Tatius' brutality (89–92) forms the counter-piece to the idyllic scenery (3–6) which abruptly follows the opening couplet and which we felt to be both a foreign body in the elegy's complex introduction and a means of providing an independent standard by which the two leading characters could be measured (7 ~ 15). Now, having almost arrived at the end, we are in a position to confirm that interpretation. Tarpeia has measured up to the standard, but has died; Tatius has been found wanting, but lives. The "pastoral" world of love and peace has proved to be a truly foreign body in the martial world which supplies the ingredients for the growth of young Rome. Tarpeia dies in isolation, voiceless, and scene as well as judgment are left to

Tatius and his opponent Romulus (both of whom think more or less in Jove's terms of honor and treason) and to the Roman Callimachus, who speaks a final distich to make sure that this poem is understood as being part of his Roman Cycle:

> From guide Tarpeia the mountain has received its name:
>> O you waking one, unjustly you own your fate's reward!

> A duce Tarpeia mons est cognomen adeptus:
>> o vigil, iniuste praemia sortis habes. (93/94)

iniustae, OCT

Mention of the name Tarpeia closes the most outward ring, referring us back to line one. The term *cognomen* likewise points to line one where the grove and tomb named by the *cognomen* have been introduced. But the term also, of course, includes our poem among the elegies announced in the Roman program by *cognomina prisca locorum* (4.1A.69). That Tarpeia was "unjustly" allowed to give her name to the place corresponds to the association of her name with the word *turpis* in line 1. She does not deserve the honor.[33] We have been led around in a full circle by the poet who finally dismisses us at the point of departure: starting from the Julian viewpoint, we have slowly approached and then entered Tarpeia's soul. After leaving her, we have now come back to condemning her.

But we are left with a cacophony. Although the reader is led safely back to the Augustan outlook in the end, it is impossible that he should have forgotten how Tarpeia argued her case and how the poet made him participate in her reasoning from within. Also, the reader has just faced Tatius' excessively brutal behavior towards her.

And there is more. If the author really deems it unjust that Tarpeia was rewarded for her treason by having a place named after her and her memory eternalized—how then will he justify what he himself has done? He has done more than contribute to the injustice by further propagating her name and incorporating it along with the illustrious ones of Vertumnus (4.2), Caesar Augustus (4.6.13), Sancus-Hercules (4.9) and Iuppiter Feretrius (4.10) in his praise of Rome's heroic growth from a she-wolf's milk (4.1A.55ff.). He has even perfected the injustice, by himself reviving the traitor, by lending her his own earlier voice with which to justify herself, and by allowing her to negate precisely the wolflike spirit of Rome's Julian mission—in the centerpiece of his poem, with a special introduction (and epilogue) which guides the reader to understanding her position and even to sympathizing with her.

The discrepancies between Tarpeia's outlook and that of her environment are too great to be harmonized, and the opposing positions are too firmly presented to allow us to subsume the one under the other. Tarpeia's loving monologue negates the elegy's overall Julian setting in a way that no other Roman Elegy even remotely does. But it is closely related to the spirit of Horos' warning against Propertius' Augustan program. Horos warned that the Roman Cycle is incompatible with the spirit of poetry and that Propertius himself would regret his enterprise; that it endangers his long-term fame for the sake of a short-term success, paid off in the currency of the day; and that Apollo's prophecy to young Propertius declared his love poetry to be an obsession which would last as long as his career as a poet.

In the Tarpeia Elegy, it seems to me, Propertius reveals that he has accepted Horos' warning. Once more he lets us hear the voice of unconditional love—in disguise. As he himself suffered both under the régime's repression and under Cynthia's fickleness, so Tarpeia suffers both under Vesta's and Rome's claims upon her freedom, and under Tatius' cruel disregard of her love. As Tarpeia's life is extinguished by a loveless environment, so Propertius the lifelong poet of love withdraws into voiceless silence—a tragic decision, because his silence means a return to his poetic vocation, which, however, cannot be actualized with Cynthia dead and the public loyalty to Octavian demanded of a poet more strict than ever.

If he then, according to Horos' prediction, regretted having undertaken his Roman Cycle in a drive for short-term fame, why did he publish that incomplete, broken-off collection at all along with the other poems in his fourth book of elegies? The answer is perhaps simple: because, under the conditions of the Zeitgeist, his short-term fame as a contemporary poet could help him to survive in the long range as the poet of his own love, and escape the threat of *damnatio memoriae*. He himself perhaps tells us so, if we are only willing to listen to his hint. When announcing his aetiological work to the contemporary public and himself as the Roman Callimachus, he asks Bacchus' help

> in order that Umbria may be swollen with pride about my books,
>
> ut nostris tumefacta superbiat Umbria libris, . . .   (4.1A.63)

What is surprising in this context is the plural: *books*. In 4.9.72 he speaks of his "book", *libro . . . meo*. Unless we assume that the new *opus* (1.67) is initially planned to comprise more than that one book (a bold assumption considering the few aetiological elegies he actually did write—they occupy about half the size of a small book), we can hardly escape the conclusion that he is taking his three earlier books along on Roman Callimachus' alleged journey to fame (in them, too, he often enough referred to Callimachus as his model). This helps to give our hypothesis its final shape.

Propertius' Roman elegies, then, must not be seen as the culmination of his career. They are a concession to his situation, in two ways. When he could no longer write personal love poetry (because of either his disillusionment or Cynthia's death or both), he seemed condemned to silence unless he ventured to lend his mature talent to a new subject. On the other hand, the official demand for participation in Augustan Poetry seems to have become an almost unbearable pressure. Both difficulties, as I said before, are solved by the proclamation of the *Callimachus Romanus*. I now ask my reader to consider seriously the suggestion that Propertius broke away from the new task because it required more self-denial than he was capable of, and to accept Tarpeia's monologue as a restatement of his earlier position, written when the new attempt had already failed, and written in tragic awareness that this position meant his own death as a poet during his physical lifetime, though perhaps eternal fame in later ages.[34] Expressing our result in terms of a person's development—apart from that of poetical skills—we have to say: Propertius did not experience a development in the sense that he changed. He did experience a temptation, at a time when he seemed to have survived his creativity as a poet and as a human being. But he overcame the temptation to change, even at the price of falling back to where he had been already. He decided to remain the same, even if it meant, paradoxically, that he had to fall silent during his own lifetime.

NOTES

CHAPTER I

1. To D. O. Ross (1975, 59ff.), a year of unrequited love is apparently not sufficient to serve as the book's opening situation: as a *love* poem, he tells us, elegy 1.1 ". . . might just as well have been the fifth of the Book, or the tenth, or the fifteenth . . .". Thus we are asked to abandon the elegy's crystal-clear surface situation in favor of joining the interpreter's hunt for hidden treasures, which consist in supposedly "programmatic" allusions (hardly verifiable from the poem's logical context), to Gallus, Parthenius, etc. Right from the start, I gladly profess to the naïveté which fails to split off a poem's "programmatic" character from its stated subject. To Sabbadini (1899, 26ff.), elegy 1.1 was "la vera sfinge properziana". He tamed the monster by performing on it an "operazione . . . veramente chirurgica": Sabbadini cut it into two poems, the "contaminazione" of which in our manuscripts he ascribed to a "redattore" (whom he apparently invented to support the chirurgic interpretation).

2. Propertius' brachylogy should not have troubled commentators: instead of "now in the midst of Baiae—and then around Baiae" he only says "in the midst of Baiae—then (*modo*)". For a different case of single *modo* without an answering *modo*, see 1.1.11 (Chapter II below).

3. For the form *Miseni*, see Enk *ad locum*; Philipp in Pauly-Wissowa, 30. *Halbband*, c. 2046.

4. Barber even considered exchanging lines 2 and 4 to improve the poem's supposedly mistaken north/south geography, whereas SB is prepared to ascribe to the poet a somewhat loose topography: "As for geography, the whole expression might be regarded as loosely describing the *Mare Tyrrhenum* off Baiae." (Fedeli [1980, 265] finds here a "digressione geografica", containing "un' amplificatio dotta".) Before blaming the textual tradition or even the poet himself for lacking

precision, an interpreter must always question his own overall understanding of the work of art.

5. If Meleager (*A.P.* 5.166, cf. Schulz-Vanheyden, 129) was his model, he "improved" it. Meleager starts out by first asking ἆρα μένει στοργῆς ἐμὰ λείψανα; *locus* (6) suggests a spatial term for rendering *in extremo . . . amore* in English.

6. The allegedly unnecessary double mention of "water" (*in unda*, *lympha*), which Propertius' style has been blamed for here ("verbal indiscipline", SB), is necessitated by what he wants to say. For *unda* (singular) standing for the plural, see the "waves" of smoke at Vergil, *Aen.* 8.257.

7. The connection is severed if one reads—with Hosius and SB—*tenetur* for *timetur* in line 18. A different interpretation is tried by Camps (I, 1966², 102). Straining the Latin text: Petersmann 1980, 120.

8. This is the meaning here of *triste*, not so much "disagreeable to Cynthia"; in the above quoted line 2.6.13 he feels "hurt" (*laedent*) as a result of his fear; here his fear gives him depressing thoughts.

9. *Tu* serves to set Cynthia off from others (contained among the *multis* and the *puellis* who came to harm at Baiae). The contrasting function of *tu* here (and in some other passages) is not recognized by Tränkle (8: "ohne einen besonderen Anlass, die angeredete Person hervorzuheben").

10. We shall face the question of "odd" distichs again when discussing elegies 1.1, 1.7, and others.

11. Recently, Richardson has declared the *quod*-clause dependent on *conscia Roma*, taken as a vocative: "You, Rome, who are privy to what would keep me here". This seems to raise more problems than it solves, among them: the relation of line 2 to 3/4; the notion of "here", which is no longer in R.'s text since he takes *Roma* as a vocative (Enk's objection applies that, without the subject *Roma*, the words *moram faciat* require a complement answering the question "*Cuius rei?*"); R.'s translation of the present subjunctive *faciat* by "would keep" sounds disagreeably close to a contrary-to-fact; that the notion of *Roma* should cover not a general public but only "those friends he (i.e., Propertius) encounters on his rounds, who talk about his dejected condition" (etc.), is an unwarranted reduction in the scope of this word. See the main text (on *desidia*).

12. Petersmann (1980), following Richardson along these lines (except for disagreeing on *conscia*, 123, n. 27), feels that the poet is being encouraged to leave for *Baiae*. He then (125ff.) misses the logic of lines 3ff. as well as the precise relationship of 1.11 and 12. See also Davis 1977, 39; 43.

13. SB, however, does not clearly see the place of *desidiae* within the logical context. Its point of reference lies not so much—as SB seems to assume—in lines 3/4 as in 5/6 (cf. *consuetos . . . amores*). See the main text.

14. SB (following Enk; see also Fedeli *ad loc.*) pleads in favor of the rival interpretation "nor does she whisper sweetly in my ear", remarking that the alternative translation ("nor does her name sound sweetly") is "inappropriate here . . .". "Propertius' love, as he is at pains to show, has survived ill treatment unimpaired." This misses the poet's point; according to 1.11, his dependence on (love for) Cynthia will not change, whether she causes him to be *laetus* or to be *tristis*. The latter being the case now (in the situation of 1.12), her name does no longer sound *dulcis* to him (when he pronounces it himself? Cf. 12.14). Thus it is the larger context of

poems 11 and 12 that suggests the translation "sound sweetly": neither does Propertius enjoy her love any longer—nor does ⟨even⟩ her name sound sweetly to him: a well-put climax of discomfort. This understanding also avoids the awkwardness of *Cynthia* (6) picking up *illa* (3).

15. Cf. *Thesaurus Ling. Lat.* s.v. *fides* (*caput alterum*; II: "*actio vel facultas credendi sive confidendi*").

16. See, most recently, Petersmann 1980, 126ff. He goes too far in concluding that Gallus must be the addressee also of 1.12.

17. Lyne 1979 (not yet acquainted with the fact that the term *domina* occurs in the newly found Gallus fragment) suggests that the understanding of love as *servitium amoris* is basically Propertius' achievement, *servitium* being as real to the poet as a situation of political confinement is to Cicero. For details on refinements of the figure, see Murgatroyd 1981.

18. For reasons of methodology, the interpretations of 1.11 and 12 given in this chapter may be compared with those presented by Petersmann (1980, 112–131), who cites (9) H. Friedrich's "Epochen der italienischen Lyrik" (Frankfurt am Main, 1964) among his tools. It will be found that *Themenführung* and *Motiventfaltung*, when pursued without strict observation of *Gedankenführung*, can contribute to obfuscating rather than to clarifying the elegist's poetic design. For instance, when misunderstanding 11.9–13 as an "interessanter literarischer Versuch" (a view which reflects the preeminence ascribed by Saylor (1975) to landscape symbolism in this passage), Petersmann peremptorily censures the poet for his, the interpreter's, failure to make sense of the text, asserting "die Gedankenführung bleibt unlogisch" (117).

19. My reader will appreciate that I am not constantly reminding him of the possible difference between poetic persona and historic individual Propertius. Interpreting autobiographical poems at their face value is not the same as granting historicity to their contents in detail. For a discussion of my procedure, see last note to Chapter V.

CHAPTER II

1. Or: "infected".

2. Or: "trampled on my head" (Hubbard 1975, 15). See below.

3. *Ille* in line 12 (Rothstein sees here an example of postclassic, unemphatic use of the demonstrative pronoun) and in the next line is used emphatically, stating the contrast to Propertius himself ("unlike myself", Postgate). A further climax is expressed by the change of position, from second half of line 12 to first word in line 13, as well as by the repetition itself: *ille . . . ille*.

4. Cf. Tränkle, p. 15 with note 2, where he twice translates *et* by "auch". On p. 16, he interprets the same as part of a climax by "sogar". This may be all right as long as it is clear that lines 11 and 12 are on fairly the same level of action. The important climax occurs when the poet moves on from these lines to the singular action described in distich 13/14. The second *modo*, although dropped and replaced (or "represented") by *et*, may nevertheless be felt and should be expressed in English—as is the case in 1.11.1–3, where the first *modo* is dropped (see Chap-

ter I; cf. *OLD* s.v. *modo*). Hering's (1970, 107, n. 32) summary is hardly invalidated by Cairns' (1974A, 94ff.) later suggestion (already declined by Housman 1888, 19 = 1972, 42) to take *modo* as "recently". Beside through *et* ("also", "too"), continuation in line 12 of the action level expressed in 11 is guaranteed by identical tense (*ibat* resumes *errabat*) and by identical acting subject (*ille*, 12, is in retrospect felt to be subject also to 11). Dropping the second *modo*, then, is a matter both of moulding (and preparing) a climax and of Propertius' well-known linguistic economy. Thus a replacement for the second *modo* (as at 1.3.41f.: *nam modo . . . rursus et . . .*) seems hardly desired here. Housman (as well as SB and others) located the need for a second *modo* (or equivalent) in the *etiam* clause (13), and, in SB's words, tried to show that "A copulative particle like *etiam* never serves the same purpose" (see also the material listed by Housman in his Commentary on Manilius, Cambridge 1937², *ad* 1.898; see also *ad* 871). But it seems questionable that the final climax of Milanion being wounded (13/14) should be at all coordinated to his erring around (11) and facing wild beasts (12). The perfect tense (*ingemuit*, 14) speaks against such a parallelizing with two preceding imperfect tenses (cf. Enk *ad loc.*). And one wonders whether the demand for a certain parallel of a second *modo* being replaced by a copulative particle (= *et*, in my account) may not overly restrain the poet's linguistic individuality.

After all, Propertius offers a wide variety of uses. He likes to collocate *modo* in both places with the same word, like *te modo . . . te modo* (4.3.7 and 8, continued by *. . . que . . . que . . . et*). In more elaborate passages, the poet works this out to (almost) full grammatical, semantical, and metrical balance, as in 1.3.21 and 23:

> *et modo solvebam . . .*
> *et modo gaudebam . . .*

Perhaps even more striking is the correspondence of 1.14.3 and 4:

> *et modo tam celeres . . .*
> *et modo tam tardas . . .*

If these passages present the ideal balance, others may be viewed as deficient modes of the ideal, as for instance *quae modo . . . et modo* (1.20.39 and 41), where the necessity of using a relative pronoun supersedes any aesthetic desire for a first *et* to balance the second. In similar fashion we can understand 1.11.1 and 3 (see Chapter I above):

> *ecquid te mediis cessantem . . .*
> *et modo Thesproti mirantem . . .*

Here, too, a desire for balance is manifest from the repeated metrical (bucolic diaeresis), grammatical (accusative of participle twice, and twice in the same metrical position) and sound (*homoeoteleuton*) pattern. What prevents the poet from making the aesthetic balance even more complete (i.e., from beginning line 1 with *et modo* or at least some other monosyllabum followed by *modo*) is the fact that the opening lines are part of a superseding logical context (consisting of two alternative questions) which must be expressed. Thus we read *Ecquid te* (*. . . cura subit*)—words which themselves will be balanced six lines later by *an te* (*. . . hostis sustulit*). Moreover, the "missing" first *modo* is, as was shown in Chapter I, easily supplied with the contrast "in the midst of Baiae—outside Baiae". Solitary second *modo* (instead of *modo* . . . *modo*) is acknowledged by Kühner-Stegmann (2.2.73) with regard to Tac. *Ann.* 4.50.4 and 6.32.1.

The question arises how far we should believe Propertius to go in dismantling and varying the aesthetic balance at the other end of the scale. Is (second) *et modo* (3.14.15) alone once more correct, or should an editor change the order of distichs? Is a case like *nam modo* . . . *rursus et* (1.3.41 and 42; continued, on a slightly different level, by *interdum*, 43) the lower limit of correspondence, or is our initial passage (1.1.11 and 12) with its *nam modo* . . . *ibat et* (and its two parallel imperfect tense forms) still acceptable? After all, there is the parallel of *et modo* . . . *et* (continued by *et*) at 2.24.11. (There, Housman and others assume a *lacuna* before line 11 to account for the "missing" *modo*.) In view of our author's stylistic range and singularity, one is inclined to side with those editors who hesitate to change the good manuscript tradition by either reading *saepe* in 1.1.12 (so again SB) or assuming (and filling) a "*lacuna*" after line 1.1.11 (Housman; see also last note in this chapter).

5. Or: "lonely".

6. For a good survey of opinions, I refer my reader to the introductory sections of Cairns' (1974A) and Hering's (1970) articles.

7. See also first note to Chapter I above.

8. Allen 1950, 255ff.

9. "Der Pentameter, der den Begriff prima *noch einmal* ausführlicher und lebendiger *wiederholt*" (Rothstein *ad loc.*; italics mine).

10. I do not deny that *primus* may occasionally be compared to an antecedent state which is not part of the number series 1, 2, 3, etc. But precise observation will show (a) that the preceding set or unit is not automatically presumed but is especially mentioned and defined, and (b) that even in such a configuration *primus* is usually understood to be the first in the *new* set, i.e., here too looks forward to what follows. Cf. Quint. 3.1.8: *Nam primus post eos quos poetae tradiderunt movisse aliqua circa rhetoricen Empedocles dicitur.* One may think that Empedocles is here seen only in relation to his "forerunners", since he seems to be followed by a new and unrelated group (*artium scriptores antiquissimi*) formed by Corax and Tisias. But, following them, Gorgias is mentioned as *Empedoclis, ut traditur, discipulus.* That is, *primus* did look forward in the direction of a consequent. Normal use, though hardly necessary to explain, is well illustrated by the adverbs *primo* . . . *deinde* . . . *tum.* A Roman audience did not understand that the word *prima* in Prop. 1.1.1 is implicitly to deny an antecedent ("there was no girl before Cynthia"). See also *venturi prima favilla mali*, 1.9.18. Even at Verg. *Ecl.* 6.1 *prima* may also indicate that the poet wishes to be seen as the first in (founder of) a new Latin genre.

11. "*Prima* und *finis* fassen die beiden Pole, zwischen denen die äusseren Ereignisse eingespannt sind. Die Wortfolge *Cynthia prima* weist auf den erzählenden Eingang des Liederbuches zurück." Petersmann 1980, 215.

12. It is of course only to the modern (not the Roman) reader that the adjective seems to "replace" an adverb. In Latin this construction (though not listed in Lewis & Short s.v. *primus*—a circumstance which has given trouble to at least one scholar) is quite natural as the following passages may show: Livy 9.6.1: *Primi consules prope seminudi sub iugum missi; tum ut quisque gradu proximus erat, ita ignominiae obiectus; tum deinceps singulae legiones.* Verg. *Aen.* 1.613/14:

Obstipuit primo aspectu Sidonia Dido,
casu deinde viri tanto, et sic ore locuta est.

Here *primo aspectu* does not mean "at first sight" (as Austin *ad loc.* seems to take the words: "it was her first sight of Aeneas"); the passage should be translated as follows: "*First* Dido was numbed by the sight" (sc., of Aeneas: this line sums up lines 588–93 of the narrative, where the hero is revealed to her eyes), "*thereafter* by the man's overwhelming sufferings" (this refers to his following address to the queen at 594ff., in which he alludes to some of his *infandos . . . labores* (597); cf. *tum* 594). Verg. *Aen.* 1.737ff.: *primaque* (sc., *Dido*) *. . . tum . . . post alii . . .* Ovid. *Ars Am.* 1.269f.:

Prima tuae menti veniat fiducia, cunctas
posse capi: capies, tu modo tende plagas.

Here the *deinde* or *tum* before *capies* must be supplied by the reader.

13. Recently, Petersmann (1980, 220), too, has pointed out a "zeitlichen Ablauf".

14. The text of Meleager's epigram (*A.P.* 12.101) is as follows:

Τόν με Πόθοις ἄτρωτον ὑπὸ στέρνοισι Μυΐσκος
   ὄμμασι τοξεύσας τοῦτ' ἐβόησεν ἔπος·
"Τὸν θρασὺν εἷλον ἐγώ· τὸ δ' ἐπ' ὀφρύσι κεῖνο φρύαγμα
   σκηπτοφόρου σοφίας ἠνίδε ποσσὶ πατῶ."
Τῷ δ', ὅσον ἀμπνεύσας, τόδ' ἔφην· "Φίλε κοῦρε, τί θάμβεις;
   καὐτὸν ἀπ' Οὐλύμπου Ζῆνα καθεῖλεν Ἔρως."

Me (so far not wounded in my chest by Desires) Myiskos
   hit with the arrows of his eyes, and shouted:
"I, I caught the insolent one. But on his eyebrows that haughtiness
   of kingly wisdom—look! I am trampling on it with my feet."
To him, when catching my breath, I said: "Dear young man, why so
                                                       astonished?
Even Zeus himself was pulled down from Olympus by Eros!"

15. Steidle 1962, 113. Cf. Fedeli (1969, 83: Propertius uses *capio* "per indicare la conquista amorosa . . ."). Alfonsi (1957, 8f.) speaks of "conquistatrice con suoi occhi". We must not uncritically equate Propertius' *cepit* with his supposed model's aggressive εἷλον ἐγώ (line 3). A major point of difference between the two poems is that, while victorious Myiskos pronounces a feeling of triumph toward his victim, no such utterance is ascribed to Cynthia in our poem. Rather, she seems to feel indifferently toward her victim (lines 21f.). Propertius transfers the active part of Myiskos to Amor, not to Cynthia.

16. Following Steidle and Fedeli, we may no longer believe that Luna was enchanted or arrested ("caught") by naked Endymion's beauty, but must assume that Endymion was a streaker who chased, outran, and finally seized ("caught") the goddess:

nudus Endymion Phoebi cepisse sororem
   dicitur . . .   (Prop. 2.15.15).

17. The "hunting metaphor" (SB) often characterizes the "prey's" rather than the "hunter's" viewpoint. A men-hunting woman like the *formosam et oculis venantem viros* of Phaedr. 4.5.4 (listed in SB's Appendix, p. 268) we can hardly use to explain Propertius' *cepit*. For Phaedrus goes on to call her a *moecha* (21; 39; 42)—a label Propertius in 1.1 is far from applying to his *domina* (cf. 21).

18. The poet cannot be held responsible for the associations a modern interpreter feels entitled to introduce. According to F. Ahl (1974, 81), "*Cynthia* is evocative of Diana *herself*. . . . Since Cynthia is the very first word of the poem, we are confronted not only with a woman, but the goddess of the hunt, the moon, childbirth, night and *all* the aspects of triformis Hecate with whom Diana is so often identified. The poet's Cynthia, then, is *beauty, death, chastity, magic, evil, coldness—* and the *very beginnings of life*." (Italics mine.) According to Ahl, "the name allows" (with the poet's permission?) "a multiplicity of innuendos." If Cynthia = Diana, the only features confirmed by the poem would be her chastity (*castas*, 5) and, in the mirror of Atalante, her (in her lover's view) deplorable disinterest in her suitor.

19. With regard to *suis*, it seems worth considering that Propertius represents Cynthia to be master of "her own" eyes—something which he himself is not any longer, for his eyes are mastered by Amor.

20. Propertius himself would use the term "wheel" in this context:

> vinceris aut vincis: haec in amore rota est. (2.8.8).

21. Schulz-Vanheyden, 123. "Triumph", W. Steidle, *AAHG* 9, 1956, 81, n.4.

22. Hanslik 1976, 189 (italics mine). Ahl (1974, 83) finds here not only love "triumphant" as the "hunter", who "presses his foot down on the head of the captured beast", but also, in a "double-entendre", "a foot in the metrical sense of verse": "Defeat by love . . . has impressed upon his mind the meter appropriate to his passion: the love-elegy." This seems hard to verify from Propertius' text.

23. Hanslik 1976, 188, n. 8.

24. Schulz-Vanheyden, 123. Nor does *pressit . . . pedibus* here, as we shall see. It has apparently escaped Schulz-Vanheyden (123; 119f.) that the poem which he for his part identifies as Propertius' presumable source for "die Geste des Fussaufsetzens", viz., *A.P.* 12.48 (Meleager: κεῖμαι· λὰξ ἐπίβαινε κατ' αὐχένος, ἄγριε δαῖμον), does by no means depict a mere *gesture* either, but an act of inflicting pain comparable to the meaning I find required in Prop. 1.1.4. See below (especially n. 29).

25. Kühner-Stegmann, *Ausführliche Grammatik der Lateinischen Sprache*, reprint Hannover, 1966, 2, 1, 84.

26. See also the passages quoted by Rothstein and Enk. In none of them is the conqueror satisfied with merely setting his foot on the victim (though his next action is not always despoiling). Bömer in his commentary on Ov. *F.* 4.858 (Heidelberg, 1958, 2, 282f.) offers a widely ranging list for the topic "Der Fuss im Nacken des Besiegten". He, too, includes passages that, strictly speaking, go beyond the gesture of victory.

27. A long list of instances is found in Schulz-Vanheyden (p. 119 with n. 24). But Schulz-Vanheyden does not distinguish between a *gesture* and an *action*, nor (and in this he differs from Hanslik) does he observe the apparent physical difference between setting one's *foot* or one's *feet* on the defeated enemy. On Prop. 1.1.4

he comments: "Das Aufsetzen *der Füsse* auf Haupt und Nacken des Gegners ist, *wie literarisches und ikonographisches Material zeigt*, eine *Geste* des Siegers, mit der er die völlige Unterwerfung des Besiegten *anzeigt*." However, his evidence does not show what he says it shows. His literary examples, anyway, mention (and, it seems to me, mean), if at all, *one* foot only (and at Curt. Ruf. 9.7.22 the foot is set on the victim to facilitate the fatal blow—not a *gesture* which "anzeigt" but an *action*!). As part of his "iconographic" evidence, he introduces a Hadrian statue, "*den linken Fuss* auf den Nacken eines Barbaren setzend", and an Aphrodite (from Pergamon), "die mit *dem Fuss* auf den Kopf des Gegners tritt." (All italics in this note mine.)

Moreover, though rejecting Gotsmich's explanation (1941, 844ff.) that this Aphrodite's action is "magical", he is silent about the alternative interpretation by Dopp and by Winnefeld (which Gotsmich summarized and tried to replace), according to which Aphrodite is stemming her foot against the defeated giant's head *in order to be better able to pull out the spear*. Apparently it escaped Schulz-Vanheyden that, if Dopp and Winnefeld are possibly right, he is not entitled to use this Aphrodite as evidence for the *gesture* of the victor ("Geste des Siegers").

The confusion in this dissertation is even heightened by the fact that, following his remarks (and mistaken evidence) on the "Geste des Siegers" (or "Gebärde des Fussaufsetzens"), the author goes on (p. 120) to consider it possible that Propertius, when writing of the "*gesture* of the victor", had before his eye a fragment (no. 9 Martini) of Parthenius in which Eros steps with *both* ($\dot{\alpha}\mu\phi o\tau\acute{\epsilon}\rho o\iota\varsigma$) his feet on the victim in order to *despoil* him ("die Spoliierung des Gegners zu erleichtern". The "spoils" here are the victim's $\phi\rho\acute{\epsilon}\nu\epsilon\varsigma$). See also the examples of spoliation in his note 27 (where "II." has to be corrected to "Il.". In note 31 on the same page, "Steidle a.a.o." is wrong and should be corrected to "Steidle 1962", since in note 28 "Steidle, AAHG 1956" had been referred to).

Clarity will not be gained if one does not distinguish between the *gesture* of and the *action* (which is part of a sequence of actions) of stepping on the defeated victim. Mention of *both* feet can be significant as indicating an action (as in Prop. 1.1.4), while mention of *one* foot *may* be indicative of the *gesture*—if it is not to be understood as "Dichtersprache". As in Ov. F. 4.663 Faunus, when stepping on the two sheepskins spread by King Numa, in all likelihood is using *both* his feet (*Faunus adest oviumque premens pede vellera duro*), so the entangled lover who experiences Amor as a pain in his neck (and is given the advice to give in and cease struggling, *desine luctari!*) probably feels the burden of Amor (cf. *A.P.* 12.48.2) standing with *both* feet on his neck (*et tua saevus Amor sub pede colla premit*, Ov. *R.A.* 530). The latter passage then combines poetic plural *colla* and poetic singular *pede* in expressing something much stronger than a mere gesture. But even *use* of *one* foot only may be more than a mere gesture. Schulz-Vanheyden's list contains an instance of Amor *torturing* Psyche (as the author, following Helbig-Speier, classifies), with his lower left leg on Psyche's body. (See W. Helbig-H. Speier, *Führer durch die öffentlichen Sammlungen klassischer Altertümer in Rom*, Band I⁴, Tübingen 1963, 804f., no. 1123.)

28. Twice (*Pont.* 4.7.48 and *Trist.* 5.8.10) the context includes the verb *calcare*, "trample". See n. 30 below.

29. Support for this view can be found in an epigram by Meleager (*A.P.* 12.48, ed. Beckby). Here the lover, lying on the ground ($\kappa\epsilon\hat{\iota}\mu\alpha\iota$), tells Eros to go ahead and step on his neck ($\lambda\grave{\alpha}\xi\ \dot{\epsilon}\pi\acute{\iota}\beta\alpha\iota\nu\epsilon\ \kappa\alpha\tau'\alpha\dot{\upsilon}\chi\acute{\epsilon}\nu o\varsigma$).

However, far from being pessimistic, he is confident that he will be able to bear (φέρειν) Eros—in spite of his *weight* (καὶ βαρὺν ὄντα). A late variant is offered by Paulus Silentiarius (*A.P.* 5.268). He reports that Eros, ever since he set his "bitter foot" (πικρὸν . . . πόδα) on the lover's chest, has been *sitting upon* (ἐνέζεται) him without moving away, his wings clipped. Both poems display the sort of longtime (cf. *donec*, Prop. 1.1.5) heavy burden Amor represents in Prop. 1.1 (cf. also, though somewhat different, 2.30.8: *et gravis ipse super libera colla sedet*). In 1.1 Amor may then be seen to stand with both his feet, i.e., with his full weight, on his victim's head, pressing it to the ground, hurting the victim. At the same time it is clear where the idea of the surviving defeated (who will be the narrator of the event) is at home: in erotic epigram.

30. The nuance of "trample" would then be comparable to *calcare*, as in *exstructos morientum calcat acervos*, Ov. *Met.* 5.88, *ense tuo factos calcabas victor acervos*, *Pont.* 4.7.47, or *imposito calcas quid mea fata pede?* (*Trist.* 5.8.10). A late Greek example of Eros "trampling" is offered by Julianus Aegyptius (s. VI A.D.) in his epigram on Praxiteles' bronze sculpture of Eros (Eros is speaking): "Bowing his proud neck under our sandals," etc. (Κλίνας αὐχένα γαῦρον ὑφ' ἡμετέροισι πεδίλοις, *A.P.* 16.203.1). Richardson translates *caput . . . pressit* by "bowed my head", perhaps in recollection of κλίνας. But one has to account for the harsh action implied in *pressit* (as well as in *pedibus*: "an immediate, sensible evocation . . . of the bodily feeling of being trampled", as Connor 1972, 53, puts it—without, however, integrating this comment into the logic of the passage).

31. The *Oxford Latin Dictionary* (s.v. *premere*, no. 15) wrongly lists this passage under "to tread or trample on", quoting as follows: *cum . . . elephas . . . eum . . . pondere suo . . . premeret*. This abbreviated quotation is misleading because—among other words—the decisive words *genu innixus* have been left out.

32. It is worth mentioning in this context that apparently there existed a convention that excluded disgracing (specifically kicking) an opponent once he was lying on the ground (especially, of course, when dead). See Fraenkel on Aesch. *Ag.* 885; Jebb on Soph. *Aj.* 1348.

33. "Indem Properz nun genau an dem Punkt, an dem sich bei dem Griechen die Pointe entwickelt, seine Vorlage radikal verlässt, macht er seinen Lesern klar: was jetzt folgt, ist nicht mehr Meleager, sondern Properz, ist gegenüber dem Epigramm neu und anders." Schulz-Vanheyden 125.

34. See Allen 1950, 265.

35. Cairns (1974A, 98), calling young Propertius an "anti-love figure", points to the parallel of Milanion (lines 9–16), who—outside our poem—is pictured as a misogynist before meeting Atalante (Aristophanes, *Lysistrata* 785–795)—"ein männliches Gegenstück zu Atalante", as Rothstein calls him.

36. One should probably not (with Rothstein, SB, Fedeli, and Wistrand, 32) tone down the converted young man's emotion to a mere disinclination. "*Odisse* ist freilich ein sehr harter Ausdruck" (Hanslik 1976, 189, seeing an allusion to *Cat.* 85: *odi et amo*; cf. Alfonsi 1957, 12).

37. These passages are among the examples Kühner-Stegmann give of the generic plural (2,2,86f.). For the difficulty of defining this use of the plural, see also Löfstedt, *Syntactica* (Malmö, 1965²) 1, 38ff., and Leumann-Hofmann-Szantyr 2,16, *Zusätze* α—"affektische (meist schmähende) Verallgemeinerung" ("affectic . . . generalization")—and β. Allen (1950, 266f.) cites Phaedria's complaint (Ter. *Eun.*

48) about *meretricum contumelias*, together with Donatus' comment "Cum uni sit iratus de omnibus queritur". In the preceding chapter we translated *mutat via longa puellas* (1.12.11) as "a long trip changes a woman."

38. The plural is occasionally used in English, too. A colleague, having spent a burdensome weekend at home, informed me one Monday morning: "The difficulty with wives, you know, is . . ."

39. Here Ahl (1974, 84) seems, at least partially, on the right track: "Perhaps this is the movement from boyhood to manhood, from innocence to worldliness, from the admiration of girlish innocence to hatred of it."

40. Cf. *Thuc.* 7.77.4: καὶ ἡμᾶς <u>εἰκὸς</u> νῦν τά τε ἀπὸ τοῦ θεοῦ ἐλπίζειν ἠπιώτερα ἕξειν (οἴκτου γὰρ ἀπ' αὐτῶν ἀξιώτεροι ἤδη ἐσμὲν ἢ φθόνου) . . .

41. Alfonsi 1957; Allen 1950; Baker 1974.

42. Lachmann, p. xxiv.

43. BB; SB.

44. Allen 1950, 266, n. 34. Allen also states that *furor* (line 7) cannot apply to Propertius' seeing prostitutes.

45. Fontenrose (1949, 381) considers it possible that poems 23 and 24 (as well as 22) amount to nothing more than a threat. See also Enk 1957, 26.

46. Enk's detailed discussion (1911, 143–150) of poem 2.24A is still valuable, especially because he emphasizes the connection of *infamis* (24.7) and *infamant* (24.10); 24A may well have to be read as a witty and appropriate response to someone who has taken the realism of 23 as "evidence" by relating its contents to the poet's real life. However this may be, no biographical "facts" can be extracted from the poem (nor from 22 or 23). See also Allen 1962, 123ff., on poems 23 and 24 and on the kind of "reality" supposedly envisaged in them.

47. BB.

48. "*Casta* cannot mean *simply* a woman who says no" (SB).

49. Evidence concerning Propertius' use of *castus* in this sense has been collected by Fontenrose (1949, 371ff.).

50. BB.

51. Fontenrose 1949, 377f. ("Cynthia, or his love for her, has taught Propertius to dislike a very different sort of woman"); Enk 1957, 27. Cf. Van Berchem 1948, 139.

A variant of Fontenrose's interpretation is offered by Wistrand (1977, 38). He has suggested that at 1.1.5 *castas puellas* "might be rendered by 'faithful girls' or 'wifely love'". But this can hardly be adapted to the poetic situation of the boy who recently awakened to love. And it, too, is subject to the general objection listed in the text.

52. CIL 4.1520.

53. BB; cf. Alfonsi 1957, 12f.

54. Fontenrose (1949, 377; 378).

55. Fontenrose 1949, 378f.; cf. Steidle 1962, 112. A peculiar variant in the Lachmann tradition is presented by Van Berchem (1948). Excluding Cynthia from the *castae* and understanding *castas odisse puellas* as "haïr les filles honnêtes" (p. 138), he is convinced "que ce sont les dérèglements de sa maîtraisse qui ont causé sa chute" (139). This is not borne out by the context, unnecessary to say.

56. Sullivan 1961.

57. Cf. Hering 1970, 103, n. 21.

58. Thus one can hardly agree with Petersmann (1980, 220) "dass das Gedicht des Anfangs den Zustand des Endes (sc., of the *Monobiblos*) meint". The disappointed lover of 1.12 can never return to being the inexperienced boy of 1.1.

59. E.g., by Cairns (1974A, 99), who, under the traditional prejudice about Cynthia's status in 1.1, rejects his own findings, viz., that mythical and mortal couple both display "conflicts between an anti-love hero and an anti-love heroine" (o.c. p. 98). See also Baker 1974, 278f.; Fedeli *ad loc.*

60. Although Wistrand (1977, 31ff.) has shown that *casta* (like *pudica*) often characterizes the "faithful", "loyal", or "devoted" wife, this does of course not exclude (not even in all of the examples given by Wistrand) that *casta* still can mean "chaste".

61. Fontenrose changes—without a basis in the Latin text—the rejection to a partial one: "Yet I cannot inspire an *equal* passion in her, so that she will love *only* me (1949, 382; italics mine).

62. Fontenrose 1949, 375f.; Steidle (1962, 113) insists "dass Cynthia eine Hetäre ist, gewiss eine von besonderer Art, aber eben doch eine Hetäre", who (according to the Milanion example) is, however, *wooed* by "ein dauerndes, intensives, aber *vergebliches Werben* des Properz" (112; italics mine).

63. The logical organization of the passage excludes changing *nam* (11) to *non* (as Weeber 1974 suggests).

64. Steidle (1962, 114) and Allen (1950, 269f.; 1962, 135f.), with whom I largely agree about the remaining part of the poem. From Alfonsi's statement "il mito è l'ideale opposto alla realtà" (1957, 14) one can derive a truth about Propertius: for him is "ideal" what is reality to others, and for them is unreal what is reality to him. Cf. Sullivan (1961, 107): "his experience is contrary to what normally happens", and Allen (1950, 270): "In Propertius' own case normal experience is reversed". It follows that the example of Milanion stresses the "unique and personal character" of Propertius' experience (Allen 1962, 136).

65. "Maggiore importanza" for Tullus (Fedeli 1969, 86) is hardly the purpose of a delayed dedication. Nor is the style of the Milanion episode elevated because its supposed Greek model was (o.c.84). Rather, the style is elevated because Milanion's fate appears praiseworthy when compared with that of Propertius. Ahl (1974, 89) believes that Propertius here is "somewhat sarcastically" countering the conventional version of the Milanion story suggested to him by Tullus. ("Da ist in den Text hineininterpretiert, was nicht in ihm steht." Hanslik 1976, 193.) See also Warden 1980, 87 ("the address to Tullus is purely formal").

66. He "avoids no toils" on his way to final success. SB is hardly right in making Milanion here an *adulescens delicatus*. His heroic endurance (including, in all probability, even fighting for the beloved and, certainly, being wounded!) distinguishes him from Propertius' helpless inactivity. Successful Milanion is not the "prototype" (SB) but the opposite of Propertius.

67. Concerning *bene facta* (fighting with the Centaur), see Hanslik 1976, 192; good: Yardley 1979; *preces* (changed to *fides* by Housman 1888, 23f. = 1972, 45f.— "Prayers! where has he said a word about prayers?"—followed by G. P. Goold 1967, 64; Hanslik 1976, 193; Yardley 1979, 131ff.) are so natural in the context that we should allow the poet to include them in his summary without having mentioned them in his narrative (thus avoiding a doublet).

68. For *tardus* meaning "slow to aid", see Genovese 1972, 143.

69. Reading *et* (at 1.1.25) means, according to Housman (1888, 33 = 1972, 52), imputing to Propertius "the stupidity of praying that Cynthia may begin to love him *and* that he may cease to love Cynthia." SB's working hypothesis (1967, 6) that "logic should not always have the last word in this text" leads him to ascribing more confusion to the distressed lover than his words actually suggest.

70. *Recte* Steidle 1962, 114; cf. Hering 1970, 111f. Thus the witches are here being offered a worthy case to prove their credibility. Shackleton Bailey (1949, 22), thinking that our poet ("with whom logical consistency is notoriously not a strong point") is simultaneously asking for help from and expressing his lacking faith in magic, looks for parallels in Latin literature of such inconsistent human behavior. But this misses the point. For a priori no help is expected to come forward from either witches or friends. Propertius is (in spite of the rhetorical form) not so much calling for help as offering the two groups a true *adynaton* as an opportunity to prove (or rather, disprove) their claims of magic power or helpful friendship. To be satisfied, he would need to see, not "tricks" of bringing down the moon, but a change in Cynthia's attitude; not advice *after* (*sero, lapsum*) the fact, but a change in his own condition. The intended outcome is, of course, that the incurability of his situation is demonstrated more clearly than ever.

The assumption of lacking "logical consistency" (SB, see above) is a dangerous hypothesis for a literary critic to make. For (like beauty) inconsistency can exist merely in the eye of the commentator. The argument of lines 19–24 may be outlined as follows: your claims of power over nature (like of being able to bring down the moon) are, in my eyes, a trick (or, to use Housman's words, "a false pretence"). Here is a real test case for you (*en agedum*) by which to prove your alleged abilities *to me*: if you can change the mind of my mistress, then I (*ego*, emphasizing) would certainly be ready to credit your craft with powers over nature (like attracting rivers and stars), i.e., I would then be willing to believe your usual claims, since you would have performed a task of much greater difficulty. (Of course the speaker does not expect the witches to solve either the greater or the smaller task, the latter of which, after all, means breaking the laws of nature.) Imperative plus *tunc* here equals "if—then".

It was left to Ross (1975, 66) to understand the witches to be *poets* (Vergil, Gallus, "the magical power of neoteric song"): "If such poetry could charm Cynthia, then Propertius would welcome it." Ross involuntarily illustrates the danger that results when an interpreter feels free to abandon the poem's surface context and logic in his search for deeper meaning. See also Chapter I, n. 1.

71. It appears easier to understand "fire" and "iron"—the usual τέμνειν καὶ κάειν—(27) as metaphors which Propertius himself subsequently (29f.) relates to the more familiar and customary remedies (though he extends them to extremes here) than to assume specialized medical language of *furor* treatment owing to a leveling "logic of metaphorization" (Cairns 1974A, 106). Nor can I see fire and iron as suggesting "servile punishment" (Lyne 1979, 129).

72. Richardson *ad loc.*; "my father's friends", Hubbard 1975, 158.

73. Allen 1950, 276; Alfonsi 1957, 18; Steidle 1962, 115.

74. See note 73.

75. See Rothstein; Enk; Ullman 1936, 170: "it seems to me to mean 'the Venus whom I serve', i.e., my particular love (note the emphatic position of *nos-*

tra), in contrast with the kindly one of verse 31 (*facili deus aure*)." Camps, un-decided between "I" (serve) and "we" (serve), compares 1.14.16ff. For similar col-locations of first person singular and plural, both referring to the same single person, cf. 1.3.21 *solvebam nostra*; 2.15.35 *possim nostros*; 3.16.1: *dominae mihi venit epistula nostrae*; 2.32.23: *nostros me laedit ad auris / rumor*; Soph. *Ant.* 734: ἡμῖν ἃ ἐμέ.

76. Cf. Allen's excellent remarks (1950, 275–277).

77. SB, stating that "Ullman's view . . . lacks warrant."

78. Allen 1950, 277; Hering 1970, 114.

79. Here is an example in our elegy of Propertius' compressed, economical use of language: two members only are mentioned of two pairs instead of all four: ear-[-hearing; approval-]-nodding. I prefer this to seeing here a god "mit den Ohren wackeln" (cf. Hanslik 1976, 197). Both Hanslik and Ahl (1974) appear to go wrong in ascribing to the poem's second half a playful character.

80. Cf. *vacem* 1.13.2. Hanslik (1976, 195) is on the right track: "Amor, der keine Erfüllung bringt". Postgate quotes 3.17.11: *vacuos nox sobria torquet amantes*.

81. Boucher 1963, 350; Cairns 1974A, 107ff.; see already Wheeler 1910, 37.

82. In a similar way, we saw the couplet 1.11.25–26 growing out of the group 17–24 and forming a sort of prophetic epilogue to it, simultaneously containing those features that would become apparent and relevant in the later situation of 1.12.

83. For other analyses, I refer my reader to Hering's survey (1970, 113f.). Again—as in 1.11 and 12—I have not been trying to find symmetry or stanzas for their own sake. Attempts of this kind, from Müllenhoff (1854) to Richmond (1928), are dealt with by Enk (1929, 146), who himself falls victim to prejudice and sys-tematization when he analyzes elegy 1.1 (1935–36, 152). See also Hubbard's sen-sible remarks and congenial structure of 1.1 (1975, 18f.).

84. See also SB *ad loc.*; Ross 1975, 60 (with n. 3)ff. Though Housman's initial problem (1888, 19ff. = 1972, 42ff.) concerned the supposed solitary *modo* (11; dis-cussed by us earlier in this chapter; see n. 4), he (and his followers) have supported the claim of a lacuna between 11 and 12 by pointing to Ovid, *Ars Am.* 2.185–192 (or 187–190, to be precise: an "imitation", according to Shackleton Bailey; Ross claims that Ovid is "obviously using the same source", o.c.62, n. 1).

I am not convinced by their argument. Ovid has just given his advice of *perfer et obdura* (Catullus would turn in his grave!) and underlined it with several ex-amples of *obsequium* taken from nature (177–184). This is followed by an illustra-tion from myth (Atalante and Milanion, 185–192). Not only are both sections of equal length (4 distichs each), they are of equal logical structure as well: in each case an introductory couplet (177/178; 185/186) summarizes the complete course of action by depicting the girl's eventual change of mind (*nec blanda satis nec . . . comis → mitis erit*; ~ *quid . . . asperius . . . Atalanta? → succubuit*; also: *perfer et ob-dura ~ meritis*). In each case the three following distichs (179–184; 187–192) illus-trate *obsequium*.

If Housman claimed that Ovid's Milanion story preserves the original number of distichs and that in Propertius' version as we read it two lines have meanwhile been lost, he should also have claimed that Ovid imitated his own imitation by writing another sequel of 4 distichs, of equally strict structure, which he prefixed to his original imitation. Would it not be more consistent to maintain that Ovid, in order to balance his own first section of 4 (= 1 + 3) distichs (177–184), "inflated" Propertius' narrative of Milanion's sufferings from two (Prop. 11–14) to three (Ov. 187–192) distichs? In this way he was able to adapt Propertius' a/b/b/a structure (9–16) to his own a/b/b/b pattern (177–184)—provided he did use Propertius as his model at all.

CHAPTER III

1. Few critics today pay attention to this claim. Solmsen (1965, 78) observed the "dual reference to life and poetry" in 1.7.5f. He also saw (o.c. p. 80) that the poet counts on a similar involvement in his readers: "He has spoken for them, has articulated their experience. This, much rather than a literary appreciation of his fine artistry or an admiration for his genius . . . , is the reason why . . . they cannot turn away from his book." See now also Petersmann's comment (1980, 64) that "die Art Properzischer Dichtung unlösbar mit der Art Properzischer Lebensführung verbunden ist."

2. *Dura*, 8, picks up *duram*, 6. In connection with *queri* (8) and *dominam* (6) all the glamour is precluded that an epic hero might draw from a victory over a *durus* enemy.

3. The epic elaboration is so artful that it has led Petersmann (1980, 68 with n. 9; see also Richardson's introductory note) to believe that Propertius here alludes to the actual *Thebais* (precisely speaking, to the wording of its proem) of the historical Ponticus (whom Ovid mentions *Tr.* 4.10.47f.).

4. Of course, we cannot be absolutely sure about the appreciation of a single Greek epic work in Propertius' time. But a fairly safe guess can be made. Though several works of the epic cycle were at some time or other ascribed to poets other than Homer, the (older) *Thebais* was attributed to the arch-poet himself as early as in the seventh century B.C. by Callinus (Paus. 9.9.5). Thus Ponticus should be seen as truly trying to rival Homer. But centuries before Propertius already, the *Thebais*, like other epic works, had moved into the background. At the great Greek festivals (Panathenaea, Olympic Games) only *Iliad* and *Odyssey* were recited. The same standard of appreciation is reflected in Aristotle's *Poetics* (1459 b 2ff.) where he pays tribute to the superiority of *Iliad* and *Odyssey*. Propertius' contemporary Vergil of course most heavily and visibly relies on the same two Homeric works. And in the excerpts from Proclus' (s. II A.D.? s. V A.D.?) *Chrestomathia* no independent Theban epic is mentioned at all (the brief summaries only serve as introductions to *Iliad* and *Odyssey*). While it is highly probable that Proclus no longer used the original works for his excerpts, Ponticus may—like Pausanias (9.9.5)—still have read the original. But the *Thebais* was almost certainly not the hallmark of Homer in this time.

5. Some scholars (Stroh 1971, 10 and 16f.; Petersmann 1980, 68; cf. 66) refer line 4 exclusively to the harsh fate that Ponticus himself, once he falls in love, is bound to provide for his epic (7.17f.). Though this is a possible (and surprising) additional point, it is a point a posteriori. The context of lines 1–4 leaves the reader, who so far has not read on, with no other possibility than to understand

that the wishful restriction (*modo*) expresses Propertius' desire that the friend's (cf. *tuis*) work may meet the "soft" fate which was denied to Homer's production. In all other respects the friend receives praise for entering in a contest with the arch-poet (the possible irony of this congratulatory statement cannot be determined before the reader gets to the understatement of lines 5–8 or even the self-praise of lines 9ff.).

6. The choice of the word *dolor* itself for Propertius' motivation gives his poetry the superior human credentials according to ancient theory. See Saylor 1971, 144. There is no indication that either the *amores* of line 5 or the pain and grief of lines 7/8 serve the purpose of winning the beloved (line 6), as Stroh (1971, 11; cf. 15; 16) assumes. Such restrictive understanding sets the stage for limiting the true scope of Propertius' poetry. See on these points now also Petersmann (1980, 69f. with n. 15).

7. Even if we take *solum placuisse* to mean that Propertius wishes to be praised as Cynthia's *only lover*, he would fill that position with her essentially by being the poet he is, as is shown by *doctae*, 1.7.11 (cf. Stroh 1971, 12 with n. 15. See also elegy 1.8). Taking *placuisse* (7.11) and *prosint* (7.14) together, Petersmann (1980, 70) finds (as has Solmsen before him, 1965, 79) that Propertius here anticipates Horace's *delectare* and *prodesse* (*A.P.* 333 f.). I am not persuaded by Hering (1982, 228) and Hodge and Buttimore (1977, 30 and 118) to understand *doctae . . . puellae* as nominative plural.

8. 2.7.19; cf. 2.1.48. These two passages settle the case for *solum* at 1.7.11 being acc. masc. and not adv., thus favoring Rothstein, SB, Camps over Schmeisser and Richardson. The two passages also advise against restricting the normal meaning of *solum* in 1.7.11, as SB thinks necessary (to him, the normal sense is "excessive in view of 7–8 and Cynthia's general character"). There is no philological restriction on a lover's wishes.

9. Maybe we should subsume here some aspects of Euripidean Tragedy. Cf. Eur. *Med.* 190–200. *Cognita* in 1.7.14 as well as *nostri* (line 24) indicate a deeper appreciation and identification on the readers' part than a mere "Dem Properz ist es auch nicht besser ergangen" (*sic* Stroh 1971, 14f., n. 19, speaking of "Trost durch Präzedenzfälle"). Already Solmsen saw: "The significant word is *nostri*" (1965, 80). Rightly Petersmann (1980, 71) emphasizes the dual effect intended by Propertius' poetry: both "im Sinne der eigenen Lebensbewältigung" and as "Lebenshilfe" for other lovers in a similar condition.

10. A reversal is also seen by Putnam 1963, 198. Hering (1982, 230; cf. 229), by wrongly separating *me laudent*, 11, and *me legat* (. . . *post haec*), 13—the former allegedly being present tense, the latter future in meaning—lays the ground for his thesis that in 1.7 two halves of equal lengths (1–12, 15–26) surround a central distich (13–14).

11. Solmsen 1965, 81, assumes only of the later, successful Propertius (the one of Books 2 and 3) that "he would no longer draw a line between himself and the Roman *ingenia*", even then hesitant in insisting "on his own kind of *ingenium*".

12. There is no need to deny (as Stroh 1971, 18ff. does) *mollem . . . versum* its Callimachean flavor, even if Propertius insists on a motivation which is completely his own. Aesthetic judgment comes in from Ponticus' part: he will have to give up calling his elegiac friend by the bad name *humilis* (21). Quadlbauer (1970, 331ff.)

has shown that *humilis* is a *Kampfwort* used by the opponents of Callimachean poetry as well as by those of Attistic oratory to denote their unpompous adversaries. For the historical uncertainty of "the quarrel between Callimachus and Apollonius", see Lefkowitz 1980.

13. 1960, *passim*.

14. See Chapter I above, pp. 10ff.

15. This momentum is overlooked by Courtney (1968, 250: "Ponticus' subjection to love can have no effect on the opinion of Propertius' poetry held by anyone but himself").

16. See also n. 1.

17. See also Putnam 1963, 197.

18. Good on this issue: Solmsen 1965. The imbalance within the otherwise parallel structure of the poem is not accounted for in the schematic outlines by Stroh (1971, 9) and Petersmann (1980, 63).

19. Wrongly Courtney charges (1968, 250): "These *iuvenes* are an irrelevant interruption in a poem solely concerned with Propertius and Ponticus". Even less congenial appears Stroh's (1971, 21, n. 41) verdict, according to which not only the distich 23f., but also the other lines on Propertius' future fame (9–14 = our section II. 1) are "dispensable" (*entbehrlich*) for the poem's main line of thought: "Sie liessen sich übrigens glatt auslösen, ohne dass man eine Lücke spüren würde". This amounts to reducing the elegist's poetic goals by declaring parts of a work superfluous or nonessential. For Stroh, the "resulting" (i.e., remaining) contrast is "then merely" (*dann eben nur*) that of success and failure in love ("Erfolg oder Misserfolg in der Liebe").

20. Current understanding (Hodge and Buttimore 1977, 134f., excepted) favors a translation of line 13 such as "Please, go and lay these depressing books aside". But it is still worth considering Hertzberg's suggestion that in line 13 Propertius is alluding to Ponticus' earlier negative criticism of his elegies, so that *tristis istos compone libellos* could be translated "compose those depressing little books (as you contemptuously labeled them before you fell in love yourself)". This gives *componere* its appropriate meaning (cf. 1.7.19). But it removes the possible reference of *tristis* to *arma . . . tristia* in 7.2 (in which case the contempt would be the elegist's). *Libellos* would favor Hertzberg.

SB objects that *tristis* "is the last epithet to be associated with the *molles chori* of erotic poetry". He points to Ovid characterizing his *Ars* as *non tristia carmina, Tr.* 2.493. SB's consideration is distinctly unfortunate because his generic approach fails to account both for the special situation of 1.9 (a haughty detractor—7.25—, not a friend of elegy, is supposed to have uttered the criticism) and for the pessimistic character of Propertius' individual poetry (e.g. 1.11.19f.: *si quid tibi triste libelli / attulerint nostri*). One cannot simply call for Ovid to explain Propertius.

Further we may say that, if Propertius' own poetry can be *tristis* as in 1.11.19f., the word will in line 9.13 not necessarily point to Ponticus' difficulties in writing elegies and mean that the latecomer's expected elegies "will be *tristes* instead of *molles*" (*sic* Allen 1974, 622).

21. Therefore, possible allusions in lines 1–4 to Meleager (Schulz-Vanheyden 127) or to Gallus (Tränkle 1960, 158) do not help us much in understanding Propertius' own plans here.

22. So also Petersmann 1980, 91f.

23. Petersmann (1980, 91f.), concentrating as usual on his method of "thematic" approach, errs in stating that no other than verbal (he speaks of "Wortwahl") connections can be found between 1.9 and 1.7 until finally in 9.9 a "thematische Anspielung" is reached. By excluding thought structure, he can only misread the context.

Referring (as does Enk; see also Hodge and Buttimore 1977, 133) the opening of 1.9 to the conclusion of 1.7, Petersmann states a "formal bemerkenswerte . . . Verklammerung" (which he tries to support by introducing an epigram by Meleager, *A.P.* 12.132) of verbal references. But 7.25/26 has also the features of a summary, wittily enhancing prospects that were outlined in greater detail within the poem's body. For the precise references, the interpreter must therefore go back to the original passages—the more so since the witticism of the last two lines may constitute a new aspect so far not emphasized (cf. *magno faenore*).

Among the instances Petersmann names he mentions that *venit* of 1.7.26 is repeated ("wiederholt") in *venturos . . . amores* 1.9.1 (and even in *supplexque venis*, 1.9.3; apparently this is a word repetition without reference of meaning!). Also, he ties *perpetuo*, 9.2, to *tardus*, 7.26. But, more precisely speaking, both *venturos . . . amores* and *perpetuo* go back farther and pick up line 7.15 with its definite future indicative which is not tempered by a *saepe* as 7.26. And *tardus* cannot be torn from its context in 7.26 and compared in isolation from it. Last but not least, Petersmann wishes to connect the loss of *libera verba* in 9.2 to the high interest (*magno faenore*) late Love is said often to exact.

Much of this amounts to a misconception about what precisely constitutes a "Verklammerung" or reference. *Venire* has many nuances of meaning, and the interpreter is not free—when he encounters the verb action defined as taking place with delay (*tardus*) and for this reason determined by excess (*magno faenore*)—to break up the context and use its elements separately for references to different statements (the coming of love; the loss of free speech; the continuance of freedom). There is no way of tying the *excessive interest* charged by latecoming Amor to the opening of elegy 1.9, since—as our interpretation will show—Ponticus in his new situation does presently not feel that he is overpaying for his *Glück*. Analysis of the logical organization will demonstrate that one misses the ironical point if one locates the complex concept of late Love's excessive demands anywhere earlier than in the elegy's second half (9.17ff.)—the logical movement of which is completely misread by Petersmann (1980, 98ff.).

24. The strictly nonliterary context of lines 9.1–4 keeps me from seeing in *libera verba* also "the freedom of *literary* expression" (Saylor 1971, 152), which is discussed later in the poem.

25. SB translates "somebody or other". As far as reading *quaevis* is concerned, it may not be quite as "idle to compare 2.16.15 *muneribus quivis mercatur amorem?*" as SB asserts, stating for his reason that in 1.9 "Propertius knows that a particular girl is involved." The same is true about 2.16.15, where the "particular" person looming behind the seemingly general *quivis* is Propertius' rival, the infamous *praetor*. See also Rothstein, BB, Camps *ad loc*. Hodge and Buttimore see several women (prostitutes) involved—and fail to explain meaningfully the growing dependence described in our poem (1977, 133ff.).

26. *Dicere* in line 6 is not necessarily limited to the meaning "diagnose the present" (hardly the prevailing task of the Chaonian doves), as Richardson *ad loc.* maintains. For Propertius does not always use *coniugatio periphrastica* in indirect questions concerning future actions: cf. 3.13.19; see also Paley *ad loc.* ("foretell"). And *dicere* in 6 is used in a context (5–8) which elaborates in *general* terms on Propertius' prophetic gift that just recently proved itself in the *specific* case of Ponticus (*Dicebam tibi*, 1).

But I do not deny that the translation "diagnose the present" makes good, perhaps even the better, sense here (Propertius, the experienced, can perceive and interpret his friend's symptoms more precisely than Ponticus himself. For the different meaning of *dicere* in close neighborhood, 9.1 and 6, cf., e.g., the adjective *patrius*, Prop. 2.7.13 and 20; Verg. *Aen.* 4.598 and 602; the verb ἔχεσθαι at Plato, *Phd.* 101 d 2 and 4)—as long as one does not assume with Rothstein and others that Propertius is intruding into what Ponticus considers his private affair. Thus Richardson apparently tries to support his thesis of an alleged secretiveness on Ponticus' part—a secretiveness not indicated in the poem's text and not likely in the light of Ponticus' implied frank objection at 25. Richardson blithely assumes *ex silentio* that Propertius "does not have to labor the point" of the affair's ("degrading" and therefore) secretive character.

But Roman everyday reality did not always and automatically correspond to moral standards (and their idealization through later classicists). After all, the existence of slave girls all over Rome is a historical truth which is hardly embellished by being viewed through the rose-tinted glasses of Comedy. To posit that "Ponticus must have tried to conceal a love affair with a slave girl" is an unwarranted assumption, at least as far as his (private) friend Propertius is concerned. The girl's status as a slave is exploited by Propertius to humiliate confirmed bachelor Ponticus, but no point is made in our poem to the effect that Propertius "has found out enough to embarrass him and proceeds to publish his discovery to the world". This approach sets the track for misunderstanding the poem's last couplet. Not to publicize a secret to the world, but to demonstrate the vital importance of elegy even and above all to epicist Ponticus is Propertius' objective. The triumphant opening, "Look, I was right!" is not sidelined by an added "For I found out". In lines 1ff. Propertius speaks like an openly admitted friend or guest of the house, not like a successful spy. See also note 36.

27. Richardson (*ad loc.*), informing us that Propertius "is not fond of the adjective *lenis*", very democratically favors *levia*, "the reading of the majority of the MSS", reproachfully stating: "Most editors prefer *lenia*". He feels that "*levia* provides a nice balance to *grave . . . carmen*". As a parallel he offers (misquoted by Petersmann 1980, 96, n. 11, who does however not seem to object to *levia*) Ov. *Am.* 2.1.21f. *elegosque levis!* Apparently Richardson has no scruples inserting the short first syllable of *levis* in a slot where prosody demands a long syllable (as offered by *lenia*). Is he aware of the difference between *lĕvis* and *lēvis*? Hodge and Buttimore opt for *levia* (1977, 134: "Love requires a smooth style"; note 7: "'*levia*' should be kept"; p. 35: "a polished style"), but their text (p. 34) offers *lenia*.

28. The alternative route (taken by Stroh 1971, 32ff.) would consist in considering the linguistic difficulties of lines 9.15/16 so unconquerable that one rather renounces the third connection between a prediction and its fulfilment (see also

Stroh's note 31 on pp. 17f.). This line of argument however is hardly convincing, since it implicitly accuses the poet of misleading his readers, e.g., by the third *nunc* at 9.15. Stroh severs *nunc* (9.15) from 7.19f. Instead, he groups it together with *necdum* (9.17) and *tum* (9.19; Stroh 26). This, of course, would be acceptable only if one followed Stroh also in denying that a new section starts at line 17.

29. Cf. Quint. 12.5.1: *accedente verborum figurarumque facili copia*. The passage is listed by SB as an example of *facilis copia*, but no hint is given by him of the context (*accedente verborum figurarumque*) which clearly is one of literary criticism. This context is, however, not negligible here.

Several commentators, among them SB himself, understand *copia*, sc., *lecti* or *puellae* ("easy access" or "ready access"; parallels provided by SB), and point to line 25 for confirmation. But at 25 the girl's readiness appears to be introduced as a *new* argument, viewed as an objection (possibly) put forward by Ponticus (Rothstein defines *sit parata* as subjunctive of indirect discourse) and now countered (26ff.) by Propertius, so that we do not expect it to double an earlier mention. For such a doublet would blunt the argument of 25ff., as, e.g., Stroh (1971, 29) admits: ". . . finden wir im Grunde noch einmal dasselbe, . . .".

Besides, the *copia lecti* interpretation offered by SB and others does not square with the rest of distich 15/16, where Ponticus is said now to be *searching* for water. Why should he be searching (*quaeris*) if he is enjoying *facilis . . . copia* (15)? The situation of Tantalus (Postgate, BB: *quaerit aquas in aquis*, Ov. *Am.* 2.2.43) does not apply to a content and satisfied lover Ponticus who will need (25) a Propertius to be made aware of his self-deception (*nec te decipiat, quod sit satis illa parata*). SB (Ponticus "is simply quarreling with his good luck") dismisses Tantalus and diagnoses a "failure to see the obvious or to know one's good fortune", illustrated by . . . *nec pleno flumine cernit aquam* (Ovid, *Tr.* 5.4.9f.). But this does not fit the situation either. For Ponticus does not think at all of looking for "water" (by strict logic: another girl!) amidst his "river" (his present love). Moreover, the text does not offer any indication that he tries "to fight against it" (sc., his love) or "is quarreling with his good luck". Shackleton Bailey's interpretation would hold only if one were willing to understand that Ponticus keeps searching for the water of epic amidst his stream of love—an unlikely mixture of moist metaphors in a poem that distinguishes between love and poetry so as to advise its addressee to adapt the type of poetry he writes to the state of love he has plunged into. But even granted this much, SB's understanding does not account for *quaeris* (different from Ovid's *cernit*). It seems most unfortunate that SB, as on line 13 above (see n. 20), so here on line 15, compares a parallel without respecting the logical contexts of the two passages. This applies also to his generic statement "Moreover, in Propertius *copia* has always an erotic context, as often in other writers." A glance only at the context shows that in our case (1.9.15) *copia* follows a question of literary criticism (13f.; see already Pasoli 1957, 60; Yardley 1981, 323) not of "erotic context". In none of SB's supposed parallels is an epic poet addressed and asked to turn to elegy. As classicists, we must learn to avoid that misconceived idea of philological democracy in which the highest number of linguistic "parallels" wins the election. Lines 15/16 do not break away from the context but are, like 13/14, concerned with the epic poet who suddenly faces the task of writing elegies. Paley and Rothstein were on the right track.

30. The poem's second half has never proved easy either. It has already been mentioned that the most recent approach (Petersmann 1980, 98ff.) with its method of tracing themes and motifs sadly misreads the section's organization. It has been a stumbling block to other methodologies as well. E.g., Skutsch (see next note) declared it to be ill motivated "padding". SB, too, in one of the rare cases where he transcends the level of line-to-line (or, rather, word-to-word) commentation (1967, 26) and tries to deal with the "connexion of thought" in 9.15–32 (*sic*), clearly runs into rough waters.

31. It is thus clear that 7.25f. is picked up by the second half of elegy 1.9 (17ff.) and must not (as is done by Petersmann 1980, 91f.; see n. 23 above) be tied too narrowly to the opening lines of 1.9 (1–4).

According to the interpretation given in the text above, there is no reason for seeing the rest of the poem (lines 17–34) as mere padding, filled in by the poet allegedly to achieve the desired number of 177 distichs for poems 6 to 14 plus 20 to 22, as Skutsch (1963, 239) believes: in lines 9.17ff., according to Skutsch, Propertius "has to take refuge in prophecy again". But why should not the poet, now that he considers stage I as fulfilled, inform his friend of stage II? Even the circumstance that Ponticus "seems by no means to be unhappy" (Skutsch l.c.) need not be a criterion of insufficient composition, but should first be considered as a paradox which the poet rather wishes to point out than conceal from his reader.

The whole idea that 1.9 is a counterpart "of very late composition" (l.c.) to 7 is unconvincing in the light of close analysis. How can three predictions and three corresponding fulfillments be composed independently from each other?

Even Skutsch's argument from metrical statistics turns against his thesis because the only case of Propertius' supposedly "early" metrical technique in elegy 1.9 (non-"iambic" ending of the pentameter, line 30) appears within the alleged padding, which—if anything—should be "late".

Both Skutsch's work and that of his followers Otis (1965) and Courtney (1968) (the latter two assume 176 distichs as the *Monobiblos*' target number instead of Skutsch's 177) indirectly support my warning that number is displayed in Propertius not for its own sake but only to present an argument more clearly. Their interest in numerical symmetries makes all three scholars underestimate Propertius' interest in logical organization. This is borne out in their unconvincing analysis of single elegies. But work like theirs should first present indisputable evidence concerning single elegies before building up schemata of a whole (or almost whole) book.

It may be noted that already Jacoby's "sicherer Blick in die Werkstätte des Dichters" (1909, 304) found a "Füllstück" (= 1.8.39–42, see o.c. p. 308, n. 2) inserted "later" by Propertius when he allegedly combined the earlier poems 1.7, 8A, 8B, 9 into a "Cyklus". But Jacoby accepted Ites' (1908, 4f.) assumption that 1.7 and 9 were written simultaneously. It should also be remarked that Skutsch's target number of 177 distichs depends (1963, 239, n. 5), on one side of his equation, on Housman's hypothesis that after 1.1.11 a distich has been lost and must be supplied by today's reader to reach the poet's original design. The erroneous character of Housman's supplement was demonstrated above (Chapter II, n. 84).

32. As *favilla*, strictly speaking, means glowing ashes, one may even understand that Ponticus thinks his danger is over already (= ashes), but Propertius

warns of the spark (*prima*) that is alive in them. The latter is confirmed by the following *tum* (19). As in 1.1.1ff., the sequence is *prima . . . tum*, and *prima* again marks the beginning of a coming development. See Chapter II, nn. 10 and 12. The logical coherence of section 17–24 forbids cutting off the distich 17/18 and placing it in the "middle" between two "blocks" of equal length (1–16 and 19–34), as Petersmann (1980, 99) does.

33. Among them are: a boy holding a bird tied to a string; the myth of the soul in Plato's Phaedrus with Amor as the charioteer; Amor taking off his wings and handing them over to the lover (Daedalus and Icarus); Amor sitting on the lover's lap, pressing an arrow into the lover's chest by hand.

Alterna manu was correctly explained by K. Prinz (1936, 93 and again 94: "*bald mit der rechten, bald mit der linken Hand*") but not integrated into the concrete context. The same can be said about Davison's identical finding (he correctly translates "now with this hand, now with that", 1948, 58). The phrase should not be watered down to mean "in turn" (Smyth 1949, 121). See also 1.11.12.

34. I.e., the poet is far from repeating at 9.25f. "noch einmal" (Rothstein) what was said at 23f.

35. "*Quare*. The argument is not very cogent, but Propertius is fond of this mode of connecting thoughts", Postgate (and many followers, except SB). Often *quare* draws, like here, the consequence from a preceding argument.

36. The situation in Catullus 6 is different. There the inquirer tries right from the beginning to trick Flavius into giving the girl's identity. In Propertius 1.7 and 9 the author's aim is to bring Ponticus to acknowledge the superiority (and difficult mastery) of elegy. The final distich stays within the same purpose—Jacoby (1914, 393ff.) collected on more than twenty pages "parallel" passages to prove that in 1.9 Ponticus is asked to reveal his girl's identity. Propertius, however, does not speak of the observer's and listener's curiosity, but of providing relief (*levat*, 34) for the loving writer's own personal agony (*pereas*, 34); not unsimilar is Hor. *Sat.* 2.1.30ff. (Stahl 1974, 51f.). Both SB and Richardson still seem to see Propertius bent on getting some sort of confession out of Ponticus. See also n. 26.

37. This is SB's suggestion, which perhaps leaves too little of the original meaning. Even when the phrase is used in a more or less formulaic fashion, the moral appeal ("eine drohende, beinah grobe Form", Rothstein; "stark unhöflich, schroff", Tränkle 1960, 165) is still felt; cf. Ov. *Am.* 3.2.24:

<blockquote>si pudor est, rigido nec preme terga genu;</blockquote>

cf. Prop. 2.12.18. An adequate translation would be "if you have a sense of shame left". But this, though admittedly possible, is not very illuminating when applied to our passage (see Enk's justified qualms. He settles for Phillimore's "if you are not past shame"), unless we feel that Propertius uses moral pressure to stimulate his friend's lacking motivation for elegy. Therefore my argument explores an alternative interpretation which gives *pudor* its full original weight (and respects *levat*). We should not go so far as to banish normal use of the phrase *pudor est* (cf. Prop. 3.13.20; Ov. *Met.* 14.18) from all *si*-clauses because there exists the formula "*si pudor est*".

38. It does not refer to the beloved as SB assumes. Our case is different from SB's examples (like *da quod amem*, Mart. 8.73.4) insofar as *in amore* is expressly

added to specify and make clear the area in which here the process of *perire* takes place. I.e., *perire* on principle is not conceived to be confined to the area of love, so that *quo pereas* must not be considered equivalent to *quod amem*. In love, the pain caused by the arrow of Amor can be eased by writing elegies; in war, the pain caused by the arrow of the enemy cannot.

CHAPTER IV

1. For the problem touched upon here, see also last note to Chapter V.

2. A detailed approach may be found in E. Lefèvre's *Propertius Ludibundus* (Heidelberg, 1966).

3. No general agreement has been reached with regard to the structure of 1.3. For discussion and rival opinions, see the comprehensive studies by Wlosok (1967) and Hering (1972). My own account is based on the desire not to hurt the syntactical groups formed by complete grammatical sentences. The thought structure hardly focuses on loving harmony and *Begegnung* (Petersmann 1978, 959).

4. Cf. 1.20.31; 22.5; 2.33.17; 4.1.47; 5.53; 11.57; for Propertius occasionally measuring single verses instead of distichs, cf. 4.2.57.

5. For a more detailed discussion, see Stahl (1968); there exists a thoughtful interpretation (including an evaluation of Propertius' loneliness) by Solmsen (1962), which takes 1.18 along the lines of 16 and 17 but does not acknowledge its own special character. For reasons of methodology, it is worth reading Stahl (1968) along with Petersmann (1980), 204ff.: immanent logic versus consideration of overriding so-called 'motifs'. Grant (1979) appears off the mark, especially on 18.24 (cf. 16.27f.).

6. Is this another prophecy or at least a presentiment expressed by the poet? We shall consider Tullus' later development at the end of our Chapter VIII.

7. My understanding is close to that of Hertzberg *ad loc.*, recently renewed by F. Cairns (1974, 155f.; see also Richardson *ad loc.*). However, Propertius does not imagine Cynthia to "pray for" (Cairns) opposing winds. Her loving kisses are an expression of gratitude for delayed departure; yet not the lover's hesitation to leave, but the adverse winds are conceived to be the cause of this delay. Thus her kisses are owed to the winds, not (as they should be) to her lover. Alternatively, I would accept Burman's (see Enk *ad loc.*) solution, translated by SB (*ad loc.*) as follows: "And say that she owed my kisses to the adverse wind (which detained me on shore)".

8. It is important to acknowledge (as Rothstein does for 1.6 and 1.19) that the single elegy sometimes presents a part only of a larger argument, the beginning of which the reader has to supply from indications the poet gives in the opening lines. But see also Hubbard 1975, 87f., on more formulaic use of this feature. In the case of 1.6, the emphatic opening denial "*Non ego nunc*" better fits the situation of echoing and parrying (*Non*) another person's taunt (or even preventing a taunt) than that of excluding a consideration of the speaker's own. Especially *ego* is aptly understood as fending off a misconception about the speaker's character. For the word *nunc* no final solution has been found. Has Tullus suggested a presently arising fear of the sea? Or does *nunc* perhaps refer to a time of seasonal storms? Both explanations would allow a more satisfactory understanding than Enk's resignation (*ad*

1.2.25). Hodge and Buttimore (1977, 110) assume a change of mind on Propertius' part.

9. Propertius' "uncomplimentary" behavior and "seeming insult to Tullus" is the more surprising since—as Cairns 1972, 4f., points out—it is not rooted in any genre precepts. Latin Elegy allows the opposite solution. In Tibullus 1.3 the lover has left the beloved woman behind in favor of traveling with his patron. Propertius' decision (and its presentation) must be taken to be completely of his own choosing. (Cairns' hypothesis, that in 1–18 the poet, regardless of context, mixes genre types not usually grouped together in this way, "so that he could demonstrate his skill and originality" [13], is unconvincing because it implicitly denies the poem a logically coherent statement comprehensible in discursive thought, thus invalidating grammatical syntax and logical conjunctions contained in the text. See also below on 31ff.).

10. Laffi (1967, 61) considers either 30/29 or 29/28 as possible; Habicht (1973, 81f.) supports the same years; see also Hubbard (1975, 43); Cairns (1974, 156ff.). Identification of L. Volcacius Tullus mentioned in the inscription (before Laffi's edition quoted as OGI 458, vol. II, p. 55 Dittenberger) as the uncle of Propertius' friend (i.e., not the nephew and friend himself) was confirmed by a new fragment found in 1954 (see Jones 1955). The new fragment is also included in Ehrenberg-Jones 1955² (reprint 1963) with no. 98.

11. Cf. Magie, vol. 1, 427f.; 440ff.; Habicht 1973, 57ff.; Atkinson (1958, 301f.) assumes a "permanent impression of the injustice of Roman rule" in Asia by the time of Octavian's final victory.

12. See, e.g., Habicht 1973, 58f. Magie (vol. 1, 441ff.), though mentioning that Octavian punished cities that had sided with Antony (Dio 51, 2.1), on the whole draws a picture of the victor's forgiveness and interest in the area's welfare.

13. For this and the following, cf. Habicht 1973, 57ff.; 80ff.; Deininger 1965, 16ff.; 36f.; 53f. Atkinson (1958, 301f.) voices doubt about the genuineness of the Asians' loyalty even as late as in the years 27 and after, counting on a "permanent impression of the injustice of Roman rule." Atkinson asks: "How could these people become convinced all in a moment that Octavian . . . was both in actual fact permanently established and in disposition mild and well-intentioned?"

14. [ἐπὶ ἀνθυ] πάτου Λευκίου Οὐολκακίου Τύλλου, lines 41f. of the inscription mentioned above.

15. Brunt-Moore (1973, 82) define imperium as follows: "imperium is a discretionary power to do what the interest of the state requires. . . . In particular, military command and jurisdiction in serious cases belong only to holders of imperium."—Already Birt (1915, 297ff.; 299f.) approached what I consider the correct interpretation of 20 and 34, but rejected it because it disagreed with his overall understanding of elegy 1.6.

16. It is true that Vergil, too, in his Georgics, expresses a preference for the vita contemplativa (or, at least, the simplicity of rural life), denouncing the pursuit of political and other goals offered by the vita activa (2.458–512). But this does not interfere with his plans of building a temple for Octavian (3.13ff.) or his tribute to Octavian's success at 4.560ff. The more remarkable is Propertius' cool indifference, which appears even singular when one brings Horace into the picture. See next chapter.

17. Atkinson (1958, 313) points out that securis in 1.6.19 cannot possibly refer

to the uncle's past consulship of 33 B.C.: "As is well known, the urban magistrates had no right to the insignia of the axes within the *fasces* during their exercise of the *imperium domi*. . . . The reference in Propertius must therefore be to a provincial *imperium*, and here it is perfectly in place."

18. See preceding note.

19. Paley's and SB's objections against Hertzberg's parallel from Juvenal (10.44: *praecedentia longi / agminis officia*) may be dropped after our investigation into the meanings of *conari*. Cp. also Holmes' (1928, 173) remarks on Octavian's triumph on August 13, 29: ". . . the conqueror on this occasion departed from established usage, his colleague and the other officers of state not preceding him, but following in company with those senators who had taken part in the campaign". Further, cf. Juvenal 7.142f.: *togati / ante pedes*; Seneca, *de morte Claud.* 3.4: . . . *se tot milia hominum sequentia videbat, tot praecedentia, tot circumfusa.* . . .

20. Both BB and Enk understand here that young Tullus had fought for Octavian and against Antony, "probably at Actium" (BB).

21. Regarding Tullus' later career, see the end of our Chapter VIII.

22. Cf. Alfonsi 1973, 302.

23. A difference of outlook comes to light also when we recall the passages we introduced earlier in this chapter, written by two of Propertius' contemporaries: while Tibullus (1.3) does leave his love to join his patron on a campaign, and while Vergil (*G.* 4.560ff.) does comment with praise on Octavian's reorganization of the East (modestly classifying his own occupation as "undistinguished leisure", *ignobilis oti*, 564—he lays no claim to one of society's value terms as Propertius will do immediately at 1.6.30), Propertius' position in 1.6 *on principle* excludes any such involvement with the representatives of the Active Life. On the "fundamentaler Gegensatz" of Tibullus and Propertius, see also Steidle 1962, 109. Petersmann, though good on Propertius' position here, seems to give more credit to Tullus' way of life than the poet does (1980, 59f.). And surely "Die private Lebensform wird gleichwertig der öffentlichen empfunden." But "der . . . werbende Ton" (o.c.61) toward Tullus is not audible to me.

24. For elegy's use in general of Roman social values in a new context, E. Reitzenstein's treatise ("Zur Sprache der römischen Erotik", 1912) is useful still today. The reversal of line 30 comes in as so natural a result of the train of thought that one feels tempted to believe that the later elaboration *militat omnis amans* (Ovid, *Am.* 1.9.1) has its earliest and original Latin precedent here.

25. The balance of *pedibus* and *remis* is destroyed by Skutsch's conjecture *remige carpes* (accepted into Hanslik's Teubner edition of 1979). See n. 27.

26. I have difficulty verifying both that distich 33/34 "évoque promagistrats et officiers romains passant en maîtres dans le monde méditerranéen", and that it shows "que Properce est sensible à la grandeur de Rome, à celle de ses hommes, à leur style" (Boucher 1965, 106). Likewise, I do not see how line 34 "témoigne de l'estime de Properce pour la domination romaine", revealing a split personality in his "alliance . . . d'une fierté impérialiste et d'un refus personnel du métier militaire" (o.c. 112). The problem (which is symptomatic) lies not with the poet but with his interpreter who cannot conceive that a contemporary author is as unaffected by and as independent from the patriotic tendencies of the opening Augustan Age as Propertius claims to be in our poem. The same must be said of the

interpretation offered by Hodge and Buttimore (1977, 115): "This poem is the closest Propertius gets in Book 1 to regretting that he is a lover and elegiac poet, rather than a man of affairs or imperial ideologue." 113: "In this poem he endorses imperialist conceptions more than amatory ones, . . .".

27. Thus the contrast between love poet and career man, wittily extended into the last section (31–36) from 19–30, provides no reason for changing the transmitted text (as Skutsch 1952, 232, wishes). Nor is it offensive that the words *accepti pars eris imperii*, highlighting the activities of Tullus, are included in the *protasis* of a long sentence (Skutsch, l.c.). For thus the main clause (35f.) is reserved for the main idea: Tullus abroad thinking of his friend at home and of his friend's harsh fate. *Et* (34) is explicative: "and ⟨in doing all this traveling⟩ you will be part of your uncle's governmental power". There is no need for Skutsch's conjecture *remige carpes* (l.c., recently accepted into the text of Hanslik's Teubner edition). See also n. 25.

Sidere in line 36, containing a nuance of fatefulness (Rothstein sees a reference to the poet's horoscope), once more points to the unchangeable character of Propertius' situation. His refusal thus receives a final note of suprapersonal firmness.

28. Cairns 1972, 5; cf. 15. See also Fedeli 1980, 173f.; 183.

29. There exists a fairly broad agreement on this structure, from Richmond and Enk (1929, 148f.) to Évrard (1974) and Burck (1981). Évrard, setting out with stylistic analysis and statistics of pronouns representing Propertius, Tullus, and Cynthia, at the latest appears to overinterpret when he, for the sake of numerical equilibrium, discounts the addresses to Tullus (lines 1 and 2) from the poem's body as appearing "surtout en raison de la dédicace du poème" (o.c. 42; cf. 43, n. 7). After that, his thesis that the end of one strophe announces the subject of the succeeding one, is hardly convincing. His rigid and static schematizations keep him from fully comprehending the poem's live and progressive, logically verifiable, movement of thought. A similar comment could be made on Petersmann's (1980, 53ff.), methodologically speaking, contrasting interpretation. (Apparently Petersmann does not know Évrard's article.) See also n. 5 above and our remarks in the preceding chapter (passim).

30. Cp. how Catullus (10 and 28) playfully voices his disappointment with his own *praetor*.

31. Let us here recall once more that Tibullus (1.3) decided otherwise, viz., to leave his girl and to follow his patron.

CHAPTER V

1. 1888, 3 = 1972, 1, 30f.

2. ". . . die Leser damit nach Hause schicken", Leo 1898, 472 = 1960, 172. Against Leo (and von Wilamowitz): Schulze-Vanheyden 36, pointing to a tension between epigrammatic setting (lines 1/2; 9/10) and elegiac middle part (lines 3–8); Birt 1915, 284.

3. o.c. 174 = 474.

4. Hodge and Buttimore even sense "a hostile note" (1977, 215); though starting with some observations similar to ours, their results (and methods) differ considerably.

5. Thus one fails to see how—without support from the words' meanings—the placement of *semper* between *nostra* and *amicitia* suggests "that their friendship is as continuous as this persistent questioning" (Hodge and Buttimore 1977, 215).

6. Cf. Hubbard 1975, 98: "Yet in the relevant years of the early twenties, when Vergil at the end of the First Georgic and Horace in, for example, Odes 1.2 were hailing Octavian as Rome's divine saviour, Propertius' book contains one mention only of his name and not a friendly one." Further, see Nethercut (1971A, 465), who points to Horace's Satires. In 30 B.C., Horace feels his powers are not sufficient *Caesaris invicti res dicere* (*Sat.* 2.1.10ff.). But he includes, as does Vergil, Octavian's praises in his book:

> Tempore quo iuvenis Parthis horrendus, ab alto
> demissum genus Aenea, tellure marique
> magnus erit . . .   (*Sat.* 2.5.62ff.)

Birt (1915, 283, following Hollstein) assumes that in the double mention of Perusia's destruction in the *Monobiblos'* two concluding poems "ein offenbarer schwerer Groll gegen Octavian" is revealed: "Daher wird dieser Machthaber von Properz 1.21 ohne jedes ehrende Beiwort nur einfach *Caesar* genannt". See also LaPenna 1977, 12: "Nel primo libro il poeta d'amore non accenna a nessun atto d'omaggio verso i vincitori e i potenti: in una certa misura un atto d'indipendenza."

7. Kiessling and Heinze; Nisbet and Hubbard seem to prefer the same date.

8. See also Nethercut 1971A, 470.

9. Perusia is *not* the home district of Tullus also. The erroneous assumption (derived from 1.22.3) made by Syme (1974, 466) has recently been revived by Hodge and Buttimore (1977, 110, n. 1; cf. 216), though expressly corrected earlier by Hubbard (1975, 24, n. 1).

10. This explanation appears more in line with the poem's increasingly saddened train of thought (as explained below) than that given by Hodge and Buttimore (1977, 217), who see (cf. *me genuit*, 22.10) the poet "identified with the land itself, which is his true ancestor", and feel that *fertilis uberibus* represents an image which "implies healing, reconciliation, the natural fertility of the land reasserting itself". No such consolation is verifiable from the text. For the larger context see also p. 120f. below.

11. See, e.g., Birt (1915): "Die Erwähnung Perusias lässt sich nur aus Tendenz erklären, und diese Tendenz kann nur gegen den Zerstörer der Stadt selbst gerichtet sein." (287); after 21, the poet in 22 "zieht ganz künstlich wieder die Erwähnung Perusias herein" (283). Mentioning Perusia instead of Assisi "ist mit Affekt gesagt", and "klingt wie eine Anklage". Thus, in answering the *qualis* question, Propertius "bekennt sich als verkappter Gegner des Octavian." "Er würde es offener und unzweideutiger sagen, wenn er den Octavian nicht zu fürchten hätte." (286). (B. does not believe that this poem could have been written still after Actium, when Octavian was the sole holder of power.)

12. As my translation shows, I do not find it grammatically possible to understand line 22.5 as expressing central Rome's harsh treatment of Italian places like Perusia (*sic* Lake 1940, 299; Nethercut 1971A, 467 et passim; see Rothstein's explanation).

13. Here, however, unavoidably, the question arises whether Octavian's spe-

cial involvement with Perusia can be neglected by any contemporary reader. See below.

14. Holmes 1928, 99, uses "the well-known story" to conjecture about Octavian's motive. Syme (1974, 212) remarks: "These judicial murders were magnified by defamation and credulity into a hecatomb of three hundred Roman senators and knights . . .", etc.

15. Cf. G. Williams' translation (1968, 177): "the grave [sic] of our country"; Putnam (1976, 100) takes the phrase to be ambiguous: "'tombs of our fatherland', the implication being that the *patria* is in some sense buried as well." Cf. Hubbard 1975, 97: "the graveyard of our country at Perusia".

16. Syme 1974, 207.

17. To the reader acquainted with 1.21, the *pulvis Etrusca* in 22.6 may well appear to be a reference to *montibus Etruscis* of 21.10 (and perhaps allude also to *Etruscis . . . aggeribus*, 21.2), thus supplying another concrete link between the two poems.

18. BB think of the great attempt described in Appian, *BC* 5.36.

19. Frothingham 1909, 348ff.; his vivid and ghastly presentation is worth reading because it helps to realize the experience the boy Propertius was exposed to, if only by hearsay. For Herrmann the allusion to the massacre seemed too bold to have been written under Octavian. Therefore, he concluded, 1.21 and 22 cannot be Propertian (1959, 751).

20. The fact that he comes *ab Etruscis . . . aggeribus* by no means signifies that he is a soldier of Octavian, as Richardson (expanding Postgate's remarks *ad loc.*?) assumes. *Agger* is not used exclusively of siege mounds or walls (such as Octavian laid around Perusia); Propertius himself (3.11.22) uses it of a defensive fortification. Besides, there were palisades of equal type erected by both sides at Perusia (. . . ὁ Καῖσαρ . . . τὴν Περυσίαν ἀπετείχιζε χάρακι καὶ τάφρῳ, . . . ἀντεπονεῖτο γε μὴν καὶ ὁ Λεύκιος, ἑτέροις ὁμοίοις χαρακώμασι καὶ τάφροις . . . , App. *BC* 5.4.33). Even if Propertius' text points to Octavian's circumvallation as the more remarkable one, it is not excluded that he merely wishes to identify the Perusine War to his reader. Richardson's inference that the two men of close relation have fought on different sides, and that in this poem one is about to kill the other, not only forces him into a new conjecture (*agnotas*, 8) and cuts the epitaph off from possibly being connected with the epilogue, but also destroys the climactic character of lines 7ff.

21. I.e., the addressee's: cf. Enk *ad* 21.6. See also Bodoh 1972, 237f. I fail to see the necessity (and possibility) of assuming here a "generic sister" who amounts to being "everyone's sister—a female mourner" (Hodge and Buttimore 1977, 212).

22. Or by Postgate's comment *ad* 21.6 ("Do not destroy her fond belief that I was killed in honourable battle")? See still Quinn 1969, 20 (she should not know that he was killed "by an unknown assailant while running away"). Kunihara (1974, 246; 248: "une morte déshonorante") not convincingly locates the supposed ignominy in the "sens péjorative" of *ignotas manus* when compared to *Caesaris ensis*: "noter l'impression de grandeur évoquée par le nom de *Caesar* et l'effet du mot poétique *ensis*" (Birt 1915, 283, we recall from n. 6 above, on the contrary saw in the bare name *Caesar*, "ohne jedes ehrende Beiwort", a sign of the poet's "Groll" against Octavian). See also La Penna 1977, 9: "meglio far credere alla sorella che egli fosse caduto sul campo di battaglia."

23. Hardly—although a "parallel" can be provided from *Anthol. Pal.* VII
550—a mere topic, as Nethercut 1968A, 143, n. 10, suggests; cf. Schulz-Vanheyden
25; 27: "geradezu etwas Tragisches".

24. ". . . sie soll das furchtbare Wie seines Todes nie erfahren", E. Reitzenstein 1936, 7; cf. p. 6, n. 8, about the "Auftrag, der dem Sterbenden so sehr am
Herzen liegt: das Los einer ihm nahestehenden Unglücklichen, soweit das irgend
möglich, zu lindern." Cf. Hommel, 1926, 988: "er soll nicht aus seinen Tränen die
geliebte Frau die besonders schrecklichen Umstände seiner tödlichen Verwundung
erraten lassen . . . , sondern ihr die Einzelheiten seines Todes, den er nach scheinbar gelungener Flucht aus der Gefahr fand, ersparen".

25. That *acta* is the appropriate Latin expression and need not be changed
was pointed out by Tränkle (1968, 567).

26. No change is required in the Latin text in line 5: see Tränkle 1968, 569.
(Some interpreters have deleted *ut*, others have understood the construction to be
like Cat. 17.5ff.; Hor. *C.* 1.3.1ff.; 1.26.25ff.; Petr. 58.12; etc.) I think Gallus'
words may include the meaning "Don't, upon escaping and making it home, die
from your wound (as I, upon escaping Caesar's swords, am now dying), i.e.: have
better luck in saving yourself than I had." This should meet the (anyway, rather
weak) objections listed by Bodoh 1972, 236.

27. That a burial should be understood to have taken place (Bodoh 1972, 241)
can in no way be verified from the text.

28. Tränkle 1968, 566, lines 2 and 4: "Wenn das letzte Distichon bedeutet,
dass die Schwester die Stelle, wo die Gebeine liegen, erfahren soll—und nur so
lässt es sich verstehen, sofern man nicht den Text ändern will—, dann kann der
Dichter vorher nicht gesagt haben, sie solle das Geschehene *nicht* erfahren." *Non
semper enim haec inter se idem faciunt*, Quintilian l.c. Besides, "das Geschehene" (*acta*)
and topographical information are not necessarily the same. Kunihara (1974, 244)
goes so far as to exclude the notion of death completely from *acta* ("acta quae facta
sunt mihi vivo"); death he sees mentioned only in the two emphasized (final position in their respective lines) words *ossa* and *mea*. Other than Tränkle, he understands 9/10 as I do: "soror sciat super montibus Etruscis dispersa esse mea ossa".
Though Kunihara too recognizes the difference of *sentiat* (6) and *sciat* (9), he is mis-
led by E. Reitzenstein's idea of "une morte déshonorante" (246). Cf. also Fedeli
1980, 495.

29. Editors generally either make both parts of Gallus' message affirmative or
both negative. See also G. Williams 1968, 176.

30. Even this particular request, viz., to conceal rather than to reveal, is,
though uncustomary, not unparalleled in Greek poetry, as Phillimore (1911, 135)
saw: *A.P.* 7.589.

31. See also Rothstein *ad loc.*; Paley *ad loc.* Butler's (1905) version ("whatever
bones she may find on the Tuscan hills are mine") did not heed Housman's hypothesis that *quaecumque* and *haec* form a "deceptive collocation" (as Housman calls
a supposed parallel he adduces, 1893, 184 = 1972 1, 294f.). Butler incurred the
notorious critic's unrelenting wrath: "Certainly the discovery that her brother had
1,000 skulls, 2,000 femora, and 26,000 vertebrae, would be at once a painful shock
to her affections and an overwhelming addition to her knowledge of anatomy"
(1905, 320 = 1972, 2, 635). It seems, however, that a supposed "deceptive colloca-

tion" can deceive him most who demands that first of all the poet get his numbers right and who silently presupposes that, after all, poetry should be an orderly business depicting orderly circumstances. Rather than leaving normal grammatical relations intact and accepting a disturbing collocation of facts, the militant critic makes the facts "acceptable" by declaring accepted grammar "deceptive". (A recent critic—Quinn 1969, 22; he prefers, as I do, to read *nec* in 6 and *at* in 9—responds in fashion: "Housman's view of 9–10 really involves monkeying with the text".) Helm (1952, 281) does not leave room either for the extraordinary circumstances: giving the short version "omnia, quae invenerit, mea sunt", he calls it mere "Unsinn". But "Unsinn" was also the term applied to Helm's forerunners Housman and Damsté (1924, 5f.) by Hommel (1926, 989). Hommel adduced the modern concept of the "unknown soldier" to explain the thrust of Prop. 1.21: when honoring the unknown, anonymous deceased individual, the bereaved are thinking of their own fallen relative whose body was never found. "Welche Gebeine die Schwester . . . auch finden mag, . . . alle haben sie Anspruch darauf, für des Geliebten sterbliche Reste gehalten zu werden." Hommel at least had a glimpse of the paradoxical situation that caused the poet to make an indefinite *quaecumque* respond to a definite *haec*. "His body was never buried (1.22.9) and so cannot have been found" (Camps 1959, 22). Siding with Housman against Hommel: Fedeli 1980, 495.

32. Still today the spectator, looking from the *Rocca* (above Assisi) across the low-lying plain (cf. *supposito . . . campo*, 1.22.9) may be struck by the full view he is offered of elevated Perugia.

33. M. Hubbard points out to me that on the alternative assumption (which I, following Enk, am hesitant to make), viz., that the *soror* is Gallus' sister, it results that she might be Propertius' mother. This would perhaps even more intensify the boy's emotional situation. Quinn (1969, 20) assumes that the two soldiers are brothers and the *soror* is their sister—a relation likewise close enough to stimulate the reader's imagination and sympathy. Birt (1915, 291) remained, to my knowledge, without followers in identifying the addressed soldier as Propertius himself.

34. Gallus' words demand concealment only as far as the *soror* is concerned. Thus Helm's objection that, if the poet has knowledge of what the *soror* is not supposed to know, the messenger "hat also offenbar die Tatsachen ausgeplaudert, die er verschweigen sollte" (1952, 279), is beside the point, and the "Rattenkönig von Unlogik" (l.c.) falls back on Helm himself, who fails to distinguish between *soror* and young Propertius.

35. See p. 105 above.

36. Richardson's statement fails to do justice to the words *mihi praecipue* (22.6). Rightly Enk quotes Passerat's interpretation: "cum aliis multis, tum mihi maxime." The reader, acquainted with the preceding elegy, knows what the poet is referring to. Congenial and sympathetic on the early—and lasting—"trauma" of the Perusine War: Levin 1982, 426f.; 436; 465; 480f.

37. The same is of course true of the epitaph poem 1.21 also. I cannot find any clue as to why *ignotas manus* (21.8) should be "sardonica ironia", allegedly concealing the true murderers (Caesar's searching soldiers) by prudently but misleadingly pointing to highwaymen (Paratore 1936, 92ff.). Without any lead given in the

text, such an interpretation remains mere phantasy. Nethercut (1971A, 469), correcting Paratore, remarks: "The fact that *Caesaris enses* stands against *ignotae manus* makes the point stronger, in a way: Caesar's name is introduced gratuitously." Still, the poem remains essentially private in character.

Likewise, I find it difficult to accept Paratore's wholesale conclusion about 1.21 "che nel doloroso epitafio sia celata un' accusa contro Ottaviano come responsabile di *tutte* le stragi *della guerra* perugina, anche di quelle commesse nei dintorni della città assediata, e quindi anche della morte di Gallo, congiunto del poeta" (o.c. p. 98; italics mine). This would turn the poet's personal affliction through politics into political poetry disguised in a personal setting. The plain information alone that his relative fought against and barely escaped Octavian's arms (*Caesaris ensis*, 21.7, is emphasized by position, as Paratore rightly saw), only to be killed on his way home, is sufficiently clear to indicate Propertius' attitude when writing the poem and his feelings when publishing the *Monobiblos*.

38. As in the foregoing chapter, we may, at least in passing, comment on a branch of present-day Latin Studies which gives first priority to considerations of genre and poetical technique.

G. Williams has treated our two poems in a chapter entitled "Imagination and Interpretation: The Demand on the Reader" (1968, 171ff.). If the poet does not make it easy for his reader to understand a poem, he, we hear, is motivated by "the poetic pleasure to be found in the mysterious, the difficult and the obscure, which gives the imagination something to work on", etc. (220). The only reasons (outside the "personal" difficulties alluded to in 1.3 or 1.18) I myself have so far given my reader for the poet's being possibly "obscure" (or "difficult") are such of political precaution—which Williams, convinced of the régime's pressure-free acceptance (cf. e.g., 50f.) does not seem to consider. Consequently, the question arises if here the literary theory may not risk losing its hold on the author's serious concerns and worries so cautiously voiced in his work.

Two formal reasons are given as making poems eligible for interpretative treatment in this chapter: (a) specifically, an epigrammatic monologue (like 1.21), especially if reluctant to reveal information about its dramatic setting, is seen to fit into the thesis that "This riddling element . . . is of the very essence of sophisticated poetry . . ." (185; cf. 171 on the technique of partial revelation). Apparently, Williams has in mind not so much a riddling element which is necessitated by the difficulty of presenting a difficult message, perhaps even in a difficult or unfavorable environment, but rather an arbitrary and playful feature. This may not even cover elegy 1.18, but how does it fit 1.21?

Let us hear the second, more general condition: there is also (b) "the *deliberate effort* by the more self-conscious poets . . . *to complicate the thematic material* of their poems by interweaving ideas and *avoiding the process of ordered exposition*" (o.c. 171; italics mine). The reader may wonder how our two poems will fare in such a world of willful complication (not to say disorder). It is impossible to go here at length into the details of Williams' genre-bound interpretations. As far as 1.21 is concerned, the only "originality" he apparently is willing to grant Propertius is that of picking a special type of epigram from the stock of existing Greek models ("completely detached from actual occasions and real life", 180)—a very special one indeed: it makes Williams the only critic to end up not with one but with two missing bodies (180) at the end of his interpretation, and in addition even with a groaning ghost ("Groans come easily to the wretched ghosts of the dead", o.c.p. 175; cf., e.g., Patroclus' shadow in the *Iliad*; see also Fedeli 1980, 486)—a revival of Birt's (1915, 290) *umbra* or Lachmann's "*eidolon*".

As far as "avoiding the process of ordered exposition" is concerned, Williams has in his way tried to turn Housman's and Leo's difficulties in dealing with our poems into a virtue: if the critic cannot think of any reason why the poem is "obscure", the reason must be sought in an alleged technique of obscuration. The consequences for the two poems are harsh: reasons of contents, organization, or actual political constellations move into the background. Since Williams cannot make any cogent sense either of the sequence 21–22 or of the parenthesis of personal lament in 1.22.6–8 within its context, he decides to have found an (alien?) footnote in one poem pertaining and "essential" (cf. 187) to another: 1.22 is said to have (p. 178) "the added function of providing an explanatory note on" 1.21 (i.e., of supplying, through its lines 6–8, the missing identity of Gallus (1.21) as being the author's relative, *mei . . . propinqui*, 22.7), because the general reading public, too, must learn what was of course known to private readers of 21 before publication: Gallus was a relative of the author's; ". . . to help him" (sc., the reader of the published poem 21) "without destroying his poem, the poet gave some essential personal information in the poem which follows" (o.c.p. 187). We are asked to believe that, in order to avoid destroying poem 1.21, the poet decides to create a patchwork in 1.22.

Thus the 2:3:3:2 design of 22 is broken up—once more again: "At least here, then, in Roman literature one poem in a collection was written partly to supplement another" (178). If the last-quoted statement appears to turn things upside down, there is reason to assume that the fault lies with the critic's theory. Let us recall and review our own findings: The "epitaph" 1.21, dedicated to a tragic event and its sorrowful implications, certainly has, in spite of its specific message, a general human appeal. As a piece of poetry, it appears rounded out and rests in itself. The "epilogue" 1.22 too presents itself as an autonomous artifact, characterizing the poet's youth as clouded by civil war and personal loss. But its emotional climax can receive concrete illumination through facts supplied by its antecedent: political partisanship (*per medios ereptum Caesaris ensis*, 21.7), familial ties (*te, parentes, soror, Gallum*, 21.5ff.) and sorrowful details, that stand behind the anonymous "my relative" of 1.22, allow the reader to understand better the poet's lasting involvement with the events around Perusia—an involvement only cautiously hinted at in the autobiographical poem 22. If one of the two "Gegenstücke" (Glücklich 1977, 46) was included in the *Monobiblos* to support the other, then this task would fall to 21. While both are equal in showing the same length, in being self-contained in poetic organization and contents, and in displaying each a verifiable train of thought of its own, 22—with its strikingly balanced 2:3:3:2 structure, its autobiographical viewpoint, and its emphasizing position at the book's end, varying the traditional *sphragis*—no doubt is the "leading" or more essential one of the two insofar as its theme is the author's own past (and present) condition. Tying the suffering persons of 21 to Propertius' life and family, as is suggested by 22.6–8, lends detail to the epilogue's emotional climax, and thus adds to our awareness of the poet's own sad experience as hinted at in 22; but knowledge of Gallus' status as the poet's relative

(22.7) can hardly add anything to our appreciation of the tragic events (and the sufferings of the victims) presented in 21.

For the sake of defining an adequate scholarly approach concerning not only the *Monobiblos* but also Propertius' later work, let us investigate the following question: How did the author of a work called *Tradition and Originality in Roman Poetry* come to misread so evident a relationship between two poems and to miss their essential human message?

One reason, of course, is the one stated earlier: his tendency to thin out hard political tensions and to look for literary traditions or "devices" instead (cf. also what Williams has to say on "*recusatio*" poetry, pp. 47 and 102). Another, equally misleading, element is that the critic's desire to establish a poetics based on stylistic "models" and similar "literary" devices tends to neglect also the logical argument by which a piece of poetry is organized—a license he shares with the "generic interpretation" we faced at the occasion of 1.6 in the preceding chapter. When, for instance, Williams dissolves the grammatical and logical context of antecedent (*si*, 22.3) and consequent (the poet's account of his home district, 22.9/10) by calling the latter a mere "appendage to the description of Perusia" (178), he deprives himself of understanding the poem's deepest concern. For the truth is that awareness of the horrors of Perusia (*si . . . tibi . . . nota*) is a presupposition for understanding the poet's own "origin": not so much geographical information as equation of home district and theater of war, as we said before.

If an evaluation can be drawn from the present case, it appears to be that the literary critic, unable to verify a poem's logical argument and tragic human message, tries to "prove" by inapposite means that his author is purposefully obscure or difficult, and proceeds to integrate his "discovery" into a hypothesized ancient literary technique—in a chapter pretentiously subtitled "The Demand on the Reader". The high-flying critic seems unaware that by his procedure he possibly deprives the poetry he deals with of its "very essence": a human message and a substantial reason for having been written. Nor does he seem to be aware that he shares a long-standing but still growing trend, viz., to reduce poetry to mechanical combination of elements labeled and classifiable by philological scholarship (a poem's political viewpoint is, at least by Augustan Interpretation, too often taken for granted and not seen to be problematical). Suffice it for us here to have, early on in our investigation, reopened an important road to Propertius' poetry and to have reclaimed two key poems for their author's poetic, i.e., in this case autobiographic, intentions. Now and then, in later chapters, we will have to concern ourselves again with similar blockades caused by learned blindness, although we will not always be as lucky as to be offered the theory that lurks behind a mistaken interpretation.

39. Polysyllabic pentameter endings do not necessarily (especially in brief, weighty poems) provide reliable dating indicators, as Hodge and Buttimore themselves see (215, n.2). Thus they do grant 21/22 considerable importance—though not in the book's context.

40. Skutsch's assumption of "padding", done by the poet for the sake of numerical equilibrium, does not rest on foundations as safe and objective as he wishes us to believe (see Chapter III, n. 31). The "law" of the pentameter ending in a disyllabic (iambic) word, supposedly observed increasingly by Propertius, is, as

we saw, violated precisely in that part of the elegy 1.9 which Skutsch has declared to be padding (i.e., late)—without trying to establish its place within the train of thought of 1.9. J. K. King's (1975–76) attempt to go beyond Skutsch and Otis by clarifying relations of contents and themes is certainly welcome. But without more indications provided from the texts themselves, one is hardly convinced that, e.g., poems 19 through 22 can be grouped together as a "cycle" because of "similarity of subject matter" (defined as "death and final separation", o.c. p. 122). Petersmann's (1980) thematic approach has not solved the problems of book composition either. Indicative (and most disturbing perhaps) is his attempt to place 7 in a "cycle" ("geschlossenen Zyklus") together with 4 to 6 (p. 65). For 7 is closer to 9 than to any of 4 to 6.

41. See, for instance, G. Luck (1961, 117f.). Helm (1957, c. 782) sees Propertius (to him a poet less serious than Catullus) living in a "leichtfertigen, lebenslustigen Zirkel gleichgesinnter jugendlicher Geniesser, die in literarischen und künstlerischen Interessen aufgehen, ohne ihrem Leben einen andern Inhalt zu geben als mehr oder minder vorübergehenden Liebschaften sich zu widmen, die sie dann zum Gegenstand ihrer meist leichten Poesien machen". Here Propertius is measured by the standards of those whom he feels to be different from himself. In this area Petersmann (1980), who often points to *Umwelt* and its function, is more congenial.

42. The following is a matter of principle, leaving aside the question whether Propertius, at the time of publishing the *Monobiblos*, had seen any Tibullan elegy at all. What scanty "evidence" there is for determining the two poets' relation may be seen from Solmsen's cautious investigation (1961; literature on details: 276, n. 4).

43. See also Nethercut 1971A, 465; 470; J. K. King 1975–76, 116; 118; Abel 32.

44. Or should we use the plural and say "loved ones"? We may wonder why he does not expressly mention his father's death before Book 4, years later. His silence does not allow us to give a certain answer. Apart from (a) hypothesizing that the wounded survivor of 1.21 (who brought home Gallus' last wishes) was the poet's father, himself bound to die from his wound soon after (so the wish for his parents to be "joyful", 21.5, would be tragic irony); or apart from (b) considering the possibility that the boy felt closer to Gallus (and Gallus' bride or wife) at that time than to his father, I see two possible answers. Either (c) that, when death struck for the first time within the family, the experience was more disturbing, especially so since it coincided with the loss of the family's home and possessions. (Besides, at the time of the second blow, the boy may have been somewhat older already, and perhaps more self-relying.) Another emotional dependence of a new kind occurred when he was old enough to fall in love. Or, (d) the epitaph poem is included mainly because of its political implications. In that case, Gallus' assassination on his way home from fighting against Octavian is to reveal the author's feelings toward the new régime. This alternative distracts from the poem's human core. My results lead me to accept (c) as most likely. J. K. King has recently indicated that the early experience may be responsible for the later refusal of an Augustan career and for the turn to love poetry (1975–76, 109; cf. 123). See also H. J. Glücklich 1977, 47.

45. Syme 1974, 466. Syme, too, points to 3.5.1.

46. There should be no doubt that *Aen.* 1.289f. refers to Octavian (Augustus), and not to his "father", C. J. Caesar. R. G. Austin in his commentary remarks: "The identity of *Caesar* is a problem. Lines 291–6 plainly refer to Augustus: is Virgil speaking of Augustus in 286–90 also?" To answer the question positively, I wish to add a new argument, drawn from the overall composition of *Aeneid* Book 1. The plot line of this book receives important impulses from Venus' changing mood and from the concern (*cura*) she feels for her son Aeneas and his men. This *cura* leads her, as on earlier occasions, up to her father's throne to ask for help ("since this worry is biting you once more again", Jove diagnoses her condition, *quando haec te cura remordet*, 261). For the present, Jove succeeds in calming down his daughter's fears (but by nighttime, we should add, her worry will be back: *cura recursat*, 662). To cheer up Venus, Jove not only employs "the facial expression with which he clears up stormy weather" (*vultu, quo caelum tempestatesque serenat*, 255), but also gives her a long prophecy about her descendants' glorious future. In doing so, he implies that it will not be before the far distant future that Venus may stop worrying about her race, i.e., may feel free from her *cura*:

> hunc tu olim caelo spoliis Orientis onustum
> accipies *se-cura*; vocabitur hic quoque votis   (289f.)

Now it seems indubitable that the time of C. J. Caesar's assassination (and supposed reception in heaven) is not apt to make Venus feel *se-cura* (290). Lines 286–290 will be a truthful prophecy to troubled Venus only if they, like the rest (291ff.), refer to the peace and security of the Augustan Age. For a more detailed account of the composition of *Aen.* 1, see Stahl 1969.

47. Cf. Birt 1915, 292.

48. See Anderson 1979, 125f.

49. I have abstained from any detailed discussion of the problem "poet and *persona*" (or whatever formula appears adequate for distinguishing between poetical *ego* and the poet's "real life"). The work of art speaks for itself, as H. Cherniss (1943) has pointed out. So one welcomes Allen's criticism (1962) of biographical interpretations with their extraction of supposedly historical details from Propertius' elegies. But we must not fall into the other extreme and forbid the poet all individual and autobiographical self-expression in his poetry—especially not against his own claims (Allen, 146: "He writes only of what he knows will be interesting to others because it is part of common experience"). If "the particular function of Roman love elegy was to give personal form to typical experience" (o.c. p. 129), may then Gallus' assassination near Perusia, too, have been nothing else but a fiction, invented to fulfill that function? Or is it more consistent to assert that, in the case of a relative's death, the autobiographical setting of sorrow is meant to reflect true-life experience, but in the case of the poet's love it is not?

We will never disentangle *Dichtung und Wahrheit* (and should not wish to). But, as we no longer take fiction as history, we should also not a priori exclude real-life personal concerns from poetry cast in an autobiographical mould. As a rule we may lay down that, as long as we are (or as any more congenial reader is) able to appreciate in an elegy of Propertius the level of reality (actuality) it claims to represent, there is no occasion to proceed to further generalization (or concretization).

Perhaps Solmsen's notion of "idealized autobiography" (1961, 276, n. 3; cf.

1962, 84) can be helpful here, as long as it allows for some truly autobiographical self-expression. Solmsen himself (1961, 277) points to the triad of experience/invention/tradition. He takes the soundly restricting position that, while the feelings expressed may be genuine, the situations depicted are, as a rule, not (1962, 82). Recently, M. L. Clarke (1976, 138), referring, among other poems, to Prop. 1.21, suggested "that the biographical approach is not so naïve as it is represented to be by our more sophisticated literary critics" (in their number, he counts A. W. Allen, M. Hubbard, G. Williams). Though it may seem that scholarship is thus coming round full circle, it will not (one hopes) return to Lachmann's way of viewing Propertius' poetry as a sort of autobiographical documentary—or for that matter, to the stage of von Wilamowitz' biographical work on Plato.

Biographical aspects can (as can historical facts) be considered fruitfully by the interpreter. After all, even Cherniss (the strictest antagonist of "the biographical fashion in literary criticism", who most stringently subscribes to "the fact that a work of art exists independently of its author . . . , that its artistic qualities . . . are not to be explained by anything outside of the work") warns that this thesis does not mean "that anyone, by reason of his humanity alone, can understand any literary work that is set before him, or that because it is a work of art with which he is concerned he need not study assiduously to acquire every instrument that may help him to comprehend the significance of the text before him" (1943, 290).

To heed this warning is especially important in cases where an author has chosen to introduce part of his life's historical (contemporary) scenery into his writings in such a way that the (auto)biographical aspects contribute to the essence of the work. The fact that Plato published the "Apology of Socrates" not anonymously but under his own name, and, further, has himself appear in it, both by name (38b6) and by implication (39c8ff.), gives the work an additional dimension. The fact that the author of the *Phaedo* expressly informs us at the outset (59b10) that he was ill and therefore not with Socrates on the day of the execution, precludes the reader from dismissing at any time the author's personal involvement in the events—an involvement which is a live and lasting ingredient of this literary creation. Thus, in denying dying relative Gallus, career-conscious friend Tullus, and even—most "literary" of the three and most difficult to assess—Cynthia the degree of historicity which their poet (possibly) included in his autobiographical poetry, the interpreter may unintentionally lose hold of the individual dimension symbolized and conveyed in the oeuvre.

Therefore I have, whenever it seemed possible, opted for the more "naïve" standpoint—leaving it to my reader's choice to reduce the actuality claimed in a specific poem to a more acceptable degree. The reader is probably more inclined to temper an interpretation by substituting "the poetical *ego*" for the poet's name than—vice versa—he is to intensify what I say by himself replacing "*persona*" with "Propertius".

CHAPTER VI

1. Wimmel 1960, 202.
2. Cairns 1979, 190. I cannot, in the present context, deal systematically with Cairns' arguments, but will have to mention them along the lines of my own inter-

pretation. Suffice it to say that—as in the case of elegy 1.6 (Chapter IV above)—his assumptions seem to me not supported by Propertius' text.

3. Boucher 1965, 135 (italics mine).

4. The later laws were known as the *lex Iulia de maritandis ordinibus*, the *lex Iulia de adulteriis* (both probably of 18 B.C., briefly before the Secular Games at which Horace's *Carmen Saeculare* represented the Emperor's intentions) and the *lex Papia Poppaea* of A.D. 9. As far as subject matter is concerned, the two last-mentioned go together and are set apart from the first. For detailed information, see H. Last 1934, 437ff.; P. Csillag 1968; Brunt 1971, 558ff.; G. Williams 1968, 553ff.; Ferrero Raditsa 1980.

5. Mommsen 1955 (1899), 691, n. 1; see also Ferrero Raditsa 1980, 296. G. Ferrero (1908, 155f.), thinking of "a law promulgated by the triumvirs at some date unknown to us", maintained that, if Augustus had passed and repealed a law within a few months, we would know about it. "It is more likely that Propertius alludes to some arrangement made by Augustus towards the close of the triumvirate, which was repealed in 28, with all the triumvirate measures, which were unconstitutional, or, in other words, had not been passed by the *comitia*." Important for our poem is that *Caesar* Octavian is seen to be responsible for the measure. Opposite to Ferrero's position: G. Williams 1962, 28.

6. Cairns 1979, 188.

7. Brunt 1971, 560.

8. Last 1934, 442, referring to Dio 56.1,2; 7,3; 10.1–3.

9. Cairns 1979, 187.

10. BB, Introduction, xxi, deducing from 2.7: "She was probably a courtesan, for (1) . . . it was impossible for him to marry her; . . . (2) he was unmarried and unwilling to marry anyone else . . . ; (3) she was unmarried, since . . . Propertius never mentions a husband;" etc.

11. Fontenrose 1949, 375.

12. Williams 1968, 529ff. "Su Cinzia i pareri sono discordi" (della Corte 1982, 551).

13. Cairns 1979, 189, n. 13.

14. Cf. Williams 1968, 534.

15. Cairns 1979, 189.

16. The last distich of elegy 2.6 is so close to the lover's attitude displayed in 2.7 that G. Luck (reading *diducet* in 2.6.41) has recently again suggested that those two lines should form the opening of 2.7 rather than the conclusion of 2.6 (Luck 1979, 77f.).

17. Scheidweiler (1960, 77) quotes from Seneca (frgm. 13.84f.): *in aliena quippe uxore omnis amor turpis est*, *in sua nimius. sapiens vir iudicio debet amare coniugem, non affectu . . . nihil est foedius quam uxorem amare quam adulteram.* Of course *licentia coniugalis* (cf. Tac. A. 11.27) is defined somewhat differently by the Stoic philosopher and by the lover Propertius.

18. "The social laws affecting Roman citizens were all designed to secure the permanence of the Italian stock, and for this reason it may be agreed that the stimulation of the birth rate was their common end." H. Last 1934, 443. This must have been true also about the situation addressed in elegy 2.7. ". . . ad Augusto, più che il matrimonio, interessara la prole" (della Corte 1982, 541; cf. 543).

19. For brief information, see Brunt and Moore 1973, 67f. Beforehand, the oath-taker had to invoke destruction upon himself and his family in case he infringed the terms. The subject was also—a similar effect resulted from the laws of adultery—encouraged to report to the authorities whatever activities seemed suspicious.

20. G. Ferrero 1909, 72.

21. Ferrero Raditsa 1980, 286f. (with notes on propagandistic literature in the 1930s).

22. G. Williams 1968, 534.

23. Mommsen 1955 (= 1899), 699 with n. 3.

24. *Aut*, 2.7.9, is (*cum pace* Scheidweiler 1960, 77) hardly to be taken as indicating an alternative here (in which case one might think of "or—in case I do not ruin my passion in marriage—that I pass your closed door", etc.), but introduces the other side of the same coin. *Ad* Verg. *Aen.* 1.369 (*sed vos qui tandem? quibus aut venistis ab oris?*) Austin remarks that *aut* "is not antithetical, but merely separative, introducing a second question more or less synonymous with the first."

25. According to a suggestion by G. Most. See also Rothstein who, however, pictures the poet as *exclusus amator* again before Cynthia's door, singing and playing his flute, as in the time before his forced marriage. But it is worth keeping in mind the alternative interpretation of lines 7–12 offered by Camps (and Paley), viz., that Propertius is depicting his marriage procession which would pass by Cynthia's house. Cf. Ov. *Her.* 12.140 (which also contains the play on *tibia* and *tuba*). In this case, *tibia* would be the flute(s) played in the procession. It should be noted, however, that *tibia* for itself does not automatically imply an allusion to a wedding (cf., e.g., Hor. *C.* 3.7.30; Ov. *Trist.* 5.1.47f.: *tibia funeribus convenit ista meis*).

26. Again we have to contradict SB. He criticizes BB's translation "if my lady's camp which I follow were a real camp of war". I quote SB: "*vera* is most naturally taken as denoting a metaphorical meaning of *castra* as distinct from the literal, not vice versa." He goes on to cite much evidence to prove his assumption. But almost all his passages differ from Prop. 2.7.15 in that they specifically state what the "real" thing is in the specific context as compared to what one customarily would understand by the word in question (e.g., *Maecenatis erunt vera tropaea fides*, 3.9.34; i.e., *tropaea* is not taken in its normal meaning but "true" *tropaea* can be understood to be *fides*). For the meaning required in 2.7.15 it is better to compare a passage like 2.9.17:

> tunc igitur veris gaudebat Graecia nuptis,

where Penelope and Briseis (the latter, though technically not married to Achilles) behave like *true* or *real* wives. Here *veris* is clearly meant to denote the literal, not a metaphorical, meaning of *nuptis*.

27. Rothstein points out that *castra* means not only the camp but also the troops that are on the march from one camp to another.

28. Rothstein came close to seeing the truth when he registered the poet's "gehobene(n) Stimmung, die dem Glanz kriegerischer Erfolge ein *ebenbürtiges* Gegenbild gegenüberstellen will" (italics mine).

29. G. Williams (1962), disturbed by the contradiction in Horace's published poetry between his official call for restoration of morality and marriage on the one

hand, and his erotic odes to girls "not burdened . . . by the chains of wedlock" (1962, 28) on the other, decided that his erotic writings were so clearly derived from Greek poetry and so far removed from real life that they could hardly be offensive to the official New Morality (cf. o.c. 42). Ferrero Raditsa has given a different answer (1980, 317) which, though more bitter, is more apt to let us see the greater responsibility and human commitment of Propertius' elegy 2.7: speaking of the Augustan "dual relation between moralistic facade and pornography", he states that Augustus "did not fear pornography (sexuality without feeling). What he feared was unpredictable love, the love which Catullus had sung and Lucretius," etc.

30. The effects which a correct reading of Propertius may have on contemporary Vergilian scholarship cannot be demonstrated here.

31. R. G. Austin, *P. Vergili Maronis Aeneidos liber quartus*, Oxford, 1966, 106.

32. The first distich of 2.1 wishes to reconcile the Roman public to the fact that the poet is publishing another *mollis liber*, i.e., the poem was written *after* the collection of Book 2 (or most of it) was considered ready for publication. This, almost unnecessary to say, goes together with the poem's programmatic character (for which see the latter part of this chapter) of firmly defining Propertius' position with regard to contemporary literary tendency.

It was an unfounded assumption by Wili (1947, 184; still accepted by Wimmel 1960, 16, n. 2) that, because of lines 30–34, the elegy was written under the *recent* impression of Octavian's triumph in 29 B.C. For the emphasis granted to the triumph does not derive from Propertius' impressionable mind, presumably arrested by a spectacular event, but is due to the fact that the triumph meant for Octavian the crowning affair of his fighting career. From the literary description of that career (25–34) the poet could hardly exclude the historical climax given it by the Emperor.

More speaks therefore against an early date of 2.1 than Fuchs' (1947, 183–84, n. 101) argument (advanced against Wili's thesis that Horace *C.* 2.12 is an answer to Prop. 2.1): "Prop. 2.1 kann nicht als Einzelstück von Horaz angehört worden sein". Wimmel's later attempt to back Wili's position by showing that 2.1 is "morphologically" younger than 2.10 (1960, 193ff., accepted by Nethercut 1972, 80) gives no proof at all of what he calls Propertius' "inner drama" (and he misreads the structure of 2.10, giving the first movement as comprising lines 1–8). Paratore (1936, 171) derived the opposite result from the existence of the two poems in the same book: "In fatti, Properzio aveva promesso da tempo ma con l'evidente proposito di non mantenere: aveva promesso nell'elegia 2.10, mentre s'era rifiutato nell'elegia 2.1".

No chronological indication can be extracted from the circumstance that Octavian is called "Caesar" in 2.1 (= "early", according to Wimmel, o.c. 193), but "Augustus" in 2.10 (= "late"). For still as late as 4.6 the Emperor may be called "Caesar": *Caesaris in nomen ducuntur carmina*: *Caesar / dum canitur*, etc., line 13f.

The only way to assign a later date to 2.10 than to 2.1 would be to revive Lachmann's thesis that 2.10 and its patriotic spirit open a new book. But, as Lachmann's successors saw, this new spirit is not borne out by the rest of the "new" book. Besides, as we shall see, restricting the meaning of 2.10 to a patriotic message is a falsification which deprives the poem of its core. A modification of Lachmann's thesis was presented by O. Skutsch (1975). Ross (1975, 118, with n. 3) likewise thinks it "probable" that 2.10 at one time was the opening poem to a Book 3.

33. Paratore (1936, 177), although not analyzing the two opposing structures the poet built into his creation, was nevertheless on the right track when speaking of "questa palese ironia, maliziosamente affermentesi nel repentino voltafaccia di v. 20" (cf. p. 171). Wimmel concedes: "Das ist freilich noch immer eine kleine Teufelei" (1960, 198). Cp. Rothstein *ad loc.*

34. This can hardly be seen as a hint (Paratore 1936, 177) that Augustus' future victories will be a less repulsive subject for the poet than his past ones (that include Perusia), which are flatly refused in 2.1.'Propertius feels the régime's coercion not as a republican but as a human being who loves his personal freedom (cf. 2.7). The advantage of future victories is that they cannot be the object of a praising epic *now*.

35. Cf. Nethercut 1972, 93: "Caesar is given Caesar's proper place—a *possible* subject for idle hours 'on leave' from Cynthia's camp". Nethercut derives the enthusiastic tone of 2.10, not so much from Augustus' supposedly great achievements, but from the poet's disenchantment with Cynthia's behavior as expressed in the surrounding elegies 2.8; 9; 11. This argument is admittedly dangerous because it could also be used to show that 2.7, since it is surrounded by heavy charges against Cynthia (2.6 and 8), is no more than an occasional fit of fading loyalty towards his mistress; but Nethercut himself appreciates 2.10 as a counterpart to 2.7 (a "startling" [o.c. 93] one, however, instead of a mitigating one), and 2.7 as a serious poem.

36. With most editors, I read *es* (instead of *est*), assuming that Cynthia is addressed directly in the first line as she is later in the poem (9; 11; 19).

37. The future character of lines 6, 12, 18 was observed by Nethercut (1972, 85).

38. Nethercut (1972, 87f.), seizing upon the same features as I do, and stressing the ambiguity of *quando* in line 8 ("when"; "since"; several commentators decide in favor of "since" alone) feels that this passage leaves the doors open both to a serious and to an ironical interpretation: "One . . . must acknowledge that both possibilities exist: a fusion of the two ideas was allowed to stand". Here I would like to bring in the poem's logical train of thought (based on grammatical sentence structure—see below) and maintain that a first or surface impression, created by the enthusiastic tone and the stunning series of time indications, is, after a second reading, to be *replaced* (not complemented) by the correct understanding that no praise is to be expected from Propertius' lips; i.e., surface and true understanding are mutually exclusive. Rothstein already sensed "dass der Dichter sich scheinbar gerade auf den Standpunkt stellt, den er in Wirklichkeit nicht einnimmt."

39. Line 6 was termed "fast zynisch" by Wimmel (1960, 196).

40. Hardly by Orpheus, as D. O. Ross (1975, 23) wishes us to understand *ille* in line 70. Ross' approach may be compared in contrast with the interpretation given in my text. Among my concerns about Ross' presentation is the question whether he gives due weight to the words *nondum etiam* at 2.10.25, *sed* and *modo* at 26, and *sic . . . ut . . . ut* at 2.13.4ff. For *etiam*, 2.10.25, compare 1.9.17. *Nondum*

etiam can here hardly be taken as "meaning the same as plain *nondum*" (Camps).

41. See end of n. 32 above. Contrary to Lachmann, Giardina (1977, 147) thinks 2.10 could function as a book's *epilogue* poem.

42. The earlier one was written shortly after the "restoration of the republic" in 28/27, when Octavian proclaimed his return to the constitution. The later elegy (2.10, dated roughly by its allusions to Britannia, India, Arabia) reflects the climate of 25 B.C. when, under the new political arrangement, *Augustus* had been "only" consul for about 2–3 years (and absent from Rome).

43. The supposed break at lines 46/47 reflects a long-standing discussion. Elegy 2.1 has seen a history of interpretations which appears strangely uniform. Ever since Heimreich (1863, extensively quoted by Enk) has split the poem up into a more joyful, optimistic earlier half and a sad and pessimistic latter one, scholars have stuck to the idea of two incompatible parts (the cut being localized at 46/47 or 56/57, and more incoherence being found in part II than in part I), usually without even looking for a logical connection. The most desperate point was reached by Damon and Helmbold, who sensed many conglomerate "parts of quite different poems" (1952, 220) in 2.1. Two more recent German investigations (Wimmel 1960; Kühn 1961), accepting and presupposing surface incompatibility, locate unity behind the scenes: Wimmel is convinced that young Propertius, being on the defensive towards Maecenas, uses *Todesnähe* to replace the apologetic *Altersmotiv* of his model Callimachus, but overutilizes it: "Properz findet in der Tat verschiedene, widersprechende Zugänge, die nun wiederum kombiniert sein wollen" (1960, 25). Kühn, finding the formal "Brücke nicht gerade sehr stark" between the two parts, likewise starts searching "welche *inneren* Gründe das Eindringen pessimistischer Gedanken verursachen" (1961, 92; italics his). Unknowingly, he adds the arch stone to a century of scholarship when scolding interpreters for looking for structural consistency in a Propertian elegy: "Die logische Verbindung der beiden Teile, die ein pedantischer Kopf erwarten würde, wird explizit nicht hergestellt" (o.c. p. 97).

44. See Wimmel, 1960, 13ff.

45. Cf. Paratore 1936, 182f.; Wimmel 1960, 37. Today there is a broad consensus that line 2.1.29 is by no means complimentary to Augustus.

46. According to Appian (5.5.49), Octavian had decided on plundering the city, and the fire was started by a mentally deranged citizen. Appian, too, appears to emphasize the inappropriate end of the ancient and dignified city: "This was the end of Perugia, which had a reputation of antiquity and dignity. For it is said to have been founded in olden times by the Etruscans among the first twelve cities in Italy." τόδε μὲν δὴ τῇ Περυσίᾳ τέλος ἦν, δόξαν ἀρχαιότητος ἐχούσῃ καὶ ἀξιώσεως· ὑπὸ γὰρ Τυρρηνῶν πάλαι φασὶν αὐτὴν ἐν ταῖς πρώταις δυώδεκα πόλεσιν ἐν Ἰταλίᾳ γενέσθαι.

47. See Kühn 1961, 90, n. 1.

48. Housman 1914, 153 = 1972, vol. 2, 882(ff.). The change in the text suggested by Housman is today accepted in Richardson's edition.

49. Ed. Pfeiffer I, p. 1, frgm. I, 1–4. Textual restorations as in the edition of E. Howald and E. Staiger (Zurich, 1955).

50. ἓν ἄεισμα διηνεκὲς ἐς βασιλήων / πρᾶξιας.

51. ἢ προτέρων ἥρωας.

52. θόρυβον δ'οὐκ ἐφίλησαν ὄνων (line 30).

53. Wimmel (1960, 27) even pictures Propertius as respectfully inventing and inserting an otherwise unnecessary distich (37/38!) in order to prevent Maecenas from feeling classified as a Telchis.

54. *Laus*, a positive value, can be seen to occupy the emphatic first position in line 2.1.47 because it *corrects* the potentially derogatory expression *conterat . . . diem* of the preceding line, which was spoken in the tone of indifference any socially elevated Roman would feel towards low-ranking professions such as shepherd, sailor, common soldier, ploughman. "A glory to end one's life in love" (47) therefore reevaluates and quickly separates the lover from those professionals who "waste" their days or "exhaust" their lifetime (46): what the lover shares with them is the lifelong inescapability (*conterat . . . diem* ~ *mori*) of the "profession", but not their lowly social situation. Without 47, line 46 would be incomplete. The same metabolic reevaluation (the corrected word there is once more *conteritur*, the correcting word *fama*) was found in 1.7.9.

55. It appears infelicitous to read lines 49/50 as an attempt to make the poet's mistress socially acceptable to Maecenas ("Cynthia soll von dem Odium der Kurtisane befreit werden, das . . . auch Properz in den Augen des Maecenas belastete", Kühn 1961, 95).

In Kühn's interpretation Propertius very much equals a schoolboy who, being charged by headmaster Maecenas with having been seen in public smoking cigars, defends himself (a) by pretending that he has smoked no vulgar brand (but carefully avoids mentioning the popular name-tag "Cynthia"), and (b) by pleading for mercy through indicating the painful and punitive reactions his intestinal system has suffered already. And in spite of lines 51–56 (or 1.12.19: *mi neque amare aliam neque ab hac desistere fas est*), Maecenas is supposed to understand that, in case of serious flaws, young Propertius may even switch brands: "In der Tat hängt die Möglichkeit, sich auf *eine* Liebesbeziehung beschränken zu können, von dem Entschluss der Geliebten ab, treu zu bleiben und den Geliebten nicht anderen Mädchen in die Arme zu treiben (vgl. *viles quaerere*, 2, 24, 9)" (1961, 94). See Baker 1970, 677ff.; Steidle 1962, 125, n. 111.

56. "Eine konsequente Fortführung des bereits in den Versen 41/46 eingenommenen Standpunkts", Steidle 1962, 125; cf. 131ff. More precisely speaking, 48b is illustrated in 49/50; 47/48a are solemnly explicated in 51–56.

57. Tentatively, one may interpret that Propertius will stay loyal to Cynthia even if

(1) facing death by poison from a refused woman (as Hippolytus from Phaedra), line 51; or (preferably) exposed to a love-philtre (as Hippolytus by Phaedra);

(2) facing the choice between metamorphosis (or worse: Homer, *Od.* 10.341) and loving another woman (as Odysseus' situation is on Circe's island), line 53;

(3) facing (like Jason's father) the prospect of rejuvenation while Cynthia grows old (line 54).

58. Tränkle (1960, 22f.) feels that lines 57f. have been formulated under the influence of Gallus.

CHAPTER VII

1. I am of course aware that love and inspiration through love may be literary conventions and clichés as well. But, as I said before (see last note to Chapter V), one can hardly reduce them to that function in Propertius. Nor could one limit Augustus' part in Propertius' work to an aesthetic convention.

2. It is possible to divide also the larger subsections further: 1–8 into 1–4 (the poet's new experience leads to thorough distrust) and 5–8 (the wide range of Amor's destructive force, confirmed through mythical examples); 13–20 into 13–16 (Propertius would sacrifice everything else for his friend) and 17–20 (but with regard to his love, his jealousy knows no limits).

3. White (1964, 65) speaks of "the almost congratulatory tone of lines 25–26", and calls the transition from 24 to 25 a "dramatic development" (o.c. 66).

4. See Shackleton Bailey *ad loc.*

5. See, e.g., Wimmel 1960, 202ff.; 212ff.

6. See Boucher 1958, 307ff. (Some doubts, though not substantial ones, may be found in Alfonsi 1963A passim); the same is true about Herrman's identification with Cilnius (anagram: Lynceus) Maecenas (1967, 139ff.). Neither suggestion offers a plausible motive for the use of a pseudonym.

7. For *licet* with subjunctive meaning "to be permitted to" (33) cf. Prop. 2.22.23; 4.1.148.

8. With Schuster, I accept *cursus* (ʂ) into the text instead of Barber's *rursus* (line 33). Hanslik (1979) likewise accepts *rursus*.

9. Interpreters have failed to see that the division is between (permitted) small and (forbidden) epic themes (division at 38:39), but *not* between a "*Heracleis*" (or whatever common heading has been assumed to unite lines 33–36) and a "Thebaid" (37–40; division at 36:37). Already Rothstein ran into self-created difficulties here, and so still did Boucher (1958, 315f.) when trying to distill works of Varius Rufus from our passage. To him 37–40 indicated "clairement une Thébaïde", "une oeuvre de grande ampleur", although no word is said in the passage about any existing work of poetry at all.

10. The reference need not be to Aeschylus' "Seven against Thebes" specifically; tragedy's swollen style appears to Callimachus as bad as that of epic (see the Callimachean passages cited by Alfonsi 1949A, 340). Direct reference to Callimachus relieves us from looking for a real-life Roman representative behind our passage.

11. For the plural *amores* "per indicare la donna amata", see La Penna 1951A, 195ff. (he does not include 2.34.48, but lists 4.4.37).

12. The way I explain it, the future *non tutior ibis* (45) is not in conflict with the fact that Lynceus has already given in to love (present tense in 25: *insanit amores*)—especially not since the exaggeration "insanely in love" is intended to be a vivid expression of Propertius' own feeling of triumph. Accordingly, there is no need to demand a "stilkritische Implikation" for line 45, as Quadlbauer (1966) does, whose division between literary criticism in hexameters 41/43/45 and true life in pentameters 42/44/46 can hardly be maintained. See the difficulty which distich 45/46 means for his scheme (o.c. 57).

13. "To be king among the girls" possibly refers to nothing more than that,

when reading his poetry (cf. *hoc . . . ingenio*, 58) at a party, Propertius arrests every woman's attention.

14. Damon and Helmbold 1952, 238.

15. Lynceus' philosophical studies (the feature by which he exceeds his forerunner Ponticus, cf. 1.7 and 9) may be seen to stand for the philosophical interest of Vergil, which is visible not only in his life (his membership in Siron's Epicurean circle) but also in his works (e.g., Silenus' song in *Ecl.* 6 or Iopas' song in *Aen.* 1).

16. A "dual purpose" is assigned to lines 59/60 also by Vessey (1970, 63). But unlike me, Vessey does not accept Propertius' Lynceus as a guide to the elegist's views on Vergil; rather, he sees in what follows a "re-alignment of prior arguments" and a "volteface": "Propertius' life-style and its literary counterpart, so forcibly expounded to Ponticus and Lynceus, is now a thing of yesterday. Propertius knows this, but he cannot escape."

17. That both the potential subjunctive and its Greek counterpart, the "future less vivid", can (apart from the customary use for a modest assertion) express a very high degree of subjective certainty is a grammatical phenomenon too rarely utilized by commentators. A convincing example is Ajax' goodbye to his son:

$$\text{῏Ω παῖ, γένοιο πατρὸς εὐτυχέστερος,}$$
$$\text{τὰ δ'ἄλλ' ὅμοιος—καὶ γένοι' ἂν οὐ κακός.}$$ (Soph., *Ai.* 550f.)

The father's wish is: more good luck for his son than he himself has had. In all other respects his son may just be like himself—and, Ajax is *certain*, he will become a noble man.

At 2.34.83, *nec . . . sim* continues *non . . . venient*, 81 (cf. *non*, 47, continued by *nec* 49). This context excludes the "subjunctive of wish", which one might otherwise suggest here for consideration. According to Propertius' practice of building distich lines, *his* and *animis*, though standing next to each other, should not be expected to belong together syntactically. As the combination *minor ore* comes without a demonstrative pronoun, so does the expression *minor . . . animis*. Thus *his* taken with *animis* would destroy the balance provided by the parallel grammatical structure; *his* resumes *haec* of 81, again resumed by *haec*, 85.

18. The difference of the two poets is defined materially, through the objects of their personal dedication. This is methodologically important to us, because here already the tracks are set for later interpretations, even as far in the future as Book 4, as an example may illustrate:

Dismissing the material aspects and concentrating on formal ones, Alfonsi (1943–44B; repeated 1945D [Chapter III] and 1954) sees Propertius in 2.1 decline an epic on the past such as an *Aeneid* (*Caesaris in Phrygios condere nomen avos*, 2.1.42) and permit only—if any at all—an epic on the present (viz., on Octavian and Maecenas, 25ff.). At the time of our passage (2.34.59–64), Propertius is said to have slowly developed a new sense of appreciation: "Properzio . . . celebra proprio, in un *excursus* di esaltazione di Virgilio . . . , l'unione di realtà e di mito, di passato e presente che è felicemente, e quasi si direbbe insuperabilmente, raggiunta nell' Eneide" (1943–44B, 464; cf. 1949A, 336: "Properzio intonerà la palinodia"). In this way, any possible issues of credo between the two authors are played down or even vanish, and a road is opened that leads to Propertius' "Vergilization" (if I may say so). Vergil's aesthetic and moral influence is said to reach its peak in Book 4: "E proprio l'elegia programmatica è tutta pervasa di spiriti virgiliani" (1943–44B, 469). Thus formalism together with attenuation of contents have cut down Propertius to a straight-minded Augustan figure—in Book 2, already, and for all the rest of his poetical career.

Elegy 2.34 proves to be a stumbling block also to Paratore's sharp-sighted attempt (1936) to define the anti-Augustan attitude of Propertius. By first taking the elegist's compliment to Vergil seriously and by then reproaching Vergil for having never returned it to Propertius (o.c. p. 207ff.), Paratore takes a roundabout path of indirect proof, which will later, as he interprets Book 4 (pp. 217ff.), keep him from finding the evidence which he so badly needs to support his thesis—even though (as my last two chapters demonstrate) Propertius' attitude is stringently presented and documented in his own words, without any need for circumstantial evidence.

The last two decades, exampled by Baker (1968B) and the recent surveys by Levin and Little (1982), have been somewhat more favorably disposed toward the idea of a Propertius who is critical of Vergil and (his) Augustanism. (This trend was hampered, however, by a tendency in Vergilian scholarship to locate opposition to Augustus within the *Aeneid* itself.) The problem, of course, has been how to evaluate Propertius' longtime development. In the 1970s, e.g., Sullivan, pointing to Pound's grotesque rendering ("Pound freely but penetratingly translated"), viewed lines 2.34.61–66 as ambiguous and their "bows to the *Aeneid*" "as another critical thrust at the Augustan poetical establishment" (1976, 24f.). Though Sullivan and I (and others) agree about a number of Propertian passages in finding them critical of the Augustan régime and its background of war (see, e.g., his selections in the chapter on "The Politics of Elegy"), I do not think that surveying elegies and listing relevant passages, without detailed interpretations of their overall contexts, can properly account for Propertius' difficulties. This is revealed especially on occasion of Book 4 where to Sullivan the poet seems purposefully to write bad poetry, e.g., the Actium poem 4.6: "The whole thing reads like a parody of court poetry" (sc., by Horace or Vergil)—an assumption by which "we are rid of some embarrassing personal and poetic aspects of this elegy in particular and Book 4 in general" (1976, 147).

By observing the long-term development of his elegy and its increasingly complex organization, my reader will be in a position to appreciate that even the "embarrassing personal . . . aspects" are an important part of the poet's human self-representation.

19. Alfonsi (1944–45, 127ff.) points to Vergil's prose draft mentioned by Donatus. Scholars have often been concerned about Propertius' apparently careless wholesale reference to the *Aeneid*. A lot of detective work has gone into the question of how much he really knew of Vergil's epic at the time of writing 2.34. A more recent investigation hypothesizes blatant ignorance on Propertius' part. Tränkle (1971, 62), upon industriously reconstructing from Ennius, Naevius, and Vergil's *Georgics* what expectations educated contemporaries might have fostered about the contents of an unpublished *Aeneid*, invites us to believe that the elegist offers nothing but his own guesswork—wrong guesswork, moreover, based on wrong inferences drawn from two passages he knew: proem and Jove's speech in Book 1. From Jove's prophecy (1.257ff.), which, like Prop. 2.34, mentions the city of Lavinium (270f.) and hints at the victory of Actium (289), Propertius is said to

have wrongly and prematurely inferred that fulfillment of the prophecy, i.e., the founding of Lavinium and the battle of Actium, would be granted broad space in the narrative of the *Aeneid*'s later books. A similar statement of inaccuracy ("accenna liberalmente al soggetto"), based on the same passages of *Aen.* 1, was made by Funaioli (1940, 109) in his polemic against Rostagni. (Boucher even claims the inaccuracy to be intended: "technique du résumé incomplet et inexact", 1965, 293.)

Neat as Tränkle's hypothesis may appear, it is open to at least two objections, one of which lies on his own level: *why* should, as Tränkle's hypothesis requires, Propertius' knowledge have been limited to Jove's oracle only (which, moreover, does not even mention the name of Actium, and mentions that of Lavinium only in a transition) and not have included other parts of the plot, either of Book 1 or of later books? If Propertius singles out the battle of Actium to characterize the *Aeneid*, is he not likely to refer to the passage where the battle is most prominent? In *Aen.* 8.671–728, the battle forms, so to speak, the climax of history, the final purpose of Aeneas' existence and toils (though unintelligible to Aeneas himself, cf. *miratur . . . ignarus*, 730), surpassed only by Octavian's final triumph celebrated at Rome. As to Tränkle's charge that Propertius mentions the founding of Lavinium although the *Aeneid* does not narrate (but only predicts) it, we must say: Propertius speaks from his own contemporary viewpoint, looking back in time: from sleeping memory, Vergil is now rousing "the walls founded on Lavinian shores". Could Propertius in this context have referred to Lavinium as not yet founded? (Besides, we must hold against Tränkle's grammatical rules, even *future* events can be expressed by the past participle: cf. the *pugnataque in ordine bella* which Vesuvius prophetically depicted on Aeneas' shield, *Aen.* 8.629).

Thus the question remains: *Why* should we follow Tränkle and limit Propertius' acquaintance with the growing *Aeneid* to proem and Jove's oracle in Book 1? Tränkle provides no answer, but expresses sympathy for Klingner's and Friedrich's analyses of Book 1, which assign an earlier date of composition to Jove's prophecy than to the surrounding parts because of "contradictions" within the plot. This however is of dubious value to his hypothesis, since the alleged contradictions result mostly from misreading Vergil's literary intentions (see Stahl 1969): it would be circular reasoning if a difficult (and misread) passage in Propertius is easily explained ("mühelos erklären", Tränkle o.c. 63) with the help of a difficult (and misread) context of the *Aeneid*, and vice versa. With this method, the truth may remain undiscovered because it is not even needed. It is superfluous to the philological mind which feels satisfied with asking Propertius for his precise reference ("*Aen.* 1, lines 257–296") and for nothing more.

How could Propertius dare characterize the vast *Aeneid* by referring to the battle of Actium, which comprises hardly 60 lines in Book 8 (and hardly any in Book 1)? asks Tränkle, and he answers: because Propertius did not yet know the *Aeneid* (at least not as fully as we know it). I doubt that this question should be answered on the level of counting lines.

Here my second objection comes in. Tränkle and his forerunners in this area tend to treat Propertius as if he were a commentator on the *Aeneid*, another but less reliable Servius, so to speak. I suggest another answer. Propertius presented the battle of Actium "gewissermassen als die eigentliche Intention" of the *Aeneid* (o.c.

61), because he, having himself been exposed to royal wishes for an epic, felt sure that the whole, vast *Aeneid* was being written for one purpose: to please the man whose final step to unrestricted power (in his own understanding) was his victory at Actium. To Propertius, the epic on Aeneas was nothing but a refined form of adulation—less direct propaganda, but no less effective. By his line "to build Caesar's name on the foundation of Trojan forefathers" (*Caesaris in Phrygios condere nomen avos*, 2.1.42) he clearly tends to characterize the *Aeneid*'s "eigentliche Intention" (and to reject it)—in terms unacceptable to Augustan Interpretation.

But, after all, Propertius may indeed, along with the description of Actium in Book 8, have had in mind Jove's prophecy on Augustus' Empire in Book 1 (Prop. 2.1.42, quoted above, may have been inspired by *Aen.* 1.288: *Iulius, a magno demissum nomen Iulo*), not because he did not yet know other parts of the *Aeneid*, but because he judged Jove's speech, like the description in Book 8, to be more revealing about the *Aeneid*'s Augustan spirit than other passages he knew of.

20. To my eye, line 2.34.66 (apart from being similar to the exalted and ridiculing line 2.1.16) would seem to recall (and ironically overinterpret) the pompous tone of a few high-flying words from the proem by which the New Homer introduces his "Roman *Iliad*" (*Aen.* 7.44f.): . . . *maior rerum mihi nascitur ordo,* / *maius opus moveo*.

21. See Chapter VIII below on 3.1.7 and our earlier remarks on 1.6.21/22 and 2.1.35; 7.5/6.

22. In a comparable way, Paratore (1957, 79ff.), judging mainly by the standard of Propertius' poetical credo, finds a difference in the treatment which Vergil's works receive from the elegist. He thinks that, with regard to Vergil's earlier works, Propertius shows himself "candidiorem et sinceriorem iudicem", but does not offer his true feelings about the *Aeneid* (cf. p. 81). Even Alfonsi (1954, 209) admits that Propertius' insight here seems "più felice" in evaluating *Bucolics* and *Georgics*. At the same time, however, he maintains that the judgment on the *Aeneid* is in line with traditional Roman understanding about historic epic. Sullivan (1976, 25) states: "Propertius, in this poem, makes his preference among Vergil's works quite apparent." But he does not observe the distinction made between *Eclogues* and *Georgics*.

23. Donatus (Suetonius) *Vita Vergilii*, 100ff.

24. Perhaps I should mention that the whole context can be naïvely misread when taken literally and without regard to overall thought structure. Wimmel (1960, 209), taking a religious approach ("das Wunder des 'augusteischen' Versöhnens und Umfassens"), has Propertius here assign divine powers and the qualities of a saviour to Vergil: Propertius "erkennt Vergil als jenen *Heils-Menschen*, dem die Vereinigung bisher unversöhnlicher Gegensätze geglückt ist, eine Einheit, an die weder Properz noch Lynceus je denken können, und die dem Vergil etwas *Göttlich-Mächtiges* gibt" (italics mine). The mere thought of Propertius ranking himself higher than Vergil makes Wimmel feel uncomfortable ("ein unbehaglicher Gedanke", o.c. p. 211).

25. It is this undertone that keeps me from finding as much positive appreciation in Propertius' judgment of the *Eclogues* as does Alfonsi (1954, 214: "L'amore idillico è semplice e schietto, non venale: ed era un ideale questo caro a Properzio . . ."). In keeping with the underlying irony, M. Hubbard suggests that 72 be

interpreted as "To Cynthia (*huic*) even Tityrus could sing and still find her un-grateful." I.e., "as in *ecl.* 10, the bucolic world can't tell the truth about real love".

26. See La Penna 1950B, 216.

27. Rothstein (1889, 8f.) has stringently shown that lines 81/82 (and *haec* es-pecially) can no longer refer to Vergil, but open the section on Propertius himself. But he found almost no followers.

28. In expecting an audience which reaches *beyond* the circle of lovers (as Roth-stein 1889, 10, observed but failed to evaluate), Propertius expressly leaves Vergil's modesty behind and exceeds the self-limitation of the *Bucolics*. Cf. *Ecl.* 6.9ff.:

> si quis tamen haec quoque, *si quis*
> *captus amore leget*, te nostrae, Vare, myricae
> te nemus omne canet;

29. I believe that Alfonsi (1943–44B, 465f.), though approaching the same identification, cannot distinctly verify it, because he underrates Propertius' inde-pendence, Also, he misjudges Rothstein's separation of *in* and *docto* (1.84) as "la falsa congettura" (465, n. 15).

30. Credit should be given to Rothstein (1889, 10ff.) for a correct linguistic explanation of distich 83/84, including the reading of *in* and *docto* as two separate words. Rothstein was kept from building a correct interpretation on this gram-matical foundation by his prejudice: because he felt that modest Propertius should here pay homage to Vergil, he took Varius (instead of Vergil) to be the defeated swan and Vergil (instead of Propertius) the successful gander, thereby invalidating his own observation (o.c. p. 9) that from 81 on Propertius is directly and essen-tially speaking about himself. This incorrect application of the correct translation was revived in Bickel's (1950) thesis that Propertius in 2.34 is upgrading Vergil at the cost of Varius: "vox invectiva Propertii de olore anseri docto cedente" (o.c. 25). Later commentators in general dismissed Rothstein's approach and returned to "amending" the Latin text. I find it encouraging that my view of the elegy's overall argument has led me back to accept Rothstein's simple explanation of the text as it is offered in the principal manuscripts.

31. See note 17.

32. I think that my interpretation has both justified Propertius' juxtaposition of Lynceus' and Vergil's antipodic careers in the same poem, and extinguished any impression of decomposition ("Eindruck der Dekomposition," Abel 1930, 59).

Alfonsi (1944–45, 118ff.) found the logical contradiction ("dato un criterio di pura logica") between the advice given to Lynceus ("turn from epic to love elegy!") and the praise of Vergil's career (from amatory poetry to epic) so intolerable that he would not allow both to be combined in the same poem. He considered lines 67–80 either a replacement ("due redazioni" o.c. 122) for 81–94 ("l'elegia fu com-posta in due tempi", o.c. 121), or at least a digression (inserted by Propertius upon hearing the protasis prefixed to the *Aeneid* [1.1.a–d]).

Already Jacoby (1905, 96n) judged the "compliment" to Vergil to be "im Zusammenhange des Gedichtes *unpassend* und *unlogisch*" (italics mine). But al-though he calls it a monstrosity ("Ungeheuerlichkeit") that Propertius sets the *Aeneid* over the *Iliad*, he takes the "compliment" seriously and fails to see Proper-tius' irony, thus missing the solution to the problem he stated.

In my own understanding, the poem's apparent contradiction is a necessary device, used by the poet to indicate the direction in which his argument would proceed if he could speak quite openly. Methodologically speaking, I believe I have found a logical criterion to distinguish two levels of speech in a poem. This will be of help in interpreting elegy 3.11 (Chapter IX below).

33. The specifically Propertian viewpoint of our section was disregarded in antiquity itself when it was used as a catalogue of erotic poets, first by Ovid and then by Quintilian and others. It is worthwhile to go through Alfonsi's lists (1943–44A, 458ff.) with an eye on this question and see how later authors kept the names but hardly the spirit of Propertius' pedigree.

34. See Chapter VIII below, on 3.4 and 5.

35. Cf. *Il.* 3.156ff.; Prop. 2.3.32.

36.   Qui quaerit Tatios veteres durosque Sabinos,
             hic posuit nostra nuper in urbe pedem.   (47/48)

Alfonsi (1949A, 339) sees here a possible joke *ad personam*: the newcomer to town (and *tumbe Parzival*, we may add) would be the historian Titus Livius himself, recent import from provincial quarters. Alfonsi (o.c. 337f.) even considers identifying the passage to which our couplet may be "un ironico riferimento": Livy's proem, in which he claims to turn to the past in order to escape watching the evils of his own time. This goes only too well with the fun Propertius makes of history in 2.1.1–16, as was shown in Chapter V above.

37. The casual appearance, to say it once more, is rooted in the dramatic setting with its vivid imagination and lively addresses (reading the poem aloud, we realize that we have to act as if Lynceus and Vergil were present). The elegy's living spirit has been misused by scholarship to construe "contradictions" instead of being correctly used as a guide to the underlying thought structure (the worst example is offered by Damon and Helmbold 1952, 238ff.: declaring our elegy "intolerable hodgepodge", they cut it into three unrelated pieces, declare as "interpolated" lines that escape their understanding, and form the remains into inconclusive "quatrains", the inconclusiveness of which opens to them the happy prospect of further slaughter in the future . . .).

CHAPTER VIII

1. See Chapter XI below.

2. It is still worthwhile reading Luck's (1957, 175ff.) circumspect explanation of the opening section. He attempts to find concrete answers (in 3.3) to the concrete questions of 3.1 by way of visualizing a consistent scenery from Propertius' hints. Luck's approach is not invalidated but rather modified by Baker's interpretation (1968A, 35ff.). Comparing 3.9.43–46, Baker concludes that, as a love elegist, Propertius in 3.1.1f. expresses desire for the same worship (*sacra*) which his models receive. For the whole complex of literary tradition alluded to in 3.1ff. (especially 3.3), see Kambylis, 1965, 125–190.

3. The most recent triumph in Rome was the Emperor's own in 29 B.C.! The political scene of the day (and its implications for contemporary writers) seems not

to exist for some scholars who distill almost every word of our text into just another *"stilkritische"* allusion to Callimachus' Alexandrian literary criticism. See, for instance, Quadlbauer 1968, 97ff. Much more to the point is Galinsky (1969, 88): "The usurpation of an epic and 'official' custom for himself and his *exiguus sermo* reflects Propertius' self-confidence." The poet's claim on a *triumphus* must be viewed in line with his habit of wresting established honors from his opponents and claiming them for himself (cf. 1.7.9ff.; [1.12.3ff.;] 1.6.30; 2.1.47; 2.7.13ff.; the last passage is evaluated by Galinsky, o.c. p. 82f.). With regard to "fame", see Brouwers 1970.

4. Nothing but a preoccupation speaks for an interpretation which limits the *scriptorum turba* of line 12 to imitators in the field of elegy. In 2.34.65 the *scriptores* addressed are foremost epic poets. Quadlbauer (1968, 100) concedes: "Aber auch andere sind nicht direkt ausgeschlossen." Of course we may also think of "converted" epicists like Lynceus (2.34) and Ponticus (1.9).

5. For the Augustan (Roman) idea of peace, cf. *Res Gestae* 13: *cum . . . esset parta victoriis pax*, etc. "*Pax* means 'pacification' as much as 'no fighting'" (Brunt and Moore 1973 *ad locum*). I cannot follow Quadlbauer (1968, 103) who finds in 3.1.17f. "ein elegantes indirektes Kompliment für den Friedensbringer Augustus." For Augustus' peace demands war poetry such as Vergil's, while Propertius' idea of peace is not recognized in Augustus' "peacetime" Rome (although it ought to be, as our passage implies). Rightly, Galinsky asserts (1969, 89): "The military preparations against the Parthians (15–16) which give rise to epic poetry, are contrasted with Propertius' poetry of *pax* (16ff.)," etc.

6. Self-confidence pervades the whole elegy. It is further expressed by the quotations from Callimachus (*Aitia*) and from Roman contemporaries. For a brief list, see Camps *ad* 3.1.

7. "Reputation", SB, Appendix, p. 295.

8. Ites 1908, 51ff.; Solmsen 1948, 105, with n. 1; Nethercut 1961, 389ff. and 1970A, 385ff.; Woolley 1967, 81; Courtney 1969, 70; Juhnke 1971, 113. This grouping should not, however, level the more substantial and much graver human concerns voiced in the pair 4 and 5 in comparison with 1–3 which move along lines of literary criticism. Cf. Jäger (1967, 74), who describes the new perspective of 4 and 5 as that of the poet facing the demands of his own time.

9. See for instance Camps' introductory remarks. A correspondence of their opening words (*Arma deus Caesar—Pacis Amor deus est*) has been observed by many interpreters. Jäger (1967, 76) has added that their concluding distichs (beside a reference of content in the latter to the earlier, seen by Ribbeck 1885, 483) correspond in form also: their hexameters are largely dedicated to the main person(s) of each poem, the pentameters to their counterparts.

10. Interpreters have shown themselves confused by the shifting addresses in this poem; but the persons addressed offer the key to visualizing a consistent situation—as may be expected of Propertius' usual fondness for clarity and logic. The elegist here pretends to be a priest who sets out by addressing Augustus' soldiers in the presence of their warlord: 1/2 characterize and announce the campaign (Caesar = third person); 3–10 indoctrinate the soldiers (= second person throughout) with their mission (once in between the priest turns directly to the present Emperor:

second person in *tua*, 4); in 11–22 the priest faces the altar and addresses the gods (= second persons in 11 and 19); during this time, he is turned away from the Emperor (= third person, 13 and 19; *hoc . . . caput* perhaps indicates a pointing gesture in the Emperor's direction); the soldiers, too, are out of sight during the prayer (= third person: *illis*, 21); only the priest himself and his personal concerns appear always in the first person because he is the one who speaks the prayer.

Wistrand's objection to the transmitted text (1977, 11ff.) that *tua iura* (4), when referred to Augustus, would make the Emperor an autocratic ruler against his wishes, must fade in the face of the *deus Caesar* of line 1 ("Such a designation is first attested here", Wistrand 17).

11. *Iuvabit tamen rerum gestarum memoriae principis orbis terrarum populi et ipsum consuluisse*, "where Livy hopes to serve Rome's history by writing it" (Camps).

12. One may of course compare the manner in which 2.10 is preceded by 2.7. For an interpretation (not without followers) that locates Propertius' opposition inside 3.4 itself, see n. 26 below.

13. It has proved difficult to weigh the two poems' individual intentions. Jäger (1967), for instance, first sees their author undecided ("in einem stark empfundenen Zwiespalt", p. 74); he also speaks of a "Dialektik der Gegensätze Zustimmung—Ablehnung" (p. 103). Later he declares the tensions between the opposites considerably lessened ("die Spannung . . . wesentlich herabgemindert") by "eine formelle Zustimmung zum Feldzugsplan des Augustus", which makes the refusal "only" personal ("welche die Ablehnung auf den persönlichen Bereich beschränkt", p. 105). But is not the problem precisely the personal one, that Propertius fervently wishes to decline what he has been urged to support so fervently? Ites felt that 3.5 offers so strong a recusatio, "*ut ipsam el. 4 revocet*", 1908, 53.

In recent literature, only Wistrand (1977, 9ff.) interprets 3.4 without any reference to 3.5. Consequently, he finds the poet "wholeheartedly" accepting Roman imperialism and only "personally" refusing "to have anything to do with it" while showing "the enthusiasm, loud and sincere but not so very deeply felt" of a national spectator "attending an international sports competition" (pp. 18f.).

14. This is Livineius' conjecture for *stant* of the MSS (the latter is kept by Barber. Ingvarsson's interpretation [1955, 165ff.] of *stant* = *sunt* does not give an adequate meaning to the context). See SB 1947, 91f.

15. Ever since 1.7.13f. and 23f.; see Chapter III above.

16. Even if Bennett (1968, 338ff.) is right in thinking that in the rest of the poem (47–60) Propertius presents himself as asking his "deified" patron to help him write an epic, such a request can hardly be serious after 45/46.

17. The claim to be born for peace and not for war (3.9.19/20) is so central in Propertius' thinking that it must be considered a grave methodological error if Boyancé (1942, 65) declares the whole subsection 3.9.7–20 "une surcharge de rédaction": "un petit poème dans le grand, une épigramme assez longue, dont le sujet n'est point sans rappeler une autre pièce addressée au même Mécène, l'ode I du livre premier d'Horace." It is a common mistake of *Parallelstellenphilologie* to infer from verbal similarities an agreement in attitude or position, or even "dependence" of one writer's attitude on the other's. Verbal similarities often result from use of the same material (situations, persons, paradigms, etc.) by two authors. Their purpose (which may include rivaling imitation, polemical reinterpretation, thematic—

and independent—use of identical subject matter, exemplification of other, more difficult contexts, etc.) must always be established by and confirmed within the context in which the interpreter reads them.

With regard to the specific section 3.9.1–20, I refer my reader to Bennett's excellent investigation (1967) of the passage both within the poem and in the light of Propertius' use of gnomes. Bennett (p. 224) fails, however, to distinguish between the broader aspect of Propertius' inborn disinclination (*naturae . . . semina*, 20) against war and his momentary excuse (fear of public failure: *turpe*, 5). By not making this distinction, Bennett (1968, 320ff.) finds Propertius ready for compromise (3.9.47ff.) where he is not.

We must not believe (as Steidle 1962, 137 does) that the poet's emphasis on peace in Book 3 is "geradezu eine neue Lebenswahl". It is as a loving being (*amantes*, 3.5.1), that he favors *pax* over *arma*.

18. Although I go along with (and even further than) Solmsen (1948, 105, n. 1) and Nethercut (1961, 395f.) in seeing the opening group of words in either poem in relation to the other poem's opening, I do not follow Nethercut's assumption of corresponding sections and of parallel key words in both poems. For these alleged parallels are not supported by parallel thought structure. Cf. Jäger 1967, 75ff.

19. See, e.g., Protagoras in Plato (*Prot.* 322a ff.). For other versions, see Nisbeth-Hubbard *ad* Horace, *C.* 1.16.3.

20. We must not—because Paetus' avarice in 3.7 seems to lack individual features, and because 3.5, too, deals with the rôle of avarice (in the area of war)—conclude with Robertson (1969, 386) that 3.5 has no reference to the poet's personal concerns either. On the contrary, 3.5 may throw some light on the character of Propertius' involvement with the subject matter of 3.7.

21. Solmsen (1948, 106 with n. 6) offers four passages from Horace's Odes to show that "the equalizing function of death" was an idea conceived under Horatian influence. But I doubt that Propertius needed help from Horace in presenting Augustus' triumph as futile. A similar point can be made about the elegist's general use in 3.1–5 of Horace's self-eternalization in Ode 3.30 (see Solmsen o.c. 106ff., among others); it was not so much a revering poetic imitation as the outcry of the isolated elegist who was afraid he would not be heard among officially sanctioned and royally promoted colleagues that made Propertius prophecy his own future fame in shrill self-praise of Horatian colors.

22. Nethercut (1961, 403) considers the identification *stulte* = Augustus possible, but decides in favor of a more general addressee (the *viri* of 4.3 or the *vos* of 5.47)—or just any "individual" (cf. o.c. pp. 396 and 406). Closest to my own findings are the results of Jäger's approach because he systematically compares corresponding elements in both elegies. With regard to 5.15/16 he remarks: "Deutlicher konnte im Hinblick auf einen vom Kaiser geplanten Feldzug Ruhm und Grösse nicht mehr abgewertet werden" (1967, 76). Before him, Ites (1908, 53f.) gave a clear picture of the corresponding features in both elegies.

23. SB.

24. Or *me iuvet . . . me iuvet.*

25. By no means should we follow Bury (1939, 7) and "amend" the transmitted text ("'To bind with the Loosener' sounds strange", *loc. cit.*).

26. The words *exitus hic vitae superest mihi* (47) pick up 23/24 (*atque ubi iam*

Venerem gravis interceperit aetas, etc.) and identify the same period of time as *tum* (25) denotes (hardly apposite: *exitus . . . vitae* = "way of leaving life", SB, Appendix). The biographical time-table leaves no gap at all. I should like to give credit to Nethercut (1970A, 397). Although not concerning himself with Propertius' condemnation of human nature, but rather taking 3.5 to be the usual *recusatio* (and the catalogue of philosophical problems a substitute for the customary promise of an Augustan epic; cf. Wilkinson 1960, 1102), Nethercut has felt that the sheer length of the "inflated" passage 25–46 hangs together with the poet's antipathy against the Emperor's campaign. In this he probably comes closer to the poet's intention than Courtney (1969, 70ff.), who, deriving the *excursus* from a Vergilian source (*Georg.* 2.458–506), thinks that Vergil serves as a "warrant" ("what better authority could be found?") when the poet proceeds from "dissociation" from the Parthian campaign (= end of 3.4) to "distaste" (= 3.5). Wilkinson (1960), in his prudent discussion of the elegist's continued resistance against Augustus, has correctly diagnosed the implications from the last couplet in 3.5 for elegy 4: "He could hardly have contrived more effectively to negative any enthusiasm a superficial reading of the previous poem might have conveyed" (1960, 1102). The immanent argument of 3.5 apparently escaped Paratore's (1936, 186ff.) search for anti-Augustan features; although seeing the implications the last distich (47/48) has both for 3.5 itself ("un enorme valore di aperta ribellione agli intendimenti fondamentali della politica del monarca") and for 3.4, he nevertheless assigns to the philosophical *excursus* the function of parodying Horace's and Vergil's philosophical aspirations rather than interpreting it in the context in which it occurs. As in 3.4 (o.c. 152ff.)—and elsewhere—he weakens the case he tries to build, looking for far-fetched allusions rather than verifying the actual consequences of a poem's argument. *Merces*, 3.4.3, for instance, according to Paratore, reveals the "spirito di preda" of Augustus' Parthian campaign—whereas in truth the poem itself, in the same line, explains the *metaphorical* use made here of the word: the soldiers' reward should be seen not in the usual booty but in their contribution to the greatness of Rome and her empire. It appears odd to me to read a second metaphor (viz., the whole campaign is predatory) into the context. In a similar way, I find it difficult to believe with Nethercut (1970A, 395) that in line 21 of 3.4 Propertius turns against Vergil's idea of *labor*, giving a "definition of *labor* as brigandage and robbery". The line expresses a point in its own context. For further considerations concerning Paratore's method, see our remarks on 3.22 in this chapter and also Chapter X below; *praeda* at 3.4.21 receives no negative connotation either from its immediate context (but see p. 200).

27. Because of this reference, Courtney sees the main purpose of 3.5 as a retraction of the promise given in 2.10: "He is now taking back what he then said" (1969, 71). In this way 3.4 becomes "a very necessary preliminary".

28. Though not proved, our working hypothesis about the poet being urged to write pro-Augustan poetry has so far consistently explained his contrasting utterances. Why else would he (unless he was a schizophrenic—a less likely hypothesis) repeatedly contradict himself in writing? We shall return to the problem in due course.

29. Nothing in the poems concerned with his ending love (3.17; 21; 24; 25) points to the new poetical beginning that will open Book 4 (not even 17, which

promises Bacchus Dionysiac poetry in case the god helps Propertius; and 3.21 points to noncreative studies in Greece, *tacito . . . sinu* (32): should he not die and open his mouth at all, it would be in lament for his lost love). We underestimate the fatal seriousness of his crisis, if we, with E. Burck (1959: "Abschied von der *Liebes*dichtung"; italics mine), see Propertius in 3.24 and 25 already defined by "Hoffnung auf neue dichterische Aufgaben und Leistungen" (o.c. 211). "Abschied von der *Dichtung*" would have been a title more appropriate to the poet's desperate situation.

30. I do not share Barber's belief that a distich is missing after line 36 of the transmitted text. See Rothstein *ad loc.* By no means can lines 37f. be forced from their abhorrent context and squeezed into the section on tourist attractions (between 10 and 11, Otto and Hanslik). This transposition destroys the poem's clear balance.

31. Cf. Hor. *C.* 3.4.21ff.:

> . . . seu mihi frigidum
> Praeneste, seu Tibur supinum,
> seu liquidae placuere Baiae.

32. For example, 3.21.11–16 refer to Propertius' request of 1.1.29ff. that his friends take him away from Rome. For more details, see now also Burck 1981.

33. When analyzing the structure of Book 3, Courtney (1970, 51f.), viewing the surface only of 3.22, states a contrast between the anti-Hellenism in 3.22 and the philhellenic journey of 3.21. Another investigation of book structure (Woolley 1967, 81), likewise taking seriously "the claim expressed in poem 22 of the superiority of Italy over Greece", puts 3.22 in corresponding contrast to the Spartan girls of easy access in 3.14, finding in 14 "praise of Sparta", "a superiority in one respect to Rome". The journey to Greece (3.21), on the other hand, is (mis)-matched to the Lycinna poem 3.15 in another "contrast" (p. 81). No indication whatsoever is given in Woolley's geometrical graph and its "panels" (o.c. p. 80) of the deeper common ground 3.21 and 22 share with each other and with Book 1. Like the unsuccessful schematic explanations interpreters have given of the *Monobiblos*, Woolley's of Book 3 is shipwrecked by its inherent disregard for the task of securing an interpretation of the single elegy, a book's construction element, in the first place. A more flexible approach to his own schematizing method is perhaps displayed in Juhnke's (1971) essay on the structure of Books 2 and 3. But it, too, offers unverified assumptions about single elegies; 3.21 and 22 are seen equally to point to "erfüllte Lebensmöglichkeiten jenseits der brüchigen elegischen Welt" (p. 116); 3.22 itself, offering "römisches Land und Leben als Überhöhung der elegischen Welt", is matched to 3.4 (the power of the Roman Empire), while 3.21 is seen as a counter-piece to 3.5 ("Flucht in die Geistigkeit", p. 121). The implications of Juhnke's assumptions are far-reaching: he is paving a one-way road, on which the Propertius of Book 3, dissatisfied with his "broken elegiac world", is unfalteringly progressing towards Augustus' Rome. One may compare also the interpretations which E. Burck has given of 3.24 and 25 (Burck 1959) and, subsequently, of the structure of Book 4 (Burck 1966). (See also the final section of this chapter and n. 29 above). Since 3.21 is doubtless serious (it shares the tendency of 3.17; 24; 25: the poet seeking liberation from the disease of his love), its contrast to the anti-

Hellenic elegy 3.22 suggests that the latter is another façade poem, the surface of which may cover up its author's true attitude. Daut's (1975) insistence on a military tone in 3.21 appears to be not in focus.

34. Brakman (1926, 77f.) takes the *ampla nepotum spes* of 3.22.41f. as an ironical allusion (made to tease Tullus) to Priam's many bedrooms and *spes ampla nepotum* in Vergil (*Aen.* 2.503), and from the stress on *aptus amor* (3.22.42) he understands "*Tullum a muliere Graeca immemorem esse reditus patriae*". Understood along these lines, the "esaltazione del matrimonio fecondo" in lines 41f. is far from being a step in "un processo catartico, che si sviluppa da una turbinosa passione verso più santi ideali di vita", as Fontana (1950, 76) would like to see it. Defining the degree of Propertius' irony or of his personal involvement is still an urgent methodological problem.

35. On the whole, Schu.-Do.'s text is more convincing here than Barber's (and Hanslik's).

36. According to Putnam (1979, 243), *ira* here (and in *Aeneid* 12, when Aeneas kills Turnus) carries a moral blemish. But this idea is perhaps (if not Stoic) more Christian than Roman. On "just wrath" and "just fury" in the *Aeneid*, see Stahl 1981, 166.

Vergilian language (and that means, of course, contents also) or spirit has been found independently from my own investigation in the two façade poems 3.22 (cp. Rothstein passim; La Penna 1951B, 50; 1977, 81f.) and 3.4 (Hanslik 1967, 187ff.), and, in addition, Horace has been adduced to confirm the Augustan attitude of 3.4 (Haffter 1970, 61). These findings are of methodological importance for judgments on Propertius' *Dichtersprache*: when intending to please the representatives of the Zeitgeist by depicting official ideology, he may be found to borrow freely from thought and linguistic achievements in Vergil's poetry. But such stylistically elevated passages should not go unchecked as if indicating a priori "Propertius at his very own". The result would be a misunderstanding like Hanslik's, who seems to take seriously Propertius' manner of appearance in 3.4: "Zwischen dem *deus Caesar* (1) und dem kleinen Menschen Properz (22) steht der Dichter als erhabener *vates* (9). Damit ist schon etwas für die grosse Struktur des Gedichtes gewonnen" (1967, 183. Cf. Woolley 1967, 81, in whose eyes the concluding distich reveals "humility—a sentiment which also finds expression in Horace"). Similarly, it is inadequate to regard poem 3.4 as difficult because of an allegedly mutilated textual tradition. The truth, as confirmed by 3.22, is vice versa: the elegist's mannered court language (his "Vergilian" style) led to misunderstanding (and possibly changing) of the original text.

We are now in a position to say a few words also about "official" court propaganda: Rothstein concludes that in 3.1.15f. (as in 2.10 and, of course, 3.4) Propertius expresses current martial expectations about the Emperor which Augustus himself never intended to fulfill. A historian, H. D. Meyer (1961), pointing to what are to him apparent misrepresentations of official foreign policy, calls the poet "naïve" (the word appears at least five times in about ten pages), since he "im Sinne des Kaisers zu sprechen glaubt" (o.c. p. 76; Meyer apparently takes 3.4 seriously and has no idea that the poet's true opinion is revealed only in the subsequent elegy). But it seems odd (and even uncritical) to assume that, in a poem written to please the court and to show the author's cooperation, His Highness would not be represented in the light and glory he himself desires to be seen in (including a few exaggerations). The naïveté would be rather with the historian who expects of and assigns to a public address the same function as to a memo circulating in the Department of Foreign Affairs. Even more inadequate than the historian's approach is that of philologists who deplore that the rhetoric of Propertius' panegyric lacks Horace's deep religious feeling toward the Emperor (see, e.g., Doblhofer 1961, 114ff.). Such a blame appears inappropriate because it leaves no room for the tragic conflict and pain under which the elegist performed his adulatory duties. The problem of whether or not the Augustan poets rightly depicted Augustus as a great conqueror is an old one (see already Ferrero 1908–1909, passim) and has been answered differently. Most revealing perhaps is the wishful self-portrait the Emperor himself sketches in his *Res Gestae* (26–33).

37. Elegy 3.17; 21; 24; 25.

38. A good example of Vergil's suggestive manner can be seen in Aeneas' words (*Aen.* 2.65f.): *accipe nunc Danaum insidias et crimine ab uno / disce omnes.* We should never forget that Augustan ideology requires a reversal of Greek national values. Since the Iulians are the divinely guided descendants of innocent Trojan Aeneas, the Greeks must be the godless aggressors of Troy. See Stahl 1981 passim.

39. In the special case of elegy 3.22, one may wonder whether, although no bridge crosses the abyss, a footpath leads around it. Much depends on the reasons that kept Tullus far from home. We know that he had become forgetful of his career. No more is indicated by Propertius (who must know more) nor perhaps could be indicated without embarrassing the noble family at Rome. But if—provided the reader would wish to continue Brakman's speculation (n. 34 above)—the reason for his stay was that he loved a *puella,* then the prospect of a career, dutiful marriage, and propagation of a family could be a deterrent on the efficacy of which the author of the Letter to Cyzicus could safely rely.

40. Cf. Hor. *C.* 3.4.21ff. (quoted above, n. 31) and Rothstein *ad loc.* Wrongly Tränkle (1960, 51; cf. 101ff.) assumes that Propertius is negative and ironical concerning Cyzicus in 3.22.1–2. Lines 3/4 are perhaps on a different level because they may already indicate the negative features of Greek myth that play an important rôle in persuading Tullus to leave Greece (27ff.).

In similar fashion, Tränkle (o.c. 102) should not tie together the words *salubris Pollucis equo* in line 26. Apart from being grammatically wrong (the dative *equo* goes with *pota,* not with *salubris*), his understanding narrows the poet's emphasis on the *general* healthiness of the *Iuturna* down to a single case and thus spoils the point of *salubris* within the train of thought.

CHAPTER IX

1. Or "through them": cf. Rothstein *ad* 1.3.44.

2. See, for instance, E. Reitzenstein 1936, 71; "lehrreich", Rothstein *ad* 2.15. See still Davis 1977, 18 ("Roman and Greek poets were especially fond of placing pairs or cycles of poems on the same subject together").

3. For a more recent discussion of these lines, see Vaio's attempt to tie them into a unit with 23–28 (1962, 237f.).

4. This applies to Barwick's interpretation (1955): in his syncrisis 2.15, being no more than a climactic variation of 14, "steigert sich . . . zu einem hohen Lied auf den Genuss sinnlicher Liebe und des Lebens überhaupt" (p. 132). Thus, in spite of correctly defining almost all of the poem's paragraphs (subsections), he completely misses its pessimism and, with it, its true meaning.

5. Stoessl 1948, 102ff.; accepted by Jäger (1967, 79ff.), who declares that elegy 14, though depicting a "later" situation than 15, nevertheless contains the "Exposition" to 15 and its "earlier" situation. Jäger's attempt to tie both elegies together is no more successful than others mentioned by him (pp. 77ff.).

6. See Tränkle (1960) 147f.: from Book 2 on, apostrophe becomes "ein Ausdrucksmittel seines Monologs".

7. Overlooking *nam*, Barwick (1955, 113) replaces the logical context, which aims at intensity of emotion, with a crude enumeration of successive events. Thus the meaning of the repetitive structural elements escapes him as it escapes Stoessl (1948, 108, with n. 10), although the latter at least sees the chiastic order of lines 3–6 and the explicatory function of lines 5/6. A decisive improvement over earlier scholarship can be found in the most recent article on 2.15 by N. Rudd (1982). Though concentrating on theme and imagery (and sometimes perhaps overstating, as on 3/4 and 5/6), Rudd usually does not lose sight of the thought structure. I am happy to record considerable agreement in his analysis and mine. The differences stem partly from the priority my interpretation gives to thought organization, partly from my viewing this elegy in the framework of Propertius' overall outlook.

8. E. Reitzenstein 1936, 77, n. 104.

9. E. Reitzenstein 1936, 78; 86f.

10. For this and related aspects, see Alfonsi 1953C.

11. See Barwick 1955, 119.

12. SB's remarks *ad locum* point in the right direction. When, however, one misunderstood the text as meaning the same as *vellem vincires*, "I wish you chained us together!", there has arisen a problem for interpreters: how could Cynthia possibly, while embracing Propertius, at the same time chain both of them together? This very technical question has vexed many a scholar's mind, and it may satisfy my reader to know that, in spite of being nonexistent, the problem has meanwhile found two solutions worth mentioning. The first (offered by Enk 1960, 125) proceeds by way of a "parallel" passage. In Petronius, a shipwrecked lover, fearing he would be separated from his beloved by the rough seas, ties both of them together with a belt around their bodies. Why should Cynthia not be able to do the same on a dry bed?

The other solution I wish to mention originates from a comparable learnedness; it has also been seen (Helm 1937, 782) that distich 25/26 may evoke the Homeric scene of Ares and Aphrodite caught in Hephaestus' fetters (*Od.* 8.266–366), and that, if this is true, there are certain implications: Ares would never like to be tied like this. But Hermes, like Propertius not the most successful of lovers, expresses his readiness to be tied even in a net twice as strong and visible to all the other gods, if only he could be close to golden Aphrodite:

$$\alpha \mathring{\upsilon} \tau \grave{\alpha} \rho \; \mathring{\epsilon} \gamma \grave{\omega} \nu \; \epsilon \mathring{\upsilon} \delta o \iota \mu \iota \; \pi \alpha \rho \grave{\alpha} \; \chi \rho \upsilon \sigma \acute{\epsilon} \eta \; \mathring{}A\phi \rho o \delta \acute{\iota} \tau \eta \qquad (Od. 8. 342).$$

This would not be an unfitting simile for Propertius himself (our interpreter feels), who, like Hermes, should very much appreciate the services of a Hephaestus, who could chain him and Cynthia together. But the *punctum saliens*, of course, lies in the fact that *velles* does not offer the figure of a Hephaestus. Therefore our textual critic (like others before him) "emends" his text to *vellet, uti* (or even *di . . . vellent*)—and misses its true meaning, just like his aforementioned colleague, the *Parallelstellen* philologist.

    A third (Jachmann 1935, 195ff.) abolished the "problem" in his own peculiar way (ably analyzed by Shackleton Bailey 1952, 12ff.); he deleted the whole passage 23–28. And a fourth (Stoessl 1948, 111) lets us in on the poet's secret: intentional obscurity ("absichtliche Undeutlichkeit"). The two Reitzensteins (R. R. 1896, 210n; E. R. 1936, 80) and Shackleton Bailey (l.c.) would allow the chain at least to be a metaphorical one, while Bury (1939, 6) even let it disappear completely (by changing *catena* into *Aetnaee*).

    13. See the passages collected in Enk's commentary. Perhaps one should consider once more Rothstein's proposal to take *in amore* with *exemplo*.

    14. "*Vesanus amor* und *verus amor* werden hier offenbar als identisch betrachtet" (Barwick 1955, 121, n. 1). In lines 29/30 *modus*, the wider notion, may contain the narrower one of *finis* in itself. One should be careful about taking both to be "here the same" as SB (Appendix, *ad loc.*) does.

    15. I hesitate to connect Propertius with a certain philosophical school (Posidonius) as does Alfonsi (1953C, 435f.).

    16. For *in* = ablative, see Rothstein *ad* 1.3.44.

    17. Nethercut (1971B, 301) finds 2.15 evidence enough for "bias against Octavian's victory." He sees Propertius' allusion to a golden age as in opposition to the Augustan golden age as proclaimed by Vergil and others. See also Paratore 1936, 199.

    18. Officially, Actium was part of a foreign not a civil war. This version could hardly be confirmed from Propertius' text. See Paratore 1936, 202 ("invincibile antipatia di Properzio per Augusto").

    19. The precise meaning of this passage is disputed. See Chapter X below.

    20. For some aspects of Antony's alleged drunkenness, see Scott 1929, 136ff.

    21. This question has recently been answered in the affirmative by Griffin (1977), who finds "a bitter truth" in 2.15.41ff., making Propertius reason: "Had he [sc., Augustus] lived like me—like Antony—the disaster of Actium need never have happened" (p. 19). To Griffin's more literary portrait of the elegist's model Antony my reader may add young Propertius' own political impressions during the Perusine War, as evaluated in Chapter V above. See also my criticism in n. 31.

    22. Thus Antony as his model does not so much help to make the poet's lifestyle more "plausible" to a Roman audience (Griffin 1977, 26), but serves as a vehicle to communicate his personal message to the public.

    23. Once again Paratore deserves credit for having seen "l'equazione Properzio = Antonio, Cinzia = Cleopatra" (1936, 197f.). But again, also, by isolating the political aspect from the context of elegies 2.15 and 16, he tends to overaccentuate it. It is, for instance, hard to believe that the elegist thought of justifying and even rehabilitating Antony from the charges which Augustan propaganda had raised against him (o.c. p. 196, n. 145), i.e., that Propertius in these two elegies committed himself to a political goal. Rather, as I shall argue below, he utilized the broadly publicized clichés of Augustan propaganda to indicate his own position: self-definition *e contrario*, which here amounts to a partial identification with the

unheroic counter-Augustus. Among recent interpreters, Griffin (1977, 18) has seen that "the poet draws a parallel between Antony and himself; and at the end of the poem he is still persevering in his 'degrading love', not breaking free". The words *quod aiunt* in the same line (35) hardly go with *surdis auribus* alone. SB's parallel (Symm. *Epist.* 9.69, in his Appendix) offers a very different word order.

24. I follow Luck's understanding (1962, 340f.; accepted by Camps), who gives the first two words only in line 35 to the interlocutor, and all the rest to Propertius.

25. If we press the text hard, we may see Antony's flight paralleled by Propertius' unmanly avoidance of the *Campus Martius* (line 34).

26. The emphatic position of *Caesaris* at the beginning of the line may also suggest a contrast to the persons mentioned earlier: Caesar's (not mine) is this kind of manly behaviour (which persons like Antony and myself, driven by Amor, lack). Attempts to make the distich more plausible by transposing it (among the latest is that of Berman 1971) have not convinced me.

27. See Chapter VIII.

28. My goal has been to verify the poet's intention on such occasions, but not (as Griffin 1977, 17 intends) to "argue that Propertius' presentation of himself in poetry as a lover—romantic, reckless and obsessed—is closely related to the figure in history of Mark Antony."

29. See Chapter XII, on 4.4.54.

30. Rightly Shackleton Bailey rejects those Augustan interpretations which set Propertius' (*nostra*) wine-cups against those of drunken Antony. SB's position was developed further by Nethercut (1971B, 299ff.), who assumed that there is no connection between wine and Actium in 2.15: "Note: it is the *bellica navis* of verse 43, not the mention of wine, which introduces mention of Actium and civil war." (o.c. p. 301). My own background study given in the text shows that, if the two opponents at Actium are at all to be associated with our passage, Propertius would rather pick Octavian than Antony as the one to exemplify the sad victories of cruel ambition.

Methodologically speaking, I would remark two things: (1) Antony is not mentioned (it is risky to drag him in here), and (2) the wine-cups, representing the Propertian way of life (*qualem . . . vitam*, 41), are shown to be the positive counterpart to criminal political ambition. This purposeful contrast—and, with it, the logical context—is destroyed if one wilfully introduces a negative version of the innocent way of life. (Position (2) above would find Paratore's consent, but not position (1). Therefore Paratore concluded that Propertius in 2.15 affirmed "il suo segreto antonianismo" (o.c. p. 202): "Properzio ha voluto copertamente protestare contro la propaganda augustea" (o.c. p. 201). This moves the elegy's center from Propertius' love to Roman politics, i.e., out of focus.)

31. It cannot be denied that Antony, insofar as he showed the same drive for power as Octavian, falls short of Propertius' ideal. In the quotation from Griffin's article in n. 21 (1977, 19) the words "like me—like Antony" thus suggest a degree of identification not warranted by the text of 2.15.

32. I wish to claim that my interpretation proves our section to form a meaningful and logically intelligible context, and in particular that, as I before accounted for the different functions of distichs 25/26 and 27/28, so now distichs 37/38 and 39/40 can be seen to be integral parts of Propertius' argument.

All these lines have a grotesquely inflated history of interpretations, some aspects of which need mentioning for methodological reasons. Condemned as "interpolated" by Jachmann (1935), they were the narrow basis for his theory on "Interpolationsforschung" and on the history of the Propertian text. Among his opponents was E. Reitzenstein (1936, 71ff.), who sensed a chance to prove the superiority of his own "psychological" method ("Gefühlsentwicklung"); it is wrong, he said, to purge the text of contradictory details, because "transparent, logical clarity" is certainly not a characteristic of Propertius ("Die durchsichtige, logische Klarheit auch des Einzelnen . . . ist jedenfalls nicht ein Charakteristikum des Properz," etc., o.c. p. 86). But Jachmann found enthusiastic support from outside the strictly philological field: B. Croce backed him as being in agreement with the requirements of esthetics ("Filologia ed estetica", 1936). Following Croce, Bernardini Marzolla (1955) castigated Reitzenstein for inadequately relying on *Gefühl* (*sentimento*) in his criticism of Jachmann, and for irrationally accepting the disputed distichs as genuine in spite of their philological and esthetical insufficiencies.

All four interpreters concur with each other in denying that elegy 2.15, as offered by our manuscripts, is logically coherent. In this, they are joined by such a rational commentator as D. R. Shackleton Bailey, who, with an eye on Book 2 and, in it, especially elegies 15 and 34, is willing to make "every reasonable allowance . . . for the slipshod writing and saltatory thinking characteristic of this author". But in spite of this allowance, he feels that a further hypothesis (some sort of "literary accidents") is needed to explain the allegedly desolate condition of the text, and he asks: ". . . is it fanciful to suggest that Propertius was the kind of author to attract them [sc., the "literary accidents"]? (1952, 20).

Considering the degree of despondence displayed by the professional world, this interpreter feels lonely in his attempt not only to vindicate the poet from the charge of illogicality but to show the elegist's desire for condensed but logical presentation even of complex subject matter.

33. I do not think the last three distichs require the assumption that the fictitious time of our elegy has changed. Even if readers wish to take the reference to the petals as a direct address to Cynthia (*vides*, 52, is present tense), for which they desire a concrete chronological interpretation, an early morning hour still seems best to fit the speaker's situation.

34. I do not feel like blaming Propertius, as BB do: "The elegy is far from being perfect in point of form, and there are repetitions in the argument."

CHAPTER X

1. For this and related aspects, see also Glücklich's recent article (1977).

2. None of the changes proposed for lines 5–8 is more convincing than Barber's OCT text (and Schu.-Do.'s). SB's concern that it is not the sailor's but the doctor's or soothsayer's business "to predict death" gives too narrow sense both to *mortem* (here "death threatened by storm" is demanded by the situation) and to *praesagit* ("feeling beforehand" leaves room for protective reaction—at least in the eyes of the individual facing the danger).

3. SB, taking *nam quid* (27) = *quidnam* (rightly rejected by Hubbard 1968, 317; cf. 315), understands "the sequence of thought" as follows: "Why should I

thus accuse lesser gods and heroes of subservience to women? Jupiter, the supreme god, is himself a flagrant case." But this (though *divos* in itself no doubt can point to demigods as well as to gods) not only wipes out the separate emphasis created by the second *quid* in line 27 (which SB replaces by a mere connective "and"; rather, the new question points to a new group, viz., gods, exemplified in the following line by its highest-ranking representative, i.e., Jove). SB's understanding also makes us ask why "Jason the hero and Hercules the hero-god" (SB leaves out Achilles, alluded to between these two, 13–16) should be referred to here as belonging to different groups, whereas the preceding argument has made no such distinction and no mention that Heracles, long after the episode reported here, would one day become a "lesser god". The argument of the poem clearly moves from heroes dominated by women to an ancient example of a woman dominating states to—gods falling for women. But here the elegist, aware of the limits set to a mortal poet, stops short of becoming explicit (his mention of Jove is hardly more than an aside)—and turns to recent Roman history (29ff.). If we are worried that *raptem*, 27, may perhaps not cover heroes who *have been mentioned already*, we may easily draw from *raptem* a *raptavi* and supply it with the first *quid*-question in 27. The line offers a very condensed way of speaking.

To fill in the ellipsis indicated by *nam* (27), Hubbard (1968, 317) understands: "I adduce Semiramis, because there is no reason to confine my charges to heroes like Jason and Achilles or to demigods like Hercules", and she thinks that line 28 refers to some story (unknown to us) about Semiramis having been the first woman to serve as the wife of Zeus Belus in the temple (*suam . . . domum*) she built for him. My concern with this interpretation (grammatically, as possible as mine) would be that nothing in the—comparatively long (3D)—description of Semiramis' subjugating activities indicates that in our context she is to function as Jupiter's subjugator. In my own understanding of the passage, the poet, rather than pointing to a remote story, hints at the abundance (*seque suamque domum*) of—only too well known—evidence offered by the πατὴρ ἀνδρῶν τε θεῶν τε which he might adduce (but tactfully or wisely omits) to confirm his thesis.

4. Jäger (1967, 194ff.) is to be credited with having observed the break of content after verse 28: "Bis dahin liegt der Rede ein logisch durchaus erfassbarer Plan zugrunde, und erst von hier an wird die Gedankenfolge völlig von einem irrationalen, gefühlsmässigen Element bestimmt." On page 202, when discussing line 58 in reference to 8, Jäger is on the brink of discovering the continuation of the initial argument in the elegy's later part. Compare Griffin (1977, 18): "Propertius has allowed the logic of his own poem, if read as a unity, to push him into the role of Antony; for he says 'no wonder if I am dominated by a woman—look at Cleopatra'."

5. The distinction is important. Von Wilamowitz apparently believed that the poet felt proud and happy to serve Augustus: "Er darf . . . Kleopatras gefährliche Grösse schildern, um ihrem Überwinder zu huldigen". Read in this way, Propertius has no personal interest at stake in 3.11 because the love theme is mere ornament and embroidery: "Sehr deutlich, wie er sich abquält, den eigentlichen Stoff mit etwas Liebespoesie zu verbrämen" (1962, vol. 1, 236, with n. 1). A "new note" is heard also by Baker (1968B, 335f.; cf. 1976, 60): "Propertius' identification of self with the *arma* of Rome is a new development". But although Baker, too, underrates the poem's first part (Cleopatra's "sins against Rome are the real reason

for her introduction here"), he is occasionally more cautious about a personal political involvement of the poet, stating merely that Propertius here "is responding to Maecenas' promptings to become a literary propagandist of the regime." Baker's phrasing here, perhaps unintentionally, leaves the decisive possibility open: in spite of the increasing number of elegies in Books 3 and 4 which visibly comply with the Zeitgeist and respond to the wishes of the régime, the poet may still have reserved room within his work for expressing his own feelings and portraying the inner world of his true involvement.

Without distinguishing politically directed publicity and personal subject matter, we will not be able to interpret adequately Book 4 but would, like Baker, have to endorse the traditional hypothesis of a one-way "development from the poetry of love to the poetry of politics" and "a sense of service to the state" (Baker o.c. p. 324), as also expressed, for instance, in Romussi's title (1940–41) "Lo sviluppo di Properzio verso la concezione di una nuova poesia politica ed etiologica". See also Grimal 1952C and Baker 1976 (n. 18 below).

6. This relation was seen by Jäger 1967, 201. Political and erotic bondage are two forms of the same subjection to woman. (Differently: Baker 1977).

7. Dio, less reluctant than Propertius, makes no distinction between Antony and Caesar in this respect, but allows Cleopatra, when planning to enslave even Octavian, to think of both in equal fashion as her former slaves: καὶ τὸν πατέρα αὐτοῦ τόν τε Ἀντώνιον ὁμοίως ἐδεδούλωτο (Dio 51.9.5).

8. To my eye, the emphasizing position of ausa (41) is more likely meant to recall the same effect from earlier in the same poem (line 13; see Jäger 1967, 200) than to make the reader look for an outside reference (which Paratore 1936, 34, and Richter 1966, 463, n. 33, find in ausa, Horace, C. 1.37.25ff.).

9. Cleopatra's annihilation of Octavian's triumph is also admitted by Horace: thus she avoided . . . deduci superbo / non humilis mulier triumpho, C. 1.37.31f.; cf. Propertius 4.6.64–66 (Chapter XI below). Cf. Plut. Ant. 78.4. Dio says that Octavian felt admiration and pity for her, but strong grief for himself because her suicide deprived him even of "all the glory resulting from his victory" (ἰσχυρῶς ἐλυπήθη ὡς καὶ πάσης τῆς ἐπὶ τῇ νίκῃ δόξης ἐστερημένος), 51.14.6. This accounts well for Propertius' vicit victorem . . . virum, but not for the candida forma of Penthesilea's corpse. While the feature of her enslaving beauty for itself might be taken to hint at Cleopatra capturing C. J. Caesar, this interpretation cannot explain the words ausa . . . oppugnare, etc., and victorem, because Caesar and Cleopatra did not wage war against each other prior to their affair. Unless we assume a mixture, it appears safer to see Octavian reflected in victor Achilles.

10. Cp. Léon-Marcien 1956, 333, with n. 15.

11. Dio leaves out no opportunity to show her alleged power over Caesar, from their first meeting (Caesar "was enthralled right away", εὐθὺς ἐδουλώθη, 42.35.1) and her influence with him (e.g., 42.44.3), through to the offense which her presence in Rome and in Caesar's house caused his fellow Romans: "But the greatest charge laid against him by all was because of his love for Cleopatra—not the affair back in Egypt (for that was hearsay), but the one in Rome itself." πλείστην δ'οὖν ὅμως αἰτίαν ἐπὶ τῷ τῆς Κλεοπάτρας ἔρωτι, οὐ τῷ ἐν τῇ Αἰγύπτῳ ἔτι (ἐκεῖνος γὰρ ἠκούετο), ἀλλὰ τῷ ἐν αὐτῇ τῇ Ῥώμῃ, παρὰ πάντων ἔσχεν (43.27.3).

Commentators on Prop. 3.11.45f. point to Cleopatra's wish to come back to

Rome with Antony and rule and exercise jurisdiction on the Capitoline Hill, as expressed in her frequent oath: ποιεῖσθαι τὸ ἐν τῷ Καπιτωλίῳ δικάσαι. (Dio 50.5.4. The oath is among the reasons why Rome declares war upon her, according to Dio). I would find it hard to assume that the prospect—true or fabricated—of her return to Rome should not revive the memories and once more arouse the feelings created by her first stay, when she was the dictator's mistress. "Di fatto sembra sicuro che Cleopatra volesse realizzare mediante Antonio ciò che avrebbe voluto ottenere già al tempo di Cesare: associarsi al governo dell'impero romano . . ." (Paladini, 1958, 262, n. 5). Propertius may well allude to her former stay through mention of her alleged desire to return.

12. Taking the pentameter (56) as part of Cleopatra's speech does more justice to *assiduo* (the word plays no part in SB's plea for Paganelli's version "elle dit et le vin . . . ensevelit sa langue"). Is, when applied by Augustan propaganda, *lingua* really "a pointless taunt" (as SB feels)? Cf. *fremitu . . . inani*, 2.16.37.

13. At this point, my reader may desire to compare my thesis about two contradicting arguments in 3.11 with a more conventional interpretation. I would refer him to the fourth chapter of Alfonsi's book (1945D, 54ff.), because it, although unintentionally, well reveals the sociological preoccupations and spiritual traditions which have dominated Latin studies for decades (not to say for centuries). They have, as I have indicated before, often prevented the development of an adequate interpretative method and of literary categories applicable to our author. Instead, Propertius was measured according to the standards set by contemporary Augustan court propaganda (which he did not wish to comply with, but which many of his interpreters found it easy to agree with), or he was even judged by Roman traditions later than his own time (i.e., unknown to him but familiar and essential to his interpreters).

Alfonsi sees fit to rough in all the problematical poems I have interpreted (3.4; 5; 11; 22) and smooth them over by the familiar plane of "development", from "passionalità morbosa e violenta" in Book 2 to participation in the supposed new mood of his time, part of which is "speranza di rinnovamento universale". Thus, Book 3 is "insomma da una parte il tramonto di un amore, dall'altra l'affermarsi di nuove idealità in una ricerca di eticità che è pur essa affermazione di vittoriosa conquista" (p. 54). No wonder, then, that Alfonsi is able to dissolve Propertius' dilemma of personal poetry and public pressure expressed in elegy 3.11 into a pre-stabilized harmony: "Infine specialissimo rilievo merita la elegia 11ª dove appunto i due elementi, l'erotico-mitologico e lo storico-contemporaneo cercano di fondersi completamente" (p. 66). In this manner, "passaggio dalla poesia erotica ad un'altra quasi epica o meglio civile" (p. 65) defines the road allegedly traveled by the poet in Book 3, and (mature) interpretative tautology is substituted for (puerile) methodology: "credere che i poeti *augustei* potessero essere, contro *Augusto*, è puerile e superficiale affermazione" (p. 68; italics mine). In the hands of this interpreter (and others), Propertius has no choice but to be an Augustan in spirit. (Wherever this "classical" spirit is seen to be lacking, one may point to a scientific fact going along with such lack, viz., his alleged postclassical use of Latin grammar and style, or his insufficient rendering of his Greek sources, as for instance in elegy 1.1, or even his presumed illogicality.) For another, rather circumspect, one-way interpretation of 3.11, see Baker 1976. ("Rather is the progression in this poem of a single, linear kind," etc., p. 58. The exempla guide the progression "from the initial love theme to panegyric", p. 59).

14. So also Hubbard 1968, 318.

15. Nethercut 1971C, 435.

16. Hubbard 1968, 318.

17. Propertius worked out the Augustan façade so well that Paladini (1958) ranks his account of Actium in 3.11 and 4.6 as even closer to "la versione aulica" or "la vista ufficiale" than Horace or Vergil: "Il poeta ha in sostanza espresso perfettamente quella che era l'interpretazione augustea dei fatti, cioè li ha collocati nella luce in cui il Cesare voleva fossero proiettati." (p. 464). Binder (1971, 183) can even illuminate a scene in *Aeneid* 8 by the help of Prop. 3.11 ("Der gleiche Gedankengang liegt der Schildbeschreibung Vergils zugrunde").

18. I wish to mention two other attempts to see in elegy 3.11 more than its Augustan surface.

The first is that of Paratore (1936), whose book on the political elegist, republican and anti-Augustan, is founded on his interpretation of 3.11. Paratore, after stating a Propertian "tecnica" of writing poems the ending of which contradicts their beginning (p. 12), evaluates the series of mythological examples (9–26) as a bridge which helps the poet to move from the subjective and private sphere of the beginning to the poem's objective center, viz., the opposition of Augustus/Rome and Cleopatra/Egypt: "un esempio tipico della più matura tecnica alessandrineggiante di Properzio" (o.c. p. 16). I do not feel that it is a compliment (rather, it is a lame excuse) to credit the poet with using Alexandrian learnedness for gluing together what does not fit: "Questi (sc., accenni mitologici) debbon fare da ponte di passaggio tra l'elemento subiettivo e l'elemento storico della poesia, e debbon quasi *legittimare la giustapposizione*" (italics mine) "del secondo accanto al primo" (o.c. pp. 16f.). By confining the mythical element to an ornamental function instead of first investigating the function of its contents, Paratore is ranking style over logic and so deprives himself even of the evidence there is for his thesis—as he does in the case of 3.22 (Chapter VIII above) or of Book 4 (where he resorts to the inconclusive "evidence" that mention of destroyed Veii in 4.10.27ff. stands for the poet's home-area town Perusia; o.c. pp. 222f.). Instead of analyzing the argument of the elegy, he decides to make a detour: the fact that Propertius treats Cleopatra with more abuse than Horace does makes him infer that the elegist degraded the Egyptian queen in order to denigrate Octavian's victory over her. Paratore's failure to see (a) why Propertius in 3.11 must insist that Cleopatra was indeed a powerful woman, and (b) that an exclusively political interpretation leads away from the core of Propertius' poetry, has probably for a long time blocked further investigation in the right direction.

Paratore's position has been at the basis of several articles by Nethercut. With regard to 3.11, Nethercut (1971C) arrives at what he calls "the ironic or whimsical" (p. 439) reading of 3.11, an important feature of which is that (since "wit is born from dislike", 442) Propertius was prompted "when officials were making much over the victory [sc., of Actium], to create the contrast between the last words of a besotted tongue and the glorious portrayal of Augustus' place in history" (p. 442).

Without listing my numerous objections to this difficult article, I take delight in attacking its basic position, viz., that Propertius "remains detached from what he writes" (p. 439) and that "he addresses his thoughts to the male, Octavian, and his success in retaining his independence (and that of Rome) from a personal and political *domina*" (p. 438). The "major regard of 3.11" is seen to be the poet's "concern with the freedom of men from the tyranny of women" (l.c.)—as if Propertius were here fighting for the liberated male and not for the opposite, viz., recognition as a human value of male dedication to a woman. Like Paratore's attempt to find a second meaning behind the Augustan façade, so Nethercut's is a priori shipwrecked, because both still follow Augustan Interpretation in looking for their leading categories in the poem's royal latter half and do not pay sufficient attention to the logical train of thought in the earlier part.

An interesting by-product of this misconception is the following. Nethercut, too, wishes to secure a broader meaning for the list of mythical women (9–26). But instead of finding the list helpful in ascertaining Cleopatra's position in the poet's original argument—with the mythical passage revealing what could not be said openly in the ensuing political passage—Nethercut (pp. 421ff.) explains the political Cleopatra of lines 27–46 in the Augustan context with the help of the mythical examples (without giving any reason why the poet should resort to enigmatic speech). His result is that "what Propertius is celebrating here is not . . . Augustus' military victory over the forces of Cleopatra". "The victory celebrated here is that of Augustus over Cleopatra as over an enchantress, powerful in love" (p. 426). Support is sought for this thesis through another major misconception: the figure of Heracles spinning wool for Queen Omphale is interpreted as pointing to Augustus (in spite of Nethercut's strange admission that "unlike Hercules . . . Augustus is able to protect his city from anyone, even from a woman").

In this way, the distortion of the poem's basic idea—from a justification of dedicated love into the opposite—is completed. It is hardly necessary to add that Nethercut, too (like Paratore), has provided no method when it comes to interpreting those passages of Book 4 where the poet pursues his own and personal train of thought behind an elaborate Augustan facade.

A detailed critique of Nethercut's method in interpreting 3.11 was given by Baker (1976). But Baker's own assumptions (a) that the erotic opening lines do not set the tone for the whole poem (p. 56), and (b) that (in this Baker agrees with Camps) the love theme here is only a "peg" for the new patriotic tone (p. 60), do not go together with my own findings. See also n. 5 above on Baker 1968B.

CHAPTER XI

1. This is, with few exceptions, *communis opinio* among scholars today. With regard to Book 4 and its special introduction (elegy 1), see, for instance, Becker 1971, 474f.; Burck 1966, 409 ("als eines der letzten des vierten Buchs entstanden und als Einleitungsgedicht für dieses Buch konzipiert"); Michelfeit (1969, 359); Pasoli 1967B, 4. Exceptions to this opinion are based on the assumption that Book 4 in its transmitted form is too self-contradictory to be capable of a meaningful interpretation. My argument in this and the following chapter will provide a new account of the book's alleged discrepancies between announcement and ensuing contents.

2. Williams 1968, 53. The traditional view of Imperial Interpretation is less critical, not only in that it takes the sincerity of Propertius' confession in 4.6 for granted, but also in that it presupposes similar taste and convictions on the interpreter's part. See, for instance, Eisenhut (1956, 128): "Das Gedicht ist die religiöse Rechtfertigung der irdischen Sendung des Augustus. Es ist eine *zurückhaltende* und *feinsinnige* und gerade darum *echte* Göttlichpreisung des Augustus" (italics mine). Cf. Gatti 1952, 154f. (Propertius celebrates Actium "degnamente"). Williams' blame of lacking seriousness is met head on by Johnson (1973): Propertius is purposefully funny in 4.6 and parodies Vergil by showing that the *Aeneid*'s description of Actium "is finally silly because Augustan propaganda about the battle of Actium was silly, and the battle itself was pretty silly" (162; cf. 160; 163; 167). But parody, though easily enough suggesting itself to the reader of a later age, appears excluded both by the poem's homogeneously adulatory surface (no ambiguity, no irreverent twinkling of the author's eye is indicated) and by its close relation to the other protestation of loyalty given in 4.1A. See also note 18 to Chapter VII.

A survey of more recent literature on 4.6 may be found in P. J. Connor (1978, 1ff.). Connor himself tries to elaborate and vary Johnson's interpretation. I refrain from dealing in detail with what Levin (1982, 473ff.; cf. 479) has termed "a band of 'Young Turks'" (including Sullivan, Nethercut, Hallett, the early Richardson, and, to a degree, apparently Levin himself). Their guesses about Propertius' ways of undercutting his national elegies (e.g., by intentionally writing inferior poetry) to my eye are not sufficiently grounded in close observation and interpretation of the text. See also Little 1982, 304, n. 177. I do not maintain that Propertius assumed that everybody took his protestations of loyalty to Augustus' program as coming naturally.

3. See also *Aen.* 8.678.

4. Richter (1966, 455ff.) would rather see Octavian's own divinity confirmed here, and he changes the transmitted text accordingly. But the point is (see Rothstein and Camps) that adulation is even more refined if C. J. Caesar's divinity receives confirmation from his "son's" achievement. Richter exchanges cause and effect when he understands that in the transmitted text "die grosse Weltstunde zu einem Subsidium für die Deutung des Phänomens Caesar . . . herabsinkt" (p. 455). He wrongly adduces (454; 457; 460) lines 61/62 in support of his thesis, overlooking the words *circa libera signa*.

5. For the special rôle Apollo played in Augustan court propaganda (family god of the Julians and personal protector of Octavian) and for Propertius' contribution in 4.6 to the official picture, see Léon-Marcien 1956, 342ff.; also, see Paladini 1958, 466ff. Pillinger (1969, 192) says that 4.6 "is as much a hymn to Apollo as a glorification of Augustus, or . . . a hymn to both at once, the glory of Augustus being prefigured in the brilliance of Apollo".

6. We observe a fine point. While Agrippa the admiral is—in spite of his continuing high position—deleted from the battle of Actium in 4.6, the two little sons (*pueros*) he has with the Emperor's daughter are accorded future Parthian victory (4.6.82). This corresponds to "the right arm undefeated in war" (*Aen.* 6.878f.) Vergil accords to the Emperor's nephew and prospective successor (Marcellus) regardless of the fact that Marcellus' life hardly extended beyond his boyhood years (cf. *puer*, *Aen.* 6.882; and see Stahl 1981, 177 n. 29).

7. A possible allusion of 4.6.42 to the oath mentioned in *R.G.* 5.3 is rightly listed (though not evaluated) in SB's Appendix. My reader encountered the oath at the occasion of elegy 2.7 (Chapter VI, at n. 19).

8. Pillinger (1969) rightly judges 4.6 to be "Propertius' most elaborate and enthusiastic endorsement of the imperial house and mission" (p. 190). He admires both the adroit hymnic transition from public (praise of Actium) to private sphere (poets' banquet) with its Hellenistic utilization of Apollo's polar attributes (the warrior god turns into the *citharoedus*), and the overall imitation of Callimachus' hymn on Apollo. If he in addition hears "a tone of admiration and respect with no hint of servile adulation" and finds the topic of Augustus' divinity "discreetly handled" (p. 199), we shall not dispute a matter of taste. But that Callimachus' formal design may have "tempered" (!) the poet's "personal enthusiasm" is in no way suggested by Pillinger's Callimachean material. Nor can the material prove that the poem's "balance of sentiment" (?) "probably reflects Propertius' own maturing views on the meaning of the *pax Augusta*" (l.c.). The equation of "maturity = pro-Augustan attitude" is not a result of the—otherwise illuminating—investigation of Callimachean influences, but existed before or beside it in the researcher's mind. Even an interpreter of so strongly Augustan attitude as E. Burck is aware that Propertius does not join the other poets at the banquet when they sing of war (1966, 412). Burck terms Propertius' withdrawal a "Verzicht"—a "beglückend freie und . . . eindeutige Verknüpfung und Lösung". "Unambiguous"—yes, indeed. But "blessedly free"? Clearly, we have to watch more than Callimachean style and "resignation" to read the poet's heart.

9. The viewpoint chosen by Propertius is Augustan also in the metaphorical sense. To understand the flattery involved in pointing to "these golden temples" (5) etc., we should compare Augustus' pride in his building program (*R.G.* 19–21). Suetonius (*Aug.* 28) reports the Emperor as boasting that he turned a city of bricks into one of marble. For my interpretation, it makes no difference whether Propertius is actually on the Palatine Hill or viewing it from the opposite side (Capitoline Hill) or from below, walking around: as long as there is no doubt about his being chiefly and centrally concerned with the Emperor's hill. With regard to the site of the Apollo Temple, see Guey 1952 and the controversy between Richmond (1958, 180ff.) and Bishop (1956, 187ff.). Cp. also Van Sickle 1975, 126ff.; Zanker 1983.

The increasing importance of the temple for Augustus himself is once more documented by *Aeneid* 8 (720ff.); it is on its threshold that the Emperor is depicted accepting the gifts of the nations. Around 18 B.C., even "The Sibylline Books, which contained the 'fate of Rome', were transferred from the Capitoline Temple of Iupiter to the Palatine Temple of Apollo," etc. (Rowell 1975, 191).

10. The structure was well brought out in Dieterich's analysis (1900, 192–202).

11. SB is mistaken in gathering "parallels" to show that *res* in line 30 points to "Tatius' wealth". The *section* is on *state* business! Cf. Marr 1970, 160 (*rerum* = "business"). Here (as elsewhere) SB's method would preclude the poet from introducing a notion that was not expressed by another writer before (or after) him.

12. As in 1.6.22 and 1.21.9, one may consider reading *at* instead of *et* in 4.1.35.

13. See Rothstein and Camps *ad loc.*

14. More fully formulated: "for a better destiny . . . to this land ⟨than if you had sent them elsewhere⟩". Taking *melius* to be "simply the equivalent of *bene*" (SB) disregards the given context. Nor is Mair's example, quoted by SB, convincing: oracular λώιον καὶ ἄμεινον does imply awareness of an alternative (the "ritualistic" question "whether if he do so and so, it will be for him λώιον καὶ ἄμεινον" demands the complement ⟨than if he abstains from doing so and so⟩).

15. Surely lines 46f. are "suggestive of" (SB) *Aen.* 8.608ff. (Venus bringing Aeneas' new arms). This, however, should not induce us to change *Caesaris* to *coniugis* (SB), but to appreciate Propertius' politically precise reading of the *Aeneid*: Aeneas prefigures Augustus. Thus Propertius makes Vergil's implicit equation Aeneas = Augustus explicit. Cf. MacLeod 1976, 143: "Aeneas is fused with Augustus". For *sui*, 46, cp. *pulchra origine, Aen.* 1.286.

16. *Melius* (39) and *felix* (48) correspond, giving the value judgment under which the poet wishes each time the following lines (39–47; 48–54) to be read. While the arriving Trojans experience fulfillment of a fate-ordained process, Italy proves fruitful to their cause. For Troy's enemies, (i.e., the Greeks) this development acquired a negative meaning (cf. the value term *male* at 53), turning their earlier victory to disaster. Since it is the positive final *results* of the historical development from poor to rich, from defeat to victory, from weakness to power which the poet is interested in here rather than the *omens* that envisaged this development (the omens only confirm to the observer a posteriori that Rome's Julian destiny was fate-ordained all along), I would hesitate to emphasize an idea of "nostalgia" for the past (MacLeod 1976, 141; 145) in 4.1.1–56. The poet's dilemma was rather an adulatory one: to show how the Emperor's interest in ancient cults and customs was outperformed by the splendid way in which he revived those objects of his interest.

The religious and oracular context of 48–54 favors the active meaning of *felix* in 48 over the intransitive alternative; this will be confirmed by lines 55f. which appreciate Italy's contribution to the Trojan-Julian cause. One may also see a relationship between *Ilia tellus* (53) and *felix terra* (48).

17. See Chapter VIII on 3.22, with note 38 on p. 208.

18. My interpretation assigns a meaningful function to the section instead of declaring it a parenthesis. See Camps; Waszink 1960, 788 (". . . si poetam . . . illuc unde abierit—de ipsa enim urbe Roma agere sibi proposuerat—*rediisse* statuerimus"); on p. 800, Waszink, having completed his investigation of section 37–56, paraphrases the last distich in it as follows: "Sed ut ad *ipsam urbem Romam*, quam hoc carmine celebrandam suscepi, *revertar*: altrix nostra, lupa Martia, in quantam magnitudinem moenia lacte tuo orta creverunt!" But up to now Propertius' subject has been "urbs Roma" only insofar as present-day golden Rome is the latest stage and most apparent manifestation of the Julian world mission, which once started from Troy. We would miss the section's purpose in the Propertian train of thought if we felt that Aeneas is introduced here by association, so to speak: "poetam de primordiis imperii Romani agentem a lupa Romulea ad Aeneae iter, Romanae magnitudinis vere originem habendam, *facile delatum*" (o.c. p. 788, italics mine). It should be *necessario delatum* because the striking phenomenon which Augustan Rome presents serves as an eye-opener to recognize the Julian texture of history itself . . .

19. "Pious", used earlier to characterize Aeneas saving his father (44), shows a religious attitude toward Julian Rome on the poet's part.

20. The contents of line 60 prevent us from taking *conari* here (as at 1.6.19, cf. Chapter IV) to mean "to set out to do."

21. I shall refrain from working this higher consistency into an interpretative system and derive from "das 'römische' 4. Buch" the author's Augustan attitude (so Burck 1966, 414—"Die feierliche und verantwortungsbewusste Haltung des Dichters", 412, and passim). For my reading of the earlier books has taught me to expect (and my following chapter will, I hope, convince my reader) that stylish political confessions may appear in conspicuous places not for their own sake but to help the author's other, less political works to be published and to survive (*nostris . . . libris*, line 63, is plural and therefore comprises Books 1–3 also!). In the same fashion, my interpretations of 2.34 and 3.22—a "Roman" poem made to order—warn me not to derive from the prominence of Vergilian "sources" in the national poems (especially 1A; 6; 11) clues to the author's personal convictions. "Seit langem aber lebte Properz dem Erscheinen der Aeneis entgegen". This judgment by Becker (1971, 478) is hardly warranted by a critical reading of 2.34. Nor is the following: ". . . machte er sich nach dem Jahre 19 *mit Leidenschaft* die Aeneis zu eigen" (l.c., italics mine).

22. Doubts concerning the customary edifying interpretations have been voiced by La Penna (1951B, 86ff.; cf. 1977, 94f.), Celentano (1956, 53), Curran (1968, 134), and Paduano (1968, 25, with n. 18); odd: Hallett 1973, 119. Personal regards motivating the author are suggested also by Eisenhut's essay (1949, 57: a poem addressing the husband of the deceased).

CHAPTER XII

1. Today there is no question that A and B belong together, if not as two halves of the same poem (= *communis opinio*), so at least as "two separate but related poems" (Sandbach 1962, 267).

2. *fides* = "fulfillment", SB (Appendix, p. 310); Becker (1966, 447) calls *fides* here a "Leitwort."

3. Cf. Becker 1966, 447.

4. For the textual difficulties involved (how can Horos, 121f., divine the poet's native place if Propertius has already mentioned it himself in 63f.?), see Sandbach's penetrating analysis (1962). He thinks Markland's is the only solution to preserve the elegy's unity: full stop at the end of line 121; no sign at the end of 122. If Horos is accorded an "abrupt appearance" (MacLeod 1976, n. 28 on p. 152 *ad* p. 145), he should at least be allowed to have overheard lines 65ff. (see our interpretation of lines 121ff.). But the name Asis(i) (125) was not mentioned by the poet before.

5. We shall probably never know whether Assisi or another city (Maddoli 1963, 300, tentatively suggests Urbinum Hortense) was the poet's birthplace. But we should not consider the whole couplet 125/126 interpolated (so again Sandbach 1962, 271f.) if it makes sense that Horos here picks up and plays upon Propertius' earlier phrasing.

6. The interpretation given in the text does not lose its validity even if *ille* is in the first place used to indicate that Horos, after "divining" features of Propertius' homeland, is now returning and referring to a well-known fact that was established earlier already.

7. This is Heimreich's (1867) understanding of 135–146, renewed recently (but alienated from the logical context) by Lefèvre 1966, pp. 431ff., and by Marr (1970, 167). Suerbaum (1964, 346) is clearly wrong in assuming that Horos' self-justification ends at line 134, and that with line 135 "beginnt der Wahrsagungsteil, die eigentliche Verkündigung des Horos". Lines 135–146 are, as I shall show in the text, still part of Horos' proof of his own qualification because they refer to identifiable elegies of earlier books. *at* (136) opens direct after indirect (*vetat*, etc., 134) discourse.

8. *Fata* (71) can hardly refer to anything other than the interpretation of Roman history Propertius has just given in 1A, 1–56, and must mean manifestations of Rome's Julian destiny (= object of his new poetry, *dicere fata*); while line 72 refers to his desire (expressed in 67f.) to be successful (= his qualification as a poet) in the new genre (*dextera* 68 ~ *dextro* 72).

Eisenhut (1961, 99) finds in line 72 a mixture of *carmen condere* and *carmen deducere*. If so, we should respect Sandbach's hint (1962, 268) that *condita sunt* is perfect tense. The threads from which the texture of Propertius' new poetry is to be formed have not been spun from a propitious distaff. *Thes. Ling. Lat.* s.v. *filum*, C, (Lackenbacher) offers no clear contemporary parallel (which perhaps can not be expected in a poet so often ahead of his time), but points to Auson. *Mos.* (396: *mollia subtili nebunt mihi carmina filo / Pierides*) and Macr. *Sat.* (5.2.8: *quod totum Homericis filis texuit Vergilius*).

9. "Dicere fata Romae" (Terzaghi 1963, 1132f., commenting on line 71).

10. For my interpretation no more is required than the usual meaning of *nunc* in a context like this ("now", i.e., "accordingly", "under the conditions outlined earlier"; cf. Marr, 1970, 167). Lefèvre (1966, 433f.), although aware of the correspondence between *tum* (133) and *nunc* (147), assumes a rare case of *nunc* with adversative and temporal force ("But now when"—*jetzt aber, da*—steering a bold course, beware!). The fact is, however, that he needs an adversative meaning as early as line 147 for another reason, of which he apparently is not aware: his treatment of lines 147–150 as a homogeneous unit makes him disregard the final adversative contrast (recognizable by the shift of grammatical construction) between lines 147–149 (*licet* plus subjunctive) and line 150 (imperative). His imprecise understanding of Propertian *licet with subjunctive* (its correct translation is "to be free to", as in 2.34.33: 2.22.23) in turn leads him to a metaphorical (instead of concrete) reading of lines 147–149. Lefèvre's interpretation was accepted by Nethercut (1968B, 92).

11. Nethercut 1970B, 116.

12. Like all the astrological investigations, also the most recent one (Marquis, 1973) rests on the unquestioned assumption that 4.1B.150 represents "an astrological code" (p. 127).

13. A detail makes this interpretation attractive: philologists have had difficulty in making sense of the *terga* of the Cancer at Prop. 4.1.150. SB points out

that one would usually speak of the *bracchia Cancri* and assumes a confusion with *terga Leonis*. Nethercut (1968B, 97) seems to think that by granting notice to "the *terga* of the crab, rather than its distinctive claws" Propertius points to the reverse side of the coin. The claws, however, are equally well visible on the coin as is the back: the viewer, looking down on the crav from above, sees its back and its extended claws, which try to encircle and catch a butterfly in front of (and perhaps slightly above) the Cancer. The coin in itself supplies no reason why the poet should identify the Cancer by its back and not by its claws.

The reason why Propertius emphasizes the *back* of the Cancer is that it is opposed to its *belly*: "Now any astrologer worth his charts would know that when we look up at the constellation of the Crab we see, not its back, but its belly" (Marquis 1973, 130). Marquis therefore assumes that with *sinistra* a position "beyond", or north of, Cancer is hinted at by Propertius. I do not think this is the solution. Rather, by making up an astrological paradox (i.e., pointing to the invisible back instead of the belly visible in the sky), the poet indicates that he is leaving the sphere of astrology ("Cancer's back is of no moment astrologically," Nethercut, 1970B, 116). It is left to the thinking reader to locate the *terga Cancri* (viz., on the coins down here in Rome). A photograph can be found on plate 2, no. 13, in Mattingly 1923, a description on p. 11 of the same work. According to Mattingly (1930, 58f.), the golden coins were struck in 18 B.C. Deonna (1954, 47) dates them around 19 B.C. Grueber (see Deonna 1954, p. 67, n. 2) dates them in 14 B.C. Deonna (1954, 47f.; 64f.; 66) attempts to find an interpretation of the coin in connection with Capricorn, Augustus' sign of conception. This would not seem to be Propertius' concern in 4.1.150, because he would rather wish to point to the money itself. But it is worth mentioning that the butterfly often stands for soul and immortality. The front of the coin shows the "laurelled head of Augustus" (Deonna 1954, 47; wearing an oak-wreath, according to Mattingly 1923, 11).

14. For other attempts (besides Rothstein's) to understand line 7 without changing the transmitted text, see Grimal, 1951, 205, n. 2; Wellesley 1969, 98 (on *praecingit*; see also 97: "Water for sacred use must be pure and running, so that Tarpeia will draw it at its first emergence in the woods, whereas Tatius may be presumed to water his horses lower down in greater proximity to his camp in the later *Forum Romanum*.").

15. It is impossible for me (and probably fruitless) to discuss the many attempts at exchanging distichs. They usually create more trouble than they claim to remove. For example, SB's decision to have line 2 followed by 9–14 not only deprives the reader of understanding the poem's differing viewpoints. I fear that his claim ("The poem now progresses naturally".) subjects literary levels of fiction to rhetorical rules of prose exposition: the *ecphrasis*-character of 3ff. (*lucus erat*, etc.) naturally (in terms of Roman poetry) amounts to a *neuer Einsatz*.

Beyond this, SB's transposition forces him to let consecutive distichs end on the same word (*Iovis*, 2 and 10: he can cite only two other examples out of over 2,000 distichs!). And his demand that "Tatius and his *vallum*" "should" appear "after some mention of the campaign", seems idle considering the indication already given in line 2.

16. Interpreters usually do not show themselves sensitive to this change. A

rare exception deserves being quoted here: ". . . we are left exposed to an emotional dialectic, a tug of war between our sense of morality and the claims of Rome's glory, and our experience of the vitality of Tarpeia's love." (Warden 1980, 103). As for the poet's own decision on this "dialectic", see our discussion later on in this chapter.

17. The lilies, too, are—as K. Wellesley (1969, 99), quoting Preller, has again pointed out—a sign of her sin: flowers are forbidden to a Vestal.

18. Evening, but not morning, as SB, following BB and once again unaware of the long-range context, would persuade us. The thoughts expressed in her monologue develop over long hours from evening to predawn (63f.).

19. In line 33 the wishful relocation was indicated by the word *sedeam*. The author had described her in 29 as *residens* so that 33 should be understood with a supplement: "Would that I might sit as a prisoner at your hearth ⟨over there as I am now sitting here on the hilltop⟩." Tarpeia integrates elements of her objective situation into the wishful scenery she is developing.

20. Already in 19 B.C., when (on the occasion of Augustus' return from the east) the Senate set up the *Ara Fortunae Reducis* in the Emperor's honor, it was the *Vestal virgins* who were (along with the *pontifices*) ordered to make annual sacrifices at the altar. The day was called *Augustalia* (*Res Gestae* 11)—a good indicator of how contemporaries were asked to see the Vestals, i.e., Rome's survival, tied to Augustus. Tarpeia's action cannot be viewed separately from the Vestals' function in the time of Propertius and his readers.

21. Nothing is wrong with *tua*, as long as we do not understand with SB that in lines 53 and 54 "Tatius is incited to take Romulus' place as king of (and in) Rome", where the parenthesis "(and in)" is an arbitrary addition to the Latin text. As we saw from Tarpeia's "good-bye" to Rome and its mountains (35f.), she expects to leave the area. Her wish is to accompany Tatius to his own country after his victory. Rome, her "dowry", will then be his vassal state. Not only the distich preceding 55f. but the poet's long-range design has to be consulted for deciding whether textual emendation is called for or not.

22. Reaction of Augustan interpretation to this passage is divided.

Alfonsi finds here more a moralizing use of an anti-Roman tradition than "atteggiamento antiaugusteo" (1949B, 160; cf. 1945D, 46). After all, according to Alfonsi, Propertius had not yet politically matured (and given in to Vergil's influence) at the time he wrote Book 2. In Book 4, Alfonsi finds "un altro orientamento spirituale del poeta", taking the praise of the she-wolf in 4.1A.37f. and 55f. to be his final word in the matter: by this "self-correction", the poet supposedly wished to indicate clearly his "mutazione di posizione". By making Tarpeia (who is "ostile a Romulo" and "nemica di Roma") voice his former thoughts, Propertius proves that he himself has dissociated himself from that position. See also Alfonsi 1953B.

Hanslik, denying that Propertius ever had any negative feelings towards Octavian, finds that passage of 2.6 (35f.), which deplores the neglect of religion, so truly Augustan that he concludes the rest of the poem must also be written in the spirit of the Augustan reforms. Pointing out that in 28 B.C. Octavian considered preferring the name "Romulus", not "Augustus", for himself, Hanslik finds that Propertius sometimes does not have a lucky hand ("Non ha . . . la mano sempre felice") in his well-meaning contributions to Augustanism, especially in his lines on licentious Romulus (2.6.19–22): "Questi versi del 28 sono da considerare piuttosto infelici" (1972, 99).

Hanslik's line of interpretation leaves no door open to the poet for ambiguity, not even within the narrow limits set by the régime.

23. This contrasts, of course, with *sine matris honore*, 53, and line 54 as a whole.

24. *nuptae* (59, perhaps we should read *raptae?*) shows that—along the lines of the traditional interpretation—in the less preferable case, too, she hopes to achieve some kind of social recognition for her status as Tatius' beloved (after all, the Sabine Women, apparently her model, likewise achieved full marital status after having first been ravished). Of course, *nuptae* can be a vocative: the ravished one addressing the happier married ones. Another consistent interpretation is to assume that only lines 57–58 contain the alternative to marriage, and that lines 59–62, completing an a–b–a thought movement, return to the first alternative, picking up lines 55f. as the terms *nuptae* (59) and *Hymenaee* (61) show. Psychologically understandable, her thoughts thus take her from the desired future (queen in King Tatius' country, 55f.) back to the present (wedding and peaceful solution of the war for Rome, 59ff.). In fact, the immediate step to take (wedding, 61f.) appears last in the series from future prospects to required action.

25. See the new interpretation suggested in n. 24.

26. The interpretation given above should be contrasted with two other existing ones:

(1) The "Augustan" view, which holds that Propertius himself condemns Tarpeia (e.g., Alfonsi 1945D, 78: ranking her love higher than her duty is against the will of fate which is justice: "e la giustizia è la vittoria di Roma").

(2) The technical and philological view, which searches for the ingredients of a literary (here: Alexandrian) tradition: Pillinger (1969, 176, n. 12) remarks: "In the etiological poem on Tarpeia . . . one of the chief interests of the poet is the delineation of the emotional state of the heroine distressed by a πάθος ἀμήχανον". This makes the elegy hardly more than a rhetorical exercise.

27. We must be careful when understanding sexual overtones (*Somnus* as "symbolic lover", Lyne 1971, 376f.) in the language of lines 67f. The terms *furiis* and *accubuisse* are explained in the following distich (*nam*, 69) in terms of Tarpeia's relation to Vesta, not to Tatius. Perhaps one might say that the two terms in line 68 belong to the sexual sphere insofar as Tarpeia's expectation was thwarted (*nescia*): she did not see the bedfellow she expected, but saw other (*novis*) ones.

28. See Stahl 1969, 539f.

29. There is no indication in the poem that Tarpeia's is a "truly *felix culpa*"— necessary for Rome's later Julian grandeur—as Baker (1968B, 344) and Grimal (1953, 28) assume.

30. For the possibility that Propertius in 71/72 may purposefully mix the figures of Amazon and Bacchant, and in doing so draw on Vergil's presentation of Dido (the warrior queen turning into the woman madly in love), see Warden 1978.

31. But see the alternative interpretation suggested in n. 24.

32. Goold's (1966, 98) transposition of 17f. to follow 92 overlooks that *dos apta*, 92, wants to correct the inappropriate *dos* of 56. An additional reference for

apta (viz., to violated Vesta of 18) would obfuscate the clear context, especially since Tarpeia's "crimes" have just been listed (87f.).

33. Goold (1966, 88f.), reading *iniustae* in line 94 (and *Tarpeium* in 93), translates: "Vigilant One, an unjust portion is your requital", explaining "that is, in having your hill named after a traitress". I hesitate to follow him in identifying *vigil* as Jupiter ("in all the verses of this poem there is one, and only one, mention of vigilance, in 85f: Iuppiter unus / *decrevit . . . invigilare*"). We should not, in narrow philological fashion, stick to related words only (*vigil—invigilare*), but accept the whole situation as given by the poet: lines 79 to 85 wish to make clear that (Jupiter and the poor watchdogs excepted) at this time Tarpeia is the only living being awake (and, in a perverted sense, watchful) in all of Rome. Her requital rather than Jove's is "an unjust portion".

34. Having ascertained the vital importance of the Tarpeia elegy for the poet's self-representation, we are now in a position to comment on certain interpretations of 4.1B. It neither announces a return to former love poetry (which does not appear in Book 4 anyhow) nor does it indicate hesitation (from fear that his poetic skills might not be sufficient for the grandeur of Roman national poetry); nor does 1B owe its position behind 1A to a posthumous editor (*sic* Festa 1926–27, 245): 1B contains the guarded admission that Propertius resigned before carrying his Julian program to its end.

Sandbach (1962, 267) thinks the only condition under which a unitarian view of 4.1A and B can be upheld is to take Horos to be "an excuse for not carrying out *in full* the programme suggested in 57–70". But Sandbach is not inclined to accept this condition as possible.

Rothstein was more certain: Propertius ". . . hatte den Plan aufgegeben und veröffentlichte nun in seinem letzten Buche, dem er dadurch den Charakter eines endgültig abschliessenden Nachtragbuches gab, einige wenige schon zur Ausführung gelangte Elegien aus diesem nicht vollendeten Werke, indem er in dem Einleitungsgedichte zugleich seinen Plan darlegte und das Aufgeben des Planes begründete" (*Erster Teil*, p. 13).

But even Rothstein was neither aware of the deeper reasons why the poet cancelled his Roman program nor of the fact that he does tell his readers about these reasons—under the masks of Horos (especially that dubious line 150) and Tarpeia.

BIBLIOGRAPHY

LEADING EDITIONS

Barber, E. A. *Sexti Properti carmina*. Scriptorum classicorum bibliotheca Oxonien-
sis. 2d ed. Oxford, 1960. (All quotations are made from this text.)
Hanslik, R. *Sex. Propertii elegiarum libri IV*. Bibliotheca scriptorum Graecorum et
Romanorum Teubneriana. Leipzig, 1979.
Schuster, M. *Sex. Propertii elegiarum libri IV*. Bibliotheca scriptorum Graecorum et
Romanorum Teubneriana. Leipzig, 1954. 2d ed. edited by F. Dornseiff, Leip-
zig, 1958. (Quotations agreeing with this text are always marked by name.)

EDITIONS AND COMMENTARIES

d' Arbela, E. *Elegiarum libri IV*. Milan, 1967.
Bonazzi, G. *Propertius resartus. Elegiarum libri a diuturna interpolatione redempti*.
Rome, 1951.
Butler, H. E. *Propertius, with an English Translation*. London, 1952.
Butler, H. E., and E. A. Barber. *The Elegies of Propertius*. Reprint. Hildesheim,
1969.
Camps, W. A. *Propertius. Elegies*. 4 vols. Cambridge, 1961–67.
Enk, P. J. *Sex. Propertii elegiarum liber I (Monobiblos)*. 2 vols. Leiden, 1946.
———. *Sex. Propertii elegiarum liber secundus*. 2 vols. Leiden, 1962.
Fedeli, P. *Properzio. Elegie. Libro IV*. Bari, 1965.
———. *Sesto Properzio. Il primo libro delle elegie*. Florence, 1980.
Giardina, G. C. *Sex. Properti elegiarum liber II*. Corpus scriptorum Latinorum Para-
vianum. Torino, 1977.
Hertzberg, G. A. B. *Sex. Aurelii Propertii elegiarum libri quattuor*. 3 vols. Halle,
1843–1845.

Lachmann, C. *Sex. Aurelii Properti carmina.* Leipzig, 1816.
Paley, F. A. *Sex. Aurelii Propertii carmina. The Elegies of Propertius.* London, 1872.
Pasoli, E. *In Properti Monobiblon Commentationes.* Bologna, 1957.
————. *Il libro quarto delle elegie.* 2d ed. Bologna, 1967. (Pasoli 1967A)
Postgate, J. P. *Select Elegies of Propertius.* Reprint. London, 1968.
Richardson, L., Jr. *Propertius. Elegies I–IV.* The American Philological Association Series of Classical Texts. Norman, Okla., 1976.
Richmond, O. L. *Sexti Properti quae supersunt opera.* Cambridge, 1928.
Rothstein, M. *Die Elegien des Sextus Propertius.* 3d ed. 2 vols. Dublin, 1966.

HANDBOOKS AND BIBLIOGRAPHIES

Bailey, D. R. S. *Propertiana.* 2d ed. Amsterdam, 1967.
Harrauer, H. *A Bibliography to Propertius.* Bibliography to the Augustan Poetry, vol. 2. Hildesheim, 1973.
Phillimore, J. S. *Index verborum Propertianus.* 2d ed. Darmstadt, 1961.
Schmeisser, B. *A Concordance to the Elegies of Propertius.* Hildesheim, 1970.
Smyth, G. R. *Thesaurus Criticus ad Sexti Propertii Textum.* Leiden, 1970.
Tränkle, H. *Die Sprachkunst des Properz und die Tradition der lateinischen Dichtersprache.* Hermes Einzelschriften, 15. Wiesbaden, 1960.

SECONDARY LITERATURE

The following list is a selection which concentrates on literature mentioned in the notes. Abbreviations are those of *L'Année Philologique.* Abbreviated references used in the text are given in parentheses.

Abel, W. "Die Anredeformen bei den römischen Elegikern: Untersuchungen zur elegischen Form." Diss., Berlin, 1930.
Ahl, Frederick M. "Propertius 1, 1." *WS* 87 (1974): 80–98.
Alfonsi, L. "Appunti properziani." *RIL* 75 (1941–42): 310–318.
————. "Nuovi appunti properziani." *RIL* 76 (1942–43): 143–153.
————. "Appunti Properziani." *AIV* 103 (1943–44): 451–465. (Alfonsi 1943–44A)
————. "Properzio e Virgilio." *RIL* 77 (1943–44): 459–470. (Alfonsi 1943–44B)
————. "Di Properzio II 34 e della protasi dell' Eneide." *RFIC* 22–23 (1944–45): 116–129.
————. "L'amore-amicizia negli elegiaci latini." *Aevum* 19 (1945): 372–378. (Alfonsi 1945A)
————. "Il pensiero della pace nell' elegia latina." *ScCatt* (1945): 61–68. (Alfonsi 1945B)
————. "Note properziane." *Aevum* 19 (1945): 357–371. (Alfonsi 1945C)
————. *L'elegia di Properzio.* Milan, 1945. (Alfonsi 1945D)
————. "Note properziane." *AC* 18 (1949): 335–352. (Alfonsi 1949A)
————. "Note properziane." *GIF* 2 (1949): 159–167. (Alfonsi 1949B)
————. "Nota properziana." *Hermes* 80 (1952): 115–117.

————. "Elegiaca. Properzio III 5.35." *Latomus* 12 (1953): 155–157. (Alfonsi 1953A)

————. "Elegiaca. (Prop. IV 4)." *Latomus* 12 (1953): 275–281. (Alfonsi 1953B)

————. "Elegiaca. Teoria properziana dell' amore." *Latomus* 12 (1953): 432–436. (Alfonsi 1953C)

————. "Il giudizio di properzio sulla poesia vergiliana." *Aevum* 28 (1954): 205–221.

————. "La donna dell' elegia latina." In *Ut pictura poesis. Studia latina P. J. Enk septuagenario oblata*, edited by P. de Jonge, et al., 35–44. Leiden, 1955. (Alfonsi 1955A)

————. "Note properziane." *Hermes* 83 (1955): 379–384. (Alfonsi 1955B)

————. "La prima elegia del I° libro di Properzio." In *Miscellanea Properziana*. Atti dell' Accademia Properziana del Subasio, 5.5, 7–20. Assisi, 1957.

————. "Properzio e Atene." *GIF* 16 (1963): 289–292. (Alfonsi 1963A)

————. "La 34a elegia del 2° libro di Properzio e il poeta Lynceo." *Maia* 15 (1963): 270–277. (Alfonsi 1963B)

————. "Propertiana." *Aevum* 47 (1973): 302–304.

Allen, A. W. "Elegy and the Classical Attitude Toward Love. Propertius I 1." *YClS* 11 (1950): 253–277.

————. "Sunt qui Propertium malint." In *Critical Essays on Roman Literature I: Elegy and Lyric*, edited by J. P. Sullivan, 107–148. London, 1962.

————. "A Piece of Advice." *Hermes* 102 (1974): 621–622.

————. "An Epexegetic *et* in Propertius." *Glotta* 60 (1982): 129.

Anderson, R. D., P. J. Parsons, and R. G. M. Nisbet. "Elegiacs by Gallus from Qaṣr Ibrîm." *JRS* 69 (1979): 125–155.

Atkinson, K. M. T. "The Governors of the Province Asia in the Reign of Augustus." *Historia* 7 (1958): 300–330.

Bailey, D. R. S. "Interpretations of Propertius." *CQ* 41 (1947): 89–92.

————. "Propertiana." *CQ* 43 (1949): 22–29.

————. "Some Recent Experiments in Propertian Criticism." *PCPhS* 182 (1952–53): 9–20.

Baker, R. J. "Propertius 3.1.1–6 Again. Intimations of Immortality?" *Mnemosyne* 21 (1968): 35–39. (Baker 1968A)

————. "*Miles annosus*: The Military Motif in Propertius." *Latomus* 27 (1968): 322–349. (Baker 1968B)

————. "*Laus in amore mori*. Love and Death in Propertius." *Latomus* 29 (1970): 670–698.

————. "Propertius' *Castae Puellae* (I 1,5)." *RhM* 97 (1974): 277–279.

————. "Propertius, Cleopatra and Actium." *Antichthon* 10 (1976): 56–62.

————. "Beauty and the Beast in Propertius 1.3." In *Studies in Latin Literature and Roman History*, vol. 2, edited by Carl Deroux, 245–258. Collection Latomus, 168. Brussels, 1980.

Barber, E. A. "Sex coniecturae Propertianae." In *Miscellanea Propertiana*. Atti dell' Accademia Properziana del Subasio, 5.5, 21–24. Assisi, 1957.

Barsby, J. A. "The Composition and Publication of the First Three Books of Propertius." *G&R* 21 (1974): 128–137.

Barwick, K. "Zur Interpretation von Properz II 15 und 14." *Philologus* 99 (1955): 112–132.

Beard, M. "The Sexual Status of Vestal Virgins." *JRS* 70 (1980): 12–27.

Beaujeu, J. "Étude d'un texte latin." *LI* 21 (1969): 180–186.

Beck, J. W. "De loco Propertii conclamato (C.IV 4.55)." *Mnemosyne* 41 (1913): 338–340.

Becker, C. "Horos redselig? Zu Properz IV,1." *WS* 79 (1966): 442–451.

———. "Die späten Elegien des Properz." *Hermes* 99 (1971): 449–480.

Bennett, A. W. "*Sententia* and Catalogue in Propertius (III 9, 1–20)." *Hermes* 95 (1967): 222–243.

———. "The Patron and Poetical Inspiration. Propertius III 9." *Hermes* 96 (1968): 318–340.

Berchem, D. van. "Au dossier d' *Ille ego*." *REL* 20 (1942): 69–78.

———. "Cynthia ou la carrière contrairiée. Essai sur la condition sociale des poètes latins." *MH* 5 (1948): 137–154.

Berman, K. "A Note on Propertius II 16.41/42." *CPh* 66 (1971): 110–112.

Bernardini Marzolla, P. "Tre elegie di Properzio." *Maia* 7 (1955): 163–183.

Bickel, E. "Varii carmen epicum de actis Caesaris et Agrippae. Critica in laudem Pisonis." *SO* 28 (1950): 17–43.

———. "Caesar Augustus als Achilles bei Vergil, Horaz und Properz." *RhM* 99 (1956): 342–364.

Bicknell, P. "Propertius I, 1, 19–22." *Latomus* 32 (1973): 629.

Binder, G. "*Compitalia* und *Parilia*. Properz IV 1.17–20." *MH* 24 (1967): 104–115.

———. *Aeneas und Augustus. Interpretationen zum 8. Buch der Aeneis*. Beiträge zur Klassischen Philologie, 38. Meisenheim, 1971.

Birt, Th. "Die Fünfzahl und die Properzchronologie." *RhM* 70 (1915): 253–314.

———. *Die Cynthia des Properz*. Leipzig, 1921.

Bishop, J. H. "Palatine Apollo." *CQ* 50 (1956): 187–92.

Bodoh, J. J. "Propertius I. 21." *AC* 41, 1972: 233–241.

———. "Contrast in Propertius I 6." *Emerita* 41 (1973): 379–401.

Boll, F. "Zu Properz IV 1." *ARW* 10 (1907): 157–158.

Boucher, J. P. "L'oeuvre de L. Varius Rufus d'après Properce II 34." *REA* 60 (1958): 307–322.

———. "Le second livre de Properce." *REL* 41 (1963): 101–106.

———. "Properce et Callimaque." *REL* 42 (1964): 273–276.

———. *Étude sur Properce. Problèmes d'inspiration et d'art*. Bibliothèque des Écoles françaises d'Athènes et de Rome, 204. Paris, 1965.

Bowersock, G. W. *Augustus and the Greek World*. 2d ed. Oxford, 1966.

Boyancé, P. "Surcharges de rédaction chez Properce." *REL* 20 (1942): 54–69.

Brakman, C. "Propertiana." *Mnemosyne* 54 (1926): 77–80.

Brenk, F. E. "Tarpeia Among the Celts; Watery Romance from Simylos to Propertius." In *Studies in Latin Literature and Roman History*, vol. 1, edited by Carl Deroux, 166–174. Collection Latomus, 164. Brussels, 1979.

Brouwers, J. H. "Properce et la gloire." *Mnemosyne* 23 (1970): 42–61.

Brunt, P. A. *Italian Manpower 225 B.C.–A.D. 14*. Oxford, 1971.

Brunt, P. A., and J. M. Moore. *Res Gestae Divi Augusti. The Achievements of the Divine Augustus*. Oxford, 1967. Reprint, Oxford, 1973.

Burck, E. "Römische Wesenszüge der augusteische Liebeselegie." *Hermes* 80 (1952): 163–200.

————. "Abschied von der Liebesdichtung (Properz III 24 und 25)." *Hermes* 87 (1959): 191–211.

————. "Zur Komposition des vierten Buches des Properz." *WS* 79 (1966): 405–427.

————. "Sextus Propertius: Elegie II 5." In *Antike Lyrik*, edited by W. Eisenhut, 431–450. Darmstadt, 1970.

————. "Liebesbindung und Liebesbefreiung: Die Lebenswahl des Properz in den Elegien 1.6 und 3.21." In *Vom Menschenbild in der Römischen Literatur*, vol. 2, edited by E. Lefèvre, 349–372. Heidelberg, 1981.

Bury, R. G. "Notes on Propertius." *PCPhS* 172–174 (1939): 6–7.

Butrica, J. L. "The Earliest Inaccurate Citation of Propertius." *AJPh* 102 (1981): 327–329.

Cairns, F. *Generic Composition in Greek and Roman Poetry*. Edinburgh, 1972.

————. "Some Observations on Propertius I 1." *CQ* 24 (1974): 94–110.

————. "Some Problems in Propertius I 6." *AJPh* 95 (1974): 150–163.

————. "Propertius on Augustus' Marriage Law (2.7)." *GB* 8 (1979): 185–204.

Cameron, A. "Propertius 1.1. and Constantine the Sicilian." *CPh* 74 (1979): 58–60.

Campagna, G. "Un disticho di Properzio su Tarpeia." *A&R* N.S. 3 (1922): 124–126.

————. "Sulla composizione di un'elegia properziana." *AIV* 83.2 (1923–24): 259–264.

————. "Elementi del mito di Tarpeia in Properzio." *RF* (1926): 363–371.

————. "Le elegie romane di Properzio." *AIV* 85 (1929): 1253–1286.

Camps, W. A. "Propertius I 21." *PCPhS* N.S. 5 (1959): 22–23.

————. "Propertiana." *CR* 11 (1961): 104–106.

Catin, L. "Properce et Cynthie." *BAGB* (1957): 4, 27–52.

Celentano, L. "Significato e valore del IV libro di Properzio." *AFLN* 6 (1956): 33–68.

Cherniss, H. F. "The Biographical Fashion in Literary Criticism." In *University of California Publications in Classical Philology*, vol. 12, 279–291. Berkeley, 1943. (= *Selected Papers*, edited by L. Tarán, 1–13. Leiden, 1977.)

Clack, J. "*Non ego nunc* (Propertius I.6): A Study in Irony." *CW* 71 (1977): 187–190.

Clarke, M. L. "Latin Love Poets and the Biographical Approach." *G&R* 23 (1976): 132–139.

Claussen, W. "On the Date of the First Eclogue." *HSPh* 76 (1972): 201–205.

Commager, S. *A Prolegomenon to Propertius*. Lectures in Memory of L. Taft Semple, University of Cincinnati, 3d ser. Norman, Okla., 1974.

Connor, P. J. "*Saevitia amoris*. Propertius, I 1." *CPh* 67 (1972): 51–54.

————. "The Actian Miracle: Propertius 4.6." *Ramus* 7 (1978): 1–10.

Copley, Frank O. *Exclusus Amator. A Study in Latin Love Poetry*. American Philological Association Philological Monographs, 17. Madison, Wisconsin, 1956.

Courtney, E. "The Structure of Propertius' Book I and Some Textual Consequences." *Phoenix* 22 (1968): 250–258.

————. "Three Poems of Propertius." *BICS* 16 (1969): 70–87.

————. "The Structure of Propertius Book III." *Phoenix* 24 (1970): 48–53.

Croce, B. "Filologia ed estetica (a proposito della El.II, 15 di Properzio)." *Critica* 34 (1936): 296–302.

————. "E. Reitzenstein: *Wirklichkeitsbild und Gefühlsentwicklung bei Properz.*" *Critica* 35 (1937): 378–379. (Review)

Cronin, P. A. "Sigmatism in Tibullus and Propertius." *CQ* 20 (1970): 174–180.

Csillag, P. "Das Eherecht des Augusteischen Zeitalters." *Klio* 50 (1968): 111–138.

Curran, L. C. "Propertius IV 11. Greek Heroines and Death." *CPh* 63 (1968): 134–139.

Damon, P. W., and W. C. Helmbold. "The Structure of Propertius' Book II." In *University of California Publications in Classical Philology*, vol. 14, 215–254. Berkeley, 1952.

Damsté, P. H. "De Propertii Elegia I 21." *Mnemosyne* 52 (1924): 1–7.

————. "De Propertii elegiarum libro IV." *Mnemosyne* 56 (1928): 214–219.

Daut, R. "Zu Properz 3, 21." In *Classica et Iberica. A Festschrift in honor of Joseph M. F. Marique*, edited by P. T. Brannan, 293–302. Worcester, Mass., 1975.

Davis, J. T. "Propertius I 21–22." *CJ* 66 (1971): 209–213.

————. *Dramatic Pairings in the Elegies of Propertius and Ovid.* Noctes Romanae, 15. Bern, 1977.

Davison, J. A. "Propertius I 9.23–24." *CR* 62 (1948): 57–58.

Day, A. A. *The Origins of Latin Love Elegy.* Oxford, 1938.

Deininger, J. *Die Provinziallandtage der Römischen Kaiserzeit von Augustus bis zum Ende des Dritten Jahrhunderts n. Chr.* Munich, 1965.

della Corte, F. "Le leges Iuliae e l'elegia romana." In *ANRW*, 2.30.1., edited by Wolfgang Haase, 539–558. Berlin, 1982.

Deonna, W. "The Crab and the Butterfly." *JWI* 17 (1954): 47–86.

Desiderei, S. "Il preziosismo mitologico di Properzio." *GIF* 11 (1958): 327–336.

Dieterich, A. "Die Widmungselegie des letzten Buches des Propertius." *RhM* 55 (1900): 191–221.

Dittenberger, W. *Orientis Graeci Inscriptiones Selectae.* Vol. 2. Leipzig, 1905.

Doblhofer, E. *Die Augustuspanegyrik des Horaz in formalhistorischer Sicht.* Heidelberg, 1966.

Dornseiff, F. "Horaz und Properz." *Philologus* 87 (1932): 473–476.

Dumézil, G. "Propertiana." *Latomus* 10 (1951): 289–302.

Ehrenberg, V., and A. H. M. Jones. *Documents Illustrating the Reigns of Augustus and Tiberius.* 2d ed. Oxford, 1955. Reprint, Oxford, 1963.

Eisenhut, W. "Die poetische Situation in der Cornelia-Elegie des Properz (IV 11)." *WJA* 4 (1949): 53–59.

————. "Die Einleitungsverse der Elegie IV 6 des Properz." *Hermes* 84 (1956): 121–128.

————. "*Deducere Carmen.* Ein Beitrag zum Problem der literarischen Beziehungen zwischen Horaz und Properz." In *Gedenkschrift für G. Rohne*, edited by G. Radke, 91–104. Aparchai, 4. Tübingen, 1961.

————. *Virtus Romana. Ihre Stellung im römischen Wertsystem.* Studia et testimonia, 13. Munich, 1973.

Elisei, R. "Sesto Properzio." *MC* 1940, Appendix 12–40.

Enk, P. J. *Ad Propertii carmina commentarius criticus.* Zutphen, 1911.

————. "Lucubrationes Propertianae." *Mnemosyne* 57 (1929): 145–159.

————. "Lucubrationes Propertianae. *Mnemosyne* 3 (1935–36): 149–164.

————. "Propertiana." *Latomus* 14 (1955): 31–42.

————. "The Unity of Some Elegies of Propertius." *Latomus* 15 (1956): 181–192. (Enk 1956A)

————. "Adnotationes criticae ad Propertium." *SIFC* 27–28 (1956): 114–118. (Enk 1956B)

————. "De vero Propertii erga Cynthiam amore." In *Miscellanea Properziana*. Atti dell' Accademia Properziana del Subasio, 5.5, 25–30. Assisi, 1957.

————. "Propertiana." *RCCM* 2 (1960): 124–129.

Ernout, A. "Propertiana." In *Ut pictura poesis. Studia latina P. J. Enk septuagenario oblata*, edited by P. de Jonge et al., 66–74. Leiden, 1955.

Erren, Manfred. *Enallage Adiectivi, Substantivi, Verbi in der Monobiblos des Properz.* Prague, 1974.

Évrard, E. "Properce, I 6." *LEC* 42 (1974): 39–49.

Fedeli, P. "Osservazioni sullo Stile di Properzio." *SIFC* 41 (1969): 81–94.

Ferrero, G. *The Greatness and Decline of Rome.* Vols. 4 and 5. New York, 1908–1909.

Ferrero Raditsa, L. "Augustus' Legislation Concerning Marriage." In *ANRW*, 2.13, edited by Hildegard Temporini, 278–329. Berlin, 1980.

Festa, N. "Properzio." *Cultura* 5 (1925–26): 443–454.

————. "Properzio e la poesia alessandrina." *Cultura* 5 (1925–26): 481–492.

————. "La poesia romana di Properzio. I primi saggi." *Cultura* 6 (1926–27): 145–155. (Festa 1926–27A)

————. "La poesia romana di Properzio. Il poema mancato." *Cultura* 6 (1926–27): 241–246. (Festa 1926–27B)

Flach, D. "Das literarische Verhältnis von Horaz und Properz." Diss., Giessen, 1967.

Fontana, M. "Properzio e il matrimonio." *GIF* 3 (1950): 73–76.

Fontenrose, J. "Propertius and the Roman Career." In *University of California Publications in Classical Philology*, vol. 13, 371–388. Berkeley, 1949.

Frank, R. I. "Augustan Elegy and Catonism." In *ANRW* 2.30.1, edited by Wolfgang Haase, 559–579. Berlin, 1982.

Frothingham, A. L. "Propertius and the Arae Perusinae. A New Interpretation of Elegy I. 21." *CPh* 4 (1909): 345–352.

Fuchs, H. "Rückschau und Ausblick im Arbeitsbereich der lateinischen Philologie." *MH* 4 (1947): 147–198.

————. *Der geistige Widerstand gegen Rom in der antiken Welt.* 2d ed. Berlin, 1964.

Funaioli, G. "*Ille ego, qui quondam . . .* e Properzio II 34." *A&R* 42 (1940): 97–109.

Gaar, E. "Die Komposition der *Regina Elegiarum*." *BBG* 65 (1929): 240–246.

Galinsky, K. "The Triumph Theme in Augustan Elegy." *WS* 82 (1969): 75–107.

————. "Augustus' Legislation on Morals and Marriage." *Philologus* 125 (1981): 126–144.

Gatti, C. "Un epigramma sulla battaglia d'Azio." *PP* 7 (1952): 149–157.

Genovese, E. N. "Propertius' *Tardus Amor*." *CJ* 68 (1972): 138–143.

Gilmore, G. D. "Two Notes." *MH* 33 (1976): 51.

Giorgialberti, V. *Properzio elegiaco dell' amore e poeta augusteo.* Rome, 1935.

Glücklich, H. J. "Zeitkritik bei Properz." *AU* 20 (1977): 45–62.

Goddard, H. "Propertius, Cynthia, and Augustus." *CR* 37 (1923): 153–156.

Goold, G. P. "Noctes Propertianae." *HSPh* 71 (1966): 59–106.

Gotsmich, A. "Die 'grausame' Aphrodite am Gigantenfries des Pergamener Altars." *AA* (1941): 844ff.

Grant, J. N. "Propertius 1.18." *Phoenix* 33 (1979): 48–58.

Griffin, J. "Propertius and Antony." *JRS* 67 (1977): 17–26.

———. "Genre and Real Life in Latin Poetry." *JRS* 71 (1981): 39–49.

Grimal, P. "Notes sur Properce, I." *REL* 23 (1945): 110–119.

———. "Études sur Properce, II. César et la légende de Tarpeia." *REL* 19 (1951): 201–214.

———. "Le IVe livre des Elegies de Properce et la politique d'Auguste." *CRAI* (1952): 258–261. (Grimal, 1952A)

———. "Properce et la légende de Tarpeia." *REL* 30 (1952): 32–33. (Grimal, 1952B)

———. "Les intentions de Properce et la composition du livre IV des *Elegies*." *Latomus* 11 (1952): 183–97, 315–26, 437–450. (Grimal, 1952C)

———. *Les intentions de Properce et la composition du livre IV des Elegies*. Collection Latomus, 12. Brussels, 1953.

———. "Properce et les Exploits de Sémiramis." *RPh* 4 (1981): 21–23.

Guey, J. "Avec Properce au Palatin: Légendes et Promenade (ad Prop. IV 1. 1–56)." *REL* 30 (1952): 186–202.

Guillemin, A. "Properce, de Cynthie aux poèmes romains." *REL* 28 (1950): 182–193.

Habicht, Chr. "Die augusteische Zeit und das erste Jahrhundert nach Christi Geburt." In *Le cult des souverains dans l'Empire Romain*, edited by W. den Boer, 41–99. Entretiens sur l'antiquité classique, 19. Geneva, 1973.

Haffter, H. "Das Gedichtbuch als dichterische Aussage. Überlegungen zu den Elegien des Properz." In *Festschrift Karl Vretska*, edited by D. Ableitinger and H. Gugel, 53–67. Heidelberg, 1970.

Haglund, E. "Ad Propertii III 11.40." *Eranos* 30 (1932): 46–47.

Haight, E. H. "Another note on Propertius I 22." *CPh* 35 (1940): 426.

Hallett, J. P. "Book IV: Propertius' *recusatio* to Augustus and Augustan Ideals." *HSPh* 76 (1972): 285–289. (Diss. summary)

———. "The Role of Women in Roman Elegy: Counter-cultural Feminism." *Arethusa* 6 (1973): 103–124.

Hamilton, J. P. "Observations on the Cornelia Elegy." *CQ* 51 (1957): 134–138.

Hanslik, R. "Textkritik in Properz Buch IV." *Hermes* 91 (1963): 178–190.

———. "Properz III 4." *WS* 80 (1967): 183–189.

———. "Storia e storia della cultura nelle elegie di Properzio." *A&R* N.S. 17 (1972): 94–102.

———. "Zum Ersten Gedicht der Monobiblos des Properz." *WS* 89 (1976): 186–198.

Harmon, D. P. "The Poet's Initiation and the Sacerdotal Imagery of Propertius 3.1–5." In *Studies in Latin Literature and Roman History*, vol. 2, edited by Carl Deroux, 317–334. Collection Latomus, 168. Brussels, 1980.

Hartman, J. J. "De prima Propertii elegia." *Mnemosyne* 46 (1918): 105–110.

———. "Propertiana." *Mnemosyne* 49 (1921): 337–351.

Helm, R. "E. Reitzenstein: *Wirklichkeitsbild und Gefühlsentwicklung bei Properz.*" *PhW* 57 (1937): 778–787. (Review)

———. "Properz, I 21." *RhM* 95 (1952): 272–283.

———. "Propertius." In *RE*, 23.1, edited by A. F. von Pauly and Georg Wissowa, 757–796. Stuttgart, 1957.

Hering, W. "*Quid haec elegia sibi velit, non ita facile dictu.* Ein Beitrag zum Verständnis von Properz I 1." *Philologus* 114 (1970): 98–117.

———. "Properz I 3." *WS* 85 (1972): 45–78.

———. "Die Monobiblos als Gedichtbuch." *ACD* 9 (1973): 69–75.

———. "Form und Inhalt in der frühaugusteischen Poesie." In *ANRW* 30.1, edited by Wolfgang Haase, 181–253. Berlin, 1982.

Herrmann, L. "P. J. Enk: *Sex. Propertii Elegiarum liber I.*" *AC* 15 (1946): 339. (Review)

———. *L'age d'argent doré.* Paris, 1951.

———. "Gallus et Lupercus." *Latomus* 18 (1959): 751–754.

———. "Lynceus." *GIF* 20 (1967): 139–145.

———. "*Sex superant versus.* (Pseudo) Properce, Élégies IV 2.57/8." *Latomus* 27 (1968): 617–21.

Hodge, R. I. V., and R. A. Buttimore. *The 'Monobiblos' of Propertius.* Cambridge, 1977.

Holmes, T. R. E. *The Architect of the Roman Empire.* 2 vols. Oxford, 1928–1931.

Hommel, H. "Der 'Unbekannte Soldat.' Zu Propertius I 21, 9–10." *PhW* 36 (1926): 988–990.

Housman, A. E. "Emendations in Propertius." *JPh* 16 (1888): 1–35.

———. "The Manuscripts of Propertius, I, II." *JPh* 21 (1893): 101–160, 161–197.

———. "H. E. Butler: *Sexti Properti opera omnia.*" *CR* 19 (1905): 317–320. (Review)

———. "A Transposition in Propertius." *CQ* 8 (1914): 151–155.

———. *The Classical Papers.* Edited by J. Diggle and F. D. R. Goodyear. 3 vols. Cambridge, 1972.

Hubbard, M. "Propertiana." *CQ* 18 (1968): 315–319.

———. *Propertius.* New York, 1975.

Ingvarsson, E. "Zu Properz III 5.2." *Eranos* 53 (1955): 165–171.

Ites, M. "De Propertii elegiis inter se conexis." Diss., Göttingen. Bielefeld, 1908.

Jachmann, G. "Eine Elegie des Properz, ein Überlieferungsschicksal." *RhM* 84 (1935): 193–240.

———. "Eine Studie zu Properz." In *Festschrift für F. Schulz*, vol. 2, 179–187. Weimar, 1951.

Jacoby, F. "Zur Entstehung der römischen Elegie." *RhM* 60 (1905): 38–105.

———. "Zur Arbeitsweise des Properz. (I 7–9)." *Hermes* 44 (1909): 304–309.

———. "Drei Gedichte des Properz." *RhM* 69 (1914): 393–413; 427–463. (= *Kleine Philologische Schriften*, vol. 2, edited by H. J. Mette, 216–265. Berlin, 1961.)

Jäger, K. "Zweigliedrige Gedichte und Gedichtpaare bei Properz und in Ovids *Amores.*" Diss., Eberhard-Karls-Universität, Tübingen, 1967.

Johnson, W. R. "The Emotions of Patriotism: Propertius 4.6." *CSCA* 6 (1973): 151–180.

Jones, A. H. M. "L. Volcacius Tullus, Proconsul of Asia." *CR* N.S. 5 (1955): 244–245.

Józefowicz, B. "Die literarischen Beziehungen zwischen Horaz und Properz." *Eos* 62 (1974): 79–92.

Juhnke, H. "Zum Aufbau des zweiten und dritten Buches des Properz." *Hermes* 99 (1971): 91–125.

Kambylis, A. *Die Dichterweihe und ihre Symbolik. Untersuchungen zu Hesiodos, Kallimachos, Properz und Ennius.* Diss., Kiel. Bibl. d. Klass. Altertumswiss. N.F. 2. Reihe. Heidelberg, 1965.

Karsten, H. T. "Propertii Elegia IV 4." *Mnemosyne* 43 (1915): 357–364.

Khan, H. A. "Sea-Symbolism in Propertius I 11." *AAntHung* 16 (1968): 253–256.

King, J. K. "Propertius' Programmatic Poetry and the Unity of the *Monobiblos.*" *CJ* 71 (1975–76): 108–124.

———. "Sophistication vs. Chastity in Propertius' Latin Love Elegy." *Helios*, N.S. 4 (1976): 69–76.

———. "Propertius 2.1–12: His Callimachean Second Libellus." *WJA* N.F. 6b (1980): 61–84.

———. "The Two Galluses of Propertius' *Monobiblos.*" *Philologus* 124 (1980): 212–230.

———. "Propertius 2.2: A Callimachean *multum in parvo.*" *WS* N.F. 15 (1981): 169–184.

Knoche, U. "Zur Frage der Properz-Interpolation." *RhM* 85 (1936): 8–63.

Krahner, L. "Versuch einer Analyse der Elegie des Properz IV 1 v. 1–70. ed. Hertzb." *Philologus* 27 (1868): 58–87.

Krappe, A. H. "Die Sage von der Tarpeja." *RhM* 78 (1929): 249–267.

Kraus, W. "Zur Idealität des 'Ich' und der Situation in der römischen Elegie: Tibull, Erstes Buch, Zweite Elegie." In *Ideen und Formen. Festschrift für Hugo Friedrich*, 153–163. Frankfurt, 1965.

Krokowski, J. "Elegie und Epigramm: Properz I 1." *Eos* 55 (1965): 142–145.

Kühn, J. H. "Die Proömion-Elegie des zweiten Properzbuches." *Hermes* 89 (1961): 84–105.

Kunihara, K. "Propertiana. I 21." *REL* 52 (1974): 239–250.

Laffi, U. "Le iscrizioni relative all' introduzione nel 9 a.C. del nuovo calendario della Provincia d'Asia." *SCO* 16 (1967): 5–98.

Lake, A. K. "A note on Propertius I 22." *CPh* 35 (1940): 297–300.

La Penna, A. "Movimento e ritmo epigrammatico nelle elegie di Properzio." *Maia* 3 (1950): 9–15. (La Penna, 1950A)

———. "Properzio e i poeti latini dell' età aurea." *Maia* 3 (1950): 209–236. (La Penna, 1950B); *Maia* 4 (1951): 43–69 (continuation).

———. "Note sul linguaggio erotico dell'elegia latina." *Maia* 4 (1951): 187–209. (La Penna, 1951A)

———. *Properzio. Saggio critico seguito da due ricerche filologiche.* Florence, 1951. (La Penna, 1951B)

———. "De tertii libri Propertiani prooemiis." *Maia* 7 (1955): 134–135.

———. *L'Integrazione difficile. Un profilo di Properzio.* Piccola Biblioteca Einaudi, 297. Torino, 1977.

Last, H. "The Social Policy of Augustus." In *The Cambridge Ancient History*, vol. X, edited by S. A. Cook, F. E. Adcock, M. P. Charlesworth, 425–464. New York/Cambridge, England, 1934.

Lefèvre, E. *Propertius ludibundus. Elemente des Humors in seinen Elegien.* Diss., Kiel, 1962. Bibl. d. Klass. Altertumswiss. N.F. 2. Reihe, 15. Heidelberg, 1966.

————. "Form und Funktion der Einleitungselegie des vierten Buches des Properz." *WS* 79 (1966): 427–442.

————. "L'Unità dell' elegia Properziana." In *Colloquium Propertianum.* Atti dell' Accademia Properziana del Subasio, 25–51. Assisi, 1977.

Lefkowitz, M. R. "The Quarrel between Callimachus and Apollonius." *ZPE* 40 (1980): 1–19.

Lejay, P. "Properce et l'astrologue." *JS* 13 (1915): 492–508.

————. "Les élégies romaines de Properce." *JS* 14 (1916): 215–222; 261–271; 297–307.

Lenz, F. K. "Ovids dichterisches *Ingenium.*" *Altertum* 13 (1967): 164–175.

Leo, F. "Das Schlussgedicht des ersten Buches des Properz." *GGA* (1898): 469–478. (= *Ausgewählte Kleine Schriften II*, 169–178. Rome, 1960.)

————. "Elegie und Komödie." *RhM* 55 (1900): 604–611.

Léon-Marcien, F. "L'interprétation de la bataille d'Actium par les poètes Latins de l'époque Augustéenne." *LEC* 24 (1956): 330–348.

Levin, D. N. "Propertius, Catullus and Three Kinds of Ambiguous Expression." *TAPhA* 100 (1969): 221–235.

————. "Hellenistic Echoes in Propertius' First Elegy." *GB* 3 (1975): 215–221.

————. "War and Peace in Early Roman Elegy." In *ANRW* 2.30.1, edited by Wolfgang Haase, 418–538. Berlin, 1982.

Lieberg, G. *Puella divina. Die Gestalt der göttlichen Geliebten bei Catull im Zusammenhang der antiken Dichtung.* Amsterdam, 1962.

————. "Die Muse des Properz und seine Dichterweihe." *Philologus* 107 (1963): 116–129; 263–270.

————. "Die Mythologie des Properz in der Forschung und die Idealisierung der Cynthia." *RhM* 112 (1969): 311–347.

Lilja, S. *The Roman Elegists' Attitude to Women.* Annales Acad. Scient. Fennicae, Ser. B, 135, 1. Helsinki, 1973.

Little, D. "Politics in Augustan Poetry." In *ANRW* 2.30.1, edited by Wolfgang Haase, 255–370. Berlin, 1982.

Luck, G. "The Cave and the Source. On the Imagery of Propertius III 1.1–6." *CQ* 51 (1957): 175–179.

————. *Die römische Liebeselegie.* Heidelberg, 1961.

————. "Beiträge zum Text der römischen Elegiker." *RhM* 105 (1962): 337–351.

————. "Notes on Propertius." *AJPh* 100 (1979): 73–93.

Lucot, R. "Sur Properce IV 1.8.33." *Études classiques* 2 (1948): 121–124.

————. "A propos de l'astrologue de Properce." In *Mélanges offerts à V. Magnien,* 65–68. Toulouse, 1949.

————. "Vertumne et Mécène." *AFLT (Pallas)* 1 (1953): 65–80.

————. "Propertiana." *AFLT (Pallas)* 2 (1954): 97–104.

————. "*Domus Remi.* (Properce IV 1. 9–10)." *Pallas* 5 (1957): 63–70. (Lucot, 1957A)

————. "Mécène et Properce." *REL* 35 (1957): 195–204. (Lucot, 1957B)

————. "Propertiana." *REL* 47 (1969): 335–346.

————. "Gallus et Lupercus." *Pallas* 17 (1970): 109–114.

Lyne, R. O. A. M. "Propertius IV 4.65 sqq. and Pind., Pyth. 9, 23 sq." *Hermes* 99 (1971): 376–378.

———. "Servitium Amoris." *CQ* 29 (1979): 117–130.

Mackay, L. A. "Umbrian Rimbaud." *G&R* 17 (1970): 177–183.

MacLeod, C. W. "Propertius 4, 1." In *Papers of the Liverpool Latin Seminar 1976. Classical Latin Poetry. Medieval Latin Poetry. Greek Poetry*, edited by F. Cairns, 141–153. ARCA Classical and Medieval Texts, Papers and Monographs, 2. Liverpool, 1977.

Maddoli, G. "Ancora sulla patria di Properzio." *PP* 18 (1963): 295–301.

Magie, D. *Roman Rule in Asia Minor to the End of the Third Century After Christ*. 2 vols. Princeton, 1950.

Magueijo, C. "Comentario a Propércio, I 1.1–6 e 25–26." *Euphrosyne* 3 (1969): 201–205.

———. "Propércio I, 22." *Euphrosyne* 6 (1973–74): 133–143.

Marquis, E. C. "Propertius IV 1.150 and the Gate of Cancer." *WS* N.F. 7 (1973): 126–133.

Marr, J. L. "Notes on Propertius IV 1 and IV 4." *CQ* 20 (1970): 160–173.

Mattingly, H. "*Mutatis mutandis.* (Prop. II 10.23)." *CR* 26 (1912): 49–50.

———. *A Catalogue of the Roman Coins in the British Museum. Coins of the Roman Empire in the British Museum. Vol. 1: Augustus to Vitellius*. London, 1923.

———. "The Date of Virgil's Death. A Numismatic Contribution." *CR* 44 (1930): 57–59.

Meyer, H. D. *Die Aussenpolitik des Augustus und die augusteische Dichtung*. Cologne, 1961.

Michelfeit, J. "Das augusteische Gedichtbuch." *RhM* 112 (1969): 347–370.

Miller, J. F. "Propertius 2.1 and the new Gallus Papyrus." *ZPE* 44 (1981): 173–176.

———. "Callimachus and the Augustan Aetiological Elegy." In *ANRW* 30.1, edited by Wolfgang Haase, 371–417. Berlin, 1982.

Mogni, V. "Spunti epici nei primi tre libri delle Elegie di Properzio." *GIF* 1 (1948): 220–242.

Mommsen, Th. *Römisches Stafrecht*. Leipzig, 1899. Reprint, Graz, 1955.

Müller, R. "Motivkatalog der römischen Elegie." Diss., Zurich, 1952.

Murgatroyd, P. "*Servitium Amoris* and the Roman Elegists." *Latomus* 49 (1981): 589–606.

Murray, R. J. "The Attitude of the Augustan Poets toward *Rex* and Related Words." *CJ* 60 (1965): 241–246.

Nencini, F. "Properzio e Vario Rufo. (Prop. II, 24, 83–84)." *MC* (1935): 119–120.

Nethercut, W. R. "Ille parum cauti pectoris egit opus." *TAPhA* 92 (1961): 389–407.

———. "Propertius I 21. 5–6." *CPh* 63 (1968): 141–143. (Nethercut, 1968A)

———. "Elegiac Technique in Propertius IV 1.71–150." *WS* N.F. 2 (1968): 92–97. (Nethercut, 1968B)

———. "Notes on the Structure of Propertius, Book IV." *AJPh* 89 (1968): 449–464. (Nethercut, 1968C)

———. "The Ironic Priest. Propertius' Roman Elegies, III 1–5. Imitations of Horace and Vergil." *AJPh* 91 (1970): 385–407. (Nethercut, 1970A)

———. "The Astrological Significance of Propertius IV 1.150. A Reexamination of *sinistra*." *WS* 4 (1970): 110–117. (Nethercut, 1970B)

———. "The *sphragis* of the *Monobiblos*." *AJPh* 92 (1971): 464–472. (Nethercut, 1971A)

———. "Propertius II 15.41–48; Antony at Actium." *RSC* 19 (1971): 299–301. (Nethercut, 1971B)

———. "Propertius III 11." *TAPhA* 102 (1971): 411–443. (Nethercut, 1971C)

———. "Propertius, Elegy II 10." *SO* 47 (1972): 79–94.

———. "Propertius 2.18: 'Kein einheitliches Gedicht . . .'." *ICS* 5 (1980): 94–109.

———. "Propertius 1.21.5: the Elision of *servato*." *RhM* 124 (1981): 325–331.

O'Sullivan, J. N. "Propertius 1.1 and Callimachus, *Lyrica*, Fr. 228?" *CQ* 26 (1976): 107–109.

Otis, B. "Propertius' Single Book." *HSPh* 70 (1965): 1–41.

Paduano, G. "Le reminiscenze dell' Alcesti nell' Elegia IV 11 di Properzio." *Maia* 20 (1968): 21–28.

Paladini, M. L. *A proposito della tradizione poetica sulla battaglia di Azio.* Collection Latomus, 35. Brussels, 1958, and *Latomus* 17 (1958): 240–269; 462–475.

Paratore, E. *L'elegia III 11 e gli attegiamenti politici di Properzio.* Palermo, 1936.

———. "Virgilio Georgico e Properzio." *A&R* 10 (1942): 49–58.

———. "Properzio." *StudRom* 4 (1956): 625–638.

———. "De Propertio Vergiliani carminis iudice." In *Miscellanea Propertiana.* Atti dell' Accademia Properziana del Subasio, 5.5, 71–82. Assisi, 1957.

Pasoli, E. "De Properti libro quarto." *Euphrosyne* N.S. 1 (1967): 3–21. (Pasoli, 1967B)

———. "Prop. 4, 1, 17–20." *Euphrosyne* 3 (1969): 47–57.

———. "Alia de Prop. IV 1, 17 sqq." *Latinitas* 18 (1970): 18–26.

———. "Bemerkungen zur Poesie des Properz." *Altertum* 17 (1971): 80–92.

Petersmann, G. "Properz 1.3." *Latomus* 37 (1978): 953–959.

———. *Themenführung und Motiventfaltung in der Monobiblos des Properz.* GB Supplementband, 1. Graz, 1980.

Phillimore, J. S. "Notes on Propertius." *CR* 25 (1911): 135–138.

Pillinger, H. E. "Some Callimachean Influences on Propertius, Book IV." *HSPh* 73 (1969): 171–199.

Pope, M. "*Quid si non* . . .—An Idiom of Classical Latin." *Phoenix* 36 (1982): 53–70.

Postgate, J. P. "Propertius IV 1, 31 (a personal explanation)." *Philologus* 62 (1903): 480.

Pratt, K. J. "Roman Antimilitarism." *CJ* 51 (1955): 21–25.

Prinz, K. "Properz-Lesungen." *WS* 54 (1936): 85–100.

Putnam, M. C. J. "W. A. Camps: *Propertius, Elegies, Book I.*" *AJPh* 84 (1963): 195–200. (Review)

———. "Propertius I.22: A Poet's Self-definition." *QUCC* 23 (1976): 93–123.

———. "Propertius 3.22: Tullus' Return." *ICS* 2 (1979): 240–254.

———. "Propertius and the New Gallus Fragment." *ZPE* 39 (1980): 49–56.

———. "Propertius' Third Book: Patterns of Cohesion." *Arethusa* 13 (1980): 97–113.

Quadlbauer, F. "Non tutior ibis. Zu Properz II 34,45." In *Hans Gerstinger—Festgabe zum 80. Geburtstag. Arbeiten aus dem Grazer Schülerkreis*, 53–68. Graz, 1966.

———. *Properz III 1.* *Philologus* 112 (1968): 83–118.

————. *"Non humilem . . . poetam.* Zur literargeschichtlichen Stellung von Prop. I 7.21." *Hermes* 90 (1970): 331–339.

Quinn, K. "Practical Criticism. A Reading of Propertius I 21 and Catullus 17." *G&R* 16 (1969): 19–29.

Raditsa. *See* Ferrero Raditsa, L.

Ramaglia, L. "Properzio e le elegie romane." *RSC* 2 (1954): 191–204.

Randall, J. G. "Mistresses' Pseudonyms in Latin Elegy." *LCM* 4 (1979): 27–35.

Reitzenstein, E. *Wirklichkeitsbild und Gefühlsentwicklung bei Properz.* Philologus Supplementband 29, 2. Leipzig, 1936.

————. "Die Cornelia-Elegie des Properz (IV 11). Eine Formuntersuchung und ihre Ergebnisse für die Textkritik." *RhM* 112 (1969): 126–145.

————. "Über die Elegie des Propertius auf den Tod der Cornelia." In *Akademie der Wissenschaften und der Literatur*, Mainz, Abh. d. geistes- u. sozialwiss. Kl. 1970, 6, 405–463. Wiesbaden, 1970.

Reitzenstein, R. "Properz-Studien." *Hermes* 31 (1896): 185–220.

————. *Zur Sprache der römischen Erotik.* SB Akademie Heidelberg 1912, 12. Abhandlung.

————. "Zu Properz IV 1." *Hermes* 50 (1915): 474–475.

Ribbeck, C. "Zur Erklärung und Kritik des Properz." *RhM* 40 (1885): 481–505.

Richmond, O. L. "Propertius and the *Aeneid.*" *CQ* 11 (1917): 103–105.

————. "Palatine Apollo Again." *CQ* 52 (1958): 180–184.

Richter, W. "Divus Julius, Oktavianus und Kleopatra bei Aktion. Bemerkungen zu Properz 4, 6, 59ff." *WS* 79 (1966): 451–465.

Robertson, F. "Lament for Paetus. Propertius 3.7." *TAPhA* 100 (1969): 377–386.

Romussi, B. "Lo sviluppo di Properzio verso la concezione di una nuova poesia politica ed etiologica." *Philologus* 94 (1940–41): 175–196.

————. "Rapporti tra la poesia erotica del IV libro di Properzio e quella dei libri precedenti." *RFIC* 71 (1943): 57–65.

Ross, David O. *Backgrounds to Augustan Poetry: Gallus, Elegy, and Rome.* Cambridge, 1975.

Rothstein, M. "Properz und Virgil." *Hermes* 24 (1889): 1–34.

Rowell, Henry Th. *Rome in the Augustan Age.* Norman, Okla., 1975.

Rudd, N. "Theme and Imagery in Propertius 2.15." *CQ* 32 (1982): 152–155.

Rutledge, A. C. "Propertius' Tarpeia. The Poem Itself." *CJ* 60 (1964): 68–73.

Sabbadini, R. "L'elegia prima del libro primo di Properzio." *A&R* 2 (1899): 26–29.

Sandbach, F. H. "Propertius I 21." *PCPhS* (1937): 12.

————. "Notes on Propertius." *CR* 52 (1938): 211–215.

————. "Some Problems in Propertius." *CQ* 56 (1962): 263–276.

Saylor, C. F. "Propertius' Scheme of Inspiration." *WS* N.F. 5 (1971): 138–160.

————. "Symbolic Topography in Propertius 1.11." *CJ* 71 (1975–76): 126–137.

Scheidweiler, F. "Schwierige Properzstellen." *Hermes* 88 (1960): 75–82.

Scholz, U. W. "Zu Properz IV, 1, 17ff." *RhM* 112 (1969): 37–48.

Schulz-Vanheyden, E. "Properz und das griechische Epigramm, mit einem Exkurs: Paulus Silentiarius und Properz." Diss., Münster, 1969. Münster, 1970.

Scott, K. "Octavian's Propaganda and Antony's *De Sua Ebrietate.*" *CPh* 24 (1929): 133–141.

Shackleton Bailey, D. R. *See under* Bailey, D. R. S.

Sickle, J. van. "Propertius *vates*. Augustan Ideology, Topography, and Poetics in Elegy IV, 1." *DArch* 8 (1974–75): 116–145.

Skutsch, O. "Emendationum trias Propertiana." *Mnemosyne* 5 (1952): 232–235.

——. "The Structure of the Propertian *Monobiblos*." *CPh* 58 (1963): 238–239.

——. "Readings in Propertius." *CQ* 23 (1973): 316–323.

——. "The Second Book of Propertius." *HSPh* 79 (1975): 229–233.

Sluiter, Th. H. "De Sex. Propertii elegia I 21." In *Ut Pictura Poesis. Studia Latina P. J. Enk septuagenario oblata*, edited by P. de Jonge et al., 189–194. Leiden, 1955.

Smyth, W. R. "Interpretationes Propertianae." *CQ* 43 (1949): 118–125.

Solmsen, F. "Propertius and Horace." *CPh* 43 (1948): 105–109.

——. "Propertius in his Literary Relations with Tibullus and Vergil." *Philologus* 105 (1961): 272–289.

——. "Three Elegies of Propertius' First Book." *CPh* 57 (1962): 73–88.

——. "On Propertius I 7." *AJPh* 86 (1965): 77–84.

Stahl, H. P. "Doppeldeutigkeit bei Properz (Elegie 1, 18)." *Poetica* 2 (1968): 438–450.

——. "'Verteidigung' des ersten Buches der Aeneis." *Hermes* 97 (1969): 346–361.

——. "Peinliche Erfahrung eines kleinen Gottes. Horaz in seinen Satiren." *A&A* 20 (1974): 25–53.

——. "Aeneas—an 'Unheroic' Hero?" *Arethusa* 14 (1981): 157–177.

Steidle, W. "Das Motif der Lebenswahl bei Tibull und Properz." *WS* 75 (1962): 100–140.

Stoessl, F. "Die Kussgedichte des Catull und ihre Nachwirkung bei den Elegikern." *WS* 63 (1948): 102–116.

Stroh, W. *Die römische Liebeselegie als werbende Dichtung*. Amsterdam, 1971.

Sudhaus, S. "Lautes und leises Beten." *ARW* (1906): 185–200.

Suerbaum, W. "Der Schluss der Einleitungselegie zum 4. Properzbuch. Zum Motiv der Lebenswahl bei Properz." *RhM* 107 (1964): 340–361.

Sullivan, J. P. "*Castas odisse puellas*. A Reconsideration of Propertius I 1." *WS* 74 (1961): 96–112.

——. *Ezra Pound and Sextus Propertius*. Austin, Tex., 1964.

——. "Propertius. A Preliminary Essay." *Arion* 5 (1966): 5–22.

——. "The Politics of Elegy." *Arethusa* 5 (1972): 17–34.

——. *Propertius: A Critical Introduction*. Cambridge, 1976.

Sweet, F. "Propertius and Political Panegyric." *Arethusa* 5 (1972): 169–175.

Syme, R. *The Roman Revolution*. Reprint. Oxford, 1974.

Tadic-Gilloteaux, N. "A la recherche de la personnalité de Properce." *Latomus* 24 (1965): 238–273.

Terzaghi, N. "Propertianae quaestiunculae selectae." In *Studia Graeca et Latina (1901–1956)*, edited by N. Terzaghi, 1116–1134. Torino, 1963.

Townend, G. "Propertius among the Poets." *G&R* 8 (1961): 36–49.

Tracy, V. A. "The Poet-Lover in Augustan Elegy." *Latomus* 35 (1976): 575–581.

Tränkle, H. "Zur Textkritik und Erklärung des Properz." *Hermes* 96 (1968): 559–582.

——. "Properz über Vergils Aeneis." *MH* 28 (1971): 60–63.

Ullman, B. L. "H. E. Butler and E. A. Barber: *The Elegies of Propertius.*" *CPh* 31 (1936): 169–170. (Review)

Vaio, J. "The Authenticity and Relevance of Propertius II 14, 29–32." *CPh* 57 (1962): 236–238.

Verstraete, B. C. "Propertius' Use of Myth in Book II." In *Studies in Latin Literature and Roman History*, vol. 2, edited by Carl Deroux, 259–268. Collection Latomus, 168. Brussels, 1980.

Vessey, D. W. T. C. "Nescio quid maius." *PVS* 9 (1969–1970): 53–76.

Volkmann, H. *Res gestae divi Augusti.* 3d ed. Kleine Texte für Vorles. und Übung., 29–30. Berlin, 1969.

Wallace-Hadrill, A. "Family and Inheritance in the Augustan Marriage-laws." *PSPhS* 207 (1981): 58–80.

Warden, J. "Another Would-be Amazon: Propertius 4.4. 71–72." *Hermes* 106 (1978): 177–187.

————. *Fallax Opus: Poet and Reader in the Elegies of Propertius.* Phoenix Supplement, 14. Toronto, 1980.

Waszink, J. H. "Propertianum." In *Hommages à L. Herrmann*, 786–800. Collection Latomus, 44. Brussels, 1960.

Weeber, K. W. "Properz 1.1.11." *RhM* 117 (1974): 183–186.

Wellesley, K. "Propertius' Tarpeia Poem (IV.4)." *ACD* 5 (1969): 93–103.

Wheeler, A. L. "Propertius as *Praeceptor Amoris.*" *CPh* 5 (1910): 28–40.

White, R. E. "The Unity of Propertius 2.34 and 3.20." In *Laudatores temporis acti: Studies in Memory of W. E. Caldwell*, edited by M. F. Gyles and E. W. Davis, 63–72. Chapel Hill, 1964.

Wilamowitz-Moellendorf, U. von. *Hellenistische Dichtung in der Zeit des Kallimachos.* Reprint. Berlin, 1962.

Wili, W. "Die literarischen Beziehungen des Properz zu Horaz." In *Festschrift für Ed. Tièche zum 70. Geburtstage*, 179–196. Bern, 1974.

Wilkinson, L. P. "Propertius III 4." In *Studi in onore di Luigi Castiglioni*, vol. 2, 1091–1103. Florence, 1960.

Wille, G. "Zum Aufbau des zweiten Buches des Properz." *WJA* N.F. 6a (1980): 249–267.

Williams, G. "D. R. Shackleton Bailey: *Propertiana.*" *JRS* 47 (1957): 240–247. (Review)

————. "Four Notes on Propertius." *CR* 8 (1958): 6–9.

————. "Some Aspects of Roman Marriage Ceremonies and Ideals." *JRS* 48 (1958): 16–29.

————. "Poetry in the Moral Climate of Augustan Rome." *JRS* 52 (1962): 28–46.

————. *Tradition and Originality in Roman Poetry.* Oxford, 1968.

————. *Figures of Thought in Roman Poetry.* New Haven, 1980.

Wimmel, W. *Kallimachos in Rom. Die Nachfolge seines apologetischen Dichtens in der Augusteerzeit.* Hermes Einzelschriften, 16. Wiesbaden, 1960.

————. "Apollo-paupertas. Zur Symbolik von Berufungsvorgängen bei Properz, Horaz und Calpurnius." In *Forschungen zur Römischen Literatur. Festschrift K. Büchner*, edited by W. Wimmel, 291–297. Wiesbaden, 1970.

Wistrand, E. *Miscellanea Propertiana.* Studia Graeca et Latina Gothoburg. 38, Acta Univ. Gothoburg. Göteborg, 1977.

Wlosok, A. "Die dritte Cynthia-Elegie des Properz." *Hermes* 95 (1967): 330–352.

Woolley, A. "The Structure of Propertius Book III." *BICS* 14 (1967): 80–83.

Yardley, J. C. "*Preces et benefacta*: Propertius 1.1.16." *Maia* 31 (1979): 131–133.

———. "Paulus Silentiarius, Ovid, and Propertius." *CQ* 30 (1980): 239–243.

———. "Ponticus' Inspiration: Propertius 1.9.15." *AJPh* 102 (1981): 322–325.

Zanker, P. "Der Apollontempel auf dem Palatin. Ausstattung und politische Sinnbezüge nach der Schlacht von Actium." In *Cittá e Architettura nella Roma Imperiale*. Atti del Seminario del 27 Ottobre 1981 nel 25° Anniversario dell' Accademia di Danimarca. Analecta Romana Instituti Danici, Suppl. 10, 21–40. Copenhagen 1983.

Zetzel, J. E. G. "The Earliest Transposition in Propertius." *AJPh* 101 (1980): 314–315.

SUBJECT INDEX

(select passages only)

INDEX OF LATIN WORDS

Compositor: G & S Typesetters, Inc.
Text: 10/12 Janson
Display: Janson, Augustea, Augustea Inline
Printer: Thomson-Shore, Inc.
Binder: John H. Dekker & Sons